Westminster Abbey

The Lady Chapel of Henry VII

Westminster Abbey

The Lady Chapel of Henry VII

EDITED BY

Tim Tatton-Brown and Richard Mortimer

THE BOYDELL PRESS

© Contributors 2003

All Rights Reserved. Except as permitted under current legislation
no part of this work may be photocopied, stored in a retrieval system,
published, performed in public, adapted, broadcast,
transmitted, recorded or reproduced in any form or by any means,
without the prior permission of the copyright owner

First published 2003
The Boydell Press, Woodbridge

ISBN 1 84383 037 X

The Boydell Press is an imprint of Boydell & Brewer Ltd
PO Box 9, Woodbridge, Suffolk IP12 3DF, UK
and of Boydell & Brewer Inc.
PO Box 41026, Rochester, NY 14604–4126, USA
website: www.boydell.co.uk

A catalogue record for this book is available
from the British Library

Library of Congress Cataloging-in-Publication Data
Westminster Abbey : the Lady Chapel of Henry VII / edited by Tim
Tatton-Brown and Richard Mortimer.
   p. cm.
Includes bibliographical references and index.
   ISBN 1-84383-037-X (Hardback : alk. paper)
   1. Henry VII's Chapel (Westminster Abbey) – History.   2. Architecture, Gothic – Conservation and restoration – England – London.   3. Henry VII, King of England, 1457–1509.   4. London (England) – Buildings, structures, etc.   I. Tatton-Brown, T. W. T.   II. Mortimer, Richard.
   NA5470.W5W38 2004
   726'.8'0942132 – dc21   2003012675

This publication is printed on acid-free paper

Printed in Great Britain by
The Cromwell Press, Trowbridge, Wiltshire

Contents

List of illustrations	vii
Acknowledgements	xi
Abbreviations	xiii
Introduction *Tim Tatton-Brown and Richard Mortimer*	1
Barbara Harvey The monks of Westminster and the old Lady chapel	5
Roger Bowers The musicians and liturgy of the Lady chapels of the monastery church, c.1235–1540	33
Margaret Condon God Save the King! Piety, propaganda and the perpetual memorial	59
Margaret Condon The last will of Henry VII: document and text	99
Christopher Wilson The functional design of Henry VII's chapel: a reconstruction	141
Tim Tatton-Brown The building history of the Lady chapels	189
Andrew Reynolds An archaeological survey of the vaults of Henry VII's chapel	205
Julian Munby The roofs of Henry VII's chapel	215
Jacques Heyman The structure of the high vault of Henry VII's chapel	219
Charles Tracy The Henry VII chapel stalls and their eighteenth-century re-modelling	227

Julian Munby
An appendix on the carpentry of the stalls   253

Phillip Lindley
'The singuler mediacion and praiers of al the holie companie of Heven':   259
sculptural functions and forms in Henry VII's chapel

John Physick
The royal, the great and the good: the history of the later monuments   295

Thomas Cocke
Henry VII chapel: the royal connection   315

Tim Tatton-Brown and Richard Mortimer
The earlier restorations   327

Donald Buttress
Restoring the chapel, 1991–6   343

Index   357

Illustrations

All images are of Henry VII chapel, Westminster Abbey, unless otherwise stated.

Colour plates

I. (A) Exterior view looking north, 1996 (Dean and Chapter of Westminster)
    (B) Exterior view, Thomas Malton, 1796 (by courtesy of Donald Buttress)
II. Interior looking west, Charles Wild, c.1825
III. Interior looking east, formerly attributed to Canaletto, c.1740 (Dean and Chapter of Westminster)
IV. (A) The vault from below (Dean and Chapter of Westminster, photograph David Lambert)
    (B) The tomb of Henry VII and Elizabeth of York, detail of effigies, looking north (Dean and Chapter of Westminster, photograph David Lambert)
V. The interior looking east (Dean and Chapter of Westminster)
VI. The tomb of Henry VII and Elizabeth of York, detail of tomb-chest, looking north-west (Dean and Chapter of Westminster, photograph David Lambert)
VII. (A) The annual reading of the indenture in the chapter house (Margaret Condon)
    (B) The abbot and convent present the indentures bipartite to the king. The artist has emphasised the indented head of the document. (Margaret Condon)
    (C) The tomb of Lady Margaret Beaufort, looking south-west (Dean and Chapter of Westminster)
VIII. The king's copy of the indentures bipartite showing the foundation indenture, damask lining of the chemise cover, and seal skippets (Margaret Condon)

Black and white plates

1.	The Stonyhurst cope, woven for the Lady chapel of Henry VII (Victoria and Albert Museum)	70
2.	Will and sign-manual of Henry VII (Copyright PRO)	100
3.	Scene at the deathbed of Henry VII (Copyright British Library)	102
4.	Detail of north side of triumphal arch, partly overlapped by eighteenth-century extension to choirstalls (Christopher Wilson)	149
5.	Painting on east wall of St Faith's chapel, Westminster Abbey (Dean and Chapter of Westminster)	151

6.	Axial chapel looking south-east (Christopher Wilson)	161
7.	Axial chapel, detail of base of central image niche on north wall (Christopher Wilson)	162
8.	Axial chapel, south wall, graffiti on blind tracery below image niches (Christopher Wilson)	163
9.	North radiating chapel, detail of east wall (Christopher Wilson)	167
10.	Pier between north and north-east radiating chapels (Christopher Wilson)	168
11.	Main arcade arch, south side of eastmost rectangular-plan bay (Christopher Wilson)	169
12.	Warwick, St Mary, closet on south side of chancel (Christopher Wilson)	170
13.	Windsor Castle, St George's Chapel, north side of sanctuary showing closet (Christopher Wilson)	172
14.	Chantry enclosure looking down and to the south (Christopher Wilson)	176
15.	South range of choirstalls, detail of canopies (Christopher Wilson)	180
16.	Detail of south return stall and west wall (Christopher Wilson)	184
17.	Hinge in central arch of nave vault, just north of mid-span (Dean and Chapter of Westminster, photograph David Lambert)	221
18.	Northern pendant of central arch looking west, January 1995 (Jacques Heyman)	223
19.	Northern quatrefoil of the central arch looking east (Jacques Heyman)	224
20.	North range of choirstalls (Christopher Wilson)	228
21.	Dignitaries' stall canopy on south side (Charles Tracy)	230
22.	Front panelling of dignitaries' stall on south side (Charles Tracy)	231
23.	North-west entranceway to stalls (Charles Tracy)	234
24.	Eighteenth-century misericord in second block of stalls from west, north side (William Mason)	235
25.	Eighteenth-century misericord from back stall in third block from west on north side (William Mason)	235
26.	Eighteenth-century misericord supporter from back stall in third block from west, south side (William Mason)	236
27.	Stall canopywork, detail (Charles Tracy)	240
28.	Pomegranate fruit and foliage misericord supporter (sixteenth-century) (Charles Tracy)	241
29.	Underside of desking: detail of Tudor badges (William Mason)	241
30.	Front edge of stall desking (Charles Tracy)	241
31.	Backing of substalls: detail (Charles Tracy)	242
32.	View of underside of stall desk tops: detail (William Mason)	242
33.	Tongres, Notre-Dame: retable with Life of the Virgin (The Conway Library, Courtauld Institute of Art)	243
34.	Tessenderloo, St Martin: pulpitum (The Conway Library, Courtauld Institute of Art)	245
35.	Aarschot, Onze Lieve Vrouwkerk: pulpitum (The Conway Library, Courtauld Institute of Art)	246
36.	Winchester Cathedral, Lady chapel stalls: decorative carving on desk front (Charles Tracy)	247
37.	Winchester Cathedral, Langton chapel: canopywork, detail (Charles Tracy)	248

38.	Ardingly church, West Sussex: former rood screen (Charles Tracy)	248
39.	Ardingly church, West Sussex: detail of dado panelling (Charles Tracy)	249
40.	Detail of tracery on front of dignitaries' enclosure, south side (Charles Tracy)	250
41.	Stall backs, south side: detail of tracery head (Charles Tracy)	250
42.	Stall backs, south side: detail of upper portion of dado panelling (Charles Tracy)	251
43.	Ardingly church, West Sussex: detail of upper part of rood screen (Charles Tracy)	251
44.	Tomb figures of Henry VII and Elizabeth of York (Dean and Chapter of Westminster)	268
45.	Saint John the Evangelist, from the tomb grate (Dean and Chapter of Westminster)	272
46.	Christ, from easternmost bay (Dean and Chapter of Westminster)	279
47.	Saints Wilgeforte and Barbara (Dean and Chapter of Westminster)	283
48.	Saints Catharine (left) and Margaret, from south aisle (Dean and Chapter of Westminster)	285
49.	Saints Jerome (left) and Ambrose (Dean and Chapter of Westminster)	289
50.	Princess Sophia, monument by Maximilian Colt, 1606: detail (Dean and Chapter of Westminster)	302
51.	Mary queen of Scots, monument by William and Cornelius Cure, 1612: detail (Dean and Chapter of Westminster)	303
52.	John Sheffield, duke of Buckingham, d.1721, monument (Dean and Chapter of Westminster)	309
53.	George Monck, duke of Albemarle, d.1670, monument (Dean and Chapter of Westminster)	310
54.	Antoine Philippe, duc de Montpensier, d.1807, monument: detail (Dean and Chapter of Westminster)	312

Figures

1.	Plan of Westminster Abbey showing position of Lady chapel	xv
2.	Plan of the Lady chapel of Henry VII	xvi
3.	Plan by John Thorpe, redrawn by William Burges	xvii
4.	Isometric view of the vault	xviii
5.	Reconstructed plan of the Old Lady chapel	24
6.	Plan showing reconstruction of arrangement of fittings as intended by Henry VII	142
7.	South aisle, outer wall	144
8.	South elevation of central vessel with (partially inaccurate) reconstruction of screens to royal closets	147
9.	Bath Abbey, south elevation of east arm, detail of drawing by J. Carter	148
10.	Windsor Castle, St George's Chapel, plan of Lady chapel and part of east arm	155
11.	Durham Cathedral, plan showing shrine of St Cuthbert and adjacent altars	157

12.	Plan showing reconstruction of arrangement of fittings intended by Henry VII (J. Perkins)	158
13.	Longitudinal section of Henry VII's chapel and eastern arm	159
14.	South-east radiating chapel, north-east wall	165
15.	North aisle, east end, shown as if before the introduction of post-medieval tombs	166
16.	Richmond Palace, view by A. van der Wyngaerde	174
17.	South range of choirstalls and screens to south royal closets	178
18.	Interior looking east	182
19.	Transverse section showing construction sequence (Tim Tatton-Brown)	195
20.	Section of west wall	198
21.	Location of the sample areas (Andrew Reynolds)	207
22.	(A) Plan of the main vault sample (Andrew Reynolds)	208
	(B) West-facing section of the junction between the western and eastern sections of the main vault (Andrew Reynolds)	208
23.	Displaced moulding stones (Andrew Reynolds)	209
24.	Proposed reconstruction of the initial design of the main vault (Andrew Reynolds)	210
25.	Plan of the easternmost vault of the north aisle (Andrew Reynolds)	211
26.	The roof structure above the sample area of the north aisle (Andrew Reynolds)	212
27.	A hanging voussoir, by Wilars de Honecort	220
28.	Cross-section of the vault	220
29.	Hinge and Sabouret crack in a quadripartite vault (Jacques Heyman)	222
30.	Hinging deformation of central arch (Jacques Heyman)	222
31.	Plan of top side of the four bays of the nave vault (Jacques Heyman)	225
32.	Plan of the clergy stalls showing construction periods (Charles Tracy)	229
33.	Title page designed after Jean Bernard Honoré Toro and another artist, c.1728 (Victoria and Albert Museum)	238
34.	Stalls, early eighteenth-century drawing by Nicholas Hawksmoor (Dean and Chapter of Westminster)	239
35.	Substructure of stalls (Julian Munby)	255
36.	Drawing of proposed shrine monument to Henry VI (Copyright British Library)	263
37.	High altar	275
38.	Plan showing figure sculptures (Phillip Lindley after J.T. Micklethwaite)	281
39.	Design by Edward Pierce for a monument to the second duke of Buckingham, d.1687 (Copyright The British Museum)	300
40.	Elizabeth I, monument	304
41.	George Villiers, duke of Buckingham, d.1628, monument	307
42.	Entrance to the tomb of Henry VII, 1869, from a drawing by George Scharf	316
43.	Plan showing burial vaults, by Hubert Poole, c.1870 (Dean and Chapter of Westminster)	318
44.	Installation of Knights of the Bath, 1812	322
45.	Plan of the roof showing sequence of repairs (Tim Tatton-Brown)	335

Acknowledgements

Colour plates:
Dean and Chapter of Westminster: IA, II, III, V, VIIC; Dean and Chapter of Westminster, photographs by David Lambert: IVA–B, VI; Donald Buttress: IB; Margaret Condon: VIIA–B, VIII

Black and white plates:
Dean and Chapter of Westminster: 5, 44–54; Dean and Chapter of Westminster, photograph by David Lambert: 17; British Library: 3; The Conway Library, Courtauld Institute of Art: 33–5; Jacques Heyman: 18–19; William Mason: 24–6, 29, 32; Charles Tracy 21–3, 27–8, 30–1, 36–43; V & A Picture Library: 1; Christopher Wilson: 4, 6–16, 20.

Abbreviations

Astle	T. Astle, *The Will of King Henry VII*, 1775
BL	British Library, London
BN	Bibliothèque Nationale, Paris
Britton	J. Britton, *Architectural Antiquities of Great Britain*, 5 vols., 1807–20
Camden	W. Camden, *Reges, Reginae, Nobiles et alii in Ecclesia Collegiata B. Petri Westmonasterii Sepulti*, 1600
CChR	*Calendar of Charter Rolls*, HMSO 1903–
CClR	*Calendar of Close Rolls*, HMSO 1892–
CLR	*Calendar of Liberate Rolls*, HMSO 1917–
Cocke, *900 Years*	Thomas Cocke, *900 Years: the Restorations of Westminster Abbey*, 1995
Colvin, *HKW*	H.M. Colvin et al., *The History of the King's Works*, 6 vols., 1963–82
Cottingham	L.N. Cottingham, *Plan, Elevation, Sections and Specimens of Henry VII's Chapel, Westminster*, 2 vols., 1822–5
CPL	*Calendar of Papal Letters*, London and Dublin 1893–
CPR	*Calendar of Patent Rolls*, HMSO 1901–
Customary	E.M. Thompson, ed., *The Customary of the Benedictine Monasteries of St Augustine, Canterbury, and St Peter, Westminster*, 2 vols., Henry Bradshaw Society 23, 28, 1902–4
Dart	J. Dart, *Westmonasterium, or the History and Antiquities of the Abbey Church of St Peter's Westminster*, 1723
EHR	*English Historical Review*
Emden, *Oxford*	A.B. Emden, *A Biographical Register of the University of Oxford to AD 1500*, 3 vols., Oxford 1957–9
Foedera	*Foedera, Conventiones, Literae et cujuscumque generis Acta Publica etc.*, ed. T. Rymer, 20 vols., 3rd edn, 1735–45
Harvey, *EMA*	J.H. Harvey, *English Medieval Architects*, Gloucester 1984
Harvey, *Estates*	B. Harvey, *The Estates of Westminster Abbey in the Middle Ages*, Oxford 1977
Inventory	*An Inventory of the Historical Monuments in London*, i, *Westminster Abbey*, Royal Commission on Historical Monuments (England) 1924
JBAA	*Journal of the British Archaeological Association*
JEH	*Journal of Ecclesiastical History*
Jones and Underwood	M.K. Jones and M.G. Underwood, *The King's Mother. Lady Margaret Beaufort, Countess of Richmond and Derby*, Cambridge 1992
L&P Henry VIII	*Calendar of Letters and Papers, Foreign and Domestic, Henry VIII*, ed. J.S. Brewer, J. Gairdner and R.H. Brodie, HMSO 1864–1932
Lethaby, *Craftsmen*	W.R. Lethaby, *Westminster Abbey and the King's Craftsmen*, 1906

Lethaby, *Re-examined*	W.R. Lethaby, *Westminster Abbey Re-examined*, 1925
Micklethwaite, 'Imagery'	J.T. Micklethwaite, 'Notes on the imagery of Henry the Seventh's chapel, Westminster', *Archaeologia* 47, 1883, 361–80
Missale	J. Wickham Legg, ed., *Missale ad Usum Ecclesie Westmonasteriensis*, 3 vols., Henry Bradshaw Society 1, 5,12, 1891–6
Neale and Brayley	J.P. Neale and E.W. Brayley, *The History and Antiquities of the Abbey Church of St Peter, Westminster*, 2 vols., 1818–23
Perkins, *Worship and Ornaments*	J. Perkins, *Westminster Abbey, its Worship and Ornaments*, 3 vols., Alcuin Club vols. 33–4, 38, 1938–52
PRO	Public Record Office, London, now the National Archives
RCHM	Royal Commission on Historical Monuments
Reign of Henry VII	*The Reign of Henry VII*, ed. Benjamin Thompson, Harlaxton Medieval Studies 5, Stamford 1995
RIBA	Royal Institute of British Architects
Rosser, *Medieval Westminster*	G. Rosser, *Medieval Westminster 1200–1540*, Oxford 1989
Rot. Parl.	*Rotuli Parliamentorum*, 6 vols., 1832
RS	Rolls Series
Salzman, *Building in England*	L.F. Salzman, *Building in England down to 1540*, Oxford 1952
Sandford	F. Sandford, *A Genealogical History of the Kings of England and Monarchs of Great Britain*, 1677
Scott, *Gleanings*	G.G. Scott, *Gleanings from Westminster Abbey*, Oxford 1863
Stanley, *Historical Memorials*	A.P. Stanley, *Historical Memorials of Westminster Abbey*, 5th edn 1882
Stone, *Sculpture*	L. Stone, *Sculpture in Britain: the Middle Ages*, Harmondsworth 1972
TRHS	*Transactions of the Royal Historical Society*
VCH	*Victoria County History*
WAM	Westminster Abbey Muniments
WD	WAM, Muniment Book 11, 'Westminster Domesday'
Westlake	H.F. Westlake, *Westminster Abbey*, 2 vols., 1923
Whinney	M. Whinney, *Sculpture in Britain 1530–1830*, 2nd edn, Harmondsworth 1988
Wilson, *Westminster Abbey*	C. Wilson, P. Tudor-Craig, J. Physick and R. Gem, *Westminster Abbey*, New Bell's Cathedral Guides, 1986

Place of publication is London unless stated otherwise.

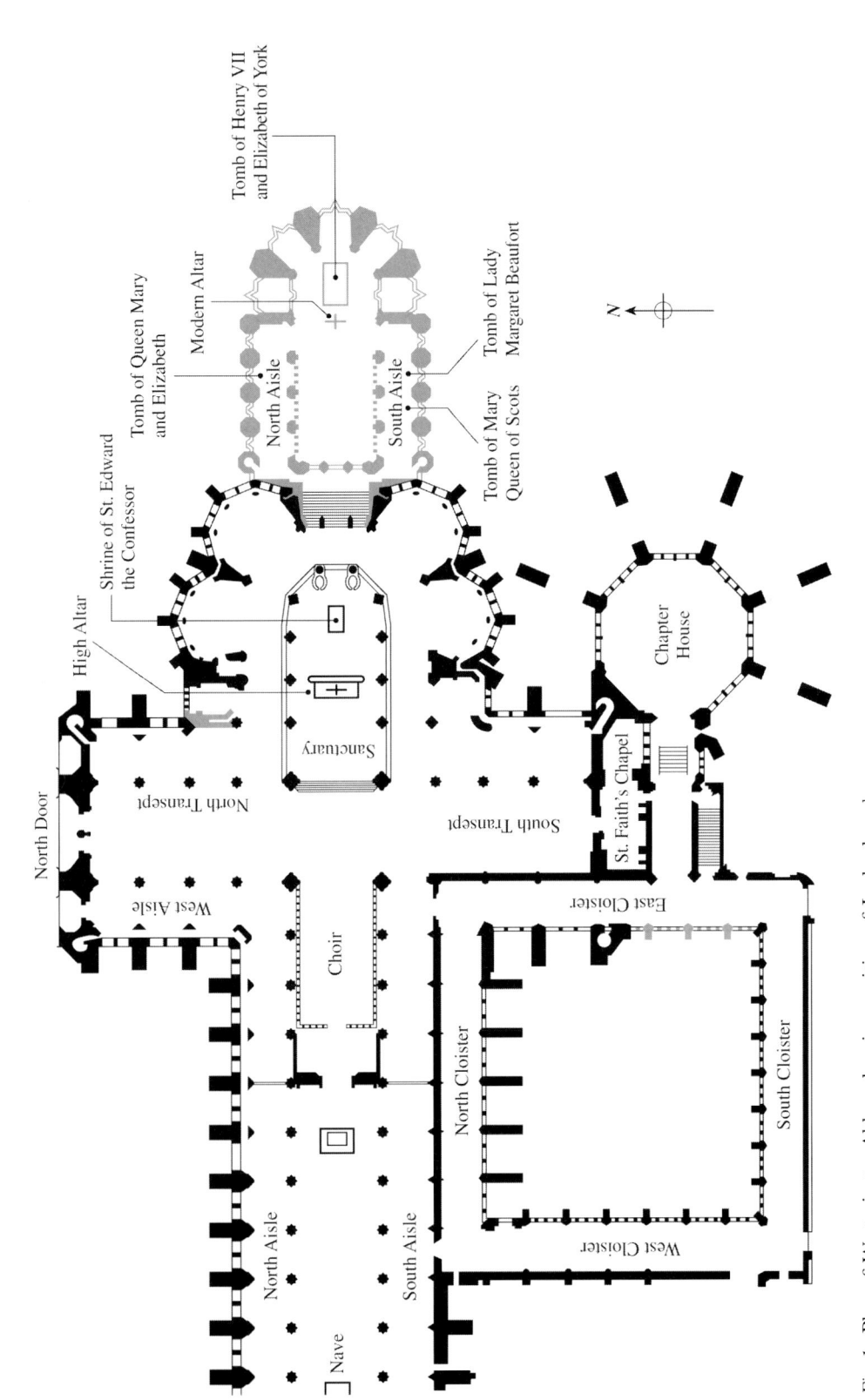

Fig. 1. Plan of Westminster Abbey showing position of Lady chapel.

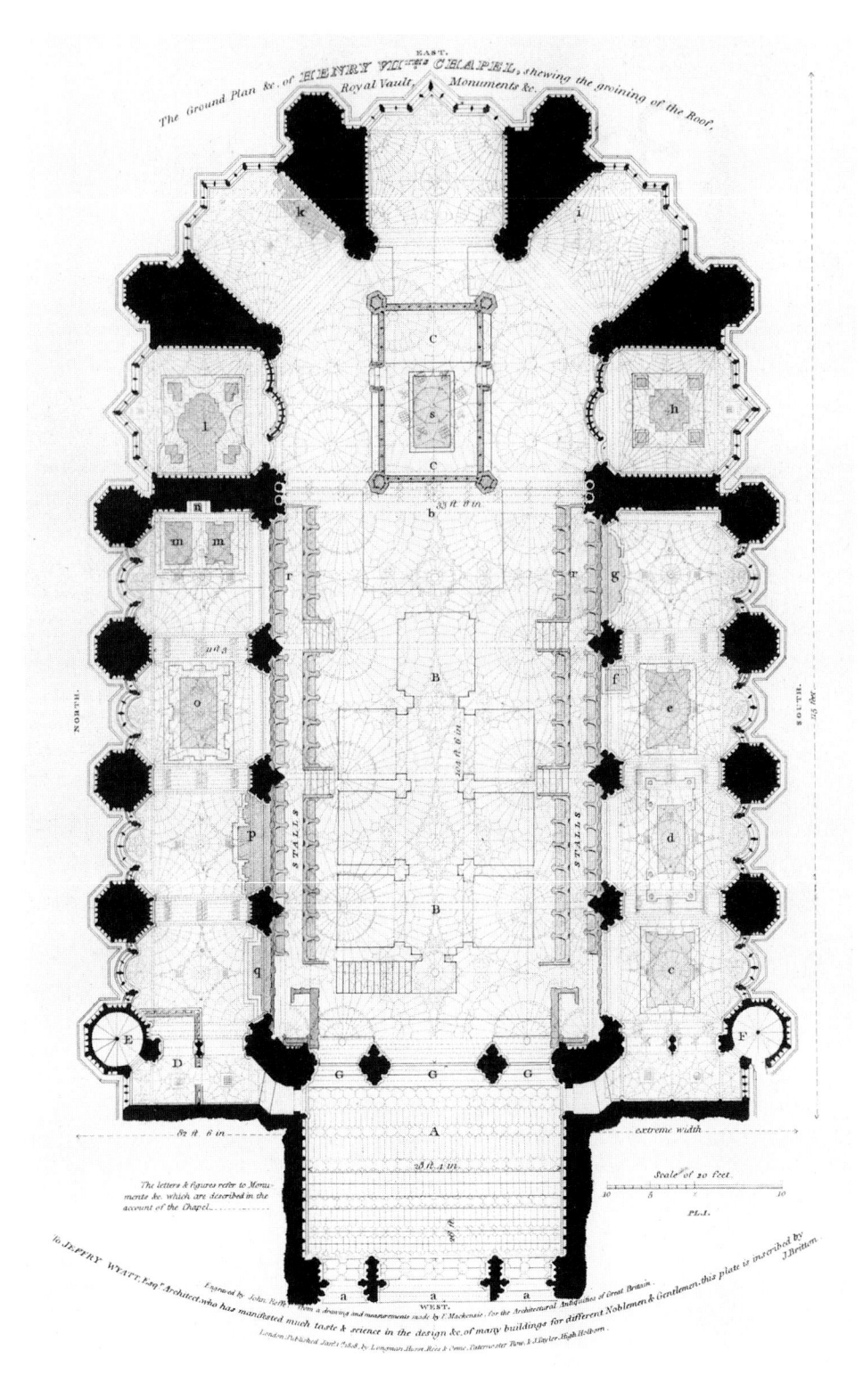

Fig. 2. Plan of the Lady chapel of Henry VII.

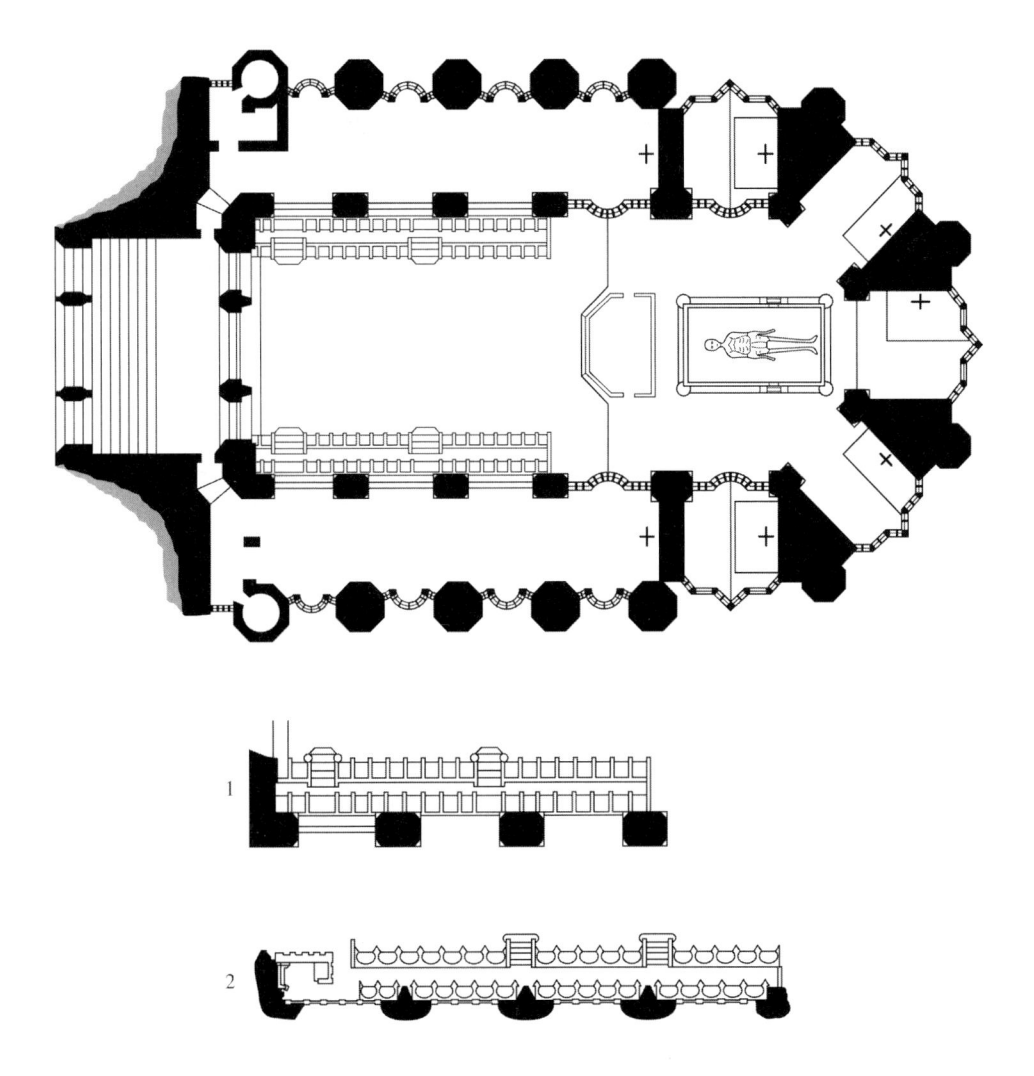

Fig. 3. Plan by John Thorpe, redrawn by William Burges. (Scott, *Gleanings*, 82)

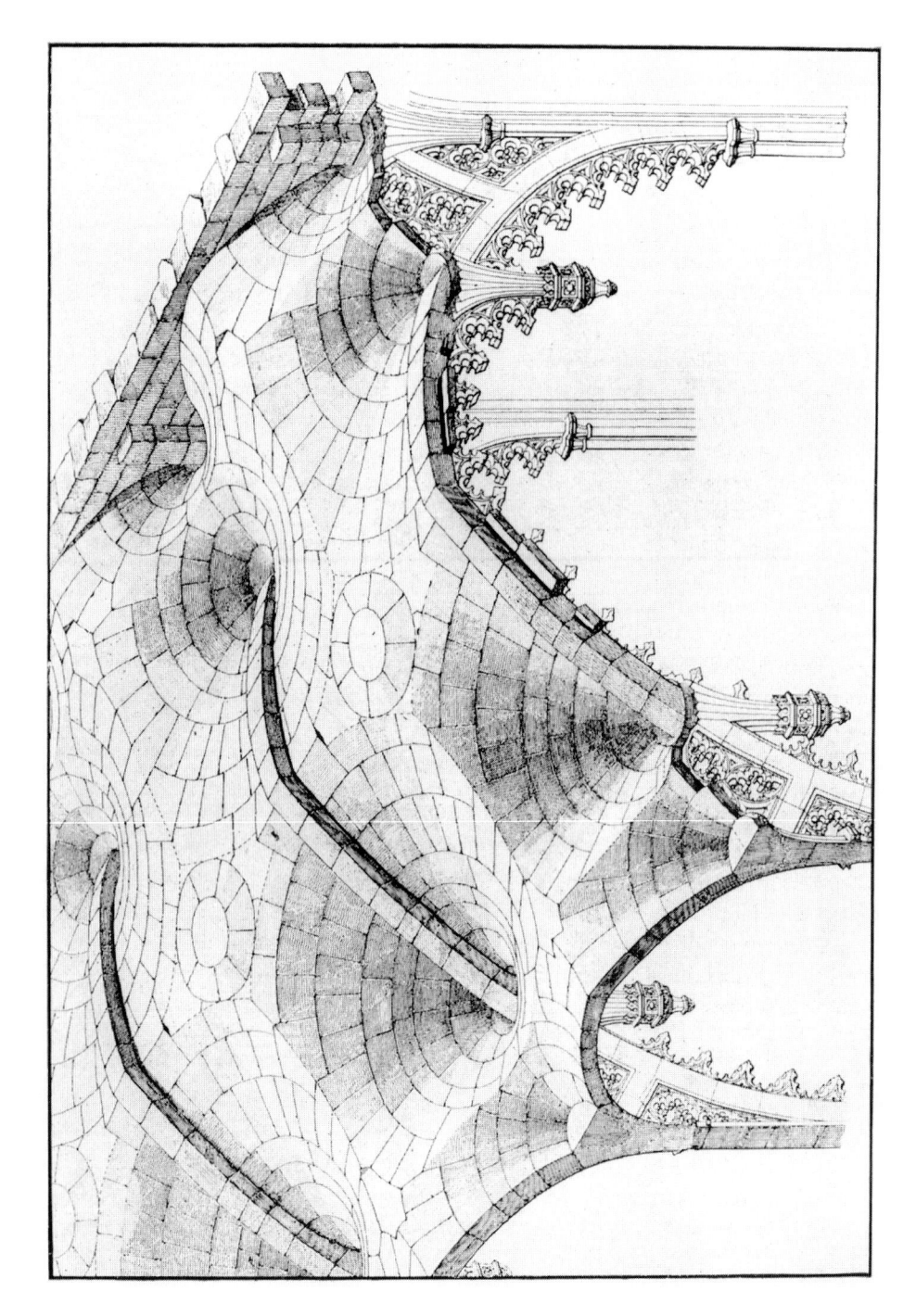

Fig. 4. Isometric view: the vault is constructed entirely from jointed masonry, rather than from ribs and panels. (From R. Willis, *Transactions of the Royal Institute of British Architects*, 1st ser. 2, 1837–42)

Introduction

TIM TATTON-BROWN and RICHARD MORTIMER

HENRY VII's Lady chapel at Westminster Abbey is surely one of the world's most famous buildings, and one of the most praised. As early as 1545 John Leland called it 'the wonder of the entire world', *miraculum orbis universali*.[1] In the seventeenth century Francis Bacon thought it 'one of the stateliest and daintiest monuments of Europe',[2] and in 1723 John Dart described it as a 'stately and surprizing structure'.[3] It is especially the vault which has been admired – in 1909 the architectural historian Francis Bond roundly declared it to be 'the most wonderful work of masonry ever put together by the hand of man'[4] – but the undulating glass screens that form the lower windows, and the remarkably complete array of original sculpture are also regularly singled out for praise.

Such an admired building has duly received its share of attention from historians and architectural writers. The complex history of Henry VII's foundation and the chapel's function as a burial place of royalty were discussed by the early writers on Westminster Abbey such as Dart and Widmore,[5] but it was not until the nineteenth century that the building itself began to be described and analysed in detail. The first to do so was John Britton, whose 'Essay towards the history and description of King Henry the Seventh's Chapel at Westminster' (1809) was accompanied by an excellent measured plan (Fig. 2) and some fine engravings, including elevations and drawings of the vault.[6] The large-scale restoration of 1809–22 was followed by Cottingham's two volumes of very detailed measured drawings of the chapel and its architecture,[7] but it was Robert Willis, in his brief discussion of the high vault in 1842[8] who first started to analyse a part of the building (Fig. 4). The below-floor archaeology, mainly

---

1 See Christopher Wilson, 'The designer of Henry VII's chapel, Westminster Abbey', in *Reign of Henry VII*, 133 n. 1 for the origin of this quotation.
2 Francis Bacon, *Henry VII*, quoted in Stanley, *Historical Memorials*, 145.
3 Dart i, 32.
4 F. Bond, *Westminster Abbey*, 1909, 134.
5 Dart i, 32–3; Richard Widmore, *An History of the Church of St Peter, Westminster, commonly called Westminster Abbey*, 1751, 119–22 – 'so fine a work, that authors both then, and since that time, seem to have contended who should praise it the most' (p. 119).
6 Britton ii, 9–51.
7 Cottingham.
8 R. Willis, 'On the construction of the vaults of the middle ages', *Transactions of the Royal Institute of British Architects* 1 part 2, 1842, 53–4.

of the burial vaults, was explored by Dean Stanley,[9] while the surviving statues were first looked at from an art-historical point of view by J.T. Micklethwaite in 1883.[10] Another of the Abbey surveyors of the fabric, W.R. Lethaby, discussed aspects of the architectural history and decoration (1906 and 1925), while in 1924 the Royal Commission on Historical Monuments published its full description and inventory of the building and its contents earlier than 1714.[11] Jocelyn Perkins's survey of the liturgical history of the chapel over 400 years, published in 1940, was the first attempt to study the use of the building and furnishings in their ecclesiastical context.[12] Meanwhile the evidence for the earlier thirteenth-century Lady chapel was studied by Westlake.[13] In 1975 Howard Colvin published a fine new history of the construction of the chapel and its surviving original contents, and a number of other papers on aspects of the chapel have been published in the last few decades.[14]

Despite this substantial literature, there remain aspects of the chapel's history and architecture that have not been studied at all, and others that have not been studied for a long while; a comprehensive new look at the building, its contents, its functions, and the purposes of its builders is now needed. The recent external restoration and internal cleaning provided a unique opportunity to study much of the stone structure, including the famous statuary and pendant vaults, at close quarters, and this book incorporates some of the results of that experience. In October 1995, when the works were completed, a seminar was held at the Society of Antiquaries of London, and some of the following essays were originally given as papers on that occasion.

We stress the fact that this building is the Abbey's Lady chapel. Henry VII's chapel was literally fitted over an existing building, and over an existing institution nearly three hundred years old. We begin with papers on the institutional background – the cult of the Virgin at Westminster Abbey, the financial aspect of the chapel and its endowment, its liturgy, the music to which the liturgy was set, and the musicians who sang it, and who continued to sing in Henry VII's chapel up to and after the Reformation. Henry VII physically replaced the old chapel and vastly increased its endowment and personnel so as to ensure his own perpetual memorial. His motives and developing intentions are the next focus, for which his will is essential evidence: we take the opportunity to publish Dr Condon's new edition of this document, the first since the eighteenth century. The founder's intentions were not carried out quite as planned, and the impact on the building of the complex history of its birth and development are next examined, by way of an enquiry into how the building actually functioned as a chapel.

The building itself and its contents are naturally the focus of the largest group of papers, beginning with the history of its construction, and going on to examine the

[9] Stanley, *Historical Memorials*, 499–526, Appendix, 'Account of the search for the grave of James I'.
[10] Micklethwaite, 'Imagery'.
[11] Lethaby, *Craftsmen* and *Re-examined*; *Inventory*.
[12] Perkins, *Worship and Ornaments* ii, 149–215.
[13] H.F. Westlake, 'Westminster Abbey: the Old Lady Chapel and its relation to the romanesque and gothic churches', *Archaeologia* 69, 1920, 31–46.
[14] Colvin, *HKW* iii, 210–22. More recent work includes H.J. Dow, *The Sculptural Decoration of Henry VII Chapel, Westminster Abbey*, Durham 1992; Richard Marks, 'The glazing of Henry VII's chapel, Westminster Abbey', *Reign of Henry VII*, 157–74; Christopher Wilson, 'The designer of Henry VII's chapel, Westminster Abbey', *ibid.*, 133–56.

external roof structure and the famous vault with the advantage of knowledge gained from the recent restoration. New information also contributes to fresh looks at the stalls and the sixteenth-century tombs and sculptures, which are among the great glories of the chapel and a large part of its raison d'être. The later sculpture is easily overlooked, despite the size of many of the pieces, but they have their own interest and complex restoration history.

Restorations of the chapel itself are the final focus. It is remarkable that so much has survived – in fact, unique in this country, and an exploration of attitudes to the chapel goes far to explain why this is so. The chronology and extent of earlier restorations are then traced, leading to an account of the most recent works by the Abbey's surveyor who directed them.

This book is published in the year of the 500th anniversary of the start of work on Henry VII's new Lady chapel. The building and its contents are as much admired as ever, and we hope to help satisfy readers' interests with what follows. While we have attempted to be as comprehensive as possible, we are aware that some aspects remain unexamined, and have no illusions that the last word will ever be said on this magnificent and complex creation. The present volume can perhaps be best described, following Britton, as 'essays towards a new history and description of the chapel'.[15]

---

[15] The editors would like to thank Christine Reynolds for much help with the illustrations, Marie-Louise Sharpin and Mandy Glass for help with computer literacy, and the contributors for their patience.

The Monks of Westminster and the Old Lady Chapel

BARBARA HARVEY

KING HENRY III, who was then a boy of thirteen, laid the foundation stone of the old Lady chapel of Westminster Abbey on 16 May 1220, the vigil of Pentecost and the day before his coronation in the abbey church.[1] Abbot William Humez (1214–22) and the monks of Westminster, who had embarked on the new work at their own expense, could ill afford such an ambitious undertaking. In their view, however, the chapel was a necessity if the worship of St Mary the Virgin, which had attained a place of central importance in their devotional life, was to have a worthy setting: the existing Lady altar in the abbey church no longer seemed adequate for this purpose. Yet an account of the old Lady chapel must begin with the old Lady altar and the Marian devotion at Westminster which brought both altar and chapel into existence. The subsequent loss of the iconography of the old abbey church, the church built by St Edward the Confessor, means that we depend entirely on written sources in this initial enquiry.

The Marian devotion and the old Lady altar

By 1220, the five major feasts of St Mary the Virgin were enshrined in the abbey's kalendar. In monastic worship, feasts were distinguished from ordinary, or ferial, days by additions to the Divine Office, of which the most onerous was the reading of

[1] Matthew Paris, *Chronica Majora*, ed. H.R. Luard, 7 vols., RS 1872–83, iii, 59; and for the building of the Lady chapel, see H.F. Westlake, 'Westminster Abbey: the old Lady chapel and its relation to the romanesque and gothic churches', *Archaeologia* 69, 1917–18, 31–46; Westlake i, 61–8; Colvin, *HKW* i, 131–3; P. Binski, *Westminster Abbey and the Plantagenets: Kingship and the Representation of Power, 1200–1400*, 1995, 10–13; for the old Abbey church see R.D.H. Gem, 'The romanesque rebuilding of Westminster Abbey', *Proceedings of the Battle Conference*, iii, ed. R. Allen Brown, 1980, 33–64, 203–7. I wish to thank the Dean and Chapter of Westminster for permission to use their muniments, and Dr Richard Mortimer, Keeper of the Muniments, and Miss Christine Reynolds, Assistant Keeper, for their unfailing help. I am also greatly indebted to Dr Roger Bowers, Mr Timothy Tatton-Brown, Dr Tony Trowles and Dr Christopher Wilson, each of whom read and commented on earlier versions of this chapter, to Professor Nicholas Vincent, for his generous help at the final stage, and to Professor Richard Pfaff for advice on liturgical points. The year of account, which occurs in this chapter, began and ended at Michaelmas. Thus, unless otherwise stated, 1388–9 began on 29 September 1388 and ended on 28 or 29 September 1389.

twelve lessons instead of the normal three at the night office.[2] Distinctions among feasts of twelve lessons, which were themselves very numerous, tended to vary with the monastery. At Westminster, and following a common practice, feasts of this kind were divided between those on which monks present in choir wore copes at high mass and those on which they wore albs. Eventually, the more important among the former were distinguished from the less important by the number of cantors assisting the precentor at the invitatory in the Divine Office: was the number seven, four, two, or one? This method of grading was evidently well established by the 1260s, when it is mentioned in the abbey's only surviving Customary: this was begun in 1266 and probably finished before 1270.[3] A small number of feasts in copes, and eventually ten, were given the status of so-called principal feasts and marked with every possible elaboration of office and liturgy: it was, for example, on these days that the precentor was assisted by seven other cantors. By the early thirteenth century, as we learn from a kalendar of this period, the Annunciation (25 March), Assumption (15 August), Nativity (8 September), and Conception (8 December) of St Mary the Virgin were observed as feasts in copes, and despite the silence of the kalendar on this point, the Assumption may already have attained the status of principal feast.[4] The Purification (2 February) was observed as a feast, although its grading at this time is uncertain.[5]

The feast of the Conception, which had been celebrated in Anglo-Saxon England, though perhaps not widely, was removed from the kalendars in some monasteries after the Norman Conquest, as its theological implications became for a time controversial. By 1130, however, as we learn from a letter of Osbert of Clare, it was again observed at Westminster.[6] The other feasts of the Virgin which have been mentioned had doubtless been observed here, with greater or less ceremony, throughout the history of St Edward the Confessor's foundation, and quite possibly by the monks of St Dunstan's foundation in the late tenth and early eleventh centuries; to our knowledge, they were observed in other Benedictine foundations of that early period.[7] We do not know when the monks of Westminster began to recite the Little Office of the Virgin or any part of it. By 1250, however, this was a common addition to the daily office in Benedictine houses. It was permissible to recite parts of it in private, and

---

[2] Now generally referred to as 'Matins', but formerly as 'Nocturns'. The hour prescribed in the Rule of St Benedict (cap. 8), was the eighth hour of the night in winter (about 2a.m.) but earlier in the summer. In the later middle ages, midnight was the common hour.

[3] *Customary* ii, 33, and for a refinement, *ibid.*, 29. For the date of this source, see n. 26 below. For the monastic grading of feasts, including the basic division into 'simple' and 'double', of which the distinctions mentioned in the text were refinements, see J. Harper, *The Forms and Orders of Western Liturgy from the Tenth to the Eighteenth Century*, Oxford 1991, 53–4, and J.B.L. Tolhurst, *The Monastic Breviary of Hyde Abbey, Winchester*, vi, Henry Bradshaw Society 80, 1942, 146–7.

[4] London, BL Royal MS 2 A. xxii, fos. 5–10; printed in *Missale* iii, 1385–96. The actual number assisting the precentor on feasts in copes is not indicated in this kalendar.

[5] E. Mason, ed., *Westminster Abbey Charters, 1066–1214*, London Record Society 25, 1988, no. 191; *Customary* ii, 92.

[6] *Letters of Osbert of Clare, Prior of Westminster*, ed. E.W. Williamson, Oxford 1929, no. 7. Osbert's letter can be dated 1128x30. For comment, see *ibid.*, 11–13, and E. Bishop, *Liturgica Historica*, Oxford 1918, 244–7. For the earlier history of this feast, see M. Clayton, *The Cult of the Virgin Mary in Anglo-Saxon England*, Cambridge 1990, 42–50, and for the hesitant acceptance in the twelfth century of the doctrine of the Immaculate Conception of the BVM, R.W. Southern, *Saint Anselm: a Portrait in a Landscape*, Cambridge 1990, 432–6.

[7] Clayton, *Cult of the Virgin*, 30–40, 50, 92–3.

Abbot Humez's monks may have finished their day, as their successors in the 1260s would finish theirs, with a private recitation of compline of the Virgin in the dormitory just before each monk got into bed.[8] They may also have found a place in their liturgy for the Marian antiphon *Salve Regina*, and thus prepared the way for its use later in the century as a votive antiphon sung in choir after compline of the day.[9] We can be confident that the monks of Westminster had long followed the common Benedictine practice of celebrating a votive mass of the Virgin on Saturdays.

In the course of the twelfth century, however, a number of Benedictine communities instituted a daily votive mass of the Virgin, and from an early date this seems to have been celebrated ceremonially, and not quickly and quietly, as in the case of a monk's private mass or even the morrow mass of the community. Inevitably, the new development made demands on the furnishing and fabric of the churches in question. On a feast day of the Virgin, the high mass, sung at the high altar, became a Mary mass. For a daily mass of this kind, a separate Lady altar was a necessity, and a Lady chapel to house it soon appeared desirable. By the early thirteenth century, the monks of Westminster may actually have possessed a Lady altar for a considerable period, for the benefit of monks who wished to say their private masses at such an altar, and to provide a focus for Marian devotion on the part of pilgrims and other visitors to their church. At least one episcopal indulgence now encouraged pilgrims to come to the abbey on the principal feasts of the Virgin, and residents of the growing town of Westminster may have needed no such incentive to come.[10] What was new in the years around 1200 was the flurry of activity then in evidence to build up an endowment for the Lady altar and so ensure the existence of an income to cover, in particular, the cost of candles.[11] This activity suggests that the daily votive mass of the Virgin may itself have been new at Westminster at this time.

The initiative in seeking an endowment for the Lady altar was taken by Br Robert de Molesham, who was at one time precentor and warden of the altar and retained his enthusiasm for this undertaking as prior (c.1191–1200+); and Molesham may also have been the prime mover in the decision to celebrate a Lady mass every day. His devotion to the Virgin was expressed – whether in his own lifetime or after his death is not recorded – in the designation of the 9th December, the day following the feast of

---

[8] *Customary* ii, 140; and for this office, see S.E. Roper, *Medieval English Benedictine Liturgy: Studies in the Formation, Structure and Content of the Monastic Votive Office, c.950–1540*, 1993, 81–4, and N. Morgan, 'Texts and images of Marian devotion in English twelfth-century monasticism and their influence on the secular church', in *Monasticism and Society in medieval Britain*, ed. B. Thompson, Stamford 1999, 124–5. For a convincingly cautious view of the possibility that Paris, BN MS lat. 10433, which contains the office and the *Salve Regina*, is a source for liturgical practice at Westminster c.1200, see C.M. Kauffmann, *Romanesque Manuscripts, 1066–1190*, 1975, no. 89.

[9] *Customary* ii, 201, where it is implied that the antiphon had previously been used at Westminster in a different way. See also Roper, *Liturgy*, 146–9, and n. 8 above.

[10] An indulgence granted by Walter of Coutances, archbishop of Rouen 1184x1207 (WD, fo. 390v).

[11] WAM 17375; Mason, *Charters*, nos. 327, 329, 346, 356 etc. For the expressed belief of the abbot of St Albans c.1225 that a daily sung mass of the BVM was normal in great churches, see *Gesta Abbatum Monasterii Sancti Albani*, ed. H.T. Riley, 3 vols., RS 1867–9, i, 284–5, cited in R. Bowers, 'The Lady Chapel and its musicians, 1210–1559', in *Winchester Cathedral: Nine Hundred Years, 1093–1993*, ed. J. Crook, Chichester 1993, 247–8. See also on the Lady mass, F.Ll. Harrison, *Music in Medieval Britain*, 4th edn, Buren 1980, 77–80. In this chapter, and in accordance with Harrison's terminology, 'Lady mass' indicates the daily votive mass of the Virgin, and 'Mary mass' the high mass on a Marian feast.

the Conception, as his own anniversary.[12] But the first explicit reference to a daily mass of the Virgin at Westminster occurs in the grant by Abbot Humez and the convent of Westminster of spiritual benefits to those who should contribute to the new work in the Lady chapel.[13]

Where, then, was the Lady altar, soon to be known as the 'old Lady altar', to distinguish it from the new altar in the Lady chapel? Since in a monastic church the position of an altar and the use made of it were intimately related features of its life, the question is of more than antiquarian interest. A miracle story preserved in a thirteenth-century collection contains the earliest surviving description of the location of the altar and the image of the Virgin and Child which was displayed there.[14] The mother of a blind child received a vision in which the Virgin sent her to the warden of the Lady altar with the instruction that he moisten the child's eyes with water that had been used to wash the feet of the image. The warden, an exceedingly devout monk named Stephen, obeyed, and, to the amazement of all who were present – a very large company, since the day was the feast of St Peter, to whom the abbey church was dedicated, and that of St Paul (29 June) – the child's sight was restored. The story probably relates to Stephen de London, who was proctor of the Lady altar in the early years of Henry III and is mentioned as precentor in 1233. The altar, as we are told, in this source, was on the north side of the church, and in 'a higher place'.[15]

Although this witness has not been mentioned in modern discussion of the site of the old Lady altar, it has been generally agreed for other reasons that the altar was situated on the north side of the abbey church. The exact site, however, has proved harder to determine.

H.F. Westlake, who brought to the discussion an intimate knowledge of the abbey's obedientiary records, identified the old Lady altar with the altar which is mentioned in the sacrist's accounts for 1363–5 and said variously in these sources to be at (*ad*) or outside (*extra*) the north door of the abbey church.[16] In this he differed from

---

[12] *Customary* ii, 92; and for Robert de Molesham, see also E.H. Pearce, *The Monks of Westminster*, Cambridge 1916, 46, and E. Mason, *Westminster Abbey and its People, c.1050–c.1216*, Woodbridge 1996, 92. Pearce dates Molesham's priorship by the presence of William Longchamp, bishop of Ely 1189–97, in the witness-list of one of his leases. However, since it appears that Molesham succeeded William Postard as prior, the *terminus a quo* is 9 Oct. 1191, the date of Postard's election to the abbacy; and if, as seems likely, he is the Prior 'R' of Mason, *Charters*, no. 345, his term extended into the abbacy of Ralph Arundel (1200x1214). Molesham retained the wardenship or proctorship of the Lady altar when he became prior, but quite possibly not as a permanency. See Mason, *Charters*, nos. 347 and 442, where the phrases *tunc custos* and *tunc precentor Westmonasterii et eiusdem altaris procurator*, which are used of him, may mean that he held the office at the time of the transactions referred to in the charters but not when the latter were executed.

[13] WAM LVIII (WD, fo. 507v).

[14] London, BL Royal MS 6 B. X, fos. 39–40r; H.L.D. Ward, *Catalogue of Romances in the Department of Manuscripts in the British Museum* ii, 1893, 645 (no. 6). The archaic reference to Westminster Abbey as a church belonging to the city of London and situated *in suburbio ab occidentali parte civitatis* suggests that this text is a layered one, drawing on earlier material. I owe my knowledge of it to Professor Vincent.

[15] *Est et altare ab aquilonali parte in editiore loco regalis basilice ad honorem et laudem nominis Dei titulo eiusdem regine celorum celebriter dedicatum, ubi utraque ymago et matris et filii iocundum spectantibus prebet intuitum* (BL Royal MS 6 B. X, fo. 39v). I am indebted to Professor Michael Winterbottom for advice on the meaning of this passage. For Stephen de London, see Pearce, *Monks*, 53. He occurs as precentor in 1233 (*CLR 1226–40*, 334).

[16] WAM 19621–3, 19626, 19629–30; Westlake i, 19–20, and ii, 344. Remarkably, the plan of the abbey church and monastery at the end of Westlake ii places the altar in the north nave.

W.R. Lethaby, who, following, as he believed, the Customary, located the altar in the nave, on the north side, and aligned it with the Holy Cross altar, the principal nave altar, and with the Holy Trinity altar on the south side. Since the Holy Cross altar could with confidence be placed some little distance west of the entrance to the choir, the traditional site for a nave altar with this dedication, Lethaby by implication placed the old Lady altar near the junction of Henry III's new work with the old nave.[17] The compiler of the Customary does in fact refer to the three altars in the same passage and notes the sacrist's obligation to provide a candle at each by day and night, but he does not say explicitly that the three were a group in any other sense. In the year after the publication of Westlake's volumes, the Royal Commission on Historical Monuments concurred, though silently in its map, in the nave hypothesis.[18]

The altar referred to in 1363–5 was in the chapel then existing outside the central portal of the north transept façade. This chapel is mentioned for the first time in 1354–5. It was demolished in the 1660s, but is shown in Wenceslas Hollar's etching of the north elevation of the church c.1654. It was a small but high structure and can be assigned to the mid-fourteenth century on stylistic grounds.[19] The chapel housed an image of the Virgin, and we can safely identify this with the image outside the north door referred to by the sacrist in 1338.[20] Evidently, at this earlier date the image was then in the north porch, which did not yet have the chapel as an addition to its central portal. It seems very likely that the image was placed here because there was already a Lady altar in the porch.

The two central doors of the north transept façade were the ceremonial entry into the church from the Palace of Westminster, and the gate situated some way beyond it, which also served as the principal entry to the sanctuary, was known to the monks as the 'king's gate'.[21] The door used by ordinary traffic was almost certainly the door adjoining the ceremonial entry on the west side. But ordinary traffic must always have been carefully regulated, since the north transept, which lay beyond, gave access to other parts of the church, and we should consider the building of the chapel outside the north transept façade with this in mind. The chapel was well placed to serve the needs of the growing number of residents in the sanctuary and promote the peace of the abbey itself by enabling them to hear a Lady mass without entering the church: it

---

[17] *Customary* ii, 45–6, Lethaby, *Craftsmen*, 26. In choosing the north side, however, Lethaby was influenced by later references to an altar by the north door. Westlake differed not only from Lethaby, but also from Robinson, who located the altar in an apse of the old abbey church, on the north side (J.A. Robinson, 'The church of Edward the Confessor at Westminster', *Archaeologia* 62, 1910–11, 89–90).

[18] *Inventory*, map at end.

[19] WAM 19623. Among many reproductions of the etching, Cocke, *900 Years*, illustration 16 (p. 34), and T. Tatton-Brown, 'Westminster Abbey: archaeological recording at the west end of the church', *Antiquaries Journal* 75, 1995, fig. 2 (p. 180) are cited here. For the chapel, see also Wilson, *Westminster Abbey*, 43, where the date c.1358–62 is suggested for its construction.

[20] WAM 19621.

[21] Colvin, *HKW* i, 137. For repairs to the paving *apud portam magnam sanctuarii vocatam le Kyngesgate* in 1441–2, see WAM 19685. The ordinary entry from the Palace was a postern gate near the monastic infirmary which gave access to a door in the south-east corner of the south transept of the abbey church. This was the *kyngesdore* referred to in the sacrist's account in 1442–3 and said to be on the east side of the church (WAM 19692). But the *porta regia* where the monks, wearing copes, greeted the king in Nov. 1387 may be identical with the central portals of the north transept façade. On this occasion, the way from the *porta regia* into the church was carpeted. *The Westminster Chronicle, 1381–94*, ed. L.C. Hector and B.F. Harvey, Oxford 1982, 208; cf. *ibid.*, 416.

was perhaps made chiefly for them. Indulgences in the name of many different bishops, ratified by Ralph de Stratford, bishop of London, on 19 September 1349, as the monastic community pulled itself together after the death of 50% or more of its members in the plague epidemic of that year, encouraged its use by a wider public at a calamitous moment.[22] The offerings recorded in the sacrist's accounts imply that for the next twenty or thirty years this chapel was a focus of popular devotion in the abbey and in this respect second only to the shrine of St Edward the Confessor.[23]

Since the old Lady altar came into existence before the beginning of Henry III's new work in the abbey church, it can only with great difficulty be identified with the altar in the chapel outside the north transept façade, for the façade belonged to the new work, and the association between altar and façade was very close. Equally, the fact that the chapel survived the completion of the new work means that we cannot safely locate it in any other part of this work. A position in the old nave, but near the junction of this with the new work, is the likely one: the altar was in fact on the north side of the nave. The reference in the miracle story to its location in 'a higher place' remains very puzzling but may mean that the altar itself was unusually high – a feature enabling as many people as possible among all those present on a busy day to see the image of the Virgin and Child which they had come to venerate.[24]

If, as suggested above, the miracle story relates to Stephen de London, who was proctor of the Lady altar in the early thirteenth century, it shows that the altar was indeed accessible to the laity at that date and that the monks, to whom we must attribute the story, wished to publicise its merits.[25] Yet with the exception of the story itself, which may have continued to circulate long after the event, the reference to the altar in the abbey's Customary is the latest to survive, and as we have seen, this source was probably completed before 1270.[26] The fate of the altar may have been decided by a very practical consideration. The new work in the nave was suspended on the king's death in 1272, by which date it extended to, and included, the fifth bay of the present church.[27] The new sacristy adjoining the north nave and built to the king's specifications, was approached by a door in this bay. It seems likely that the altar was found to be too near the inevitable daily traffic through this door for devotional use, and dismantled for this reason.

[22] WD, fo. 409r. The indulgences were evidently obtained by Br John Mordon, sacrist, who is described as *procurator* of the chapel. For the tradition that Abbot Simon de Bircheston and twenty-six monks died in the epidemic, see *The History of Westminster Abbey by John Flete*, ed. J. Armitage Robinson, Cambridge 1909, 128.

[23] WAM 19623–39 (providing totals for sixteen years). See also B. Nilson, *Cathedral Shrines of Medieval England*, Woodbridge 1998, 229, and below, 13.

[24] See n. 15 above.

[25] Above, 8.

[26] *Customary* ii, 45–6. The date for the inception of this work (1266) derives from the damaged colophon of the sole, fifteenth-century, manuscript (*ibid.*, vi). Decrees of Abbot Ware dated, respectively, 1270 and 1275, read like interpolations in the original text and thus tend to confirm a date for completion of the latter before 1270. References to Henry III in terms suggesting that he was deceased may also represent interpolations. *Ibid.*, 45, 92, 226–7. On the transitional nature of some of the arrangements recorded in the Customary, see Robinson, 'The church of Edward the Confessor', 89–90. For the story of the miraculous cure of the blind boy in an early-fifteenth-century manuscript, see M.R. James, *A Descriptive Catalogue of the Manuscripts of Sidney Sussex College, Cambridge*, Cambridge 1895, 86 (no. 38).

[27] Colvin, *HKW* i, 144, and fig. 22. The fifth bay lacked clerestory and vault (*ibid.*, 150). For the final stages of Henry III's new work, see Binski, *Westminster Abbey and the Plantagenets*, 29–33; and for the romanesque nave west of this point, Tatton-Brown, 'Archaeological recording', 174–5.

Long before these events, the monks of Westminster acquired relics of the Virgin, and their treatment of these sheds useful light on the role in Marian devotion which they envisaged, first for the old Lady altar, and subsequently for the old Lady chapel. Writing in the mid-fifteenth century, John Flete attributed all but one of the Virgin's relics to royal donors, among whom St Edward the Confessor, the monastery's second founder, was the most important and the most recent.[28] When Flete wrote, the distinction between relics and images was not sharply drawn; indeed, it had long been obscured by the practice of making images of relics which themselves became objects of veneration. The exceptional 'relic' mentioned in a previous sentence was in fact an ivory image of the Virgin, said to have been dear to St Thomas of Canterbury and to have been given by him to St Edward the Confessor. Flete intended his readers to understand that Thomas Becket gave the image to the shrine in the abbey church to which the Confessor's body was translated in 1163, two years after his canonisation. Becket was present at the translation and took away, as his perquisite, the stone which had covered Edward's tomb. But the failure of Richard of Cirencester, a monk of Westminster, to mention the gift in the account of the translation which he wrote c.1370, suggests that the tradition may have been of quite recent growth when Flete compiled his list of relics some fifty or sixty years later.[29]

The gifts attributed by Flete to the Confessor included milk and hair of the Virgin, the only corporeal relics in the list, and a number of secondary relics – that is, artefacts or objects owned by the Virgin or associated with her in other ways. In general, from the ninth century onwards, corporeal relics gained in esteem on the part of the faithful at the expense of the secondary kind. Even in the late middle ages, however, corporeal relics of the Virgin were still outnumbered by secondary relics. This being so, the preponderance of the latter kind in the collection at Westminster tells us little or nothing about the date at which this had been put together. Among the secondary relics at Westminster was the Virgin's girdle, believed to be efficacious for women in child-birth. This, as Flete tells us, was made by the Virgin with her own hands, used by her during her lifetime, and given by her to St Thomas the Apostle before her Assumption. It is scarcely necessary to say that late medieval testimony about the early history of any relic deserves a sceptical response. Moreover, girdles of the Virgin were common features of medieval relic collections. Yet the belief that the girdle had been so intimately associated with the Virgin may explain why, of all her relics at Westminster, it was the girdle that seems to have attracted the greatest attention: this was a secondary relic, but of no ordinary kind.[30]

In the thirteenth and fourteenth centuries, the monks' practice of lending this relic from time to time to women of high status, including at least two queens, testifies to the fame which it then enjoyed, and since great distances were sometimes involved, may have served to spread this more widely. In 1242, on the earliest recorded occa-

---

[28] *Flete*, 69–70.
[29] Richard of Cirencester, *Speculum Historiale de Gestis Regum Angliae*, ed. J.E.B. Mayor, 2 vols., RS 1863–9, ii, 325–6; and for the translation see F. Barlow, *Thomas Becket*, 1986, 95. Later relic lists mention two ivory images of the Virgin (WAM 9477–8, 9485; Westlake ii, 500).
[30] For niceties of distinction and the long-term growth in prestige of corporeal relics, see N. Hermann-Mascard, *Les Reliques des saints: formation coutumière d'un droit*, Paris 1975, 65–9, and for the many supposed girdles of the Virgin in existence by the early sixteenth century, E. Duffy, *The Stripping of the Altars: Traditional Religion in England c.1400–c.1580*, Yale 1992, 384.

sion of such a loan, the girdle was sent to Gascony for the benefit of Henry III's queen, Eleanor of Provence, who gave birth later in the year to their daughter Beatrice.[31] In the late thirteenth century, however, the monks, wishing, it appears, to promote this relic in a way not previously attempted, obtained a number of indulgences offering remission of penance to those who should come to the abbey church to venerate it. Other relics are also mentioned, and, taken together, the indulgences seem to show that the girdle belonged to a small group regarded by the monks as the most precious in their entire collection. Beside the girdle, this included the ring of St Edward the Confessor, the imprint of Christ's foot, relics of the Crucifixion, and, most precious of all, the relic of the Holy Blood of Christ given by Henry III in 1247.[32] The abbey's relics were normally kept at the shrine, although, with the sacrist's good will, they might be kept at any altar in the abbey church, including, of course, the high altar, and temporary display elsewhere, or by the community of monks in procession, was a regular feature of the liturgical round each year. Some of the outstanding group of relics to which the girdle belonged may have been among those displayed at the altar of the Holy Trinity and altar of St John on Good Friday and the feasts of St Peter and St Paul (29 June) and St Peter in Chains (1 August) in 1338, and very likely in other years too.[33] It seems possible, however, that this small group, or several items in it, normally occupied the place of honour on or very near the altar standing at the head of the shrine – the altar where Edward I, Queen Eleanor, and the Lord Edward venerated relics and made offerings in April 1290.[34] Whatever the exact location, later references to the shrine-keeper's 'quire' containing collects and Gospel readings for the girdle suggest that this relic was normally kept at the shrine.[35]

Many indulgences, promoting, as it was hoped, the cult of the Holy Blood at Westminster, achieved little or nothing in the end.[36] Were the monks perhaps more successful in the case of the girdle? At the end of the middle ages, this was one of a number of relics in the abbey or in other religious houses confiscated by Henry VIII's commissioners on the grounds that they were venerated by 'the people'.[37] In the fifteenth and early sixteenth centuries, the offerings at the shrine of St Edward which the abbey sacrist recorded in his accounts year by year were, in sum, small – too small for it to seem at all likely on the basis of this evidence that any relic kept there was

---

[31] *Customary* ii, xviii, 73. For the loan to Philippa of Hainault, Edward III's queen, in 1338 and again in 1354, see N. Vincent, *The Holy Blood: King Henry III and the Westminster Blood Relic*, Cambridge 2001, 169–70.

[32] WD, fos. 398–9. The bishop of Bethlehem's indulgence in 1292 omits St Edward's ring but includes the point of a nail used at the Crucifixion. For the estimate of eleven years as the total remission offered in indulgences relating to the Virgin's girdle see *Flete*, 74; and for the relic of the Holy Blood, Vincent, *Holy Blood*, 7–19, 31–81.

[33] WAM 19621.

[34] London, PRO, C 47/4/4, fo. 41v. For the suggestion that the relic of the Holy Blood was kept at the high altar, see Vincent, *Holy Blood*, 170–1. For the well recorded arrangement of relics at Durham cathedral priory, which provides a useful reminder that such arrangements were carefully planned, see *Liber de Reliquiis, 1383*, in *Extracts from the Account Rolls of the Abbey of Durham*, ed. J.T. Fowler, 3 vols., Surtees Society 99–100, 103, 1898–1901, ii, 425–40.

[35] WAM 9477–8; cited in Vincent, *Holy Blood*, 169 n.

[36] *Ibid.*, 133–6.

[37] C.A. Wriothesley, *A Chronicle of England during the Reigns of the Tudors, from AD 1485 to 1559*, ed. W.D. Hamilton, 2 vols., Camden n.s. 11, 20, 1875–7, i, 31.

now an object of devotion on a significant scale.[38] The sub-sacrists, however, who had special responsibility for the shrine, kept accounts that were distinct from those of the sacrist himself, but of these not a single example survives.[39] Quite how many visitors the shrine now attracted is at present an open question.

From an early date, images of the Virgin were probably more popular with pilgrims and devout visitors of all kinds to the abbey church than her relics in the strict sense. In common with the relics, however, they waxed and waned in popularity, and in the later middle ages they generally waned. Thus after the first heady years in the life of the chapel at the north door, when offerings at the image of the Virgin might, it appears, exceed £20 per annum – a sum suggesting that 5,000 people or more made offerings here in the course of the year in question – each decade witnessed a decline, until, at the end of the century, only a few shillings per annum were received.[40] In the very small chapel of Our Lady of the Pew, in the north ambulatory, which probably served as the chantry chapel of Mary of St-Pol, countess of Pembroke (d.1377), offerings declined in the course of the 1380s and 1390s from a few pounds to a few shillings per annum.[41] In the Lady chapel itself, the gift from Edith Twylly in the late fifteenth century of two kerchiefs for the image of the Virgin reminds us that offerings might be made in kind as well as cash. Edith was the wife of John Twylly, the chapel clerk and rent-collector.[42] But money offerings for all purposes in the chapel amounted to only a few shillings per annum at the end of the thirteenth century, when they are first recorded, and as far as we know they did not rise subsequently.[43] Here, perhaps, decline had already taken place from a much higher level attained when the chapel and the image were both new.

Nevertheless, the difference between the total sums offered in the Lady chapel in the late fourteenth century and those offered in the chapel at the north door c.1350–80 is striking and not robbed of its significance for this period by the possibility that the Lady chapel may have attracted relatively larger offerings in the past. As the monks of Westminster of this period intended, the image of the Virgin at the north door was an object of popular devotion, and so too was the hair shirt of St Thomas of

---

[38] Nilson, *Cathedral Shrines*, 229–31; Harvey, *Estates*, 44–5.

[39] B. Harvey, *The Obedientiaries of Westminster Abbey and their Financial Records, c.1275–1540*, Westminster Abbey Record Series 3, Woodbridge 2002, 170.

[40] WAM 19623, 19626–59; Nilson, *Cathedral Shrines*, 229. For the suggestion that, in the later middle ages, a normal offering at a shrine in England consisted of a sterling penny, see *ibid.*, 114–15. So-called great pennies were used for royal offerings at masses and redeemed by royal officials at the rate of 7d in the case of the king's offering and 5d in the case of the queen's; for examples, see London, PRO, E 101/396/2, fos. 29v–30, E 101/414/3, fo. 30r, and for the practice, N. Vincent, 'The pilgrimages of the Angevin kings of England 1154–1272', in *Pilgrimage: the English Experience from Becket to Bunyan*, ed. C. Morris and P. Roberts, Cambridge 2002, 30. For the oratory or chapel of St Mary de le Pew in or near the St Stephen's chapel in the Palace of Westminster and the image of the Virgin there, see *CPR 1367–70*, 325, and *CPR 1391–6*, 244; and for its elusive site, see, most recently, E. Howe, 'Divine kingship and dynastic display: the altar wall murals of St Stephen's chapel, Westminster', *Antiquaries Journal* 81, 2001, 261 and n., 264 and n.

[41] WAM 19639–59; Nilson, *Cathedral Shrines*, 229. Note, however, the short-lived but marked increase in offerings at this image c.1480.

[42] WAM 23258. For John Twylly and his wife, Edith, see below, 20–2; and for the several kinds of offering which relics in general attracted, Hermann-Mascard, *Les Reliques*, 275–9.

[43] WAM 23917ff.

Hereford which they also displayed there.[44] But clearly, in the Lady chapel, the popular cult of images and relics now had little place, if any: the image of the Virgin in this chapel and the relics that were, to our knowledge, kept there, were intended to enhance worship for which no popular dimension was envisaged. The practice of displaying the Virgin's girdle at the shrine in preference to the chapel points to the same conclusion. Though hesitantly, for the evidence is imperfect, we can say that the old Lady altar, which had the openness of a typical nave altar to the laity, was to this extent unlike the altar in the old Lady chapel.

The endowment and income of the old Lady chapel

The old Lady chapel, begun in 1220, was finished c.1245, towards the end of the abbacy of Richard de Berking (1222–46), who chose it as his place of burial.[45] At or very near the inception of the new work of the chapel, Abbot Humez and the convent of Westminster granted confraternity to all who should contribute to it, and a share in thirteen masses to be offered in the abbey church each week for the living and twenty to be offered each week for the dead. Of the thirteen, three were to be votive masses of the Holy Spirit, seven of the Virgin – these were evidently the daily masses of the Virgin introduced a generation earlier – and three of saints whose relics were in the abbey church.[46] Very few of the names of those who were inspired by this grant to contribute to the capital cost of building the chapel are recorded. We know only that without the assistance of Henry III the monks could not have completed the building when they did.[47]

Once in use, the chapel needed an income, to be provided ideally by an endowment, and here we are better informed. It was an easy matter to deflect the endowment of the old Lady altar to the use of the new one, but more was needed, and by gift and purchase the abbot and convent of Westminster slowly acquired an amount that seemed adequate at the time. The key figures in this enterprise were a succession of wardens of the chapel, each no less dedicated a fund-raiser, it appears, than Robert de Molesham. By the end of the thirteenth century, the chapel owned properties and rents in the town of Westminster and the City of London which yielded an income of c.£20 per annum.[48] Many obedientiaries at Westminster had more, and outside the cloister a landed income double this in amount was now considered necessary to maintain a knight – a member of the aristocracy of thirteenth-century England, if at

---

[44] WD, fo. 409r.
[45] WD, fo. 566v; *Flete*, 106.
[46] WAM LVIII (WD, fo. 507v).
[47] Colvin, *HKW* i, 131–2. See also N. Vincent, 'King Henry III and the Blessed Virgin Mary', forthcoming. (Professor Vincent has kindly allowed me to read this important essay in advance of publication.)
[48] Rosser, *Medieval Westminster*, 52; and for Westminster c.1300, *ibid.*, 19 (fig. 4). Most of the property in question was probably acquired before 1279, when the Statute of Mortmain placed an embargo on the acquisition of real property by religious which proved hard to evade for c.20 years; see S. Raban, *Mortmain Legislation and the English Church, 1299–1500*, Cambridge 1982, 189–90.

times only just a member – in the way of life appropriate to his degree.[49] With only £20 per annum, the warden of the chapel could afford no extravagance. But since his heaviest recurring outlay at this date was on wax, which could normally be purchased for, at most, 9d per lb, the sum was adequate for his needs.[50]

Much of the property comprised in the endowment was acquired, not by gift, but by purchase or exchange, a strategy enabling the warden to put together compact holdings with a potential for development, some of which were situated very near the abbey, in Long Ditch and Tothill. In the twelfth and thirteenth centuries, however, those who sold property to a monastery might be numbered among its benefactors and rewarded, as other benefactors were, with spiritual benefits. We are probably to understand in such cases that the vendors had agreed to part with property they would gladly have kept, or preferred the monastery to other purchasers offering a higher price. The case of Matilda Brand exemplifies the package of cash and prayers that the warden of the Lady chapel might offer for properties which he coveted. Matilda, who owned houses in the town of Westminster, was in debt to Jews and others at her death, which probably occurred before 1240. Br Ralph de Gloucester, when warden of the Lady chapel, acquired the houses from her executors in return for a lump sum of eleven marks (£7 6s 8d) and an undertaking to discharge Matilda's debts and meet the cost of daily masses for her soul for a period of two years.[51]

The warden's determination to acquire properties in Westminster and London ensured that townsmen and citizens of these places were the dominant groups among all those who gave or sold real property to the Lady chapel. Some were well-to-do servants of the Abbey or the Palace of Westminster, if not, like Odo the goldsmith, a servant of each in turn. Odo, from whom the warden of the Lady chapel twice purchased rents in Westminster, was reeve of the abbot's liberty in Westminster early in the thirteenth century and subsequently Henry III's clerk of works in the palace.[52] George de Samford, who obtained spiritual benefits for himself and his family in or shortly before 1305, in return for a grant to the chapel of land in Eye, in present-day Mayfair and Pimlico, was a royal serjeant-at-arms; so, too, was his uncle, Thomas de London, who was apparently buried in the chapel.[53] Others – as, for example, John, a tailor of Charing, from whom the warden acquired a rent of 4d per annum during the abbacy of Richard de Berking – may have been as ordinary as the references to them now suggest.[54] Invisible at this distance of time, but always to be imagined in the

---

[49] P. Coss, *The Knight in Medieval England, 1000–1400*, Stroud 1993, 103; M. Powicke, *Military Obligation in Medieval England*, Oxford 1962, 103–10.

[50] For purchases of wax @ 9d per lb in 1298–9 and 1299–1300, see WAM 23179. In 1299–1300, the price is described as high and apparently explained by a lack of confidence in the currency. For the price of wax more generally, see J.E. Thorold Rogers, *A History of Agriculture and Prices in England* i, Oxford 1866, 446, 454.

[51] WD, fo. 545. For the date of this transaction, see Rosser, *Medieval Westminster*, 336.

[52] Mason, *Charters*, nos. 425, 442. For Odo, see also Colvin, *HKW* i, 101–2, and Rosser, *Medieval Westminster*, 26, 328 and n.

[53] WD, fo. 563v. (I have assumed that the warden's undertaking to provide a slab for Thomas de London's place of burial shows that it was in fact in the Lady chapel.) For Thomas, see *CClR 1288–96*, 474. Another Thomas de London, mentioned in the king's service in the 1280s and 1290s, was a member of the Order of St Thomas of Acon.

[54] WD, fo. 513r.

background, are those who gave the money enabling the warden to build up his portfolio of properties.

Towards the end of the fourteenth century, however, the financial needs of the Lady chapel were transformed by the decision taken by the abbot and convent at this time to employ a professional cantor and professional singing-men for its choir. Walter Whitby, the first cantor, or master of the choir, was appointed in 1384–5, initially to train the singing-boys who already formed part of it. The first singing-men were appointed in 1393, and their number quickly rose from three to six.[55] By 1399, the total cost of the stipends, and, in most cases, livery of clothing to which the cantor and the six singing-men were entitled was c.£50 per annum. This sum amounted to between two and three per cent of the abbey's net annual income and represented a mushroom growth at a time when, in the short term, annual expenditure exceeded income by a significant margin.[56] Moreover, in 1397–8, the very year in which the number of singing-men was doubled, nine novices were received to profession – a number without known precedent in the fourteenth century, and quite possibly large for any year in the abbey's history.[57] In consequence, there were now nearly sixty monks in the community, although the norm for many years had been forty-eight.[58] Yet monks, like singing-men, could be maintained only if income for the purpose was available. The rise in the number of singing-men and the rise in the number of monks probably took place with the active encouragement of Richard II, the abbey's patron, and in the expectation that he would assist with the expenses so incurred. Richard in fact gave generously to the new work in the nave of the abbey church, which was taken in hand shortly before the beginning of his reign, and to the shrine of St Edward the Confessor; and to the abbey's existing store of fine vestments he added some of exceptional splendour and value.[59] But plans to augment the income of the abbey further for other purposes were cut short by his deposition in 1399: not even the anniversary which he had founded for himself and Anne of Bohemia six

---

[55] For Whitby, who is described as a clerk (*clericus*), see WAM 18999, 19871–5, 23187–8, Bowers, 'The Lady Chapel and its musicians', 248, and *idem*, 'To chorus from quartet: the performing resource for English church polyphony, c.1390–1559', in *English Choral Practice 1400–1650*, ed. J. Morehen, Cambridge 1995, 17. While at the abbey, Whitby was entitled to meals and for a time took these at the table of Richard Excestre, a former prior living in retirement in a private chamber (WAM 19371–2). At the time of his death in 1396–7, Excestre employed a *clericus commensalis*, and Whitby may have held such an appointment in this small household earlier.

[56] Stipends in 1399 amounted to £47 per annum, and the cost of the livery to which five of the singing-men were entitled may be estimated at c.£2 15s per annum. See WAM Reg. Bk i, fo. 86v, and for the cost of the various garments given as livery at Westminster in this period, WAM 19879–84. The stipend of £10 per annum of John Tyes, the cantor, probably included a payment in lieu of livery: cf. the livery @12s per annum received in the 1380s by Walter Whitby, the first cantor (WAM 19871–5). The cantor and singing-men received small gratuities on special occasions, but no account has been taken of these or of the cost of the recreation (i.e. light refreshments), which they also received on occasion, in estimating the total cost to the abbey of employing them. For the abbey's income c.1400 and the excess of expenditure over income, Harvey, *Obedientiaries*, xxvi, 132.

[57] WAM 23729–30. Cf. Pearce, *Monks*, 126–8, where eleven monks are listed for the first time in 1397–8. Of these, however, R. Shiplake and W. York probably entered in the previous year.

[58] B. Harvey, *Living and Dying in England, 1100–1540: the Monastic Experience*, Oxford 1993, 73.

[59] N. Saul, 'Richard II and Westminster Abbey', in *The Cloister and the World: Essays in Medieval History in Honour of Barbara Harvey*, ed. J. Blair and B. Golding, Oxford 1996, 200–4. See also Bowers, 'To chorus from quartet', 17–18.

years previously was yet properly endowed.[60] These circumstances, and the accession of Henry IV, a king whose attitude towards the abbey was distinctly cooler than that of his predecessor, made economies inevitable. These affected not only the Lady chapel choir, which was swiftly reduced in size, but also the number of monks in the community at Westminster, which was allowed to fall to the old norm of forty-eight or thereabouts.[61]

These developments lend an air of crisis to the history of the Lady chapel in the years around 1400. When, however, the abbot and convent of Westminster decided to employ a cantor and, a little later, singing-men, they evidently agreed that the cost of the arrangements they had in mind, which were on a more modest scale than those actually in place by 1399, would be a charge, not on the funds of the Lady chapel itself, but on conventual funds in a more general sense. It was to be shared among a number of obedientiaries, each of whom would contribute to a fund to be administered for this purpose by the precentor, the official responsible under the abbot for chant in the Lady chapel, as for that in the choir of the abbey church. Contributions to a fund of this kind appear in the accounts of the obedientiaries in question in the 1380s and 1390s.[62] The crisis in the abbey's fortunes in 1399 was real enough. But the new financial arrangements relating to the Lady chapel weathered the storm and were still in place a century later: indeed, they provide one of the threads of continuity between the life of the old chapel and that of the new Lady chapel built by Henry VII. As, *mutatis mutandis*, often happened in monastic administration, the contribution of each obedientiary participating in the scheme became standardised in amount. Thus in the fifteenth century, the cellarer and sacrist each contributed £5 6s 8d (eight marks) per annum and the monk-bailiff £2 13s 4d (four marks). The warden of the Lady chapel himself contributed £4 5s 4d per annum – a puzzling sum, larger than six marks but smaller than six-and-a half which it is now impossible to rationalise.[63] The precentor's fund from all sources amounted to c.£20 per annum.

In this late period, therefore, the endowments so laboriously acquired by Robert de Molesham and his successors provided only a proportion, though a substantial one, of the income needed to maintain the standard of worship to which the monks now aspired in their Lady chapel. In the late fifteenth century, near the end of the chapel's life, the warden's net income, which came almost entirely from rents, contributed c.70% of the total sum available in principle each year for all the needs of the chapel,

---

[60] G.O. Sayles, 'The deposition of Richard II: three Lancastrian narratives', *Bulletin of the Institute of Historical Research* 54, 1981, 267–8, translated in C. Given-Wilson, *Chronicles of the Revolution, 1397–1400*, Manchester 1993, 162–7; and see also *idem*, 'The *Manner of King Richard's Renunciation*: a "Lancastrian narrative"?', *EHR* 108, 1993, 365–70. For the endowments of the anniversary, see also Harvey, *Estates*, 397.
[61] Harvey, *Living and Dying*, 73; and for changes in the choir, see below, 43.
[62] e.g. WAM 18999, 19001–4 (almoner), 19372–7 (infirmarer), 19651–7 (sacrist), 23342–5 (warden of churches).
[63] For contributions in the period 1425–50, see WAM 18890, 18892–4 (cellarer), 23373–94 (warden of churches), 19414–17, 19419, 19421–7 (infirmarer), 23214–26 (warden of Lady chapel), 18630–55 (monk-bailiff), 19667–99 (sacrist); and in the period 1475–1500, WAM 18897–18907 (cellarer), 23412–22 (warden of churches), 19457–79 (infirmarer), 23250–7, 23259–60, 23262–9 (warden of Lady chapel), 18673–87 (monk-bailiff), 19723–32, 19734–55 (sacrist). (These sequences include many duplicate accounts.)

and other obedientiaries, through the medium of the precentor's fund, c.30%.[64] However, the warden's income in this period came in part from leasehold rents in the town of Westminster which had been acquired since 1450. Towards the middle of the fifteenth century, when his income was smaller but the contributions of other obedientiaries identical in amount to those recorded later, his contribution to the total funds available was proportionately smaller (c.60%) and theirs larger (c.40%).[65] In the late middle ages, the abbey's income was in general administered more flexibly and with less attention to departmental boundaries than previously, and appropriately so, since many of the latter had been drawn in the twelfth century. But nowhere was the new attitude more conspicuous than in the remodelling of the finances of the Lady chapel, especially in the testing years around 1400.

The warden and his assistants

As custodian of a cherished part of the monastery's devotional life and a sizeable portion of its urban properties, the warden of the Lady chapel was a figure of some importance to his fellow monks. But he was not the busiest of obedientiaries, and during the early years of the chapel's existence, as we learn from the abbey's Customary, it seemed possible to prescribe for him a daily routine closely resembling that of a claustral monk: he was to attend the morrow mass and high mass as well as the regular hours in the abbey church, and the daily chapter.[66] A tall order, we may think, despite the saving words 'when at home' in the prescription, for the warden had the care of the chapel, its altar and images, its books, candles, and vestments, as well as its property. But at this time, the Lady mass may have been the only regular observance in the chapel itself. The hour of this mass, at which the warden would normally have been present, though not necessarily as celebrant, is not recorded. If, however, there could be even an expectation, whether realised or not in practice, that he would attend the high mass in the abbey church each day, the Lady mass must have been sung either earlier or later in the morning. A fortuitous reference to the saying of private masses in the chapel after the Lady mass points to the earlier time as the correct one.[67] If so, the Lady mass was over before mid-morning. Nor were the long

---

[64] Actual sums 1475–1500: warden's net income, c.£50 per annum; contribution of other obedientiaries, c.£20 per annum. In practice the costs of the Lady chapel did not consume the entire £70 per annum in this period, and at the annual audit of obedientiary accounts part of the warden's income was sometimes made over to other obedientiaries in greater need.

[65] Actual sums 1425–50: warden's net income, c.£33 per annum; contribution of other obedientiaries, c.£20 per annum. For the warden's leasehold rents in Westminster after 1450, see Rosser, *Medieval Westminster*, 343 (App. IV, D). Prices, though subject to short-term fluctuations, remained relatively low for most of the fifteenth century (*Agrarian History of England and Wales* iii, ed. E. Miller, Cambridge 1991, 437 (fig. 5.2)). Thus the sums mentioned in the text represent actual changes in the warden's income.

[66] *Customary* ii, 93, 96. For the development of the Benedictine *horarium* down to the thirteenth century, see D. Knowles, *The Monastic Order in England*, 2nd edn, Cambridge 1963, 448–53, and *idem*, *The Religious Orders in England* i, Cambridge 1948, 280–1; and for the *horarium* at Westminster in the later middle ages, Harvey, *Living and Dying*, 154–9.

[67] For the purchase of two keys for the use of monks saying private masses after the Lady mass, see WAM 23226; these were probably keys to a double lock on the aumbry. At St Augustine's Abbey, Canterbury, the Lady mass was apparently celebrated before terce (*Customary* i, 412).

absences which now characterised the life of several other obedientiaries to be anticipated in the warden's case, since he could inspect nearly all the properties in his care in the space of a single day and without sleeping away from the monastery. Day by day, he had more time at his disposal than many other obedientiaries and may have devoted much of it to the Divine Office, the primary occupation of a claustral monk.

At the end of the thirteenth century, the warden was somewhat busier. The inventory made when Henry de la Rye succeeded Reginald de Hadham as a warden in 1304 lists among the chapel service-books two psalters, a diurnal, and a breviary said to be secured to a *pulpitum*; the latter was probably a lectern or reading-desk.[68] From these details we may infer that some hours of an Office were now recited in the chapel, although quite possibly these were only the day hours, and we do not know how many monks participated. Moreover, it is likely that the votive Lady antiphon, referred to c.1266 as a new departure in the monastery, and then sung in choir after compline of the day, was now sung in the chapel – its natural setting, as it may have been thought.[69] Nevertheless, when the warden sent a substitute to take his place on the rota of celebrants at high mass in the abbey church and on the rota of readers at meal-times in the refectory, as he did in 1298–9 and again the following year, he may have been influenced quite as much by a sense that this was the appropriate way for an obedientiary to behave as by his actual commitments in the Lady chapel, for these were still relatively light.[70]

In the later middle ages, a number of wardens were pluralists, combining their duties in the Lady chapel with duties in other departments. Among the busiest of these were perhaps Thomas Arundel and John Waterden, each of whom held the wardenship and precentorship concurrently in the late fifteenth century, and in Waterden's case for as long as four years (1485–9).[71] The precentor had oversight, not only of chant in the abbey church, but also of the monastery's writing office. The closing decades of the fifteenth century were a period of further innovation in music in the chapel, and in Waterden's case, if not in Arundel's, this circumstance may explain the decision to combine the two offices in a single person for the time being – in effect, to give the precentor control, under the abbot, of the affairs of the Lady chapel.[72]

Occasionally, however, the chapel received the undivided attention of a heavy-weight administrator, and most notably when Peter Combe was appointed warden. When his first term as warden began in 1395, Combe had already served as archdeacon, treasurer and monk-bailiff, warden of the monastery's appropriated

---

[68] WAM 23180; and for this inventory without the preamble and sections relating to goods in the warden's domestic quarters, Westlake ii, 502–3. For *pulpitum* as reading-desk in a late-fourteenth-century contract, see Salzman, *Building in England*, 449.

[69] Above, 7.

[70] WAM 23179. The bout of illness mentioned in these accounts. from which the warden recuperated at Paddington, probably explains the appointment of a subwarden in these years and the choice of Gilbert Ravel, a senior monk, for the post.

[71] Pearce, *Monks*, 147–8, 158. Exclusive of Arundel and Waterden, six of the thirty-eight wardens appointed in the period 1350–1500 (i.e. 16%) had to our knowledge served previously as precentor or would do so later. For lists of each official, see *ibid.*, 195–6, 203; each, but especially that relating to the precentor, has gaps.

[72] Below, 47–9.

churches, kitchener, warden of the new work, and warden of manors forming the endowment of Eleanor of Castile's anniversary at the abbey.[73] For the next three years, he served concurrently as warden of the Lady chapel and sacrist and thus had responsibility for every altar in the abbey church, as well as the shrine, the abbey's large collection of relics, and extensive properties in London and Westminster. During his second and third terms as warden (1401–3 and 1407–c.1411), he held no other office. Combe had been professed in the early 1360s and when appointed warden of the Lady chapel for the second time, in 1401, may have been about sixty years old and glad to shed some of his responsibilities. Even so, the fact that he was now allowed to devote himself exclusively to the duties of warden implies that these were exceptionally difficult years in the chapel – as, indeed, we know they were.[74]

The warden was assisted by a clerk (*clericus*), and the use of this word tells us that the servant in question was literate and had a certain proficiency in Latin: he had received a clerkly education.[75] By the thirteenth century, laymen sometimes possessed these qualifications without finding it necessary to seek even minor orders, much less any of the major ones, from a bishop in order to employ them gainfully. The status, in this sense, of the clerk of the Lady chapel is never in fact clarified until the late fifteenth century, when the post was held by one John Twylly. In a lease of property in the sanctuary which he and Edith, his wife, received from the warden of the chapel in 1490, Twylly is described as a yeoman of Westminster.[76] Clearly, he was a layman. But we can assume that the clerk named Richard who served in the new Lady chapel at Westminster in the second decade of the sixteenth century and is described as a chaplain (*capellanus*) was a priest, for this was the normal meaning of 'chaplain' at this time.[77] We should not assume that changes in the status of the clerk – changes represented in this case by a quantum leap from lay to priestly – were confined to the years around 1500: in some degree they may have been a feature of arrangements at an earlier date. It is, however, likely that the typical clerk of the Lady chapel belonged to the very large number of unbeneficed clergy who existed in late medieval England, many of whom managed to find a livelihood in religious houses, including Benedictine monasteries. Indeed, without them many of the latter would have found it difficult to celebrate all the chantry masses to which they were now committed.[78]

Whatever his ecclesiastical status, the clerk of the Lady chapel was both scribe and

---

[73] Pearce, *Monks*, 109.
[74] Above, 16–17.
[75] *Customary* ii, 91. On the meaning of *clericus* in twelfth- and thirteenth-century England, see M.T. Clanchy, *From Memory to Written Record: England, 1066–1307*, 2nd edn, 1993, 225–30.
[76] WAM Lease Bk 1, 46.
[77] WAM 23286–7. Richard is styled [rent-]collector here, but this official and the clerk of the chapel were now certainly one and the same. He may have been Twylly's immediate successor.
[78] For the employment of secular priests and other secular clergy at Westminster Abbey, see e.g. WAM 18878, 19356, 19621, and *Customary* ii, 180; and for the expectation that this practice would continue in the new Lady chapel, *CPL* xviii, nos. 115, 118, and below, 30. For the wider context, see C. Burgess, 'Strategies for eternity: perpetual chantry foundation in late medieval Bristol', in *Religious Belief and Ecclesiastical Careers in Late Medieval England*, ed. C. Harper-Bill, Woodbridge 1991, 23; H.M. Colvin, 'The origin of chantries', *Journal of Medieval History* 26, 2000, 166–73; R.N. Swanson, *Church and Society in Late Medieval England*, Oxford 1989, 46–50; and S. Townley, 'Unbeneficed clergy in the thirteenth century', in *Studies in Clergy and Ministry in Medieval England*, ed. D.M. Smith, Borthwick Studies in History 1, 1991, 55–7.

general factotum, and from the beginning he may have acted as rent-collector, although it is envisaged in the Customary that the warden will do this in person.[79]

Down to the mid-fourteenth century, the clerk's most important duty was attendance at the Lady mass, and, almost certainly, for most of this period, if not for longer, he served the mass on ferial days. His obligations as a server explain why he was provided with a surplice.[80] Inevitably, he was an important figure in security arrangements in the chapel, and a role of this kind is hinted at in the fifteenth century, when he is named as a participant in the formal delivery of the goods of the chapel to new wardens when they assumed office.[81] Ultimately, the warden was responsible for the goods, but no doubt in practice the clerk looked after them. The theft from the chapel of an alb, chasuble, stole, fan, corporal, and a corporal case, on the Friday before Palm Sunday 1487 suggests that this may normally have been a demanding part of his job.[82]

The clerk's wages of a half-penny a day (15s 2½d per annum) in the later thirteenth century, rising to a penny a day (£1 10s 5d per annum) in the mid-fourteenth, were probably given in lieu of *mensa* (cooked food as distinct from bread and ale): this was a common purpose of daily wages paid to household servants. If so, we can assume that he was now non-resident. His stipend, a payment in addition to his wages, rose from 6s 8d per annum at the end of the thirteenth century to £1 per annum c.1360, a substantial stipend for this period at Westminster.[83] His livery of clothing, first mentioned at the beginning of the fifteenth century, was for many years of the modest kind considered appropriate for a servant ranking as a groom in the monastic household, and it was valued at 6s 8d per annum.[84] These details, however, may give a misleading impression of the total earnings of the clerk of the Lady chapel, since his employment in one department of the monastery may well have smoothed the path to employment in others and to opportunities in the neighbourhood of the monastery. John Twylly, who has already been mentioned, held a so-called tenement consisting of ten cottages at Charing Cross, and two tenements in the sanctuary on lease from the warden of the Lady chapel, and owed the warden far more in rents than he received for his services as clerk. He probably derived a substan-

---

[79] *Customary* ii, 91.
[80] WAM 23180 (Westlake ii, 502); *Documents Illustrating the Activities of the General and Provincial Chapters of the English Black Monks, 1215–1540*, ed. W.A. Pantin, 3 vols., Camden 3rd ser., 45, 47, 54, 1931–7, i, 99. In 1373–4, a *puer* received a stipend of 6s 8d for lighting candles in the Lady chapel for a year, and this may be an early reference to the employment of boys from the almonry school at Westminster to serve the Lady mass (WAM 23186; and for the practice generally in Benedictine monasteries, see R. Bowers, 'The almonry schools of the English monasteries, c.1265–1540', in *Monasteries and Society in Medieval Britain*, 189–94, 208–9).
[81] WAM 9479, 23258, 23261. On each occasion, the clerk was John Twylly.
[82] WAM 23261.
[83] For the clerk's wages and stipend c.1300 to 1400, see WAM 23179–23198. The 'stipend' of £2 13s 4d per annum paid to John Chaundhors, clerk of the chapel, in 1373–4 may represent wages of £1 10s 5d per annum and an actual stipend of £1 3s 4d per annum, with a few pence deducted to make a round sum of four marks (WAM 23186). A stipend, in the sense of a cash payment in addition to wages, is not mentioned in the warden's accounts subsequently but may have been paid from another source. For the emoluments of the monastery's servants more generally, see Harvey, *Living and Dying*, 163–77.
[84] Livery @ 6s 8d per annum for the clerk is first mentioned in 1411–12 and @ 10s per annum for the first time in 1470–1 (WAM 23204, 23244).

tial income from sub-leasing and may have discharged some of his duties as clerk by deputy.[85]

For the succentor, as perhaps for the average clerk, duty in the Lady chapel represented only part of a normal day's work. This official, who was invariably a monk, was the precentor's deputy, and he shared in the precentor's responsibility for the regulation of chant in the abbey church. But he was especially charged with making up the rotas naming the monks who were to have individual parts in the daily Office and with the immediate care of the service-books – and of all books in the monastery, these received the hardest use.[86] We can assume that, in addition to the rotas needed by the monks in choir, the succentor also compiled those needed in the Lady chapel. These included one naming the six monks who were to attend the Lady masses – presumably for a week, the common period for which a liturgical duty of this kind was performed. It was particularly appropriate to entrust him with this task, since the monks on this rota evidently provided the choir for the period in question.[87] His reward was a stipend of 6s 8d per annum from Lady chapel funds. The continuance of this payment in the fifteenth century, and, indeed, the doubling of the amount in the 1450s, seem to show that there was still work for him to do and points to the continuing importance of the monks themselves in the music of the chapel in this late period.[88]

The environs and interior of the chapel

It will already be clear that the old Lady chapel needed large premises in addition to the chapel itself: indeed, it is hard to fit the entire complex into the space which seems to have been available. The domestic quarters, which are referred to variously in the mid-fifteenth century as office and hospice, may have been a separate structure from the chapel itself. If so, they were probably situated in the garden or at a greater distance from the Lady chapel, south of the monks' cemetery and in the vicinity of the infirmary chapel and cloister. If in the latter position, they were conveniently near the precentor's office, which was adjacent to the infirmary.[89] In the hall, the equipment inventoried in 1304 included baskets for distributing alms, as the warden was bound to do on the principal feasts of the Virgin and the anniversary of Robert Molesham. Much later, in the mid-fifteenth century, three so-called chambers are mentioned, and each of these may have been, not a single room, but a set or, at the very least, a room divided into cubicles. We can assume that the warden, if not a pluralist holding more than one office in the monastery and possessing better quarters elsewhere, occupied one of the chambers. The second and third may have existed for the occasional convenience of the cantor, the singing-men, or others involved in the

---

[85] WAM 23260–74. The tenements in the sanctuary were at the north door of the church. For Twylly, see above, 20, and for subleasing in the sanctuary, Rosser, *Medieval Westminster*, 77–80.
[86] *Customary* ii, 38. For a succentor's duties in the wider monastic scene, see Harrison, *Music in Medieval Britain*, 39.
[87] *Customary* ii, 91.
[88] WAM 23181–23229, and for the increase to 13s 4d per annum c.1458, see WAM 23230.
[89] Harvey, *Obedientiaries*, xxxiii.

life of the chapel but living at a distance from the monastery.[90] The existence of a larder, which was itself large enough to be described as a *domus*, implies that some meals were now served on the premises, and points to a degree of withdrawal on the part of the warden from the common life of the monastery greater than that found necessary in the first century of the chapel's history.[91] A red worsted hanging mentioned in 1447–8, when repairs were necessary, may have been one of a set imparting cheerfulness as well as warmth to his day-time quarters.[92]

If the domestic quarters were free standing, the vestry must have given immediate access to the chapel, perhaps on the south-west side. This room possessed a chest, where 'evidences' – that is, charters and other kinds of deeds – and precious objects were kept: this was made the more secure in 1489–90 by reinforcing the bottom and fitting two new locks. The register of evidences or deeds made in 1398–9, the first of its kind, as we are told, that the chapel ever possessed, was probably kept here.[93] The aumbry, where sacred vessels were kept, was situated in the inner vestry, and this, like the aumbry itself, was kept under lock and key.[94] When the goods of the Lady chapel were inventoried in the late fifteenth century, the chapel's service-books were listed among the sacred vessels – the prick-song book, for polyphony, and quires of plainsong among the basins and the candlesticks.[95] This suggests that, in accordance with common practice elsewhere, the books were kept with the vessels in the aumbry. In winter, a fire was lit in the vestry fireplace, so that monks celebrating mass could warm their hands.[96] The presence of a weight and tripod for candle-making among the utensils in the warden's hall in 1304 suggests that in this period the chandler employed by the warden did his dangerous work here or nearby.[97] But plenty of storage space must have existed in the vestry for the candles themselves, and much more was needed for vestments, altar furnishings, and the like.

On entering the chapel in any period at a time of day when all the candles were lit, even a regular visitor may have been arrested for a moment by the brilliance of the spectacle, for the interior was, in Westlake's words, 'a blaze of light and colour'.[98] It was also impressive in scale, for the length of the chapel was c.75x100ft and the internal width 28ft (Fig. 5). Its height was not that of the original design, but that to which it had been raised in 1256, so that the chapel might be integrated into Henry III's new work in the abbey church. In volume, the chapel probably resembled the contemporary Lady chapel at St George's, Windsor, which still survives, together with

---

[90] For the hall and the distribution of alms, see WAM 23180 and *Customary* ii, 92; for the chambers, WAM 23225; for *officium* and *hospicium*, WAM 23226, 23232. In 1398–9, the warden purchased boards and nails for a bed for John [Tyes], the cantor, when he should sleep on chapel premises (*pro lecto domini Johannis cantoris infra capella iacentis*) (WAM 23196).

[91] WAM 23225; and see above, 18–19.

[92] *In emendacione de le hangyng de rubeo wursted infra officium viijd.* (WAM 23224).

[93] For the chest, see WAM 23262, and for the register, for which ten skins of parchment were purchased, WAM 23196. One of the locks for the chest was a so-called hanging-lock.

[94] For the purchase of keys for each in 1489–90, see WAM 23262.

[95] WAM 23258, 23261.

[96] See e.g. WAM 23196, and for the fire-place (*caminum*), for which bellows (*j. sufflator*) were purchased in 1400–1, WAM 23198.

[97] WAM 23180; and for a guide to the under-explored process of candle-making, see C. Furness, *How to Make Beeswax Candles* (British Bee Publications, Geddington, n.d.).

[98] Westlake ii, 347 (a description relating to the chapel in the fourteenth century).

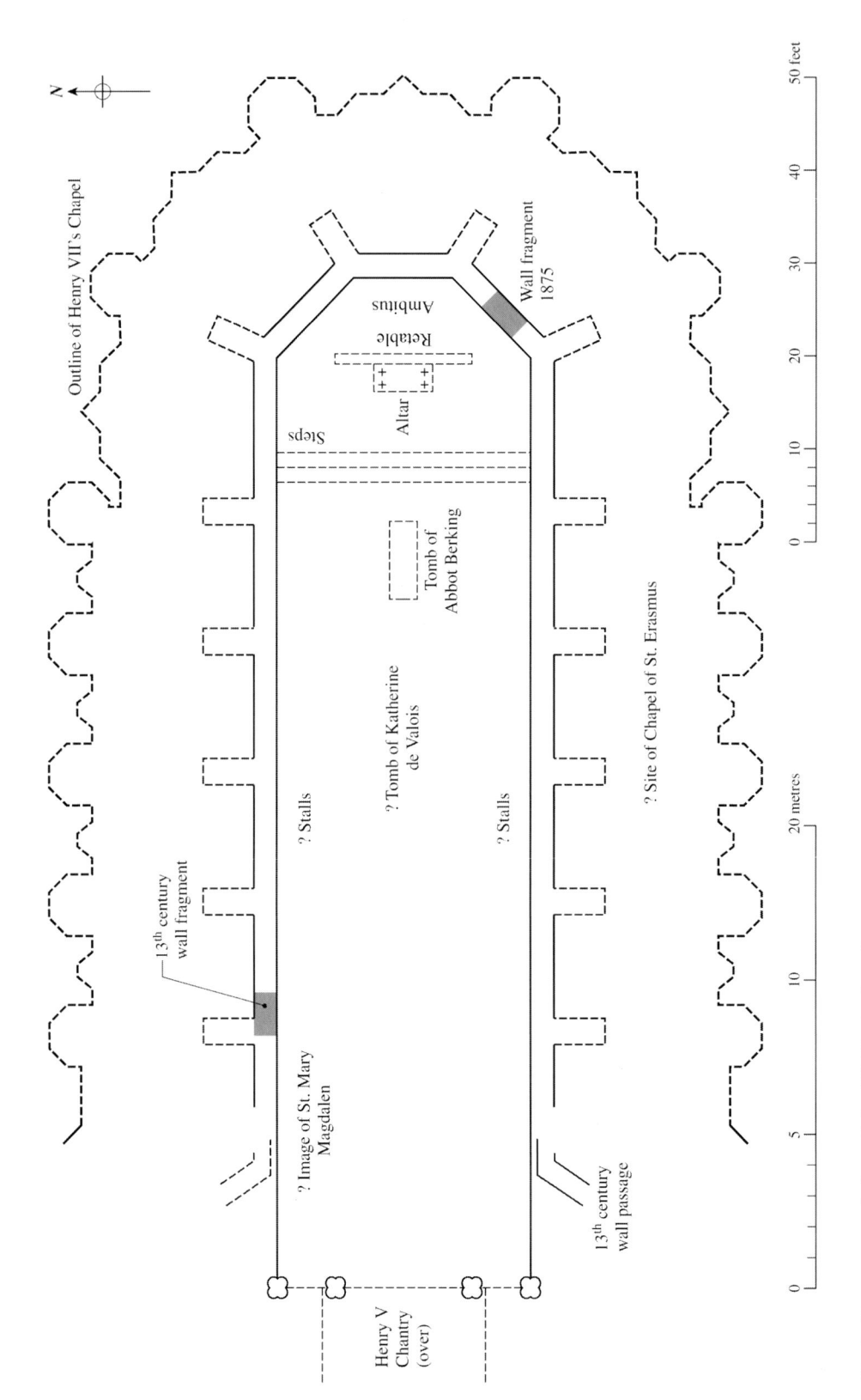

Fig. 5. Reconstructed plan of the Old Lady chapel.

a thirteenth-century vestibule (Fig. 10).[99] The warden's earliest surviving accounts and the inventory made in 1304, eked out by the earlier Customary, enable us to form an impression of the interior at the end of the thirteenth century.[100] The altar stood clear of the east end of the chapel, from which it was separated by an *ambitus*, or passage. On either side of it were identical columns, each having at the top an angel bearing a candle in its hands. The curtains at each side were of embroidered silk. A beam, placed above and in front of the altar and running the width of the chapel, carried twenty candles, each weighing five pounds. A hanging lamp, the successor to that placed at the old Lady altar for which the sacrist had been responsible, burnt by day and by night.[101] The so-called frontal, made to hang before the panel which was itself before the altar, and one of the altar cloths were of *pannum de aresto*, an oriental fabric. The altar, as the inventory seems to show, had a retable and this consisted of more than one panel; these were probably the two *tabule depicte* costing £80 and given by Henry III in 1258. Two cloths existed for these: one, striped or panelled like the frontal, was made of a fabric which is not specified; the other, probably for Lent, was of linen.[102] At the Lady mass on ferial days, the celebrant apparently wore a white chasuble or a red one, but we are not told on what grounds one might be preferred to the other on the day in question. The so-called principal chasubles – by which we should probably understand those worn on Sundays and on the Virgin's principal feasts – were decorated with, respectively birds and fish, and a tunic and dalmatic decorated with dragons and birds may have been reserved for these days. Making a rare reference to the materials of which vestments were made, the inventory records the fact that one of the 'principal' albs was of silk.

In a tabernacle above and behind the retable was the feature to which it was intended that every eye should travel: an image of the Virgin and Child, the Virgin in a silk gown and wearing brooches and rings, and both Virgin and Child wearing silver-gilt crowns. The *ambitus* separating the altar from the east end of the chapel was lit by fifty candles. A late reference (1369–70) to a window evidently at the east end as a window 'behind' the image perhaps implies that the latter was quite near the window in question, and if so the *ambitus* may have been on a modest scale.[103] If, however, the chapel's reliquaries were kept behind the altar – and this is their likely position – the *ambitus* gave access to them and was important for that reason among others.[104] At the foot of Berking's tomb, which was raised and before the altar, stood two candelabra. A painted door gave access to the garden, known as 'St Mary's garden'; door and garden were probably on the south side of the chapel. More

[99] I am indebted to Mr Tatton-Brown for the measurements given in the text and for the analogy with the Lady chapel at Windsor.
[100] WAM 23179, 23180 (Westlake ii, 502–3); *Customary* ii, 91–3.
[101] The candles were apparently on a lesser beam which was itself on the main beam (WAM 23179r; and for the lamp at the old Lady altar, see above, 9).
[102] . . . *unum pannum stragulatum et alium pannum lineum ad cooperiend' superiores tabulas altaris sub pedibus ymaginis beate Marie* (WAM 23180; Westlake ii, 502). For the *tabule depicte*, costing 120 marks (£80) and given by Henry III in 1258, see *CLR 1251–60*, 424; *CPR 1247–58*, 613. See also Binski, *Westminster Abbey and the Plantagenets*, 153; and for altars and retables in this period, Bishop, *Liturgica Historica*, 30.
[103] *In emendacione unius fenestri retro dictam ymaginem* [sc. *beate Marie*], *ut in ferramento, vitro et opere, xxxiiijs. viijd.* (WAM 23185).
[104] For the reliquaries, see WAM 23180 (Westlake ii, 502), where two wooden *tabule* and two small *loculi*, each of the four containing relics, are listed.

conspicuous, perhaps, were the two organs, one at the sanctuary steps, the other in a raised position, on or against a wall of the chapel, and possibly in a loft.[105] Yet neither instrument need have been large. It is likely, too, that a lectern, which would have been needed for readings at the Lady mass, stood at the sanctuary steps on the north side. But the lectern to which a breviary was attached was probably in the choir itself.

All this the visitor saw on entering the chapel at the end of the thirteenth century. Two centuries later, towards the end of the chapel's life, the spectacle was in many respects different, although the differences relate more to furnishings and vestments than to the fabric. On the south side, some light may have been lost through the construction of the chapel of St Erasmus. This chapel, the gift of Elizabeth Woodville, Edward IV's queen, though apparently not in the Lady chapel, was adjacent to it and may have given rise to the pentice (*penteys*) repaired at the warden's expense in 1498–9.[106] In the Lady chapel, altar furnishings, and vestments were now typically of damask or baldachin, and the inventories of this period convey a stronger sense than existed previously that certain colours were appropriate to certain days and seasons. Thus some at least of the 'cotidian' vestments used on ferial days were green, and on these days the image of the Virgin was apparently dressed in a mantle of green sarsenet.[107] Moreover, the chapel now possessed a complete set of black vestments, the gift of Piers Beawpee. Piers, who may have had connections with the Palace of Westminster and resided in the precinct, no doubt intended that his gift should be used at funerals and anniversaries, and perhaps initially at his own.[108] Before the altar, instead of Richard de Berking's tomb, there was now a level (*planum*) marble slab, probably with a brass for the inscription which is recorded by John Flete. The tomb had been levelled in 1397–8, when the warden paid £5 for the new slab, and the date is sufficiently near the arrival of singing-men in the chapel for a connection between the two events to seem likely. We are never told where the singing-men were seated or where the lectern, at which they sometimes sang, was placed. If, however, they and monks participating in the chant in this period were normally stationed at the sides of the chapel and the cantor in the middle – and this is the likely arrangement – the cantor may have found the tomb in its existing form an inconvenience when he attempted to rule the choir.[109] Forty years later, some of the advan-

---

[105] ... *unum par organorum inferius super gradum; aliud par maiorum organorum superius in muro* (WAM 23180; cf. Westlake ii, 502). One of the organs had been removed by 1363–4, when an enclosure (*clausura*) was made on the site. The parclose made near (*prope*) the altar in 1369–70 at a cost of £3 12s 8d may have replaced the earlier enclosure; if so, the organ in question was that at the sanctuary steps. See WAM 23184–5. For the door into the curtilage or garden of the Lady chapel, see WAM 23179.

[106] WAM 23268. For the purchase of 21,000 bricks to make a wall around this chapel, see WAM Muniment Book i (Liber Niger), fo. 93r, and for the short life of the chapel, Westlake ii, 350–1.

[107] For the vestments and other furnishings of this period, see the inventories made in 1483, 1485, and 1489 (WAM 9479, 23258, 23261), and for the growth of conventions relating to the seasonal use of liturgical colours in the late middle ages but continued absence of uniformity, W. St J. Hope and E.G.C. Atchley, *English Liturgical Colours*, 1918, 17–22.

[108] Piers was probably of the same family as Edward Beaupie, marshal of the king's hall and parishioner of St Margaret's church, Westminster, for whom see F. Kisby, 'Courtiers in the community: the musicians of the royal household chapel in early Tudor Westminster', in *Reign of Henry VII*, 241. Cf. the gift of vestments as a feature of chantry foundations in parish churches (C. Burgess, ' "For the increase of Divine Service": chantries in the parish in late medieval Bristol', *JEH* 26, 1985, 61–4).

[109] For the new slab, see WAM 23195; for the inscription and an unfavourable view of the destruction of

tages gained by the levelling of Berking's tomb were probably lost by the erection of that of Katherine of Valois, who was buried in the chapel in 1437, for the tomb-lists on which we rely at this point agree in placing her tomb in the middle of the chapel. Berking's tomb, as we learn from John Flete, had been of marble and finely ornamented. Katherine's, by contrast, was unimpressive: if it were to be moved, it was said when a burial place for her son, Henry VI, was under consideration, it might be 'more honorable apparellyd' in its new place.[110]

Less conspicuous, even so, in the general aspect of the chapel than the tomb of Katherine of Valois, but of greater significance in its life, was the image of St Mary Magdalen, symbol of penitence, which had been placed here in the 1420s. An existing image of this saint at the foot of Simon Langham's tomb in the chapel of St Benedict marked the fact that Langham died on her feast day (22 July), in 1376. The decision, some fifty years later, to associate another with worship in the Lady Chapel suggests that the monastic community itself was now caught up in devotion to St Mary Magdalen with an intensity not previously experienced. It is possible that there was now a side altar dedicated to this saint, and such a feature could explain an otherwise puzzling convention which the warden now followed in his accounts. From this time onwards, when recording his expenditure on oil each year, he apparently distinguished that used in the lamp above the image of St Mary Magdalen from that used in the lamp 'in the chapel', the latter being the lamp above the altar: to him the image of the Magdalen was not quite 'in the chapel'.[111]

If the fittings and furnishings of the chapel had changed since 1300, so had the environment, for in the intervening period the monks of Westminster had permitted, and themselves participated in, the development of the abbey sanctuary as an urban site, crowded with shops and tradesmen's premises of every kind. Now, even the Lady chapel garden, on the south side of the chapel, and looking towards the private cemetery of the monks, was to some extent a built-up area. The tenement leased to Geoffrey Chaucer shortly before his death in 1400 was in the Lady chapel garden.[112] The town of Westminster may have been a little less populous in 1500 than it had been in 1300, but the sanctuary was much more so.

---

the former tomb, *Flete*, 106; for the singing-men's lectern (*le deske*), which was repaired in 1489–90, WAM 23262; and for choir seating in collegiate and monastic churches, Harper, *Western Liturgy*, 36–8.

[110] WAM 6389**, cited in Westlake ii, 358; and for the tomb-lists, Harvey, *Estates*, 366–9.

[111] For the first reference to the new image, see WAM 23214; for the representation of St Mary Magdalen at Langham's tomb, Westlake i, 125; and for the many-faceted devotion to this saint in the middle ages, G. Constable, *Three Studies in Medieval Religious and Social Thought: the Interpretation of Mary and Martha: the Ideal of the Imitation of Christ: the Orders of Society*, Cambridge 1995, 72–86, 128–9. The so-called 'chapel of St Mary [the Virgin] and St Mary Magdalen' referred to in and after 1506 was probably a chapel elsewhere in the abbey church in which the images of these saints were placed at a certain juncture during the building of the new Lady chapel (WAM 23273–23315). In the event, the temporary lodging apparently became the permanent home for both images.

[112] WAM LVII; and on the building of houses and shops in the sanctuary in the fourteenth century, and the demographic background, see Rosser, *Medieval Westminster*, 68–9, 155–8, 167–76.

Worship in the old Lady chapel

Nearly everything mentioned in this account of the old Lady chapel existed primarily for the sake of the daily Lady mass and the celebration of the Virgin's feasts. Even the obtrusive tombs had been placed in the chapel at the request of those most intimately concerned because it was the centre of the Marian devotion in the monastery; and the image of St Mary Magdalen, the conspicuous exception to the concentration of attention on the Virgin, was so placed that it could be regarded as not quite 'in the chapel'. To the five feasts that were already celebrated when the abbey possessed a Lady altar but not a Lady chapel, two were later added: the Oblation (21 November) apparently in the 1370s or 1380s, and the Visitation (2 July) in the 1440s, an early date for this feast in England.[113] On feasts of the Virgin, special altar furnishings, vestments, and sacred vessels were used, and new candles lit; and if the prescribed custom was observed, the celebrant at the Lady mass was, not the warden himself or a deputy named in all probability on one of the succentor's rotas, as on other days, but one of the *custodes ordinis* – that is, one of the senior monks who shared in the disciplinary functions of the prior.[114] Except in number, the feasts of the Virgin were the equivalent in the chapel of the ten principal feasts observed in choir. In the late fifteenth century, the use of torches, the largest candles in the chandler's repertory, on the feast of Corpus Christi, and the practice of decorating them with waxen flowers, which is first mentioned in 1489–90, suggest that this feast was now accorded the same status.[115]

The decision to build a Lady chapel, and the development there of a distinctive style of liturgy, enriched by the participation of a professional cantor and singing-men, and, at times, singing-boys, reflect the vitality of Marian devotion at Westminster in the later middle ages and the monks' determination that this should be articulated with the utmost dignity and beauty. Paradoxically, these things would not have been possible, and similar developments would not have taken place in a considerable number of other Benedictine houses, had not overall monastic observance itself been in decline. By the thirteenth century, the common life which lay at the heart of Benedictine observance – a life in which monks prayed together, ate together in one refectory, and as far as possible, slept in the same dormitory – was fast shrinking into a way of life for the monks who were not too busy, too distinguished, or too senior to be held to its requirements, and not even this observant minority took all meals in common.[116] Lady chapels, with their autonomous liturgies, performed with the assistance of a rota of monks who could scarcely have participated unless relieved

---

[113] Recreation for monks on the feast of the Oblation is first mentioned in the warden's accounts in 1387, but no account survives for the period 1374–87. The Visitation is first mentioned in 1448, but after a gap in accounts covering the relevant part of the year since 1440. See WAM 23187, 23224; and for the new feasts, R.W. Pfaff, *New Liturgical Feasts in Later Medieval England*, Oxford 1970, 47, 107.

[114] *Customary*, ii, 91.

[115] WAM 23262ff. The practice was continued in the new Lady chapel where, in 1534–5, the flowers are identified as roses (WAM 23314).

[116] For the norms of monastic life down to c.1300, see J. Burton, *Monastic and Religious Orders in Britain, 1000–1300*, Cambridge 1994, 159–86; and for some of the irregularities that won widespread acceptance in the thirteenth century, Knowles, *Religious Orders* i, 280–5, 287–9, and J.R.H. Moorman, *Church Life in England in the Thirteenth Century*, Cambridge 1946, 334–49.

of some part of the normal obligations of claustral monks, fitted easily into this development which, indeed, they did something to promote.

But who beside the warden and his assistants, the monks on the rota for the week, and, in due course, the singing-men and singing-boys frequented the old Lady chapel at Westminster during the two and a half centuries of its existence? The chapel replaced the old Lady altar in the nave as the principal focus of Marian devotion in the abbey and may at first have possessed some of the accessibility of the latter to the laity and others not of the monastic household: to pilgrims, sightseers, and local residents. Indeed, the promise of spiritual benefits made by Abbot Humez and his monks to those who should contribute to the new work of the chapel implies a willingness to allow donors to see what their gifts had enabled the monks to build.[117] Yet in the longer term, the monks did little to promote a wider interest in the chapel. The indulgences encouraging pilgrims and visitors of any kind to attend mass in the Lady chapel which many bishops granted in or about 1344 were probably obtained on the initiative and at the expense of a single monk. He was Philip de Brightwell, for whom and for whose parents, William and Agnes, prayers were solicited.[118]

For most of its history the old Lady chapel was essentially a private chapel – private, that is, to an extent that could never be true of the old Lady altar in the nave of the abbey church, the area traditionally open to the laity. This status was perfectly consistent with use of the chapel for funerals and anniversaries and other occasional services, and with the admission of favoured individuals to its ordinary worship. William Hateclyff (d.1480), Edward IV's secretary, who lived in the sanctuary and asked in his will for burial in the chapel may have known it well as a place of worship.[119] His request is one of many intimations we have of the close association existing between the chapel and the Palace of Westminster. It is possible, too, that Robert Drope (d.1485), who gave the chapel some fine vestments and an altar cloth with frontal was a familiar figure in the chapel. Drope was a London draper and one of the creditors of the feckless Abbot Norwich at the time of the latter's resignation in 1467. He and Alice, his wife, though parishioners of St Michael's, Cornhill, where he was buried, were for many years corrodians of the Abbey and held a tenement at the north door of the abbey church on lease.[120] But with rare exceptions, of which the

---

[117] Above, 14.
[118] WD, fo. 407v. Note, however, that the list of indulgences in this source is incomplete (Vincent, *Holy Blood*, 133, 160 n.). For offerings in the Lady chapel, see above, 13, and for the chronology of indulgences in England into which any particular examples must now be fitted, N. Vincent, 'Some pardoners' tales: the earliest English indulgences', *TRHS* 12, 2002, 23–58.
[119] A.B. Emden, *A Biographical Register of the University of Cambridge to 1500*, Cambridge 1963, 292–3; and for Hateclyff's supposed burial on the right side of the altar in the chapel, see the tomb-list in London, BL Egerton MS 2642, fo. 323r. However, other lists do not mention the tomb, and it is open to doubt whether Hateclyff was actually buried in the chapel. For his house in the sanctuary, see WAM 19738.
[120] Harvey, *Living and Dying*, 250–1; and for his gift to the Lady chapel see WAM 9479, 23258, 23261. On his death, his tenement at the north door passed to John Twylly (WAM 23260; and for Twylly, see above, 21–2). For Drope's will, in which he left £20 for the repair of the Abbey church and requested that a requiem mass be celebrated for his soul by the monks of Westminster, see PRO, PCC Milles 4. (I owe this reference to Professor Caroline Barron.)

interment of Katherine of Valois, after a requiem mass at the high altar in the church, may have been one, the visitors were never allowed to grow into a crowd.[121]

In this respect, as in many others, the monks' conception of the old Lady chapel was apparently different from Henry VII's conception of the new one. If all went as Henry intended, the new chapel would house the shrine of the canonised Henry VI, and the shrine itself would become the focus of a new cult and a magnet for sightseers. In building the chapel, however, Henry VII thought of himself as well as his uncle and predecessor on the throne; thus the chapel was to contain his chantry chapel and be the scene of his well attended anniversary each year. For the monk-priests and secular priests who should celebrate requiem masses and offer prayers for the king and others in the chapel, he obtained the most generous of all indulgences, the *Scala Coeli*, so called because it offered penitents benefits first associated with the chapel of S. Maria Scala Coeli outside the walls of Rome.[122] But Henry also intended that the prayers of larger numbers than would participate in the anniversary or chantry masses would help to ease the path of his soul through Purgatory. Accordingly, on the same occasion in 1504, he obtained exceptional indulgences for all the faithful who, being confessed, should come to the chapel and pray for the king on any Sunday in Lent or on Good Friday, although on Good Friday they would be much greater than on other days.[123] Moreover, Henry obtained plenary indulgence, renewable annually in the individual case, for all visiting the chapel on the feast of the Ascension or on the vigil and praying for him there; and it was envisaged that confessors, whether regular or secular priests, might be occupied for four days in hearing the confessions of those wishing to claim the benefits of this indulgence. When the Ascensiontide indulgence was first brought into use in 1506, seven hundred copies were printed by Richard Pynson for the warden of Henry VII's foundation.[124]

In the long run, and partly for reasons which could not have been foreseen c.1500, things turned out very differently: Henry VI was never canonised, and indulgences ceased to have any place in the life of the Lady chapel at Westminster, or in that of the abbey church itself. Yet it seems clear that in the mind of its founder the new Lady chapel was to be accessible, on occasion, to the faithful coming from outside the cloister and precinct in numbers which have no parallel in the history of the old chapel. Did the monks of Westminster feel twinges of regret as they contemplated the privacy and the control of events they were to relinquish in exchange for the body of Henry VI – a possession which they had long coveted – a magnificent new Lady chapel, and the huge endowment promised for Henry VII's chantry and anniversary? Or did they regard the approaching changes as a necessary, even exhilarating, process

---

[121] For the offerings of cloth of gold etc. made at Katherine's funeral, see WAM 19678.

[122] *CPL* xviii, no. 118; *Foedera*, V (iv), 212. For the *Scala Coeli* indulgence, see Morgan, 'The Scala Cœli indulgence and the royal chapels', in *Reign of Henry VII*, 86–7; for Henry VII's anniversary, which included weekly as well as annual observances, Harvey, *Estates*, 30, 399; and on current tensions between monasteries and their patrons in the late medieval period, which are to some extent exemplified in Henry VII's relationship with Westminster Abbey, B. Thompson, 'Monasteries and their patrons at foundation and dissolution', *TRHS* 4, 1994, 115–21.

[123] *CPL* xviii, no. 118.

[124] (WAM 24241*). For the indulgence, see *CPL* xviii, no. 115. To obtain the benefits, it was also necessary to make an offering for the upkeep of the chapel. Cf. Sixtus IV's indulgence (1476), printed by Caxton, which had been sold for the benefit of the new work in the abbey nave (G. Rosser, 'A note on the Caxton *Indulgence* of 1476', *The Library*, 6th ser. 7, 1985, 256–8).

of modernisation, resembling in this respect the building of the old Lady chapel in the now distant past? But of course, these two responses to the situation that arose as Henry VII's plans took shape were not mutually exclusive. Many who were present on 24 January 1503, when Abbot Islip and others laid the foundation stone of the new Lady chapel on behalf of the king may have felt drawn in some measure to each.[125]

---

[125] Colvin, *HKW* iii, 211.

The Musicians and Liturgy of the Lady Chapels of the Monastery Church, c.1235–1540

ROGER BOWERS

The first Lady chapel and the monks' observance of Lady mass and antiphon, c.1235–1384

IN ANY GREAT monastic church such as that of Westminster Abbey there were two principal sites in which during the later medieval period divine service was offered on a corporate basis. These were the principal quire and the Lady chapel. In the quire the complete daily round of divine worship, consisting of high mass and the eight services of the Office, with a host of ancillary observances, was performed and sung in a ceaseless cycle by the community of monks. The ritual, ceremony and verbal texts of the Latin liturgy which they followed were those prescribed for the Western church as a whole, as also was the plainsong chant to which these services were sung. All was observed in Westminster's local manifestation of Benedictine Use.

Meanwhile, at the far east end of the church lay the chapel of the Blessed Virgin Mary, of which the foundation stone had been laid by Henry III in 1220. A building of noteworthy size (Fig. 5),[1] its construction appears to have been completed only in 1245–6, though the chapel was roofed during 1234 and could have been consecrated for use soon after.[2] Here each day a smaller and more select body of executants gathered somewhat before mid-morning each day to observe the devotion for which the Lady chapel had been built, the daily votive mass of the Virgin, or Lady mass.

Each day this took probably some forty to forty-five minutes to perform. It was a standard mass of the usual nineteen to twenty consecutive sections,[3] whose particular texts rendered it votive to the Virgin Mary.[4] The texts of the ordinary were unchanging. Irrespective of the liturgical rank formally appointed to the day, Lady

---

[1] Above, 23–7. It is a pleasure to record my thanks to the Keeper of the Muniments and his staff for their unfailing helpfulness during the preparation of this chapter, and to the British Academy, whose award of a Research Readership during 1991–3 furnished the opportunity for the conduct of most of the research informing it.

[2] Westlake, 57–9, 344–50.

[3] John Harper, *The Forms and Orders of Western Liturgy from the Tenth to the Eighteenth Century*, Oxford 1991, 113–25.

[4] No late medieval gradual of Westminster Abbey survives. However, details which can be gleaned from the Westminster Abbey Consuetudinary dated 1266 and the 'Litlington Missal' of 1382–4 can be

mass always enjoyed the status of a festal mass. Consequently, even in Advent and Lent the Gloria was never omitted; the Credo was performed on all days except (in effect) ferias and minor feasts, and, in particular, a sequence was always sung.[5] In respect of the propers, the Benedictine sources agree on presenting four sets of ritual for the Lady mass, changing with the seasons of the year.[6]

Many of the verbal texts of these masses can be identified as having been appropriated from high mass of the day for the five principal feasts of the Virgin (Annunciation, Assumption, Nativity, Conception and Purification), and it may fairly be assumed that their associated chants were imported with the texts. Consequently, in every likelihood the character of the ceremony, text and chant heard every day in the Westminster Lady chapel can be appreciated as having differed in no material manner from that heard in quire at high mass of the day.[7]

Seemly observance of such a mass required the presence of at least a small chorus of competent singers in addition to the celebrant and his altar assistants. The Consuetudinary dated 1266 explained how the endowments and estates of the chapel and the conduct of the services within it were to be managed by a monk-obedientiary entitled Warden of the chapel;[8] in particular, Lady mass was always to be performed 'with appropriate honour'.[9] To this end, it was to be observed by the Warden (or a deputy acting in his stead) and a team of six monks nominated from day to day for the purpose. Such a disposition ensured the presence of a celebrant, his two assistants (deacon and subdeacon) at the altar, and two monks per side to sing the chant.[10] On the five principal feasts of the Virgin each year the mass may well have been attended by other monks in addition, for whose 'recreation' afterwards quite substantial sums were reserved.[11] So inaugurated, Lady mass continued to be sung daily in the original Lady chapel and its successor right up to the dissolution in 1540, and indeed beyond it until the abolition of the Latin liturgy, first in 1549–53 and permanently from 1559.

---

    amplified with matter drawn from the handful of equivalent documents surviving from other Benedictine houses to yield a likely conspectus of the content and character of Lady mass as celebrated at Westminster. See *Customary*; *Missale*; *The Ordinal and Customary of the Abbey of St Mary, York*, ed. J.B.L. Tolhurst and the Lady Abbess of Stanbrook, Henry Bradshaw Society 73, 75, 84, 1934–50, i, 56–8; Roger Bowers, 'The musicians of the Lady chapel of Winchester cathedral priory, 1402–1539', *JEH* 45, 1994, 210–27, at 212–14.

[5] *Missale*, cols. 490, 498–9; Frank Ll. Harrison, *Music in Medieval Britain*, 2nd edn, London 1963, 57, 78–9. The 'Litlington Missal' does not advert to the Kyries and Sequences of the Lady mass; in respect of late medieval Benedictine use, these appear in fullest detail in *Ordinal of St Mary, York* i, 56–8.

[6] These were 'Rorate celi desuper' (Advent to Christmas), 'Salve sancta parens' I (Christmas to Purification), 'Salve sancta parens' II (Purification to Easter, and Trinity Sunday to Advent), and 'Salve sancta parens' III (Easter to Trinity Sunday). *Missale* ii, cols. 1119–29. For the preface used at Lady mass, see *ibid.*, col. 508.

[7] A distant but not misleading impression of the character of the chant of the Lady mass can be drawn from inspection of the music set to any of the Lady mass texts in a modern service book such as the Liber Usualis (e.g. *The Liber Usualis with an Introduction and Rubrics in English*, Tournai 1938, wherein the modern votive masses of the Virgin appear on pp. 1263–72).

[8] *Customary* ii, 91–3.

[9] 'cum debito honore': *ibid.* ii, 91.

[10] Also in attendance was the 'clerk' of the Lady chapel, for whom see Harvey, above, 00. After the general fashion of his kind, he served as a general assistant and factotum in keeping the chapel cleaned and its furniture and fittings maintained; it is unlikely that he contributed to the performance of mass other than, perhaps, as server.

[11] WAM 23179 (1298/9) – 23186 (1373/4), *Curialitates* or *Exhennia*.

Concerning the content and conduct of liturgical observance at this early period, much can be inferred from an inventory of the goods of the chapel taken in 1304.[12] For the use of the celebrant there were provided one new missal and one old. For the singers there were supplied nine small books, well bound, 'of the sequences and other chants'.[13] Probably these were special compilations of Lady mass plainsong for both ordinary and proper, taking the place of full graduals.[14] The books provided indicate that the daily Office of the Virgin was also observed in the chapel.[15] In its fullest form, this consisted of a complete office of eight services parallel to the Office of the Day;[16] almost certainly, even in a great monastery such as Westminster, all was merely recited and not sung. Such observance, however, renders especially likely the use of the Lady chapel as location also for the performance each day, following Compline in quire, of a liturgical observance of particular significance for the future, namely the antiphon (followed by a collect) votive to the Virgin Mary and sung before the chapel's principal image. At Westminster this practice in 1266 was a recent innovation; the particular antiphon prescribed, with its chant, was the ubiquitous 'Salve regina, mater misericordie'.[17]

The intensity of contemporary devotion to the Virgin Mary in England not only procured the elevation of the daily Lady mass to permanently festal status; it also ensured that the solemnity of its celebration be particularly marked wherever possible by the enhancement of its music with items sung not in the conventional plainsong but in polyphony, some improvised according to conventional rules, other specially composed. Much the greater part of English composition surviving from the later thirteenth and fourteenth centuries is of pieces for use at the Lady mass.[18] It extends particularly to discrete settings of the five movements of the Ordinary, and also to both the sequence itself and to settings of original Marian texts similar in character to the liturgical sequence, which it was permitted to substitute for the latter when desired.[19]

From so prominent a monastery as that of St Peter, Westminster, it is not at all surprising that there should survive from an early date evidence of the cultivation of

---

[12] WAM 23180; printed in Westlake ii, 502–3.

[13] *Ibid.*: *unum novum missale et aliud vetus . . . ix parvos libros de Sequenciis et aliis cantibus bene ligatos.*

[14] Such volumes would indeed have consisted primarily of settings of the sequences, by far the bulkiest item in any aggregate collection of Lady mass chant for the year. The inventory also lists the conventional vestments used by those attending each day at mass, namely albs and amices for the monks, and a surplice for the 'clericus' of the chapel. Presumably the very much richer vestments of the celebrant were kept under conditions of greater security by the sacrist.

[15] The service-books included two psalters, a 'jornale' (that is, a diurnale, a service-book drawn from the breviary and containing the day-time Hours), and a breviary fixed on the pulpitum of the chapel, which therefore appears to have been the location from which the lessons were read.

[16] Except for a rotating series of psalms for matins, its texts were limited to just three sets, changing with the season of the year. Harper, *Form and Orders*, 133–4; *Missale* iii, cols. 1321–35.

[17] Described as *ex moderno et non ex veteri usu*: *Customary* ii, 201; cf. Harrison, *Music in Medieval Britain*, 81–2. For the principal image of the Virgin, see above, 14.

[18] See Harrison, *Music in Medieval Britain*, 104–55; John Caldwell, *The Oxford History of English Music 1: From the beginnings to c.1715*, Oxford 1991, 34–107.

[19] Frank Ll. Harrison, 'Music for the Sarum Rite: MS 1236 in the Pepys Library, Magdalene College, Cambridge', *Annales Musicologiques* 6, 1958, 99–144, at 121.

polyphony among the members of the monastic community at the quire service,[20] and from a relatively early period there is evidence also that, on days suitably festal, the abbey enhanced its performance of Lady mass in the Lady chapel both with the music of vocal polyphony and with the organ. The 1304 inventory of the goods of the Lady chapel records a considerable collection of items of written polyphony.[21] It possessed no fewer than eight *rotuli* – individual scrolls – containing polyphonic music (*de organo*),[22] while a further five scrolls containing 'sequences' alone and listed with the first eight may well also have contained polyphony both to genuine sequences and to kindred Marian texts. The five quaterns 'of music' (*de Cantu*) may well also have contained polyphonic settings, while nine great quaterns of the gift of the monk Alexander de Pershore[23] were still blank, but evidently were intended to have music copied into them. These traditions were maintained, and before his death in 1383/4 the monk Robert Wynwyk, perhaps one of the monastery's expert singers, had donated to the Lady chapel a further volume of polyphony.[24]

The chapel also contained in 1304 two organs,[25] an unusual feature for so early a period; organs in monastery Lady chapels appear otherwise not to be encountered at a date earlier than the 1380s.[26] One instrument, the smaller of the two, stood on the choir step, and seems likely to have been a modest positive.[27] The other was a 'great organs', fixed to and suspended upon the wall above, painted cloths being extended to either side; there appears to be no other record in England at this time of an organ located in such a position. However, the manner in which the church organ was used to enhance the liturgical service at this period is not known and, overall, the scanty records of the chapel indicate little beyond the ongoing routine observance of the Lady mass throughout this period.

---

[20] For incidental (and by no means exhaustive) references to the performance of two- and three-part polyphony during the quire service on festivals, see Consuetudinary of 1266: *Customary* ii, 33–4; cf. Harrison, *Music in Medieval Britain*, 113. Of no surviving polyphonic music of this period does Westminster Abbey appear to provide a likely provenance. The muniments do contain three manuscript fragments of polyphony (WAM 12185, 33327, MS 101); however, all are wrappers or binding-strips to documents and volumes of external origin which entered the archives or library long after the expiry of their useful life, as music performed long before at some other, unknown, location.

[21] WAM 23180 (printed in Westlake ii, 503): *v quaternos scriptos de Cantu. ix quaternos magnos non scriptos de dono A. de Persore. viij Rotulos de organo. v Rotulos de Sequenciis.*

[22] For singing from manuscript rolls at this time see Christopher Page, 'An English motet of the fourteenth century in performance: two contemporary images', *Early Music* 25, 1997, 7–32.

[23] Monk, occurs 1284–1311; in the latter year he was precentor. E.H. Pearce, *The Monks of Westminster*, Cambridge 1916, 62.

[24] WAM 23193, *Expense necessarie*. In 1376 Wynwyk had been warden of the Lady chapel: Pearce, *Monks*, 110, 195.

[25] WAM 23180: *unum par Organorum inferius super gradum aliud par maiorum Organorum superius in Muro cum ij pannis depictis circa eadem [sic] extentis.*

[26] Roger Bowers, 'The performing ensemble for English church polyphony, c.1320–c.1390', in *Studies in the Performance of Late Mediaeval Music*, ed. Stanley Boorman, Cambridge 1983, 161–92, at 182 n. 51.

[27] The expenditure of 10s 0d in 1363–4 for wooden boards to make an enclosure 'where the organs used to stand' may mark the occasion of the removal of the smaller organ from its former position to another. WAM 23184, *Minute*.

The inauguration of a professional Lady chapel choir, 1384–1399

The practice of professional music-making at Westminster Abbey began in 1384. The capacities to compose, copy and perform polyphonic music probably were valued to at least a respectable extent among the monks of this period; nevertheless, polyphony was by no means essential to the liturgical service, and the likelihood is that its performance and cultivation were always the preserve of just a few enthusiasts. The Black Death of 1348 might thus constitute a catastrophe capable of extinguishing these capacities altogether. Certainly such an eventuality had occurred by 1356–7,[28] when the abbey, evidently bereft of monks who understood the theory, notation and practice of polyphony, needed to employ a secular musician from beyond the precinct wall to restore the tradition.[29] And towards the end of the century, as among the employers of the most prominent secular choirs the enhancement of the mass of the Virgin with elaborate music was beginning to gain an ever greater importance, the decision was taken to employ a professional secular musician on a permanent basis thenceforth, primarily to be in charge of the performance of the music of divine service executed in the Lady chapel.

At Michaelmas 1384, towards the end of the abbacy of Nicholas Litlington (1362–86),[30] the abbey took into its employment one Walter Whitby, providing to him annually a robe furred with lambswool and a salary of £4 per year.[31] At Michaelmas 1388 Whitby was succeeded by Walter Braytoft,[32] a priest and canon of the Augustinian house of Holy Trinity, Aldgate, London.[33] Braytoft remained in the abbey's employment until at least Easter 1393, receiving a stipend of £4 per year.[34]

Although never identified as such in the abbey archives, both were in fact prominent church musicians of their period. Early in 1396 Whitby became a singing-man of the Chapel Royal, where he continued to serve Richard II and Henry IV until at least 1406.[35] As well as singer he was also an organ-player, receiving at Christmas

---

[28] WAM 18984, *Allocaciones: Allocatur eidem ijs viijd pro expensis j clerici existentis in Elemosinaria et docentis confratres nostros ad cantum fractum.*

[29] Perhaps to ensure that the reception that year of an important relic of St Benedict was effected with an appropriate level of solemnity. (I am grateful to Mrs Brenda Tew for this suggestion.)

[30] Litlington's commission for the creation of the magnificent high altar missal which was executed 1382–4 and, bearing his name, still survives in the abbey library, is further evidence of his attention to the expedition of matters liturgical at this time. J.A. Robinson and M.R. James, *The Manuscripts of Westminster Abbey*, Cambridge 1908, 7–8, quoting account of Abbot's Treasurer 1383–4: WAM 24265*, *Expense nove missalis.* Further references to the creation of this manuscript to be found in the following year's account (WAM 24266) appear generally to have been overlooked.

[31] WAM 19871–5, *Empcio liberate.* WAM 18999, *Expense necessarie.* WAM 23187–8, *Soluciones et stipendia.* WAM19371, A/c Infirmarer 1387/8, *Minuta cum aliis expensis factis.*

[32] WAM 23188, *Soluciones et stipendia.*

[33] In 1372 (probably at the age of nineteen or twenty) Braytoft had been ordained subdeacon: *Registrum Simonis de Sudberia, diocesis Londiniensis, A.D. 1362–1375*, ed. R.C. Fowler, C. Jenkins and S.C. Ratcliff, 2 vols., Canterbury and York Society 34, 37, 1927–8, ii, 116, also 63 (I owe this reference to Miss Barbara Harvey). Evidently he now possessed licence to absent himself from his home monastery to pursue a career in professional church music.

[34] WAM 23188, 23190–2, *Soluciones et stipendia.* WAM 23188, *Firma tenementorum cum pastura.* WAM 19373, *Decime.* WAM 19374–6, *Soluciones et stipendia.* WAM 19651, *Soluciones forinsece.*

[35] PRO E 101/403/10, fos. 39v, 44v; E 404/511/296; E 404/511/374; E 101/404/21, fo. 44v. BL MS Harley 319, fo. 46r. Whitby's name is absent from the next surviving Chapel Royal list (1413: PRO, E 101/406/21, fo. 27r), and does not recur thereafter.

1406 a gratuity of 13s 4d for playing in St George's Chapel, Windsor.[36] During 1395–6 Braytoft became master of the choristers at Lincoln cathedral, where he remained until some point following 1408.[37]

Whitby's appointment at Westminster in 1384 appears to have been the earliest such venture at any English monastery. No surviving document elucidates the precise function which he and Braytoft were engaged to perform at the abbey. Nevertheless, the manner in which each received half of his total cash stipend from the warden of the Lady chapel indicates clearly that it was there that their principal service to the monastery was being conducted. Hereby, that is, the abbey secured the services of a trained and able singer who was obliged to be present with the monks deputed to attend upon the daily celebration of Lady mass in order to stiffen and lend distinction to the singing of its music. Probably, however, Whitby and Braytoft also fulfilled another function, for within the period of their employment at the abbey there also occur references to the presence within the monastery of some number of singing-boys, a group never here enumerated but probably not exceeding four or so.

As may be shown to have occurred contemporaneously also at the cathedral priories of Ely and Norwich, certain of the boys of the almonry grammar school had lately begun to be deputed to attend, doubtless as servers, upon the daily celebration of mass in the Lady chapel.[38] At Westminster in 1364 the Warden had made a gratuity of 6s 8d to 'the boys of the chapel' to help to amplify their feast on St Nicholas' day, and during 1373–4 a boy had been paid 6s 8d for his work during the year lighting the altar-candles at mass.[39] Given the availability now of a professional musician as teacher, it took no very great leap of the imagination to conceive a plan to form from among the boys of the almonry school a small choir to enhance not only the ceremony of the mass but the performance of its chant as well. Reference to the existence of such singing-boys (*pueri cantatores*) occurs during 1389–90, and to one singing-boy (*puer de eisdem cantoribus*) during 1392–3.[40]

Probably in 1384, that is, there was pioneered at Westminster the inauguration of a choir of a kind which was to become the norm for monastery Lady chapel choirs in general during the following century.[41] This consisted of a qualified secular master and a group of singing-boys trained by him, whose principal duty was to attend daily

---

[36] Account of Treasurer, 1406/7: Windsor, St George's Chapel, MS xv.34.24, *Stipendia officiariorum cum rewardis*.

[37] A successor is known to have been in office by 1413. Archives of the Dean and Chapter of Lincoln: Lincolnshire Archives Office, MSS Bj 2/8, fo. 119v; A.2.29, fo. 2r; A.2.30, fo. 4r; Bj 2/10, fo. 132r. Roger Bowers, 'Music and worship to 1640', in *A History of Lincoln Minster*, ed. D. Owen, Cambridge 1994, 47–76, at 55, 75.

[38] Roger Bowers, 'The almonry schools of the English monasteries, c.1265–1540', in *Monasteries and Society in Medieval Britain*, ed. B. Thompson, Harlaxton Medieval Studies vi, Stamford 1999, 177–222, at 208–9.

[39] WAM 23184 verso: *Expense anno xxxix°*. WAM 23186, *Soluciones et stipendia*.

[40] WAM 24540, *Empcio forinseca*. WAM 19651, *Soluciones forincece*. E. Pine, *The Westminster Abbey Singers*, London 1953, 15, asserted the existence of a reference to singing-boys relating to the year 1388. Unfortunately he gave no reference, and no entry which could have given rise to this assertion has yet been found.

[41] Harrison, *Music in Medieval Britain*, 40–4, 185–94; Bowers, 'The musicians of the Lady chapel of Winchester cathedral priory', 214–35; Bowers, 'The almonry schools of the English monasteries', 208–13.

at Lady mass, participating with the attending monks in rendering its plainsong with all the decorum and distinction that such a group could achieve. Boys' voices were not used in composed polyphony at this time, but as well as singing plainsong they could contribute descant improvised to the chant according to conventional rules; the master and monks, meanwhile, enhanced the mass with such polyphony of men's voices as the monks could manage.

Such a level of capacity sufficed to satisfy the aspirations of the likely founder of the Lady chapel choir, Abbot Litlington. In March 1393, however, and upon an initiative attributed within the monastery expressly to the new and music-loving abbot William Colchester,[42] the choir was favoured with an expansion enabling it to offer a musical contribution of a wholly professional character, in a manner directly comparable to that being developed contemporaneously at the most enterprising of the established cathedral and collegiate choirs and household chapels of royalty and the aristocracy.

At Lady Day 1393 there was brought into effect a new *ordinacio* initiated explicitly by 'the lord William, now abbot'.[43] No copy of the text of this ordinance is known; however, its basic provisions may be deduced. Under its terms no fewer than seven, and in all probability eight, of the obedientiaries began to put into a pool managed by a nominated monk a sum of 40s 0d contributed annually by each.[44] Thus was provided a pool of £16 0s 0d, collected for distribution as stipend to a group of professional singers, commonly designated as the *cantores seculares*.[45] Since Whitby and Braytoft had each in turn received a cash salary of £4 0s 0d per year (excluding extras for livery and board), it seems very likely that this level of salary continued to apply, and that the pool of £16 0s 0d per year was intended to provide for an ensemble of four voices, the usual number at this period for specialist groups of singers.[46] The overall result was the establishment of a small self-contained choir consisting of a master and probably three other adult voices, with a still unidentified number of boys, probably four.

Of the names of the singing-men few are now known. Neither 'Richard the singer' of 1393/4 nor the unnamed singer who received subsidised board in 1392/3 can be further identified.[47] However, their colleague Henry Drayton, on whose livery in

---

[42] It is clear from the surviving accounts of his household that Colchester personally took enormous pleasure in music. See accounts of abbot's household 1387–1419: WAM 24537–8, 24540, 24542–9, *Dona data*. WAM 19875, *Expense forincece cum donis datis*, WAM 24268–9, *Dona data*.

[43] WAM 18732, *Exhennia*; WAM 23340, *Exhennia*.

[44] These were the warden of the Lady chapel, the sacrist, the almoner, the infirmarer, the cellarer, the chamberlain, and the warden of the churches. To these should almost certainly be added the monk bailiff, who was making this payment by the time of the earliest surviving account of this obedientiary, 1413–14. See, respectively, WAM 23192, *Vadia et stipendia*; 19651, *Soluciones forinsece*; 50733, *Stipendia et vadia*; 19380, *Minuta*; 18878, *Expense forinsece*; 18732, *Exhennia*; 23340, *Exhennia*; 18627, *Exhennia*.

[45] The first payments to this group of singers were made during 1392/3, in respect of the half-year beginning at Lady Day, which may be taken to have been the occasion of its inauguration. WAM 18732, *Exhennia*; WAM 23340, *Exhennia*.

[46] Roger Bowers, 'To chorus from quartet: the performing resource for English church polyphony, c.1390–1559', in *English Choral Practice 1400–1650*, ed. J. Morehen, Cambridge 1995, 1–47, at 11–20.

[47] WAM 50733, *Minute: in iiij virgis [panni] emptis pro j gowna facta Ricardo cantori precepto domini abbatis, pro virga xviijd – vjs*. Four yards is less than the usual allowance for the gown of an adult; given that this payment was made by the almoner, the possibility remains open that Richard was one of the singing-boys from the almonry school. WAM 23192, *Expense necessarie*.

1393–4 the treasurers caused 8s 0d to be spent,[48] had been admitted by Christmas 1395 as a singing-man of the Chapel Royal of Richard II, whose successor he continued to serve at least until Christmas 1408.[49]

The locale of the singers' employment was primarily the Lady chapel;[50] their function there was to give their attendance at Lady mass, where lights were provided at the desks from which they sang.[51] However, on each of the ten 'principal feasts' of the year the adult singers contributed also to the performance of service in the principal quire,[52] lending distinction and finesse to the rendering by the monks of high mass and the major offices. Doubtless the specialist singers contributed to the services in which they participated not only professionally accomplished plainsong, but also the special distinction of polyphonic music. For such a function they needed a written repertory. During the first full year of the group's operation, 1393/4, the existing volume of polyphonic compositions used in the Lady chapel, donated by Robert Wynwyk, was augmented with unidentified settings occupying sixteen folios of vellum, and in its expanded form was then re-covered and re-bound ready for use.[53]

In September 1397 the group of professional adult singers was expanded in number again, from (probably) four to seven, and substantial increases were effected in their levels of pay. In the event, this phase was to be of only brief duration. The transience of its existence, however, should not obscure the remarkable endeavour that was being essayed in the Westminster Lady chapel at this time, which appears to have been the establishment of a Lady mass choir staffed according to the model presented by the contemporary manner of the observance of Lady mass by such a body as the Chapel Royal or a major collegiate church.

Abruptly at Michaelmas 1397 the salary pool established for the singing-men was increased from £16 0s 0d per year to no less than £47 0s 0d.[54] This sum was appointed to pay a group totalling seven, and there yet remains record, with full details of vocal designation and remuneration, of the names of the group during the last days of Richard II, 21 June to 29 September 1399.[55] For this period it yields the

---

[48] WAM 19879, *Expense forinsece cum donis datis*.

[49] PRO E 101/403/10, fo. 43v (Drayton's name is last on the list as the most recent recruit); E 101/405/22, fo. 38r. His name is absent from the next surviving list, that for summer 1413: E 101/406/21, fo. 27r.

[50] To the warden of the Lady chapel they were the *Cantores in choro et in Capella beate marie*: WAM 23192, *Vadia et Stipendia*; 23196, *Exhennia et Soluciones*.

[51] WAM 23193 (1393–4), stock account on verso.

[52] E.g. WAM 50733, *Stipendia et vadia*. The 'ten principal feasts' (Christmas, St Edward, SS Peter and Paul, the Assumption, St Peter ad Vincula, All Saints, and the Translation of St Edward, with Easter, Pentecost and Trinity) were a recognised group of the ten major occasions of the liturgical year, already designated as such by the time of the Consuetudinary of 1264: *Customary* ii, 101, 246.

[53] WAM 23193, *Expense necessarie: Et in ligatura et coopertura unius libri organici quondam ex dono fratris R. Wynwyk cum Augmentacione iiij quaternorum vocatorum velym, in toto vijs xd*. See also above, n. 24.

[54] WAM 23346–7, *Exhennia*; 19004, *Stipendia et vadia*; 19386–7, *Minuta*; 23195–6, *Soluciones forinsece*; 18881, *Expense forinsece*; 19657, *Expense et soluciones forinsece*. Of the chamberlain and monk bailiff, for whose offices no accounts have survived for either 1397–8 or 1398–9, it appears that the share of one probably remained fixed at £2 0s 0d, while the other rose to £3 0s 0d; such a presumption allows the whole £47 0s 0d per year now being paid to the corps of seven voices (see Liber Niger, fo. 86v) to be accounted for.

[55] *Anno regni regis Ricardi secundi xxiij° Isti fuerunt Cantores seculares in Ecclesia Westmonsteriensi*: WAM Liber Niger, fo. 86v. See Appendix (57 below).

most detailed anatomy of a small ensemble of professional singers available in respect of any location in Europe. The performance responsibilities appended to each of the singers' names leaves no doubt that the principal qualification and capacity of each was the knowledge and skill to perform composed polyphonic music.

The highest-paid member of the ensemble, John Tyes,[56] enjoyed no livery allowance, but a handsome salary of £10 0s 0d per year. He was designated as *organista*; certainly this term meant 'singer of polyphonic music', and in this case probably meant with equal validity 'organ-player'. Tyes probably served also as master of the singing-boys; certainly it was to be both master of the Lady chapel singing-boys and organist that he was appointed to the staff of Winchester cathedral at Michaelmas 1402,[57] and the high rate of pay he had been enjoying at Westminster strongly suggests that these were the functions he had been fulfilling there likewise. John Byfeld, his responsibility designated as 'tenor', was paid annually £6 13s 4d, with livery of two tunics and a fur; William Causton, whose vocal designation was not given, was remunerated exactly as was Byfeld.

Of the remaining four, John Grede received £6 13s 4d without livery, John Barker and Peter Pleford £6 0s 0d plus livery, and John Browing £5 0s 0d plus livery. Barker and Pleford were career church musicians, who fifteen years earlier had been singing-boys together in the household chapel of Thomas Arundel, bishop of Ely.[58] The responsibility and function of each of these four was designated 'treble'. This term (a vernacular rendering of the Latin *triplex*, meaning 'three-fold') had not yet attracted its modern association with the boy's unbroken voice, but was the designation given to the performer of a particular part in the contrapuntal web of polyphonic music, namely the upper part in three-part music required to render the harmony 'three-fold'.[59] Polyphony at this period was composed within an overall compass of thirteen to fifteen notes only; boys' voices were not involved in its performance, and the voices ('trebles') performing the top part in the standard three- and four-part music of the day were adult voices, probably closely akin to the modern male alto.

The group of singers also included a small team of boys now expressly enumerated at four,[60] very probably their number since inauguration in 1384. The boys would not have been expected to do more than to sing the plainsong of Lady mass, and – individually, and if taught to do so – to extemporise descant to plainsong at appropriate points in the service. They were also available to help in serving the celebrant. For such purposes a team of four would have been entirely adequate, and indeed the same number was appointed for the Lady chapel choir of Winchester cathedral on its inauguration under Tyes in 1402.[61]

---

[56] In 1371 a boy of London diocese named John Tyes had received the first tonsure, probably as a child of seven or eight years: *Registrum Simonis de Sudberia*, ed. Fowler, Jenkins and Ratcliff, ii, 108 (I owe this reference to Miss Barbara Harvey).

[57] Bowers, 'The musicians of the Lady chapel of Winchester cathedral priory', 217–21.

[58] Accounts of household, 1381–4: Cambridge University Library, MSS EDR D(5)2, m. 3v, and D(5)6, m. 2v; also PRO E 101/400/28(2), m. 2v. Bowers, 'To chorus from quartet', 17 and n. 43.

[59] *Ibid.*, 15–16 and n. 33; Bowers, 'The performing ensemble for English church polyphony', 178–9 and n. 38.

[60] WAM 23196, *Expense necessarie: Et dat' pueris cantantibus in capella per vices hoc anno xiijd*. WAM 23197, *Expense necessarie: In expensis iiij puerorum cantorum per tempus visus diversis vicibus viijd*.

[61] Bowers, 'The musicians of the Lady chapel of Winchester cathedral priory', 217–19.

The duties of the enlarged ensemble during 1397–9 probably differed not at all from those of their predecessors since 1393. The principal site of their work remained the Lady chapel of the monastery,[62] from the revenues of which were met the costs of the surplices which, as seculars, they wore when routinely present at service.[63] Moreover, they made particular contribution to the celebration of Lady mass on Christmas Day, in recognition of which the Warden paid gratuities of 12d in 1398, and in 1400 18d for the singers' recreation afterwards.[64]

For the two years 1397–9, therefore, the independent choir of secular singers based on the Lady chapel consisted of a master, six other adult singers and four boys. An insight into the music routinely performed by the adults is yielded by the surviving compositions of its Master, John Tyes. These are a three-part setting of Gloria and a four-part setting of Sanctus,[65] both of which would have been suitable for either Lady mass in the Lady chapel or high mass in quire. Scoring in four parts (for two high voices, one middle, and one low) was the most opulent available at this period, and the list of 1399 yields a unique insight into contemporary methods of performance. The provision of four voices designated 'treble' permitted the master to appoint two to sing each of the two upper parts, while to Byfeld was allocated the foundation part designated *tenor*. Causton was available to perform the middle voice, while Tyes was at liberty to join in on whichever of the two lower parts seemed the more suitable and amenable to doubling.[66] Meanwhile, the Lady chapel organ also remained available for use at service.[67] Altogether, this body of singers certainly possessed the resources, and almost equally certainly the expertise, to perform in the Lady chapel and in the quire any of the most exacting and demanding music of its period. Westminster Abbey was bidding fair to emerge as a location able to compare with any for the degree of enterprise and musical ostentation with which the daily Lady mass was offered.

Almost certainly the particular constitution of the choir had not been determined by accident. In character and dimensions it bears probably a strong resemblance to the sub-groups of experts within the choirs of such bodies as the Chapel Royal by whom were undertaken their performances of polyphony. The respect and affection borne by Richard II towards the abbey is well known, as is his cultivated patronage of the arts and his particular projection of those possessing potential to enhance the image of kingship.[68] The creation of a body of singers at Westminster Abbey which could contribute to the splendour of kingship on the not infrequent occasions of Richard's visits of state may well have constituted a potent motive for this aggrandisement of the Lady chapel choir.[69] Certainly, it seems intensely suggestive

---

[62] For the levelling of the tomb of Abbot Richard de Berking during 1397/8, probably to yield space immediately west of the altar for the singers to occupy, see above, 26.

[63] WAM 23196, *Empcio stauri, Expense necessarie*.

[64] WAM 23196, 23198, *Expense necessarie*.

[65] *The Old Hall Manuscript*, ed. M. Bent and A. Hughes, 2 vols. in 3, Corpus Mensurabilis Musicae 46, Rome 1969–73, i, 32–5, 369–72.

[66] Further, see Bowers, 'To chorus from quartet', 15–18.

[67] WAM 23196, 23197, 23198 *Expense necessarie*.

[68] N. Saul, 'Richard II and Westminster Abbey', in *The Cloister and the World: Essays in Medieval History in honour of Barbara Harvey*, ed. J. Blair and B. Golding, Oxford 1996, 196–218.

[69] For Richard's concern that his visits to the abbey be distinguished by contributions to the ceremony

that the abrupt termination of its expanded personnel and the succeeding return to former levels of staffing should so perfectly coincide with the detention and deposition of the king at Michaelmas 1399.

Retrenchment and restoration, 1399–1422

With effect from 29 September 1399 the enlarged pool of finance, which had been paying stipend to the singers at the rate of £47 0s 0d per year, was abruptly reduced by more than half, to £22 13s 4d.[70] By Michaelmas 1407 it had been reduced yet further, to £21 6s 8d.[71] The lean but – even by secular standards – complete choral force maintained between 1393 and 1399 was being shrunk and transformed into something quite different, a body no longer resembling a choir based on secular models staffed by both men and boys.

The more than halving of the pool at Michaelmas 1399 appears to have been accompanied by a directly corresponding reduction in the number of adult singers. During 1413–14 the making of three new surplices sufficed for them,[72] and it is probable that it was to this number that reduction in the autumn of 1399 had been made; three was the working minimum, allowing three-part polyphony to be undertaken one voice to a part. John Grede remained, and was still in the monastery's service during 1405–6;[73] at Michaelmas 1402, however, John Tyes departed to inaugurate a Lady chapel choir at Winchester cathedral.[74] Moreover, of the singing-boys there is now no trace whatever. Not a single reference to boys of the Lady chapel choir can be found after December 1400,[75] and it is clear that from about that time until March 1480 the choir was of adult voices only. The degree of contraction imposed on the choir after 1399 evidently cost it entirely what were – at this period – its least essential members.

This period of retrenchment lasted for the duration of the reign of Henry IV who, perhaps as a reaction from the degree of devotion bestowed upon it by his predecessor, exhibited no particular concern for the Abbey. Henry V, however, proved to be a vigorous patron, who from the moment of his coronation hastened in particular to expedite work on the re-building of the nave.[76] Apparently coincident with his accession in March 1413 there also appeared a restored degree of momentum in the cultivation of its music.

By Michaelmas that year there had been initiated a programme of piecemeal increases in the several contributions made to the pool which, apparently by 1419, had raised it from £21 6s 8d to £29 12s 0d.[77] This increase would have permitted the

---

made by his own Chapel Royal, see *The Westminster Chronicle, 1381–1394*, ed. L.C. Hector and B. Harvey, Oxford 1982, 314 (1388), 450 (1390), 508–10 (1392).

[70] WAM 19006, *Stipendia*; 19659, *Soluciones forinsece*; 18733, *Exhennia*; 18882, *Expense forinsece*; 19389, *Minuta*; 23198, *Exhennia*; 23348, *Exhennia*.

[71] WAM 19394–5, *Minuta*; 23201–2, *Stipendia et expense necessarie*; 23203, *Vadia et Stipendia*.

[72] WAM 23206, *Expensis in capella*.

[73] WAM 23201, *Stipendia et expense necessarie*.

[74] Bowers, 'The musicians of the Lady chapel of Winchester cathedral priory', 217–18.

[75] WAM 23197, *Expense necessarie*.

[76] Westlake i, 188–90.

[77] The infirmarer's contribution, expressly on the orders of the abbot (still William Colchester), was at

group to be raised in number to the standard four, which probably by now had occurred. The Lady chapel duly remained the focus of the duties of the group of secular singing-men,[78] and up-dating their repertoire of polyphony was now made a priority. During 1415–16 the warden paid out 20s 0d to the monk John Walden 'for a new volume of settings in polyphony'; the exact nature of Walden's contribution to the creation of this book was not specified, but 20s 0d sufficed to procure a substantial volume.[79] Further, in the same year of 1415–16 the existing organ of the Lady chapel gave way to a new instrument. Its cost of £9 0s 0d would not have bought anything very elaborate – just a conventional positive with, perhaps, three or four ranks providing sufficient tonal capacity to justify its being called a 'great organs'.[80]

A new musical impetus was now felt in the principal quire as well as in the Lady chapel. Most noticeably, during 1413/14 there began the piecemeal accumulation of a substantial volume of polyphonic music for use in the quire of the abbey church, not least, no doubt, for use by the team of secular singing-men when present in the monks' choir on the ten principal feasts discussed above.[81] The total expenditure of 73s 1d would have furnished a very fine and ample volume.[82] At much the same time, moreover, there was being made for the quire of the abbey church in 1414/15 a new great organ, to the cost of which one obedientiary's contribution was 20s 0d.[83]

Probably it was not by mere coincidence that this sudden burst of restored initiative in the cultivation of music at the Abbey occurred in the immediate wake of the accession of Henry V. Although he could not emulate his father as an actual composer of polyphonic music,[84] Henry V was energetic in promoting its performance as an expression of regal and ceremonial grandeur, and probably also of doctrinal and liturgical orthodoxy at a time of intense suppression of the Lollard heresy. He doubled in number the personnel of the Chapel Royal he had inherited,[85] and also

---

Michaelmas 1413 raised by 13s 4d to 66s 8d per year; this increment, in effect, was then back-dated to Christmas 1412. WAM 19407, *Minuta*. WAM 23206, *Vadia et stipendia*; 23366, *Exhennia*; 18889, *Expense forinsece*; 18736, *Minute*; 18628, *Exhennia*; 19663, *Expense forinsece*; 19027, *Stipendia*.

[78] It is in the accounts of the warden of the Lady chapel that by far the greatest number of references to the singing-men occur, and expressed as a proportion of total income, the warden's contribution to the singers' salaries was by far the greatest of all eight contributors.

[79] WAM 23209, [*Allocaciones super compotum*]: *Et eidem [computanti] xxs solut' Fratri Johanni Walden pro novo libro organorum*.

[80] WAM 23209, *Recepcio forinseca: Idem respondit pro veteris [sic] organis venditis Cs. Expense in capella: Solut' pro aliis Novis Organis Factis hoc anno pro Capella in parte solucionis maioris summe xls.Soluciones Forinsece: Et solut' pro Organis magnis novis xxs.* [*Allocaciones super compotum*]: *allocat' ei xxs pro novis organis factis hoc anno*.

[81] See above, 40 and n. 52.

[82] During 1413/14 20s 0d was spent on the creation of this volume, 13s 1d in 1414/15 and 40s 0d in 1415/16. WAM 18554 (1413–14) [*Allocaciones*]: *De quibus allocantur ei . . . xxs pro factura cuiusdam libri organici pro choro*. WAM 18556 (1414–15), [*Allocaciones*]: *De quibus allocantur ei . . . xiijs jd pro factura libri organici*. WAM 18557 (1415–16), [*Allocaciones*]: *De quibus allocantur ei . . . xls solut' pro factura novi libri organici*.

[83] WAM 18556 (collector of Westminster rents), [*Allocaciones*]: *De quibus allocantur ei . . . xxs solut' pro novis magnis organis factis*.

[84] Though commonly identified as Henry V, the composer 'Roy Henry' is most plausibly to be identified with his father Henry IV, actually described by one contemporary as 'in musica micans' (Harrison, *Music in Medieval Britain*, 221). In reality, it seems no more likely that Henry V was the composer of this arcane and intellectual music than that, for instance, Lord Nelson was in his spare time an accomplished amateur composer of string quartets.

[85] Roger Bowers, 'Choral establishments within the English church, 1340–1500', unpublished Ph.D. dissertation, University of East Anglia 1975, 4028–9.

undertook an injection of impetus into the cultivation and performance of polyphonic music by the choir of St George's Chapel, Windsor.[86] The manner in which this latter enterprise coincided exactly in time with comparable developments at Westminster suggests that the latter also may have been the result of direct royal initiative, conveyed to and implemented by a happily compliant Abbot Colchester.

The fifteenth-century choir, 1422–1480

Throughout the period following the interment of Henry V in the Abbey in 1422 the principal characteristic exhibited by the Lady chapel choir up to 1480 was one of stability, its personnel established at a membership of four singing-men.[87] After 1422 the annual pool was never reduced from its figure of £29 12s 0d; rather, the ongoing vitality of this department of the abbey's functions is suggested by the manner in which this sum was, from time to time, enhanced by small but permanent increments.[88] So amplified, the pool retained these levels of contribution right up until the Dissolution.[89]

The rate of pay offered to the singing-men was generous, and the very few names which have been preserved show that the abbey was able to attract the services of skilled practitioners. Indeed, the frequency with which these turn up at other points in their careers either earlier at St George's Chapel, Windsor (where until 1479 rates of pay were lower), or later at the Chapel Royal or St Stephen's Chapel, Westminster, is strongly suggestive of the prevalence of a rather cosy pattern of progress and promotion among these four choirs enjoying royal association and patronage.[90]

As possessor of so very singular a name, Thomas Thomas, a singing-man during 1450–1,[91] may be understood to be the man so named who by Michaelmas 1435 was already a lay clerk, master of the choristers and organ-player of St George's Chapel, Windsor, vacating these offices on 25 March 1439.[92] Since there was no monk of that

---

[86] Roger Bowers, 'The music and musical establishment of St George's Chapel in the fifteenth century', in *St George's Chapel, Windsor, in the Late Middle Ages*, ed. C. Richmond and E. Scarff, Windsor 2001, 171–214, at 179–80, 183–5.

[87] WAM 19683, 19685, 19687, 19692, *Expense forinsece*; 19687, 19727, *Expense in Ecclesia*; 23239, 23251, *Expense necessarie*. During 1436/7, when instead of his usual 40s 0d the almoner paid only 30s 0d as contribution to the singers' stipends, it was particularly noted that only three singers had been in office that year: WAM 19043, *Stipendia*.

[88] During the reign of Henry VI the warden of the new work 'had to pay a share of the costs of the secular singers': Westlake i, 190. WAM 23080, collector of Westminster rents 1462–3, *Expense forinsece*.

[89] The last surviving accounts of all nine obedientiaries involved show that the sums paid in the final days of the monastery had not been altered from those established by 1422. Monk bailiff 53s 4d (WAM 18714), infirmarer 66s 8d (WAM 19502), cellarer £5 6s 8d (WAM 18958), chamberlain £4 0s 0d (WAM 18827), warden of the churches 53s 4d (WAM 23451), almoner 40s 0d (WAM 19154), sacrist £5 6s 8d (WAM 19837), warden of the Lady chapel £4 5s 4d (WAM 23317), collector of Westminster rents 13s 4d (WAM 23178).

[90] It has not been possible to show if the John Bedyngham who was an employee of the abbey between 1440 and 1450 and returned briefly in 1453/4 (WAM 19684–7, 19694–5, 19698–700, 19704, *Vadia et Stipendia*) can be identified with the composer of that name, principal musician of St Stephen's Chapel, Westminster, in 1457.

[91] WAM 19700, *Expense in Ecclesia*.

[92] Bowers, 'The music and musical establishment of St George's Chapel', 188–9, 214.

name, the Richard Pridias who in 1460 received payment as a music scribe may readily be identified as one of the singing-men,[93] and may well be identifiable also with the Richard Prideaux who in 1451/2–1454 had been a lay clerk of St George's, Windsor, where also he had been rewarded for his diligence as a copyist of polyphonic music.[94] At Christmas 1448 John Barbour, 'Synger', took up residence in Sanctuary Yard; at Easter 1450 he vanishes from the record, but only because the abbey had agreed that he should thenceforth occupy his home rent-free, as a mark of its appreciation for his 'assiduous service'.[95]

English composition at this time enjoyed at large an enviable reputation for the novelty of its harmony and the grandeur of its conception. Little detailed information can now be found to illuminate precisely the content and manner of performance by the Lady chapel singers at Westminster; nevertheless, their pay was generous and their circumstances favourable, and their maintenance of a broad and challenging repertory from among the three- and four-voice settings of votive antiphons and masses of this period, may well be imagined.

For the singing-men the performance of polyphonic music remained an enduring priority, and with it the supply of books from which it was sung. Some idea of the singing-men's repertory may be gained from the manner in which in 1460 16d was paid to Richard Pridias for 'the noting of a mass of St Dunstan in a chapel book'.[96] This enabled them to perform, from their principal volume of polyphonic music and most probably at high mass in the monks' quire, what appears likely to have been a *cantus firmus* mass composed for use on the feasts of the saint celebrated as the abbey's primary founder. In 1483 two books of polyphony were in the care of the Warden and the clerk of the chapel; one at least was described as 'old' and evidently had been in use during much of the previous period.[97] As well as the books of polyphony, the organ of the Lady chapel was kept in use and repair, paid for at regular intervals up to 1465.[98] Its role at service remains obscure but was evidently significant, and eventually this manifestly deteriorating instrument was succeeded by a new during 1470–1.[99]

The singers remained based principally in the Lady chapel, the warden accounting for the consumption of candles provided for 'the singers and the celebrants' at mass.[100] Their contribution was recognised in a way characteristic of their employers. On the five principal feasts of the Virgin, to which in 1400 was added the Oblation,[101] Lady mass was celebrated with especial dignity reinforced by the presence of

---

[93] WAM 23232, *Expense necessarie*. WAM 19066–70, *Firme domorum*.
[94] Bowers, 'The music and musical establishment of St George's Chapel', 188–92.
[95] WAM 19698, *Firme infra sanctuarium, Custus domorum*; 19699, *Firme infra sanctuarium*.
[96] WAM 23232, *Expense necessarie: Et solut' Ricardo Pridias pro notacione unius misse de servicio sancti Dunstani in libro Capelle xvjd*. The payment seems too large to relate to the copying of merely the plainsongs of the propers of a mass of St Dunstan into the chapel's gradual.
[97] WAM 9479, also 23258 (1485), 23261 (1489): Item a prykked song boke . . . iij olde books of which oon is of prykked song and the other ij of playne song.
[98] WAM 23225–6, *Custus domorum [sic]*; 23230, 23239, *Expense necessarie*.
[99] WAM 23244, *Expense necessarie*. During 1475–6 the warden raised 10s 3d by selling 41 lb of metal, being an assemblage of old organ pipes. WAM 23250, *Recepcio forinceca: De xlj lb metalli de veteris pipes [sic] organorum precio libri iijd – xs iijd*.
[100] WAM 23221, 23223, stock account on verso; 23224–55, *Empcio stauri*.
[101] WAM 23201 *et seq.*, *Stipendia et expense necessarie* or *Expense necessarie*.

extra members of the monastic community.[102] From 1405 onwards it was recorded that the singers had begun to share with the monks in the refreshment provided on each occasion, to which in 1447–8 was added the feast of the Visitation.[103]

Meanwhile, the duties of the singing-men in reinforcing the monastic choir on the ten principal feasts continued throughout this period. Some of their singing in quire was done from a lectern, placed probably *in medio chori*, for use at which the sacrist in 1440–1 supplied a new stool.[104] If, as seems very likely, the function of the singers was to perform on feast-days polyphonic settings of the ordinary of high mass, and perhaps a motet at its conclusion, this would have been undertaken from a manuscript placed on such a lectern. It is possible that on the ten feasts the role of one of the secular singers included playing the organ in the monks' quire.

By now the services of the singing-men were also coming into demand for functions elsewhere in the church. Starting in 1431, and as a consequence of some specific benefaction, they were deputed to attend upon certain of the monks singing vespers and mass in the chapel of St Thomas on the feasts of both the martyrdom and the translation of St Thomas Becket and St Edmund.[105] The identity of the founder of this devotion has not been discovered. Moreover, between 1414 and 1418 the almoner had rewarded annually certain of the monks and the secular singers on the feasts of St Margaret and St Anne.[106] Probably this remuneration was in respect of their helping to honour the patronal festival by participating in the parish church of St Margaret (of which the almoner was rector) and the almonry chapel of St Anne in a celebration of mass. From 1435 until 1450 certain of the monks, with the secular singing-men, resumed this practice in respect of St Margaret's.[107] In their capacity as parishioners the singing-men may indeed have contributed much to a cultivation of music there; probably it is no accident that St Margaret's is one of the earliest parish churches in England whose services (from the 1470s onward) are known to have been regularly distinguished with the singing of polyphonic music.[108]

1480–1540: The amplified chorus of 1480 and its transfer to the new Lady chapel, 1512

It was in 1480, under the abbacy of the industrious John Estney, that a new horizon of enterprise was vested in the Lady chapel choir by means of the addition to its personnel of one entire new section. This step was taken in order to modernise the ensemble and to enable it to tackle a whole new repertory of polyphonic music that had developed in earnest during the previous fifteen years or so.

Until lately, polyphonic music for the church service at large had normally been

---

[102] WAM 23184 *et seq.*, *Exhennia et recreacio fratrum*. See above, 34.
[103] WAM 23224, *Expense necessarie*.
[104] WAM 19682, *Custus domorum*; 19684, 19692, *Expense in ecclesia*.
[105] WAM 18580, 18582: *Firme, Resolucio reddituum, Expense forinsece, Liberacio denariorum*; 23096, *Expense forinsece*.
[106] WAM 19019,19020,19022, *Minute*.
[107] WAM 19676,19683 *et seq.*, 19699, *Expense in Ecclesia*; 19044, 19047, *Minute*.
[108] As early as 1474/5 the churchwardens acquired a volume of 'pricksong', to which working additions began promptly to be made: Fiona Kisby, 'Music and musicians of early Tudor Westminster', *Early Music* 23, 1995, 223–40, at 226–7.

composed for the solo voices of just three or four adult males (altos and tenors), within an overall compass of two octaves. However, in about the early 1450s composers began to expand upon this traditional ensemble by adding to it both boys' treble and adult bass voices, and by composing for performance not just by specialist soloists but by all the members of a choral ensemble. By thus creating music engaging an overall compass extending to three octaves and a second, composed for a five-part chorus employing the voices of both boys and men, the composers were creating what has been considered ever since to be the unique and quintessential sound of English cathedral music. Tentatively begun in the 1450s, such composition by the mid-1460s was becoming standard, though set alongside and not replacing composition for men's voices alone.[109]

This was music which was speedily perceived at the greater monasteries as constituting a development in devotional practice fully worthy of adoption and replication, for its capacity to lend both dignity and beauty to the service.[110] However, the monastic environment offered only limited opportunities for its introduction; the engagement of a musical repertory involving the participation of young boys wholly external to the community of habited monks was necessarily confined to services sung in locations other than the principal quire. The locale most readily available for its adoption was evidently the Lady chapel, where its deployment at service offered particular gratification, enabling monastic communities closely to imitate their secular counterparts in devoting much of their cultivation of polyphony to adoration and veneration of the Virgin Mary.

Such music the four men's voices of the Lady chapel ensemble were not constituted to tackle. Consequently, with effect from 25 March 1480 the choir was modernised and augmented by the addition of a team of six boy's voices.[111] Once again, the boys were drawn from the obvious source, the resident scholars of the almonry grammar school.[112] To one of the singing-men was paid an increment of stipend, amounting to 13s 4d per year, to be emolument for his work as their master.[113]

Lady chapel inventories surviving from the 1480s indicate the manner in which this development involved no change to the historic content or nature of the work undertaken by the choir.[114] It continued to meet twice each day in the chapel just as before, supplementing with its music the devotions of the monks enatbled to offer the two principal observances conducted there,[115] the morning Lady mass and the evening antiphon. At the Lady mass the boys and singing-men combined with the

---

[109] Bowers, 'To chorus from quartet', 20–31.
[110] Bowers, 'The almonry schools of the English monasteries', 208–13.
[111] Among that minority of Lady chapel choirs which were of the Westminster type, of men's voices alone, the earliest yet known to have been augmented at this period with a team of boys' voices is that of Worcester cathedral priory, in 1478 on the initiative of John Alcock, bishop of Worcester: Bowers, 'Choral institutions within the English church', 6047–55.
[112] Within the grammar school the team of singing-boys was perceived from 1507 onwards as a somewhat distinct group, for whom separate provision of livery was made: WAM 19115, *Minute et expense necessarie*.
[113] Paid to the Master *pro erudicione puerorum cantancium*: WAM 19087–19154 (Almoner, 1479/80–1538/9), *Stipendia famulorum*.
[114] WAM 9479 (6 October 1483), 23258 (1 October 1485), 23261 (18 October 1489).
[115] Each inventory duly lists the stock of albs and amices required by all the altar party, as well as the chasubles supplied for the celebrant and tunicles and copes for deacon and subdeacon. Contrary to a

monks in the performance of its plainsong, and contributed the rendering in elaborate polyphony of the five constituent movements of the Ordinary (including the Kyrie), and of the Alleluia and sequence of the proper. In the late afternoon or early evening the choir attended upon the monk or monks appointed to observe the daily votive antiphon and collect addressed to the Virgin Mary, commencing this devotion with their performance of an elaborate polyphonic setting either of the text of 'Salve regina', as actually stipulated in the Consuetudinary, or of any other of the Marian antiphon texts commonly deputed to the composers of this period. It may be noted that at this time there existed certain monks who possessed the capacity actually to share with the secular singers the function of singing polyphonic music. One such was Edward Botiller, whom in 1489 the abbot commended as possessing 'competent lernyng and understondyng, and can syng bothe playn songe and prikked song'.[116]

As the fifteenth century closed the Lady mass and its singers were about to be favoured by the building of a lavish new chapel, and just as in earlier generations the interest and patronage of Richard II and Henry V had generated influences leaving a constructive mark on the history of Lady chapel music at the abbey, so also did that of Henry VII now. By late 1497 he had decided to create at Westminster a chapel to be the site both of his own tomb and chantry and of the shrine of Henry VI; he resolved to conjoin with these objectives an expression of the intensity of his piety towards the Virgin Mary, by demolishing the old Lady chapel and replacing it with a single building able to accommodate both its historic and enduring function and his own present ambitions.

The earliest sign of Henry's interest and intentions was the issue on 17 December 1497 of royal letters patent whose effect was to facilitate the establishment and maintenance thenceforth of elevated standards of musical performance for the Lady mass and evening antiphon.[117] The king granted powers to the monk-precentor or to his depute (meaning, in practice, the master of the Lady chapel choir) to take up for service at the abbey 'any well singing men and children, upon reasonable wages or exhibition wherewith they may be pleased', from anywhere in his realms (except for his own Chapel Royal and any other choir possessing royal exemption). He also granted the abbey exemption from any liability so to surrender any of its 'singing-men or children' to other choirs possessing like powers (his own Chapel Royal alone excepted).[118] By so granting licence to requisition the services of able singing-men and of boys already trained (a privilege never granted to any other monastic Lady

---

practice becoming common elsewhere, there is no indication that the Lady chapel choir at Westminster ever contributed at this period to the weekly Jesus mass and antiphon.

[116] WAM Register A, fo. 30v, quoted in Robinson and James, *The Manuscripts of Westminster Abbey*, 12. Indeed, among so large a body of monks it is likely that there always existed a certain number fully qualified not only to do full justice to the plainsong of the liturgy and devotions performed in the Lady chapel, but also to participate in the performance of polyphonic music by the secular singers when entabled to do so.

[117] *CPR 1494–1509*, 129–30.

[118] By 1497 such provisions were becoming quite common: see Bowers, 'The music and musical establishment of St George's Chapel', 204–6; idem, 'The cultivation and promotion of music in the household and orbit of Thomas Wolsey', in *Cardinal Wolsey: Church, State and Art*, ed. S. Gunn and P. Lindley, Cambridge 1991, 178–218, at 189–91. The payment by the sub-almoner of 10s 0d to a 'master Cornysh' in October 1522 may well have been made to William Cornysh the younger as an inducement to him not to use his powers to take a singing-boy for the Chapel Royal, where he was master of

chapel choir), the king signalled his concern that in terms of its music the observance of divine worship by the Lady chapel staff should aspire to the highest levels of artistic achievement. The effectiveness of such a privilege was evident in November 1511, when in the space of about a fortnight three new singing-boys were recruited by virtue of this commission: Richard Bemond, William Fynnes and Peter Best, all from London, the latter two from the choirs of the parish churches of St Botolph and St Olave respectively.[119]

Towards the end of 1502 the old Lady chapel was demolished, and on 24 January 1503 there was laid the foundation stone of its successor, the present Henry VII chapel. The observance of the daily Lady mass (with organ)[120] and evening antiphon was not interrupted, though the site to which they were temporarily re-located has not been determined.

It is thought that the new chapel was consecrated for use in about 1512. It was the king's original intention that the tomb of himself and his queen should lie to the west of the high altar 'a convenient space and distaunce from the grees [step] of the high Aultier'.[121] A 'convenient space' was that which allowed a clear sight of the altar from the two easternmost stalls on each side, occupied at Lady mass by the four choir monks, and which also left enough space immediately west of the step to accommodate the singing-men and boys. These were not to occupy any of the formal stalls, but to stand at desks located on the chapel floor, where mats were provided to reduce the discomfort of standing on chilly stone or tiles.[122] In the event, however, no shrine of Henry VI was ever established, and the tomb of Henry VII was located where it stands today, in a position east of the high altar which allowed ample space west of the then location of the altar-step to accommodate the singers immediately below it.[123]

From the outset it was understood that the respective personnel observing in the chapel its two distinct functions were to be entirely independent of each other. The four masses celebrated daily by monks at the tomb's chantry altar were spoken masses, so timed that three preceded daily Lady mass (begun at about 10.00 a.m.) and one followed it. At the weekly obit for the soul of Henry VII the displacement of matins of the dead, from its normal position immediately prior to requiem mass to the evening previous following Vespers,[124] is explicable by a desire not to incommode the Lady mass. The succession of the old Lady chapel by the new therefore impinged not at all on the manner of celebration of Lady mass and the observance of the evening antiphon, of which the history between 1480 and 1540 may be considered to be continuous.

---

the choristers. 'Fyrst in reward for master Cornysh on seynt Edwards day in October anno xiiij^{to} xs': WAM 33301, fo. 15r.

[119] WAM 33301, fo. 2r. The enduring value of the privilege was well recognised, and in 1535, when the original sealed text of the royal letters patent was accidentally mislaid, the abbey hastened to pay for and obtain a replacement: *L&P Henry VIII* viii, no. 291(61); Edward Pine, 'Westminster Abbey: some early Masters of the Choristers', *The Musical Times* 94, 1953, 258–60, at 259.

[120] WAM 23274, *Expense necessarie*.

[121] Will of Henry VII: Helen Dow, *The sculptural decoration of the Henry VII Chapel, Westminster Abbey*, Edinburgh 1992, 113.

[122] WAM 23290, *Expense necessarie*. See Fig. 6.

[123] See below, 154–9 and Fig 2.

[124] Indentures of 16 July 1504: *CClR 1500–09*, 139–40, 142–4, 151.

The Masters of the Lady Chapel Choir of Westminster Abbey, 1480–1540

[M = Michaelmas (29 September)]

1.	William Cornysh	25 March 1480 – 25 March 1491[125]
2.	William Park	M 1491 – M 1497[126]
3.	Robert Penn	M 1497 – M 1500[127]
4.	Thomas Watson	M 1500 – M 1502[128]
5.	John Kemp	M 1502 – M 1508 x M 1510[129]
6.	James	M 1508 x M 1510 – November 1511[130]
7.	Roger Cricktoft	December 1511 – M 1512 x M 1513[131]
8.	John George	M 1512 x M 1513 – M 1517[132]
9.	John Sylvester	M 1517 – M 1532[133]
10.	George Thaxton	M 1532 – M 1533 x M 1534[134]
11.	. . . . . . Mason	M 1533 x M 1534 – M 1534 x M 1535[135]
12.	William Green	M 1534 x M 1535 – January 1540[136]

The office of teacher of the singing-boys, and thus of master of the choir, was filled continuously from 1480 up until 1540. The duty of the master, as well as to coach the boys in the plainsong and ceremony of the services at which they were in attendance and to train them in the techniques of improvised descant, was to teach to them their parts in the extended and elaborate polyphony cultivated throughout this period. There is no indication that the boys ever joined the singing-men at service in the monks' quire on the ten principal feasts.

The choir's daily performance of Lady mass and Marian antiphon offered a reasonable chance for the maintenance of a repertory of real challenge and quality; nevertheless, compared with the full liturgical round of Salisbury use as observed by a secular church (cathedral or collegiate) or aristocratic household chapel, any monastic Lady chapel choir offered only a limited opportunity for the exercise of musical endeavour and enterprise. Among those recruited to be master at Westminster it is likely that the ablest men soon reached the point at which they felt they had achieved all they could, so prompting them to move onward to another post elsewhere that offered greater scope. None is known to have come from a comparable post prior to this appointment; several, however, are known to have proceeded to distinguished

---

[125] WAM 19087–99, *Stipendia famulorum*.
[126] WAM 19102–7, *Stipendia famulorum*.
[127] WAM 19108–11, *Stipendia famulorum*.
[128] WAM 19112, *Stipendia famulorum*. Cambridge, St John's College, MS D.91.20, pp. 43, 45.
[129] WAM 19113–15, *Stipendia famulorum*.
[130] WAM 19116, *Stipendia famulorum*; 33301, fo. 2v.
[131] WAM 19117, *Stipendia famulorum*. Here his name is given as the odd-looking 'Cretoff'; probably, however, he is to be identified with the 'Roger kryktet' to whom (apparently as incoming Master) the sub-almoner paid 5s 0d in December 1511 (WAM 33301, fo. 2v), and both appear likely to be variant spellings of the more plausible 'Cricktoft' found in e.g. WAM 23305, 23309–15, 23317 (1528/9–1536/7), *Recepte*.
[132] WAM 19118–22, *Stipendia famulorum*.
[133] WAM 19124–47, *Stipendia famulorum*. WAM 33301, fos. 7r, 8r, 11v, 15r, 16r, 16v.
[134] WAM 19148–9, *Stipendia famulorum*. On WAM 19148 Thaxton's name was incorrectly written as 'Caxston'.
[135] WAM 19149, *Stipendia famulorum*.
[136] WAM 19152–4, *Stipendia famulorum*. BL, Add. MS 40061, fo. 4r. Pine, 'Westminster Abbey: some early Masters of the Choristers', 259.

careers elsewhere following it. This feature suggests that such an appointment tended to be sought by young men near the start of their careers, who used it as a stepping-stone to finer things elsewhere.

The most celebrated of the masters of the Lady chapel choir (table, above) was the first, William Cornysh, identifiable as the elder of the two musicians of this name.[137] It is possible that he was specially recruited to fill a post newly created in March 1480, but no less likely that in fact he was then already one of the singing-men. His services were much valued by the abbey, by whom by 1489 he was being styled 'gentilman'. It rented to him cheaply a substantial mansion located in Sanctuary Yard;[138] a few days after leaving the abbey's service he, with his wife Joan, renewed the lease, and expressly as inducement for continuation of his good will he was permitted to continue paying only the much reduced rent.[139] Probably he had moved on to membership of the household chapel, distinguished but peripatetic, of some member of the aristocracy.[140] He died in 1502, and was buried in the cemetery of St Margaret's, of which his residence in Sanctuary Yard rendered him a parishioner.[141] The Almonry in 1509 possessed a silver bowl donated by William Cornysh, 'syngar',[142] apparently a memento for use at the singing-boys' table there.

Nothing other than his Westminster career is known about Cornysh's immediate successor William Park. Robert Penn had already been one of the singing-men since at least Michaelmas 1493;[143] after leaving Westminster, he occurs from February 1503 until his death in 1538 as a Gentleman of the Chapel Royal.[144] In 1502 his successor Thomas Watson likewise moved on to grander things elsewhere, as a singing-man and possibly master of the choristers of the chapel of Margaret Beaufort, mother of Henry VII.[145] She died in 1509, and by 1514, and until his death in 1523/4, Watson was master of the choir (of cathedral strength and quality) maintained by the guild of St Mary in the parish church of St Botolph, Boston (Lincolnshire).[146]

---

[137] For an endeavour to apportion the available biographical data between these two namesakes, see Roger Bowers, 'Cornysh, William', *Oxford Dictionary of National Biography*, forthcoming.

[138] Register of the common seal: WAM Lease Book 1, fo. 15r; WAM 17887.

[139] WAM Lease Book 1, fo. 49v. His widow Joan retained possession of their home in Sanctuary Yard until her death in 1519: WAM 23272–5, 23285–94, *Firme terrarum*.

[140] It may have been at the instigation of so potent an employer that from Christmas 1499 Cornysh was granted by the abbey a substantial annual pension of £5 6s 8d: WAM Lease Book 1, fo. 116r. There appear to be no compelling grounds for belief that this William Cornysh ever became a Gentleman of Henry VII's Chapel Royal (*pace* Kisby, 'Music and musicians of early Tudor Westminster', 227, 236).

[141] David Skinner, 'William Cornysh: clerk or courtier?', *The Musical Times*, May 1997, 5–17, at 9, 11.

[142] 'Item a bolle of sylver plane [plain] with a foot parcell gilte of the gift of William Comysh syngar weyng [weighing] xv unces di'. WAM 6597.

[143] Rosser, *Medieval Westminster*, 160 and n. 201. WAM 19105–19110, *Stipendia famulorum*; 23265–23268, *Expense necessarie*.

[144] Kisby, 'Music and musicians of early Tudor Westminster', 228, 232; Andrew Ashbee and David Lasocki, *A Biographical Dictionary of English Court Musicians 1485–1714*, 1 vol. in 2, Aldershot 1998, 879–80. Pine, *Westminster Abbey Singers*, 26.

[145] Cambridge, St John's College, MS D.91.20, pp. 43, 45, 106. A preliminary account of the household chapel of Lady Margaret appears in Fiona Kisby, 'A mirror of monarchy: music and musicians in the household chapel of the Lady Margaret Beaufort, mother of Henry VII', *Early Music History* 16, 1997, 203–34.

[146] At Boston he supervised the installation of a new organ built by Anthony Duddyngton in 1519/20, and received compositions from numerous contemporary composers, including in 1521/2 Thomas

John Kemp had been a singing-man of the Lady chapel since at least Michaelmas 1499.[147] His destination after leaving Westminster is not known; he continued to be remembered there, gratuities being given in December 1511 both to him and to Robert Penn.[148] The longest tenure of all was enjoyed by John Sylvester; already a singing-man of the Lady chapel in December 1511,[149] he came to enjoy sufficient distinction successfully to supplicate the university of Oxford in February 1522 for award of the degree of bachelor of music.[150] George Thaxton presently became a lay clerk of the choir and organist of St George's Chapel, Windsor, where he is found between 1547 and 1555.[151] William Grene did not need to seek promotion elsewhere to obtain work at a major secular church, since following the dissolution in 1540 he remained as the first master of the choristers of the successor new foundation cathedral.[152]

As well as six boys the full Lady chapel choir now consisted of five singing-men, for in March 1480 the mastership was created as an office additional to the established four.[153] Perhaps a retrenchment was effected while the choir was temporarily re-located during the building of the new chapel; four were recorded in December 1511,[154] a number also indicated for 1508/9.[155] However, by no later than 1515/16 there were again five,[156] a number probably restored immediately upon the consecration of the new chapel. Except for the period December 1522 – December 1523, when their number was briefly recorded consistently as four,[157] five remained the complement of singing-men thereafter.[158]

Of the singers themselves little is known beyond a few names. Penn, Kemp and Sylvester had all been singing-men prior to their elevation to the mastership.[159] It is just possible that the composer Nicholas Ludford was briefly one of their number. Probably of a local family, he rented property from the abbey between Christmas 1516 and Michaelmas 1522,[160] the latter probably marking the date of his appointment to the choir of St Stephen's Chapel, Westminster. Roger Empson, already in office by December 1522, survived to become one of the inaugural lay vicars of the

---

Ashwell. BL MS Egerton 2886, fos. 16v, 263r; 135r, 151v, 178v, 204v (Duddyngton); 204r, 207r (Ashwell).

[147] WAM 19111–19112, *Stipendia famulorum*; 23269–23271, *Expense necessarie*.
[148] WAM 33301, fo. 3r. Kisby, 'Music and musicians of early Tudor Westminster', 228.
[149] WAM 33301, fo. 3r.
[150] Emden, *Oxford*, 516.
[151] Edmund H. Fellowes, *Organists and Master of the Choristers of St George's Chapel, Windsor Castle*, Windsor 1939, 21–2.
[152] BL Add. MS 40061, fo. 4r.
[153] Four singing-men in 1476/7: WAM 23251, *Expense necessarie*. Five thereafter up to 1505/6: inventories 1483, 1485, 1489 (WAM 9479, 23258, 23261); 23260, *Empcio stauri*; 19749, *Expense ecclesie*; 23274, *Expense necessarie*.
[154] WAM 33301, fo. 2v.
[155] New surplices: 20 ells of cloth purchased instead of usual 25: WAM 23278, *Expense necessarie*.
[156] WAM 23288, *Expense necessarie*.
[157] WAM 33301, fos. 15r, 18r; 33314, fos. 6v, 6v, 7r. Also 32299, 33300 (undated but evidently directly contemporaneous).
[158] WAM 33301, fos. 7r, 11r; 33314, fo. 4v; 23296, 23304, *Expense necessarie*.
[159] See above, 52–3.
[160] Kisby, 'Music and musicians of early Tudor Westminster', 233–4. John Ludford (possibly the composer of that name) was, as a sub-tenant, a resident of a property of the Almoner during 1463/4: WAM 19070, *Custus domorum*.

new foundation in 1540.[161] Of Empson's two colleagues, Coks and Roger, nothing further is known for certain.[162] The three other singing-men sharing with Empson the top of the list by seniority at the establishment of the new foundation in 1540 may very well have been his colleagues as the last singing-men of the Lady chapel choir: Lewis Mugge, Thomas Wharleton and Thomas Youell.[163]

On all occasions for which evidence survives the number of singing-boys was six.[164] Due provision was made for a comprehensive education in music; lessons on a keyboard instrument were expedited from about 1512 by the purchase of a clavichord from Robert Hamme,[165] a Gentleman of the Chapel Royal who lived locally.[166] In 1514, to expedite their lessons in the grammar school, four primers were obtained for their use.[167] For the period 1511–24 some dozen names of singing-boys can be recovered; however, none is at present known to have proceeded to a conspicuous career in music in adult life.[168] The boys were granted enjoyment of a 'boy bishop' celebration of their own on each 6 December. However, this took the form primarily of a party; the monastic environment offered no scope for involving them in the liturgical solemnities proper to Holy Innocents' day (28 December).[169]

From two sources it is possible to glean some direct impression of the character of the music performed by the Lady chapel choir in these final decades of its separate existence. The inaugural master, William Cornysh, is now recognised as among the foremost composers of his generation;[170] four works survive complete, and a fifth is completable. 'Ave Maria, mater dei' and 'Gaude virgo, mater Christi', each for four men's voices, are composed in a style at once both concentrated and compact, the

---

[161] WAM 33301, fo. 15r. BL, Add. MS 40061, fo. 4r.

[162] WAM 33301, fo. 15r. Roger's wife: WAM 33301, fos. 16r, 19v. Coks may very well be identifiable with Thomas Cocke, singing-man, whose will was proved in the Westminster Commissary Court in 1531: Kisby, 'Music and musicians of early Tudor Westminster', 237.

[163] BL, Add. MS 40061, fo. 4r. Thomas Youell occurs later as a lay clerk of the choir of Canterbury Cathedral.

[164] WAM 33301, fos. 2r, 2v, 4v, 7r, 7r, 8r, 11r, 11r, 15r; 32045B. The making of 28 pairs of double-soled and 14 pairs of single-soled shoes in December 1511 may indicate a short-term overlap of tenures during which there were briefly seven boys: 33301, fo. 2v.

[165] 'Item to Roberd hame for a peyr of clavycors vjs viijd'. WAM 33301, fo. 14r (undated note in hand identifiable as that of William Fitts, Subalmoner 1511–1513, deceased 1513).

[166] Ashbee and Lasocki, *Biographical Dictionary*, 538; Kisby, 'Music and musicians of early Tudor Westminster', 228.

[167] WAM 33301, fo. 4v.

[168] All from WAM 33301. For a list, see Kisby, 'Music and musicians of early Tudor Westminster', 236–7, though for 'S[teven] More' read 'Simon More', for 'B. Russell' read 'Edward Russell', for 'J[ohn] Walker' read 'T[homas] Walker' (for whom see also *ibid.*, 235), for 'J[ohn] Wappys' read 'J. Wappys', and for 'W[illiam] Whyght' read 'W. Whyght'.

[169] As well as presiding over the party the 'bishop', attended by his fellows, made the conventional tour of the neighbourhood, the singing-men providing his escort. WAM 33301, fos. 2v, 6v, 7r, 11r, 15r, 18r. WAM 32306.

[170] As first proposed by Skinner, 'William Cornysh: clerk or courtier?' Eight major works were included in the principal manuscript surviving from this period, the Eton Choirbook of c.1502–4. The Magnificat (*Early Tudor Magnificats* i, ed. P. Doe, Early English Church Music 4, 1962, 49–64) sets a text for quire Vespers, in a style whose extremes of self-consciously extrovert virtuosity might be thought to exceed those which could be realised by a small Lady chapel choir; most probably this dates from later in Cornysh's career.

former in particular exhibiting a notable suavity and elegance of melody;[171] it has achieved much popularity in recent years. The latter piece is likewise relatively brief and direct in its expression. Both may well represent the music of the evening Marian antiphon as sung in the old Lady chapel.

The settings of 'Salve regina' and 'Stabat mater dolorosa' were likewise suitable as evening antiphons.[172] Scored for the standard five-part choir of this period (treble, alto, two tenors, bass), both may well have been written between 1480 and 1491 for the full ensemble of voices at Westminster, the former indeed composed to a text actually specified for the Marian antiphon there.[173] Florid in melody, exuberant in rhythm, extended and virtuosic, these compositions make great demands on the voices of men and boys alike, and certainly stand as a tribute to the skill of the singers by whom they were performed, and of the masters by whom the singers were trained.

Of the polyphonic music sung for the ordinary of Lady mass, an insight into that being performed in about the 1520s is yielded by some fragments of manuscript which may well be of abbey provenance.[174] Both are in choirbook format, and unmistakably English. One preserves the alto part commencing a setting of Sanctus (verso), and an evidently elaborate *gymel* involving two trebles beginning the Benedictus (recto).[175] The second contains a setting of Agnus dei, probably for four voices; parts of the alto and bass remain on the verso, and of the treble and tenor on the recto.[176] Exhibiting a rhythmic character of especial exuberance, the Sanctus is probably the earlier (perhaps c.1500); in this respect, the Agnus (perhaps c.1520) is rather more restrained, though the melismatic style of word-setting exhibited by both is immensely extended and spacious.

Inventories of the 1480s list the books from which such music was performed. One choirbook, perhaps recently acquired in 1483 and containing music for the newly expanded choir, was listed simply as 'a prykkyd song boke'. It contrasted with a second book 'of prykked song' of greater age, listed as 'olde'.[177] The stock of polyphony was increased in December 1511 by the purchase of 'a pryksong booke of masses antems and other songs',[178] a mixed collection of compositions typical of the repertory of a Lady chapel choir. To use such books of polyphony the singers gath-

---

[171] *The Eton Choirbook*, ed. Frank Ll. Harrison, 3 vols., Musica Britannica 10–12, 2nd edn, London 1967–73, iii, 57–8, 59–62.
[172] *Ibid.* i, 116–23; ii, 137–48.
[173] See above, 35.
[174] WAM, MSS 102A–B, 103. In England such settings of the Latin mass were rendered redundant in 1549, and as unwanted waste these leaves were incorporated into the English bindings of contemporary theological books imported from abroad, MSS 102A–B into D.2.31 (Paris, 1549), and MS 103 into F.1.15 (Paris, 1545).
[175] WAM MS 103.
[176] WAM MSS 102A and 102B, which fit together to create a continuous vertical strip. The clef of the highest voice (C1, not present but implied by flats applied to pitches *b* and *e*, each doubled at the respective octave) is unusual; the legend 're wo·', 're way', or 're fo·' appearing beneath all instances of a *minor color* figure consisting of a blackened breve and two blackened minims defies all attempts at comprehension.
[177] WAM 9479, 23258, 23261. Regarding the books used at service, the texts of all three inventories are identical.
[178] WAM 33301, fo. 3r.

ered round a single lectern provided for the purpose.[179] For the plainsong of Lady mass, sung from the desks,[180] the inventories included four graduals and two other 'olde' books, supplemented by two unbound quires each containing the service of a feast recently introduced, respectively the Visitation and the Oblation.

In its capacity as primarily the Lady chapel, the new Henry VII chapel was furnished from the start with at least one organ. Like its distant predecessor of 1304,[181] the last 'great organ' of the old Lady chapel had not stood on the chapel floor but had been suspended in some elevated location on an interior wall, to which access was gained by steps which had required repair in 1489/90.[182] In all likelihood this had been the established and permanent location of the successive great organs of the old chapel, and in all probability this convention was preserved in the new. Amongst this building's astonishing prodigality of decoration, the west interior wall above the entrance doorways stands out as the sole plane space remaining bare and unadorned by anything other than elementary blind arcading (Plate II). It appears certain that it was always intended and expected that some elaborate item of furniture or equipment should be installed against and obscuring this wall, and the great organ of the chapel and its ancillary loft is the obvious candidate. However, all that is now known of this instrument is its propensity to require repair.[183]

The Lady chapel singers also performed elsewhere within the Abbey and even in the immediate neighbourhood beyond the precinct wall. On 7 December 1530 the probate of the will of John Potter, an officer of the Abbey treasurer, brought into effect his request that on every Friday for one year following his death 'the syngers of our lady masse of the monastre of westm[inster]' should sing before some image of St Peter within the abbey church 'in suche maner as shall please them, playne songe or other wise', a prayer beginning 'Iuste iudex, Jesu Christe', followed by a collect and further prayer.[184] Members of the choir continued to contribute on suitably festal occasions to the performance of elevated music at services in the neighbouring parish church of St Margaret.[185] Such influences might flow two ways. It is possible that the content and nature of music-making at service in the Lady chapel was enhanced by the availability, if sought, of advice and even participation from any of the distin-

---

[179] *Et in j pecia ferri pro emendacione lectrine pro Cantatoribus in Capella et in clavis ad eundem [sic] ijd*. WAM 23250, *Expense necessarie*.
[180] *Et in emendacione lez deske[s] pro Cantatoribus in Capella predicta xijd*. WAM 23262, *Custus Reparacionis Capelle*.
[181] See above, 36.
[182] *Et in emendacione graduum euncium ad organa in dicta Capella vjd*. WAM 23262, *Custus Reparacionis Capelle*.
[183] WAM 23305, 23314, 23315, *Expense necessarie*. It is noteworthy that among the very ample and detailed dissolution inventories of 1539–40 none was made relating to the goods and furniture of the Lady chapel (see Mackenzie E.C. Walcott, 'The inventories of Westminster Abbey at the Dissolution', *Transactions of the London and Middlesex Archaeological Society* 4, 1875, 313–64). Evidently, no interference with ongoing intercession for the soul of Henry VIII's father or with the conduct of Lady mass and antiphon was intended or expected to arise merely from the dissolution of the monastery.
[184] For distribution to the participants, Potter instructed that 20d per week be delivered by his executors 'to thands of the maister of the children syngers'. PRO, PROB 11/23, frame 190r (24 Jankyn).
[185] Kisby, 'Music and musicians of early Tudor Westminster', 226; Skinner, ' "At the mynde of Nycholas Ludford": new light on Ludford from the churchwardens' accounts of St Margaret's, Westminster', *Early Music* 22, 1994, 393–413, at 396; Rosser, *Medieval Westminster*, 272–3.

guished musicians who made Westminster their home, such as Henry Abyndon, Richard Ede, and several members of the Chapel Royal.[186]

In the intensely musical nation which England had become by 1539–40 the monastic Lady chapel choirs, given their limitation to two observances per day, were no longer among the most conspicuous of the country's many contributors of choral endeavour to realisation of the beauty of holiness in divine worship. Nevertheless, the Lady chapel choir of Westminster Abbey was one of only a dozen or so which boasted a comprehensively professional membership of both men and boys, and, especially in the sixteenth century, the abbey's royal associations, plus the centrality of its locale and its ability to offer high rates of pay, certainly were factors militating in favour of genuinely elevated standards of performance. The government of Henry VIII appreciated the value of the Lady chapel choirs sufficiently strongly to instruct that in the case of any re-founded institution its choir was not to be dissolved along with the parent monastery. Rather, the Westminster Abbey singers of January 1540 were retained to become the nucleus of the choir of twenty-six men and ten boys and their master then provided for the collegiate church of St Peter in Westminster, by whom the daily Lady mass and votive antiphon continued to be observed in the Lady chapel for so long as the Latin service continued, and by whose successors the music of divine worship has been sustained in the abbey church ever since.

Appendix

The Singing-men of the Lady Chapel Choir, 23 Richard II (22 June – 29 September 1399)

Anno regno regis Ricardi secundi xxiij°. Isti fuerunt Cantores seculares in Ecclesia Westmonasteriensi, scilicet:
Johannes Byfeld Tenor habuit hoc anno pro stipendiis suis x marcas cum ij Tunicis et una furrura
Item Johannes Tyes organista habuit absque vestura x li
Item Willelmus Causton habuit x marcas et vesturam et furruram sicut J. Byfeld
Item Johannes Barker Treble habuit ix marcas cum vestura et furrura ut supra
Item Johannes Grede Treble habuit x marcas absque vestura et furrura
Item Petrus Pleford Treble habuit ix marcas cum vestura et furrura ut supra
Item Johannes Browing Treble habuit Cs cum j vestura absque furrura

Summa preter vesture et furrure [sum total not entered]

WAM Liber Niger, fo. 86v

---

[186] Kisby, 'Music and musicians of early Tudor Westminster', 223–40. However, reports that these residents included, 1502–5 and 1513–19, William Cornysh the younger, master of the choristers of the Chapel Royal, appear to be mistaken, resting on misunderstanding of the entries recording the continued occupation of the elder Cornysh's home by his widow (*relicta*): note 139 above, and WAM 23272–5, 23285–94, *Firme terrarum*.

God Save the King! Piety, Propaganda, and the Perpetual Memorial[1]

MARGARET CONDON

THE PLAT, or drawing, signed by Henry VII's own hand, for the design of the Lady chapel to be built at St Peter's, Westminster, and the *schema*, in the form of a plat similarly signed, for the glazing of the windows of the new chapel, are not known to survive. What does survive, however, in addition to the magnificent chapel, unified in concept and regal in execution, is the intellectual map of the king's intentions, spiritual and temporal, in directing and funding the building itself. These are formally embodied in his last will, dated 31 March 1509, three weeks before his death, and in the remarkable series of indentures, finalised between July and December 1504, founding the chantry in the chapel, an almshouse at Westminster, and other prayers, suffrages and endowments, both at Westminster and in other religious houses and institutions of his realm. The building of the chapel, of which the foundation stone was laid on 24 January 1503, his burial at Westminster on 11 May 1509, and the erection of his tomb after 1512 (albeit displaced from the site originally specified), were the culmination of a process which had begun more than a decade before. Together, in the repeated terminology of both the will and the indentures, the chapel and the services it was to support were to be a perpetual memorial whilst the world should endure.

---

[1] This paper was originally drafted in 1996. Since that time adverse circumstances have conspired against any substantial update of the text, although mature reflection suggests other avenues to be pursued. I am indebted to Dr R.E. Archer, Miss E.A. Danbury, Dr M.R. Foster, Dr E.M. Hallam and Dr Richard Mortimer for their comments on earlier versions of this chapter and for their support and encouragement, and to Miss Barbara Harvey who first drew my attention to the warden's accounts of Henry VII's foundation in the abbey. Thanks are due also to Dr Mortimer and to Miss Christine Reynolds of Westminster Abbey Muniment Room, and the late Mr Ken Wilcocks and the repository staff of the Public Record Office for their assistance in making available manuscripts which are still regarded as being among the particular treasures of their respective archives. Other debts are acknowledged in the footnotes.

The development of the king's project

The will and the indentures signpost a process begun as early as 1494, and continuing after Henry VII's death. By 1494 the king had begun to plan for his posthumous memorial, which was to be enhanced by its close physical association with the cult of Henry VI.[2] He commenced the rebuilding of the Lady chapel of St George's Chapel, Windsor, in preparation for his own future burial there, and by 1501 work had begun on his tomb. Papal bulls obtained between 1494 and 1498 indicate that the many elements of Henry VII's eventual memorial were already present in broad outline in the Windsor phase of the project – not only a perpetual chantry and the association with Holy King Henry, but also the sufficient endowment, the special privileges of indulgence, even a hospital or almshouse outside the walls.[3] But in 1498 the monks of both Chertsey and Westminster disputed Windsor as Henry VI's preferred place of rest and a conciliar enquiry found in Westminster's favour.[4] In consequence, Henry VII turned the focus of his efforts to Westminster, and the building work at Windsor was largely completed by other hands.[5]

On 26 July 1498 the king set his seal to a solemn promise. He was to obtain from the pope a bull for the translation of Henry VI, and to change and alter in favour of Westminster all those things which, to the laud of God, and to the honour of the holy body of his uncle, he had begun or had intended to do at Windsor. For this, and for the costs of the translation, Westminster was required to contribute £500, spread over three years. This amount, whose payment is recorded in the account of the abbey's sacrist for 1500–1 as a payment for the removal of the body, continued to skew the sacrist's account for some years to come; the imbalance was partially redressed only in 1509–10 by the substantial offerings made at Henry VII's own funeral, that of his mother, and the coronation of his son.[6] But Henry VI has now no place in the secular or sacred imagery of the chapel and is easily forgotten. Iconoclasm has removed the holy man's statue, although a graffito identifies its niche and thus the site of his altar in the easternmost apsidal chapel.[7] By the assumed decision of his son, Henry VIII, Henry VII's own tomb stands on the likely intended location of a shrine for Henry VI, and is itself thus displaced from the place of honour before the high altar specified in his will of 1509. The promised translation remains unfulfilled. The promise was renewed by the king's will but, in contrast to the clear, specific, and effective arrangements for his own memorial, the translation of Henry VI was expressed as no more than a pious hope. It waited at the least on the completion of the chapel; but depended still more on the particular processes of the papal curia, ultimately outside his control. Despite his genuine commitment, the hoped-for canonisation had not

---

[2] Henry VII regularly made an offering at Windsor to Holy King Henry as well as St George; a practice continued by Henry VIII.
[3] *Foedera* xii, 563–6; Colvin, *HKW* iii, 308–15.
[4] Colvin, *HKW* iii, 309–10; WAM 6389*; 6389**; 6389***; printed with related documents in Stanley, *Historical Memorials*, 3rd edn, 1869, 600–17.
[5] Colvin, *HKW* iii, 308–15.
[6] WAM 19756, 19768; agreement WAM 6389***, printed in full in Stanley, *Historical Memorials*, 615–16.
[7] The siting of Henry VI's altar, chapel and shrine is discussed in C. Wilson, below, 154–9. Wilson has also identified an image of Henry VI in the carving of the prior's stall.

been achieved by the time of his death and the case, already flawed, was not pursued thereafter with the same tenacity.[8] Yet that anticipated translation of a canonised familial saint profoundly influenced the ground plan of the chapel and, during Henry VII's life, the implied association with Henry VI's supposed sanctity was a continuing strand in the construction of Henry Tudor's own memorial. It was further extended by his will through the bequests for the completion of the chapel of Henry VI's foundation at King's College, Cambridge;[9] the special bequest to Henry VI's altar at Westminster;[10] and even in the completion of Henry VII's most innovative project, the hospital of the Savoy, whose imagery included a painted statue of Holy King Henry.[11]

The enquiry as to Henry VI's preferred place of burial proved, however, to be the crucial catalyst for the alteration and enlargement of Henry VII's design. The king formally accepted the advice of his council on 26 July 1498. At some time between that date and the death of Abbot Fascet in the autumn of 1500 an agreement was reached between Henry VII, Fascet and John Islip, the then prior, on the terms of a perpetual chantry and associated suffrages, culminating each year in anniversary services. It may safely be assumed that, as at Windsor, this memorial was to be associated with a rebuilding of the existing Lady chapel. Other works were to be associated with the enterprise. The king declared his intent to build an almshouse besides the monastery, to be overseen by the monks, and indicated that the chantry centred on Westminster would be mirrored annually elsewhere within the realm. For these 'foreign obits' the abbot and convent were to act as treasurers, issuing an annual dole in payment. It is tempting to suppose that negotiations towards furthering this agreement were the principal topic of discussion when, on 11 June 1501, Henry VII dined with John Islip, George Fascet's successor, in the abbot's lodgings at Cheyneygates.[12]

By July 1502 the essential terms had been worked out. On 7 July, by indenture under the sign manual and privy seal (now missing) made between the king and Islip, the abbot and convent were granted the college of St Martin le Grand, Luffield priory, and other lands and revenues spiritual and temporal to an estimated annual value of nearly £400. The grants, allowing revenues to be taken until Michaelmas 1503 from dates which commenced variously from Michaelmas 1500 to Michaelmas 1502, were 'towards thexecucion and fulfillenge of suche parte of the kinges laste will as herafter is declared . . .'. The abbot was to make account in February following for the revenues actually received, and either restore to the king any over-payment, or to receive from him full recompense for any shortfall. The

---

[8] For the cult and the appeals for canonisation, B.P. Wolffe, *Henry VI*, 1981, 351–8; S. Anglo, *Images of Tudor Kingship*, 1992, 70–3. For the cult of Henry VI as peace maker, an element of which is embedded in Henry VII's own presentation of himself in his memorial services, see S. Walker, 'Political saints in later medieval England', in *The McFarlane Legacy: Studies in Late Medieval Politics and Society*, ed. R.H. Britnell and A.J. Pollard, Stroud 1995, 94–8.

[9] PRO, E 23/3, fo. 11v. All references to the will are to the original manuscript. A full text of the will was published as *The Will of Henry VII*, ed. T. Astle, 1775. A revised text is included in the present volume.

[10] A pair of silver gilt candlesticks additional to the bequests of vestments and plate made to all the altars within the chapel. PRO, E 23/3, fos. 14, 14v.

[11] WAM 63509; R. Somerville, *The Savoy*, 1960, 18.

[12] WAM 33320, fo. 35. The original agreement with Fascet is lost, but lies behind the text discussed below.

conditions of the grant were broadly those to which the abbot and convent would agree in 1504 with the exception of payments for the foreign obits and for fifty-eight weekly and periodic sermons, both of which were specifically excluded from this interim agreement. The date of the anniversary to be observed was not specified, since behind this summary document lay the detailed, but now lost, agreement with Abbot Fascet and Prior Islip. Crucially for the dating of the text of the indentures of 1504, this deed of 1502 included the provision for an annual dole of £3 7s 4d 'for the redenge of the saide papiers and of the Indentours whan they shalbe engrosed in the chapitre house . . .'.[13]

When finally engrossed those indentures were a somewhat different document. The agreement with Islip enabled the immediate commencement of some part of the king's device, but was afterwards revised. It had not even been complete of itself. The annual cost of the almsmen's gowns and pittances is an addition, possibly in the king's own handwriting. Two years on other services showed an increase of provision, and perhaps of requirement: the ceremony for the anniversary was almost certainly enlarged, its emphasis altered, and its date changed. Demonstrable increases in cost between 1502 and 1504 include, for example, twenty rather than twelve pence apiece for the scutcheons for the almsmen's robes, and 13s 4d rather than 10s as remuneration for each of the fifty-eight sermons.

On 16 July 1504, eighteen months after the foundation stone of the Lady chapel had been laid, indentures bipartite and septipartite, collectively embodying the terms of the king's foundation, were sealed and acknowledged, separately and together, in the abbey's chapter house by, or on behalf of, the two main parties.[14] Three days before, the abbey had been granted its customary privileges in all the lands of the new endowment, and on 15 July its title was further secured through the pardon of alienations and donations, effectively buttressing the earlier mortmain licences.[15] Finalisation of the long cherished agreement triggered a major release of funds in the week of 19 July. The books of the king's Chamber record the transfer of £5,000 upon an indenture, £579 13s 2d in recompense of an overspend on the abbot's account for the chapel, and £300 by way of prest.[16] However broken down, these large sums are one more indication of the size and urgency of the king's investment. In terms of both its requirements and its endowment it far exceeded earlier royal foundations at Westminster.[17] This was deliberate. The agreements of 1504 make specific reference to Richard II's anniversary; and Islip, both as abbot and as a former warden of the manors which endowed the foundations of Queen Eleanor, Richard II and Henry V would have been closely familiar with their terms.

[13] WAM 6634. For the limited financial benefit derived from St Martin's Le Grand, where services still had to be maintained, and an anniversary observed, Harvey, *Estates*, 198–9, 399.
[14] For the sealing of the indentures septipartite, which appears to have been staggered, see below, 79–80. There is no particular reason to suppose that the king, who had removed from Westminster to Greenwich on 13 July, was present.
[15] *CPR 1494–1509*, 245, 303–5, 364, 365, 374–9.
[16] BL Additional MS 59899, fo. 62.
[17] See table and references in Harvey, *Estates*, 33–6.

The will

Various strands of intent can be teased out from the king's will. The thirteenth century Lady chapel which preceded Henry VII's new chapel in the abbey of St Peter was the place of burial of Katherine de Valois, widow of Henry V, daughter of Charles VI of France, and, by her marriage to Owen Tudor, the king's grandmother. By linking Katherine's burial with his own new enterprise, there is an association with the victories of Henry V in France; with the English claim to the French throne; and with Henry VII's supposed descent (as with any other English king) from St Louis IX,[18] as well as an overt act of familial piety in honouring the king's paternal grandmother.[19] Burial at Westminster would confirm, in death as in life, the king's dynastic legitimacy. It was the place where Henry, as other kings, had received his solemn anointing and coronation, and was the place of 'commen sepulture' of kings.[20] Not only did the abbey of St Peter's, Westminster house the body and shrine of Saint Edward, King and Confessor (claimed by the king in life as one of his accustomed 'avowries', and unmistakeably appropriated as a patron by means of legacies in the king's will) but, on Henry's initiative, his new chapel was to house the body of a new saint, Henry VI, his uncle of the half blood. A near life-size image of Henry Tudor, armour clad and holding the actual crown circlet won at Bosworth, was to kneel in propinquity to the one at the crest of Edward's shrine; the king's mortal remains would lie in proximity to the other once the body of the as yet uncanonised Henry VI had been transferred from Windsor to its new resting place.[21] One continuing strand in the political propaganda of the reign proclaimed the legitimacy of Henry VII as direct and rightful heir of the last Lancastrian king, whose supposed sanctity lost nothing in the re-telling.[22] The proposed shrine could be expected to attract pilgrims, and the founder attract the reflected glory, both as benefactor and in the familial honouring of the holy man's duly authenticated wish concerning the place of his burial. The great chapel itself, like the chapel it replaced, was to be named in the honour of the Virgin, to whom Henry VII had repeatedly declared his devotion. Hers was the last mass which Henry heard in life;[23] and the liturgy for the principal feasts

---

[18] Thus, for example, the claim in the schema for Henry VII's window in the Greyfriars church, Greenwich, that the king was lineally descended from Louis IX and son to him in the ninth degree, BL Egerton MS 2341A, B.

[19] By 1460, according to depositions made in 1498, some of Henry VI's household had felt that Katherine's tomb should be upgraded. In the event, however, after an exhumation consequent on the rebuilding of the old Lady chapel, Katherine's embalmed corpse remained above ground and awaiting reburial until 1778, becoming in the meantime a target for souvenir hunters. She was reburied in the chantry of Henry V in 1878: Stanley, *Historical Memorials*, 3rd edn, 601, 160, 171; *idem*, 8th edn, 1896, 133, 134.

[20] PRO, E 23/3, fo. 1v. This was also a consideration explicitly made by Richard II in his own foundation at the abbey, on which Henry VII was well informed: WAM 9472; *CChR 1341–1417*, 347–8, 375–80; and below, 85–6.

[21] For the image, PRO, E 23/3, fos. 14–14v; below, n. 32; P. Lindley, *Gothic to Renaissance: Essays on Sculpture in England*, Stamford 1995, 57–8. For the suggestion that the chapel itself consciously echoed the setting of Edward's shrine, see below, 160

[22] S. Walker, 'Political saints', 79, 85–7, 98; and the eschatological Anglo, *Images of Tudor Kingship*, 61–73.

[23] *The English Works of John Fisher*, ed J.E.B. Mayor, Early English Text Society, Extra Series, 27, 1876, 274.

of the Virgin, taken in pre-determined rota through each week, was to be used for the first mass of each day celebrated within the chapel by his chantry priests.[24]

There was to be no doubt as to the identity of the benefactor. The chapel would be entered through gates bearing the king's arms, badges, and emblems, endlessly repeated in both the sculptural decoration and the glazing of the chapel;[25] and even in its less durable furnishings (e.g. Plates 1, 29).[26] Priests wearing vestments adorned with the king's badges would daily offer divine service for Henry VII himself within a chantry enclosure heavily encrusted with those same emblems; weekly and occasional sermons would invoke the king's name; and even the most benighted of his subjects, coming to receive alms, would be reminded of the name of the giver, and asked to offer prayers for his welfare in life, and his soul after death. It was a commemoration in which the king's subjects, great and small, were to be exhorted to share whether by reason of specific obligation, or by summons by bells or from the pulpit, or at certain times of the year through the enticement of plenary remission of sin obtainable by fulfilling the conditions of indulgences whose conditions included prayers for the king.[27] In Henry VII's original design, confirmed by his will but altered in its posthumous execution, his tomb commanded the place of honour 'in the myddes of the same chapell, before the high aultier, in such distaunce from the same, as it is ordred in the plat made for the same chapell, and signed with our hande'.[28]

The will leaves absolutely no doubt as to the secular scale of Henry VII's piety. It contained the customary provision for the payment of the king's debts, for the welfare of his servants, and, despite a disclaimer against outrageous pomp and ceremony, for a regal funeral. But its balance was weighted towards funding works of charity, devotion and intercession for the good of the testator's soul. Although it also included a

---

[24] *CClR 1500–1509*, 140.
[25] PRO, E 23/3 fos. 2v–3. For the glazing scheme, see R. Marks, 'The glazing of Henry VII's Chapel, Westminster Abbey', in *Reign of Henry VII*, 157–74, and works there cited, proposing a thematic treatment of the Old and the New Law, the hierarchy of the heavenly hosts, and including a narrative of the Virgin, as well as the ubiquitous and overwhelming heraldry. The comments of Andrew Martindale on Margaret of Austria's mausoleum constructed by her after 1506 in the church of St Nicholas of Tolentino, Brou, are also pertinent. Heraldry outweighs the New Testament scenes in the glazing, and carved stone and monuments give constant reminders of Margaret and her dead husband, Philibert of Savoy; and, as at Westminster, a private closet was provided for the patron: A. Martindale, 'Patrons and minders: the intrusion of the secular into sacred spaces in the late middle ages', in *The Church and the Arts*, ed. D. Wood, Oxford 1992, 143–78, esp. 146–9; for Henry VII's closet, see below, 167–73.
[26] WAM 6612: although in this late inventory of 1617 only a hearse cloth, decorated with portcullises, and a hanging for the choir, with red and white roses, can be confidently associated with Henry, his mother or his son by reason of their iconography, they, and other items mentioned, but for which the evidence of association is more tenuous, are suggestive of a once much larger accumulation. Detailed descriptions of some of these can be recovered or extrapolated from the 1540 dissolution inventory of the abbey itself: although the section covering Henry VII's chapel is now missing, a few entries were made (in error) in the main inventory, PRO, LR 2/111 (printed M.E.C. Walcott, 'The inventories of Westminster Abbey at the Dissolution', *Transactions of the London and Middlesex Archaeological Society* 4, 1869–74, 313–64); and from the post mortem inventory of the goods of Henry VIII, where at least some of the plate and ecclesiastical textiles there described are likely to have had an origin in the chapel: *The Inventory of King Henry VIII*, ed. D. Starkey, 1998, i, *passim*.
[27] *CClR 1500–1509*, nos. 389–90; *CPL*, xviii, no. 115.
[28] PRO, E 23/3, fo. 2.

substantial provision for the marriage of his youngest surviving daughter, Mary, that provision had least preference in the order of priorities; was conditional on the availability of funds; and was envisaged only as a safeguard in case parliament refused to fund the expense of the dowry, which had been guaranteed by treaty in 1507.[29]

The total cost of the king's will is unknown. Although payments to underpin the various legacies had been made since about 1500, the last weeks of the king's life show an accelerated level of activity. Expenditure authorised by the will, but for which pre-payments were made in March and April 1509, before the king's death, include £5,000 for the completion of the chapel at King's College, Cambridge, 10,000 marks for the hospital of the Savoy, and £2,500 to Westminster itself, to be taken in addition to a further £2,500 then being in the abbot's hands.[30] After meeting the cost of the funeral the account of John Heron, Henry's treasurer of his chamber, ended in a technical superplus,[31] that is, an excess of expenditure over income: although it is important to remember that the Chamber treasury, although the most important, was not the only treasure house under the king's immediate control, and moreover that plate and bullion were, in this context, no more than convertible currency.[32] At a literal level, this paper bankruptcy (for it is nothing more) could have been taken as fulfilment of the king's intention: the final clause of his will conventionally directs that any treasure not expended on legacies, obligations, and other charitable deeds specified in the will should be distributed at the discretion of his executors for the welfare of his soul.[33] It was not the dead king's intention, however, that those great works of piety and dynastic display should remain incomplete. It is a tribute to the faith kept by the executors, and by his son, and a political statement of intent and dynastic affirmation, that so much of the will was eventually put into execution. It is also an indication of the substance of the king's earthly treasure. The accounts of John Heron record several very large payments to the executors in the early years of the new reign, totalling £60,000 by March 1512.[34] Since it is clear that these were payments by instalment, they suggest a compromise between the executors and the king's council, between whom there was a considerable overlap, to determine the resources which were to be devoted to the performance of the late king's will. Despite a prior feoffment on the lands of the duchy of Lancaster, for example, the receipts of each year continued to be paid in full directly to the receiver general of the duchy and

---

[29] For the proxy marriage and treaty guarantees, PRO, E 23/3, fos. 16–17 and below, nn. 140–1. In the event, in 1514 Mary married Louis XII of France.

[30] Below, 'The last will of Henry VII', 104, 107.

[31] £89 13s 10½d, PRO, E 36/214, p. 348.

[32] Thus, for example, the plate and bullion handed via Robert Fenrother, one of the masters of the Mint, to John of Utrecht (Vantryke, VanUtrike), to make the king's harness 'in silver' on 16 April 1509, PRO, E 36/214, p. 344. Whether this was for one of the images mentioned in the will, or for use at the exequies, is unclear, although the first interpretation is strengthened by analogy with the Walsingham image of 1507, PRO, E 36/214, fos. 85v, 103; see also D. Grummit, 'Henry VII, chamber finance, and the new monarchy', *Historical Research* 72, 1999, 229–43.

[33] PRO, E 23/3, fos. 18v–19. There is an apparent change of ink, although not of hand, in the will at this point, although in the present poor condition of the document it would be unwise to assume this as a point of substance.

[34] PRO, E 36/215, pp. 36, 125, 138, 169. Other payments for specified purposes were made by Heron on direct warrant or, as with the distribution of alms, had been incorporated into the account for the funeral expenses.

thence into the king's chamber; the reduction in value to the chamber itself is accounted for by an increased subvention to the new king's household and not to the execution of the old king's testament.[35] The executors' accounts do not survive, and little more than half of the £60,000 can be firmly accounted for, including at least a further £15,000 for King's and the Savoy, and £2,500 for the king's tomb and the high altar of his new chapel.

The indentures

The last will, signed and sealed in 1509 (Plate 2), is, however, only one part of a documentary equation. It takes for granted, and indeed makes specific reference to, agreements made almost five years before between the king and the abbey of St Peter's, Westminster.[36] These agreements had been embodied in a series of four indentures bipartite made between the king and the abbot and convent of Westminster, and an indenture septipartite made in the first instance between the king and the abbot and convent of Westminster as principals, but with the five other parts binding two bishops and their chapters, the chapters of the royal free chapel of St Stephen Westminster, and of the cathedral of St Paul, London,[37] and the mayor and commonalty of London, as guarantors for the foundation of a chantry, an anniversary, and other services to be centred on the new Lady chapel, still under construction, and for the foundation and maintenance of an almshouse adjacent to the precincts of the abbey. A complementary series of twenty indentures quadripartite set out the responsibilities to be undertaken by the abbot and convent for the maintenance and payment of an annual dole for a series of 'foreign obits', that is, annual anniversaries, with services paralleling those in the abbey, to be held elsewhere in the king's realm, and bound the celebrating communities to observe their form, specifying in considerable detail the prayers, liturgies, and processionals to be used. To these indentures also the city stood guarantor, with a right and obligation to levy a penalty, graduated according to the wealth of the house, in the event of default.[38]

The inseparable connection between the indentures and the will in establishing the perpetual memorial was recognised by parties other than the king. The official Repertories of the city of London, in recording the formal act of sealing of the several volumes comprising the indenture septipartite on 18 July 1504, identify the books as those 'conteynyng the testament and laste wille' of Henry VII.[39] The cost, too, cannot be determined from the will alone. Even before the legacies made in the final will for

---

[35] PRO, DL 28/6/7–10.

[36] PRO, E 23/3, fos. 6–6v.

[37] The bishopric was vacant. William Barons, the Master of the Rolls responsible for overseeing the sealing of the indentures, was promoted to London in November 1504.

[38] King's copies and some third party indentures in PRO, E 33/1–25; Westminster's copies in BL Harleian MS 1498 and WAM 57070–82; abstracts of texts from their enrolment on the Close Rolls of Chancery in *CClR 1500–1509*, nos. 389–94, 532; for other references and list of the parties to the indentures see Appendix, below, 95–7.

[39] Corporation of London Record Office (CLRO), Repertories 1, fo. 161. For Peter Le Neve, two centuries later, see below, 'Will of Henry VII', 101–2 n. 8.

the completion and furnishing of the Lady chapel and the king's tomb, nearly £15,000 had been expended on the building works, with a further £500 for the almshouses associated with Henry's foundation.[40] An entry of 16 December 1502 in the books of the treasurer of the king's chamber records the transfer of a lump sum of £30,000 for the purchase of lands for the endowment of Westminster; although it is difficult to explain by means of the surviving documents quite so large a payment for this cause alone, and individual purchases continued to be recorded as outgoings in the king's books. It is far more likely that this very large sum was reserved and chested up for later disbursement over time, and that it represents the estimated cost of the whole enterprise: an impression reinforced both by the entry following, for thirteen pairs of trussing coffers, and by analogy with the funding of the Savoy.[41] The foundation indentures suggest that more than £5,000 had been expended by July 1504 on the endowment,[42] in addition to the loss to the crown of patronage inherent in the transfer of the spiritualities. The king bore the cost of the altar furniture, mass books, and vestments; and of obtaining from the papal curia bulls of both confirmation and of privileges, over and above the abbey's contribution to the latter. The king's will brought further gifts. They included two important relics, a piece of the Holy Cross and the leg and foot of St George.[43] The reliquary for the latter was branded, like the chapel, with an unmistakeable remembrance of the immediate benefactor: the case was further embellished with the king's badges of a red rose and two portcullises, before being presented to St Edward's shrine.[44] A rich set of vestments of unknown, but extraordinary value, numbers and workmanship had been made at the king's own cost between about 1500 and 1505 and was bequested directly to the abbot and convent.[45] Appropriately he transferred also, for use at the high altar of the Lady chapel, the greatest image of the Virgin then being in his own jewel house (estimated in 1540 at a massive 422½oz), besides other plate.[46] Despite the increasing ill-health of Henry's later years, it is clear, from the scale of the undertaking, from the efforts required to secure a sufficient endowment within a short compass of time, and from the richness of the associated artefacts, that the imminence of death alone was not the determinant of the timetable.

One aspect of this great enterprise is easily overlooked. The various indentures bipartite and quadripartite as they survive in their present and final form include a significant change of plan for those services to be held in the king's lifetime, with a shift of emphasis from an intercessory celebration in constant awareness of death to a commemorative requiem in its shadow. One clue is a clause in the king's will. This

---

[40] Colvin, *HKW* iii, 207, 213.
[41] *Excerpta Historica*, ed. S. Bentley, 1823, 129, from Craven Ord's extracts from the books, BL Additional MS 7099; original entry BL MS Additional 59899, fo. 7v. For the Savoy, Colvin, *HKW* iii, 201–2.
[42] Harvey, *Estates*, 199–202, analyses the breakdown of this sum.
[43] PRO, E 23/3, fo. 14. St George had been received from Louis XII and paraded with great pomp in April 1505, *The Great Chronicle of London*, ed. A.H. Thomas and I.D. Thornley, 1938, 329; *Memorials of King Henry the Seventh*, ed. J. Gairdner, RS 1858, 82–3. In addition to the large fragment mentioned in the will, another piece of the cross had come with the suppression of Luffield priory, and was retained by the king, WAM 2997.
[44] WAM 9485, printed in Westlake ii, 501.
[45] PRO, E 23/3, fo. 15; and see below, 68.
[46] PRO, E 23/3, fos. 14, 14v; LR 2/111, fo. 47.

included a bequest to the abbot and convent of Westminster of twenty-nine copes, and the vestments for the priest, deacon, and sub-deacon, fashioned in cloth of gold and wrought with red roses and portcullises.[47] Such was their extraordinary magnificence that they would be borrowed by Henry VIII for use at the Field of the Cloth of Gold, and he appropriated half the set on the dissolution of the abbey (Plate 1).[48] The abbot would normally be expected to officiate at the anniversary mass; if, as in 1508, a bishop took that place, the abbot and prior might be expected to serve as deacon and subdeacon respectively. The number of priests available and present within the monastic community varied, reaching the mid thirties, but in the crucial years between 1504 and 1506 a maximum of twenty nine monk priests were paid for their attendance, receiving a higher rate than the monks professed but not yet priests, novices and the *conversi*, or lay brothers.[49] The initial congruence of numbers surely suggests an intention that the copes were to be used at the anniversary, as well as on more secular state occasions; and the period in which the garments were fashioned follows the chronology of the memorial. Six copes of the richest possible version of 'riccio sopra riccio' cloth of gold, were completed by Antonio Corsi of Florence by 1500. The bulk of the remainder were delivered by Lorenzo and Ieronimo Bonvisi in 1502, although work on the embroidery of the copes and other vestments continued until 1505.[50] The original indentures agreed between the king and abbot Fascet, and confirmed by Islip in July 1502, must have envisaged prayers for a living king and queen, with an annual requiem to coincide perhaps with the anniversary of his coronation, 30 October, much as Richard II had intended in his first foundation in the abbey.[51] The psalms and responses prescribed for daily use by the whole monastic community point in a similar direction: a recognisable variant is included in the Accession day service added to the book of Common Prayer; whilst verses from Psalm 20 had been incorporated into the fronts of the Garter stalls which were part of Edward IV's work at St George's, Windsor, which was to be *his* funerary chapel.[52] The collect, secret, and post communion prayers to be observed in the king's lifetime were taken with relatively little variation from the coronation service itself.[53] Other evidence, payment by the treasurer of the king's chamber for a hearse costing

---

[47] PRO, E 23/3, fo. 15.

[48] Westlake ii, 311; PRO, LR 2/111, fo. 17; Starkey, *Inventory of Henry VIII*, no. 8863; L. Monnas, 'New documents for the vestments of Henry VII at Stonyhurst College', *Burlington Magazine*, May 1989, 345–6, including illustrations; see also Starkey, *Inventory of Henry VIII*, no. 8871, for two altar frontals with angels, clouds, and the king's badges, with the motto '*Dominus meus adiutor*', which are likely to have come from the chapel.

[49] WAM 24238, 24241*. But thirty-four in 1502, twenty-six in 1505, and in the thirties from 1516, WAM 24236, 24240, 24242–24250. For the vigil services on the eve the monks were to be 'revested' in the manner used for Richard II's anniversary: for Richard II's six copes, including one of great magnificence with the arms of the king and queen, PRO, LR 2/111, fos. 13–15.

[50] Monnas, 'The vestments of Henry VII at Stonyhurst College: cloth of gold woven to shape', *Bulletin de Liaison du CIETA* 65, Lyon 1987, 69–80 (with author's manuscript correction of first date); L. Monnas, 'New documents', 345–9.

[51] *CPR 1388–1392*, 470.

[52] A.F. Sutton and L. Visser-Fuchs, 'Chivalry and the Yorkist Kings', in *St George's Chapel, Windsor, in the Late Middle Ages*, ed. C. Richmond and E. Scarff, Windsor 2001, 128, drawing attention to the message of the victory of God's anointed in war.

[53] See below, 85–6.

£58 16s 7d and settlement of the abbot's reckoning for the chapel in the week of 11 November 1502, and £191 13s 4d paid the week following to Lewis de Fava for two lengths of black and white cloth of gold in quantities appropriate to a hearse cloth, points to three possible dates for the first anniversary service: 30 October, or All Saints or All Souls, November, 1502.[54] But on 11 February 1503 Elizabeth of York died in the aftermath of childbirth. Celebration was no longer appropriate; and those anniversaries held within the king's lifetime were to be held on the anniversary of the death of a much loved wife and queen. As with Richard II, the foundation documents are altered by that stark reality.

The great series of indentures which founded both the services and the related suffrages intended as a perpetual chantry and memorial for the well being and souls of Henry VII (d.1509), his wife, Elizabeth of York (d.1503), his parents, and his children are, like the chapel itself, the product of a mixture of a deeply seated religiosity and of dynastic affirmation, emphasising the king's lineage and status, and the fealty and homage owed him in death as in life. The texts, with minor differences of orthography, are preserved as of record on the Close Rolls of the reign.[55] Study of the original indentures as artefacts, however, and recourse to their full text rather than the generally excellent modern abstract, adds a further dimension towards understanding the totality of the king's vision. Yet perhaps only the king himself, John Islip, abbot of Westminster, and the several Chancery clerks responsible for the sealing and enrolment of the indentures ever saw the documentary archive in all its awesome entirety. Unusually, all the indentures were intentionally written and created in codex form: that is, they are bound volumes rather than flat sheets of parchment (e.g. Plate VIII). The nature of an indenture was that it recorded a binding legal agreement in a format which had some built in safeguard against forgery or non-observance, and which, by way of the seals appended or applied interchangeably each to each, required the formal and deliberate assent and acknowledgement of all the parties. In the case of the Westminster indentures this meant the writing, with rubrication in colour and gold leaf, illumination, binding, and sealing of eight indentures bipartite, annexed together and bound to form two volumes, sleeved in a fabric chemise and embellished with goldsmiths' work – a total of 258 written folios plus the blank bifolia that covered each separate indenture before they were gathered and annexed together to form the two volumes;[56] and similarly the writing, illumination, binding, embellishment and sealing of the seven volumes which made up the indenture septipartite, itself a document of twenty-eight written folios to each part.[57] All (where they survive) have illumi-

---

[54] BL Additional MS 59899, fos. 3, 4.
[55] PRO, C 54/365, 368; full calendar in *CClR 1500–1509*, nos. 389–94, 532. Two entire rolls were devoted to the enrolments.
[56] This appears to true of the king's copy, PRO, E 33/1, although the volume has been disturbed. The interleaves of the Westminster volume, BL Harleian MS 1498, are of fine ruled parchment, too clean to be covers.
[57] PRO, E 33/1 (Plate VIII), BL Harleian MS 1498 (indentures bipartite); PRO, E 33/2, king's copy of indenture septipartite. The indenture septipartite formerly belonging to the chapel of St Stephen's, Westminster, BL Additional MS 21112 (purchased in 1855 at Sotheby's, lot 1889, from the library of Charles Meigh) no longer has its chemise binding, whereas that of St Paul's, housed in the cathedral library, is in superb condition. The pages of the indenture bipartite have a text block approximately 185x130mm (height x width) on a page 380x245mm; the indentures septipartite approximate to 185x140mm on a page 380x250mm. A detailed technical description of the construction of the inden-

Plate 1. The Stonyhurst cope, woven for the Lady chapel of Henry VII, now in the Victoria and Albert Museum (British Province of the Society of Jesus and Stonyhurst College).

nations of some quality which reflect not only the nature of the indentures which they adorn, but also the interrelationships of the parties to those agreements.[58] Eighty volumes, four to each indenture, and each of fourteen or more written folios, formed the whole sequence of the indentures quadripartite.[59]

In their cumulative consequence the documents are unique. Like the chapel, they can be read at various levels of meaning. Even their fabric outer covers make a statement: velvet was frequently the fabric of choice for prestige bindings well into the seventeenth and even eighteenth centuries; whilst one recent commentator has suggested that the choice of a chemise cover for the foundation indentures was, by this date, unusual, and likely to be a deliberate choice of style precisely suited to the reverential nature of the text.[60] Whilst it would be foolish to pretend that the docu-

tures bipartite and septipartite, giving measurements for the oak boards and chemises of the two volumes belonging to the king, PRO, E 33/1, E 33/2 (boards 393x267mm and 397x281mm respectively) in F. Bearman, 'The significance of two late medieval textile chemise bindings in the Walters Art Gallery', *Journal of the Walters Art Gallery* 54, 1996, 163–87. The bindings of both volumes were disturbed in the nineteenth century in order to effect repair.

[58] For the illuminations, see below, 77–80, and Plates VIIA–B; and J. Backhouse, 'Illuminated manuscripts associated with Henry VII and members of his immediate family', in *Reign of Henry VII*, 176–8, commenting on the 'splendid vulgarity' characterising manuscripts produced in England in this period. See also K.L. Scott, *Later Gothic Manuscripts 1390–1490*, 1996, ii, 365 for other works by the same illuminator.

[59] Not all now survive. Those of the City of London, twenty in number, are lost; Westminster's archive is incomplete; the king's series complete but damaged; and of the third party indentures only ten of the original twenty are thought to be extant. For references, see Appendix, 95–7. The indentures quadripartite approximate to 130x100mm on a page 315x225mm; and see *Fifth Report of the Royal Commission on Historical Manuscripts*, 1876, Appendix, 436 for the volume belonging to Christchurch, Canterbury; and *Illuminated Manuscripts in the Bodleian Library*, ed. O. Pächt and J.J.G. Alexander, iii, Oxford 1973, nos. 1171, 1172.

[60] Bearman, 'Late medieval textile chemise bindings', 163–87; see also J. Storm van Leeuwen, 'The well-shirted bookbinding: on chemise bindings and Hülleneinbände', in *Theatrum Orbis Librorum: Liber*

ments are in the first rank of manuscript production, the fact remains that they still command extraordinary attention whenever they are in use, five hundred years after their first making. The king cared, and cared passionately about the Westminster project: the magnificence of the king's device extended even to these largely hidden, but absolutely fundamental, records of his foundation. The chapel is instantly familiar, as is the chantry grate begun in the king's lifetime and the tomb commissioned after his death. So too, increasingly if belatedly, are the vestments given in 1509. The one surviving cope is one of the two or three most outstanding pieces of renaissance weaving still extant (Plate 1).[61] In contrast, the indentures, save for one often reproduced miniature, remain surprisingly undervalued. Yet they describe the inner life of the chapel. It is in that conviction that the text which follows pauses to look at their physical format as well as their written substance.

The indentures were designed to impress (Plate VIII). All nine volumes were similarly bound. The outer covers of the chemise are of heavy velvet, with an inner lining of rich Florentine or Luccan damask, now faded, woven in a typical pineapple design which, however, differs between the two instruments. Both the outer chemise and its brocade lining are carefully seamed along the vertical – the join is staggered – suggesting the use of fabric of standard, and thus fairly narrow, loom width.[62] Cords and tassels of silk and gold and silver thread ornament the outer seams and corners, in red and gold for Westminster in both volumes of the indentures bipartite, and in green, white, silver and gold for the king in the indentures septipartite. The velvet might now be loosely described as burgundy; but in the extraordinarily full description entered in the memoranda of the chamberlains of the Exchequer in 1505, when they took custody of the two volumes which remained with the king, the colour is named as purple.[63] Certainly the purple of the *imperium* would fit with what we know – or presume – of Henry VII's image of himself, and with the closed crown imperial which adorns the central boss on the covers of both indentures, as it had the signet seal used throughout the reign, and the coinage progressively from the late 1480's, and was to do in the ornament of Westminster, King's, and the Savoy.[64]

The slightly smaller indentures quadripartite have a binding of thonged oak boards covered with blue velvet, the colour of royal mourning,[65] with a simple hinge

---

Amicorum presented to Nico Israel on the Occasion of his Seventieth Birthday, ed. T. Croiset van Uchelen, K. van der Horst and G. Schilder, Utrecht c.1989, 277–304, esp. 293–4.

[61] The cope was on display in 2002 in the British Galleries of the Victoria and Albert Museum. The author is indebted to Lisa Monnas for generously sharing her extensive knowledge of late medieval textiles.

[62] On loom widths see L. Monnas, 'Vestments of Henry VII . . . woven to shape', 74, and L. Monnas, 'Loom widths and selvedges prescribed by Italian silk weaving statutes 1265–1512: a preliminary investigation', *CIETA Bulletin* 66, 1988, 35–44. Lisa Monnas's as yet unpublished work on the chemises takes into account loom width and is likely to suggest an alternative Italian origin for the damask, based on informed technical considerations.

[63] *The Antient Kalendars and Inventories of the Exchequer*, ed. F. Palgrave, 3 vols., 1836, iii, 76.

[64] Cf. Anglo, *Images of Tudor Kingship*, 119: but a limited audience does not preclude a personal projection of kingship. The genealogical window ordered by Henry VII for the convent of the Observant Franciscans at Greenwich required two images of the king: both were to have the closed crown imperial and, in the larger image the king, holding both the hand of his queen and his orb and sceptre, was to be clothed in robes of purple, being his habit royal of estate, BL Egerton MS 2341A, B. See also C. Challis, *The Tudor Coinage*, Manchester 1978, 47–51.

[65] Thus A.F. Sutton and L. Visser-Fuchs, *The Reburial of Richard, Duke of York, 21–30 July 1476*, Richard

and hasp closure,[66] and are embellished front and back with pierced metalwork and bosses in the form of the king's badges of portcullis and rose. The velvet, with its silk threads and close pile, is of extremely high quality. Despite this, these books exhibit an uneasy marriage of immediate opulence combined with economy in execution which may simply reflect on the large number of volumes and speed of completion required. The top edge of each cover is slashed to allow the fabric to mimic, once turned down, the indented top edge of the binding boards. It is clear from variations in the colours of the selvedges that they were cut from at least three, and perhaps four, different lengths of cloth. Most covers have at least one selvedge, and some are made up, with patching which cannot entirely be explained away, from more than one piece of fabric.[67]

In the twenty indentures quadripartite, originally eighty volumes in all, the parts even of a single instrument have readily discernable differences of decorative detail and considerable variation in their border design.[68] The first page of each has an illuminated initial letter and a border in Flemish style with, variously, Henry's badges, foliage, flowers, and other ornament, or stylised acanthus leaves, and generous use of gilding. The illuminations follow a pattern, but are the work of more than one hand, Their heavy-handed imagery asserts a propriety apposite to the purpose of the text, and ranges in accomplishment from tolerable competence to the barely second rate.[69] The common elements are the inclusion of the king's badges of the red rose and portcullis in the borders, and the incorporation into the initial letter 'T' with which each text commences of his coat of arms and supporters of the greyhound and red dragon dreadful.[70] The background to the heraldry is dimidiated in the Tudor colours of

---

III Society 1996, 6, 9, 18–19; A.F. Sutton and L. Visser-Fuchs, 'The royal burials of the House of York at Windsor: Princess Mary, May 1482 and Queen Elizabeth Woodville, June 1492', *The Ricardian* 11, 1999, 455, 457, citing a herald's account; cf. J. Woodward, *The Theatre of Death*, Woodbridge 1997, 19, citing evidence from the end of the sixteenth century and identifying the colour as purple.

[66] Most of the clasps are flat metal; others have the rose and portcullis, e.g. PRO, E 33/18.

[67] A particularly good example is the cover removed from PRO, E 33/25. This has two different edges, a left-hand selvedge of green silk threads, and a bottom edge of red, blue, and gold, with a clear indication of the weave. For patching, see, e.g., PRO, E 33/8. All the fabric covers were examined in the course of preparing a revised finding aid for use in the Public Record Office although some of the findings were too detailed for incorporation into the final list. They have also been studied in much greater depth by the textile historian, Lisa Monnas, whose 'The textile covers of the Foundation Indentures for the chapel of Henry VII (1485–1509)' is still forthcoming. Velvet bindings, worked with gold, were being produced by the printer Berthelet for Henry VIII in the 1540s for approximately 3s a volume: *The Libraries of King Henry VIII*, ed. J.P. Carley, 2000, 227–45. For the seals, all of which were, or had become, detached by the mid-nineteenth century, see PRO, E 33/26/1–65; SC 13/I 90; SC 13/I 91 and SC 13/H 82, the latter identified and described in R. Graham, 'The seals of the Cluniac monastery of Bermondsey', *Surrey Archaeological Collections* 39, 1931, 80 and pl. 28.

[68] See, e.g., PRO, E 33/9, 10 (King's and London, Austin Friars) and more markedly in E 33/15, 17 (King's and London, Friars Preachers).

[69] See also Backhouse, 'Illuminated manuscripts associated with Henry VII', 177, on the limited artistic value of these texts.

[70] On Henry VII's badges, especially the re-identification of the dragon, and their simple but effective visual mnemonics, Anglo, *Images of Tudor Kingship*, 34–6, 56–60, 79–81. One volume now in public custody appears to have been repainted in the seventeenth century, PRO, E 33/23. Peter Le Neve is the most likely culprit. Similar motifs, in a different arrangement, decorate a separate agreement for suffrages made between the king and the chapter of St Swithin's, Winchester: H. Maas, 'Zwei spätmittelenglische Texte der Bremer Stadtbibliothek', *Festschrift zum XVI. Neuphilologentag in Bremen vom 1. bis 4. Juni 1914*, Heidelberg 1914, 71, discussing Staats- und Universitätsbibliothek Bremen, MS

white and green, as are the silk cords which carry the great seal, pendant to all save the king's copies. The text blocks preserve the form only of an indented relationship.[71] Sufficient margin was allowed at the head of each page to write the alphabet sequentially and then indent that edge, bisecting the letter forms: but it is the letter base that has been retained across the series. It is possible, however (unless simply fortuitous), that some vestige of a traditional indenture is preserved by the oak covers, likewise indented at the head, which occasionally show good matches. The seals pendant interchangeably to each more reliably guarantee the interrelationship of each instrument's four parts. The seals are contained in silver skippets (Plate VIII), some, but not all, of which are engraved with a form of words to identify the party sealing. Those protecting the great seal are embellished with the king's badges.

Whilst many of the bosses which decorated the series of eighty indentures quadripartite are essentially mass produced emblems in brass, no doubt similar in type to those ordered by the king's mother in 1501, at a price of 13d each,[72] the furniture of the volumes of the indentures bipartite and septipartite is good goldsmith's work.[73] The bosses, which display the king's arms and badges, are of silver gilt enamelled and champlevé, with the greyhound and dragon worked in the round. The catchplates and clasps of the composite volumes of the indentures bipartite are attached to a silk braid and looped cord pull, and include both dynastic reference, in the form of the double red rose, and an angel, redolent of the imagery that would be employed in the sculpted corbels of the king's new chapel at Westminster. The indentures septipartite are less elaborately closed with engraved hinges and clasps of silver gilt enamelled to represent the double rose. In the king's copy of the indentures bipartite the silver seal skippets have central bosses enamelled with coats of arms for the common seal of the abbey, pendant on red and gold cords. Westminster is similarly identified in the king's part of the indenture septipartite. A brief form of words, engraved or pounced in classical epigraphic style, identifies the remaining seals. A similar arrangement once held for the other six volumes of the set, only two of which are known to survive: these have been less well served by the passage of time.[74] The companion volume of the indentures bipartite, formerly the property of Westminster Abbey and thus sealed with the king's great seal, has skippets of silver and silver gilt in two different styles, with central bosses of roses of silver gilt, enamelled, and of the crown imperial on each lid; and bosses of the Beaufort badge of the portcullis in worked gold on the base, pendant on cords of green, white and gold, a Tudor scheme continuing in the cord pull of the volume's closure. When this latter volume passed from the abbey's ownership after 1540 it was reserved for Henry VIII, and at the time of that king's death remained on an upper shelf in his 'lytle study', a magpie-nest next to his 'olde bedde chambre' in the palace of Westminster.[75]

---

a.49; I am indebted to Dr Thomas Elsmann, Keeper of Manuscripts and Rare Books, Bremen, for assistance with this manuscript and the Maas edition.

[71] Astle, 70.

[72] St John's College, Cambridge, MS D 102.2, pp. 15–17.

[73] Cf. M. Campbell, 'English goldsmiths in the fifteenth century', in *England in the Fifteenth Century*, ed. D. Williams, Woodbridge 1987, 45–50, on the limited survival of work of this period.

[74] St Paul's Library (unnumbered MS) retains four skippets or part skippets; all the seals had been removed from BL Additional MS 21112 by the time of its acquisition.

[75] Now BL Harleian MS 1498; the catalogue of the Harleian manuscripts records that it came into the

Little can be said with any degree of certainty concerning the crafting of the books: there are simply too many ambiguities in the chamber accounts.[76] Not even the craftsman of the silver and silver gilt bosses, clasps, and skippets is known beyond doubt. No single goldsmith enjoyed exclusive patronage; and marks resembling roman numerals on some of the skippets from the indentures quadripartite, and the absence of marks on others, suggest more than one maker.[77] In late June and July 1504 the goldsmiths John Mundy and Bartholomew Rede, the latter also one of the wardens of the mint, were paid upon invoice by John Heron, the king's treasurer of the chamber, the amounts being £38 18s 4d and £126 1s 2d respectively.[78] The timing suggests a connection with the indentures bipartite and septipartite, which would have required a total of ninety bosses and sixty-four skippets,[79] as well as the finely worked clasps; and Rede was paid on 26 July, two days after the general ratification of the indentures septipartite. The same week's expenditure included payments to the clerks of the Master of the Rolls,[80] to the king's serjeants Humphrey Coningsby and John Kingsmill, the learned counsel assisting with the legal process, and to their clerks; with smaller payments going to clerks of the Exchequer and the Common Pleas.[81] It is possible, but perhaps unlikely, that the relatively small payment to Quentin Poulet, the king's librarian, of 9s 1d, was for the insertion of the dating clauses added to the books at the time of sealing, or for those late textual additions which reflected the changing primacy in each particular part of the instrument of the several parties to the indentures septipartite, or for some other more physical part of the undertaking.[82] More certainly eighteen months earlier Poulet had been responsible for writing out in roll form the original indentures for the foundation of the almshouses;[83] and from the general pattern of the king's expenditure on books and stationery he was almost certainly responsible for sub-contracting or executing the bindings. Negotiations for and writing of the twenty indentures quadripartite was a second major undertaking completed only towards the end of 1504. It required complex arrangements for

---

collection through the gift of Sir Thomas Hoby. See also Starkey, *Inventory of King Henry VIII* i, nos. 11036, 15906, 16747, and more conveniently in Carley, *Libraries of King Henry VIII*, 285.

[76] Crimson velvet was purchased in March 1504 at 16s a yard, although at 45 yards the amount is excessive for the nine chemises; three years earlier velvet in a more appropriate quantity had been purchased for nearly three times this price. Payments to Quentin Poulet in March 1501 for book clasps look too early to be relevant, unless the 'King's book' refers to an earlier recension of the indentures, BL Additional MS 59899, fo. 48v; PRO, E 101/415/3, fo. 46; but a payment of 14s to Stephen 'case maker', BL Additional MS 59899, fo. 56, may be for the boxes described below, 75 and n. 88.

[77] E.g. PRO, E 33/26/7 'ii'; E 33/26/9 '+'; E 33/26/14 'xiii'; E 33/26/35 'vii'.

[78] BL Additional MS 59899, fos. 60, 62v.

[79] Five of the indentures were sealed with eight seals, two with seven, and two with five. Price comparison is difficult, the nearest equivalents perhaps being the six silver gilt pixes commissioned from William Horne in December 1503 at a cost of £4 13s 4d, BL Additional MS 59899, fo. 41v, and the pixes commissioned by the king's will in 1509, priced at £4 each, PRO, E 23/3, fo. 15v. It is, of course, possible that Horne's commission was for skippets, which might help explain differences in their design.

[80] William Barons, appointed bishop of London in November of the same year.

[81] BL Additional MS 59899, fo. 63; see also fos. 6, 6v for other payments to the two serjeants.

[82] BL Additional MS 59899, fo. 62v. For example, the preface to the sealing clause in the St Stephen's copy of the indenture septipartite is an addition in a hand other than the engrossing hand of the main document, reflecting the primary position of the dean and canons in relation to that particular part of the indenture, BL Additional MS 21112, fo. 26v.

[83] BL Additional MS 59899, fo. 12.

sealing and for acknowledgement of the deeds in Chancery which mirrored those adopted for the indentures septipartite, and which continued over more than a month from 20 November and to 26 December of the same year.[84] Two hundred and forty silver skippets were required to contain the seals which were appended interchangeably each to each.[85] It is perhaps not surprising that, when the clerks of Chancery came to enrol these repetitive, but slightly varying, texts they occasionally nodded, especially in respect of the only house of nuns.[86]

Consistency in ensuring, as far as was humanly possible, the perpetual observance of the memorial extended even to the arrangements for the preservation and safe custody of the original documents. The king's parts of the two principal volumes of the foundation, the indentures bipartite and septipartite, were transferred to Exchequer custody on 25 February 1505[87] in two boxes or forcers of cuir-cisclé (cut leather).[88] The elements of the design, different for each, are the portcullis, with the royal coat of arms surmounted by the closed crown imperial, and with the double rose of Lancaster; that is, with the king's badges which feature so prominently in the bindings and illuminations of the indentures which they were designed to contain. Stylised foliage fills much of the remaining space. An internal quilted lining of crimson silk may originally have given greater opulence, as well as protection to the volumes.[89] They share with only the Treaty of Calais of 1360, and the ransom documents for David Bruce, king of Scotland, for which a pair of specially commissioned and decorated chests had been provided in 1361,[90] a format with an element of propaganda as well as archival integrity.

More conventional provision was made for the indentures concerning the foreign obits. Both parts of a pair of iron-bound and leather-clad standards, or travelling chests, survived until 1985: the King's or Exchequer chest in the museum of the Public Record Office and Westminster's in the abbey library.[91] Despite the deterioration of its leather covering, the Westminster exemplar retains almost intact the

---

[84] *CClR 1500–1509*, no. 532; CLRO Journal 10, fo. 328v (minute not entered); CLRO Repertory 1, fo. 161. See also below, 80.

[85] *CClR 1500–1509*, no. 532; the abbey contributed £7 for the skippets for its seals, an amount that seems insufficient for the sixty required: WAM 24240. Rede and Nicholas Warley were paid £43 6s 8d and £104 7s 9d on 2–3 January 1505, but the timing means that these payments could as easily have been for New Year's gifts, for which Mundy was specifically paid a week later, BL MS Additional 59899, fos. 74, 75.

[86] The enrolment, PRO, C 54/369, was the work of several clerks. The abbess of Syon was turned into a man, *ibid.* mm. 31–2.

[87] Palgrave, *Kalendars and Inventories* iii, 76–8.

[88] PRO, E 33/28, 29. The first is illustrated in G.D. Hobson, *English Binding before 1500*, Cambridge 1929, pl. 41a; where it is described as 'good second class work', *ibid.*, 50. I am indebted to Mr F. Bearman for this reference. For Steven 'casemaker', see above, n. 76.

[89] Palgrave, *Kalendars and Inventories* ii, 333; neither silk lining now remains. The source is Arthur Agarde, who was able to spend but little time in the dark and closely guarded Chapel of the Pyx, and it is possible therefore that he mis-read the chemise. In 1504/5 the abbey also made proper provision for a chest for its copies of the king's books, at a cost of 34s 4d, and it is likely that this was the chest described below: WAM 24240, and nn. 91–2.

[90] C. Jenning, *Early Chests in Wood and Iron*, Public Record Office Museum Pamphlets 7, 1974, and the study by present author incorporated as an introduction to the class list of E 27 (typescript in PRO).

[91] Jenning, *Early Chests*, 3, 5; Palgrave, *Kalendars and Inventories* ii, 334; *29th Report of the Keeper of Public Records*, 1987, 21, records the loss of the PRO chest at a time of refurbishment of the Chancery Lane PRO building. See also above, n. 89.

internal divisions and parchment labels which identify the twenty individual volumes by the name of the third party, the particular religious house or body corporate undertaking the performance of the anniversary.[92] Both chests were lined with pink or red linen or buckram. This same material is found on the raised floor of the Westminster chest, which is slotted to receive the internal wooden partitions. Since the books being placed in these standards were put directly into the chests without other form of protection the lining was entirely appropriate, and appears to be original. It does not, as has sometimes been suggested, predicate a change of use for the chests themselves.[93]

The two-part indentures

The crucial document is the composite volume of four indentures bipartite annexed within single covers and sealed for that reason with five, rather than four, seals. When, on 4 November 1504, John Islip, abbot of Westminster, came into Chancery to take his oath on the Gospels to observe the king's foundation, he brought, as he was required to do, the abbey's part of these indentures with him, even though the text had been enrolled on the Close Rolls of Chancery of the previous regnal year, and held the book in his hand whilst making his oath.[94] Each of the two counterpart volumes, which together make up the instrument, contains the foundation indenture itself, ordaining and describing the liturgical memorial to be observed in the abbey and the Lady chapel, and other associated privileges and charitable works, and naming the endowment to support those services; an indenture of ordinances to be followed by the almsmen placed under the abbey's tutelage and the provision to be undertaken by Westminster for their material needs; an indenture of abstract summarising the terms of the foundation and the financial penalties that would be incurred by non-performance of any of its clauses; and an indenture of penalties detailing the way in which those fines might be levied, and acknowledging that the abbot and convent were so bound.[95] This last indenture was, in effect, an inspeximus of a related document, the indenture septipartite, made between the king, the abbey, and other outside interests, which provided a guarantee for the whole.

Although the indentures individually and collectively bear a date of 16 July 1504, that date, variously written, is an insertion in an otherwise completed text, suggesting

---

[92] I am indebted to Dr Richard Mortimer, Keeper of the Abbey's muniments, for the opportunity to examine the chest; photographs in PRO, PRO 30/26/253.

[93] The PRO chest has been linked to Margaret Beaufort, an assumption grounded on her death at Westminster at a time when she was housed in the abbot's lodgings: *Public Record Office Museum Catalogue*, ed. D. Gifford, HMSO 1974, 88. But another similar standard of approximately the same date remains among the abbey's possessions, and by the mid-sixteenth century they were a recurrent item of Exchequer expenditure for archival purposes: PRO, E 407/68.

[94] *CClR 1500–1509*, no. 437. A similar requirement, for an oath to be taken in the chapter house and witnessed by a notary, was agreed by the prior of St Swithin's, Winchester, for himself and every new prior thereafter: Maas, 'Zwei Texte', 73.

[95] PRO, E 33/1; BL Harleian MS 1498; contemporary abstract of the financial obligations incurred by the abbot and convent, and of penalties for non-performance, in WAM 6637; see also *CClR 1500–1509*, nos. 392–4.

that they had been written, illuminated, and then bound, well in advance.[96] Each of the four indentures begins with an illuminated page, with a historiated initial precisely related to the text that follows, and a border richly ornamented with the king's badges. In the king's part of the indentures bipartite the illustrations with which the first and last indentures commence thus show the abbot and convent of Westminster kneeling before Henry VII to present the volume to the king.[97] The book is clearly and recognisably depicted in its bound form, with pendant tassels. In Westminster's copy these illustrations are somewhat clumsily reversed to show, correctly, Henry VII proffering the copy sealed with the great seals to the abbot and convent.[98] It is possible that the artist has reinforced his message by indicating the venue as Star Chamber, the formal meeting place of the king's council whose advice and expertise, formally or informally given, undoubtedly underpinned the whole process. The setting is preserved throughout the sequence, except for the third miniature, described below.[99] The second indenture, the ordinances of the thirteen poor men, opens with an initial which shows the abbot and convent, in company with the almsmen offering the whole volume to the king. The almsmen's sleeves are emblazoned with the king's badge of a crown imperial surmounting a rose, displaying the nature of their service. The king is enthroned; the other parties kneel in an attitude of subservience and prayer.[100] The third miniature, heading the indenture of abstract, is perhaps the most telling. It describes in pictorial form that annual reading intended to secure the perpetual observance of the king's memorial in all its original strength and effect. This indenture was to be read in open chapter in the presence of a senior law officer of the crown within the two days before the celebration of the anniversary. An annual reading of foundation charters was a common enough provision: the intrusion of laymen into privileged space most certainly was not. The community is shown assembled in their chapter house (Plate VIIA). The book is open (and clearly recognisable by its distinctive binding and tassels) on a lectern, and is being read by a monk before the assembled company. This includes not only the abbot and convent but also the full assemblage recounted by the indenture of the chief justice of the King's Bench, the king's attorney, the recorder of London, and the steward of the abbey's lands.[101] In practice, this full gathering of outsiders in company with the convent is a chimera born of artistic licence. Even for

---

[96] In Westminster's copy the whole of the dating clause of the first three indentures is an insertion; in the fourth only the day and the month. In this case the year runs continually with the text, intruding into the margin, for which appropriate allowance was made in the decoration which is ragged along its inner right-hand length allowing for this and other textual overspill on the page; BL Harleian MS 1498, fo. 98.

[97] PRO, E 33/1, fos. 5, 107. The PRO volume has two series of foliations, both imperfect. One, in red ink, dates from the Chapter House; the other is a modern foliation in pencil. The numbering used here was derived by a count that included in the sequence the blank covers enclosing each separate indenture.

[98] BL Harleian MS 1498, fos. 1, 98.

[99] The indentures note that Edmund Tudor's chantry was to be established in a form to be devised by the council; the foreign obits, the subject of the later indentures quadripartite, were to be appointed by the king.

[100] PRO, E 33/1, fo. 65; BL Harleian MS 1498, fo. 59. Illustration from Westminster's copy in Backhouse, 'Illuminated manuscripts associated with Henry VII', 177, and pl. 45. The appointed robes were actually russet rather than black. *CClR 1500–1509*, 146.

[101] PRO, E 33/1, fo. 83; BL Harleian MS 1498 fo. 76.

the first reading taking place after the formal engrossment and sealing, for which the precentor of the abbey took the lectern, only the chief justice of the King's Bench, John Fyneux, and Edmund Dudley, steward of the abbey's lands, gave their attendance.[102] The text itself required the attendance of the king's attorney or recorder only as substitutes should the chief justice be unable to attend; and for all years for which accounts survive their presence seems not to have been required.[103]

At least once a year the two part indentures were thus actual working documents, although abstracts were made for day to day reference. Use of the composite volume on such formal occasions was facilitated by permanent bookmarks of worked silver and gold thread which protruded from the side of the blank page preceding each of the four indentures. They are intact in the abbey's volume; in the king's copy only those marking the first and third indentures remain.[104]

The seven-part indentures

The wide ranging commitments undertaken by the abbey were underpinned by the original indenture of penalties, the indenture septipartite. This briefly rehearses the various elements of the abbey's obligations and then sets out the fines for non-performance on any occasion of each of the separate clauses to which the abbot and convent stood bound, and the procedure for the levy of those penalties in the event of default. For example, omission of the weekly sermon incurred a fine of five marks; failure to ring the bell for the chantry mass one mark; to deliver charcoal to the almsmen twelve pence. Failure to read the indenture of abstract would incur the very large fine of £100.[105]

As its name implies, the indenture was seven times replicated. One volume, each of an opulence equivalent to the two-part indentures, remained with each of the seven chief parties named. The extreme degree of outside supervision and legal enforcement that these documents represent is the most novel, yet characteristic, aspect of the king's chantry provision. The first and second parties were Henry VII and the abbot and convent of Westminster. The third party to the agreement, with primary responsibility for initiating proceedings for the recovery of the specified financial penalty in the event of default, was the mayor and commonalty of the city of London acting for themselves and their successors in perpetuity. In default of action by the city the responsibility for securing the fine and Westminster's adherence to the terms of its agreement passed successively (for that part in default only) to the other parties to the indenture. These were, in the order named, fourthly, the dean and canons of St Stephen's, Westminster; of the fifth part, the dean and chapter of St Paul's; of the sixth part the bishop of Winchester; and the prior and convent of St Swithin's,

---

[102] WAM 24240.
[103] Accounts of the attendance for the reading and the anniversary were included in the wardens' accounts for the chapel, WAM 24236–50; 28043; for distributions to named monks for their part see, e.g., WAM 5256B, 5260B.
[104] PRO, E 33/1, fos. 4, 82; BL Harleian MS 1498 (the blank pages are not foliated).
[105] Abstract and list of penalties in *CClR 1500–1509*, nos. 391, 392; for the originals, see Appendix, below, 95.

Plate IA. Exterior view looking north, 1996.

Plate IB. Exterior view, Thomas Malton, 1796.

Plate II. Interior looking west, Charles Wild, c.1825. (WAM CN.10.II.15)

Plate III. Interior looking east, formerly attributed to Canaletto, c.1740.

Plate IVA. The vault from below.

Plate IVB. The tomb of Henry VII and Elizabeth of York, detail of effigies, looking north.

Plate V. The interior looking east.

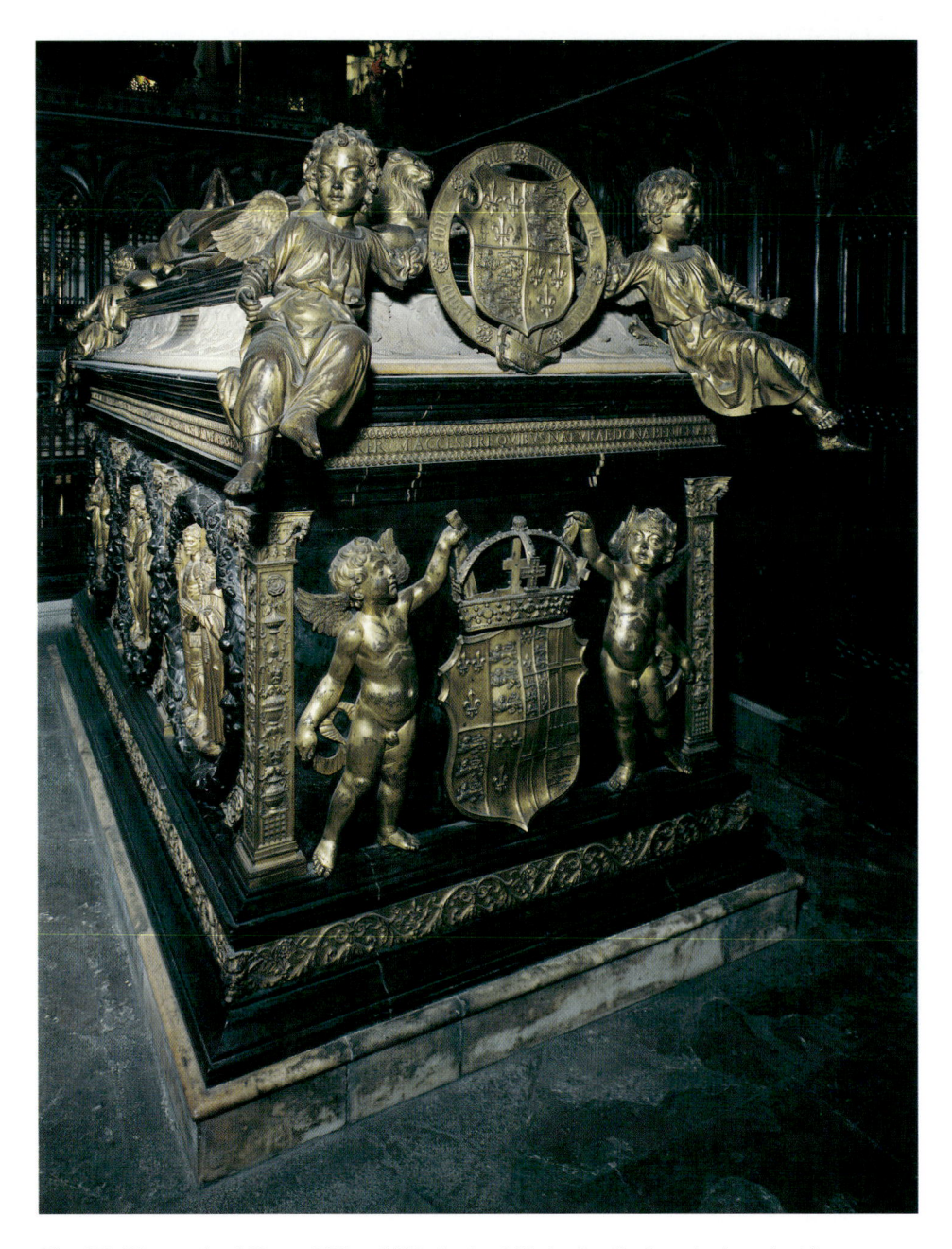

Plate VI. The tomb of Henry VII and Elizabeth of York, detail of tomb-chest, looking north-west.

Plate VIIA. The annual reading of the indenture in the chapter house. (PRO, E 33/1, fo. 83)

Plate VIIB. The abbot and convent present the indentures bipartite to the king. The artist has emphasised the indented head of the document. (PRO, E 33/1, fo. 5)

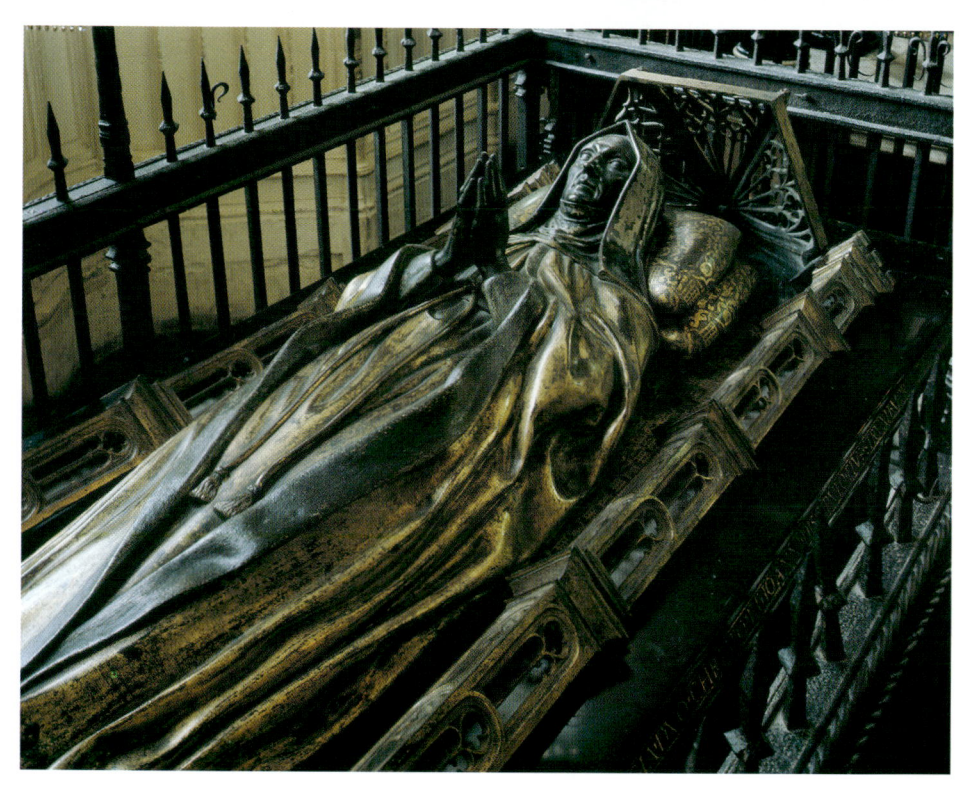

Plate VIIC. The tomb of Lady Margaret Beaufort, looking south-west.

Plate VIII. The king's copy of the indentures bipartite showing the foundation indenture, damask lining of the chemise cover, and seal skippets. (PRO, E 33/1)

Winchester; and of the seventh part the archbishop of Canterbury, and his cathedral chapter. All the above acted for themselves and their successors in perpetuity. The fine accrued to the city or other party suing.

The clergy named are cited only by office in the text. As individuals, however, the immediate signatories were bound to the king by bonds of long service. Edward Underwood, dean of St Stephen's, had been the queen's confessor. Dean only briefly, he died before the end of the year, and was succeeded by Thomas Hobbes, king's chaplain and one of the king's councillors.[106] Robert Sherborne, dean of St Paul's, had earlier been the king's secretary. Still a trusted councillor, he was most recently the king's orator in Rome.[107] Richard Fox's service to Henry VII pre-dated the reign. He had been keeper of the privy seal since 1487, bishop of Winchester since 1501 after a succession of other preferments, and would emerge as the most active and dominant of the executors after 1509. William Warham, archbishop of Canterbury, was the king's chancellor, appointed after a decade as Master of the Rolls and then keeper of the great seal, and would be appointed supervisor of the king's will.

The reasons for London's involvement can only be guessed at. Whilst the advantages to the king are obvious, the assent of the city to the policing of the agreements is less easily explained. The dominant concern expressed in the repertories and journals of the Common Council at this period is the protracted negotiations over the confirmation of the city's charter; and may lead us to guess, although it would be unwise to be dogmatic, that their potentially onerous involvement in the memorial process was part of the price which London was prepared to pay for confirmation of its charter and traditional liberties.[108] Certainly this would be a primary motive when, two years later, the wardens and fellowship of the major livery companies swiftly and unanimously agreed to take part in perpetuity in an annual commemorative service to be held in the king's new chapel at Westminster, on the occasion of the appearance in the exchequer of the mayor and sheriffs of London for the swearing of their oaths concerning their office.[109]

The frontispiece to the king's copy of the indenture septipartite[110] shows all the parties kneeling before the king, offering him the bound volume with its distinctive binding (Plate VIIB). It is reasonable to suppose that then, as now, the chemise concealed the seals that formally signified the assent of each of the parties to the obligations they had undertaken. This illustration, although true to the text, is an anachronism. The minutes of the proceedings of the Common Council of the city of

---

[106] Cf. *CPR 1494–1509*, 388 (and the original enrolment), which names the dean as John; but the date of Edward's death corresponds with that of Hobbes's appointment, Emden, *Oxford* iii, 1930–1.

[107] W.E. Wilkie, *The Cardinal Protectors of England*, Cambridge 1974, 76–7. His primary mission was to obtain the dispensation for the marriage of Prince Henry to Katherine of Aragon, but some time after 6 July he was forced to leave Rome empty handed.

[108] CLRO, Journal 10, Repertories 1, 2, *passim*; especially Repertory 1, fos. 149, 150.

[109] CLRO, Repertory 2, fo. 10v, 6 July 1506; the Crown's assent to the election of the mayor and sheriffs, and their delivery of an ancient quit rent, was a customary ceremony regulated by an order entered on the Exchequer memoranda rolls of 7 Edward III: see PRO, PRO 22/82, pp. 147–8. Similar considerations may have moved both the universities of Oxford and Cambridge, and the merchant tailors of London, in giving their agreement to observe anniversaries and services mirroring those at Westminster: cf. *Epistolae Academiae Oxon* ii, ed. H. Anstey, Oxford Historical Society 36, 1898, 672–3, 680–1; *CClR 1500–1509*, 248.

[110] PRO, E 33/2.

London, and the repertories of the Court of Aldermen indicate that the common seal of the city was affixed to the six copies to which their seal was to be put only on 18 July; on 24 July 1504 powers were given to certain aldermen to present these books to the king and to receive from him the seventh part indenture, which was to be retained in the Guildhall. In practice the six previously sealed indentures were handed over by the city's common serjeant to the Master of the Rolls at the Guildhall on 24 July, at a solemn ceremony in which the Chancery court sat in the Guildhall to record the formal acknowledgement of sealing and the petitionary process leading to the enrolment of the indenture on the close rolls of Chancery.[111] It might be reasonable to assume that the mayor, William Capell, and his fellows received, in return, their copy of the indenture sealed under the great seal and those of the other five principals plus the two supporting cathedral chapters. Certainly the frontispiece to that part of the indenture septipartite which was to remain with St Stephen's, Westminster, showed the dean and canons kneeling before the king in Star Chamber to receive their copy, without the other parties being present.[112] But the arrangements were still more complex, and both text and illustrations are misleading. If credence is given to the records of the city of London, then the city's retention for nearly a week of the six indentures already sealed on 16 July with the king's great seal and the common seal of the abbey provides a gloss on the indenture text and is some indication of the importance attached by Henry to the city's part as guarantors. By this scenario the other parties named are unlikely to have set their seals to the documents before 24 July when Chancery, in the persons of the Chancellor or the Master of the Rolls, with their attendant clerks, sat successively (but in unknown sequence) at Westminster, where William Warham, the archbishop of Canterbury (and Lord Chancellor) and Richard Fox, bishop of Winchester, made their formal acknowledgement; in the chapter of St Stephen's, Westminster, and in the chapter of St Paul's, as well as in the Guildhall. The common seal of the chapter of Canterbury may have been added only on 3 August, at Canterbury: the dating clause recording the text of the chapter's *acta* authorising the sealing, and their acknowledgement of the deed 'in Chancery' being inserted in the king's copy of the indenture, and also in those of St Stephen's and St Paul's, in a humanist, non-curial hand.[113] The date of sealing by the prior and convent of St Swithin's, Winchester is unclear. There is a blank, still unoccupied, left for the dating clause in all these indentures, including the king's; but the enrolment on the Close Rolls records that the chapter gave their assent on 19 September before the abbot of Hyde and John Kingsmill, by virtue of a writ of *dedimus potestatem*. There must be at least a suspicion that this was retrospective validation, obtained from a body that had in 1503 agreed to perform the king's suffrages and receiving, in turn (but at a later date) limited freedom from the mortmain laws.[114]

---

[111] CLRO, Journal 10, fos. 318, 318v; CLRO, Repertory 1, fo. 161; and see *CClR 1500–1509*, 156.
[112] BL Additional MS 21112, fo. 1.
[113] PRO, E 33/2, fo. 28; *CClR 1500–1509*, 156; BL Additional MS 21112, fo. 27; St Paul's, Library MS. I am indebted to Jo Wisdom of the Chapter Library for checking the St Paul's manuscript for me.
[114] PRO, E 33/2, fo. 28v; *CClR 1500–1509*, 156; BL Additional MS 21112, fo. 27v; so also in the St Paul's manuscript. The 1503 agreement may be one reason why, unlike St Paul's and St Stephen's, there was no separate grant by way of the indentures quadripartite: Winchester Cathedral Library, Register of the Common Seal, ii, fo. 15r; a (?) draft remains among the cathedral archives; further agreement, with privileges, but with date and text incomplete in an otherwise apparently finished and

The four-part indentures

The services at Westminster were the high point and the most visible element in a veritable cathedral of prayer. In the eighteenth year of the reign (1502–1503): that is, at the point at which the arrangements with Westminster for a perpetual memorial on a truly regal scale were gathering momentum, a retrospective record was made in Chancery of a number of grants of confraternity and agreements with various religious communities for prayers and services to be offered for the king's welfare in life, and for the good of his soul after his death.[115] The grants, made variously to the king, to the king and his consort, Elizabeth, or to the king, queen, and the king's mother, Margaret Beaufort, countess of Richmond, range in date from 1486 to 1502. Some, particularly the award of 1499 by King's College, Cambridge, closely mirror the Westminster provision. The king's agreement, both subliminally and explicitly, emphasised also the connection with Henry VI. In the period between the first commencement of the services at Westminster and the sealing of the formal indenture of foundation in July 1504 at least a further twenty-five religious houses granted the king the performance of services in his life in the same manner as at Westminster, and an obit of the most solemn kind on the announcement of his death. Other such agreements followed, encouraged and underwritten by constitutions of the synods of both archdioceses.[116]

The foundation at Westminster took this cumulative process one stage further. Formal agreements were made with the two universities, the deans and chapters of St Stephen's, Westminster and St George's, Windsor, with houses of each order of friars and other favoured religious orders or major houses in London and elsewhere, including the monks of St Augustine's, Canterbury and St Albans, the Carthusians of the London Charterhouse, and the Brigettines at Syon. In return for an annual dole, for which the abbot and convent of Westminster, and the mayor and corporation of London, were to act as treasurers, wardens, and trustees the communities were to observe an anniversary in perpetuity. The terms were formally engrossed in the series of twenty indentures quadripartite.[117] The indentures specify the prayers and ceremonial to be used, and the intentions for which they were to be offered. Both mirror those observed at Westminster itself. The largest payments, of £10 per year, went to

---

illuminated manuscript, Staats- und Universitätsbibliothek Bremen, MS a.49; edition of the English section of the text of the Bremen MS, Maas, 'Zwei Texte', 72–5. I owe the Winchester references to John Hardacre, curator of the cathedral archives, and Dr Thomas Elsmann. Neither grant appears on the admittedly imperfect Close Rolls of the reign.

[115] *CClR 1500–1509*, 197. The nature of the deeds, and the dedicatees, is not clear in the otherwise full calendar of the grants, and reference needs to be made to the enrolment, PRO C 54/363.

[116] *CClR 1500–1509*, 647, including a reference to Canterbury's decision, made between February and May 1504; A.F. Pollard, *The Reign of Henry VII from Contemporary Sources*, 3 vols., 1914, iii, 254–5; see also the allusion and legacy in Henry VII's will, E 23/3, fo. 8v. It is probable that the enrolment of these grants provided the documentary basis for the schedule to the will missing (if it was ever attached) by at least 1600, BL Harleian MS 297, fo. 16.

[117] For references and a list of the houses see Appendix, below, 95–7; brief and not entirely accurate abstracts in *CClR 1500–1509*, 532, from PRO, C 54/368. For the close relations maintained by both the king and his mother with Syon, N. Beckett, 'Henry VII and Sheen Charterhouse', in *Reign of Henry VII*, 117–32.

the two universities. Both still retain, not only their parts of the indentures, but also a physical memorial of the regality of the occasion, hearse cloths of cloth of gold, heavily embroidered with the king's badges. Whereas the arrangements made with the various religious houses and chapters are primarily a testimony to the king's confidence in the efficacy of prayer, involving the whole convent or chapter in an anniversary mass centred round a cloth-covered hearse, and requiring also from every priest a mass of requiem on the day, the annual obits held at Oxford and Cambridge were, as at Westminster, very public occasions. They were to be held in the university church of each. At both, a hearse, covered with the best stuff the university could provide, was to stand before the high cross.[118] After the mass the members of the university, headed by the chancellor, if present, were to process to the lighted hearse singing the *Libera me*, the *De profundis*, and the specially appointed collects.[119] Despite the wording of the indentures, which was standardised across the entire sequence, it seems inconceivable that these magnificent hearse cloths were not provided by the king himself.[120]

The endowment

The scale and nature of the memorial required by the agreement with Westminster demanded equally impressive, directed, and secure financial provision. Begun by Easter 1501[121] the initial endowment was an interim grant. By the following year it included the manors of Halton, Alkborough, and Burton Stather, and other lands in the county of Lincoln which, although they would form part of the permanent endowment, were initially granted by George, Lord Bergavenny, for a period of three years only from Michaelmas 1502, pending completion of a complex exchange of lands involving Maurice Lord Berkeley as a fourth party. In agreeing to the arrangement, made 1 March 1503, the abbot specifically reserved his position on signing and sealing any formal agreement concerning either the foundation at Westminster or the foreign obits until such time as the abbey's title was 'made sure'.[122] The first formal account of John Islip as warden for the foundation, made for the year ending in Michaelmas 1503 but including payments made earlier than the year of account, included also the manors of Remenham, Berks, and Broadwater, Sussex, neither of which appear in subsequent accounts.[123] Although Islip himself surveyed Broadwater in 1504/5, these two manors seem not to have formed part of the permanent endow-

---

[118] This seems to imply, and this receives some support from the accounts, a processional with the university's cross.

[119] PRO, C 54/368. The entries in *CClR 1500–1509*, 532, are neither sufficiently full nor wholly accurate.

[120] At Cambridge the costs of observing the anniversary in 1505 include a payment for carriage of a funeral pall, the only year in which such a payment appears: *Grace Book B*, ed. M. Bateson, 2 vols., Cambridge Antiquarian Society, Luard Memorial Series, Cambridge 1903–5, i, 203; the same account includes a payment for writing out the special collects required. The Oxford pall is on open display in the Ashmolean museum. For the Cambridge pall see below, 93–4.

[121] *CPR 1494–1509*, 201, 245 (grant in frankalmoign and licence to appropriate the free chapels of Stanford and Upper Lambourn, Berks., both parcel of the duchy); see also bulls allowing transfer of Windsor's intended endowment to Westminster, 20 January 1500, PRO, SC 7/4(1).

[122] WAM 14650.

[123] WAM 24236; duplicate in WAM 24237.

ment.[124] What is certain is that this initial tranche of lands and spiritualities enabled the commencement of the ordinary commemorative and votive services later the same year, and the inauguration of the university scholarships integral to the king's chantry provision.[125]

The acquisition of the endowment was manipulated by the king even more closely than at first sight seems apparent; and the forced pace stands in contrast with that of Henry V's foundation, made only in 1445, more than twenty years after that king's death, and the incomplete endowment for that of Richard II, interrupted by his deposition and violent death.[126] Luffield priory had been in Henry's hands since 1494 and had at first been intended for the endowment of St George's, Windsor.[127] St Martin's was a royal chapel, of which the dean was James Stanley, younger son of Thomas, earl of Derby, the third husband of the king's mother. The suppression of both, and of the college of Tickhill, parcel of the duchy of Lancaster, required papal licence. The drafts for the bulls appear to have been prepared in England for presentation to the Curia, and their passage perhaps eased by a flow of funds, primarily for other purposes, for the use of the pope.[128] Various advowsons, tithes, and other spiritual benefits were permanently alienated from the duchy of Lancaster, held in right of the crown, but not joined to it. The balance of the endowment, however, was to be acquired by Westminster directly, allegedly on an open land market. A fair price was paid.[129] Yet the king's guiding hand is apparent even in the purchase of Fen [in Fishtoft] and Scrane [in Freiston], Lincs., from William Esyngton. A deed signed by Islip 14 December 1503, agreeing to acquire the lands for the performance of the will of Henry VII, is in fact written on the reverse of a waste memorandum in the hand of John Heron, Henry's treasurer of his chamber. The memorandum is clearly of matters pertaining to the business of the king; and it includes, without further elaboration, an entry for the payment of £504 13s 4d. This was the outstanding balance of the purchase price.[130] The deed is witnessed by Humphrey Coningsby, serjeant at law and one of the king's councillors, as well as one of the learned counsel acting for the abbey;[131] and the actual conveyance was effected through a group of men, headed by Bishop Fox, who might loosely be termed the king's feoffees.[132] In November and December of the previous year the king had bought out other interests in both Fen and Remenham, rewarding Coningsby and his clerks, and John Kingsmill, for their

---

[124] WAM 24240; title to both had been obtained, somewhat heavy handedly, by Reynold Bray, who possibly intended to transfer them to Westminster, M.M Condon, 'From caitiff and villain to Pater Patriae: Reynold Bray and the profits of office', in *Profit, Piety and the Professions*, ed. M.A. Hicks, Gloucester 1990, 154–6.
[125] See below, 86, 89.
[126] See Harvey, *Estates*, 33, 198–202.
[127] *Luffield Priory Charters, Part 1*, ed. G.R. Elvey, Buckinghamshire Record Society 15, 1968, ix; an inventory of the goods was taken by Richard Empson in 1496. Empson was granted the lease by Westminster in December 1504, WAM 3007.
[128] *CPL 1495–1503*, xxv–xxvi, from WAM 6633; *Excerpta Historica*, 128 (original PRO, E 101/415/3, fo. 101v).
[129] Harvey, *Estates*, 200–2.
[130] WAM 14708*.
[131] *Ibid.*
[132] *CPR 1494–1509*, 342.

services.¹³³ The arrangements made for a complex exchange between George, Lord Bergavenny and Maurice Berkeley under pressure from the king, the aim of which was to release lands for the endowment of the king's foundation, were to be scrutinised by the king and his council on a tight timetable in anticipation of the summons of a parliament. The costs and charges relating to the conveyance were to be borne by the king.¹³⁴ The purchase of land in Plumstead, Kent, and in Manewden and elsewhere in Essex, in support of the endowment, is unlikely to be fortuitous. The vendor, John Cutte, the king's receiver of his duchy of Lancaster, and subsequently both under-treasurer of the Exchequer and one of the king's executors, was a client of Reynold Bray, one of he king's most senior and most loyal councillors. William Cope, the king's cofferer, whom the king paid for Plumstead in December 1499, in what is probably a related transaction, had been Bray's servant since the 1470's. The enabling role played by Bray remains obscure, but may be inferred both from his prominent part in the inauguration ceremony and by his release of lands to Margaret Beaufort in 1501, in assistance to the endowment of her Westminster chantry. It is possible that his contribution to the king's foundation was distorted by his death on 8 August 1503, little more than two weeks after the licence to him and his feoffees to grant Broadwater and Remenham to Westminster had passed the great seal; the lands are known to have passed to his heirs.¹³⁵

Augmentation of the endowment continued beyond 1504, and the accounts suggest an active and informed interest on the part of Abbot John Islip, and some continuing cost to the abbey. Although Henry VII's memorial was onerous in terms of both spiritual obligation and expenditure, it was also of critical importance to the augmentation and maintenance of the abbey's income;¹³⁶ and in the extensive negotiations for the confirmation of the abbey's charters in the first years of the reign of Henry VIII specific confirmation was sought of his father's foundation.¹³⁷ At several points in the negotiations prior to 1504 Islip reserved the convent's position on signing agreements or effecting the provisions of the Foundation until such time as the endowments promised by the king had been securely put in place. His accounts for 1503–1504 show a continual itinerary to meet with the king and his council concerning the foundation.¹³⁸ The abbey customarily retained a number of the king's legal counsel¹³⁹ and, in securing the endowment to the abbey, common recourse was had by both king and abbot to Thomas Frowyk, Humphrey Coningsby and John Kingsmill, serjeants at law, with further advice being sought, for the securing of the spiritualities, from Drs Bothe and Taylor.¹⁴⁰ The advice and service given by Edmund Dudley, steward of the abbey's lands, and one of its regularly retained learned

---

[133] BL Additional MS 59899, fos. 4v–6.
[134] WAM 14650.
[135] Condon, 'Reynold Bray and the profits of office', 146, 148–9, 152–6; payment by the king to Cutte June 1503, BL Additional MS 59899, fo. 28. For Margaret Beaufort's chantry, transferred like the king's from Windsor to Westminster and ultimately established in the south aisle of the Lady chapel, M.K. Jones and M.G. Underwood, *The King's Mother*, Cambridge 1992, 207–9.
[136] Harvey, *Estates*, 33–5, 52–3, 67–8, 399.
[137] Negotiations for confirmation, WAM 23005–6; *L&P Henry VIII* i, 448, 485.
[138] WAM 24240; above, 61–2, 82.
[139] Treasurer's accounts, e.g., WAM 19996–20000, 23001–6.
[140] WAM 24240.

counsel, for which he, as others, was rewarded by Islip from the revenues of the foundation,[141] may have been one of the factors which brought Dudley to the king's notice, and his subsequent career first as speaker of the parliament which met in January 1504, and then as a leading member of the king's Council Learned.

Liturgical commemoration: the perpetual memorial

The foundation indenture, that is, the first of the indentures bipartite, required the monks of Westminster to maintain in perpetuity prayers for his safety and well being as king, and for the salvation of his soul, specifying precisely the prayers, sequences and psalms to be used. The agreement bound the whole convent to a daily memorial which intruded into the regular services, adding to the high mass collects and other prayers for Henry as founder. During the king's life all chapter masses were to include the anthem *Domine salve fac regem nostrum Henricum Septimum* in the sung responses to be made by the celebrant and the choir. Whilst there is nothing liturgically unusual in this essentially psalmaic response, which translates in common parlance as 'God save Henry the Seventh our king', it was a prayer which Henry had made his own, and which gained in strength through its repetition. The anthem is first found as a motto in charters of Henry VI. It was continued under the Yorkist kings and appears again, more forcefully, under Henry VII, where it is found in English as well as in Latin.[142] The psalms ordained to be said or sung during the canon of the mass, and the responses, garnered from the psalms with minimal alteration to name Henry VII, were carefully chosen. They recall his coronation and triumph, including in full the 'Coronation Psalm', Psalm 21(20), sung during the anointing with the holy oils. By analogy they remember also the tribulations of his reign, his desire for the peace and prosperity of his realm, and his trust in and intercession for the saving grace of God. Repeatedly the celebrant and choir were to ask, in the words of David, for preservation of the king from his enemies, and for their discomfiture, ending with a plea for peace and prosperity.[143] The same basic themes, with a plea for the blessing of eternal life, run through the specially appointed collect, secret and post communion prayers. These, too, were a close variant on the coronation service, with a strengthened prayer for peace.[144] After the king's death both the psalms and the prayers were to be

---

[141] WAM 24240; identified as steward in the accounts of the Treasurer, WAM 19996–20000, 23001–4; he first appears as retained counsel in the account of the monk bailiff 1499–1500, WAM 18687.

[142] For the adoption and deliberate use of the motto by Henry VI and Henry VII see E.A. Danbury, 'The decoration and illumination of royal charters in England, 1250–1509: an introduction', in *England and her Neighbours 1066–1453*, ed. M. Jones and M. Vale, 1989, 174–7.

[143] Psalms 20(19) and 21(20) were to be said or sung in full; the responses were Psalm 68(67) v. 1; Psalm 20(19) v. 10, naming Henry the Seventh as the king to be prayed for; Psalm 20(19) v. 2; Psalm 61(60) v. 3, slightly altered; Psalm 89(88) v. 23; Psalm 41(40), v. 2 and Psalm 122(121) v. 7. I am indebted to Miss E.A. Danbury, and especially to the splendid web concordance (now sadly discontinued) maintained by Richard Goertz of Brown University, for assistance in identifying the Vulgate texts used. For Psalm 21(20) '*Dominus in virtute tua letabitur rex*' and the Coronation service, L.G. Wickham Legg, *English Coronation Records*, 1901, 92, 232; Henry VII, like Richard II before him, placed particular emphasis on this sacring in his choice of Westminster for burial. See above, 68–9.

[144] Text of the collect, secret and post communion prayers of the coronation service, in Legg, *Coronation Records*, 102–6.

replaced by others more appropriate to the commemoration of and intercession for the dead. The justified sense of repeated danger, of intercession for, and divine intervention in, the king's preservation and good estate, is one of the repeated undercurrents of the reign. It appears again in the king's will, and was firmly incorporated into the memorial services to be held in the king's lifetime.

The collect for the living king was widely observed and distributed, both in manuscript and print: not only at Westminster but by specific agreement or general injunction throughout the churches of his realm.[145] At Westminster itself, failure to observe the collects or psalms would incur a fine of 40s for each default. The collect was printed at the king's command, almost certainly by Richard Pynson, who, also, at the king's request, published a Sarum missal before the end of 1504. This included certain 'novis officiis non parum necessariis': votive masses which included an office and mass of the Virgin, of *Salus Populi* – and a '*Missa pro Rege*' whose proper included those same prayers.[146]

In addition to the conventual daily remembrance and invocation, Westminster was to observe a weekly obit which included the customary vigil, with a requiem and a distribution of alms on the day,[147] and was to relocate those services to the chapel once built. Over and above this corporate obligation, a chantry was to be maintained by three monks dedicated to that service, whose numbers were to augment the normal complement of the abbey. It was the king's intention that, ultimately, his chantry monks should be university educated to the degree of bachelor or doctor of divinity, and part of his endowment was to be directed to funding three new scholarships at Oxford, in addition to those customarily funded by the abbey itself.[148] The king understood, however, that only the three most senior monastic officers, the abbot himself, the prior, and the monk bailiff, were so qualified, and that those offices had prior claim. Since the chantry was to take immediate effect, and had, indeed, been in place since 1502, in the interim three professed monks without such qualifications were to be appointed until such time as the conditions could be fully met.[149] The

---

[145] See above, 81. The collects etc. were not new in 1504, but at Westminster their close affiliation to the *Liber regalis* gave them a particular resonance; and from 1503 the king made extraordinary efforts to secure their observance throughout the realm.

[146] Payment for new collects, 24 November 1503; prest for the printing of mass books, paid to Pynson 12 July 1504, and printed in December, *Excerpta Historica*, 131, 132 (original BL Additional MS 59899, fos. 38, 61); *Missale ad usum insignis et preclare Sarum . . . adiunctis . . . aliquibus novis officiis non parum necessariis* (STC 16179) second foliation esp. fos. 19v–20; some copies of the missal were printed on vellum, and it is plausible, at least, that some were intended for the chapel (and see the cycle below, n. 150); for the collect see also H. Reynolds, *Wells Cathedral: its Foundation, Constitutional History and Statutes*, Leeds c.1880, 208, 212; a recognisable variant is entered in the so-called Beaufort hours, BL MS Royal 2 AXVIII, fo. 240v. By the will of Margaret Beaufort, this volume was to be chained in the Chapel: Jones and Underwood, *The King's Mother*, 240.

[147] For the distribution of Henry VII's alms at Westminster, both for the weekly obit and at the anniversary, B. Harvey, *Living and Dying in England 1100–1540*, Oxford 1993, 23–33; by the 1520s Henry VII's weekly alms had, however, been diverted to the support of the song school, *ibid.*, 32 n. 94.

[148] The scholarships had been in place since 1502, below, 89.

[149] John Ashley, Henry Jones and Robert Humfrey were designated as the first chantry priests. All had been priests for at least ten years, and were to rise in the abbey's hierarchy. Ashley was Kitchener, one of the abbey's lesser offices, from 1503; Humfrey acted as Treasurer from 1503 in succession to William Borowe, who transferred to Chertsey, WAM 24236; WAM 23002; E.H. Pearce, *The Monks of Westminster*, Cambridge 1916, 169–70, 172.

indenture sets out the terms of the chantry, naming the prayers to be used, which were to mirror those being said communally and severally at the chapter mass, and the liturgical cycle that was to be observed. His priests were to pray for the king's good estate in life, and his soul after death, and for the souls of his wife, parents, and children, with an alteration in the forms of the collects and other prayers after the death of the king's mother in order to include her by name.

Whilst the prayers followed customary liturgical practice in the quiet use of Latin, the chantry monks fulfilled both an intercessory and a public function. At the lavatory of the mass, that is, the point at which the celebrant ritually washed his hands in a symbolism of purity and inner cleanliness before proceeding to pray for the acceptability to God of the sacrifice about to be offered by all present, and for the intercession of the saints for the salvation of all so celebrating, they were to turn to any lay congregation being present asking them, in English, to pray for the king's prosperous estate in life, and that of his realm. After the king's death, and likewise in English, they were to request prayers for the good of his soul, and those of his wife, children, and parents. Each day the masses, which followed in an appointed order, were those of the feasts of the Virgin, taken in rotation, of requiem, and of the calendar of the church's year. All were to be attended by the king's almsmen, whose distinctive robes and shoulder scutcheons of the king's badges proclaimed the nature of their service, and the identity of the principal beneficiary. Between the second mass, of requiem, and the third, the priest warden of the king's almsmen would likewise offer mass, with dedications on a different weekly cycle but closing, like the chantry priests, on Saturdays with the liturgy for the commemoration of the Virgin.[150] Until the completion of the chapel and tomb enclosure, which would incorporate an altar, the chantry was to be sited under the lantern of the church, between the high altar and the choir, and was to be accompanied by a display of lights around the hearse, conventional in numbers but pedantic in extravagance, more fully explored in Christopher Wilson's article.[151] The premature death of Elizabeth of York meant that the priests celebrated at the tomb of the queen, temporarily buried in a vault under the lantern, and the warden's accounts include payments for the erection and maintenance of railings and hangings around her tomb.[152] At Easter both hearse and altar were to be relocated to a side chapel in the south aisle, near the altar of St Benet; and incidental expenses arising from the regular observance of the chantry from 1502 include the purchase of a chest in which to place the ornaments of the altar.[153]

The most solemn service of all was to be a requiem held on the anniversary of the death of the queen, 11 February, during Henry's lifetime, and, after his death, of his own burial. It was to be an occasion of secular pomp and circumstance, as well as sacred memorial and intercession. It required the attendance of the Chancellor, Treasurer, Master of the Rolls and all the justices, and the mayor of London, with the two

---

[150] On Sundays the Holy Trinity; Monday of Angels; Tuesday of the Holy Ghost; Wednesday of *Salus populi* (a mass for 'any necessity' – effectively for forgiveness and salvation); Thursday *De Corpore Christi*; Friday of Jesus; and Saturday of the Commemoration of the Virgin. See also the Pynson missal, above, n. 146.
[151] Wilson, below, 175–7; and see below, 90–1.
[152] WAM 24236–24241*; *Great Chronicle*, 322.
[153] WAM 24236.

sheriffs and the recorder, or principal law officer, of the city. All were to be paid for that service. In the default of attendance of any of these, there was to be a distribution of alms to prisoners in lieu, in addition to the general almsgiving of £20 on the day.[154]

Other directly intercessory and commemorative clauses of the agreement included the foundation of an almshouse, placed under the tutelage of the monks of Westminster, for thirteen poor men, to include one priest, plus three serving women. The inmates were not only to be pensioners of the crown but were to play an important part in the chantry services, in addition to a regime of prayer for the king within the almshouse itself.[155] The indentures emphasise their primary duty of prayer and intercession for the king and his dynasty, and their duties were to be publicly displayed on painted tablets placed in both the almshouse and the Lady chapel.[156] Sermons, endowed in perpetuity, were to be made within the abbey weekly, and at certain named festivals, either by one of the king's chantry priests or by some other 'famous doctor' of Oxford or Cambridge. The preacher was to invite prayers for the prosperous estate of the king and his realm in life, and of his soul, those of his wife and family, and all Christian souls after his death. During the sermon nearest to the anniversary the preacher was to remind his audience of the time and place, inviting prayers and attendance. This invitation was also to be made annually, on the continually renewed initiative of the abbot of Westminster, by the preacher at St Paul's Cross, a specific payment being allowed for that purpose. The tolling of bells further encouraged participation in both the services and for the distribution of alms. Three indulgences (previously given in favour of Windsor) were attached to the foundation. That of *Scala Coeli* was primarily for the king's own benefit in his lifetime, but available to all souls prayed for after his death; a Lenten and an Ascensiontide indulgence (700 copies of which were printed by Richard Pynson in 1507 and distributed in subsequent years) were available to all who fulfilled their conditions, including prayers for the king in life or death, and an offering for the upkeep of the chapel.[157] A chantry was to be maintained in the Grey Friars, Carmarthen, for the soul of Edmund Tudor, the king's father, Westminster acting as paymaster. The abbot was further charged with making annual payment to eighteen other houses or chapels, and to the two universities, for maintenance of commemorations which were to be specified by indentures still to be completed. This latter obligation was formalised by the series of

---

[154] See also below, 90–1; for the almsgiving, Harvey, *Living and Dying*, 31–2.
[155] For the almshouses, Colvin, *HKW* iii, 206–10. For the Ordinances, *CClR 1500–1509*, no. 390.
[156] The first tablets were provided in 1504/5 at a cost of 58s 8d, WAM 24240.
[157] *CPL* xviii, nos. 115, 118; Wilkie, *Cardinal Protectors*, 60; N. Morgan, 'The Scala Coeli indulgence and the royal chapels', in *Reign of Henry VII*, 82–103; since Henry VII's priests were allowed to undertake other chantries once they had fulfilled their duties to the king, the indulgence *Scala Coeli* may effectively have been available to others beside the king even in Henry's lifetime; original in PRO, SC 7/26/29 and copy of Alexander VI's grant of 1502, confirmed in 1504 by Julius II, PRO, SC 7/64/78; WAM 24241*; later accounts show the posting of the indulgence. The warden's account for 1516 records work done for the coming of Henry VIII 'ad indulgencias' in a year in which the anniversary would fall on Whit Sunday and would therefore be brought forward, normally to the Saturday preceding. Does this indicate the completion of the tomb? WAM 24242; although Henry VIII regularly sought the privilege, PRO E 36/215, pp. 59. 185, 318, 377, 446. Unambiguous mention of the king's offering at the anniversary mass (by the hands of a third party) is made in 1511 and 1512, PRO E 36/215, pp. 118, 184.

twenty indentures quadripartite, sealed in November and December 1504. To these twenty separate indentures, too, the abbot and convent became parties.[158]

Whilst much of Henry VII's foundation at Westminster, although undoubtedly born of a deep and enduring religious faith, is focused primarily on his own perceived spiritual needs, and as a personal and dynastic memorial to be maintained and overtly displayed in perpetuity, there was also some understanding of the convent's own needs beyond mere remuneration.[159] Two *conversi*, or lay brothers, were to be added to the abbey's normal complement, only part of their time being claimed by their assigned duties of the maintenance of lights and assistance at services in the Lady chapel.[160] Partly to ensure suitably qualified monk priests for his own services, but primarily to secure the quality and increase the number of monks suitable and of sufficient calibre for the governance and management of the abbey's affairs, three scholarships, to be held in the king's name, were founded at Oxford. These were to lead to the degree of bachelor of divinity, with provisions for a period of further study, to a maximum of three years, to allow advance towards a doctorate, and for replacement as vacancies occurred. The warden's accounts duly show the payment of a bursary to Thomas Barton, Thomas Jay and William Bothe as the first of the king's scholars, supported as such since the interim agreements of 1502. Whether these particular monks in course of time succeeded to the duty of prayer is not known, since only the first of the series of warden's accounts records the names of the chantry priests.[161] Bothe died in 1507/1508, but the fact that Jay's preferment within the abbey was rapid from 1514, and that both Barton and Jay eventually rose to the office of prior[162] was a full realisation of the dual intention of the king's bursaries. The timetabled duties of the priests allowed for the employment of men of calibre, whose employment accords with Henry VII's belief in the increased efficacy of the prayer of the most spiritually able. This clearly mattered to the king: over and above the requirements of his chantry and memorial, by 1505 he had installed Dr Brian Darley, newly qualified as a doctor of theology, as a chantry priest at St Edward's shrine, and beneficed him with a canonry in the collegiate church of Tamworth, Staffordshire, void by the resignation of one of his own household chaplains.[163]

The remaining clauses of the foundation indenture specified the oaths to be made by each successive abbot and prior to observe the conditions of the indenture, and rehearsed the endowment of the abbey with lands, advowsons, and specie to be invested in land, in order to fund the whole. A separate clause confirmed the appropriation of St Martin's, where a solemn anniversary was to be held as in the abbey.

---

[158] PRO, E 33/3–25; abstract in *CClR 1500–1509*, no. 532; acquittances for payments 1505–33 in WAM 27969–28036. For the names of the third parties, and a list of surviving documents, see Appendix, below, 95–7.

[159] For an analysis of the similar interplay of forces in respect of Henry VII's patronage of the Carthusian priory of Sheen, which has some lessons for Westminster, see Beckett, 'Henry VII and Sheen Chartcrhouse', 117–32.

[160] For the king's encouragement of *conversi*, D. Baker, 'Old wine in new bottles: attitudes to reform in fifteenth century England', in *Renaissance and Renewal in Christian History*, ed. D. Baker, Oxford 1977, 206–7.

[161] WAM 24236–24241*.

[162] Pearce, *Monks*, 32, 177, 178; Emden, *Oxford*, s.n.

[163] BL Additional MS 59899, fos. 73, 87; *CPR 1494–1509*, 394; A.B. Emden, *Biographical Register of the University of Cambridge to 1500*, Cambridge 1963, 177.

The king promised both spiritual and temporal reward in the form of the papal bulls of indulgences, licence for the exhumation and transfer of Henry VI, and confirmation of the king's foundation. A key provision required an annual reading within two days antecedent to the major anniversary of the indenture of abstract, the third of the four indentures bipartite. A *non obstante* clause secured the agreement of the abbot and convent to those elements of the foundation which were contrary to the rules or customs of their order, including the dispensation of the chantry monks from participation in the conventual mass where the timing overlapped with that appointed for the king's service, and the presence of laymen in the chapter house for the reading of the abstract.

What has to be envisaged and extrapolated from these texts is the centrality of the hearse and subsequently of the tomb, not only in the services, but also as the hub and focus of a constantly renewed processional. The ceremonial and dynastic impact of the hearse was one which was familiar to contemporaries[164] and would be further secured, in the case of Henry's tomb, by the hearse-like structure of the bronze enclosure begun in the king's own lifetime. At the anniversary mass the foreign presence, that is, those lay dignitaries specified in the foundation indenture, including and headed by the principal officers of state, the Chancellor and the Treasurer of England, was required to go after the offertory to the hearse or its tomb replacement, once complete. Standing about the hearse or tomb they were then to say the *De profundis* Psalm 130(129). At this point, their service done, and in accordance with customary funerary practice, they were allowed to leave. After the sung mass of requiem to be observed each week, which, after the chapel had been built, was to be said at the high altar of the chapel with the convent being seated in their places in the choir, all were then to go in procession to the hearse or tomb, singing the responses of the *Libera me* as they went or stood about, then following on in speech or chant with the *De profundis*, and those special collects and prayers appointed by the king and particularly specified in the indentures. Such large processionals would have gathered around rather than within the enclosure whose pierced walls gave good visual access to the tomb and its attendant altar, whilst the great lights soared above this hearse-like structure on prickets and basins integrally incorporated into the design: although in practice an ordinary hearse appears to have been used, at least for the anniversary services.[165] Even the vestments contributed to this finely crafted liturgical theatre. At the weekly obit the celebrant wore a cope of black damask, furnished with orphries of cloth of gold, with the king's badge of a crowned rose embroidered on the hood; and we may at least infer that the richer cope wholly of cloth of black cloth of gold (inventoried in 1540) was to be similarly used for the anniversary.[166] At the visits of any reigning king, or the queen, or dukes or earls of the king's blood (upon proper

---

[164] See A.F. Sutton and L. Visser-Fuchs, *The Reburial of Richard, Duke of York, 21–30 July 1476*, Richard III Society 1996, 3–6, 18–19, 33–6.

[165] This view of the enclosure was reached independently by the present author and by Dr Christopher Wilson, but is further explored by him below, 175–7. Some idea of the commanding effect of this intended *chapelle ardente* can be derived from the illustration of the hearse used for Abbot Islip's funeral in 1532, for which see *The Obituary Roll of John Islip*, ed. W. St John Hope, *Vetusta Munimenta* vii pt iv, 1906, pl. xxii.

[166] PRO, LR 2/111, fos. 18, 18v.

warning) as well as at high mass and evensong of major feasts, and also during the weekly obits, thirty tapers were to burn about the tomb always well above the height of a man, since once reduced to five feet, they were to be replaced: the full set of 100, newly made at twelve pounds and nine feet, was to be used at the anniversary. Four tapers, initially of eleven feet, but allowed to waste to six feet before replacement, stood continually burning about the tomb.[167] At the anniversary massive torches, their bowls blazoned with the king's badges, were to be carried by the almsmen, supplemented by other poor men, to a total of twenty-four; four of these torches were in weekly use for the obits. On a Saturday, after evensong, the king's almsmen received their weekly pittance at the tomb. Their days began with an assembly in the almshouse chapel, and prayers for the king, after which they, too, were to process to the tomb, two by two, for the first of the three chantry masses.

The memorial in place

Although the chapel may have been substantially complete by 1509, the work was to continue after Henry VII's death. The liturgical and charitable memorial, however, was fully effected in the king's own lifetime, and continued without interruption at least until the religious changes of the latter part of the reign of his son. Both the chantry priests and the almsmen commenced their service in 1502, in which year also the abbey observed some form of anniversary service. The numbers of the almsmen gradually increased from an initial complement of three in June 1502, to five in August, and twelve by the middle of November, receiving in time for the feast of All Saints their first annual livery of robes embellished with scutcheons of the king's badges. The first of the sermons appears to have been made on 7 May 1503, from which date the abbot of Westminster, as warden of the foundation, dated his regular payments for this purpose.[168] The first of the anniversary services conducted according to the formulae of the final agreement took place in 1504, presumably, as the indentures would require, on or about 11 February, the first anniversary of the death of Elizabeth of York.[169] The presence included the abbot, prior, forty five brothers, monks professed but not priests, and novices, seven *conversi*, and all the required foreign presence, that is, the chancellor, William Warham, the treasurer, Thomas, earl of Surrey, the chief justices of both King's Bench and Common Pleas, the Master of the Rolls, five other justices, the long serving Chief Baron, William Hody; and the mayor, sheriffs, and recorder of London. By the following year, the whole spiritual and legal edifice of the memorial was in place, and the warden's accounts record the solemn reading of the foundation charter and the obligations incurred by the abbey. The papal bulls which buttressed Henry VII's earthly endowment of land with grants of indulgences, confirmed his foundation of the chapel, and

---

[167] Their position was specified as the middle of the sides of the tomb: surely the reason for the prominent pierced brackets and prickets incorporated at that position in the chantry canopy. Their size and status is not clear from the abstract in *CClR 1500–1509*, 144, and reference needs to be made to the original manuscripts.
[168] WAM 24236.
[169] Observed almost certainly on 10 February this year: see below, 92.

gave him faculty to translate the body of Henry VI, were sealed only in May 1504, and it is probable that their reception in England was the final determinant of the timetable enacted in July 1504.[170] Similarly, it may not be entirely accidental that neither the bull of confirmation intended for Westminster itself, and eventually handed over to the abbey, nor the king's parts of the indentures bipartite and septipartite, deposited in the Exchequer, were placed into their final custody until February 1505, after that first formal reading and associated performance of the anniversary.[171]

Although it cannot be certain beyond doubt that Henry himself participated in the anniversary services, Bernard Andre, Henry's blind court poet, tells of the enormous solemnity and reverence with which Elizabeth's anniversary was regularly observed. There are other pointers also. On the anniversary date between 1504 and 1509, Henry was most usually at Westminster itself or at his favourite palaces of Richmond or Greenwich, both within easy reach of Westminster by barge.[172] In 1504, February 11, the day of the queen's obit, fell on a Sunday. Islip's accounts indicate that the anniversary was observed that year in the manner that would be formally agreed under the terms of the indentures bipartite, sealed only the following July. In those years on which the anniversary fell on a Sunday, it was to be kept on the Saturday immediately preceding; and the accounts of the king's chamber duly but belatedly record a payment for the king's offering at Westminster for that date.[173] In 1508, when Henry was too ill to leave Richmond, he sent his chamberlain, Giles, Lord Daubeney, as his representative. Daubeney sat in the place of honour, above a large presence of lords spiritual and temporal. On this occasion the bishop of London presided at the altar.[174] Although in 1506 the king spent 11 February at Windsor, he remained within his secret chamber, in contrast to the public activity of surrounding days, and dined privately with his guest, Philip, king of Castile. Ten days later both kings dined with Islip at Westminster; and included the tomb of Elizabeth of York in their official itinerary.[175]

---

[170] The king's accounts include without further explanation a payment on 5 July 1504 to Master Peter (Carmeliano, the king's Latin secretary) for two of the pope's servants, BL Additional MS 59899, fo. 60v; for the bulls, *CPL* xviii, nos. 113–15, 117–20; originals PRO, SC 7/26/23–25, 29 dated 20, 23 May 1504. The endorsements on the bull directed to Westminster itself may include a note in the king's own handwriting, PRO, SC 7/26/23.

[171] WAM 6638, warrant of 17 February 1505; above n. 87; that the indentures were deposited in the chapel of the Pyx, the traditional strong place where both the regalia and royal wills were held, reinforces a sacral and testamentary view of the documents; and it is because Richard II's will was so deposited in that king's lifetime that his will has been preserved.

[172] 1504 Westminster; 1505 Greenwich; 1506 Windsor; 1507, 1508 Richmond; 1509 Hanworth, near Richmond, and probably already ill. Expenses of the king's traverse included in the sacristan's account 1504–5, WAM 19760, payment to Neale, the king's bedeman, 13 February 1505, BL Additional MS 59899, fo. 78.

[173] BL Additional MS 59899, fo. 47.

[174] *Memorials of . . . Henry the Seventh*, 108–9.

[175] *Ibid.*, 301–3; WAM 24241*.

After the king's death

By the time of the king's death in 1509 the future of his memorial must have seemed secure into perpetuity. The chapel itself, although not yet finished was, in its essentials, substantially complete, and already a source of interest and curiosity for those sufficiently privileged to obtain access.[176] When, in 1520, the council of Henry VIII entertained some French ambassadors they were taken, at their own request, and with Islip as their guide, to see the notable things done in the chapel and at the Savoy.[177] That consequent sense of awe, wonder and celebration of the king and his dynasty, transcending even the borders of his realm, were surely also part of the king's design. The services and ceremonial, sacred and secular, both at Westminster and elsewhere, were being regularly observed with, indeed, a dual commemoration in 1509, the first taking place on 11 February, the anniversary of the death of Henry's queen, and the second on 11 May, the date that would obtain for the future, being that of the king's own burial.[178] At Westminster, services for Henry III and for Eleanor, Edward I's queen, had been observed for more than two centuries, and that for Richard II was a paler precursor, still honoured, of Henry VII's own provision. All this was known to, or could be assumed by, the king, and his confidence in the arrangements so carefully made is implicit and explicit in his will of March 1509. Yet within thirty years much of that edifice of ritual and intercession had been dismantled. Holy Trinity, Aldgate, was dissolved in 1532, by reason of its alleged impoverishment, and its lands and revenues surrendered directly to the Crown.[179] The other twelve religious houses bound to Henry VII's service followed as a result of general dissolution between 1536 and 1539. The abbey of Westminster itself was dissolved in 1540. The legislative framework of the Reformation gradually removed the endowment of colleges and chantries, and cast doubt on the efficacy of intercession for the souls of the dead. Although in the immediate aftermath of dissolution the newly constituted college of dean and canons which replaced the monastery continued to observe the anniversary, and was funded at an annual rate of £40 for that purpose, the reduced level of funding suggests that it was the ceremonial which was being observed for the good of the dynasty, and that the commemoration had been stripped of its more charitable aspects.[180] At Cambridge the last payment received from Westminster had been made in 1539 but it, too, continued for a time to observe the anniversary, maintaining the services and ceremonial at their former level. In 1544 the university successfully petitioned the king for renewed funding, proffering their copy of the indenture quadripartite in evidence and support of the claim.[181] Thus supported, observation of the obit continued until 1547, then fell into abeyance with the religious changes under

---

[176] See Wilson, below, 141.
[177] W.J. Loftie, *Memorials of the Savoy*, 1878, 98–9.
[178] For the double memorial at Cambridge in 1509, *Grace Book B*, 236–7.
[179] E. Jeffries Davis, 'The beginning of the Dissolution: Christchurch, Aldgate, 1532', *TRHS*, 4th ser., 8 (1925), 127–42; for the short-lived plan to use its revenues for the endowment of an almshouse, PRO, E 135/8/48.
[180] *L&P Henry VIII*, xviii pt 2, 123–4.
[181] *Grace Book B*, ii, 245, 247, 224; *L&P Henry VIII*, xix pt 2, 422; the £10 was assigned on the revenues of the Court of Augmentations, abolished in its turn in 1554.

Edward VI, only to be resumed in 1554 under the catholic Mary. Discontinued finally from 1558, the pall had an after-life as a canopy for Elizabeth I on her visit to Cambridge in 1564: an event which one commentator has speculated secured the pall's preservation from a sale of vestry goods the following year.[182] Displayed until recent years in Great St Mary's, the university church, the cloth of gold with its rich embroidery memorialised Henry VII for those who paused to recognise the king's unmistakable insignia. Although despite vicissitudes the Westminster almshouses continued to fulfil a charitable purpose well into the eighteenth century, the functional symbolism identifying their founder, and the almsmens' primary duty of prayer, had been gradually eroded and removed.[183]

There remains, however, the dynastic propaganda deliberately and physically incorporated into the Lady chapel, and into the crafting of the indentures of 1504, without which the chapel itself cannot be fully understood. The first is inescapable to any visitor to the chapel and, although diminished in quantity by time and wanton destruction, has lost nothing of its impact; the second still has some force in that those indentures which still survive are numbered by their present custodians among their more significant and precious treasures. The Lady chapel at Westminster is entered through great bronze and brass-clad gates wrought with the king's 'badges and cognissaunces';[184] the intellectual gateway, so often neglected, is through the indentures, adorned and enhanced with that same purposeful heraldry.

An Appendix lists, as far as they have been traced, all surviving copies of the various indentures. The author is indebted to the custodians of these indentures for their ready assistance. The twenty one volumes which once pertained to the city of London are, however, thought to have perished in the Great Fire of 1666.

---

[182] Hugh Tait 'The hearse cloth of Henry VII belonging to the University of Cambridge', *Journal of the Warburg and Courtauld Institutes* 19, 1956, 294–8.
[183] Their later history is briefly summarised in Colvin, *HKW* iii, 209–10.
[184] For the gates, Scott, *Gleanings*, 92–3.

Appendix I

Surviving Parts of the Indentures of Henry VII's Foundation

Indentures Bipartite

(Foundation indenture; almshouses; indenture of abstract; inspeximus of indenture of penalties)

Party to indenture	Reference
King	PRO, E 33/1
Westminster	British Library, Harleian MS 1498

Indentures Septipartite

(Indenture of penalties)

Party to indenture	Reference
King	PRO, E 33/2
Westminster	—
Canterbury	—
Winchester	—
St Paul's, London	St Paul's Cathedral Library
St Stephen's, Westminster	British Library, Additional MS 21112
City of London	Assumed lost in 1666

Indentures Quadripartite

(Foreign Obits)

Name of third party	King's (PRO)[+]	Westminster	Third Party[++]	London[*]
Abingdon Abbey	E 33/3 Abbey Seal: E 33/26/1	WAM 57070	—	—
St Alban's Abbey	E 33/4 Abbey Seal: E 33/26/2	WAM 57071	BL Harleian MS 28	—
Bermondsey Abbey	E 33/5 Abbey Seal: SC 13/H82	WAM 57072	[Sale catalogue, Ellis & Co., Bond Street]	—
Cambridge University	E 33/6	WAM 57073	UA Luard 147[*] UA Seals 18	—

+ Surviving Seals mostly in E 33/26: few of those of London and Westminster can be associated with particular indentures; wrappers in E 33/27 indicate the indentures having seals c 1840.
++ Loose Great Seal SC 13/I 90 and loose Westminster and London seals in E 33/26.
* Assumed lost in the Great Fire, 1666.

Canterbury, St Augustine's	E 33/7 Seal: SC 13/I91	WAM 57074	—	—
Canterbury, Cathedral	E 33/8	WAM 57075	Canterbury Cathedral Archives, DCc/Ch Ant W.48a	—
London, Austin Friars	E 33/9 Friary Seal: E 33/26/16	WAM 57076	PRO, E 33/10	—
London, Carmelites	E 33/11 Friary Seal: E 33/26/17	—	PRO, E 33/12	—
London, Charterhouse	E 33/13 Charterhouse Seal: E 33/26/18; London Seal: E 33/26/19	WAM 57077	—	—
London, Christchurch *alias* Holy Trinity	E 33/14 Seal: E 33/26/20	—	—	—
London, Friars Preachers	E 33/15 Skippet without seal: E 33/26/21	WAM 57078	PRO, E 33/17	—
Westminster, St Stephen's	E 33/16 Seal: E 33/26/25	—	—	—
London, St Mary Grace's	E 33/18 Seal: E 33/26/23 London Seal: E 33/26/24	WAM 57079	Bodleian Library, MS Rawlinson C370	—
London, Grey Friars	E 33/19 Friary Seal: E 33/26/22	—	—	—
London, St Paul's	E 33/20 St Paul's Seal: E 33/26/33	WAM 57080	Bodleian Library, MS Barlow 28	—
Oxford University	E 33/21 University Seal: E 33/26/29 London Seal: E 33/26/30	—	University Archives, MS WPβ.I.1	—
Rochester Cathedral	E 33/22 Rochester Seal: E 33/26/31 London Seal: E 33/26/32	WAM 57081	—	—

Sheen Priory	E 33/23	—	—	—
Syon Abbey	E 33/24 Abbey Seal: E 33/26/27	WAM 57082	—	—
Windsor, St George	E 33/25	—	—	—

In addition to the indentures described above, an agreement for 1503 between the king and prior and chapter of Winchester, for services as at Westminster, is preserved in the Staats- und Universitätsbibliothek Bremen, MS a.49. Like the indentures quadripartite, it commences with an illuminated initial 'T'. The binding is stamped leather. I am indebted to Dr. Thomas Elsmann, Keeper of the Manuscripts and Rare Books Department of the Staats- und Universitätsbibliothek Bremen for information concerning this document.

The Last Will of Henry VII: Document and Text

MARGARET CONDON

Introduction

AS CHRISTOPHER WILSON notes elsewhere in this volume, the will of Henry VII has always been seen as the central text for an historical interpretation of the Lady chapel of the Abbey church of St Peter, Westminster. A full text of the will has been in print for more than two centuries – one reason, of course, for its historiographical primacy over the foundation indentures for the chantry in the chapel: for although the will's editor, Thomas Astle, himself drew attention to the latter they have moved into common currency only since 1963, when an extended abstract was incorporated into the final published volume of the long series of calendars of the Close Rolls of Chancery.[1] But although widely if selectively quoted, the edition of the king's will produced by Thomas Astle in 1775 is not easily accessible outside a major academic library; whilst the Westminster references are distributed at discrete intervals through the lengthy text. The volume was privately printed for Astle and is relatively scarce.[2] Surprisingly, there is no copy in the Public Record Office, the custodian of the original manuscript will, even though the library of that office inherited a number of important archival texts from the former Tower Record Office,[3] where Astle himself had been keeper of the Records. A full text of the will, revised against the original manuscript, is therefore presented here as an adjunct to the essays

---

[1] Astle; the original document is PRO, E 23/3; *CClR 1500–1509*, 138–55; cf. *Catalogue of the Harleian Manuscripts in the British Museum*, Record Commission 1808, ii, 74–8. The description of the foundation indentures published by Astle, and the extended entry in the second volume of the catalogue of the Harleian manuscripts (1st edn 1759–62, revised and extended edn by Record Commission 1808–12), although punctilious and containing a superb physical description of the foundation indentures, were no real substitute for a full or detailed abstract text. A revised transcript of most, but not all, of the will entries relating to Westminster, with an introduction which was highly critical of Astle's work, was included by Edward Brayley in 'An Historical and Architectural Account of King Henry the Seventh's Chapel at Westminster', in Neale and Brayley, 6–8, 17 (separate pagination). Brayley also included a description and a list of contents of the foundation indentures, plus a short extract in full transcript (taken from BL Harleian MS 1498), *ibid.*, 11–16.

[2] The British Library has three copies, one presented more than twenty five years after first publication; of the Bodleian Library's three, two came in with the collections of Francis Douce and John Gough Nichols, eminent antiquaries in their own right.

[3] They can be identified by their distinctive bookplate.

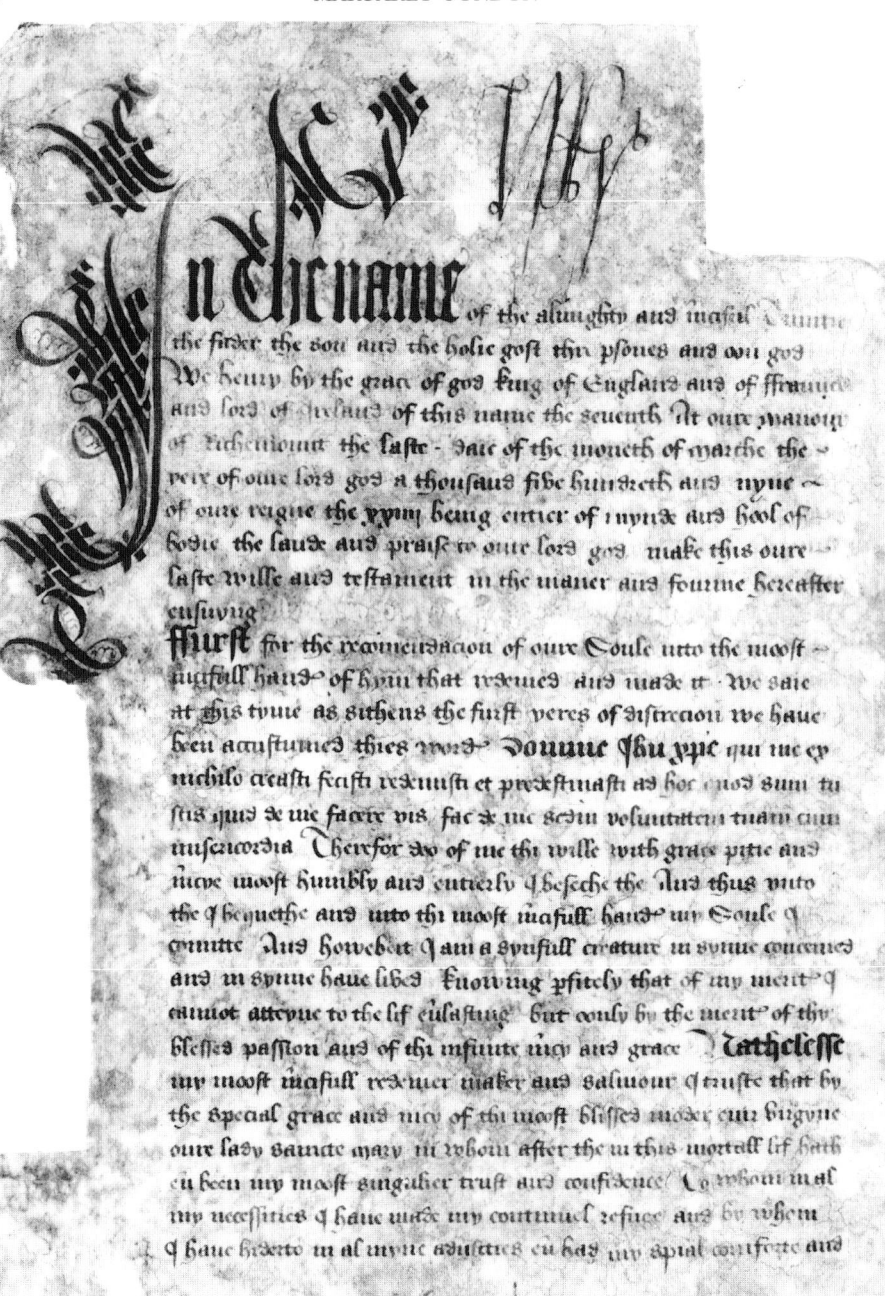

Plate 2. Will and sign-manual of Henry VII. (PRO, E 23/3, fo. 1)

in this volume; with an introduction which treats of the will primarily as a documentary object rather an offering a detailed exegesis, much of which would be foreign to the subject matter of this book. For the same reason, the will text is annotated sufficiently to identify persons and dates, but does not essay a comparative or extended treatment.[4] The will bears scholarly re-examination, and Henry VII's will and its execution have been addressed in its wider perspective in a paper which is to be published elsewhere.[5]

The small, much damaged will of Henry VII (Plate 2) is one of only four survivors of an ancient accumulation of original royal wills once stored in the Treasury of the Exchequer where, under the nominal custodianship of the treasurer and chamberlains, they were held under conditions of maximum security and secrecy.[6] From the fourteenth century the medieval treasury was centred on the chapel of the Pyx, in the cloisters of Westminster Abbey, although records deposited in the Exchequer were also stored in both the palace of Westminster and in the Tower; and in the sixteenth century the number of buildings collectively comprising the treasury expanded, not least by the addition of the chapter house of the Abbey, which was fitted up for record storage in the latter part of the reign of Mary I. Until its despoliation under the Commonwealth the Pyx, however, remained at the heart of the system. Two strong doors, with their five locks, and closely guarded access to the keys, stood guarantee to the security of the records, regalia, and other items of value stored there. In 1610 Arthur Agarde, deputy chamberlain of the Exchequer, specifically remarked on the preservation in the Pyx of the wills of Henry VII and Henry VIII, their immediate companions being the three 'golden leagues', treaties with solid or worked gold seals, a measure of the regard in which the royal wills were held.[7]

By the mid-eighteenth century most records from the Pyx, as from other treasuries of the Exchequer, had been consolidated in the chapter house. The will of Henry VIII was certainly there by 1694, housed in one of the great wooden chests; and although not specifically mentioned it seems probable that Henry VII's will, too, had been so transferred.[8] Eight chests were still in the chapter house in 1807, their

---

[4] Summary biographies of most of the persons mentioned in this will may be found in standard works of reference such as the *Complete Peerage*, ed. G.E. Cockayne; Emden, *Oxford*; *History of Parliament 1439–1509: Biographies*, ed. J.C. Wedgwood, 1936; *History of Parliament: The Commons 1509–1558*, ed. S.T. Bindoff, 3 vols., 1982.

[5] M.M. Condon, 'Authority beyond the grave: the will of Henry VII revisited', paper presented to the Fifteenth Century Conference, Bristol, 2001, forthcoming.

[6] PRO, E 23/1–4. The others are the wills of Richard II and Henry VIII, and the so-called second will of Henry V. Other royal wills survive in near contemporary or later copies including, in some instances, entries in episcopal or other registers. For royal wills deposited in the Treasury in the thirteenth and fourteenth centuries, but no longer known to be extant in the original, *The Antient Kalendars and Inventories of the Exchequer*, ed. F. Palgrave, 3 vols., 1836, i, 108. A revised edition of *A Collection of All the Wills . . . of the Kings and Queens of England*, ed. J. Nichols, 1780, to include all the extant medieval royal wills, is in course of preparation.

[7] *Antient Kalendars and Inventories* ii, 316, 332–3; the history of the treasuries and the chests in which documents, including the wills, were held is explored by the present author in an introduction to the class list of E 27 (typescript in Public Record Office).

[8] In December 1694 Peter Le Neve, as part of his work on the ancient records, drew up a memorandum entitled 'notes on the chests', which is a brief and selective inventory of chests and their contents as existing at that date, PRO, E 192/25 pt 2. Le Neve, better known as an antiquary and as Norroy herald, was, as deputy chamberlain of the Exchequer (1684–1712), one of the official custodians of

Plate 3. Scene at the deathbed of Henry VII. (BL Add. 45131, fo. 54)

contents by now somewhat shuffled, but still including the royal wills and the foundation documents of Henry VII's chantry at Westminster.[9] It is to this period of incarceration within the chests kept on the ground floor of the chapter house that both series of documents almost certainly owe their physical disintegration.[10] All four royal wills were finally transferred to the Public Record Office, Chancery Lane, when the

---

the records. A somewhat cryptic note by Peter Le Neve entered some time after 1702 on the flyleaf to the illuminated *Abbreviatio* of Domesday Book (which he misdates by several centuries) supposing that the illuminations inserted in the *Abbreviatio* are by the same hand as the exemplification of Henry VII's will almost certainly refers to the foundation indentures rather than the will of 1509, PRO, E 36/284, flyleaf.

[9] PRO, OBS 1/693, fos. 8v–11 (chests 4 and 5 are not inventoried).

[10] Edward Brayley in 1818 pointedly remarked that the series of indentures quadripartite had rotted from this cause: Brayley, 'Henry the Seventh Chapel', 16 n.; for the problems of both the Pyx and the Chapter House, Stanley, *Historical Memorials*, 379. In 1847 Frederick Devon, Assistant Keeper in charge of the record office in the Chapter House, commented ruefully but forcefully on the effect of keeping documents for any length of time in locked chests, without exposure to the air, re-iterating William Illingworth's charge to the Record Commissioners that the records were, in consequence, 'crumbling into dust': PRO, PRO 4/3 pp. 197–9; PRO 4/6, pp. 81–2.

Chapter House was cleared in 1859.[11] They were moved again, to what is now the National Archives at Kew, once Chancery Lane closed in 1996, continuing their long history in secure storage and public custody.

Text and content

The will of Henry VII is dated 31 March 1509, three weeks before the king's death, which occurred late in the night of 21 April (Plate 3). It is a powerful document that has invited extreme comment.[12] But the will is typical of the man, can be shown to have earlier parallels in its parts, if not in its totality of vision and provision, and more importantly is the logical culmination of preparations begun over a decade before. It is possible to read it largely as a precise embodiment of the king's wishes, and it at times captures the king's authentic voice. Yet although it appears to include some late revision expanding the compass of his charitable bequests, and may have been coloured by the penitential mode of the king's last weeks,[13] it would be unwise to read either language or content uncritically as a form of *obiter dicta*. The king's will is a construct evolved, probably, over time and in more than one revision. Much of it is cast in the form of a legal document drawn up by the king's secretariat, well versed in his manner of thought and mode of expression, working to a formula or from a variety of formal instruments going back a decade and more. It is consciously referential to even earlier precedent. If its language accurately captures the king's deep and genuine piety, his concern for the hereafter, both sacred and secular, and his careful preparation for an enduring memorial, its actual words reflect – at times word for word – those documentary origins. For example, the whole section concerning the feoffment on the lands of the duchy of Lancaster, made to the use of the king's will, is a construct drawing on the documents that had formulated that trust. That the listing of lands, rights, and revenues should be particular and should follow the wording of an earlier deed is unsurprising. But even the phrases concerning the insecurity and uncertainty of the world are not those of a deathbed utterance. They belong to the preamble of the parliamentary act of 1504 which revised the list of feoffees seised to the use of the king's will. More tellingly, the expression of loyalty to his long term supporters and companions of Bosworth and later crises, at first reading an intensely personal declaration, so closely mimics the similar provisions of Edward IV's will of 1475 that there can be little doubt that the text of the latter was in front of the king or his advisers when this particular clause was first drawn up.[14] Henry VII's will, in turn,

---

[11] *21st Report of the Deputy Keeper of Public Records*, 1860, xiii–xiv.

[12] J.P. Cooper, 'Henry VII's last years reconsidered', *Historical Journal* 2, 1959, 112–13; R.L. Storey, *The Reign of Henry VII*, 1968, 63; for a more temperate view, N. Beckett, 'Henry VII and the Sheen Charterhouse', in *Reign of Henry VII*, 117–32, especially 120.

[13] For the influence of and close contact between the king and his confessor in the last two months of the king's life, 'Sermon sayd in the cathedral chyrche of Saynte Poule . . . the body being present of the moost famous prynce Kyng Henry the VII', *The English Works of John Fisher*, ed. J.E.B. Mayor, Early English Text Society, Extra Series, 27, 1876, 271–6.

[14] *Rot. Parl.* vi, 444–6, 521–2; R. Somerville, *History of the Duchy of Lancaster* i, 1953, 276–7; text of will of Edward IV, S. Bentley, *Excerpta Historica, or Illustrations of English History*, 1833, 377–8.

served, with appropriate and sometimes unctuous elaboration, as a source document to draw up agreements with third parties in order to effect its provisions.[15]

Principal among the long considered concerns given formal expression in the will are the provisions for the completion of the Lady chapel which Henry had begun at Westminster, for his burial there, for the continued and conspicuous use of his bequests of vestments bearing his badges, of altar goods, relics, and votive images, and for a continual and continued edifice of prayer and other spiritual observances intended not only for the good of his soul, but also as a perpetual memorial to be observed at Westminster and more widely throughout his realm. Arrangements for the king's funeral were remitted to his executors, who were also to oversee the completion of his tomb. Funding was confirmed to two other major building projects, the proposed hospital of the Savoy, barely commenced and not yet endowed, and to the completion of Henry VI's foundation of King's College, Cambridge, where work on the chapel had resumed by 1508. The king's reign-long patronage of the Franciscan Observants and the Carthusians was given further material substance in return for prayer. There are other bequests also which can be loosely designated as charitable giving, including a generous distribution of alms which was ordered to be made between the days of death and burial, and a like provision of £2,000 for the repair of named highways. Both bequests differ only in their scale of munificence from customary testamentary formulae observed by many of the king's subjects. There are further legacies ordained to the abbot and convent of Westminster themselves, including £333 6s 8d given towards the abbey's own current building works; and a generous sop to Cerberus in the form of a rich votive image of St George given to St George's Chapel, Windsor, where a decade and a half before the king had intended his burial place.[16] There is a statement of intent supporting the marriage of his younger daughter, Mary, to Charles of Burgundy, the future Emperor; of loyalty to his long-term supporters; and, as has often been singled out for comment, provision for redress to his subjects of things done and exactions taken by him, or in his name, should such actions be proven unjust. The execution of the will was to be financed from the king's substantial treasure and by the feoffment on the lands of the duchy of Lancaster, to stand good until the will had been fulfilled in all its parts. Any residue of treasure was to be expended for the good of his soul.

The will signed and sealed in 1509 was not the first made by Henry VII, although it is the only text to survive. Revision of testamentary dispositions was, then as now, by no means an uncommon practice. Henry's mother, Margaret Beaufort (d. 29 June 1509) made a whole series of wills during the last seven or eight years of her life, each year causing the previous will to be read to her, and renewing and revising it as neces-

---

[15] See particularly the preamble to the agreement with King's College, Cambridge: R. Willis and J. Willis Clark, *Architectural History of the University of Cambridge*, Cambridge 1886, i, 476–8. The indenture names the king and the provost and scholars as the parties, the latter were then bound for due performance to both the king and his executors. The provost of King's had been in negotiation with Henry VII's Council for the two weeks preceding the agreement.

[16] The king could do no less: Edward IV had given a rich reliquary of the saint's skull (described in the Dissolution inventory), PRO, E 36/113, fo. 43v; see also Anne. F. Sutton and Livia Visser-Fuchs, 'Chivalry and the Yorkist Kings', in *St George's Chapel, Windsor, in the Later Middle Ages*, ed. C. Richmond and E. Scarff, Windsor 2001, 128.

sary.[17] The m[...] [...]l will of Henry's son and successor, Henry VIII, was
an amalgam o[...] [...]er texts and dispositions;[18] and
the same can [...] the extant texts is
instructive.[19] [...]ade a will in 1492
before he left [...] so done in 1504 in
the light of c[...] [...]e year of a revised
feoffment to [...] [...]t with Westminster,
and of the p[...] [...]ges that of 1509.[20] It
is known th[...] [...] year Henry VII lay
seriously ill [...] signet was paid forty
shillings fo[...] [...] May for writing the
will in par[...] [...]lsey, two of the king's
chaplains, [...] [...]asses at six pence the
mass, a fu[...] [...]ervant – a forerunner
of the 10[...] [...]n of the gravity of the
king's illn[...]

In 15[...] [...]t Hanworth, a recently
acquired [...] [...]hmond (Fig. 16), which
lay less [...] [...]bout the beginning of
March.[...] [...],000 masses to be said in
Londor[...] [...] rood of Chester. 8,000
masses [...] [...]t of 13 March, and 2,000
masses [...] [...] March.[24] On 6 April one
Richa[...] [...]ment.[25] Individual clauses
of th[...] [...]he text had been finally

---

[17] Jo[...]

[18] J.J[...] [...]ll – a forensic conundrum', *Historica[...]* [...]s: a comment', *Historical Journal* 37,
1994, 891–900; L.W. [...], [...]isions of 1546–7', *Historical Journal*
37, 1994, 901–14.

[19] Texts in *Foedera* ix, 289–93, and P. and F. Strong, 'The last will and codicils of Henry V', *EHR* 96, 1981, 79–102.

[20] *Rot. Parl.* vi, 521–2; G.R. Elton, 'Henry VII: a restatement', in *idem, Studies in Tudor and Stuart Politics and Government* i, Cambridge 1974, 70–1. For a contemporary and later view of the Westminster agreements as Henry VII's 'testamentum', above, n. 8, and Condon, 'God save the king', above, 66.

[21] S.B. Chrimes, *Henry VII*, 1972, 313–14; PRO, E 36/214, pp. 141, 156.

[22] PRO, E 36/214, p. 147; unless the entry in Heron's book was considerably in arrears, this payment, unlike the alms given to prisoners, was rather more than a customary Lenten observance: cf. *Works of John Fisher*, 272.

[23] For Hanworth, where the king was rebuilding the house and making a pleasure garden from 1507, although title to the estate was not finally confirmed until 1515, Colvin, *HKW* iv, 147–9. Apart from a short excursion to Esher and Chertsey, the king lay at Hanworth from mid-January until the end of February. There is a gap in his known itinerary from 27 February to 1 March.

[24] PRO, E 36/214, pp. 325–7, 329, 343; further payments for intercessory prayers were made on 10 April, by which time it was clear that the king was unlikely to survive. Taken in conjunction with other payments being made at this time by John Heron to forward the execution of the king's testament, it is tempting to interpret the payment for 10,000 masses as at least insurance securing the *post mortem* provision, even if according to John Fisher's funeral sermon a quota of 10,000 masses was Henry's regular Lenten investment: *Works of John Fisher*, 272.

[25] PRO, E 36/214, p. 343.

completed, signed and sealed. For example, on 14 March two London goldsmiths, John Mundy and Nicholas Worley, were paid £500 for making pyxes; and an equal sum was paid by the king's treasurer of the chamber to two more goldsmiths, Robert Amadas and William Kebill, on 2 April.[26] There can be little doubt that these payments, made in the king's lifetime, were for the silver gilt pyxes, ornamented with the king's badges of the red rose and portcullis, that were to be distributed under the terms of his will to every parish and religious house in which the sacred vessels were of wood or base metal.[27] With the will signed, several major legacies were paid out before the king's death on the authority of his will, which identified them as payments 'before the hande'.[28]

The manuscript

Henry VII's will is in book form, written on parchment in a good chancery hand (Plate 2). At over 13,000 words and thirty-seven written pages it is longer than the will of any other English medieval king. The manuscript is a quality fair copy text, commencing with an elaborated initial and strapwork embellishment of its two opening words, but containing a number of copyist's errors, whose continuance uncorrected is in itself a comment on the king's failing powers.[29] The manuscript is now damaged, not only by its legacy of ancient damp and mould, but also by deliberate excisions from its margins that are probably the by-product of an uncouth repair. Much of the page surface is covered by the silk used to strengthen the fragile parchment: with consequent further reduction in the document's legibility.[30]

---

[26] PRO, E 36/214, pp. 327, 342.

[27] PRO, E 23/3, fo. 15v; none is known to exist: C.C. Oman, *English Church Plate 596–1830*, 1957, 25. According to the will, a pattern had already been delivered to Heron and the Master of the Jewel House. If made, the pixes are likely to have resembled the skippets on the Westminster counterpart of the foundation indenture, BL Harleian MS 1498.

[28] Below, 107. John Heron's accounts record them as paid in pence and, in the terms of the indenture with King's College, the king 'utterly and absolutely forsaketh, refuseth and renounceth for evermore' all property in the money. Willis and Clark, *Architectural History* i, 477.

[29] This is particularly true of the homoeoteleuton which has resulted in the designation of Thomas Lovell as the king's secretary, PRO, E 23/3, fo. 17v; and the failure to note Giles Daubeney, the king's former chamberlain, as 'deceased' (d. 21 May 1508), the latter an error which is as likely to arise from a cramped and incomplete insertion over an erasure (since the text elsewhere correctly notes the demise of Geoffrey Simeon, dean of the Chapel, d. 20 August 1508) as to point to a derivation from a will text of 1507. Daubeney's name immediately precedes that of William Hussey (d.1495), the point at which the insertion commences. The failure to complete the date of the proxy marriage of his daughter, Mary, to Charles of Burgundy (17 December 1508) is also surprising. By contrast, Henry had himself amended a gardener's name in the accounts for his wife's funeral in 1503 and his chamber accounts, for example, offer numerous instances of his pedantic attention to written detail.

[30] Edward Brayley in 1818 favourably reported the will as recently repaired and bound at the direction of John Caley (Secretary of the Record Commission, sub-commissioner with responsibility for the arrangement and repair of records and, from 1818, Keeper of the records in the Chapter House). Brayley, 'Henry the Seventh's chapel', 8. Repairs of this date were done by essentially unskilled labour, although some of those labourers became proficient through practice: and despite their sometimes barbaric methods their consolidation of fragile records has the great merit of securing their survival. The document, PRO, E 23/3, has since been separated into three parts. Parts 2 and 3 are the tooled leather binding and archive box of Caley's intervention. Part 1 is the manuscript will, sewn within re-

The dating clause for the writing of the will and its ratification by the king is incorporated in the preamble to the will text but was initially left incomplete. The day and the year are thus pre-planned insertions in a previously written document. Both the month, March, and the place, Richmond, appear to be written continuously with the main body of the text: most probably a pointer to the date of final compilation of the will of 1509, although a carry over from the lost text of 1507 cannot be entirely ruled out. At various points in the body text gaps were left by the scribe to allow for the later entry of dates, mostly of indentures still to be drawn up, which would document pre-payment of bequests before the king's death. Some such entries, including the financial provision for the hospital of the Savoy, remain incomplete. Although payments to support the legacy were made within a week of the final sealing, and before the king's death, the required indenture was not made until 1510, and then with parties other than those named in the will itself.[31] In other instances, such as the payment of £5,000 for the finishing of King's College, Cambridge, the date of the indenture [31 March] was subsequently inserted; and the books of the treasurer of the king's chamber duly record this payment two weeks later.[32] The latest date to be inserted in the will itself is 13 April, three days after the final seal was applied. Appropriately this entry recorded an indenture documenting the transfer of funds for the completion of the king's chapel at Westminster.[33]

The will is signed at the head and at the end with the king's sign manual, the latter serving as the authority for sealing in the manner specified in the text: that is, with the privy seal and signet, with the king's own personal signet of the eagle, and with the great seal (Plate 2). This last was in the keeping of the Chancellor, William Warham, Archbishop of Canterbury, who was also appointed supervisor of the will. Henry's will had been signed on the day before Palm Sunday: that is, not only within a vacation between legal terms but at the commencement of Easter week, the high point of the church's year. The archbishop was away from court, and on 9 April one of the regular messengers of the chamber was paid for taking the king's will to him at Canterbury.[34] The final clauses of the will contain the revised legal dating at Canterbury, on 10 April 1509, the date on which the will was authenticated with the great

---

placement parchment covers. Caley's repairers appear to have separated and trimmed each folio along the binding edge, pasting each after further trimming into a parchment window which enabled rebinding of the whole in scrapbook form. Individual leaves thus vary in size, but suggest approximate folio dimensions of 264mm x 240mm (h x w) for the original manuscript. The seal cords are doubled round the spine and oversewn to secure them to the document.

[31] Payment on 16 April by deposit in the Mint, PRO, E 36/214, p. 344; the indenture was made with the abbot and convent of Westminster rather than the Dean and Chapter of St Paul's; Colvin, *HKW* iii pt 1, 201–2. This account corrects the chronology in R. Somerville, *The Savoy*, 1960, 9–33. On the background and decade of preparation which lay behind the project, D. Thomson, 'Henry VII and the use of Italy: the Savoy Hospital and Henry VII's posterity', in *Reign of Henry VII*, 104–16. Deposit in the Mint is likely to be a euphemism for some form of money changing exercise. Many of the early payments in support of the will were, usefully, in pence, and in this respect the timetable for the Savoy was less critical than other major projects. For a cautionary note on interpreting the Chamber accounts, D. Grummit, 'Henry VII, Chamber finance, and the New Monarchy', *Historical Research* 72, 1999, 229–43.

[32] Willis and Clark, *Architectural History* i, 476–8; PRO, E 36/214, p. 344.

[33] PRO, E 23/3, fo. 3.

[34] PRO, E 36/214, p. 343.

seal;[35] the whole being 'signed' in conventional Chancery fashion by John Yonge, Henry's Master of the Rolls, and one of his executors.[36] This completion of the sealing of the will, and its formal enrolment in Chancery, completed the predetermined diplomatic process.[37] The foot of the final page is marked with an indication of that enrolment.

Three of the will's presumed four seals are still attached. The great seal, pendant on triple plaited cords, is impressed in natural wax. The impression of the privy seal, with its distinctive Prince of Wales feathers, is damaged. It has as its reverse an impression of the signet seal which, although imperfect, shows clearly the king's badges of the SS of Lancaster, the red rose, and the Beaufort portcullis: and the thumbprint left when impressing the seal into the softened wax. This seal composite is in red wax, and is appended by green and white cords, the Tudor colours.[38] A second pair of pendant cords now lacks any seals or (at least to the naked eye) any evidence of sealing. The missing seal is that of Henry's personal signet seal of the eagle, of which no specimen is known, and for which the will provides the primary evidence. The diplomatic of the sealing clause implies that this, like the departmental seals, was to be affixed by another hand, the king's sign manual serving as the authorising warrant. Logic might suggest that it was the intended occupant of the remaining cords: although it may be significant that there is a hole in the apparently sound parchment adjacent to the king's closing sign manual. Equally Henry's official signet, normally in the custody of his Secretary, may, as with the will of Richard II, itself have been intended for the empty cords. As already noted, it has actually been applied as a counterseal to the Privy Seal: in itself a not uncommon practice, if unexpected in this context.

The official enrolment of the king's will almost certainly survives. It is not now to be found on or among the Close Rolls of Chancery, but in a manuscript acquired by the British Library in 1899 from the sixth earl of Hardwicke.[39] The roll, endorsed '*Ultima voluntas Regis Henrici Septimi*' is written in a chancery hand. Internal evidence, based on the insertion of dates in blanks left in the text, suggests that the document was written between 31 March and 10 April 1509, respectively the dates on which the original was signed and sealed with the great seal. The date of signing of the original will [31 March 24 Henry VII] is entered continuously with the text, and those amendments to the original which had arisen out of corrected clerical error are likewise incorporated. However, other insertions of dates are insertions as in the original, and

---

[35] The date is supplied from Astle's edition. The document is damaged at this point and the '10' is missing. Astle's reading is confirmed by BL Additional MS 36273B, for which below, 108–9.

[36] Yonge's own tomb, erected after his death in 1516, includes fragments of worked stone salvaged as waste from the workshop carvings made for the king's chapel at Westminster: C. Galvin and P. Lindley, 'Pietro Torrigiano's tomb for Dr Yonge', *Church Monuments* 3, 1988, 42–60; one piece of carved stone remains *in situ* in the tomb, but two substantial fragments, both in the style of the angel frieze, are now PRO, SC 16/30, 31; for the constant intercourse between Yonge and Abbot Islip in 1509–10, WAM 33324.

[37] Precedent for enrolment in Chancery is far from clear, although Rymer's transcripts record a Chancery origin for Edward IV's will of 1475: BL Additional MS 4615, fos. 1–22.

[38] Seals illustrated in Chrimes, *Henry VII*, pl. 7, but incorrectly captioned: 7a is actually the privy seal, not the great seal, which is pl. 7b (obverse and reverse).

[39] BL Additional MS 36273B. Philip Yorke, the first earl, had been Lord Chancellor for nearly twenty years, 1737–56.

the final sealing clause is, in its entirety, an addition. The balance of probability is that the document is the official Chancery enrolment of the will and, as such, of itself commands authority.[40]

The edition of 1775

The eighteenth century was one of record publication, and in the last quarter of the century transcripts of the two other original king's wills in Exchequer custody, those of Richard II and Henry V (earlier published by Thomas Rymer, historiographer royal, with some errors in transcription or of proof reading) were made for John Nichols by George Rose and Abraham Farley, the antiquarian-minded keepers of the records in the chapter house.[41] Nichols's edition of the will texts appeared in 1780; it had been preceded, five years earlier, by an edition of the will of Henry VII, published privately by Thomas Payne for its editor, Thomas Astle. Astle was an antiquary widely respected for his scholarship and his understanding of the public records, serving both on committees concerning the records and becoming, first, chief clerk of the Record Office in the Tower and then, in 1783, succeeding to the keepership there. Nichols paid tribute to Astle's 'judicious preface and appendix' and excluded the will from his own edition of will texts which he concluded, instead, with one version of the will of Henry's mother, Margaret Beaufort. Forty years later, however, Edward Brayley was less complimentary about Astle's labours.[42]

From 1770 Thomas Astle had been one of the editors of the *Rotuli Parliamentorum*, and his correspondence in respect of that work offers useful insights into his working methods and his essential respect for his exemplars, as well as both his weaknesses and his strengths as an editor.[43] The preface to his edition of Henry VII's will made use of his familiarity with the parliament rolls, and his references to the legislation of Henry's parliaments presented to Astle's contemporaries the product of recent and still unpublished research.[44] A useful appendix, acknowledged to Humphrey Wanley (d.1726), analyses both the contents and the structure of the Westminster copy of the foundation indenture for Henry VII's chantry and almshouses at Westminster (British Library MS Harley 1498). Wanley's catalogue of the Harleian manuscripts, continued by other hands, had been in print since 1762, but Astle's easy familiarity with Wanley's work could draw on his early employment on the catalogue index and in

---

[40] There is also a contemporary, or near contemporary, copy of the will on paper in book form in the archives of St John's College, Cambridge. The location suggests that this paper copy may have been made for Margaret Beaufort, or possibly John Fisher, as executor. It has not been collated with the present text. Cambridge, St John's College, MS D.22.12.

[41] Nichols, *Wills . . . of the Kings and Queens*, 191–202, 236–43. The transcripts provided by Rose and Farley for Nichols, and preserved in the Bodleian Library, are far more accurate than Nichols' sloppy text would suggest.

[42] Nichols, *Wills . . . of Kings and Queens*, 355; above, 99 n. 1.

[43] M.M. Condon and E.M. Hallam, 'Government printing of the public records in the eighteenth century', *Journal of the Society of Archivists* 7, 1984, 365–70, 380.

[44] The final volume, including the parliaments of Henry VII, was printed only in May 1776 and not distributed until the following year; and it was not until 1783 that the universities received copies.

preparing the text for publication.[45] The tone and absence of any other acknowledgment in the will preface suggests that Astle was the transcriber, as well as the editor, of the will text, a correlation that, at this date, cannot always be assumed. In particular, scholarly access to documents in the custody of the Exchequer chamberlains and their sometimes temperamental deputies was discretionary, and subject to the payment of fees, and in many instances transcripts were made by the custodians of the records, and not by the enquirer.[46] Astle's work on the rolls of parliament, and his connections, may have given him privileged status. Equally, the practice of the editors of the parliament rolls had been to take pre-existing transcripts as a basis for their work, although their frequent inaccuracy compelled recourse, where possible, to the originals: it is thus by no means impossible that Astle's starting point, or the spark to his interest, was a heavily corrected early seventeenth century transcript in the Harleian collection.[47] One thing is certain. Astle's interest in Henry VII extended well beyond the will. His personal manuscript collection appears at some stage to have included two of the central documents of Henry VII's last decade. These are the original account book of the treasurer of the king's chamber for 1502–5, a volume heavily annotated by the king himself and including most of the critical references concerning payments for the king's chantry at Westminster, and the extract and fair copy chamber accounts and memoranda kept by John Heron's clerks for part of the same period.[48]

Astle's edition has been maligned. In practice, however, actual mis-readings of the *sense* of the text, or omissions of words, are few although, as Edward Brayley long ago noted, the renderings of individual words do not stand close scrutiny.[49] Most pages of the edition offer examples of variation from the orthography of the original; but many of the deviations fall into certain easily defined, but not always consistently applied, channels. These include the doubling of final 'l' in accordance with standard spelling; separation of elisions and crasis in the text into the component words, sometimes with changes in spelling; omission of 'u' when indicated by a superscript abbreviation; and omission of the 'e' in abbreviated plurals and possessives, or the replacement of that 'e' by a possessive apostrophe foreign to fifteenth century usage. Astle's text is peppered with capital letters which accord with the conventions of his day rather than the usage of his exemplar; the convention which is observed in the present text follows modern editorial practice, tending to minimise the use of capitals. Neither is an exact rendition of the original. What Astle's edition does not do – nor

---

[45] *Catalogue of the Harleian Collection of Manuscripts . . . preserved in the British Museum*, ed. H. Wanley, D. Casley, W. Hocker and C. Morton, with an index by T. Astle, 2 vols., 1759–63; the entry is repeated in the Record Commission edition, *Catalogue of the Harleian Mss* ii, 74–8. The indenture had been a gift to Harley from Sir Thomas Hoby. The unsigned preface, which may also be by Astle, allots a longer space to a fulsome description of the indenture than to any other one manuscript, and is followed by a description of the indenture quadripartite formerly belonging to St Albans (BL Harleian MS 28); preface repeated in the Record Commission edition, 20–1; cf. BL Additional MS 62775.
[46] Condon and Hallam, 'Government printing', 348–88, *passim*.
[47] BL Harleian MS 297, fos. 8–27. The manuscript is part of a collection ascribed to Ralph Starkey (d.1628) or his amanuenses. The orthography is too far removed from Astle's text to be his actual source.
[48] BL Additional MSS 51899, 21480.
[49] Above, 99 n. 1; for example, Geoffrey Elton refers to 'Astle's not altogether accurate edition', Elton, 'Henry VII: a restatement', 70 n.

should it be expected from the practice of his day – is to note insertions or erasures as they occur in the original text.[50]

As previously noted, most of the will's clauses relating to Westminster were included in full transcript by Edward Brayley in his monograph on the chapel (in a text which is generally superior but itself begins with a minor omission). Extensive extracts from the entire will, based on Astle's text but with spelling modernised, were included by Sir Harris Nicolas in his *Testamenta Vetusta* (1826) which, whatever its demerits, made the substance of this and other wills available to a much wider audience.[51]

Note on editorial practice

The document has deteriorated significantly in the two centuries since Astle published his work. In some instances the text is actually missing; in others, it is now illegible; and marks of abbreviation (most usually indicating a doubled 'm' or 'n') are often not easily visible, even with the assistance of ultra-violet light. Actual damage has been noted, and Astle's reading has been silently accepted in such instances. For the badly damaged last page, which contains the various dating clauses, specific acknowledgement is made of readings supplied from Astle's edition, simply because of their importance for any evaluation of the document itself. The readings, if not the orthography, can be confirmed from the contemporary enrolment of the text, British Library Additional MS 36273B. Capitalisation and punctuation are those of the editor, and not of the original text, which uses both with restraint. In a few instances of ambivalence the original punctuation and word order provide an essential guide to the sense, producing a variant reading from that adopted by Astle. Abbreviations have been extended; and 'u' and 'v' used in accordance with modern practice. The occasional vestigial thorn is given its modern equivalent but is recorded in the footnotes.

The enrolment of the will, British Library Additional MS 36273B, includes a number of different copyist's errors, and much variant orthography. Neither have been noticed or collated with the original text. Words and phrases added with a caret in the original run continuously in the copy. Deliberate insertions in the original, other than those arising from error, have, however, been compared with the relevant entries in the enrolment and footnoted accordingly.

---

[50] A letter from John Strachey to John Topham, in the absence of Astle, concerning the printing of the parliament rolls would suggest that some at least of Astle's conventions were regarded as 'best practice' at the time: BL Additional MS 33711, fos. 293–4, printed in Condon and Hallam, 'Government printing', 388.

[51] N.H. Nicholas, *Testamenta Vetusta*, 2 vols., 1826, i, 26–36. The papers of William Lowndes, Secretary of the Treasury 1695–1724, include a shorthand copy of Henry VII's will which can only be termed an archival curiosity, PRO, T 48/23, but is one indication of a continuing interest in the will in the years before publication.

The Will of Henry VII: Text of PRO, E 23/3

edited by Margaret Condon

H R

In the name of the almighty and merciful Trinitie, the Fader, the Son, and the Holie Gost, thre Persones and oon God. We, Henry, by the grace of God King of England and of Fraunce, and Lord of Ireland, of this name the Seventh, at oure manour of Richemount the *laste*[1] daie of the moneth of Marche, the yere of oure Lord God a thousand five hundreth and *nyne*,[2] of oure reigne the *xxiiij*,[3] being entier of mynde and hool of bodie, the laude and praise to oure Lord God; make this oure last Wille and testament in the maner and fourme hereafter ensuyng.

Furst, for the recommendacion of oure soule into the moost mercifull handes of Hym that redemed and made it, we saie at this tyme, as sithens the furst yeres of discrecion we have been accustumed, thies wordes '*Domine Jhesu Christe, qui me ex nichilo creasti, fecisti, redemisti et predestinasti ad hoc quod sum, tu scis quid de me facere vis, fac de me secundum voluntatem tuam cum misericordia.*' Therefor doo of me Thi wille with grace, pitie and mercye, moost humbly and entierly I beseche The. And thus unto The I bequethe, and into Thi moost mercifull handes my soule I committe. And howebeit I am a synfull creature, in synne conceived, and in synne have lived, knowing perfitely that of my merites I cannot atteyne to the lif everlasting, but oonly by the merites of Thy blessed passion, and of Thi infinite mercy and grace. Nathelesse my moost mercifull Redemer, Maker and Salviour, I truste that by the special grace and mercy of Thi moost Blissed Moder evir Virgyne, oure Lady Saincte Mary, in whom after The in this mortall lif hath ever been my moost singulier trust and confidence, to whom in al my necessities I have made myne continuel refuge, and by whom I have hiderto, in all myne adversities, ever had my special comforte and *(fo. 1v)* relief, wol nowe in my moost extreme nede, of her infinite pitie take my soule into her handes, and it present unto her moost dere Son: whereof swettest Lady of Mercy, veray Moder and Virgin, Welle of Pitie, and surest refuge of al nedefull; moost humbly, moost entierly, and moost hertely I beseche The. And for my comforte in this behalve, I trust also to the singuler mediacions and praiers of al the holie companie of Heven; that is to saye, aungels, archaungels, patriarches, prophetes, apostels, evaungelistes, martirs, confessours, and virgyns. And specially to myne accustumed avoures I calle and crie, Sainct Michaell, Sainct John Baptist, Saint John Evaungelist, Saint George,

---

[1] Inserted into space left in text. Written continuously in BL MS Add. 36273B.
[2] Inserted into space left in text. Written continuously in BL MS Add. 36273B.
[3] Inserted into space left in text. Written continuously in BL MS Add. 36273B.

Saint Anthony, Sainct Edward, Saint Vincent,[4] Saint Anne,[5] Saint Marie Magdalene, and Saint Barbara; humbly beseching you, not oonly at the houre of dethe soo to aide, soccour and defende me, that the aunciente and gostely enemye, ner noon other evill or dampnable esprite, have no powar to invade me, ner with his terriblenesse to annoye me; but also with your holie praiers, to be intercessours and mediatours unto our Maker and Redemer, for the remission of my synnes and salvacion of my soule.[6]

F[or][7] the Kinges Sepulture

And forasmoche as we have received oure solempne coronacion, and holie inunccion, within our monastery of Westminster, and that within the same monasterie is the commen sepulture of the kinges of this Reame; and specially bicause that within the same, and amonges the same kinges, resteth the holie bodie and reliquies of the glorious King and Confessour Sainct Edward, and diverse other of our noble progenitours and blood, and specially the body of our graunt dame of right noble memorie Quene Kateryne, wif to King Henry the vth, and doughter to King Charles of Fraunce; and that we by the grace of God pourpose right shortely to translate [8]into the same[8] (fo. 2) the bodie and reliquies of our uncle of blissed memorie King Henry the vj[th]. For thies, and diverse other causes and consideracions us specially moevyng in that behalf, we wol that whensoevir it shall please our Salviour Jhesu Crist to calle us oute of this transitorie lif, be it within this our Royaume, or in any Reame or place withoute the same, that our bodie bee buried within the same monastery: that is to saie in the chapell where our said graunt dame laye buried, the which chapell we have begoune to buylde of newe in the honour of our blessed Lady. And we wol that our towmbe bee in the myddes of the same chapell, before the high aultier, in such distaunce from the same, as it is ordred in the plat made for thesame chapell, and signed with our hande. In which place we wol, that for the said sepulture of us and our derest late wif the Quene, whose soule God pardonne, be made a towmbe of stone called touche, sufficient in largieur for us booth. And upon the same, oon ymage of our figure, and an other of hers, either of theim of copure and gilte, of such faccion, and in

The Kinges Chapell

The Kinges towmbe

The Kinges ymage

---

[4] St Vincent Ferrier: canonised 1455; the patron saint of Vannes, in Brittany, where Henry VII had once sheltered as an exile. In 1502 Henry VII had sent a rich chasuble and two altar frontals to the cathedral at Vannes (the town of Vincent's death and the site of his shrine). His image figures on one of the medallions adorning the king's tomb, where he is paired with St Edward. He is also represented in the statuary of the north chapel and the main vessel of the Lady chapel itself. See R. Griffiths, *The Making of the Tudor Dynasty*, Gloucester 1985, 172–3; J.T. Micklethwaite, 'Notes on the imagery of Henry the Seventh's Chapel, Westminster', *Archaeologia* xlvii pt 2, 1883, 377.

[5] The position of St Anne in the list of female saints suggests, and the iconography of the tomb interprets, that St Anne, the mother of Mary, is intended. She is shown on the tomb with her emblem of the book with which she taught the Virgin to read. Confusingly, the king's mother, Margaret Beaufort, famously wrote to her son on 'thys day of Seynt Annes, that y dyd bring ynto thys world my good and gracious prynce, kynge and only beloved son', referring to it as the day of the king's nativity: but St Agnes *secundo* is meant. For St Anne/St Agnes, see Jones and Underwood, 74.

[6] All feature in the iconography of the tomb and chapel; banners of the king's avowries accompanied his body on its way to the grave. The later practice is tellingly illustrated in the Obituary roll of John Islip, where the abbot's avowries attend his deathbed, and their banners accompany his hearse, *The Obituary Roll of John Islip*, ed. W.H. St John Hope, Westminster 1906, pls. XXI, XXII.

[7] MS damaged.

[8] 'into the same' added at end of line.

suche maner, as shalbe thought moost convenient by the discrecion of our executours, yf it be not before doon by our self in our daies. And in the borders of the same towmbe bee made a convenient scripture, conteignyng the yeres of our reigne, and the daie and yere of our decesse. And in the sides, and booth endes of our said towmbe, in the said touche under the said bordure, we wol tabernacles bee graven, and the same to be filled with ymages, specially of our said avouries, of coper and gilte.[9] Also we wol that incontinent after our decesse, and after that our bodye be buried within the said towmbe, the bodie of our said late wif the Quene bee translated from the place where it nowe is buried,[10] and brought and laide with oure bodye in our said towmbe, yf it be not soo *(fo. 2v)* doon by our self in our daies. Also we wol, that by a convenient space and distaunce from the grees of the high aultier of the said chapell, there be made in lenght and brede aboute the said tombe, a grate, in maner of a closure, of coper and gilte, after the faction that we have begoune; whiche we wol be by our said executours fully accomplisshed and perfourmed.[11] And within the same grate at oure fete, after a convenient distaunce from our towmbe, bee made an aultier in the honour of our Salviour Jhesu Crist, streight adioynyng to the said grate. At which aultier we wol certaine preistes daily saie masses, for the weale of our soule and remission of our synnes, under such maner and fourme as is couvenaunted and aggreed bitwext us, and thabbot, priour, and convent of our said monasterye of Westminster; and as more specially appereth by certaine writinges indented made upon the same, and passed, aggreed and concluded, betwix us and the said abbot, priour, and convent, under our grete seale, and signed with our owen hande, for our partie; and the convent seale of the said abbot, priour, and convent, for their partie, and remayneng of recorde in the rolles of our Chauncellary.[12]

And if our said chapell and towmbe, and oure and our said wifes ymagies, grate and closure, be not fully accomplisshed and perfitely finisshed, according to the premisses, by us in our lif tyme; we then wol, that not oonly the same chapell, tombe, ymagies, grate and closure, and every of theim, and al other thinges to theim belonging,

Marginalia: The grate for the towmbe

Marginalia: The finisshing of the Kinges Chapell, ymagies, grate and closure

---

[9] This instruction was met by the bronze gilt medallions mounted within the circular wreaths, carved with astonishing virtuosity in the brittle stone, of the north and south sides of the touchstone (Tournai marble) tomb chest (Plate VI). The Virgin and Child and St Christopher are additions to make up the number. All are in a classical, not a gothic, idiom. For a recent discussion of the tomb, P. Lindley, *Gothic to Renaissance: Essays on Sculpture on England*, Stanford 1995, 54–62, 70–1. As is well known, the tomb was not erected in the place identified by the will, and the change in location is reflected in the vaulting of the chapel. A large boss of the king's arms directly identifies the site of the tomb beneath. More remains to be written about this tomb and its construction; and at least in the present author's mind there remains a question mark as to where the king was first buried.

[10] Elizabeth of York was initially buried in a temporary vault under the lantern of the abbey church: above, 87. Since the heralds are quite specific that on 11 May 1509 the king was laid to rest beside her, either he, too, was placed in the same temporary grave or the executors had authorised a change of plan so that both were placed in the vault where they now lie, whether or no they were its intended incumbents.

[11] Begun probably in 1505, Colvin, *HKW* iii, 219; see also below, 175–7. Marks incised into the uprights and tracery of the enclosure in a logical sequence of slashes and zeros facilitated its reconstruction around the tomb chest.

[12] PRO, E 33/1; BL MS Harley 1498; *CClR Henry VII 1500–1509*, no. 389; above, 76–8, 87.

with al spede, and assone after our decease as goodly may be doon, bee by our executours hooly and perfitely finisshed in every behalve, after the maner and fourme before rehersed, and sutingly to that that is begonne and doon of theim. But also that thesaid chapell be desked, and the windowes of our said chapell be glased, with stores, ymagies, armes, bagies *(fo. 3)* and cognoisaunces, as is by us redily divised, and in picture delivered to the priour of Sainct Bartilmews besides Smythfeld, maistre of the workes of our said chapell.[13] And that the walles, doores, windows, archies and vaultes, and ymages of the same our chapell, within and without, be painted, garnisshed, and adorned with our armes, bagies, cognisaunces, and other convenient painteng, in as goodly and riche maner as suche a werk requireth, and as to a kinges werk apperteigneth. And for the more sure perfourmance and finisshing of the premisses, and for the more redye payment of the money necessary in that behalf, we have delivered in redy money before the hande, the some of v m^l li, to the abbot, priour and convent of our said monastery of Westminster, as by writinges indented betwixt us and theim, testifieng the same payment and receipte, and bering date at *Richemount*[14] the *thretene*[15] daie of the moneth of *Aprill*,[16] the xxiiii[17] yere of our reigne, it dooth more plainlie appiere. The same five thousand poundes and every parcel therof, to be truly emploied and bestowed by thabbot of our said monastery for the tyme being, aboutes and upon the finisshing and perfourmyng of the premisses from tyme to tyme, as nede shall require, by thadvise, comptrollement and oversight of such persones as we in our live, and our executours after our decesse, yf they be not doon in our live, shall depute and assigne, without discontynuyng of the said werkes or any parte of theim, till thei be fully performed, finisshed, and accomplisshed. And that the said abbot of our said monastery for the tyme being be accomptable for themployeng and bestowing of the said some of v m^l li. upon the said werkes, to us in our lif, and to our executours after our decesse, for such parcell therof as shall reste not accompted for before that, and not imploied ner bestowed upon the said werkes after our decesse, as often and when soo ever we or they shall calle hym thereunto, as it is more largly *(fo. 3v)* conteyned in the said indentures. And in case the said v m^l li. shall not suffice for the hool perfourmance and accomplisshment of the said werkes, and every parcell of theim, and that thei bee not perfitely finisshed by us in our life daies; we then wol that our executours from tyme to tyme, as necessitie shall require, deliver to the said abbot for the tyme being, as moch money above the said v m^l li. as shall suffice for the perfite finisshing and

---

[13] William Bolton. For a reconstruction of the glazing scheme, proposing a thematic treatment of the Old and the New Law, the hierarchy of the heavenly hosts, and including a narrative of the Virgin, as well as the ubiquitous and overwhelming heraldry, R. Marks, 'The glazing of Henry VII's Chapel, Westminster Abbey', *The Reign of Henry VII*, 157–174, with a survey of the literature at 157, n. 1.
[14] Inserted into space left in text; also an insertion in BL MS Add. 36273B.
[15] Inserted into space left in text; also an insertion in BL MS Add. 36273B.
[16] Inserted into space left in text; also an insertion in BL MS Add. 36273B.
[17] Now illegible: supplied from Astle. Written continuously with the text in BL MS Add. 36273B. The account book of the Treasurer of the King's Chamber records a payment of £2,500 above £2,500 already in hand under the date of 15 April 1509, PRO, E 36/214, p. 344.

	perfourmyng of the said werkes, and every parte of theim; thesame money to be emploied and bestowed upon the perfite finisshing and perfourmyng of the said werkes, by the said abbot for the tyme being, by the foresaied advise, oversight, comptrollement and accompte, without desisting or discontynuyng the same werkes in any wise, till they and every parcell of theim as before is saied, be fully and perfitely accomplisshed and perfourmed, in maner and fourme before rehersed.
For the Funerallis	And astouching our funerallis, thentierment of our body, and chargies of our sepulture, we remitte theim to the discrecion of the supervisours and executours of our testament, wherein we wol thei have a special respect and consideracion to the laude and praising of God, the welth of our soule, and som[ewhat][18] to our dignitie roial; eviteng alwaies dampnable pompe and outeragious superfluities. For the susteigneng and bering of the which chargies, we wol that our executours take of our redy money remaignyng in our coffers, or of our plate, juelx, goods or debtes, asmoche as shalbe necessarie or requisite for the same; all which expenses funerallis we wol be doon and perfourmed, furst and before all other thinges, of what condicion soo evir thei bee.[19]
The x m^l masses	Also we woll, that furthwith and ymmediatly after our decesse, whensoevir it shall please God soo to dispose of us, beit within this our Reame, or in any other Reame or Contrey without the same; *(fo. 4)* our executours with al diligence and spede that goodly may be doon, cause to be saied within our said monastery, our citie of London, and other places next adioinyng to the same, for the remission of our synnes, and the weale of our soule, x m^l masses; wherof we woll xv^c bee saied in the honour of the Trinitie; M^{l}M^{l}V^c in the honour of the v woundes of our Lord Jhesu Crist; M^{l}M^{l}D in the honour of the v Joies of our Lady; ccccl in the honour of the ix ordres of aungelles; cl in the honour of the patriarches; DC in the honour of the xij Apostellis, and m^{l}m^{l}ccc, which maketh up the hool nombre of the said x m^l masses, in the honour of All Sainctes. And that the said masses and every of them, bee saied and doon as above, at the ferrest within oon moneth next and ymmediatly ensuyng the knowlege of our said decesse. And that every preist saieng any of the said masses, have for every of theim soo by hym saied, vj d., the which in the hool amounteth to the somme of ccl li.
The distribucion of almose	We wol also that[20] yf we decesse within this our Reame, that then betwix the houre of our deceasse, and thende of the daie of our sepulture, be destributed in elemose for the weale of our soule, two thousand poundes; and yf it shall fortune us to disceasse in any place without this our Reame, we wol that then assone as goodly may be doon, and at the ferrest within oon moneth next and ymmediatly

---

[18] MS damaged.

[19] Performed, according to the record of John Heron, Treasurer of the Chamber to both Henry VII and Henry VIII, at a cost of £8,474 4s 6d, although this sum includes more than £2,000 in alms, for which the will makes separate provision, PRO, E 36/214, p. 348; Funeral Accounts PRO, LC 2/1, fos. 87–144, briefly calendared in *L &P Henry VIII*, I, 20; the various heralds' accounts include the one printed in J. Leland, *Antiquarii de Rebus Britannicis Collectanea*, ed. T. Hearne, 2nd edn, iv, 1774, 303–9; abstracts in *L&P Henry VIII*, I pt i, 19–21.

[20] Initial thorn.

after that our said executours shalhave furst notice of oure decesse, bee distributed in elemesse for the weale of our Soule, the same M^{l}M^l li.; wherof we wol that M^{l}D li. bee distributed amonges such poore folkes as may travaile to aske elemose, that is to saye, to every of theim iiij d.; and of thoder D li., CC li. to be dealte within oure citie of London, the suburbes of the same, and our monastery and towne of Westminster, amonges lame, blinde, bedred, and moost nedye folkes of thesame, which may not travaile to aske elemesse; and (*fo. 4v*) thoder CCC li. to be dealte amonges the miserable prisoners remayneng in any prisone within our said citie or the suburbes of the same, or of our toune of Westminster, condempned for debt or other cause, where the dutie and damages excede not iiij li., or suche as remayne in prisonne oonly for lack of payment of their fees: to thentent thei doo praie to almighty God for the remission of our synnes, and salvacion of our soule. And that the same D li. to bee distributed amonges the same lame, blinde, nedy, and the said prisonners in fourme before rehersed, within the same tyme. And in this partie we hertily desire our executours to thinke and considere howe necessarie, behoofull, and howe profitable it is to dede folkes to bee praied for, entierlye requiring theim, that in the distribucion of the said elemesse, they exhorte and moeve the poore people that shall receive the said elemose, devoutly and by name to praie for us and the weale of our soule, soo that oure soule may fele that as thei loved us in our life, soo thei may remembre us after our deceasse; and for the true execucion herof, we charge their conscience as thei woll aunswere therefor before God.

And for the more redy and sure paiement of the said M^{l}M^{l}CCL li., we have delivered in redy money before the hande, to thabbot, priour and convent of our said monastery of Westminster, the same some of M^{l}M^{l}CCL li., as by writinges indented betwixt us and the said abbot, priour, and convent of our said monastery of Westminster, testifieng the same payment and receipte, and bering date at [——][21] the [——][22] daye of the moneth of [——][23] the [——][24] yere of our reigne, it doeth more plainly appere; thesame M^{l}M^{l}CCL li. saufly and surely to bee kept by the said abbot, priour, and convent for thesame causes oonly, and to thentent before rehersed, and not to bee delivered to any persone, or for any cause, or at any tyme, but oonly for the causes abovesaied; and to our executours incontinently after our deceasse, as it ys (*fo. 5*) more largely expressed in the said indentures. And if it shall fortune by any chaunce, or by the disposicion of our Lord God, oure bodye to be entered and buried in any other place withoute oure said monastery within this our Reame or in any other place without this our Reame; we woll neverthelesse that the said x m^l masses bee fully saied, and thesaid M^{l}M^{l}CCL li. plenarly paied and distributed, for the remission of our synnes, and

---

[21] Blank in text. Also blank in BL MS Add. 36273B.
[22] Blank in text. Also blank in BL MS Add. 36273B.
[23] Blank in text. Also blank in BL MS Add. 36273B.
[24] Blank in text. Also blank in BL MS Add. 36273B. The distribution of alms was actually done by the king's chaplains under the direction of the king's almoner, each chaplain taking responsibility for a particular section of the specified alms-giving on various dates between 27 April and 11 May, PRO, LC 2/1, fos. 112v–113; PRO, SP 1/1, fos. 21–21v, 25, 26.

	the weale of our soule, after the maner and fourme, and within the tyme, and within the places above rehersed: Soo that thesaid money bee emploied oonly aboutes thesame, and to noon other use, ner for noon other matier whatsoever it may bee.
The payement of the Kinges debtes	Also we wol that all our debtes, furst a[nd][25] before al other charges, our funerallis, and costes of our enterement and sepulture oonly excepted, with all possible spede and diligence after thei appere due, iustely and truly bee contented and paied by the handes of our executours, wherewith we charge theim as thei wol aunswere for us
For restitucions and s[ati]sfactions[26] for wronges	before God, and discharge our conscience. And also if any persone, of what degree soevir he bee, shewe by way of complainte to our executours any wrong to have been doon to hym by us, oure commaundement, occasion or meane, or that we helde any goodes or landes which of right ought to apperteigne unto hym: we wol that every such complainte be spedely, tenderly and effectuelly herde, and the matier duely and indifferently examyned, by the moost Reverende Fader in God tharchebusshop of Caunterbury that nowe is,[27] or that hereafter for the tyme shalbe; the Reverende Faders in God Richard, Bisshop of Wynchester,[28] the Bisshops of London[29] and Rochester,[30] that nowe bee, or hereafter for the tyme shalbe; Thomas, Erle of Surrey our Tresourer general;[31] George, Erle of Shrewesbury, Steward of our House;[32] Sir Charles Somerset, Lord Herberd, oure *(fo. 5v)* Chambrelaine;[33] the chief Justices of our Benche and Comon place that nowe bee, or that the tyme of our decesse shalbe;[34] Maister John Yong, Maistre of the Rolles of our Chauncery;[35] Sir Thomas Lovell, knight, Tresourer of our House;[36] Maistre Thomas Routhall, our Secretary;[37] Sir Richard Emson, knight, our Chancellor of our Duchie of Lancastre;[38] Edmund

---

[25] MS damaged.

[26] MS damaged.

[27] William Warham, archbishop of Canterbury (1503–32), Keeper of the Great Seal 1502–4, Chancellor 1504–15, supervisor of the will of 1509.

[28] Richard Fox, bishop of Winchester (1501–28), keeper of the Privy Seal since 1487. Also an executor.

[29] Richard FitzJames, bishop of London (1506–22), king's almoner 1495–7. Occasions on which he preached before the king include the funeral of Elizabeth of York. Also an executor.

[30] John Fisher, bishop of Rochester (1504–15). Also an executor. Preached the funerary sermon at St Paul's on 10 May 1509 whilst the king's body lay in state on its way to Westminster.

[31] Thomas Howard, earl of Surrey. Treasurer 1501–22, created duke of Norfolk 1514. Also an executor.

[32] George Talbot, earl of Shrewsbury. Steward of the household since 1502.

[33] Charles Somerset, Lord Herbert; created earl of Worcester 1514. Made Chamberlain of the Household in succession to Giles Lord Daubeney, 1508. Also an executor.

[34] John Fineux, Chief Justice of the King's Bench (1495–1525) and Robert Rede, Chief Justice Common Pleas (1506–1519). Both also named among the king's executors.

[35] John Yonge, Master of the Rolls since 22 January 1508. Also an executor. Died 25 April 1516. His tomb, also by Pietro Torrigiano, has direct associations with the workshops for the king's chapel, above, 108 n. 36.

[36] Like Richard Fox, Thomas Lovell was one of Henry VII's longest-serving councillors. Treasurer of the Household by 1502, having previously been treasurer of the Chamber. Also an executor. For Lovell's omnicompetence, S.J. Gunn, 'Sir Thomas Lovell (c.1449–1524), a new man in a new monarchy', in *The End of the Middle Ages*, ed. J. Watts, Stroud 1998, 117–53.

[37] Thomas Ruthall. Made bishop of Durham in June 1509. Also an executor.

[38] Chancellor of the Duchy of Lancaster since 1505, and a leading figure in the policies of Henry VII's last years. Also an executor. Arrested within three days of Henry VII's death; charged with treason, and executed 1510. See S.J. Gunn, 'The accession of Henry VIII', *Historical Research* lxiv, 1991, 278–87.

Dudley, squier;[39] our Attourney, that at the tyme of oure decesse shalbe;[40] our Confessour, the Provincial of the Freres Observauntes;[41] and Maistre William at Water, Deane of our Chapell,[42] or any vj or theim at the leest, and iij of our executours. And in caas by suche examinacion it can be founde, that the complaint be mad of a grounded cause in conscience, other then mater doon by the course and ordre of our lawes, or th[at][43] our said executours, by their wisdoms and discrecions, shal thinke that in conscience our soule aught to stande charged with the said matier and complaint: we wol then that as the caas shall require, he and thei bee restored and recompensed by our said executours, of such our redy money and juelx as then shall remayne, and for lack therof, of suche revenues as we shall hereafter appointe, aswel for that cause, as for the contentacion of our said debtes, yf any suche shal fortune to be. And to thentent that no suche persone, ne any other whereunto we shal after our deceasse stande indebted, have cause of ignoraunce of this our wille and mynde, we wol that our executours within iij monethes next and ymmediatlye folowing our decesse, at the ferrest, cause open proclamacions to bee made in every shiretoune, and iij or iiij other of the best burghes and market townes, of every shire within this our Reame; that if any man can for any cause reasonable, clayme any debt of us, or shewe that we have wronged hym in any maner of wise, that might or shulde charge our conscience as before is saied, that he reasorte to our said executours, and the said examiners, in such place as after their (fo. 6) discrecion shalbe appointed; and then and there to be redely herde and aunswered, as reason and conscience shal in that parte require. And howbeit that thofficers of oure House and Warderobe for the tyme being have continuelly had for the bering of the charges of thesame so large and sure assignementes,[44] that we trust there is litle or nothing owing in that behalf; yet forasmoche as we wold gladly that every of our subgettes shuld be truly and iustely contented of al that we owe unto theim, we wol that if any persone prove before our executours that any dutie is owing unto hym for the charges of our said Houshold and Warderobe, then our said executours take suche provision for his contentacion, that he be paied by the handes of thoes officers of our House and Warderobe, in whose tyme the said dutie grewe or shuld

---

[39] Also an executor. Like Empson, Dudley was arrested in the immediate aftermath of the king's death, and for the same reasons, real and alleged. For his appeal to this committee for correction of certain matters 'for the helpe and Reliefe of his [Henry VII's] soule . . .', in discharge of this trust, C.J. Harrison, 'The petition of Edmund Dudley', *EHR* lxxxvii, 1972, 82–99.

[40] John Ernley, king's attorney (1507–19); appointed Chief Justice Common Pleas 1519.

[41] The format suggests that these are intended to describe one rather than two people, but is unclear. In 1504 the king's confessor had been John Burnell, friar observant. The vicar provincial of the friars observant in 1508 was named as Stephen Baroms. *CPL*, vol. xviii, ed. M. Haren, 155; *CPR 1494–1509*, 568. In the event neither seems to have participated in the work of the committee.

[42] William Atwater, dean of the Chapel of the Household since 1508; bishop of Lincoln 1514–21.

[43] MS damaged.

[44] *Rot. Parl.* vi, 497–502; amended by warrant 1501, PRO, E 404/83 22 June. On the security of these assignments money was actually advanced by John Heron by way of prest out of the revenues of the Chamber in order to secure an adequate cash flow to the Cofferer of the Household, independent of delays in realising the fixed assignments. The king thus had reason for confidence in the security of his credit.

	have been paied; orellis, for default therof, to be paied unto theim by their owen handes, of our said goodes and revenues.
The couvenauntes betwixt the King and thabbot of Westminster etc	And for the fournisshing, maynteynyng and perfourmyng of certain diverse couvenauntes and aggrementes, concernyng more plainly and particularly the specialties of this our Wille and testament, passed and accorded betwixt us, and the said abbot, priour, and convent, by writing indented and sealed upon both parties, and entred of recorde in the rolles of oure Chauncery: that is to say, for the wages and charges of oure iiij chauntry monkes; thexhibicion and finding of iij monkes, scolers to the Universitie of Oxonford, there to studie in science of divinitie; the rewardes of prechers, for saying of certain sermons every Sonday throughout the yere, and at certaine festes, and other daies, within our s[aid][45] monastery; the keping of our Anniversarie and wekely obite within our said monastery, and the distribucion of elemosse that shalbe doon at thesame; the mainteyneng of certain tapers, torches and lightes, to brenne at thesaid Anniversarie and wekely obites contynuelly and perpetuelly, whil the werld shall endure, aboutes our towmbe; the finding of certain converses by us encreased (fo. 6v) within the said monastery; the maynetenaunces of certain forrein anniversaries, to be holden for us in diverse cathedral churches, conventual and collegiat churches, and the two Universities of Oxonford and Cambrige; the sallary of the chauntry preist, that we have perpetuelly founded and ordeyned to singe for the soule of my lord our fader, in the house of the Grey Freres in Caermerden in Wales; and the finding of xiij poor men, and the iij poor women, that we have perpetuelly establisshed in oure elemesse house, by us buylded within our said monastery of Westminster, with diverse other charges to the same belonging and depending, and seremonies to the same apperteignyng, as more largely in the said writing indented is specially expressed and declared: we have yeven, graunted and amortised, for evir and in perpetuitie, certain landes spirituall and temporall to the yerely value of M^l marces and above in full recompense, aswel of almaner of charges concernyng the premisses conteined in thesaid writinges indented, as also for al casualties and evictions, if any such should hap ne hereafter.[46]
For the founding of Hospitalles	And forasmoch as we inwardly considere, that the vij workes of Charite and Mercy bee moost profitable, due, and necessarie, for the salvacion of mans soule, and that the same vij workes stande moost comonly in vj of theim: that is to saie, in viseting of the sik; mynistring mete and drinke and clothing to the nedy; logging of the miserable pouer; and burying of the dede bodies of cristen people: We therefor gretely tendring thesame, and considering that the next way to doo and execute the said vj werkes of P[itie][47] and Mercy, ys by meanes of keping, susteynyng and maynteynyng of commune hospitallis, wherin if thei be duly kept, the said nede pouer people bee lodged, visited in their siknesses, refresshed with mete and drinke, and if nede be with clothe, and also buried yf thei fortune to die within thesame; and understanding also that there be fewe or

---

[45] MS damaged.
[46] *CPR 1494–1509*, 374–9; Harvey, *Estates*, 198–202, 425–7; above, n. 12.
[47] MS damaged.

noon suche commune hospitallis within this our Reame *(fo. 7)* and that, for lack of theim, infinite nombre of pouer nedie people miserably dailly die, no man putting hande of helpe or remedie; we therefor of our grete pitie and compassion, desiring inwardly the remedy of the premisses, have begoune to erecte, buylde and establisshe a commune hospital in our place called the Savoie besides Charingcrosse, nigh to our citie of London; and thesame we entende with Goddes grace to finisshe after the maner, fourme and faction of a plat which is devised for thesame, and signed with our hande; and have endowed with landis and tenements to the yerely value of D marces above al reprises, to bere, maynteyne, and susteigne therewith, aswel oon hundreth beddes garnisshed, to receive and lodge nightly oon hundreth pouer folkes, as also a certain nomber of preistes, and other ministres[48] and servitours, men and women, as suche a matier shal require, to have the keping, ruling, and guyding of thesaid hospitall and pouer folkes, and ministring unto theim metes, drinkes, and other necessaries; and also to doo, execute, and perfourme diverse other thinges within [our][49] said hospitall, to the laude of God, the weale of our soule, and the refresshing of thesaid pouer people, in daily, nightly and hourely exployting the said vj workes of mercy, pitie and charite, after suche statutes and ordenaunces as we entende to make for the better ordring and directing of thesaid hospitall. And if this be nat fully and perfitely finisshed, perfourmed, and doon, or that thesaid statutes be not entierly made, by our self in our lif, we wol that then al the premisses and every of theim bee doon by our executours assone as goodly may be doon after our decesse. And for the buylding of thesaid hospitall, and furst provision of cc beddes fully garnisshed for the said c poor men, bokes, chalices, vestmentes, aultreclothes, aultre tables, and other implementes necessarie for our said hospital, the chapel of thesame, and other houses of offices to thesame hospital belonging, and for the more redye payment of the money that shalbe requisite for the furnisshing of the *(fo. 7v)* same, we have delivered in redy money before the hande, the some of ten thousand marces, to the Dean and Chapitre of oure cathedral church of Pawlis within our citie of London, as by writinges indented betwix us and theim, testifieng the same payment and receipt, and bering date at [———][50] the [———][51] daie of the moneth of [———][52] the xxiiij yere of our reigne, it dooth more plainly appere. The same ten thousand marces, and every parcel therof, to be truly emploied and bestowed by suche a persone or persones, as we in our lif shall depute and appointe to be maister of our werkes by our lettres in fourme of a plakarde, signed with oure hande and sealed with our signet; or if the said werkes bee not doon and finisshed in our lif, as our executours, after

[48] MS 'mistres'.
[49] MS damaged.
[50] Blank in text. Also blank in BL MS Add. 36273B.
[51] Blank in text. Also blank in BL MS Add. 36273B.
[52] Blank in text. Also blank in BL MS Add. 36273B. For the Savoy, R. Somerville, *The Savoy*, London 1960, 9–33; in the event this money was deposited in the Mint 16 April 1509 and transferred in April 1510 to the abbot and convent of Westminster, the abbot thereafter acting as custodian for this and subsequent transfers of funds; Colvin, *HKW* iii, 201.

our decesse, by their writing shall depute and assigne to be maistre of the said werkes, aboutes and upon the finisshing and perfourmyng of thesaid workes, and for provision of the said beddes, bookes, chalices, vestimentes, aultreclothes, aultre tables and implementes, as nede shall require, by the device, comptrollement and oversight of suche persons as we, or our s[aid][53] executours, in maner beforesaied, shall depute and assigne, without discontynuyng of the said workes or any parte of theim, till they bee fully perfourmed, finisshed and accomplisshed.[54] The said ten thousand markes to be delivered by thesaid Dean and Chapitre, by bille and billes indented, to the said maister of our said werkes in our lif, and aftre, in maner beforesaied, by such parcellis and particuler sommes from tyme to tyme, as the necessitie of the said workes shall require, and as shalbe desired and required by the said maister of our said werkes, with suche persones as shalhave the controllement and oversight of the same, to thentent above rehersed, by indentures to be made betwixt thesaid Dean and Chapitre, and the said maistre of our werkes, testifieng the delivering and receipt of thesaid particuler somes of money.[55] And that aswel the said Dean and his successours, for the delivere of *(fo. 8)* [the said][56] particuler sommes to the said maistre of our werkes, by the desir [a]nd[57] requeste beforesaied, as also thesaid maistre for themployng and [be]stowing[58] of the said some of tenne thousand marces and every parcel therof, of and upon the premisses, be accomptable to us in our lif, and to oure executours after our decesse, for such parcell therof as then shall reste not emploied ner bestowed upon thesaid premisses and provision aftur our deceasse, as often and whansoevir we or thei shal calle theim therunto, as it is more largely expressed in the same indentures. And in caas thesaid x m^l marces shall not suffice for the hool perfourmance and accomplisshment of the premisses and every parcell of theim, and that thei be not perfitely finisshed by us in our daies; we then wol that our executours from tyme to tyme, as necessitie shal require, by like indentures, and upon like accompte, deliver to the said Dean and Chapitre for the tyme being asmoch money above the said x m^l marces as shall suffice for the perfite finisshing and perfourmyng of the premisses, and every parte of theim; the same money to be emploied and bestowed upon the perfite finisshing and perfourmyng of thesaid premisses, by the said maistre of our werkes, by thesaid oversight, comptrollement and accompte, without desisting or discontynuyng of the same werkes in any wise, till thei and every parcell of theim as before is saied bee fully and perfitely accomplissed[59] and perfourmed in maner and fourme afore rehersed.

---

[53] MS damaged.
[54] This project was indeed managed by the executors, Richard Fox, bishop of Winchester, assuming the senior role. William Holgill was the master of the works.
[55] A number of these original indentures survive, in addition to the accounts for 1512–19, and some authorising warrants: Colvin, *HKW* iii, 202–3; PRO, CRES 2/1703.
[56] MS damaged.
[57] MS damaged.
[58] MS damaged.
[59] *Sic.*

THE LAST WILL OF HENRY VII 123

And in likewise, if it be[60] not doon by our silf, we wol that our said executours make two semblable commune hospitallis, aswel in fourme and faction, as yerely value in landis, nomber of preistes, ministres, servauntes, beddes for pouer folkes, and statutes and ordenaunces: the oon of theim to be made in some convenient place in the suburbes of our citie of Yorke, and the other in the suburbes of our city of Coventre, either of theim as nigh to the same cities as conveniently may be doon. And that oure executours for the perfourmyng and fournisshing of the same take of *(fo. 8v)* our said money, juelx, plate and revenues, for either of the sai[d two][61] hospitallis, twenty thousand markes, which is fourty thousand markes in the hool.[62]

The Kinges suffragies

Also where as diverse and many, and almoost al the cathedral churches, seculers and regulers, abbaies, priouries, and collegiat churches of this our Reame, wherof, for the more clere notice of theim, the names been expressed in a cedule to this our Testament annexed,[63] have geven and graunted, every of theim aparte by hym self, by their dedes sealed with their chapitre and convent seales, and also have bounden theim by writinges indented betwixt us, under our grete Seale, and theim under [*their*][64] said chapitre and convent seales, to doo, rede, saie and singe for us, aswel in our life, as after our decesse, in perpetuite, and while the world shall endure, certain orisons, praiers and suffrages, as in the said writinges is more plainly conteigned; and for the which we have geven and graunted to theim by our said writinges indented bitwext us and theim certain grete and large confirmacions, pardons, licences, and other grauntes, to the grete weale, prouffite, suertie and quietnesse of the said churches, abbeys, priouries and colleges, as in likewise is conteigned in the said writinges indented betwixt us and theim. Yet of our more ample grace and favour, and to thentent that ymmediatly aftur oure decesse, thei shuld the more singulerly and tenderly have our soule specially remembred in their good praiers; and also have the better cause hertily to pray for our soule, in their said quotidian orisons, praiers and suffrages, as thei bee bounden to doo by their said writinges, we wolle that our executours, assone as conveniently may be doon after our decesse, cause to be delivered to every of the principall and chief heed rulers and governours of thesaid cathedrall churches, abbeys, priouries and collegiat churches, seculer and reguler, vj s viij d; and to every chanon seculer and reguler, monke, vicaire and ministre within thesame, being preist, iij s iiij d; *(fo. 9)* and to every other such chanon, monk, vicaire and ministre not being preist, xx^{ti} d; tenderly requiring and charging theim, at the deliveraunce and receipt of thesame, to have our soule affectuously remembred in their said dailly orisons, praiers and suffragies, and the rather for the memoriall that thei have of us at that tyme.

The repairing of High wayes

Also we wolle, that our executours bestowe and emploie, with as goodly spede after our deceasse as conveniently may be doon, M^{l}M^l li

---

[60] 'be' interlined with caret.
[61] MS damaged.
[62] This is the first and last that is heard of the hospitals.
[63] Not annexed. See above, 81, 86.
[64] Understood. Not in MS.

upon the newe making and repairing, where nede shal require, of such highe waies and brigges as hereafter folowe; that is to saye, upon the newe making or repairing of the high wey and brigges betwixt oure castell and towne of Windesore, and our manour of Richemount; [65]the high wey and brigges betwixt the same our manour of Richemount and Saint Georges church besides Suthwark; the high wey and brigges betwixt the same Saint Georges church and our manour of Grenewich; and the high wey betwixt thesame our manour of Grenewich and the citie of[65] Caunterbury. All which high waies, we wol be substancially diched upon booth sides, where thei may be conveniently so doon, wel and surely graveled, and reised upon a good height, with such a brede and largenesse as two cartes may passe the oon by the other, or booth togeders. And the said two thowsand poundes, as farre as it wol goo and extende, to bee emploied upon the same, and upon noon other thing, in the moost sure and substancial maner that can be devised by our executours, or such as thei shal depute and assign to the same, if it be not doon by our self in our life tyme.

The provision for the Lordes and other that have truly served the King
Item, forasmoche as diverse of the lordes, aswel of our blood as other, and also knightes, squiers, and diverse our true lovyng subgettes and servauntes, have faithfully assisted us, and diverse of theim put theim in extreme ieobardie of their lives, and losses of their landes and goodes, in servyng and assisting us, aswel aboutes the recovery of our right and Reame of England, as at diverse other[66] seasons and tymes of ieobardy *(fo. 9v)* in consideracion wherof, we have made unto diverse of theim grauntes, some of landis, tenementes and offices, and some of offices, fees and annuities. We wol and require and straitely charge our sone the prince, and other oure heires, that every lord, knight, squier and other, havyng any thing of our graunt what soever it be, that he and his heires have and enioie every graunt soe by us made for any of the said consideracions or any other cause, according to the tenures, fourme and effect of every of thesame, without any maner lette or interuppcion of our sone, or any other our heires.

The Kinges feoffament of his Duchie of Lancastre
And where as by auctoritie of oure Parliament holden at Westminster the xx[ti] daie of the moneth of February, the vij[th] yere of our reigne,[67] it is amonges other thinges ordeyned, established, and enacted that John, then Archebisshop of Caunterbury, Primat and Chaunceller of all England, decessed;[68] Thomas, then Archebisshop of Yorke, decessed;[69] Jasper, then Duke of Bedford, decessed;[70] Piers, then Bisshop of Winchestre, decessed;[71] John, then Bisshop of Ely,

---

[65] 'the high wey ... the citie of' inserted into too small a space ?over erasure.
[66] 'other' interlined with caret.
[67] *Rot. Parl.* vi, 444–6.
[68] John Morton, archbishop of Canterbury and Chancellor (1486–1500); made cardinal 1493. Died 15 September 1500.
[69] Thomas Rotherham, archbishop of York (1480–1500), Treasurer of England 1485–6, died 29 May 1500.
[70] Jasper Tudor, earl of Pembroke and duke of Bedford, the king's uncle; died 21 December 1495.
[71] Peter Courtenay, bishop of Exeter (1478–87), bishop of Winchester (1487–92); died 22 September 1492. Keeper of the Privy Seal 1485–87.

decessed;[72] Richard, then Bisshop of Exon, nowe Bisshop of Winchester;[73] Edmond, then Bisshop of Rouchester, now Bisshop of Sarum;[74] Thomas, Erle of Arondell;[75] John, Erle of Oxonford;[76] George, Erle of Shrewesbury;[77] Thomas, Erle of Surrey;[78] John, then Viscount Welles, decessed;[79] John, then Lord Dynham, Tresourer of England, knight, decessed;[80] Giles, Lord Daubeney, knight;[81] William [82]Husee, knight, decessed;[83] Oliver King, clerk, decessed;[84] John Cheyney, knight, decessed;[85] Gilbert Talbot, knight;[82,86] Thomas Mountgomery, knight, decessed;[87] Reinald Bray, knight, decessed;[88] John Savage, knight, decessed;[89] James Blount, knight, decessed;[90] Richard Guldeford, knight, decessed;[91] Thomas Lovell, knight;[92] and John Risley, knight,[93] from the said xx daie of February the said vijth yere of oure reigne, holde, enjoie and possede, the honour, castell and lordeship of Lancastre and Clidrowe, with the membres and appurtenaunces of the same, and al manours, lordeships, landes, tenementes, rentes, reversions (fo. 10) services, possessions and hereditamentes, parcell of the Duchie of Lancastre, within the countie of Lancastre, with their appurtenaunces; and the Countie Palatyne of Lancastre with thappurtenaunces, and al liberties, fraunchesies, jurisdiccions, privilegies, lawes, custumes, and al other thinges to thesame Countie Palatyne and other premisses and every parcell of theim belonging and apperteynyng, or parcel of the same; the honours, castellis, lordships and maners of Pountfret,

---

[72] John Alcock, bishop of Worcester (1476–86), bishop of Ely (1486–1500); died 1 October 1500.

[73] Richard Fox, successively bishop of Exeter (1487–92), Bath and Wells (1492–94), Durham (1494–1501), and Winchester (1501–28); and see above, n. 28.

[74] Edmund Audley, bishop of Rochester (1480–92), Hereford (1492–1502), Salisbury (1502–24).

[75] Thomas Fitzalan, earl of Arundel; his wife (d.1491) had been aunt to Elizabeth of York; the earl himself was one of the godfathers of Prince Arthur. Also an executor.

[76] John de Vere, earl of Oxford; restored 1485, and one of Henry VII's principal supporters.

[77] Above, n. 32.

[78] Above, n. 31.

[79] John Welles, Viscount Welles, the king's uncle of the half-blood and, by reason of his marriage to Cecily, one of Edward IV's daughters, also the king's brother-in-law. Died 8 February 1499.

[80] John Dinham, Lord Dinham. Treasurer 1486–1500; died 7 January 1501.

[81] Giles Daubeney, Lord Daubeney. Chamberlain of the Household 1495–1508; died 21 May 1508.

[82] 'Husee . . . . Talbot, knight' inserted over erasure.

[83] William Hussey, Chief Justice of the King's Bench (1481–95); died 8 September 1495.

[84] Oliver King, king's secretary 1487–95, bishop of Bath and Wells (1495–1503); died 29 August 1503.

[85] John Cheney (Lord) Cheney; died 30 May 1499.

[86] Gilbert Talbot, younger son of the second earl of Shrewsbury. Commanded Henry's right wing at Bosworth and frequently employed by him thereafter. Lieutenant of Calais 1507. Died 19 September 1516.

[87] Thomas Montgomery; died 2 January 1495.

[88] Reynold Bray, Chancellor of the Duchy of Lancaster and one of the king's principal councillors and few real confidantes. Died 5 August 1503.

[89] John Savage. Killed at the siege of Boulogne, 1492. See S. Chrimes, *Henry VII*, London 1972, 336.

[90] James Blount. As Captain of Hammes responsible for the escape from prison of the earl of Oxford in 1485, both joining Henry Tudor against Richard III. Died 1492.

[91] Richard Guildford. Controller of the Household 1493–1505; died 6 September 1506 whilst on pilgrimage in the Holy Land.

[92] Above, n. 36.

[93] John Risley, one of the work-horses of the king's council; died 1512. See R. Virgoe, 'Sir John Risley, Courtier and Councillor', *Norfolk Archaeology* xxxviii, 1982, 140–8, esp. 144–6.

Tykhull, Knaresburgh and Pikering, with the membres and appurtenaunces; and al manours, lordeships, landes, tenementes, rentes, reversions and services, parcel of the Duchie of Lancastre in the counties of York and Notingham with their appurtenaunces; the honour, castell, lordship and manour of Tudbury, with thappurtenaunces; and al manours, lordships, landes, tenementes, rentes, reversions and services, parcel of the Duchie of Lancastre, in the counties of Staff' and Derby, with their appurtenaunces; the honour, castell, lordship and manour of Bolingbroke, with the membres and appurtenaunces; and al other manours, lordships, landes, tenementes, rentes, reversions and services, parcel of the Duchie of Lancastre, within the countie of Lincoln' with thappurtenaunces; the manour and lordship of Long Benyngton', parcel of the Duchie of Lancastre in the countie of Lincoln, with thappurtenaunces; and al castellis, lordships, manours, landes, tenementes, rentes, reversions and services, parcel of the Duchie of Lancastre, in the Counties of Norf' and Suff', with their appurtenaunces, to theim and to their heires for evermore: to thentent that thei, their heires, and the heires of every of theim, shall for certain grete and reasonable causes in the same acte expressed, bee and stande feoffees of every parcel of the said honours, castellis, lordships, landes, tenementes, rentes, reversions, services, possessions and hereditamentes, with their membres and appurtenaunces, liberties, fraunchesies, iurisdiccions, privilegies, lawes, and custumes, for the paiement of our debtes, avauncement of our children nat preferred, dedes of charitie, and memorialx to be had and doon for us, to the laude and honour of God, and the welth of our soule, and the perfourmyng (fo. 10v) and execucion of al that by our laste Wille we have and shall elles ordeign and dispose to be doon with the same, as in the said acte it is more plainly expressed.

And forasmoche as diverse and the grettest nombre of the said persones named in the said acte, sithe the making of the same, be decessed, and the [94]casualtie of this world is suche,[94] and life is as uncertaine to suche as survyve, as was to theim nowe departed; and for that it was thought right, requisite and necessarie, for the better and more sure perfourmance and execucion of this our said Wille, to renewe and encrease a more nombre of honourable personages, to have ioinct and as full and plaine and large auctoritie and powair with the said personnes rehersed overliving, and to be with theim adioyned in the premisses and every parte therof, as the said persones soo decessed had. It was therefor afterward, by auctoritie of another parliament, holden at Westminster the xxv daie of the moneth of January, the xix[th] yere of our Reigne,[95] amonges other thinges enacted, ordeyned, and establisshed, by the advise of the Lordes spiritual and temporall, and the Comons in the same parliament assembled, that William, nowe Archebisshop of Caunterbury, Primat and Chaunceller of al England;[96] Thomas, Archebisshop of Yorke,

---

[94] 'casualtie . . . world' possibly written over an erasure.
[95] *Rot. Parl.* vi, 521–2.
[96] William Warham. Above, n. 27.

decessed;[97] Edward, Duke of Buckingham;[98] Richard, nowe Bisshop of Winchester;[99] William, Bisshop of Duresme, decessed;[100] William, Bisshop of Lincoln;[101] Edmond, Bisshop of Salesbury;[102] Geffrey, Bisshop of Chestre;[103] John, Abbot of Westminster;[104] Charles, Lord Herbert;[105] John Fyneux, knight;[106] Thomas Frowik, knight, decessed;[107] Geffrey Simeon, clerc, decessed;[108] William Barons, clerc, decessed;[109] Thomas Rowthale, clerc;[110] Edward Poynynges, knight;[111] Henry Vernon, knight;[112] John Mordaunt, decessed;[113] James Hobart;[114] Richard Emson,[115] Humfrey Conyngesby,[116] and John Kingesmele,[117] sergeauntes at the lawe, stande and bee seased ioinctely with the said persones surviving, of and in al the castellis, manours, lordeships, landes, tenementes, rentes, reversions, services, possessions and hereditamentes, with other premisses before remembred, and to bee and stande in like astate, auctoritie and powair, and under like maner, fourme, and condicion, of the premisses, and of every parte of theim (*fo. 11*) and to the same uses and ententes, as the said personnes nowe being dede, had, shuld or might have had in the premisses, or any parte therof, yf thei had contynued in plain life; and as if the said personnes nowe of newe named had had a ioinct estate, and had been ioinctly named, with the said survivours in the said acte, with the personnes that nowe survive. And over this it was enacted, ordeigned, and establsshed by

---

[97] Thomas Savage, dean of the Chapel of the Household 1489–92; bishop of Rochester (1492–6), London (1496–1501), York (1501–7); died 2/3 September 1507.

[98] Edward Stafford, duke of Buckingham. Afforded the status of an executor in the accounts for Henry VII's funeral, although not named as such in the will. He was, however, principal mourner.

[99] Richard Fox. Above, nn. 28, 73.

[100] William Sever, bishop of Carlisle (1495–1502), Durham (1502–1505); died 1505.

[101] William Smith, bishop of Coventry and Lichfield (1492–6), Lincoln (1496–1514). Moved from the service of Margaret Beaufort before 1485 to that of Henry VII; president of the council of Arthur, prince of Wales. Also an executor.

[102] Edmund Audley. Above, n. 74.

[103] Geoffrey Blythe, bishop of Coventry and Lichfield (1503–31).

[104] John Islip, abbot of Westminster (1500–32) and a central figure in the execution of the king's will in respect of the Lady chapel, Westminster.

[105] Above, n. 33.

[106] Above, n. 34.

[107] Thomas Frowick, Chief Justice Common Pleas (1502–6); died 7 October 1506.

[108] Geoffrey Simeon, dean of the Chapel of the Household (1501–8); died 20 August 1508.

[109] William Barons, Master of the Rolls (1502–4); bishop of London (1504–1505); died 10 October 1505.

[110] Thomas Ruthall. Above, n. 37.

[111] Edward Poynings. Best known as Deputy of Ireland 1494–6 under Henry, duke of York; successively lieutenant, constable, deputy warden and, in 1509, warden of Dover; became controller of the household to Henry VIII in 1509.

[112] Henry Vernon, a former councillor, controller and treasurer of Prince Arthur; died 13 April 1515.

[113] John Mordaunt, Chancellor of the Duchy of Lancaster (1503–4); died 5/6 September 1504.

[114] James Hobart, king's attorney (1486–1507) when replaced by John Ernley; died 24 February 1517.

[115] Above, n. 38.

[116] Humphrey Coningsby, king's serjeant-at-law; a colleague of Reynold Bray and closely involved in the legal processes concerning the king's chantry at Westminster. (Justice King's Bench 1509–33; died 1535.)

[117] John Kingsmill, king's serjeant-at-law; involved, although to a lesser extent than Coningsby, in the legal processes concerning the king's chantry. (Justice Common Pleas 1504–9; died 11 May 1509.)

the same auctorite, that what tyme and whansoevir that the said William, Archebisshop of Caunterbury; Thomas, Archebisshop of Yorke;[118] Richard, Bisshop of Winchestre; William, Bisshop of Duresme, decessed;[119] and Edmond, Bisshop of Salesbury,[120] or any of theim, hereafter shall fortune to decesse, or any of their sees to be voide by any other waies, that thei that soo shall succede theim or any of theim in the said sees and bisshoprikes, and every of theim, and their successours, and the successours of every of theim, shalhave successively for evir, like auctorite and powiar so to doo, ordre, execute and perfourme our said Wille, and every parte therof, ioinctely with the other that shal survive, as the same Bisshops shuld, ought, or might doo, in, to and for the same, yf thei had contynued in plain life, and as if the said persones that soo shal succede, had had their plain possessions in their said sees and bisshoprikkes, the tyme of the said xxv daie of the moneth of January, the xix[th] yere of our Reigne, and had been wel and perfitely named in the acte made for this entent in the said parliament holden the said xxv day of the said moneth of January. We wol that ymmediatly after our decesse our executours, without let or contradiccion of our said sone the Prince, our said feoffees, or any other persone, take, levie, and perceive al the rentis, prouffites, revenues and emolumentes comyng and growing of the said honours, castellis, lordships, landes, tenementes, rentes, reversions, services, possessions and hereditamentes, with the membres and appurtenaunces, liberties, fraunchesies, iurisdiccions, privileges, lawes, and custumes, or of any parcell of theim; and the same prouffites, rentes and emolumentes, over and above the *(fo. 11v)* charges of the lawe, and of right issuyng or paiable of the same, thei emploie and truly bestowe aboutes and upon the payeng of our debtes, restitucions of wronges, and the full and entiere perfourmyng and executing of this our present Wille, and every thing conteyned in the same.

The finisshing of the Church of the Newe College in Cambrige	Also where oure uncle of blissed memorie, King Henry the Sixt, to the laude of God, and thencreace of cunnyng and doctrine in the lawes of God, to the edificacion of our feith, and the weale of Cristen soules, founded and endued a famous college in our Universitie of Cambrige called the Newe College, and in the same beganne a grete and large churche, for divine service to bee saied and doon in the same by the fellowes of the said College: which church restith as yet unperfited and unfinisshed, litle or nothing wrought or doon thereupon syns the deceasse of our said uncle; saving that nowe of late, to the honour of God, the weale of our soule, and for the singuler trust that we have to the praiers of our said uncle, for the grete holynesse of life and vertue that he was of in erthe; we have at

---

[118] Savage died 2/3 September 1507; his successor, Christopher Bainbridge, was translated from Durham to York by papal provision 22 September 1508 and was included among the king's executors although his involvement was limited and, to a large extent, he was an absentee, dying in Rome in 1514.

[119] Sever was succeeded by Christopher Bainbridge after a vacancy of more than two years; but after Bainbridge's translation to York in September 1508 the see was again vacant, and remained so at the time of Henry VII's death. Thomas Ruthall, one of the king's executors, was provided to Durham 12 June 1509, receiving the temporalities on 3 July.

[120] It may be relevant that the bishop of Salisbury was the ordinary with responsibility for Windsor.

oure propre costes and charges caused workmen in a good nombre to worke upon the advauncement of the building of the same churche, intending by Goddes grace incessantly to contynue the same, til the said church be perfitely buylded and fully finisshed.

And for the more sure perfourmance and perfite finisshing of thesaid church, and other the premisses, and for the more redy paiement of the money necessarie in that behalve, we have delivered in redy money before the hande to the provost and scolers of oure said College, the some of five thousand poundes, as by writinges betwixt us and theim testifieng the same payment and receipte, and bering date at *Richemount*[121] the *laste day of Marche*[122] the xxiiij yere of our Reigne, it doth more plainly appere; the same v m^l li, and every parcell thereof, to be truly emploied and bestowed by the said provost, and other provostes of the said College for the tyme being, upon, to,[123] and for the buylding and finisshing of the said churche, from tyme to tyme as nede shal *(fo. 12)* require, by thadvise, comptrollement and oversight of suche personnes as we in our life, and our executours after our decesse, if it be not doon in our life, shall depute and assigne, without discontynuyng the said workes or any parte of theim, till thei bee fully finisshed, perfourmed, and accomplisshed, as farre as the said some of money of v m^l li shall extende. And that the said provost that nowe is, and that hereafter shalbe, bee accomptable for themployeng and bestowing of the said v m^l li upon the said workes, to us in our lif, and our executours after our decesse, for such parcell therof as shall reste not accompted for before that tyme, and not emploied nor bestowed upon the said workes, as often and whan soever we or they shall calle hym therunto, as it is more largely expressed in the said indentures. And in case thesaid v m^l li shal not suffice for perfourmance of[124] accomplisshment of the said werkes and every parcell of theim, and that thei be not perfitely finisshed by us in our daies, we than wol that oure executours from tyme to tyme, as necessite shal require, deliver to the said provost for the tyme being asmoch money above the said v m^l li as shall suffice for the perfite finisshing and perfourming of the said workes, and every parte of theim, the same money to be emploied and bestowed upon the perfite finisshing and perfourmyng of thesaid workes by thesaid provost for the tyme being, by the foresaid advise, oversight, comptrollement and accompte, without desisting or discontynueng the same werkes in any wise, till thei, and every parcell of theim, as before is saied, be fully and perfitely accomplisshed and perfourmed, in maner and fourme before rehersed. And that thesaid provost for the tyme being, for such somes of money as shalbe delivered to hym by our executours to the entente above rehersed, bee accomptable to theim as often and whansoevir thei shal require.[125]

---

121 Inserted into blank left in text. Similarly inserted in BL Add. MS 36273B.
122 'last day of marche' inserted into blank left in text. Similarly inserted in BL Add. MS 36273B. For the indenture, R. Willis and J. Willis Clark, *Architectural History of the University of Cambridge*, Cambridge 1886, i, 476–9; Colvin, *HKW* iii, 188–9.
123 'to' inserted with caret.
124 *Sic.* [*rectius* ?and].
125 For the later history of the building works, Willis and Clark, *Architectural History* i, 478–503, 608–19;

The bequest for the finisshing of the Church of Westminster	Also we geve and bequeith to the perfourmyng and finisshing of the newe church of the monastery of Saint Petre of Westminster, wherin we received our holie coronacion and inunccion, five hundreth markes. *(fo. 12v)*
The bequeste to the Freres Observauntes	Also where we alwaies have had a speciall confidence and truste in the devoute praiers of the Freres Observauntes of this our Royaume, for our good and prosperous estate in this present life, and that we be veray desirous to have the same for the weale of our soule, and the remission of our synnes, after our decesse: to thentent they may have the better cause, and the more largely bee bounden hertely and devoutely soo to doo, we wol that our executours bestowe and emploi to the behove of our house of the freres of Grenewich, being of our foundacion, for the closing of their gardyne and orcharde with a brikewall, or aboutes other thinges as by the fader and the rulers of the said House shalbe thought moost consonant to the laude of God, helth of our soule, and the weale of thesaid House and freres, two hundreth poundes. And soo to the house of Richemount being in likewise of oure foundacion, two hundreth poundes. And to every of the houses of the said Observauntes of Caunterbury, Suthampton and Newe Castell, c marces. The same somes of money to be emploied and bestowed by our said executours upon such thinges as by the faders and rulers of thesaid houses shalbe thought moost consonant to the laude of God, helth of our soule, and the weal of the said houses and freres. And also to either of the Chartrehouses of London and Shene, fourty poundes.[126]

And over this, where as the said Freres Observauntes have no possessions, nor other goodes moevables nor immovables, wherewith to susteigne and maynteigne neither their lives with mete, drinke and clothing, nor for the renewing of their bookes, chalices, vestimentes, and other ornamentes necessarie and convenient for the service of God, nor for the reparacions of their churches and houses, but oonly of the almons, devocion and charite of Christian people, whereby though the same freres be some tymes and for the more partie sufficiently after their necessite succoured, releved and purveied: yet know we experimently by the secrete conversacion that we have had with thesaid freres, that had ne been other privie souccours and releves, diverse *(fo. 13)* tymes made to theim in their extreme [nedes],[127] thei had diverse and many tymes be in manifest perill of ruyne, and daungier of perdicion for lack of fode. The whiche inconveniencies and daungiers we, for our long contynued devocion towardes Saint Fraunces their patrone, and oure charitie towardes thordre of the said freres, inwardly considering, and gretely desiring in due tyme to provide the remedie, wol and ordeigne that our executours within vj monethes next after our deceasse at the farrest, and without lengar delaie, committe and betake to the priours, dean', conventes and chapitre hereafter named the sommes hereafter

---

Colvin, *HKW* iii, 189–95; see also F. Woodman, *The Architectural History of King's College Chapel*, London 1986, *passim*.

[126] For Henry VII and the Carthusians see N. Beckett, 'Henry VII and Sheen Charterhouse', *Reign of Henry VII*, 117–32; for the Observants, A.G. Little, 'Introduction of the Observant Friars into England', *Proceedings of the British Academy* 10, 1921–3, 458–65; Colvin, *HKW* iii, 196.

[127] MS damaged.

ensuyng, by indentures in due fourme to be made betwixt our said executours, and the same priours, dean', conventes and chapitre, and to thuse hereafter also folowing: that is to saie, that our said executours, in maner and fourme beforesaied, deliver to the priour of Caunterbury for the tyme being, two hundreth poundes, to thuse and behouf of the convent of the Freres Observauntes of the same Caunterbury; to the priour of the Chartrehouse of London, two hundreth poundes, to thuse and behove of the convent of Freres Observauntes of Grenewich; to the priour of the Chartrehouse of the Shene, five hundreth marces, to thuse and behove of the convent of the Freres Observauntes of Richemount; to the priour of the cathedral churche of St Saint Swithin of Winton', cc li, to thuse and behove of the convent of the Freres Observauntes of Suthampton'; to the priour of the cathedral church of Saint Cuthbert of Duresme, cc li, to thuse and behouf of the said Freres Observauntes of Newe Castell; and to the dean and chanons of the cathedral church of Lincoln, cc li, to the use and behove of the convent that by our souccour and aide is newly begoune in the towne of Newark, in our countie of Notingham.[128] The same somes, and every parcell of theim, to bee delivered by the said priours, dean, conventes and chapitre to thuse of the said conventes of Freres as before is saied, to such persones, at such tymes, and by (fo. 13v) such parcellis, and in suche maner and fourme, as to the Provincial of the said Freres, and wardeyn of the convent that shall nede it for the tyme being, shalbe thought moost expedient, and as thesaid Provincial and wardeyn shall require and desire; the same somes of money to be emploied to thesaid behove, and to such uses, as to the same Provinciall and convent shalbe thought moost necessarie, and to noon other.

And that our said executours, at the deliveraunce of the said somes of money, require and charge theim to have our soule contynuelly remembred in their devoute praiers, observaunces and ceremonies, soo that by the great mercy of our Salviour it may be partener of thesame. And that the said two houses of Richemount and Grenewiche cause to be saied for the remission of our synnes, and the weale of our soule, D masses; and the said iiij houses of Caunterbury, Suthampton, Newcastell and Newarke, every of theim, ccc masses; and either of the said Chartirhouses cc masses; the same masses to bee hooly saied by the brederne of thesame houses, assone as thei shall mowe goodly and conveniently doo aftre oure deceasse.

The garnisshing of the aultier within the Kinges grate	Also we wol that our executours, except it bee perfourmed by oureself in our life, cause to be made for the overparte of the aulter within the grate of our tombe a table of the lenght of the same aultre, and half a fote longer at either ende of the same, and v fote of height with the border, and that in the myddes of the overhalf of the same table, bee made the ymages of the Crucifixe, Mary, and John, in maner accustumed; and upon both sides of theim, be made asmany of the ymagies of our said advouries as the said table wol receive; and under the said Crucifixe, and ymages of Marie and John, and other advouries, bee made the xij Apostels. All the said

---

[128] These legacies were paid in instalments of 500 marks, PRO, E 36/214, p. 348; E 36/215, p. 21; *L&P Henry VIII*, I pt i, 58, 115. For the site at Newark, *CPR 1494–1509*, 567–8.

table, Crucifixe, Mary, John, and other ymages of our advouries and xij Apostellis, to be of tymbre, covered and wrought with plate of fyne golde. (*fo. 14*)

The bequeste of the same aultier Also we geve and bequethe to the aulter within the grate of our said tombe our grete pece of the Holie Crosse, which, by the high provision of our Lord God, was conveied, brought, and delivered to us from the Isle of Cyo[129] in Grece; set in gold; and garnisshed with perles and precious stones; and also the preciouse relique of oon of the legges of Saint George, set in silver parcell gilte, which came to the handes of our broder and cousyn Loys of Fraunce, the tyme that he wan and recovered the citie of Millein, and geven and sent to us by oure cousyne the Cardinal of Amboys, [Legate][130] in Fraunce: the which pece[131] of the Holie Crosse, and leg of Saincte [George][132], we wol be set upon the said aulter, for the garnisshing of thesame, upon al principal and solempne festes, and al other festes, aftour the discrecion of oure chauntery preistes singing for us at the same aulter.[133]

Also we geve and bequeth to the same aulter, if it be not doon by our self in our life, oon masse booke hande writen; iij sutes of aultre clothes; iij paire of vestementes; a chales of gold of the value of oon hundreth marces; a chalece of silver and gilt of xx[ti] unces; two paire of cruettes silver and gilt of xx unces; two candilstikkes silver and gilte of c unces; and other two candilstikkes silver and gilt of lx unces; and iij corporaces with their cases; vj ymages, oon of Our Lady, a nother of Saint John Evaungelist, Saint John Baptist, Saint Edward, Saint Jerome, and Saint Fraunceys, every of theim of silver and gilte, of the value of xx[ti] markes; and oon paire of basons silver and gilt of the same value; a bell of silver and gilte of the value of iij li vi s viii d, and a pax brede of silver and gilte, of the value of iiij marces.

The bequest to the high aultier within the Kinges Chapell Also we bequethe to the high aultre within our said chapell of Our Lady, called Our Lady aultre, the grettest ymage of Our Lady that we nowe have in our Juelhouse,[134] and a crosse of plate of gold upon tymber, to the value of c li. And to every other aulter being within our said chapell (*fo. 14v*) of Our Lady, bee thei of the sides of the same, or in any other place within the compasse of the same, two sutes of aultier clothes, two peire of vestimentes, two corporaces with their cases; oon masse booke; oon chalice of silver and gilte, oon peire of cruettes silver and gilte, oon belle silver and gilte, and two peire of candilstikkes silver and gilte, oon of theim for the high aulter, and thoder for the aulter of our said uncle of blessed memorie King Henry the vj[th]. And we wol that the said vestiments, aultre clothes, and other ornamentes of our said aultres, bee soo

---

[129] Chios, a Genoese possession.
[130] MS damaged. Supplied from Astle.
[131] 'pece' inserted with caret.
[132] MS damaged. Supplied from Astle.
[133] For St George, *Memorials of King Henry VII*, ed. J. Gairdner, Rolls Series 1858, 82–3; wrongly ascribed by the Great Chronicle to Maximilian. George d'Amboise ruled Milan for Louis XII for three years after its recapture in 1500 and was proxy for its investiture to Louis by Maximilian in 1505. See also above, 67.
[134] Estimated in 1540 at 422½oz, above, 67.

embrowdred and wrought w[ith][135] our armes and cognisaunces, that thei may by the same bee knowe[n of our][136] gifte and bequeste. And as for the price and value of theim, our [mynde i]s,[137] that thei bee of suche as apperteigne to the gifte of a Prince; and therfor we wol that our executours, in that partie, have a special regarde and consideracion to the lawde of God, and the welthe of our soule, and oure honour Roial. Savyng alweies, that if we in our daies by our life provide the said vestimentes and ornamentes, that then our executours bee not in any wise charged with theim after our deceasse.

An Image of the King to be made and sette upon Sainct Edwardes Shryne

Also we wol that our executours, yf it be nat doon by our self in our life, cause to bee made an ymage of a king, representing our owen persone. The same ymage to be of tymber, covered and wrought accordingly with plate of fyne gold, in maner of an armed man; and upon the same armour, a coote armour of our armes of England and of Fraunce enameled, with a swerd and spurres accordinly.[138] And the same ymage to knele upon a table of silver and gilte, and holding betwixt his handes the crowne which it pleased God to geve us, with the victorie of our ennemye at our furst felde. The which ymage and crowne, we geve and bequethe to Almighty God, our blissed Lady Saint Mary, and Saint Edward, King and Confessour; and the same ymage and crowne in the fourme afore rehersed we wol be set upon, and in the myddes of, the creste of the shryne of Saint Edward, King, in suche a place as by us in our life, or by our executours *(fo. 15)* after our deceasse, shalbe thought moost convenient and honourable. And we wol that our said ymage be above the kne of the height of thre fote, soo that the hede and half the breste of our said ymage may clierly appere above and over the said crowne; and that upon booth sides of thesaid table be a convenient brode border; and in the same be graven and writen with large lettres, blakenameled, thies wordes **REX HENRICUS SEPTIMUS.**[139]

The bequest to the College of Wyndesore

Also we geve and bequethe to Almighty God, our Lady his blessed Moder, and Saint George, within oure college of Windesore, and to the Dean and chanons of the same College that nowe be, and that hereafter shalbe, for a perpetuel memorie there to remaigne while the world shal endure, and to be set upon the high aulter of the said College, at the daies of solempne festes, and such other tymes as the Deane and chanons of our said College shall thinke convenient and honourable, a grete ymage of Saint George, of gold, peysing ccxl unces, garnisshed with rubies, perles, saphires, diamondes, and other stones, the which ymage is now in our Juell house.

---

[135] MS damaged.

[136] MS damaged.

[137] MS damaged. Supplied from Astle. There is every reason to suppose that these various gifts of vestments, books and plate were effected; incomplete lists of both plate and vestments may be identified in the imperfect dissolution inventory (which largely omits the goods of the chapel) and it seems possible that some may subsequently have passed to the direct ownership of Henry VIII, although it would be unwise to assume universal Westminster origin simply on the evidence of dynastic badges mentioned in the inventories of that king's goods. PRO, LR 2/111, fos. 15, 47, 54, 55.

[138] *Sic.*

[139] For a discussion of the crown of Bosworth, M.K. Jones, *Bosworth 1485, Psychology of a Battle*, Stroud 2002, 22, 158–60, 170–3. For the kneeling effigy, whether or no it was made in the precise manner specified, Lindley, *Gothic to Renaissance*, 57–8. See also below, n. 141.

The bequeste to the monastery of Westminster	Also we bequethe and geve to God and Saint Petre, and to thabbot, priour and convent of our monastery of Westminster that nowe bee, and that hereafter shalbe, for a perpetuell memorie, there to remaigne, while the world shal endure, the hoole sute of vestimentes and coopes of clothe of gold tissue, wrought with our badgieus of rede roses and poortcoleys, the which we of late at our propre costes and charges caused to be made, bought and provided at Florence in Ittalie: that is to saie, the hoole vestementes for the preist, the deacon and subdeacon, and xxix copes of the same clothe and worke.[140]
A image of the King to be made and sette at Saint Thomas shryne at Caunterbury	Also, if it be nat perfourmed by our self in oure life, we wol that our executours cause an ymage of silver and gilt, of like faction and weight, as is the ymage that we have caused to bee made to be offred and sette before Our Lady at Walsingham, to be made with this scripture *(fo. 15v)* SANCTE THOMA, INTERCEDE PRO ME. The same image for a perpetuell memorie to bee made, offred and sette, before Saincte Thomas of Caunturbury, in the metropolitan churche of Caunterbury, in suche place as by us in our life, or by our executours after oure deceasse, shalbe thought moost convenient and honourable, and as nigh to the shrine of Sainct Thomas as may bee: and that upon booth the sides of the table wherupon our said ymage shal knele be a brode border; and in the same graven and writen with large lettres, blake enameled, thies wordes REX HENRICUS SEPTIMUS.[141]
The bequeste of certaine Chalices and Pixes for the holie Sacrament	Item, forasmoche as we have often and many tymes, to our inwarde regrete and displeasure, seen at oure Jen[142] in diverse and many churches of oure Reame, the Holie Sacrament of the aulter kept in ful simple and inhonest pixes, specially pixes of copre and tymbre, we have appointed and commaunded the Tresourer of our Chambre,[143] and Maistre of our Juelhous,[144] to cause to be made furthwith pixes of silver and gilte, in a greate nombre, for the keping of the Holie Sacrament of thaultre, after the faction of a pixe that we have caused to be delivered to theim. Every of the said pixes to be of the value of iiij li, garnisshed with our armes, and rede roses and poortcolis crowned: of the which pixes [we][145] wol, that to the laude and service of God, thonour of the Holie Sacrament of thaultre, the weale of our soule, and for a perpetuell memorie of us, every house of the iiij ordres of freres, and in likewise every parisshe church within this our

---

[140] L. Monnas, 'New documents for the vestments of Henry VII at Stonyhurst College', *Burlington Magazine*, May 1989, 345–9. Even in its much altered state, the one surviving cope, on display in 2002 in the British galleries of the Victoria and Albert Museum, can only be described as breathtaking.

[141] The absence of the executors' accounts means that it is not known whether the Canterbury effigy was ever made: it is not traceable in the Dissolution inventories, but I have not examined the local accounts which might yield incidental clues. However, In July and November 1507 John Arnolde, goldsmith, was paid £14 toward making of the king's image and harness; PRO, E 36/214, fos. 85v, 103. I am indebted to Christopher Wilson for reminding me of these references. If this can be interpreted as the Walsingham image, then it makes it more likely that the payment of 16 April 1509, plate and bullion handed via Robert Fenrother, one of the masters of the Mint, to John of Utrecht (VanUtrike) to make the king's harness 'in silver' on 16 April 1509, PRO, E 36/214, p. 344, was for one of the votive images rather than for use in the exequies.

[142] Thus in both PRO, E 23/3 and BL Add. MS 36273B. Eyes.

[143] John Heron.

[144] Henry Wyatt.

[145] MS damaged.

THE LAST WILL OF HENRY VII 135

Reame, not having a pixe, nor noon other honest vessell of silver and gilte, nor of silver ungilted, for the keping of the said Holy Sacrament, have of our gifte in our life oon of the said pixes, assone and spedely as goodly may be doon. And if this be nat perfourmed in parte or in all in our lif, we then wol, that that shall rest not perfourmed in our life, bee perfourmed by our executours within one yere at the farrest next after our decesse.[146] *(fo. 16)*

The bequest for the mariage of my Ladye Mary the Kinges doughter

Also where as for the more assured conservacion and encreace of the state, and honour of us, our heires and successours, and of our Reame, and thadvauncement of the prosperitie, utilitie and comoditie of our subgiettes, it is by our conducte and moyne couvenaunted, accorded and concluded, betwixt us on the oon partie, and the moost sacrede Prince Maximilian, elect Emperour, aswel for hymself and in his owen name, and as then King of Romains, as also as graundfader, tutor and governour of the persone, landes, and contreis, of the right high and mightie Prince Charles, Prince of Spayne, Archiduc of Austrich, Duc of Burgoyne, Braban', etc, and Counte of Flaundres, etc, his nepheu, and the same Charles Prince of Spayne, by thassent of his said tutour, and the right noble Princesse the Lady Margarete, Duchesse of Savoie, awnte to the said Prince, on thoder partie, for mariage by Goddes grace to be had, and solempnely in the face of the Churche to be contracted, betwixt the said Prince of Spaine, and oure moost dere doughter the Lady Mary, at suche tyme as thesaid Prince of Spaine shalbe of such perfite and full age, as the lawes of the Churche require for that pourpose, under such maner and fourme, and in suche tyme and place, and with suche condicions, as in the treatie therupon passed and concluded betwixt the commissioners of bothe sides, and afterwarde aswel by us as by the said Emperour, Prince of Spayne and Duchesse, by our and their several lettres patentes, under our and their grete seales, subscribed with our and their handes, ratified and confermed, it appereth more ample and at lenght.[147] According whereunto spowselles by wordes of the present requisite, due and convenient in that behalve, by our moynes, and at our right grete costes and charges, have been solempnely and openly contracted betwixt the said Prince of Castell, by his proctour[148] in that partie sufficiently constituted, ordeigned and deputed, on the oon partie, and our said doughter in her persone on thoder partie, in our manour of Richemount, the [——][149] daie of the moneth of Decembre, in the xxiiij yere *(fo. 16v)* of our reigne, our self in our persone, and thambassadours of the said Prince of Castell, with many other of the moost honourable lordes spirituall and temporall, ladies, and other nobles of our royaume in a grete nombre then being present, with diverse and many moost solempne and honourable justes, tourneys, festes, and other triumphes and ceremonies, to such an acte

---

[146] Above, 106.
[147] *Foedera* xiii, 171–215, 219–32, 236–9.
[148] John, Lord Berghes, Maximilian's Chamberlain.
[149] Blank in text. Also blank in BL MS Add. 36273B. The proxy marriage had taken place on 17 December 1508.

convenient and requisite, ensuyng the said contracte of espowsellis, and by a long space of tyme contynuyng and enduring.[150]

And where as we, for the dote and mariage of our said doughter, over and above the costes of her traduccion into the parties of Flaundres, and furnisshing of plate and other her arraiment for persone, juelxs, and garnisshing of her chambre, which wol extende to no litle some nor charge, must paie and content to the said Prince of Spaine thesome of fifty thousand poundes in redy money, at certaine termes expressed in the said treatie; for the which paiement, by thadvise of our Counsel, we have by our lettres under our grete seale, subscribed with our hande, bounden our self, our heires and successours, reames, landes, countreis, and al other goodes moevable and imovable, and in like wise the persones and goodes of all and every our subgettes, movables and imoevables, where soever thei shalbe founden; and that in likewise the maire and felliship of our Staple of Calais have, at our desire, bounden theim and their successours for the paiement of the said some;[151] we undoubtedly truste and have our full confidence, that the thre estates of our Reame, according to the lawes and aunciient custumes provided, and inviolably tyme oute of mynde observed and used, for the mariage of the kinges children of the Realme, shal and wol by auctoritie of Parliament, sufficiently ordeyne and provide for the full paiement and contentacion of thesaid LM^l li to the said Prince of Spayne, according to the pourpourte of thesaid treatie; and see us and our said Staple discharged of the said bandes and obligacions. Considering specially, that the perfection of the said mariage shall (fo. 17) redounde to the grettest honour, suertie, tranquillitie, reste, peace, proufitte and commoditie, universally and particularly, of our said Reame and subgettes, and that thei and their goodes, by our said bande as before is saied, stande bounden for the same.

And in case it soo fortune, as God defende, that the said mariage, by the dethe of the said Prince of Castile, or by any other chaunce or fortune whatsoever it be, take not effect, but be uttrely dissolve and breke, or that our said doughter be nat maried by us in our life, nor after the same have sufficient provision for her dote and mariage by the said thre estates; we then wol that our said doughter Mary have for her mariage, fifty thousand poundes, paiable of our goodes, yf somoch remaigne after the perfourmance of such thinges and charges as in this our Wille is above and before expressed and specified. Which thinges and chargies, we wol furst and before al other matiers be doon and perfourmed, of and with our said goodes as farre as thei wol extende; and that doon and fully perfourmed, yf any thing then remayne of our said goodes, we wol then that they for

---

[150] Peter Carmeliano's narrative account was published in both English and Latin by Richard Pynson at the king's command (and a Latin text was delivered to King Ferdinand in Spain), 'The Spousells' of the Princess Mary, ed. J. Gairdner, 1893, own pagination 1–35, *Camden Miscellany Vol. ix*, Camden Society, new ser., liii, 1895; *Memorials of King Henry VII*, 438.

[151] Bonds of Henry VII and of the Staple guaranteeing the dowry, PRO, E 30/1740, 1728; bonds were also taken from the king, Prince Henry, the earls of Arundel and Oxford, and the mayors and governing bodies of twelve major trading towns, including London, in case the king should raise any difficulty to prevent the marriage, and as security for the specified penalty of 250,000 crowns, PRO, E 30/1729–1733.

the payment of the said LM^l li, take of the said goodes asfarre as thei wol goo. And if the said goodes wol not perfourme the said L m^l li, we then wol that that lakketh and cannot be levied of our said goodes for the paiement of the said LM^l li bee levied of the said rentes, revenues, prouffites and emolumentes, by the handes of our executours, soo and in noon other wise, that in her said mariage she be ruled and ordred by thadvise and consent of our said sone the Prince, his counsaile, and our said executours; and soo that she be maried to some noble prince out of this our Reame.

The namyng of thexecutours of this Testament

And for the perfite execution of this oure laste Wille and Testament, we make our derrest and moost entierly beloved moder, Margarete, Countesse of Richemount,[152] the moost Reverend fader in God Christofer, Archebisshop of Yorke; the Reverend faders in God Richard, Bisshop of *(fo. 17v)* Winchestre, Richard, Bisshop of London, Edmond, Bisshop of Sarum, William, Bisshop of Lincoln, John Bisshop of Rouchestre;[153] our right trusty and right welbiloved cousins Thomas, Erle of Arundel and Thomas, Erle of Surrey, our Tresourer generall; our right trusty and welbiloved counsaillours Sir Charles Somerset, knight, Lord Herbert, our Chambrelaine; Sir John Fyneux, knight, chief Justice of oure Benche; Sir Robert Rede, knight, chief Justice of oure Common place; Maistre John Yong, Maistre of the Rolles of our Chauncery; Sir Thomas Lovell, knight, Tresourer of our Housholde; Maistre Thomas Rowthale, oure Secretarie; Sir Richard Emson, knight, Chaunceller of oure Duchie of Lancastrie; Sir John Cutte, knight, our Undertresorer general;[154] and Edmond Dudley, squier, our executours: praying and requiring, and also straitly charging theim, to put theim in their uttermoste devoirs, wele and truly in al thinges in maner and fourme afore declared, to execute and perfourme this oure laste Wille and Testament, as our special truste is in theim, and as thei wol therefor aunswere and discharge us and our soule before God.

Also we wol, that tharchebisshop of Caunterbury for the tyme being, whom we hereafter appointe to be supervisour of this our Wille and Testament, and xij of our said executours, that is to saie, the said Bisshops of Winchestre, London and Rouchestre; Charles Somerset, Lord Herbert; the said two chief Justices; the Maistre of the Rolles; Sir Thomas Lovell our Secretarie;[155] Sir Richard Emson; and Edmond Dudley, or vij of theim, yerely, in the iiij termes of the yere, as often as thei conveniently may, and as the case and necessitie shal require, and at the leest in every terme, to contynue their said assemble by the space of xij daies, in some certain place suche as thei

---

[152] Margaret Beaufort, countess of Richmond. Took precedence among the executors in the month after Henry VII's death; but died 29 June 1509.

[153] Christopher Bainbridge, archbishop of York; Richard Fox, bishop of Winchester; Richard Fitzjames, bishop of London; Edmund Audley, bishop of Salisbury; William Smith, bishop of Lincoln; John Fisher, bishop of Rochester. There is an overlap with the personnel of the commission for redress, and with the feoffees of 1504.

[154] John Cutte, undertreasurer of the Exchequer since 1505, and before that receiver-general of the Duchy of Lancaster (1492–1505) had been a close colleague of Reynold Bray. The few surviving warrants suggest that he was one of the core administrative officers for the execution of the will.

[155] *Sic*: copyist's error through homoeoteleuton for Sir Thomas Lovell, Treasurer of the Household and king's councillor, and Thomas Ruthall, the king's secretary. So also in BL MS Add. 36273B.

shal lust to appointe in our citie of London, or nigh aboutes the same, there to commoun, treate, and see, what then shall reste to be doon for thaccomplisshement of this our Wille, and plenarye *(fo. 18)* execucion of the same; and also to make a cliere declaracion what is received, what is paied, and what is owing, of the said issues, proffites and emolumentes; and the same declaracion yerely at every tyme that thei shal assemble theim togeders, to shewe to tharchebisshop of Caunterbury for the tyme being. For the tyme of which their attendaunces and businesses, we wol thei have for their costs, vj li xiij s iiij d for every daie that thei shall for the said businesse make and kepe thesaid assemble; wherof we wol thesaid Archebisshop of Caunterbury have for every daie that he shalbe present and attending to and in the said assemble, xx s; and the remanent therof to bee distributed amonges suche and asmany of our said executours, as shalbe continuelly present, and kepe the said assembles and every daie of theim, without departing thens, till thei by their comune assent and ordenaunce departe thens togeders.

| The namyng of the Surveiour of this Testament | And over this, we ordeigne and make the said Archebisshop of Caunterbury for the tyme being surveiour of this our laste Wille and Testament.[156] Willing and charging our said executours, specially the xij superattenders and every of theim, that in every matier of charge and doubte thei aske and demaunde his advise and counsaile. |

And if it fortune, that for any thing touching thexecucion of this oure Wille or any parte therof, there falle any diverse opinions, variaunces, and discordes, betwix our said feoffees, or executours, or feoffees and executours, or feoffee and feoffee, or executour and executour, we eveg[156A] then, and by theis presentes graunte to the said Archebisshop, plaine powiar and ful auctoritie; and finally we wol, that he as umpier have full powiar and auctoritie to calle, and to take unto hym, viij, or vj at the leest, of suche of our said feoffees and executours as he shall finde best disposed to the perfourmyng of our said Wille, wherewith we charge his conscience before God. And by their advises and assentes to make finall conclusion and determinacion in such matier or matiers, as the said variaunce or debate rose upon, and was moeved for; *(fo. 18v)* soo that according to his and their conclusion and determinacion, the said matiers bee determined, and the said debates utterly ceasse, in all thinges touching our feoffament or Wille.

And for the grete attendaunces, peynes, and labours, which we knowe wele our said supervisour and executours, specially the said xij principal superattenders, must have and susteigne in this behalf, we, in consideracion of the same, over and above suche somes of money as we have above assigned for their attendaunces at the termes, bequethe to our said supervisour oon hundreth poundes; and to every of our said executours taking upon hym by auctoritie of thordinarie, thadministracion and execucion of this our laste Wille and Testament, and gevyng[157] his attendaunce as before is saied, c li in redie money. The same c li to be paied in maner and fourme folowing: that is to saie, to the said Archebisshop of Caunterbury,

---

[156] William Warham.
[156A] MS 'yeve', i.e. vestigial yogh.
[157] MS 'yevyng', i.e. vestigial yogh.

and to every of our said executours gevyng his and their attendaunces as before is saied, fifty markes at thende of every halfe yere, accompted from the daie of our deceasse, till the said c li be fully contented and paied. And at suche tyme as our said Testament and laste Wille shalbe in every pointe and thing conteigned in the same fully executed and perfitely ended, we wolle, that then aswel the said Archebisshop, as our said executours, gevyng his and their attendaunces, as before is saied, have every of theim cc li, and to every of the remanent of our said executours, not named ner appointed for any of the said xij superattenders, we geve and bequethe c li. The same to be paied whan our said Wille, as before is saied, shalbe fully executed and perfitely perfourmed.

The residue of our chatellis, goods and debtes, not geven, nor bequethed, nor disposed to be employed nor bestowed, by this our laste Wille and Testament whatsoevir thei be, or in whose handes or custodie they remaigne, and to us or to any other persone or persones to our use apperteynyng, due, or belonging; we wol, that our said executours dispose (*fo. 19*) emploie and bestowe, to and upon suche uses, workes, and dedes of merite, almose, pitie and charite, and suche as may serve for the better execucion of this our laste Wille and Testament, as to theym after their discrecions shalbe thought moost plaisaunt and acceptable to God, [mo]ost[158] expedient for the redempcion and remission of our synnes, [and moost hol]some[159] and meritoriouse for our soule, wherewith we estraictely [charge thei]m,[160] their saules and consciences, as thei wol for the same ac[compte][161] and answere before God, at his h[igh daie o]f[162] Jugement.

In testimonye of all which premisses, and of every of theim, and also in witteness that thies presentes be our laste Wille and Testament, we have comaunded and caused and by warant of thies presentes, signed with oure signe manuell, wol and comaunde, aswel our privy seale, as our signet, remaynyng in the keping of our Secretary, and our privie signet of the eguell remaynyng in our owen keping, as also our g[rete sea]le,[163] to be put to thies said presentes. Dated at *Caunterbury*[164] the [x[th]][165] day of *Aprill*,[166] the xxiiij yere of our reigne.[167]

Yong[168]

H R

Irrotulatur[169]

---

[158] Document damaged: text supplied from Astle.
[159] Document damaged: text supplied from Astle.
[160] Document damaged: text supplied from Astle.
[161] Document damaged: text supplied from Astle.
[162] Document damaged: text supplied from Astle.
[163] Document damaged: text supplied from Astle.
[164] Insertion into space left in text.
[165] Document damaged: text supplied from Astle; but agrees with BL MS Add. 36273B.
[166] Insertion into space left in text.
[167] The dating clause 'at Caunterbury . . . our reigne' appears to be an addition in BL MS Add. 36273B.
[168] John Yonge, Master of the Rolls.
[169] The enrolment is no longer among the records of Chancery, housed in the Public Record Office. For the suggestion that it still survives and may be identified as BL MS Add. 36273B, based on hand-

(fos. 19v – 20) [*Blank*]

(fo. 20v) The testament of Kyng Henry the vij[170]

SEALS: –

(i) Double cord, plaited in green and white, with pendant Great Seal in natural wax.
(ii) Double cord, plaited in green and white, with pendant seals in red wax:
   (a) *Obverse*: Privy Seal [*damaged*]
   (b) *Reverse*: Signet seal[171]
(iii) Double cord [*Empty*]

---

writing and the insertion of dates in blanks left in the text, see above, 0000. As such the roll commands an authority which has not previously been recognised.

[170] Fo. 20v written in a hand of the mid-sixteenth century.
[171] Impression includes clear fingerprint. All three seals are illustrated in S.B. Chrimes, *Henry VII*, London 1972, 144, but the captions for the Privy and Great Seals (the latter from a British Library example) have been reversed. The signet of the eagle is missing.

The Functional Design of Henry VII's Chapel: a Reconstruction

CHRISTOPHER WILSON

ON 5 JULY 1508, in the course of a visit to Westminster Abbey by Edward Stafford, third duke of Buckingham, the sum of 8d was given 'to the keeper of the King's new chapel there'.[1] The purpose of this payment was not spelled out by the duke's cofferer, in whose accounts it appears, but the most likely explanation for it must surely be that the duke had succeeded in taking a look inside the great chapel whose building at the east end of the abbey church had been in progress during the previous five and a half years. If that is indeed what happened, the record of the keeper's gratuity assumes great importance on several counts. It becomes the earliest known evidence that the masonry begun in January 1503 was complete or nearly complete; it indicates that the building had already begun to acquire the reputation of a sight worth seeking out; and its description of the chapel as the king's suggests that this uniquely splendid structure was generally thought of as a product of the monarch's personal patronage and not simply as the Lady chapel of the abbey.[2]

On 12 July 1559, fifty-one years and one week after Buckingham's visit, the monastery of Westminster was definitively suppressed. The departure of the monks and the re-establishment of protestantism signalled the end of the Lady chapel's liturgical and devotional life. Henceforth the only permissible responses to the building would be ones already implicit in Buckingham's desire to view it and in the wording of the record of his tip to the keeper, namely admiration for its architecture and recognition

---

[1] *L&P Henry VIII* iii, pt i, 1867, 497. This reference appears not to have been applied to the building chronology of the chapel until now. The value of the gratuity was not totally insignificant. Compare, for example, the 8d paid to each priest-monk of Westminster attending the weekly obits of Henry VII, whose main components were three services over two days, and the 6d per day taken by an embroiderer mending a chasuble belonging to Henry VII's chantry in 1518–19; WAM 24236, 24248. For granting me full access to Henry VII's chapel during and immediately after its restoration in 1994–5, I am greatly indebted to the Dean and Chapter of Westminster, to their former Surveyor, Donald Buttress, and to Messrs Rattee and Kett, contractors for the restoration. I also wish to record my thanks to Roger Bowers and Barbara Harvey, who offered detailed and extremely helpful comments on an earlier draft of this paper, and to Nigel Ramsay, who drew my attention to Thomas Gardiner's history of England and its unique record of the dedication date of the chapel.

[2] Unsurprisingly, the building is referred to as 'the kinges new chapell' in the first and in many of the subsequent payments for its construction entered in Henry VII's own chamber accounts; BL Add. MS 59899, fo. 1 (October 1502) and *passim*; PRO, E 36/214, *passim*.

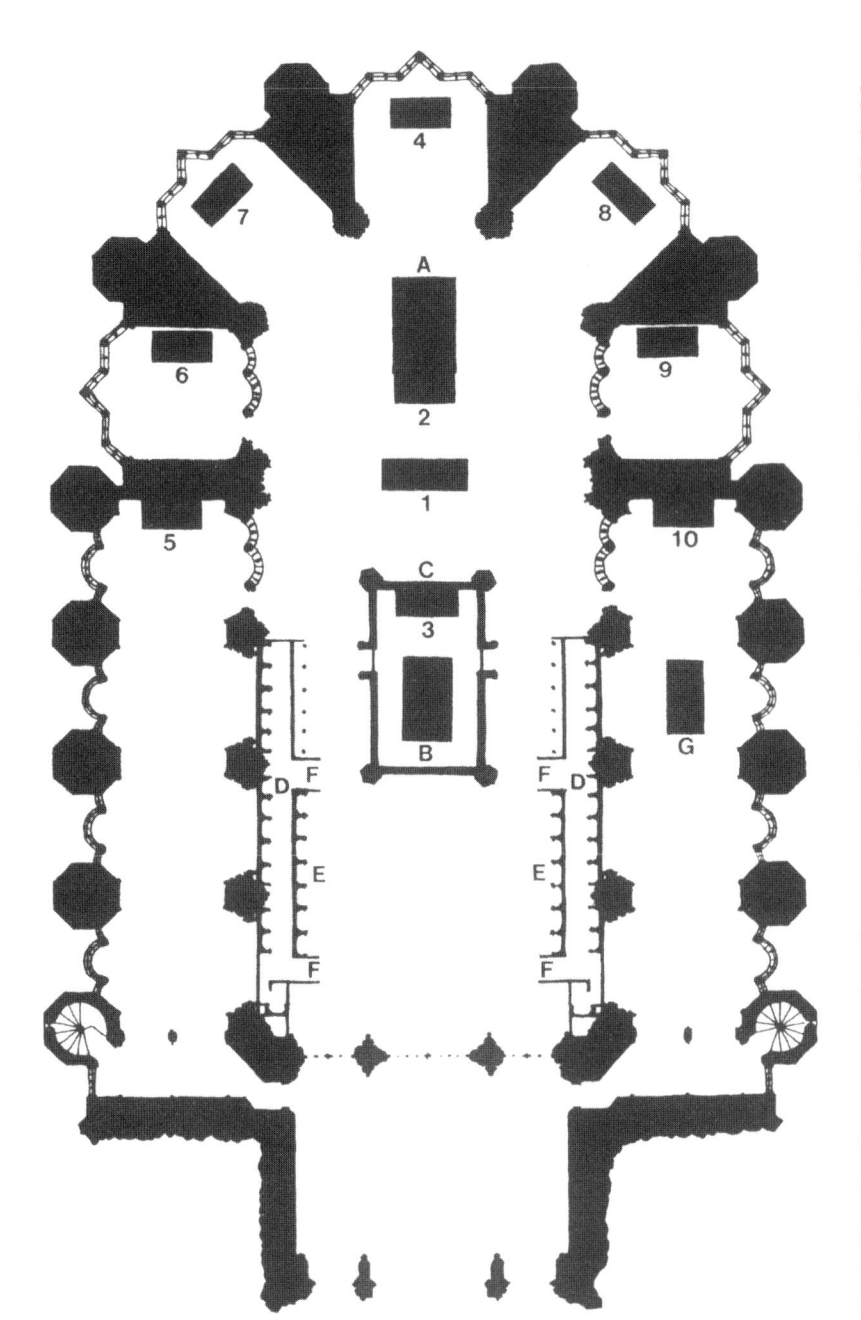

Fig. 6. Plan showing reconstruction of arrangement of fittings as intended by Henry VII. Key: *Altars*: 1. Blessed Virgin Mary (high or Lady altar); 2. St Henry; 3. the Saviour (chantry altar of Henry VII); 4. the Trinity (?) (King Henry); 5–10. dedications unknown. *Other fittings*: A. shrine of St Henry; B. tomb of Henry VII and Elizabeth of York; C. enclosure of chantry chapel of Henry VII; D. upper choirstalls; E. substalls F. access stairs to upper choirstalls; G. tomb of Lady Margaret Beaufort. Note: steps and hautepaces are not shown.

of its role as a monument to the founder of the ruling house.[3] This essentially humanistic conception of the chapel's meaning has continued to predominate down to the present day, and, together with the fact that the fabric and many of the fittings survive in a good state of preservation, it has tended to foster an impression of completeness which obscures the real nature of the multifarious functions which Henry VII himself intended his foundation to fulfil.

Only one attempt has ever been made to identify those functions and to establish how they related to the spaces and fittings provided in the chapel. This is an eight-page subsection of the second volume of Jocelyn Perkins's *Westminster Abbey. Its Worship and Ornaments*, published in 1940.[4] Perkins was sacrist at the Abbey and had been the driving force behind the installation of a near-copy of the high altar of the Lady chapel set up in 1526 – a finishing touch to the restoration carried out between 1932 and 1935. More than sixty years have elapsed since the publication of Perkins's work, and a closer look at the problems he addressed seems long overdue. The main aim of the present paper is to reconstruct as fully and precisely as possible the physical settings for those functions which Henry VII himself wished to see accommodated in the chapel's central vessel (Fig. 6). The many departures from the founder's intentions for the fitting out of his chapel in the two decades following his death will be discussed only in so far as this is necessary to reconstitute the dispositions originally planned. A further important aspect not considered, at least for its own sake, is the possible contribution made to the planning and decoration of the chapel by the king's mother, Margaret Beaufort, countess of Richmond.

It is not easy to see why so little attention has been paid to the functions of Henry VII's chapel. Admittedly, the document which reveals most about the king's wishes regarding the furnishing of the building, the will written shortly before his death on 21 April 1509,[5] has been extensively cited by most students of the chapel, but almost no use has been made of the set of indentures drawn up between the king and the abbey, dated 19 July 1504, in which is spelled out, with unique fullness, the manner of conducting all aspects of the king's commemoration.[6] The interpretation of neither document is simple since both locate rituals and their participants in relation not to the architecture but to the fittings, which, as has already been noted, do not conform to the founder's intentions. The structure of the chapel itself provides some evidence of its intended usage, but in common with all Gothic ecclesiastical buildings of the highest ambition, it embodies an architectural system whose consistent application was an end in itself and which for that reason was impinged on only minimally by functional requirements. Yet even by the standards of the grandest Gothic architecture, the chapel makes extraordinarily few concessions to practical 'on-the-ground'

---

[3] A pioneer of the view of the chapel as artistic marvel was John Leland who hailed it as 'miraculum orbis universali'; J. Leland, *Commentarii in Cygeum Cantionem*, 1545, sig. Pii. Leland's accolade is echoed twice in the effusive praise of the chapel by the Elizabethan topographer John Norden in BL Harley MS 570, fo. 35. In the second half of the sixteenth century the chapel began to be referred to regularly as Henry VII's, a usage which must have seemed fitting on account of its housing the king's tomb and its use as a mausoleum for his grandchildren from 1553 onwards.
[4] Perkins, *Worship and Ornaments* ii, 149–60. The discussion there is partially adumbrated in J. Perkins, *The Chapel of King Henry VII and its High Altar*, n.p. 1935.
[5] Above, 99–140.
[6] BL Harley MS 1498; *CClR 1500–09*, 138–57; above, 59–97.

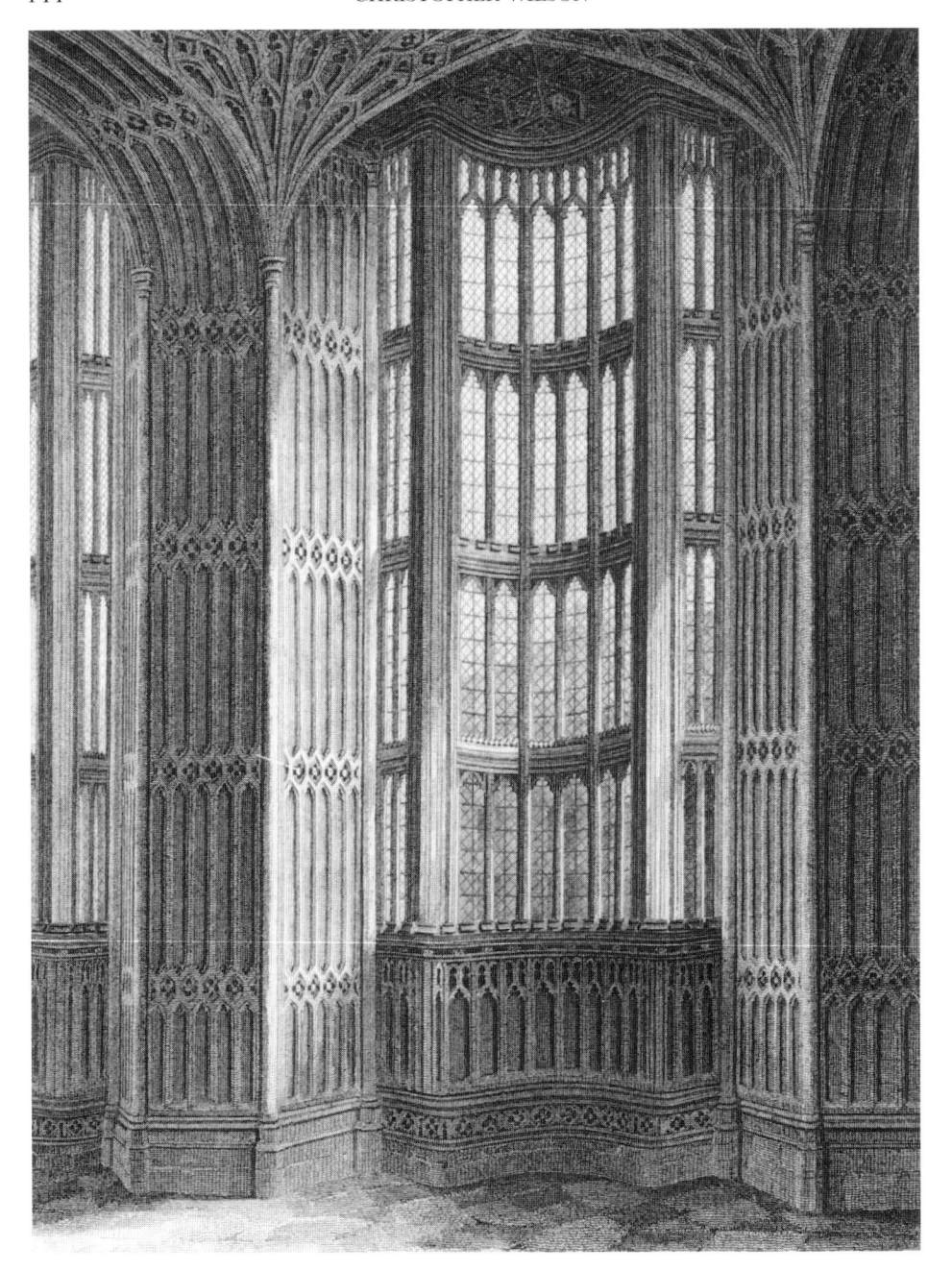

Fig. 7. South aisle, outer wall. (Britton ii, pt. ix, pl. xvi)

realities. For example, there are no piscinas or aumbries such as occur in the subordinate chapels of the vast majority of great churches, including the main abbey church at Westminster, and the near-universal feature of stone benching set against the aisle walls is discarded, for the sake, it would appear, of giving full play to the architect's novel and audacious concept of replacing conventional walls with undulating glazed screens (Fig. 7).[7] The few indications of use that the structure yields can of course be interpreted in the light of comparisons with other functionally analogous buildings or parts of buildings, but the uniqueness of the chapel's architecture inevitably makes this a less than straightforward exercise.

The Lady chapel

From the point of view of the owners of Henry VII's chapel, the abbot and convent of Westminster, its primary role was as the monastery's main chapel of the Virgin. Practically all earlier examples of Lady chapels annexed to major monastic churches or cathedrals were single vessels, usually simple rectangles in plan, in which a single altar stood against or close to the east wall.[8] Westminster's Lady chapel is exceptional in being a basilican structure containing multiple altars and in making provision for a saint's shrine to the east of the high or Lady altar.[9] The saint in question was the as yet uncanonized King Henry VI, whose enrolment among the saints had been vigorously promoted by Henry VII from early on in his reign. The position of the boundary between the Lady chapel proper and the area intended to be given over to the cult of St Henry is not at all obvious. One might expect that it would have been defined by a monumental reredos or altar screen, as in the east arm of the main church at Westminster (Fig. 1) and in every other English church possessing a major relic, but there is no sign that a structure of this sort has ever traversed the central vessel of Henry VII's chapel. Indeed the highly wrought architecture of its lateral elevations contains no plain surfaces such as would have been needed to enable the ends of a reredos to abut against the sides of the central vessel.

One of the surest clues to the former existence of an altar in a medieval church is the step at the western limit of its hautepace or platform, although in the case of the

---

[7] This lack was doubtless intended to be compensated for by the inclusion of wooden benches integral with the backs of the choir stalls, apparently a unique feature.

[8] An exception was the cruciform but unaisled Lady chapel built on the east side of the cloister of Wells cathedral from 1488 (destroyed). The three-aisled chapel built at the east end of Salisbury cathedral in 1220–5 functioned liturgically as a Lady chapel but was dedicated to the Holy Trinity and All Saints, a fact which may account for its tripartite form. At St Augustine's abbey, Canterbury, at an unknown date after 1414, a chapel of similar three-aisled form, perhaps a belated imitation of the Salisbury chapel, replaced the axial radiating chapel of the Romanesque church, whose dedication was also to the Trinity. This chapel, which is known only from its extant foundations and which may or may not have been completed, presumably retained the dedication of its predecessor. It was itself succeeded, apparently around 1500, by a single-span rectangular Lady chapel.

[9] The only basilican Lady chapels besides Henry VII's chapel belonged to a quite distinct category, namely those situated in the east arms of large basilican churches, for example the cathedrals of York, Worcester and London. Tim Tatton-Brown reminds me of the possibility that the early sixteenth-century Lady chapel of St Augustine's Abbey, Canterbury (see n. 8 above) resembled the romanesque Trinity chapel, whose site it occupied, in housing the shrine of St Augustine.

high altar of Henry VII's chapel such evidence would not suffice to fix the position exactly since the eastern limit of the hautepace is not marked in any way. The oldest known plan of the chapel, that made c.1583–1601 by the surveyor John Thorpe (Fig. 3), shows the step of the high altar hautepace somewhat to the west of the centre of the eastmost rectangular-plan bay, in much the same position as the present step dating from 1699.[10] The latter coincides almost exactly with the position of the analogous steps in the north and south aisles, which seem to be largely original, and there must be a good chance that one continuous step ran across the whole chapel at this point.[11] The hautepaces in the side aisles appear to be uniform with that formerly in the south-east radiating chapel which, it will be argued below, belonged to the first altar to be installed there (Fig. 14).[12] However, as will also be shown below, the siting of this altar, like that of three other of the radiating chapel altars, did not conform to the founder's intentions, and therefore Thorpe's rendering of the hautepaces cannot be assumed to be evidence of what Henry VII wanted; more probably it records what his executors did after his death.

The design of the central vessel includes two features which can be seen as indications that the high altar was to stand not far to the east of the step shown by Thorpe in the eastmost rectangular-plan bay. The first of these features, the triumphal arch at the west limit of the apse, is no doubt partly a device for accommodating the thick east walls of the north and south aisles (Figs. 8, 2), but a parallel may be drawn with the sanctuary at Bath Abbey, where there is a similar succession of basilican elevations by short lengths of solid walling surmounted by a tunnel vault (Fig. 9). The eastmost 'bay' at Bath is in effect a gigantic recess for the high altar, and some encouragement to accept that this was also the thinking behind the analogous feature at Westminster is Bath's close connectedness to Henry VII in terms of patronage: the builder was Bishop Oliver King, formerly Henry's principal secretary and Register of the Order of the Garter, and the designer was Robert Vertue, architect of the king's extensive works at Greenwich Manor and the Tower of London.[13] The other feature

---

[10] Only the central section of the present step, that directly before the high altar, belongs to the marble pavement donated in 1699 and shown in Dart ii, frontispiece (Fig. 17). In 1732, when the choir stalls were extended eastwards as far as the triumphal arch, the outer parts of the 1699 step were removed and replaced much further east. Thorpe's plan (reproduced in J. Summerson, *The Book of Architecture of John Thorpe in Sir John Soane's Museum*, Walpole Society 40, 1964–6, pl. 33) is most likely to have been drawn in the period 1583–1601, during which he was a clerk in the Office of Works. His rendering of the steps at the west end of the chapel is reassuringly accurate, as is that of the hautepaces in four radiating chapels, although the hautepace for an altar against the south wall of the axial chapel must be an invention. The nineteenth-century reproduction of Thorpe's plan illustrated in Fig. 3 errs in showing the axial chapel's hautepace as if for an altar against the north wall. The three-sided projection from the centre of the high altar hautepace shown in Thorpe's drawing is unlikely to be for the original altar, although there is a near-parallel in the rectangular projection of the high altar hautepace in the main church at Westminster as recorded in Abbot Islip's mortuary roll. Perhaps the projection was intended to compensate for a reduction of space for the high altar caused by the installation of Henry VII's monument in the apse.

[11] The better preserved of these is that in the north aisle, but it is clear that its southern counterpart has originally been of the same length on the east-west axis, i.e. 2.60m (8ft 6½in.).

[12] This hautepace was evidently removed in 1830, when the monument to Antoine-Philippe, duc de Montpensier was installed on the site.

[13] For Vertue's work at Bath see C. Wilson, 'The designer of Henry VII's chapel, Westminster Abbey', in *Reign of Henry VII*, 140–3.

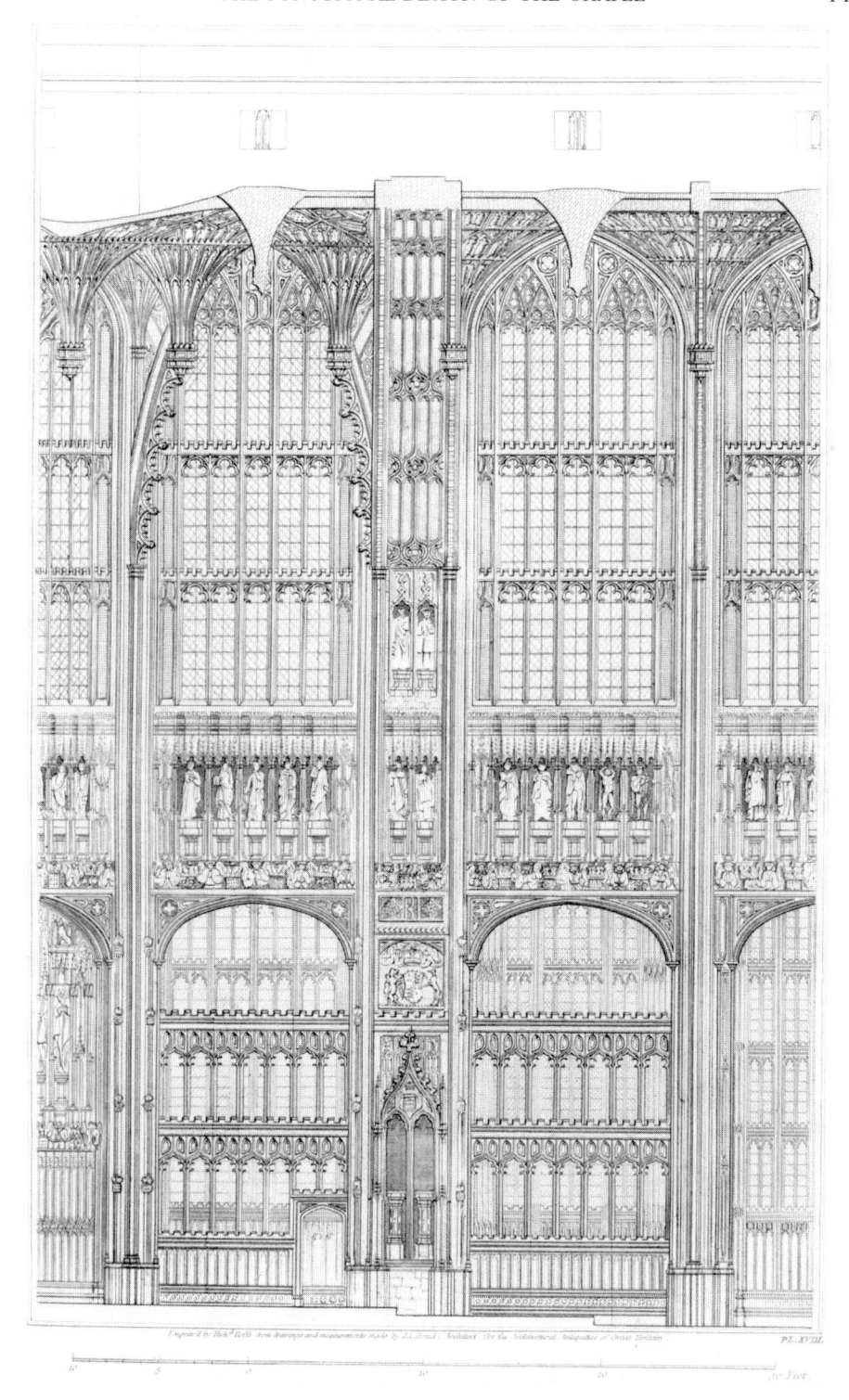

Fig. 8. South elevation of central vessel with (partially inaccurate) reconstruction of screens to royal closets. (Britton ii, pt ix, pl. xviii)

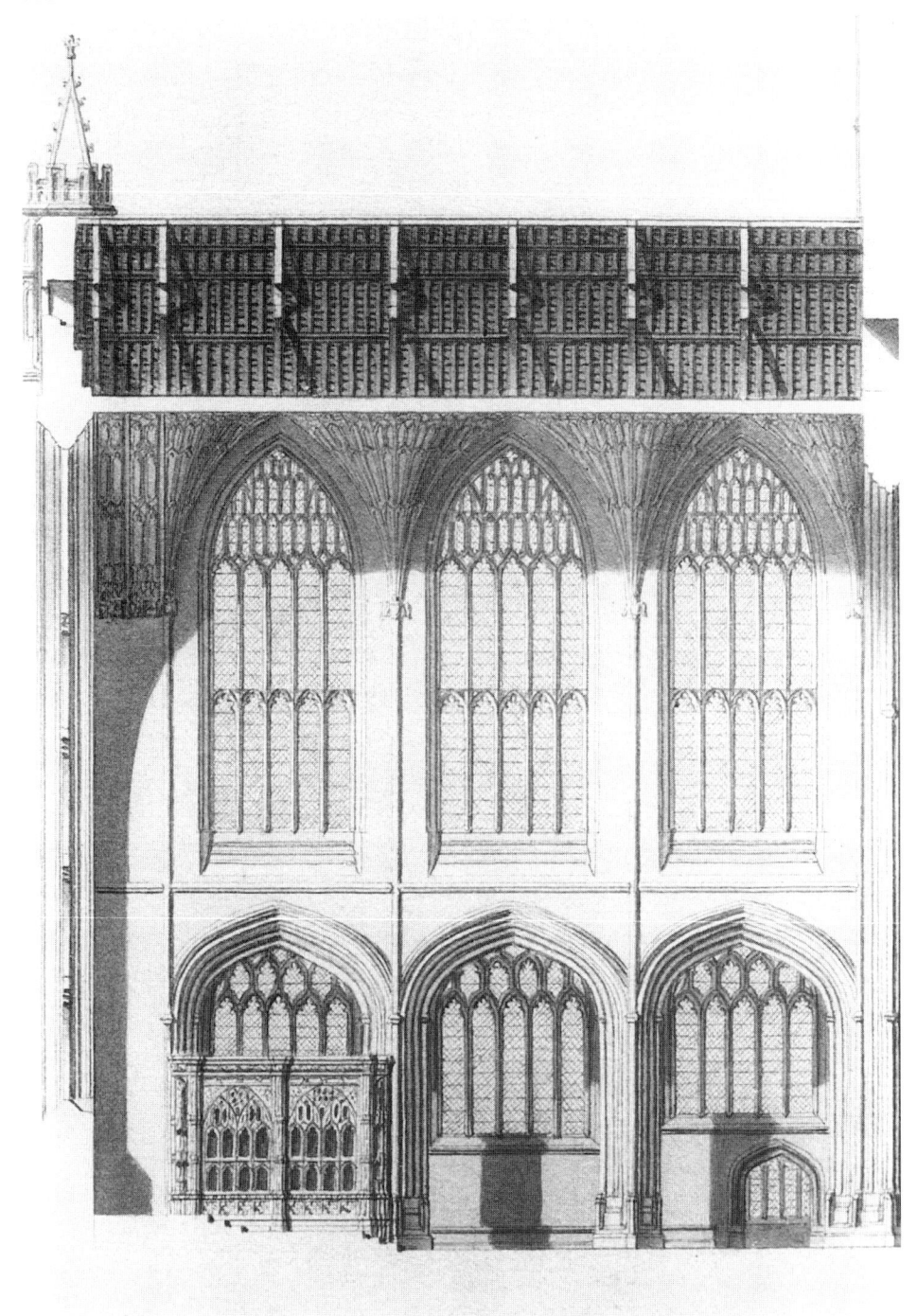

Fig. 9. Bath Abbey, south elevation of east arm, detail of drawing by J. Carter. (Reproduced as *Plan, Elevation, Sections and Specimens of the Architecture of the Abbey Church of Bath*, Society of Antiquaries of London, 1798, pl. v)

Plate 4. Detail of north side of triumphal arch, partly overlapped by eighteenth-century extension to choirstalls.

which suggests that the triumphal arch at Westminster was intended to shelter the high altar is the pairs of niches, now empty, which form the lowest zone of its decoration (Plate 4). These differ from all the many other image niches in the chapel in being almost at floor level and in being bracketed together as pairs by ogee arches. Unless the ogees are mere decorative flourishes, they suggest that the lost images were neither self-contained nor a single series but two pairs. In medieval religious iconography by far the most important double pairs of figures are of course the Annunciation and the Visitation, subjects perfectly suited to decorate the space occupied by an altar dedicated to the Virgin Mary. The unique lowness of the niches within the chapel would have symbolized very effectively the earthly setting of the events which inaugurated the Era of Grace. The omission of projecting canopies such as occur above all the other niches means that the statues which stood here would have lacked the self-contained quality which characterizes the great majority of the extant statues, and this may be another indication that the niches housed narrative pairs rather than single images.[14] The alignment of the rear of the high altar with the east edge of the triumphal arch would have placed it further east than the altars in the side aisles, thereby giving it an appropriate measure of pre-eminence. The dimensions of the intended high altar are unknown, but it can safely be assumed that the length would have been less than that of the high altar dedicated to St Peter in the main abbey church, which was around 3.35m (11ft).[15]

Since the high altar was not backed by a screen running across the chapel, the intention must have been to make it freestanding, with a relatively low dossal rather than anything worthy of the name of reredos.[16] Subordinate altars of this form must once have existed in the many greater English churches, including the main church at Westminster, where wall benches and arcading precluded the installation of altars hard up against east walls. It can almost be taken for granted that the thirteenth-century Lady chapel demolished to make way for Henry VII's chapel had arcading on its east wall, but there is clear documentary evidence proving that the altar there was surrounded by a space (*ambitus*) (Fig. 5) and that it incorporated a dossal (in the form of a painted retable) surmounted by a statue of the Virgin – a type of altar whose appearance can most readily be visualized from the still-extant late thirteenth-century painting over the altar in St Faith's chapel in Westminster Abbey (Plate 5).[17] Henry VII's will mentions a large silver-gilt image of the Virgin destined

---

[14] Of course a few of the surviving figures in the chapel form narrative groups, but considerations of overall architectural coherence dictate that their canopies are of the same type as those above the adjacent single figures.

[15] P. Binski, 'What was the Westminster Retable?', *JBAA* 140, 1987, 56, 170 n. 24.

[16] There is no evidence from late medieval England of the use of high freestanding altarpieces like those found frequently in Germany and Central Europe, which are typologically an outgrowth from the tradition of dossals and retables surmounted by one or more statues. The use in this paper of the word 'freestanding' in relation to altars denotes merely their lack of physical contact with a wall or wall-like screen behind them and does not imply continuity with the early medieval tradition of dossal-less altars.

[17] Westlake ii, 502, citing an inventory of the Lady chapel dated 11 July 1304 (WAM 23180). It is highly probable that the antependium and retable existing in 1304 were those by Peter de Hispania for which Henry III paid the very high price of 120 marks in 1258; *CLR 1257–60*, 424; *CPR 1247–58*, 613. For the St Faith's chapel painting as an altarpiece see C. Wilson, 'The Neville screen', in *Medieval Art and Architecture at Durham Cathedral*, ed. N. Coldstream and P. Draper, British Archaeological Association Conference Transactions 1977, Leeds 1980, 93–4.

Plate 5. Painting on east wall of St Faith's chapel, Westminster Abbey.

for the high altar of his chapel, and presumably it was to have perched above a dossal very much as its thirteenth-century predecessor did and as the fictive statue of St Faith still does.[18] If there was a wish to perpetuate the essential characteristics of

[18] It is not absolutely impossible that Henry VII envisaged that the high altar would incorporate the retable of 1258 from the old Lady chapel (for which see preceding note), since the difference in date between it and the new Lady chapel is not so much greater than that between the two main components of the abbey's high altar as it existed from the mid-fifteenth century to the mid-sixteenth century,

the previous Lady altar this would be somewhat surprising, for in the two and a half centuries which had elapsed since its making tall reredoses had become *de rigueur* in England to an ever-increasing extent. Apart from simple conservatism, a likely influence on the choice of altar type would have been the wish to maintain the existing hierarchy among the altars in the abbey church, and specifically to ensure that the Lady altar did not outdo the true high altar, that in the main church, which in the 1440s had acquired a stone reredos of only moderate height and elaboration. Such concern with the decorum of the abbey church as a whole is surely more readily attributable to the monks of Westminster than to the king or his advisors. Another factor may have been the architectural purism identified earlier as the root of the refusal to integrate fittings into the structure of the chapel. To have installed a solid screen behind the high altar would have severed the apse from the rest of the main vessel, thereby reducing the viewer's ability to perceive that the elevation of the apsidal bays had been made uniform with those of the rectangular-plan bays to an exceptional degree. That the wish not to compromise the architectural coherence of the central vessel was a real consideration is evident from the fact that there have never been stone canopied sedilia such as stand south of the altar in most other late medieval English Lady chapels of high ambition. During the Gloria and the Credo the priest-monks celebrating mass must have sat in comparatively simple freestanding seats.

The conduct of the daily Lady masses involved no more than a small number of monks. Always present were the warden of the chapel, the succentor and six other monks whose attendance was prescribed by a table or rota compiled by the succentor. There is no evidence that the old Lady chapel possessed stalls.[19] The stalls in the existing building, which total forty, were presumably sufficient to accommodate the larger numbers of monks present on the principal feasts of the Virgin. The six monks tabled to attend on ordinary days probably occupied the three most easterly of the main upper stalls on each side.

At Westminster Abbey, as at other major English monasteries, the music of the Lady chapel had been more up-to-date and ambitious in character than that of the main monastic choir for more than a century before the foundation of Henry VII's

---

namely a retable, probably of c.1269, and a stone screen of the early 1440s, both still extant though heavily damaged. The high altar installed in the new Lady chapel in time for its dedication in 1516 (see n. 36 below) must have been displaced when the high altar commissioned from Pietro Torrigiano in 1517 was set up in the chapel in 1526. Presumably Henry VII's precious image of the Virgin stood above the high altar until 1526, but what was done with it then is not known. It was still in the abbey at the Dissolution in 1540, together with other items of plate provided for the chapel by Henry VII; J.A. Robinson, *The Abbot's House at Westminster*, Cambridge 1911, 46.

[19] Recent discussion of the single thirteenth-century misericord incorporated into the present early sixteenth-century stalls has favoured an origin in the early thirteenth-century Lady chapel stalls rather than those made in the mid-thirteenth century for the main choir, which remained in use until 1775; P. Tudor-Craig in Wilson, *Westminster Abbey*, 139; C. Tracy, *English Gothic Choir Stalls 1200–1400*, Woodbridge 1987, 8. However, stalls are not known to have existed in Lady chapels before the later fifteenth century, and the random piecing in of old and stylistically alien woodwork by craftsmen charged with making such exceptionally ambitious stalls as those in Henry VII's Chapel would be a puzzling anomaly. The existence of substantially more stalls in the thirteenth-century abbey choir than there were monks to fill them at any time from the late middle ages onwards must have made re-use of one of the supernumerary thirteenth-century misericords there a tempting option if one of the misericords of the stalls in Henry VII's chapel had happened to suffer accidental damage.

chapel.[20] Whereas professional singers were rarely employed in the main choir, in the Lady chapel they were the chief providers of music. In 1480 the Westminster Lady chapel choir was reformed so as to be able to perform the new English style of polyphony developed in the household chapels of royalty and at the cathedral and collegiate churches, a style characterized by great virtuosity and a compass of more than three octaves. Besides a master, there were now six boys recruited from the grammar-school of the abbey almonry and three – occasionally four – singing-men, an ensemble sufficient to perform the four-, five- and six-part polyphony of the period. Any seating provided for the singing-boys and men would have consisted of no more than movable benches.[21] This appears to be in conformity with normal monastic usage but contrasts with the practice in secular foundations of allotting to the choristers substalls in front of those of the clergy. The polyphonic music of the ordinary and some of the propers of the mass, and of the votive antiphons of the Virgin performed late every afternoon, would have been sung from single copies of the music placed on a large lectern directly before the high altar. Numerous late medieval pictorial sources show the singers standing in an informal group around such a lectern. Another musical resource which was probably almost as mobile as the singers, and certainly as undemanding of permanent fittings, was the organ.[22] Doubtless a small instrument, this could have stood to one side in the sanctuary or even behind the high altar when not in use. Henry VII's concern that the music of the Westminster Lady chapel be of the highest quality is evident from his proclamation of 17 December 1497 that the abbey was to be permitted to take singing-men and boys from any other choral establishment except the Chapel Royal, which already had such rights of impressment.[23] Westminster Abbey was apparently the only monastic house ever to receive this privilege, and its granting is hard to understand unless the king had already made up his mind to abandon his plan, apparently conceived in the early 1490s, to adopt the Lady chapel of St George's, Windsor as a burial place for himself and as the site of a shrine housing the body of the canonized Henry VI. The king's council gave its formal assent to the switch to Westminster only on 5 March 1498.[24]

---

[20] The remainder of this paragraph is heavily dependent on R. Bowers, 'The performing ensemble for English church polyphony, c.1320–c.1390', in *Studies in the Performance of Late Medieval Music*, ed. S. Boorman, Cambridge 1983, 161–92; *idem*, 'The Lady chapel choir of Westminster Abbey, 1384–1540', unpublished typescript in Westminster Abbey Library, 1992; and *idem*, 'The musicians of the Lady chapel of Winchester cathedral priory, 1402–1539', *JEH* 45, 1994, 210–37; and see Dr Bowers' article, above.

[21] Bowers, 'Winchester cathedral', 227 n. 50.

[22] From at least the 1370s and 1380s most major religious institutions in England possessed a Lady chapel organ, according to Bowers, 'Performing ensemble', 182. The old Lady chapel had two organs, both apparently fixed and one certainly placed high up against a wall (see above, 36). The lack of similar provision in the new chapel would appear to be a further instance of according priority to the symmetry and systematic quality of the architecture.

[23] *CPR 1494–1509*, 129–30; above, 49–50.

[24] Stanley, *Historical Memorials*, 2nd edn, 1868, 581.

The shrine and altars of Henry VI

The first move to promote Henry VI's canonization was made some time during the papacy of Innocent VIII, which ended on 25 July 1492.[25] The process seems to have continued satisfactorily during Henry VII's lifetime but remained incomplete at his death and was ultimately to founder along with the obedience of the English church to Rome. An indenture drawn up between the king and the abbot of Westminster on 26 July 1498 states that owing to 'the singuler affeccion and devocion that his grace hath to his Uncle of blessid memory King Henry the vj[th]', he had 'lately begon to make and bilde of new the chapell of our Lady within the Collegeat church of Wyndesore entending to have translatid the body of his said Uncle in to the same and nygh unto him within the said chapell to have be buryed hymself'. However, since it had been established that Henry VI had in his lifetime indicated his desire for burial at Westminster, the king had 'determyned to convey and bring the said holy body of his said Uncle to the said Monastery of Westminster and there to be commytted to perpetuall sepulture in the chapel of our Lady within the church of the said Monastery – the which chapell oure said souverain Lord entendith to make and bilde of new and in the same not ferre from his said Uncle to be buryed hymself'.[26] There is here a rather surprising terminological looseness, although it is doubtful whether this amounts to evidence of uncertainty or confusion of purpose. The references to 'translation' and 'holy body' imply a sanctity which Henry VI had not yet formally attained despite the existence of a flourishing cult of 'good King Henry' centred on his grave in the south choir aisle at Windsor. 'Perpetual sepulture' was entirely inappropriate for a saint's relics, which it was obligatory to place in a shrine consisting of a precious metal *feretrum* set on a high stone base to whose west face was attached an altar dedicated to the saint.[27] If it was the intention to move Henry VI's body to Westminster before canonization had been completed – something which neither the indenture nor any other source makes clear – temporary burial would have been the correct treatment. Any tomb erected then would have had to stand on the main longitudinal axis and be succeeded in its role as container of the relics by a shrine – also on the main axis, but on a different site – once canonization had been promulgated.[28] There was simply no room at Westminster for a tomb as well as a shrine.[29] This potential

---

[25] B. Wolffe, *Henry VI*, 1981, 355. Henry VII's acquisition, presumably from some private individual who had offered it for sale, of 'King Harry pelow' (see below, 60) is confirmatory evidence that the king's interest in the cult of Henry VI was general knowledge by 1492.

[26] Stanley, *Historical Memorials*, 2nd edn, 1868, 585–6.

[27] Cf. the vagueness of the will's reference to the intention 'to translate the body and reliquies'; above, 113. If the intention was to use the legal device of a binomial to secure the meaning, the result can hardly be judged successful.

[28] For the early sixteenth-century design for a monument (not a shrine) which bears the later sixteenth- or early seventeenth-century inscription 'The Monument intended for Kinge Henry the sixte' (BL Cotton MS Augustus II, 1) see the entry by C. Wilson in the catalogue of the exhibition *The Glory of Gothic: Art in England 1400–1547*, Victoria and Albert Museum, London 2003, 166. See Fig. 35.

[29] An exception to the general rule that a saint's first burial site was in a different spot from his or her shrine was St Hugh of Lincoln, whose shrine was eventually erected on the site of his original grave: J.S. Alexander, 'The Angel Choir of Lincoln cathedral and the shrine of St Hugh', *JBAA* 148, 1995, 144–5. However, the treatment accorded to St Hugh's relics conformed to normal usage to the extent that their setting immediately before the translation to their definitive site was one some distance away

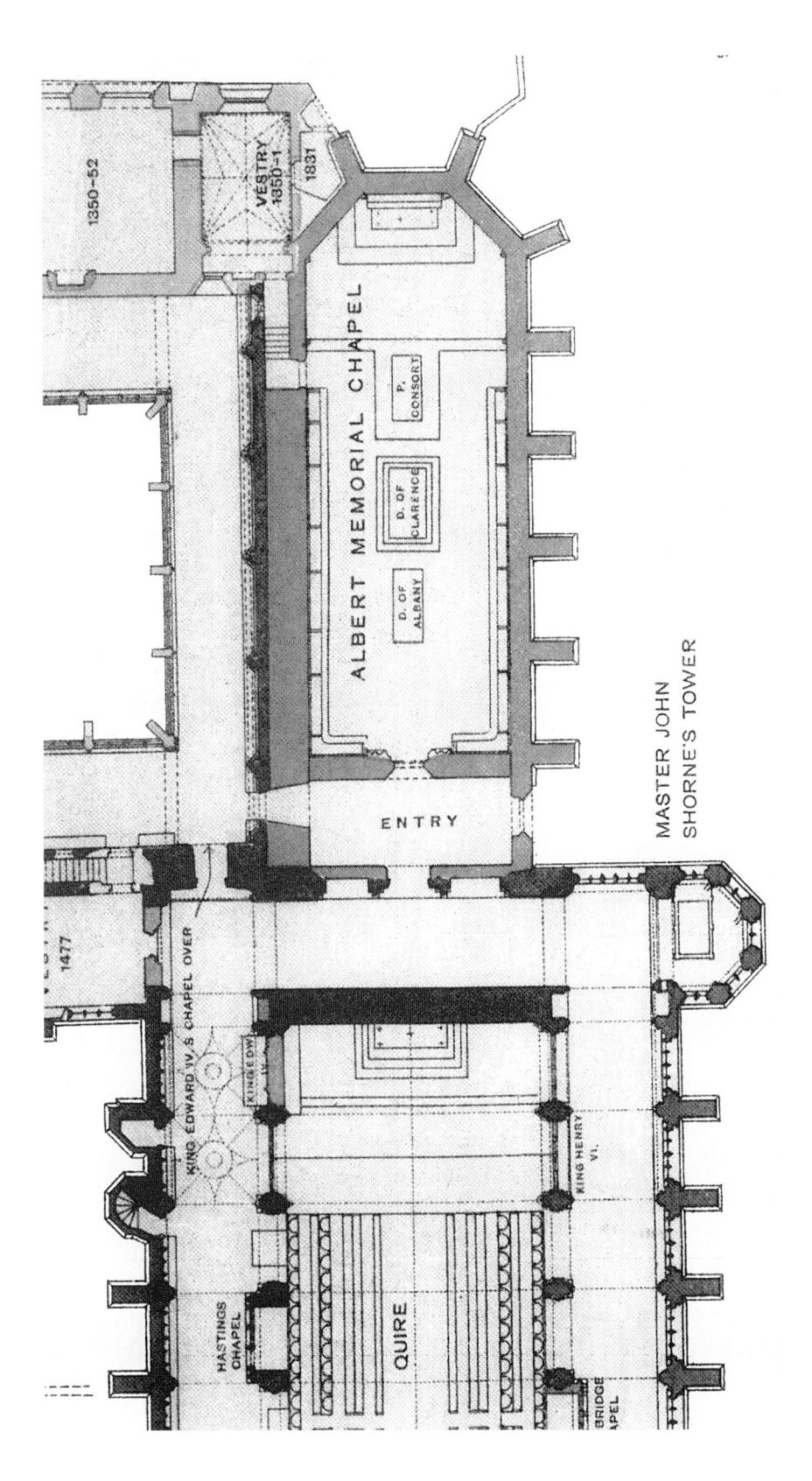

Fig. 10. Windsor Castle, St George's Chapel, plan of Lady chapel and part of east arm. (W.H. St J. Hope, *Windsor Castle*, London 1913, plan vi, detail)

problem, and also the desirability of not competing with the grave at Windsor, which could have continued to function as a subordinate cult site after the removal of the body,[30] suggest that Henry VI was to have made his triumphal entry into Westminster already a saint.

Neither Henry VII's will nor the 1498 indenture reveals where the shrine was to stand in the new chapel at Westminster. However, since the honour due to a saint normally required that his or her shrine be behind the high altar and on the main longitudinal axis, effectively the only possible site was the apse. Like the chapel's incorporation of four bays 4.16m (14ft) long on the east-west axis, its apse derives from the equivalent chapel at Windsor and was clearly meant to denote its succession to the latter as the site of the shrine of Henry VI (Figs. 10, 6).[31] At Windsor the 6.10m (20ft) length of the apse from east to west would have provided adequate room for a shrine whose base had the minimum length (including steps and the standard feature of an altar against the west end of the base) of around 3.66m (12ft),[32] but at Westminster the apse was far more spacious on account of the much wider span of the central vessel. The altar of King Henry mentioned in Henry VII's will was not the one attached to the west face of the shrine base, which would only come into being once the canonization process was complete, but rather that standing in the axial radiating chapel (see below). The setting up of two contiguous altars dedicated to the same saint would have been an extraordinary anomaly, and it can be assumed that no such duplication was ever intended. Like its counterpart next to the grave in St George's, the altar of King Henry in the axial chapel at Westminster cannot have been formally dedicated to one who was merely a prospective saint. The most likely titulus for the Westminster altar is the Trinity, the same dedication as the altars occupying the analogous positions at the east ends of St Edward's chapel in the main abbey church and of St Thomas's chapel in Canterbury cathedral. After the canonization of Henry VI, the altar in the axial chapel could have had its dedication augmented to include St Henry, but the proximity of the shrine altar, which would have had to bear that dedication, would have greatly reduced the need for such a revision. There appears to be only one near-parallel for the set-up which the translation of Henry VI into the Westminster Lady chapel would have brought into being. At Durham cathedral an altar dedicated to St Cuthbert and St Bede stood against the east wall of the church, a little way to the east of the shrine, which was sited in the usual place behind the high altar. The altar

---

from the latter. Translation from tomb to shrine in the same church normally involved only two sites. The nonaxial siting of St Hugh's shrine is also exceptional and may be due not only to the wish to re-use the first burial site but to an intention to provide for a second shrine alongside St Hugh's, namely that of Bishop Robert Grosseteste, whose canonization was no doubt expected to be completed soon after St Hugh's translation in 1280.

[30] There is no suggestion anywhere in the documents relating to discussion of the claims on Henry VI's body advanced by Chertsey abbey, St George's, Windsor and Westminster Abbey that St George's was to lose such lesser relics of the king as his hat and spur. It was not uncommon to leave behind at a first burial site some corporeal relics, and Windsor could reasonably have hoped to salvage the situation to that extent.

[31] Wilson, 'Designer of Henry VII's chapel', 148–51.

[32] Evidence that the full depth of the Windsor apse, which was planned as five sides of an octagon like Henry VII's chapel, was to be taken up with the shrine is the placing of the western exit of the passage from the mid-fourteenth century sacristy so that it gives into the easternmost rectangular bay, where the main altar could most conveniently have stood (Fig. 10).

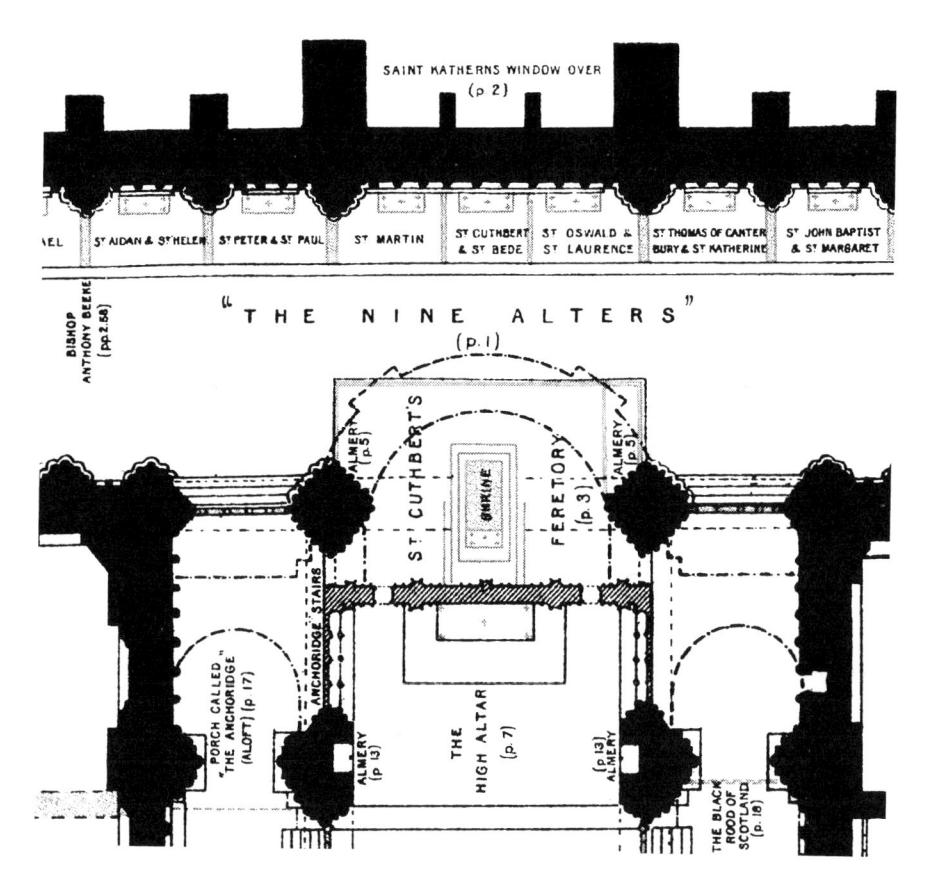

Fig. 11. Durham Cathedral, plan showing shrine of St Cuthbert and adjacent altars. (*Rites of Durham*, ed. J.T. Fowler, Surtees Society 107, 1902, plan between pp. 304 and 305, detail)

attached to the west face of the shrine base bore a dedication to St Cuthbert alone and was used only once a year, on the saint's principal feast (Fig. 11).[33] It is not impossible that Durham influenced Westminster, for Richard Fox, bishop of Winchester, one of Henry VII's executors, and a likely advisor to the king on his new chapel,[34] had occupied the see of Durham from 1494 to 1501 and, somewhat unusually, had resided for extended periods in his diocese. However, the main motive for installing the altar of King Henry in the axial chapel will not have been the wish to emulate Durham cathedral but rather the need to provide a site for the veneration of Henry VI as soon as the Lady chapel came into use. Even so powerful and determined a promotor of the cult as Henry VII could not be sure that canonization would be completed by the time the chapel was ready to be inaugurated.

The suggestion of Jocelyn Perkins that the shrine was to have stood in the axial chapel does not carry conviction. His reconstructed plan (Fig. 12) shows no altar anywhere in this chapel and thereby acknowledges, albeit unintentionally, the main

---

[33] J.T. Fowler, *The Rites of Durham*, Surtees Society 107, 1902.
[34] The influence of Fox, one of Henry VII's most trusted councillors, on the design of the king's almshouses near the west gate to the precinct of Westminster Abbey is convincingly suggested in Colvin, *HKW* iii, 209.

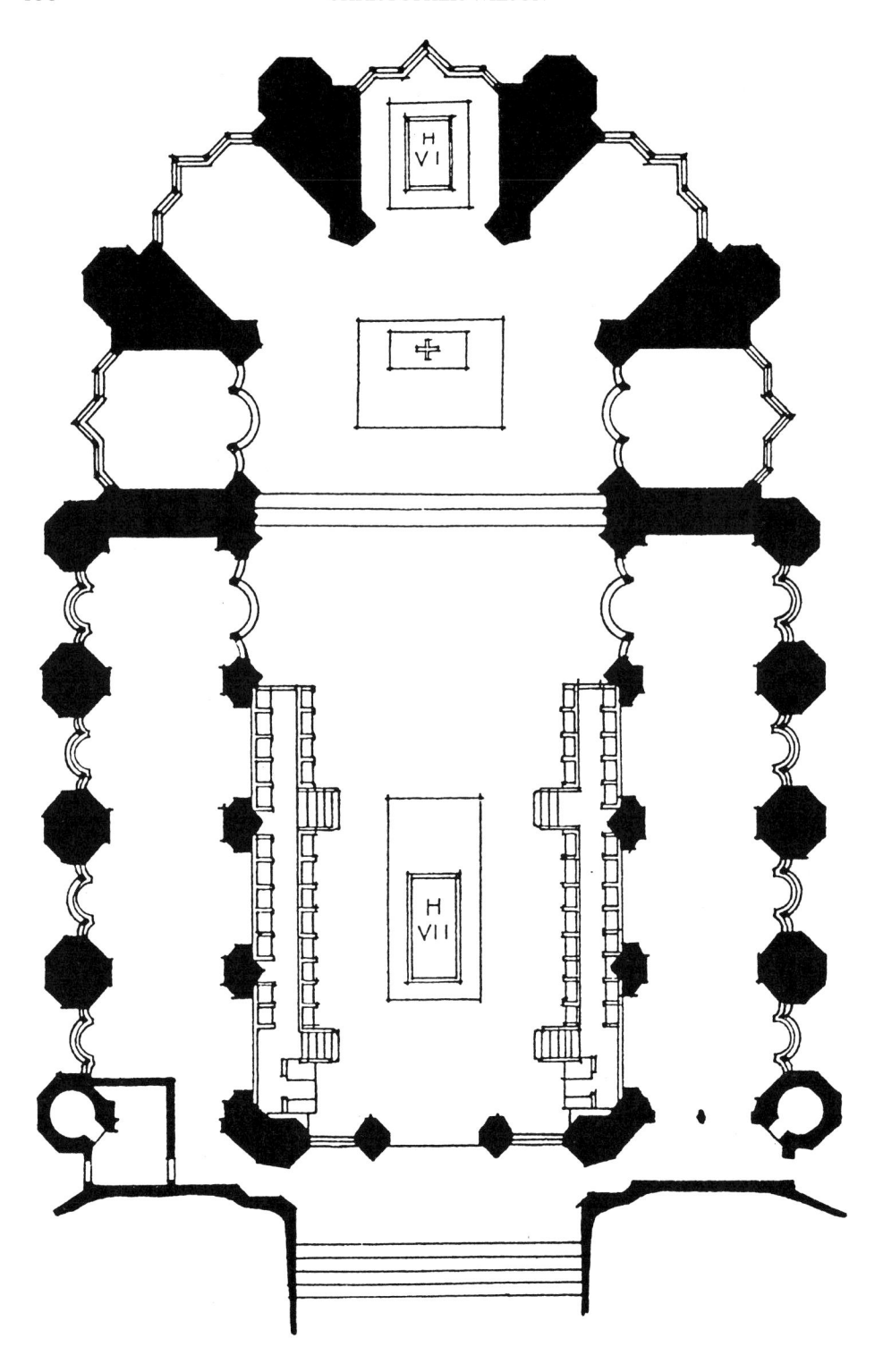

Fig. 12. Plan showing reconstruction of arrangement of fittings intended by Henry VII. (Perkins, *Worship and Ornaments* ii, 155)

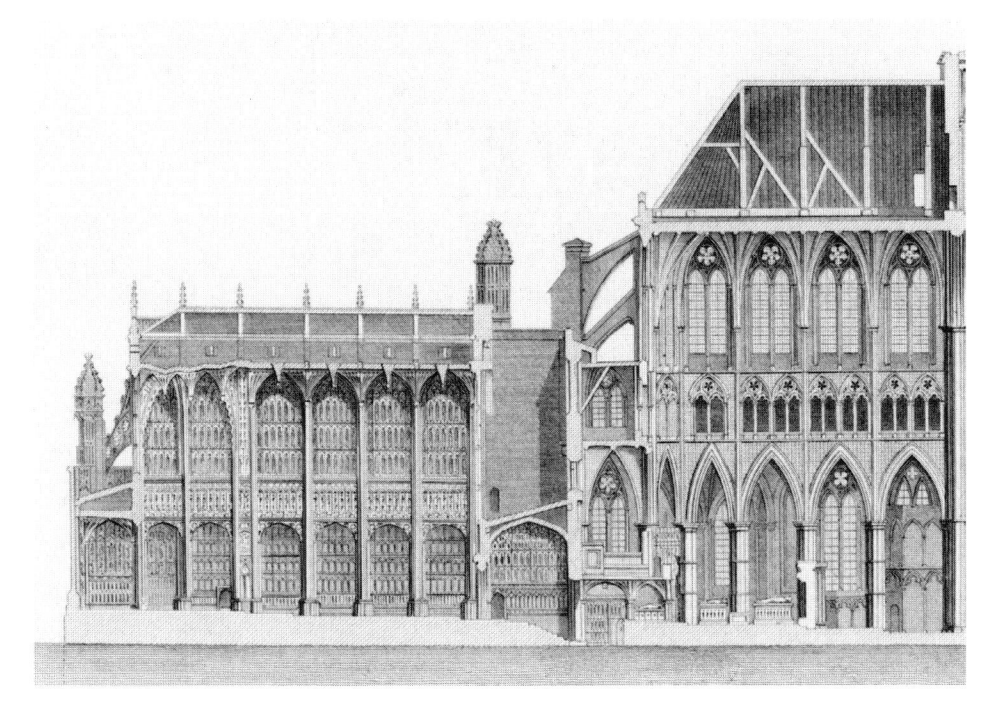

Fig. 13. Longitudinal section of Henry VII's chapel and eastern arm. (Neale and Brayley ii, pl. xlv, detail)

difficulty with locating the shrine here, namely the want of space. Like all the radiating chapels, that on the main axis is approximately 4.16m (14ft) wide and 3.96m (13ft) long, quite insufficient to house a shrine comparable to that of St Edward, whose base and steps, when in their original state, were some 2.74m (9ft) wide and 4.58m (15ft) long including the attached altar.[35] Even if St Henry's shrine was to have had a more modest complement of steps, pilgrims would not have been able to circulate around it, let alone kneel and pray in the niches which were a standard feature of major English shrine bases. The erection of Henry VII and Queen Elizabeth's monument in the apse, probably in 1515,[36] must have marked the end of any prospect that the shrine of Henry VI was to be installed in the Lady chapel.

---

[35] The length including the hautepace of the attached altar was around 5.79m (19ft). These dimensions are taken from the reconstruction in J.G. O'Neilly and L. Tanner, 'The shrine of St Edward the Confessor', *Archaeologia* 100, 1966, figs. 16–20.

[36] The erection of the chantry enclosing the monument proper has been dated to 1512 on the grounds that the elegy to Henry VII composed by John Skelton in that year was immediately suspended from it (Lethaby, *Re-examined*, 180), something for which there is no evidence, notwithstanding a much later reference to hanging tables ('tabulae pensiles') in the chapel which bore this and other poems commemorating Henry VII; Camden, sig. C4v–D2v. Skelton's poem, which dates itself to 29 November 1512, makes clear that the king's body was then in the chapel, but the reference to Henry's burial under this pile ('mole sub hac'), is surely insufficient evidence for the existence of a substantial and permanent structure over it. The likeliest moment for the erection of the chantry was shortly after the completion of the tomb commissioned from Pietro Torrigiano on 26 October 1512, the erection of which would have been greatly complicated if the enclosure were already *in situ*. Under the contract

One of the most remarkable manifestations of Henry VII's ambition as a patron is that his chapel at Westminster resembles no other Lady chapel but rather takes on the appearance of a second east arm to the abbey church. There can be little doubt that the apsidal termination, the radiating chapels, the elevated floor level (Fig. 13), and the 10.36m (34ft) span of the central vessel were conscious echoes of the setting of St Edward's shrine (Fig. 1), or that these were intended to signal that Henry VII was according honours to Westminster's second saint equal to those Henry III had bestowed on the Confessor.[37] Another feature of the projected setting of Henry VI's cult which was surely modelled on St Edward's was that the shrine and altar would have been approached not via aisles but through whatever intervals were left between the high altar and the sides of the central vessel (Figs. 1, 6). Pilgrim access to St Henry, as to St Edward, would therefore have been impossible while mass was being celebrated at the high altar.[38] The lack of physical barriers to the cult area in the form of screens has already been discussed, but just as remarkable is the absence of such standard fixtures from the entrance arches of the three eastern radiating chapels (Fig. 2). A parallel instance of the omission of a screen from the narrow entrance to a much-frequented reliquary chapel is the late twelfth-century axial chapel of Canterbury cathedral, the so-called 'corona'. Perhaps those responsible for the functional design of Henry VII's chapel were envisaging that two or all three unscreened radiating chapels would resemble the Canterbury corona in housing lesser relics of the saint whose shrine stood nearby. In May 1492 Henry VII acquired Henry VI's pillow for twenty shillings, but there is no way of knowing whether he intended this treasure to be venerated in his chapel at Windsor or its successor at Westminster.[39]

In Henry VII's will the plate, vestments and service books of the altars 'bee thei of the sides of the same [chapel of Our Lady], or in any other place within the compasse of the same' were the subject of a characteristic admonition that the executors take care to ensure 'thei bee of suche as apperteigne to the gifte of a Prince'.[40] The little room inserted as an afterthought into the vestibule to the north aisle is likely to have been a sacristy serving all these altars (Fig. 2).[41] Along with the high altar, the altar of

---

with Torrigiano the tomb was due to be completed within three years, and its erection by the end of 1515 or the start of 1516 can be inferred from the Westminster monk Thomas Gardiner's record that the chapel was dedicated the day after the birth of Princess Mary, i.e. 19 February 1516 (new style); J.G. Smyly, 'Thomas Gardiner's History of England', *Hermathena: a Series of Papers on Literature, Science and Philosophy, by members of Trinity College, Dublin* 43, 1922, 248.

[37] Wilson, *Westminster Abbey*, 71–2. The width of the central vessel measured between the pier shafts is also 34ft at St George's, Windsor, and the designer of Henry VII's chapel will have been aware of this undoubtedly deliberate correspondence with the main church at Westminster, even though in his design 34ft is the distance between the front wall planes represented by the mouldings flanking the vault shafts and continued upwards as wall ribs.

[38] The lack of access to St Edward's Chapel other than through the doors in the high altar screen has attracted surprisingly little comment from scholars. The movable wooden stair which links the north aisle and the chapel via the gap east of Edward I's tomb chest may perpetuate a medieval access point, although such an arrangement would hardly have permitted large numbers of people to circulate. Numerous eighteenth- and early nineteenth-century views show that the present Victorian stair had a late seventeenth-century predecessor.

[39] BL Add. MS 7099, fo. 10.

[40] See above, 132–3.

[41] The straight joints between this room and the masonry of the chapel proper show that it is not primary work, but its stylistic character is indistinguishable from that of the rest of the chapel. It is surprising

Plate 6. Axial chapel looking south-east.

Plate 7. Axial chapel, detail of base of central image niche on north wall.

King Henry VI is singled out as being the recipient of a pair of silver-gilt candlesticks, and clearly it was more important in the king's eyes than any of the altars in other subordinate chapels. The axial chapel now contains no physical traces of its sixteenth-century altar. It must have resembled the freestanding type posited above for the high altar, as the bay window which takes the place of a conventional east wall was too complex in plan and had glazing which extended too far down to provide a suitable backing for an altar with a dossal, the minimum embellishment acceptable in the later middle ages.[42] Both of the chapel's side walls are solid and both carry

 that a sacristy was not part of the original scheme, for the abbey's main sacristy was some way away, on the north side of the nave.
[42] The modern altar here lacks a dossal (Plate 6).

Plate 8. Axial chapel, south wall, graffiti on blind tracery below image niches.

symmetrical displays of enniched images (Plate 6). The two groups of imagery are not of equal importance, however, for the north wall, symbolically at the right hand of God, contained in its central and therefore most honorific niche a statue of the dedicatee of the chapel. King Henry's image has been removed, no doubt because his cult was obnoxious to protestant sentiment, but its niche is identifiable by the initials 'H R' remaining on its base, a token of the scruples felt by the church authorities when allowing a prospective saint to be represented in the midst of images of those whose saintly credentials were beyond challenge (Plate 7).[43] Facing King Henry in the

---

[43] Compare the surviving two-dimensional representations, where there is no nimbus and the figure is identified as *King* Henry the Sixth.

central niche on the south wall was St Peter, the dedicatee of the abbey church at Westminster. That King Henry's altar became the focus of a cult despite the absence of the relics is evident from the early sixteenth-century inscriptions scratched into the walls of the chapel. The only one fully legible before the limewashing of the interior in 1995 was that near the middle of the panelled dado of the south wall which read 'Anthony Dalbroke seru[a]ntt unto the duke off norfoke grace' (Plate 8).[44] The other radiating chapels contain no such early graffiti.

As in the axial chapel, the altars in the north-east and south-east radiating chapels were to have been freestanding. They were also to have been 'orientated' so that the windows rose directly behind them, but at a date subsequent to the completion of the structure of the chapel the panelled dados of the more easterly of their solid side walls were partly dressed back to allow the installation of altars hard up against them (Fig. 14).[45] It is possible that this was done when catholicism was restored by Mary I in 1553, but it is also quite likely that all the pre-reformation altars of the chapel had survived the imposition of protestantism in Edward VI's reign, since the high altar was certainly allowed to remain then. The high altar tolerated by Edward VI had been erected in 1526 and clearly represented a departure from Henry VII's scheme, for it displaced that incorporating the large silver-gilt statue of the Virgin mentioned in the king's will.[46] It would not be surprising if the executors had also taken it upon themselves to depart from the founder's intentions regarding the placing of the lesser altars.

The north and south chapels differ from their fellows further east in having imagery on just one of their solid walls, the east walls before which their altars were to stand. But despite the fact that their altars could be correctly orientated, they were not at first meant to have been butted up against the east walls. The obvious explanation for this deviation from normal practice – that there was a desire to make the altars in all the radiating chapels of the same freestanding type – receives confirmation from the north and south aisles, where the intention that the orientated altars be butted up against the east walls is made crystal clear by the omission of the ubiquitous wall panelling and the inclusion of areas of flat masonry tailor-made for the abutment of altars and dossals (Fig. 15). Whereas the use of the normative type of altar in the north and south radiating chapels would have undermined the sense that all five chapels opening off the apse formed a single series and were parts of a larger entity, this was not a consideration which could have any bearing on the north and south aisles, whose interiors were effectively impossible to see simultaneously with those of

---

[44] Most of the graffiti datable to the early sixteenth century on paleographical grounds are on the south wall, opposite the former image. Along with the rest of Henry VII's chapel, the axial chapel was limewashed in 1995 and its graffiti are therefore less legible than formerly.

[45] The evidence was effaced in the north-east chapel when the large monument to John Sheffield, duke of Buckingham and Normanby (d.1721) was installed against the south-east wall (Plate 52).

[46] For the silver-gilt image see n. 18 above. The altar erected in 1526, which was commissioned in 1517 from Pietro Torrigiano, may have been retained under Elizabeth I because Edward VI had been buried beneath it and it could therefore be thought of as his monument. For the destruction on 16 April 1561 of all the other altars in Westminster Abbey, including those in Henry VII's Chapel, see *The Diary of Henry Machyn, Citizen and Merchant-Tailor of London from AD 1550 to AD 1563*, ed. J.G. Nichols, Camden Society 40, 1848, 256.

Fig. 14. South-east radiating chapel, north-east wall and south radiating chapel, east wall. (Neale and Brayley i, pl. lvi)

Fig. 15. North aisle, east end, shown as if before the introduction of post-medieval tombs. (Britton ii, pt ix, pl. xii)

Plate 9. North radiating chapel, detail of east wall.

the radiating chapels. However, at some time subsequent to the completion of the structure, and exactly as in the north-east and south-east chapels, the panelling has been cut away from the east walls of the north and south chapels so as to improvise the more conventional kind of arrangement that existed from the start on the east walls of the north and south aisles (Plate 9).

The royal closets

Unlike their fellows further east, the north and south radiating chapels are separated from the main vessel by high stone screens (Figs. 2, 17). These have small doors set near the west ends of the screens rather than at their centres (Fig. 14). Clearly the purpose of these barriers was rather different from that of the screens regularly set up in front of subordinate chapels during the late middle ages, a type exemplified in the main church at Westminster. Both the smallness and the eccentric placing of the doors in the screens to the north and south radiating chapels become understandable if one postulates that the spaces beyond are not merely side-chapels but 'closets', oratories enabling members of the royal family to pray before the altar of Henry VI's shrine with some degree of privacy. Until the openwork upper parts of the screens were removed in the eighteenth century, their remarkable triple-bow form resembled closely that of the windows in the side aisles, but whereas the latter existed for their own sakes, the screens possessed a functional justification to the extent that their bold projection offered to anyone within the closets a commanding view of the central vessel of the chapel. The solid dados of the screens would not have been an obstacle

Plate 10. Pier between north and north-east radiating chapels.

Plate 11. Main arcade arch, south side of eastmost rectangular-plan bay.

to any royal personage directing their gaze and their prayers towards the shrine altar, since they would have been raised up by kneeling on a prayer desk and cushion such as were standard equipment in royal and aristocratic closets.[47] Of course the users of the closets also had the option of praying facing the altars within those spaces. The jambs of the main arcade arches to which the screens are attached confirm the royal function of the north and south chapels, for they differ from the jambs of the arches to the three eastmost radiating chapels in being encrusted with carvings of royal beasts (Plate 10). Some of these beasts are damaged and a minority are unidentifiable, but they include the leopards of the arms of England and the dragon and greyhound supporters used by Henry VII.

Virtually identical bay-window-like structures screened the eastmost bays of the side aisles until 1732, when they were destroyed to make way for an eastwards extension of the choir stalls (Figs. 8, 6, 17).[48] They too would have enabled the spaces behind them to have functioned as closets, though the external focus of devotion was in this case the high altar. The arches that enclose the screens are again given special

[47] See, besides the extensive pictorial evidence, the reference by Lancaster Herald to the cushions in the king's closet at Richmond in 1501, and the section 'Quysshyns for Estates' in the 1540 dissolution inventory of Westminster Abbey: F. Grose and T. Astle, *The Antiquarian Repertory*, 4 vols., 1807–9, 315; M.E.C. Walcott, 'The inventories of Westminster Abbey at the dissolution', *Transactions of the London and Middlesex Archaeological Society* 4, 1875, 346.

[48] See above, Tracy, and C. Tracy, *English Gothic Choir Stalls 1400–1540*, Woodbridge 1990, 52 nn. 25, 26. The payment to the mason-builder Andrews Jelfe referred to in the latter note could well relate to the demolition of the screens and the dressing back of stubs of masonry, as well as to the adjustments to the pavement referred to in n. 10 above.

Plate 12. Warwick, St Mary, closet on south side of chancel.

decoration, consisting of undercut foliage of varied patterns rather than heraldic beasts (Plate 11). The distinction may be iconographic in intent – a floral, or at least vegetal, allusion to the Virgin in the bay containing the Lady altar, and English royal beasts in that housing the altar of a saint-king. A further special feature of the arches flanking the Lady altar is that they are wider than the regular arches of the main arcades to the west. The north-west closet would probably have been that occupied by Henry VII at the anniversary masses if he had lived to see the chapel finished, for the 1504 indentures specify that both before and after his death those masses were to be celebrated at the high altar (see below, 173, 175). It is very revealing of the priorities of the king, and whoever else was responsible for negotiating with the architect to agree the final design, that the only significant disturbances to the regularity of the chapel's architecture should have been caused by those parts of the building intended to accommodate the living members of the royal family. The influence of St George's, Windsor, so pervasive in the detailing of the architecture, is almost certainly at work here too, for the one part of that building where the regular bay system is interrupted is the north side of the sanctuary, the site of Edward IV's chantry and closet (Plate 13). Although Henry VII's chapel incorporates exceptionally many royal badges, its only representations of the royal arms are those which decorate the triumphal arch, between and immediately above the screens to the two pairs of closets (Plate 4). The purpose of these splendid embellishments was clearly to underscore the privileged nature of the part of the building where they occur, and it is likely that they were intended to function as surrogates for the royal presence during the periods when the closets were not fulfilling their role of sheltering members of Henry VII's family. A near-parallel and possible source is the very large painted White Hart badge of Richard II in the analogue to the closets in the main abbey church at Westminster, the royal oratory on the west side of the south transept.

Spaces set apart for founders and their families had been a feature of palace chapels and related buildings since Antiquity, but by the mid-fourteenth century screened-off closets immediately adjacent to high altars were beginning to find favour with élite patrons. In England an influential example is likely to have been the oratory built by Edward II and Edward III high up on the south side of St Stephen's chapel in Westminster palace, but no records of its appearance have survived. The finest fourteenth-century English closet still in existence is that which Thomas Beauchamp, second earl of Warwick, provided when rebuilding his family's collegiate foundation of St Mary's, Warwick in the 1370s (Plate 12).[49] It occupies the south side of the second most easterly bay of the chancel, immediately west of the sedilia, and like the closets in Henry VII's chapel, it opens into the sanctuary at ground level. The fenestration of its outside wall was destroyed c.1443–7 in order to build a second closet opening into the north side of the eastmost bay of the Lady chapel which is better known today as the Beauchamp chapel.[50] The Beauchamp chapel closet resembles its earlier neighbour in being the most impressive example of the genre to have survived from its period. Both the Warwick closets anticipate the west pair of closets in Henry VII's chapel in containing small altars, in commanding clear views of tombs as well as of major altars, and in being entered by small doors at the west ends of their inner lateral walls. The closets in England's late medieval royal palaces have all perished, but clear evidence that the most remarkable architectural feature of the closets in Henry VII's chapel grew out of a long tradition is the record that in 1392–3 four 'baywyndowes' were made for the king's and queen's oratories in the chapel at Easthampstead, one of the hunting lodges within Windsor Forest.[51] These windows were probably glazed but that does not mean that some or all of them did not project into the chapel. Glazing, some of it movable, was originally installed in the windows of the only still extant example of a royal closet with an inward-facing bay window,

---

[49] Although not a palace chapel, St Mary's was a collegiate church under the patronage of the earls of Warwick and close to the castle which was their *caput honoris*. The rebuilding of the choir is ordered in the will of Earl Thomas I (d.1369) (W. Dugdale, *The Antiquities of Warwickshire*, 1656, 317), and the stylistic evidence confirms a dating of c.1370–80 for the design.

[50] That the Beauchamp chapel closet is known as the dean's chapel is symptomatic of a long-standing lack of awareness in England of the oratory as a medieval room-type. By contrast, one of the major surviving late fifteenth-century examples, that on the north side of the chapel of Magdalen College, Oxford, is still known as the Oratory.

[51] Colvin, *HkW* ii, 927.

Plate 13. Windsor Castle, St George's Chapel, north side of sanctuary showing closet.

that built in the late 1470s high up on the north side of the sanctuary of St George's, Windsor (Plate 13).[52]

But the strongest and most direct influence on the closets in the Westminster Lady chapel is likely to have been exerted by the chapel of Henry VII's most important new residence, Richmond Manor as reconstructed after the fire of 1497. Like their Westminster counterparts, the king's and queen's closets at Richmond flanked the chapel and shared the same floor level (Fig. 16). A parliamentary survey compiled in 1649 reveals that each had 'a fayer wyndowe opening into the chapell'.[53] Admittedly, these features are not specifically called bay windows, but the surveyors' description of the spectacular multi-storey bays on Richmond's river front merely as 'turrets' suggests that their vocabulary did not include a descriptive term for this feature.[54] The windows of the Richmond closets must have been remarkable to have earned the epithet 'fayer' from the unexcitable professionals that the surveyors clearly were, and given that Richmond, together with Henry VII's tower at Windsor, was where the Tudor vogue for complex bay windows made its début, the chances that its closet windows anticipated at least the general form of those in Henry VII's chapel must be very good. The closets themselves probably bore a striking resemblance to the aisles of the Westminster chapel as they existed down to the early eighteenth century, with the three west bays of their arcades almost completely blocked by the high choir stalls and only the eastmost bays communicating visually with the central vessel. The Richmond closets too were spaces lower than, but as long as, the chapel they adjoined; they were lit mainly by the windows in their outer walls; and they opened into the chapel only through window-cum-screens which almost certainly flanked the main altar. Such similarity in form is a strong argument for a similarity in function. However, besides housing a closet, the south aisle of Henry VII's chapel also served as Lady Margaret Beaufort's chantry and tomb chapel, aspects which lie beyond the scope of this paper. Almost certainly, it was the north aisle which was being referred to in a payment of 1523–4 for lights in 'o^r ffathers abbottes chapell w^t in the new chapell'.[55] Perhaps Abbot John Islip (1500–32) had adopted the north aisle and its altar before deciding to build his own chantry chapel in the main abbey church.

The commemoration of Henry VII

The nature and scope of the king's commemoration both before and after his death are spelled out in unparalleled detail in the indentures drawn up between the king and the abbey in 1504. Most of the elements of the commemoration were standard for their time, but their scale was without precedent. Careful provision was made for the

---

[52] Payments for the ironwork associated with the glazing occur in the building account for 1482–3: W. St J. Hope, *Windsor Castle*, 1913, 382, 405. An example of a closet with a bay window which still retains glazing is that on the south side of the sanctuary of the priory of St Bartholomew the Great, Smithfield, which bears the rebus of Prior William Bolton, master of the works of Henry VII's chapel. The screens to the closets at Westminster have never been provided with glazing grooves.
[53] W.H. Hart, 'The Parliamentary Surveys of Richmond, Wimbledon and Nonsuch, in the county of Surrey, AD 1649', *Surrey Archaeological Collections* 5, 1871, 79.
[54] *Ibid.*, 78.
[55] WAM 19836 (account of the sub-sacrist).

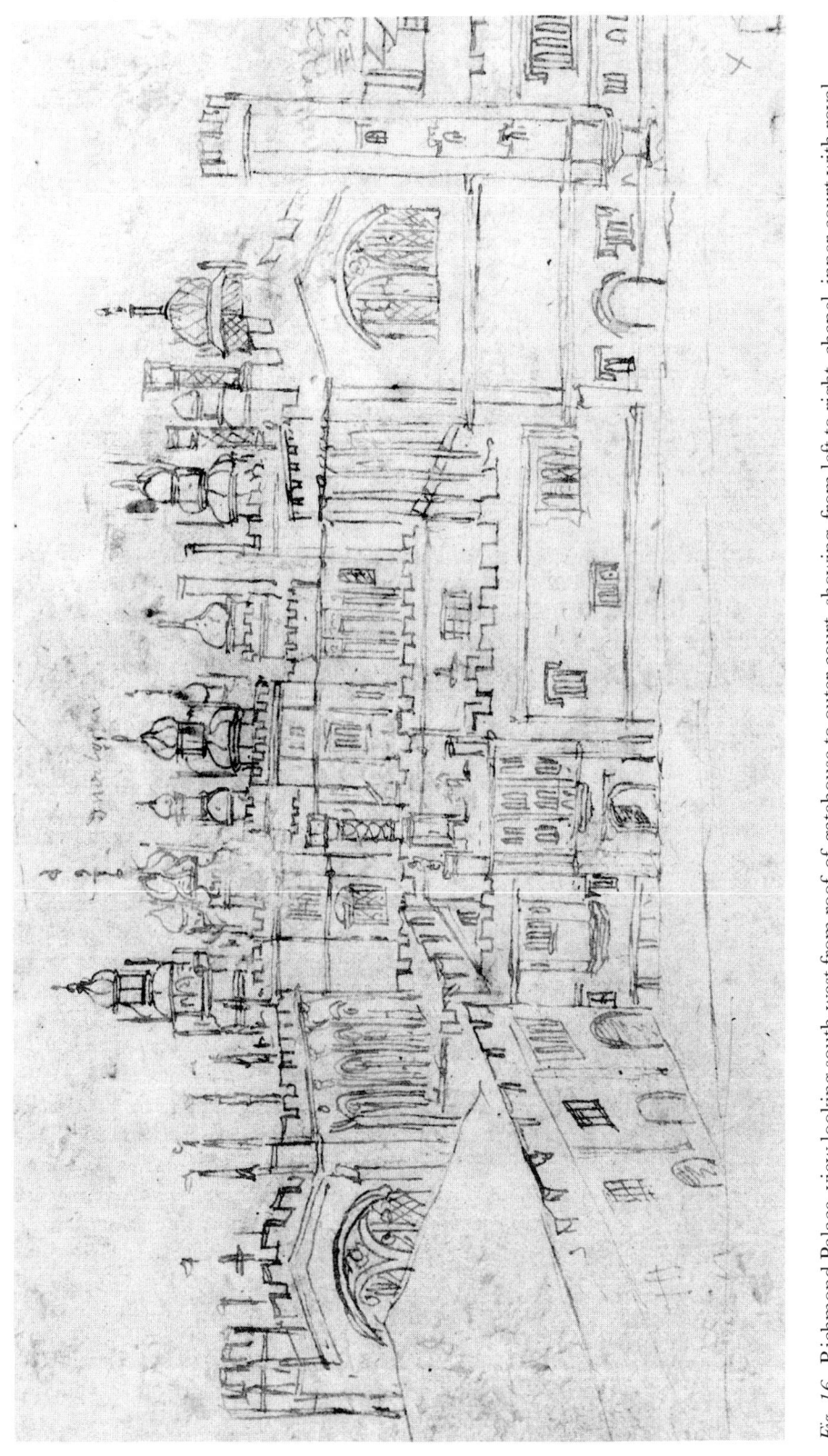

Fig. 16. Richmond Palace, view looking south-west from roof of gatehouse to outer court, showing, from left to right, chapel, inner court with royal lodgings beyond, great hall, by A. van der Wyngaerde. (Ashmolean Museum, Oxford)

execution of the rites within the choir and sanctuary of the main abbey church should the new Lady chapel not be ready for use at the king's death, as indeed proved to be the case. Only the provisions relating to the completed Lady chapel will be discussed here. Of the arrangements put into operation pending the completion of the chapel, the key points to note in this context are that the anniversary masses were to be celebrated at the high altar, that the matutinal altar on the east side of the crossing was to be used for the daily chantry masses, and that the king's temporary grave in the crossing was to be surmounted by a taper-bedecked hearse.[56]

As is made clear in the will, the bronze chantry chapel enclosing the monument of Henry VII and Queen Elizabeth was also to house an altar of the Saviour whose five-foot-high reredos was to be formed of gold-sheathed statuary.[57] All that remains of this altar is the hautepace and the horizontal bar marking the west limit of the ceilure or canopy (Plate 14). The indentures clarify that the altar was to be used exclusively for the chantry masses. These were celebrated daily at 7a.m., 8a.m. and immediately after the singing of the gospel at high mass in the main monastic choir. At the first lavatory of each mass, the monk-chaplain was to turn towards the laity present and urge them to pray for the soul of the king and queen, their children, the king's father, progenitors and ancestors, and also his mother.[58] The requiem masses held annually on the same date as the burial and weekly on the same day of the week as the anniversary were to be celebrated at the high altar of the Lady chapel. In the weekly obits, after the requiem which was normally the final part of any obit, there followed an additional component to the service, which consisted of the abbot, prior and convent standing round the tomb (meaning the tomb and chantry), singing the responsory *Libera me, domine, de morte aeterna* and saying Psalm 129(130), *De profundis*.[59]

'Upon and aboute the said tombe', one hundred tapers each nine feet (2.74m) long and twelve pounds (5.88kg) in weight were to be in place continuously, and during the anniversaries all were to be lit. During the masses at the weekly obits, during high mass on principal feasts, or whenever the reigning king or queen or a royal duke entered the monastery, thirty of the tapers were to be lit. Four of them were to burn perpetually 'aboute and upon the same tombe, that is to say in the myddes of either side and either end of the same tombe'.[60] The requirements that a hundred tapers burn at anniversaries and that four of them burn continuously conformed to established Westminster usage in relation to the commemoration of Henry III, Eleanor of Castile, Richard II and Anne of Bohemia, and Henry V.[61] Perhaps observation of careless maintenance of lights around earlier royal tombs lay behind the stipulation in the indentures that the tapers were never to be allowed to burn down below five feet (1.52m). Any failure on the part of the abbey to uphold perfectly this supremely extravagant display would incur one of a whole series of graded penalties for non-compliance that are listed in a separate section of the indentures. For example, leaving one of the four tapers at the centres of the sides unlit for half an hour during

---

[56] BL Harley MS 1498, fos. 4v–5v; *CCR 1500–09*, 140.
[57] See above, 114, 131–2.
[58] BL Harley MS 1498, fos. 4v, 102v; *CCR 1500–09*, 139–42.
[59] BL Harley MS 1498, fo. 27v; *CCR 1500–09*, 139–42.
[60] BL Harley MS 1498, fos. 21v, 30v, 109; *CCR 1500–09*, 143, 144.
[61] B. Harvey, *Living and Dying in England 1100–1540, the Monastic Experience*, Oxford 1993, 25–6.

Plate 14. Chantry enclosure looking down and to the south.

the daytime would result in a fine of 3s 4d, a significant sum.[62] All the lights planned to be around Henry VII's permanent monument were counterparts to those used earlier on his hearse in the crossing of the abbey church, and it is clear that, despite the indentures' slightly misleading use of the word 'tomb' rather than 'closure' or 'grate' (the terms used there and in the will to denote the chantry chapel), it was the latter which was intended to function as a permanent successor to the hearse over the temporary grave.[63]

The four tapers at the centres of the sides and ends were undoubtedly meant to stand on the massive brackets with crown-shaped drip pans that still occupy these positions. But how were the rest of the tapers to have been supported? Seen from floor level, the metalwork of the chantry appears complete (apart from one or two lengths of cresting and some other terminal features). However, when viewed from above (Plate 14), it becomes apparent that the openwork covings which project outwards and inwards from the top of the screenwork mask metal structures far more bulky than they would have needed to be merely to ensure the rigidity of the covings. Sitting above the screenwork, and continued down into the spandrels between the arched heads of the eight-light 'windows' which make up the screens, are long thick slabs of cast metal. Projecting at frequent intervals from the slabs are massive struts pinned into the cornices of the outer and inner covings. The cornices of the outer covings carry a deep openwork parapet, but those of the inner covings preserve only a regular series of indentations that shows they were meant to carry elements that have now disappeared. It is very likely that the prickets and drip pans for the ninety-six tapers

[62] BL Harley MS 1498, fo. 119; *CCR 1500–09*, 154.
[63] So far as I am aware, this has not been recognized before, but see Harvey, *Living and Dying*, 26 n. 71.

were to have been attached here, where their weight and that of the wax could have been counterbalanced by the parapet above the outer cornice. Numerous surviving late medieval tomb railings make provision for the support of tapers, but, needless to say, all are more modest than Henry VII's enclosure.[64] Royal examples include the iron railings of the tombs of the Black Prince and of Henry IV and Joan of Navarre in Canterbury cathedral, and the chantry chapel-like stone screen before the monument of Edward II in Gloucester cathedral. The effect of Henry VII's gilt-bronze[65] chantry surmounted by its palisade of tapers would have been breathtakingly splendid, but it is certain that this hearse function was never fulfilled. The surviving accounts for Henry's foundation reveal that after the transfer of the king's body into his chapel the hundred tapers burned on a hearse, and it is evident that this was not the same thing as 'le brasyn chapell', for both are referred to in the accounts for 1518–19. Presumably the hearse bearing the hundred tapers was of the normal type, that is, of timber and dismountable.[66]

Where did Henry VII intend his chantry chapel-cum-hearse to stand? The simple impossibility of accommodating it anywhere else allows us to be sure that it was always meant to be sited on the central longitudinal axis. All earlier chantry chapels except one had been placed laterally in relation to principal liturgical spaces. The exception is the very elaborate chantry of King Henry V inserted some sixty years previously into the east end of the Confessor's chapel in the main church at Westminster, a precedent very likely to have been noted by Henry VII and his advisors.[67] The king's will says only that his chantry was to be 'a convenient space and distaunce from the grees [i.e. step] of the high aultier', a formulation which clearly implies that it was to be west of the altar. Its precise position was to be 'as it is ordred in the Plat [i.e. architectural plan or design] made for the same Chapell and signed with our hande'.[68] Jocelyn Perkins located the chantry in the two west bays of the central vessel without giving his reasons (Fig. 12).[69] Had the chantry been set up in that position its north and south sides would have been no more than 1.59m (5ft 2½in.) away from the substalls.[70] The spaces flanking the chantry would therefore have been barely sufficient for the different groups who needed to make use of them: any laity who were

---

[64] For illustrations of many of the extant English examples see F.H. Crossley, *English Church Monuments 1150–1550*, 1921, 169–76. Crossley's text makes no mention of lights!

[65] The gilding of the chantry, which is specified in the will (above, 114), and which is said to have decayed badly by the late sixteenth century (BL Harley MS 570, fo. 35), seems to have vanished without trace. In all probability it was never carried out.

[66] WAM 24248 (sub-sacrist's account).

[67] The eventual placing of the chantry behind the high altar rather than before it, as Henry VII had intended (see below), was probably also modelled on Henry V's chantry, which stood immediately east of the altar of the Trinity, until the Reformation the main altar in the Confessor's chapel.

[68] Above, 113–14.

[69] It is curious that Perkins omits the chantry enclosure from this plan, but shows it in his plans of the chapel as completed in Henry VIII's reign and as existing in 1940; Perkins, *Worship and Ornaments* ii, 157, 159.

[70] If, as is argued below, the substalls were for the use of priest-monks at the weekly obits and anniversaries, they ough to have needed desks just as much as the main stalls behind them. Some indication of their importance to Henry VII is that the will refers to the chapel when fitted with stalls as 'desked': above, 115. However, the absence of desks to the substalls, which is documented by Thorpe's late sixteenth-century plan (Fig. 3), can be understood as a pragmatically inspired departure from the ideal made in order not to obstruct the lateral west doors of the chapel and due to the impossibility of

Fig. 17. South range of choirstalls and screens to south royal closets. (Dart ii, frontispiece, detail)

present at the daily chantry masses; the thirteen almsmen of the king's almshouse at the west end of the abbey precincts, who were required to say prayers kneeling or sitting round the chantry during the first two of those masses;[71] those who came to the chapel to take advantage of the indulgence available there at Ascensiontide;[72] and the whole convent which, as was noted above, stood round the chantry to perform the final parts of the weekly obits. If, however, the chantry were to have been set up two bays further east, where there were no substalls, the flanking spaces would have been 2.06m (6ft 9in.) wide, a dimension somewhat more adequate to the uses enumerated above.[73] At the west end of these spaces the intervals between the chantry and the more easterly of the two sets of stairs up to the main stalls would still have been narrow, about 1.28m (4ft 2½in.).[74]

The evidence which weighs most heavily against Perkins's siting of the chantry and tomb in the westmost bays is not the possible practical shortcomings of such an arrangement but the fact that it would have been at odds with late medieval English usage. The preferred position for a founder's tomb was not in the midst of the liturgical choir between the two lateral ranges of stalls but between the latter and the high altar. Among the comparatively many places where this arrangement has survived undisturbed are the Beauchamp chapel at Warwick and the collegiate foundations of Archbishop William Courtenay at Maidstone and Sir Reginald Cobham at Lingfield, Surrey.[75] In Henry VII's chapel, space on the longitudinal axis of the main vessel was limited on account of the need to accommodate a shrine chapel behind the high altar,

---

contriving satisfactory means of access to any substall desking. In purely practical terms, no desks at all were necessary as the monks would have known by heart the texts and music of the obit and anniversary (vespers, matins, mass of the dead) and of the Lady masses.

[71] BL Harley MS 1498, fos. 63–63v; *CCR 1500–09*, 151. The indentures refer to twelve of the almsmen sitting or kneeling at the sides of the tomb and the priest-almsman kneeling at the head, but here, as in relation to the tapers burning round the monument, the chantry rather than the tomb proper must be meant. The space available between the chantry enclosure and the present double tomb commissioned some three and a half years after Henry VII's death, which is much smaller than earlier English royal double tombs, would have accommodated kneeling almsmen only if their faces had been virtually pressed up against the sides and west end of the tomb chest. There would certainly never have been sufficient space for seats to enable the almsmen to sit.

[72] Their numbers were expected to be large enough to require four confessors to be in attendance: *CPL* xvii, 150–1 (no. 115).

[73] Part of the 'standing room' provided by the spaces flanking the chantry would have been under the desking of the upper stalls and between the uprights which extended from the desking to the floor (Fig. 17). The inclusion of these uprights was clearly a way of making the lower parts of the eastern stalls harmonize with the canopied substalls before the western stalls.

[74] This dimension is based on the distance separating the fronts of the lowest steps of the stairs to the east of the return stalls, which are original and which appear to have projected by the same amount as the steps of the other stairs before the latter's eighteenth- or nineteenth-century remodelling; Dart ii, frontispiece (Fig. 17).

[75] The 1439 will of John Stourton, the rebuilder of Stavordale priory, specifies burial for himself and his wife in the middle of the choir at Stavordale, between the stalls and with the desk (*lectrinum*) at the head of the tomb; F.W. Weaver, ed., *Somerset Medieval Wills*, Somerset Record Society 16, 1901, 145. Although this description of the site of the tomb might seem to imply a position well towards the west within the liturgical choir, the reference to the desk indicates that the tomb stood near the eastern limits of the stalls, for English (as distinct from continental) usage was to set the cantor's desk between the very eastmost stalls or even beyond the stalls altogether; C.S. Phillips, *Canterbury Cathedral in the Middle Ages*, 1949, 15–16, 36; Fowler, *Rites of Durham*, 14. It is suggestive that the position proposed here as the intended site of Henry VII's tomb and chantry is closely analogous to that which Henry VIII

Plate 15. South range of choirstalls, detail of canopies.

but placing the chantry east of the substalls would have made it adhere to the norm as closely as possible. It would also have recalled to a certain extent the hearse which stood to the east of the choirstalls in the main abbey church until the time came to transfer the king's commemoration into his new purpose-built chapel. Another factor likely to have influenced the placing of the tomb, and hence of the chantry, will have been the need to ensure that it occupied a site no less easterly and therefore no less honorific than that of the monument to Lady Margaret Beaufort in the south aisle. The latter was set up, apparently by 1515,[76] in the centre of the second bay from the east (Plate VII C). Of course one cannot be absolutely certain that this is where her tomb was originally intended to be, but the fact that those who took responsibility for its making were bound to the countess by the closest ties of personal loyalty[77] must provide some reassurance that the existing location is not a departure from what she, and presumably her son also, intended. The positioning of the access doors in the north and south sides of Henry VII and Queen Elizabeth's chantry indicates that their tomb-chest was always meant to occupy the west part of the enclosure, and therefore placing the tomb-chest abreast of Lady Margaret's would have brought the

chose for his own monument in the much longer eastern arm of St George's, Windsor. It too was to have had a 'grate' enclosing the tomb and a chantry altar, and its position midway between the stalls and the high altar, would have brought it similarly close to the latter; Hope, *Windsor Castle*, 484.

[76] R.F. Scott, 'On the contracts for the tomb of the Lady Margaret Beaufort . . .', *Archaeologia* 66, 1915, 370, where the regnal years of Henry VIII are incorrectly converted.

[77] These were two of her executors, John Fisher, bishop of Rochester, chaplain and confessor to Lady Margaret, and Henry Hornby, master of Peterhouse, secretary, dean of chapel and chancellor to the countess.

east end of the chantry hard up against the hautepace of the Lady altar recorded by John Thorpe (although, as was noted above, it is unlikely that the central westwards-projecting section of the hautepace shown by Thorpe belonged to the original scheme approved by Henry VII). In requiring that his and his queen's monuments be flanked by choir stalls, Henry VII was no doubt fully aware that he was departing from established English usage; and it is not impossible that his decision had been influenced by the tombs of the first two dukes of Burgundy, which together took up a very large proportion of the space between the stalls in the choir of the Charterhouse of Champmol.[78]

In the two preceding paragraphs it has been assumed that the existing choir stalls in the three west bays of the chapel adhere to Henry VII's original scheme. In the king's will they are referred to in the same sentence as the stained glass, for which designs are specifically stated to have been in existence,[79] and on the strength of that juxtaposition it would not be wholly unreasonable to infer that the form of the stalls was also settled. A possible indication that their making was well under way by the time of the king's death is the record of a payment by the duke of Buckingham the day after the visit to Westminster Abbey mentioned at the start of this paper: 'to a Fleming of Westminster, bringing certain images and showing them to my Lord, 1s.' These images are most unlikely to have been of stone,[80] and the possibility arises that the duke had encountered the carvers of the misericords, who were indubitably Netherlandish, and had invited one of their number to show him a further sample of his work.

The choir stalls incorporate three wholly exceptional features which are difficult to account for unless they were decided on when it was still intended that the stalls fulfil the unique requirement of flanking a space containing a chantry chapel (Plate 20). The most obvious of these singularities is the great elevation of the seats, without which the monks in the stalls flanking the chantry would have had hardly any sense of occupying a single liturgical space. The fact that even when skied some 1.07m (3ft 6 in.) above the floor the occupants of the more easterly stalls would still not have had a clear view of their brothers in the stalls opposite or of the liturgical action in the sanctuary may well have been used by the convent as an argument in favour of substituting for the unique and massive hearse-cum-chantry a comparatively insubstantial and dismountable hearse of traditional type. The second special feature of the stalls is the way in which they do not form continuous ranges standing in front of

---

[78] See the engraving of 1780 showing the Champmol choir looking south-west: O. Cartellieri, *La Cour des Ducs de Bourgogne*, Paris 1946, pl. 2; P. Quarré, *Claux de Werve, Imagier des ducs de Bourgogne*, exhibition catalogue, Musée des Beaux-Arts, Dijon, 1976, 99–100. The tombs of dukes Philip the Bold (d.1404) and John the Fearless (d.1419) were set up in 1410 and 1469 respectively. The few earlier English examples of monuments placed at the centres of liturgical choirs seem all to have been low structures or slabs set flush with the pavement.

[79] Above, 115.

[80] *L&P Henry VIII* iii, pt i, 497. Stone images at this period would usually be approximately life-size figures in the round or reliefs incorporated into slabs or architectural features, neither of which were safely movable without relatively expensive packing. If Buckingham had wished to inspect samples of stone sculpture he would either have gone to the workshop, which is likely to have been close to the Lady chapel, or would have paid considerably more to have them brought to him at his city of London mansion.

Fig. 18. Interior looking east. (Dart ii, frontispiece)

the main arcade piers but are broken up by the piers into runs of five.[81] This arrangement, which is not found at an earlier date in England but which occurs at several places in Germany and the Low Countries,[82] may well have been adopted at the suggestion of the Netherlandish makers of the stalls. Yet the decisive factor in its use here was surely not craft tradition but the practical necessity of maximizing the heavily used spaces flanking the chantry. Perhaps not fortuitously, the eschewal of the standard English practice of making lateral stalls form continuous ranges, and the concomitant visibility of the piers, resembled the omission of a conventional high altar reredos and sedilia in serving to promote the visual autonomy of the chapel's architecture. The inclusion of canopies which straddle the fronts of the piers and do not surmount seats (Plate 15) is a most ingenious way of adhering to the English tradition of continuous rows of canopies. The third peculiarity, the omission of a full set of return stalls, can be attributed to the decision that the west wall of the chapel contain not a single entrance, such as was to be found at the west end of every other liturgical choir in England, but a triple portal whose outer doors would have served to channel pilgrim traffic towards the gangways leading past the chantry and the high altar to the area of Henry VI's shrine (Fig. 6). The outer two doors are flanked by narrow areas of solid masonry whose purpose was clearly to accommodate the single return stalls occupied by the abbot and prior (Fig. 2).[83] This neat solution to a unique problem was upset when, at some stage in the making of the stalls too early to have left any physical traces in their fabric, it was decided to enlarge the return stalls so that they overlap the beast-bearing polygonal shafts which form the outermost parts of the rich ornamentation of the west portal (Plate 16).[84]

[81] In the westmost bay the presence of return stalls determines that there are not five regular stalls but two plus two canopies which do not shelter seats. The earliest interior views of the chapel (engraving by W. Hollar dated 1665 in Sandford, between pp. 442 and 443; Dart ii, frontispiece (Fig. 18)) show the conventional continuous arrangement, and for this reason it has been suggested that the present arrangement is a late eighteenth-century alteration: Tracy, *Choir Stalls 1400–1540*, 53. That the setting of the stalls between the piers is original is evident from the presence of specially wide canopies straddling the fronts of the main arcade piers of the chapel (Plate 16), from the exact fit of the backs of the stalls against the flanks of the piers, and from the fact that both canopies and backs are authentic early sixteenth-century work. The Sandford and Dart views probably show the conventional treatment because the drawings on which the engravings are based failed to emphasize sufficiently the intruding parts of piers, which would in any case have tended, particularly in a monochrome medium, to merge into the miasma of vertical lines needed to render the uprights of the canopies. The oil painting in the Museum of London attributed to Canaletto and reproduced in Tracy, *Choir Stalls 1400–1540*, pl. 178, has no independent topographical value as it is essentially a crib of the 1723 view and reproduces some of the peculiar errors of the latter. Dr Tracy now accepts that the interruption of the main upper seating by the piers of the main arcade is an original feature; see Tracy below, 227 n. 1.
[82] For example Cologne, Xanten and 's-Hertogenbosch cathedrals. It appears that the only earlier English stallwork which approximates to the 'interrupted' arrangement in Henry VII's chapel is that of the mid-fifteenth century in the Beauchamp chapel, Warwick.
[83] This part of the elevation of the west wall is shown with plain masonry in Cottingham ii, pls. IV, V, but with blind tracery panelling in Britton ii, pt XI, pls. I, II. Which rendering is correct cannot be ascertained as the masonry is entirely concealed by the return stalls.
[84] The fact that the abbot and prior had return stalls in the main monastic choir makes it likely that they were always intended to have such seats in the new Lady chapel. The width of the existing return stalls is close to the minimum needed to accommodate a desk and an entrance from the east, and the possibility exists that the architect and the designer of the stalls had not collaborated successfully. The omission of return stalls from John Thorpe's plan (Fig. 3) is not evidence for their absence in the late sixteenth century as Thorpe's rendering of the stalls is inaccurate in several respects.

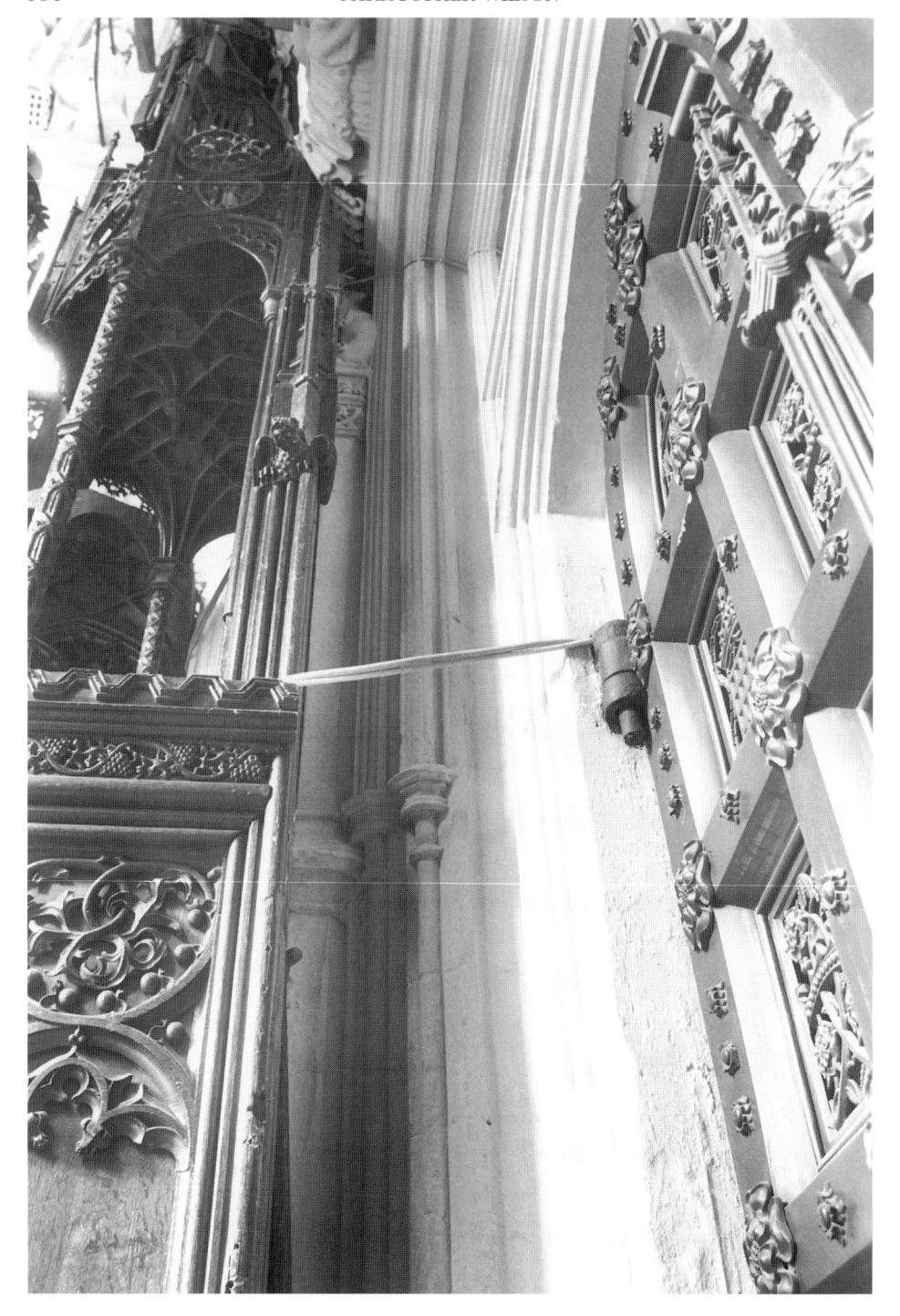

Plate 16. Detail of south return stall and west wall.

The importance of the stalls in the functional scheme is evident from their being the first fittings mentioned in the king's will after the royal tomb and chantry. Although, as was noted in the first section of this paper, a few stalls were occupied by monks participating in the daily Lady mass and many more at mass on the principal feasts of the Virgin, the strong probability that there were no stalls in the old Lady chapel suggests that the present seats were thought of as being chiefly for the use of the monks when attending the obits and anniversaries. The 1504 indentures require that the king's weekly and annual commemorations be attended by the whole convent, which was normally around fifty in the late middle ages.[85] However, the main upper stalls of Henry VII's chapel provide only for two groups of twelve monks in the lateral stalls, with the abbot and prior in the return stalls. Undoubtedly, this disposition was intended to evoke the prototype of all religious communities, Christ and the Apostles.[86] The same ideal number was also provided for in the set of cloth-of-gold copes specially commissioned by the king in Florence and bequeathed to the abbey in his will. The total number of copes furnished was twenty-nine, but three will have been for the celebrant and his two principal assistants, whose other vestments were of 'the same clothe and worke' as the copes (Plate 1).[87] Normally it was to be the abbot who celebrated at anniversaries, and on these occasions his stall would be occupied by the prior and that of the prior by the subprior or some other major obedientiary.[88] In the vigils on the day before each anniversary the abbot and prior would occupy their own stalls. Unsurprisingly, given the general laconism of the will, the purpose of these quite exceptionally splendid and costly vestments is not spelled out, but since the monks were to attend the anniversaries 'revested',[89] and since the number of copes was that needed for the occupants of the main stalls and for the celebrant and his chief assistants, there can be little doubt that they were for use in the chapel on the anniversaries.[90] It will have been the most senior monks present who wore the copes at

---

[85] The number of monks regularly participating in the services in the main choir was considerably less than fifty, but no exact figures are available; Harvey, *Living and Dying*, 73–4, 77 and n. 22. The main choir at Westminster contained sixty-four mid-thirteenth-century stalls, two of which are shown without their seats in the early eighteenth-century plan that is the earliest exact record: Lethaby, *Craftsmen*, 23; WAM (P) 916.

[86] Cf. the provision at St George's, Windsor for twenty-six canons and the same number of Garter knights; C. Wilson, *The Gothic Cathedral: the Architecture of the Great Church 1130–1530*, 218, 220. The complement of the Chapel Royal under Henry VII was also made up of multiples of thirteen. For the numbers see R. Bowers, 'The cultivation and promotion of music in the household and orbit of Thomas Wolsey', in *Cardinal Wolsey: Church, State and Art*, ed. S.J. Gunn and P.J. Lindley, Cambridge 1991, 180 n. 6.

[87] Above, 134.

[88] It is possible that the prior and one of the obedientiaries acted as deacon and subdeacon at the anniversary masses, in which case the abbot's and prior's stalls will still have been occupied by senior monks.

[89] BL Harley MS 1498, fo. 16; *CCR 1500–09*, 142.

[90] Use in the chapel is discounted in L. Monnas, 'New documents for the vestments of Henry VII at Stonyhurst College', *Burlington Magazine* 131, 1989, 349, apparently on the grounds that this would have duplicated the will's provision (above, 132–4) for vestments to be used at masses celebrated at the altars in the chapel. However, the will makes quite clear that the latter vestments were for the subordinate altars in the chapel and had yet to be acquired by the king's executors. The inclusion of twenty-nine copes in the cloth of gold set is the best evidence that it was intended principally for use on the king's anniversaries celebrated in his chapel, notwithstanding the fact that its normal place of storage was the main abbey sacristy, to judge from the reference to twenty-eight copes in the 1539

the anniversaries and sat in the upper stalls then and at the weekly obits. Yet, as the extant annual accounts for Henry VII's foundation show, many more than twenty-six monks attended the weekly obits and the anniversaries.[91] Some would doubtless have sat in the substalls, but professed monks who were not priests, and any unprofessed novices present, probably stood before the more easterly stalls or occupied benches. Certainly, the absence of eastern substalls would have allowed flexibility in the numbers of junior monks participating. At the anniversary masses considerable numbers of monks over and above the three principal celebrants would serve the altar, and it is doubtless they who are referred to in the indentures as being 'about the said high Aultier', as distinct from being 'present in the said Quere'.[92]

The dynastic mausoleum

Running along the outside of Henry VII's chantry enclosure, and repeated on the inside, are verses which tell us, among other things, that the founder of the chapel 'established a sepulchre for himself and for his wife, his children and his house'.[93] Since the composition of this inscription postdated Henry VII's death[94] there must be distinct possibility that it reflected not his but his successor's notion of the purpose of the chapel.[95] Against such an interpretation may be adduced firstly a reference in Henry VII's will, in the passage setting out his reasons for fixing on Westminster as his burial place, to the abbey as the 'commen sepulture of the kinges of this Reame',[96] and secondly the extreme improbability that in choosing to extend the fabric of this particular church he had failed to realize that he was augmenting its capacity to receive further royal burials.

Only the building itself yields any clues as to where in the chapel Henry VII was envisaging that tombs might be installed in future. Of the radiating chapels, the axial one housing Henry VI's altar was surely meant to remain unencumbered, and those flanking it are set at a forty-five degree angle and would therefore have provided too little space for correctly orientated tombs. The western radiating chapels were potentially sites for tombs, although the role of these spaces as royal closets is likely to have

dissolution inventory (Walcott, 'Inventories', 332). Confirmation of this interpretation is the correspondence between the fourteen senior clergy of the post-dissolution cathedral foundation at Westminster (bishop, dean and twelve prebendaries) who participated in the anniversary in 1541 (*L&P Henry VIII*, 17 (1542), 135 (no. 258)) and the fourteen copes left in the main abbey sacristy after Henry VIII appropriated the others in 1540 (Walcott, 'Inventories', 314).

91 WAM 24236, 24238, 24240, 24241*, 24242, 24244, 24246, 24248–50.
92 BL Harley MS 1498, fo. 16.
93 'Septim[us] Henric[us] . . . statuit . . . Sepvlcru[m] Pro se, proq[ue] sua Coniuge, prole, Domo.' There is no evidence of any intention to translate into the new chapel the bodies of any of Henry's and Elizabeth of York's children who died in infancy, or of any consideration given to burying Prince Arthur anywhere else than at Worcester cathedral.
94 It includes the king's death date.
95 A more blatant instance of Henry VIII's interference with the design of his parents' monument is the fulsome mention of himself in the inscription round the tomb-chest, which was probably composed in 1512: 'Happy in their progeny were those parents to whom, England, you owe Henry the Eighth.' (FOELICES PROLE PARENTES HENRICVM QVIB[VS] OCTAVVM TERRA ANGLIA DEBES.)
96 Above, 113.

deprived any monuments here of the desirable attribute of standing on the central longitudinal axis. The most prestigious sites of all were of course those on the main axis of the central vessel, and it is highly probable that for a period of a year or so beginning late in 1515, and again in 1525, Henry VIII intended to use for himself the space here which had originally been earmarked for his parents' monument.[97] If this was indeed the case, it follows that the relegation of the founder's chantry and tomb to the apse, and the concomitant abandoning of his plan to raise a shrine to Henry VI on that site, were due to his son. In the end Henry VIII was buried at Windsor where, perhaps with a certain poetic justice, no more than a simple inscription marks the spot. The burial which eventually launched the Westminster Lady chapel on its career as a mausoleum for Henry VII's successors and descendants, that of Edward VI in 1553, was, uniquely and bizarrely, excavated below the high altar and was therefore never marked by any monument.[98] In the opening decades of the sixteenth century the south aisle received at least one burial of a former member of Lady Margaret Beaufort's household and possibly also that of a relation, which suggests that this was regarded as the countess's chapel in the fullest sense. The north aisle, the obvious place for later royal graves other than the main vessel, was actually used for the next two burials in this category, those of Mary I and Elizabeth I. The monument to the latter highlights the main disadvantage of the aisles as receptacles for royal tombs, for it occupies an uncomfortably large proportion of the modest 3.35m (11ft) span. Presumably Henry VII was anticipating that later royal monuments would be as restrained in their dimensions as the chantry he commissioned proves he was intending to be in relation to his own tomb.[99]

[97] This explanation of the discrepancy between the intended and actual sites of Henry VII's monument was apparently first suggested by H.F. Westlake, who adduced as evidence the draft contract of 1519 for a monument to Henry VIII and Katherine of Aragon, to be made by Pietro Torrigiano, and a papal bull of 1525 which refers to the Westminster Lady chapel as if it were a proposed new foundation of Henry VIII's, but presumably meaning a new chantry foundation: Westlake ii, 478–9. Henry VIII's intention to usurp his parents' burial site may have been formed as early as 1512, when the body of his father (and probably that of his mother also) was transferred to a site within the chapel whose precise position is unknown; but the obvious moment at which to act upon such an intention was the Autumn of 1515, when the tomb of Henry VII and Queen Elizabeth was due for completion under the terms of Torrigiano's contract. An indication that the 1519 tomb project was intended for Windsor is a memorandum of 23 April 1517 recording the king's decision to be buried at St George's; Hope, *Windsor Castle*, 463, a reference which appears to have been missed by most writers on Henry VIII's monument. However, the draft contract of 1519, which mentions no site, specifies that it was up to the king to indicate where he wished the tomb should stand (W. Illingworth, 'Transcript of a draft of an indenture of covenants for the erecting of a tomb to the memory of King Henry the Eighth, and Queen Katherine his wife', *Archaeologia* 16, 1812, 86), and it therefore appears that, despite the decision reported in the 1517 memorandum, the king still intended to keep his options open.

[98] This placing recalls the early medieval treatment of saints' relics, but the resemblance is unlikely to have been in the minds of either the emphatically protestant Edward VI or his sister Mary I, who may have thought of the arrangement as a way of making it impossible to raise a monument over the burial site. See also n. 46 above.

[99] This existing tomb chest is a mere 1.52m (5ft) wide. The need for a gangway between the tomb and the chantry means that none of the designs considered by Henry VII can have been much more than 1.83m (6ft) wide.

In concluding, it should be emphasized that though Henry VII must have accepted, at least privately, that the peripheral parts of his chapel would be changed to the extent of becoming the sites of future burials and monuments, there is no reason to doubt that he thought of the central vessel and its tightly organized fittings as a complete and self-contained entity rather than as something capable of extension or reworking to suit the needs of his successors. Henry intended that the principal beneficiaries of the foundation would be: himself and his queen, who were named first in the chantry masses; his uncle, soon to be canonized and enshrined behind the high altar; the monks of Westminster, who acquired not only the most sumptuous Lady chapel in Christendom but a source of pecuniary profit;[100] and of course those laity who chose to visit the chapel to take advantage of the notable range of devotional resources marshalled there. The king's status as author of the entire project was to be proclaimed forever by the uniquely assertive placing of his almost oppressively large and splendid hearse-cum-chantry; but when the chapel was at length dedicated on 19 February 1516, nearly seven years after the king's death, the chantry had been demoted from its symbolically central position, its bronzework had been left ungilded, and it had failed to acquire the massive phalanx of tapers which were essential to its function as a permanent hearse. The Westminster monk Thomas Gardiner, whose manuscript history of England is our only source for the dedication date, was no doubt well aware that all of Henry VII's wishes had not been respected, yet this did not prevent him from hailing the foundation as 'the moste honorabull . . . that hath bene harde off . . . an insampull to all kynges crystun to provyde for ther parpetuall rememberaunsse'.[101]

---

[100] For the surplus of income over expenditure see B. Harvey, *Estates*, 33. From 1517 Abbot Islip was taking 30s for celebrating the anniversary mass instead of the 20s he had taken hitherto, which was the amount specified in the 1504 indentures: WAM 24244.

[101] Smyly, 'Thomas Gardiner's History', 246. See also n. 36 above.

The Building History of the Lady Chapels

TIM TATTON-BROWN

The old Lady chapel

THE DOCUMENTARY history for the building of the Lady chapel has been discussed in several earlier publications, most usefully by Sir Howard Colvin.[1] It is, therefore, only necessary to summarise its history here.

The foundation stone for a new Lady chapel at Westminster Abbey was laid, as Matthew Paris tells us, by the boy-king Henry III, on the Vigil of Pentecost (16 May) 1220, on the day before his coronation in the Abbey. This was only just over two weeks after Henry III had attended the final part of the ceremony for the laying of the foundation stones of Salisbury cathedral, a much grander affair.[2] At Salisbury, the large eastern chapel (dedicated to the Trinity, but always used for the Lady mass) was a rectangular aisled structure which was rapidly built so that it could be brought into use in 1225 and, it was hoped, also house the shrine of St Osmund. At Westminster, however, where money was tight and coming only from the Abbey's funds, the building of the new Lady chapel seems to have been a protracted affair, with completion only in about 1245–6. Pope Innocent's bull of 1245 refers to 'the repairs which the monks had begun in far too sumptuous a fashion, and which they were unable properly to finish'.[3] Some roofing work perhaps took place in 1234, when twenty oaks from Tonbridge forest were given by the king, and early in 1240 Henry gave 52 marks for a glass window in the chapel, but he also gave £10 in 1245 towards 'the work of the chapel of Mary', so the work was not quite complete when demolition of the old eastern arm started in July 1245. By 1246, when the work really must have been complete, Abbot Richard de Berking was buried in front of the high altar in the chapel. In July 1244 the fitting out of the subsidiary altars of St Michael and St Adrian was mentioned '*super voltam in nova capella*', and this probably refers to a lower-vaulted vestibule at the west end of the chapel on top of which were the secondary altars.[4] One final piece of documentary evidence speaks of the disposal of timber in 1256, from a roof that had been taken down, as 'the roof was to be rebuilt

---

[1] Colvin, *HkW* iii, 131–3.
[2] It should perhaps be noted that Salisbury cathedral was also to be a vast Lady chapel, as the whole cathedral was dedicated to the Virgin Mary.
[3] See WD, fo. 406. For this and all subsequent documentary references, see Colvin, *HkW* iii, 131–2.
[4] A similar situation, albeit of fifteenth-century date, survives in the Lady chapel at Gloucester.

in stone'. This was clearly to fit in with the completion of this part of Henry III's new eastern arm (the presbytery) of the abbey, but whether it means that the old Lady chapel was originally without a stone vault, or whether this was just the removal of roof timbers at the west end of the old Lady chapel in the vestibule area, is not now possible to know for certain.

The most important discovery of surviving material evidence for the thirteenth-century Lady chapel came in 1875 during tomb digging in the north-east and south-east chapels of Henry VII's chapel. In the latter was revealed an earlier wall across the entrance to the chapel, which immediately suggested that the thirteenth-century chapel ended in a three-sided apse. Various fragments of masonry beneath the stalls, which were examined in 1995, also reveal the plan of the north and south walls of the earlier chapel, and show that all the main arcade foundation-walls for the new Henry VII chapel were built around the outside of the lower walls of the earlier polygonal chapel, whose east end is really a half-octagon (Fig. 2). Only the present vestibule to the chapel is the same width (28ft – 8.5m – internally) as the old chapel. The width of the later chapel is about 33ft (10m) and below the raised principal stall (now the Grand Master's stall) in the north-west corner of the chapel can be seen a large fragment of *in situ* Reigate stone masonry that must date from the thirteenth century. Unfortunately much of the rest of the early masonry below the stalls on the north and south sides has been cut away, or obscured, by the ducting for the heating pipes.

One question that has not been resolved is that of the floor level of the earlier chapel. It seems unlikely to have been as high as the present floor-level, nor to have been as low as the ground-level outside or of the level of the eastern ambulatory of the presbytery. There were perhaps just a few steps up into the thirteenth-century vestibule, and it may be possible one day to determine the earlier floor level by entering the late seventeenth-century royal burial vault beneath the east end of the present south aisle.[5]

One other important piece of evidence for the form of the thirteenth-century Lady chapel are the blocked-up wall passages at the west end of the chapel, first properly understood and discussed by H.F. Westlake in 1918.[6] He pointed out that the wall passage, at window-sill level around the mid-thirteenth-century chevet could be followed on the south to a blocking (of early Tudor rubble) in the south wall of the vestibule. This clearly suggested that the wall-passage must have continued around the Lady chapel itself, and its level (at least in the vestibule area) indicates a lower floor level in the earlier chapel's vestibule.

It is therefore possible to reconstruct an approximate plan for the thirteenth-century Lady chapel (Fig. 5), but the detailing of the bay-divisions can only be guessed. If they were in the same positions as the present bays in the Henry VII chapel,[7] this would give a Lady chapel of five full bays with a three-sided apse on the east, and an additional bay for the vestibule on the west, containing the lower vault

---

[5] This might also reveal the extent of the external buttresses to the chapel.
[6] H.F. Westlake, 'Westminster Abbey: the old Lady chapel and its relation to the romanesque and gothic churches', *Archaeologia* 69, 1917–18, 31–46. On the north the wall-passage is blocked up much further to the north-west.
[7] This might be suggested by the awkward spacing of the 'great arch' in the eastern bay (see below).

beneath the documented subsidiary altars in the loft above. This would mean that the main 'nave' of the chapel (i.e. without the apse or vestibule) would have internal dimensions of 70ft by 28ft (21 by 8.5m), which compares closely with the thirteenth-century royal chapel at Windsor.

Another unresolved question is the form of the eastern arm of the Abbey before Henry III's total rebuilding of the mid-thirteenth century. This has also been extensively discussed in the past, and, as no new archaeological evidence has been forthcoming coming, it can be summarised fairly briefly here.

It now seems probable that the east end of Edward the Confessor's great new mid-eleventh-century church was tri-apsidal.[8] However, it is highly likely that this fairly basic east end was replaced in the mid-twelfth century by a new semi-circular ambulatory in preparation for the new raised shrine of St Edward the Confessor in the area behind the high altar that was dedicated in 1163. It is more than likely that the new shrine of 1268–9 was on, or close to, the site of the twelfth-century shrine, but without further archaeological evidence from below the floors, it will not be possible to resolve this.[9] It is, however, inconceivable that the new shrine of 1163 was just in the eastern apse of the Confessor's church, and that the new Lady chapel was built in 1220 as a free-standing chapel. Building work in the Abbey in the twelfth century is, of course, poorly documented, but the foundations of the nave, that were found in 1933, show that several modifications to the structure took place in the twelfth century.[10]

Three-sided (or semi-octagonal) apses are highly unusual in England, so that it is surely no coincidence that the three known examples of this, at Westminster, Windsor and Lichfield, are all of closely similar dimensions. It also seems likely that they were also all first built at the same time (c.1220–40), and that they might have had the same designer.[11] It is not possible to be sure of this because all three structures were completely rebuilt in the later middle ages. At Lichfield the Lady chapel was rebuilt in its present form in the early fourteenth century,[12] and at Windsor the thirteenth-century remains are fragmentary. The ultimate origin of Westminster's three-sided Lady chapel apse is presumably in France, where this form of termination for the eastern Lady chapel is common in the thirteenth century. Bayeux, Coutances and Amiens cathedrals are just three early examples which could be cited. The form developed in France to its high point at the Sainte Chapelle in Paris, which was also begun in c.1240, and has a seven-sided apse. In England most other churches of this date, like for example the east end of Salisbury cathedral, or the chancel of the new Temple church in London, tend to be of the 'hall' type with straight east ends. It is unfortunate that no architectural fragments from the thirteenth-century Lady chapel

---

[8] See discussion in R. Gem, 'The romanesque rebuilding of Westminster Abbey', *Proceedings of the Battle Conference on Anglo-Norman Studies*, ed. R. Allen Brown, 3, 1980, 33–60, and also E.C. Fernie, 'Enclosed apses and Edward's church at Westminster', *Archaeologia* 104, 1973, 235–60.

[9] In 1910 a large hole was dug by W.R. Lethaby on the south side of the original apse, but this only revealed the original eleventh-century foundation – see *Archaeologia* 62, 1910, 99.

[10] Gem, 'Romanesque rebuilding', 42.

[11] Not necessarily the same master-mason, and certainly not Henry of Reims, despite much earlier discussion of this.

[12] By William Eyton, c.1310–36, according to John Harvey, 'The origins of the perpendicular style', in *Studies in Building History*, ed. E.M. Jope, 1961, especially 150–2.

at Westminster have been found, so that it is not possible to form any idea of the fenestration or other architectural decoration of this chapel.

Sometime in the 1470s a new chapel of St Erasmus was built onto the south side of the Lady chapel at the expense of Elizabeth Woodville, Edward IV's queen. This was presumably a small structure like Henry IV's chantry chapel of St Edward the Confessor that was built onto the north side of the Trinity chapel in Canterbury cathedral in 1438–40.[13] At the west end of the Lady chapel the vestibule may well have been modified in the later middle ages and it was no doubt in the 'loft' above the vestibule vault that the organs would have been sited.[14] There was also a vestry, but it is not known where it was situated, and around the east end (and south-eastern side) of the old Lady chapel were, by the later middle ages, a garden and various buildings including Geoffrey Chaucer's tenement of 1399, and Caxton's shop from 1476.[15] These were probably close to the major route from Westminster palace to the south transept and chapter house, which seems to have run through the monks' cemetery and garden.

Henry VII's new Lady chapel

Once again, the background to the building of a new Lady chapel at Westminster Abbey has been frequently discussed. As is well known, the chapel was also originally intended to house a shrine-tomb for King Henry VI, as well as the new Tudor tombs for Henry VII, his queen, and his mother, Lady Margaret Beaufort as well as possibly his grandmother, Queen Katherine de Valois. However, in the 1490s Henry had already begun to rebuild the Lady chapel at St George's Chapel, Windsor as his own place of burial. This was close to the place of burial of Henry VI (his body had been moved from Chertsey abbey to Windsor by Richard III, in 1484), and at this time it looked as though Westminster Abbey had ceased to be a royal burial place. This was not to the liking of the abbot and monks at Westminster, and in 1498 they were able to persuade Henry VII that Henry VI had always wanted to be buried at Westminster.[16] Unfortunately the building accounts for the chapel have completely disappeared, and all we possess are the exact amounts paid out annually for the cost of the work. These very large sums are:

1502	£1,481 18s 1d	1506	£1,812 17s 0d
1503	£1,765 16s 7d	1507	£2,121 10s 7d
1504	£1,370 12s 62d	1508	£3,780 11s 11d
1505	£2,527 6s 42d	1509	£1,000 0s 0d
		Total	£14,860 13s 1d

---

[13] This chapel was not constructed until the reign of Henry VI when it was put up at about the same time as Henry V's chantry was being completed at Westminster. See F. Woodman, *The Architectural History of Canterbury Cathedral*, 1981, 178–9.

[14] The earlier altar of St Adrian seems to have disappeared. For the organs and the statue of St Mary Magdalen, which was probably in the vestibule, see above, 26–8.

[15] Rosser, *Medieval Westminster*, 8, 161, 213.

[16] Stanley, *Historical Memorials*, 146–8.

The figure for the last year is incomplete because payments ceased on the king's death on 21 April, but a further £5,000 was given to the abbot John Islip (1500–32) to pay for the chapel to be 'holly and perfectly finished in every behalve' (to quote the king's will). This means that the total cost of the building was at least £20,000.[17]

We also know that the old Lady chapel and the adjoining chapel of St Erasmus were demolished between October 1502 and January 1503, and that Richard Russell, the Abbey's master-carpenter, was paid 8d a day for seventy-three days for taking down St Erasmus's chapel. This possibly indicates that this chapel, which was only about thirty years old, was a timber-framed structure built (possibly on a brick foundation) as a large oriel on the side of the Lady chapel.[18] A group of labourers was also paid £13 4s 6d for taking away stone from the demolished structure to various places in the Abbey. Then on 24 January 1503 at 2.45p.m., as Holinshed's chronicle tells us, 'the first stone of our ladie chapell' was laid by Abbot Islip, Sir Reginald Bray (who was closely involved with the work at St George's, Windsor), Doctor Barnes, Master of the Rolls, Doctor Wall, the king's chaplain and many others. Holinshed also tells us that this stone was inscribed with quite a long Latin inscription, but which this stone was (or stones were) is not known. It is possible that the inscription was of bronze set into some blocks of the Kentish ragstone plinth, but no trace survives. Equally the inscription could have been on a large Caen stone block at the base of the plinth on the east side, but if so it was not identified in the early nineteenth century when the plinth was fully restored in Kentish ragstone.[19]

Apart from the exact date of the start of the work and the overall annual costs, very little other information is known, though it has usually been assumed, with good reason, that the work was nearing completion at the time of the king's death, and hence that all the building work took about seven seasons. We also know that the initial master of the works was Sir William Tyler, but he died in 1504, and was probably replaced not long afterwards by William Bolton, the Prior of St Bartholomew's, Smithfield, who saw the works to completion.[20] The master mason is not known, but on the strength of a famous contract of 1506,[21] and by comparing the building with other documented work elsewhere, Dr Christopher Wilson has suggested that Robert Janyns was the designer of the Henry VII chapel.[22] Earlier writers like Lethaby[23] had, however suggested that the designer was Robert Vertue (or even his brother William), and it should be noted that both Robert Vertue and Robert Janyns died in 1506. The possibility of more than one designer should also be considered, and this will be discussed further below.

---

[17] The best summary and discussion of all this is Colvin, *HKW* iii, where detailed references can be found.
[18] Was it possibly like Bishop Audley's semi-octagonal structure built 1500–7 on the south side of the Lady chapel at Hereford cathedral, though this was of stone?
[19] No repairs to the plinth were carried out in the recent restoration.
[20] Colvin, *HKW* iii, 213–14.
[21] It is an estimate for the king's tomb made by 'the king's master masons', Robert Vertue, Robert Jenyns and John Lebons.
[22] C. Wilson, 'The designer of Henry VII's chapel, Westminster Abbey', in *The Reign of Henry VII*, 133–56.
[23] Lethaby, *Craftsmen*, 225; *Re-examined*, 164.

Phases of building and building materials

Because the documentary evidence is so meagre, we need to turn to the building itself to try to work out the sequence of construction. Rather surprisingly this has not been attempted before, presumably because the early nineteenth-century external restoration was so thorough. This is certainly true,[24] although there is one area that is virtually unrestored, and that is the area of masonry on the inner walls under the aisle roofs. This area shows one major construction break, as well as one significant change in the form of the upper clerestory wall. Quite a large amount of the original timber roof trusses survive here, and it is possible to demonstrate a building sequence in this area, which will be discussed in more detail below.

Looking at the building as a whole, four main phases for the building sequence may be suggested (Fig. 19):
1. The foundations and plinth up to floor level.
2. The arcades and outer aisle walls.
3. The upper clerestory wall.
4. The aisle vaults and high vault, flyers and massive outer pinnacle turrets.

Before these are dealt with in more detail, we should look briefly at the building materials.

In 1807 the abbey mason, Thomas Gayfere, reported that the following building stone had previously been used: 'In foundation, Kentish rag: plinth Kentish stone, from Maidstone; corbels, or springing pieces, to flying buttresses, Huddlestone, Yorkshire;[25] superstructure generally, Caen, Normandy;[26] skreens to south-east and north-east chapels, Rygate stone, Surrey.'[27] He then went on to say that Bath stone would be the best stone for the restoration, and this stone now covers much, but not all, of the exterior.

An examination of the fabric of the chapel during the recent restoration has confirmed Gayfere's report, and his brief comments can be slightly amplified. The whole of the plinth is certainly of Kentish ragstone from the Maidstone area of west Kent, and the worn original masonry can be readily distinguished from the early nineteenth-century repairs in the same stone.[28] Much of the external carved masonry is, as we have seen, now of Bath stone, but in several areas masonry of Caen stone, and Magnesian limestone was seen on the outside of the chapel once the very thick layer of surface pollution had been cleaned off. The largest areas of original masonry that survive externally today are on the upper wall between the clerestory windows. Magnesian limestone, which was quarried in south Yorkshire at various quarries, including Huddlestone, is a fine hard limestone which was used in London for carved

---

[24] There is, however, still some original external masonry.
[25] John Stow, *Survey of London*, ed. C.L. Kingsford, 1908, ii, 107, writing at the beginning of the seventeenth century, had heard that the chapel was (partly) built of stone from Huddlestone in Yorkshire.
[26] Sir Christopher Wren, in his report on the Abbey, also mentions the 'tender Caen stone': S. Wren, *Parentalia, or Memoirs of the Family of the Wrens*, 1750, 299.
[27] Cottingham i, 8; Neale and Brayley, 51–2.
[28] For the sources of this stone see B.C. Worssam and T. Tatton-Brown, 'Kentish rag and other Kent building stones', *Archaeologia Cantiana* 112, 1993, 93–125. Gayfere's new ragstone has a distinct early nineteenth-century tooling.

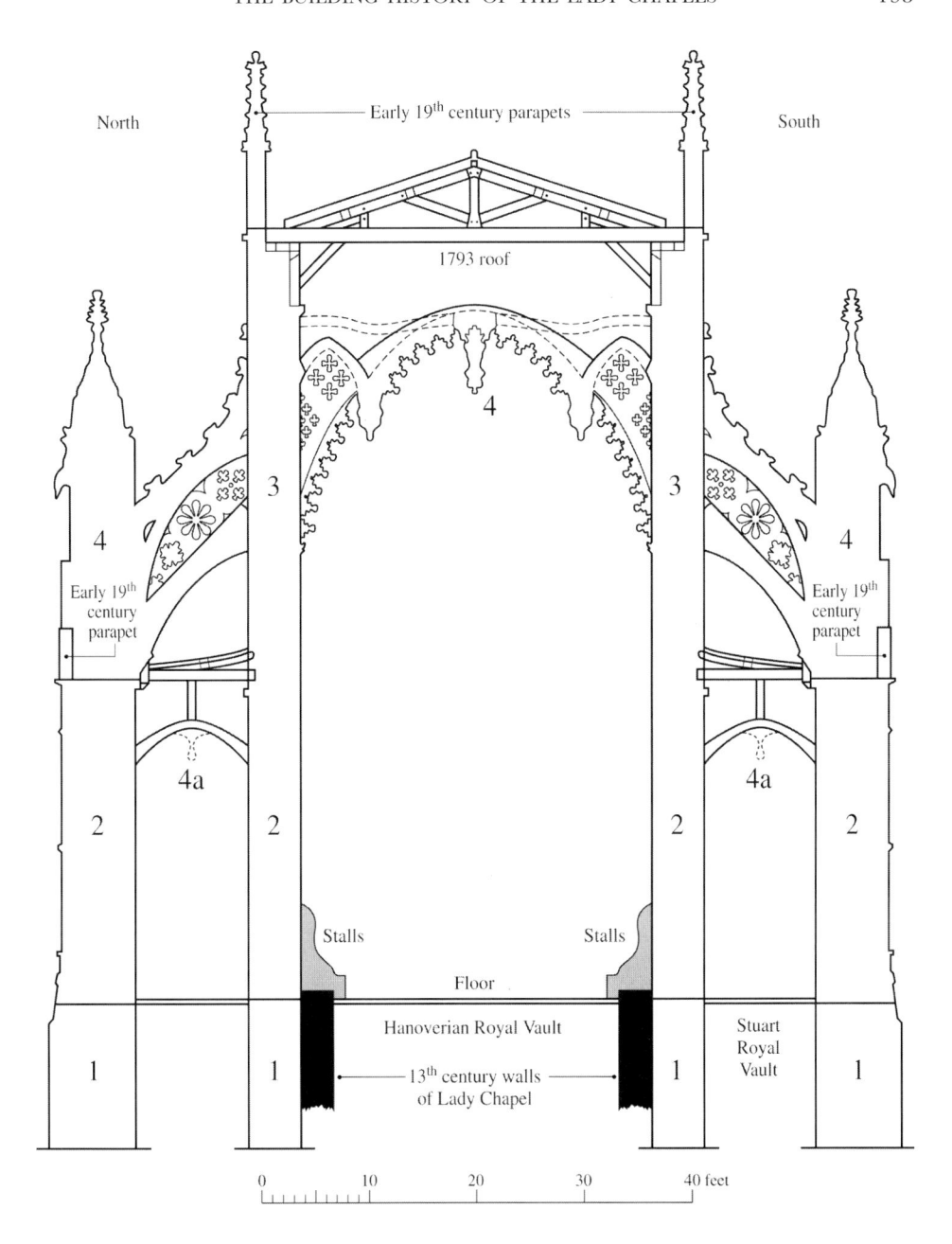

Fig. 19. Transverse section showing construction sequence.

work from the fourteenth century.[29] Its use at the Abbey could also be seen in the upper part of the west front, as well as in the west porch[30] and on the outside of the south transept, below the great rose window, where it was used to case up the Reigate stone in the mid-fifteenth century. It would have been an ideal material for the corbels and 'springing pieces to flying buttresses' as Gayfere states, though most of this has now been replaced by Bath stone. Caen stone was, with Reigate stone, the commonest building stone used in London from the eleventh to the sixteenth century.[31] However, Reigate stone is very soft (much softer than Caen), and it was realised in the later middle ages that it soon weathered very badly, so in the fifteenth and sixteenth centuries Reigate stone was mostly only used internally. This is where it is found in the Henry VII chapel both in the screens (whose upper parts were destroyed in 1806), and in quite a lot of the carved material. Reigate stone can also be seen in the walling below the aisle roofs and above the vaults. The principal internal material is, however, still Caen stone.[32]

The other principal materials that were used for the building were oak for roof trusses (and no doubt for the scaffolding), and lead which has always been the material for covering the roofs. No original lead now survives on the roofs, though until the early nineteenth century most of the original lead probably survived on the aisle roofs, as well as on the two upper western turrets of the high roof.[33] (The lead on the high roof was renewed in 1793.)

The foundations and plan

As we have already seen, the new Lady chapel was almost certainly constructed around the outside of the lowest section of the walls of the thirteenth-century Lady chapel (Fig. 5). Once the demolition work, which took place in the later autumn of 1502,[34] had reached a certain level, the inside of the old chapel must have been carefully packed with rubble and levelled up. Abbot Berking's tomb, and perhaps some other burials, were probably left *in situ*, though Katherine of Valois' coffin (still in a temporary tomb) was removed.[35] New foundations were then made in the ground outside the old chapel walls, first for the piers, which may have had foundations in the earlier buttress foundations, five on either side, which were ultimately to be the supporters of large turrets and flying buttresses. Around the east end of the chapel even more remarkable foundations were made in a triangular form, which were for solid radiating walls between the eastern pier foundations and the octagonal buttresses. This allowed five radiating chapels to be made, each having a roughly rect-

---

[29] E. Gee, 'Stone from the medieval limestone quarries of south Yorkshire', in *Collectanea Historica. Essays in Memory of Stuart Rigold*, ed. A. Detsicas, 1981, 247–55.
[30] T. Tatton Brown, 'Westminster Abbey: archaeological recording at the west end of the church', *Antiquaries Journal* 75, 1995, 171–88.
[31] Salzman, *Building in England*, 129–30, 135–6.
[32] It has been difficult to identify most of the internal stone because of the thick coatings of limewash.
[33] Dismantled in 1803 and replaced with stone in 1822.
[34] From October 1502 until the end of the year.
[35] See above, 192. Henry VII may have intended to return her body to the new chapel, as we have already seen.

angular floor plan, and this exactly reflects the plan of the larger mid-thirteenth-century chevet of the Abbey. In fact, at an early stage, it was clearly intended that the new Lady chapel should be a smaller version of the earlier presbytery with, in each case, a shrine at the focus. The radical new idea, however, was to have a continuous frieze-fenestration all the way around the outside of the lower walls, though it would, of course, be broken into by the solid octagonal turrets. Even more remarkable was the use of bow-windows (flanked by half-bows) in the aisles (Fig. 7), and double-canted (convex-concave) windows, ending at the centre in a V-shape (and in six separate planes) in the chapel windows (Fig. 2 and Plate IA). These two types of windows had just been used in a new domestic tower at Windsor Castle, which was constructed for Henry VII by the master mason, Robert Janyns, in about 1498–1501.[36] Only just before that the Lady chapel at St George's, Windsor had been rebuilt (1494–8), when it was still thought that St George's Chapel would be Henry VII's place of burial.[37] The new Lady chapel at Westminster was, therefore, an extraordinary combination of ideas from both these buildings, and it seems highly likely, as Christopher Wilson has suggested, that Janyns was the master mason for this new virtuoso work at Westminster.[38] However, Janyns died in 1506, and, as will be discussed below, it is probable that the upper (clerestory) section of the building and the vaults were designed by another master mason.

The idea of having a frieze-fenestration for the aisle and chapel was certainly planned from the beginning as the many planes of all these windows is continued right down to the ground in the high external plinth. This plinth actually has 140 different faces all the way around the outside of the chapel, and this lowest six feet is made entirely with plain Kentish ragstone ashlar, topped by a simple offset course with a hollow chamfer. Above this the building stone changes[39] but there are two more plain ashlar courses with, only above this, a large moulded string-course, which is exactly at the new internal floor level.[40] Only above this (nearly 9ft – 2.7m – above the ground) does all the fantastically elaborate Perpendicular panel work start. This is perhaps because many small buildings around the chapel were expected to obscure its lowest levels.[41] The foundations of the internal piers for the new chapel would also have been brought up to this height, perhaps with relieving arches between each pier,[42] and then all the intervening space would have been filled and packed with rubble to make what was effectively a large podium. Only later were burial vaults (getting larger with time) cut down into the packing (culminating in the large central royal vault of 1737),[43] and at this stage no crypt or undercroft was considered. To

---

[36] Colvin, *HKW* iii, 308.
[37] Colvin, *HKW* iii, 308–11. He also intended the new shrine for Henry VI to be there.
[38] Note 22 above.
[39] It is now Bath stone, but was originally either Caen or Magnesian limestone.
[40] All of this, including all the details of the mouldings, are shown in the fine measured drawings by Cottingham. No new measured drawings were made during the most recent restorations, though repairs have been marked on a new set of drawings made by Rattee and Kett.
[41] Little is known about the details of these buildings, or where exactly the boundary wall with the Palace of Westminster was situated.
[42] No details of these are known, though parts of them may be visible in the later royal burial vault in the south aisle.
[43] Below, 319 and Fig. 43. The earliest vault was Henry VII's own small burial vault, but this was unlikely to have been dug until after the chapel was complete. Dean Stanley's investigations found that it was

Fig. 20. Section of west wall. (Neale and Brayley i, pl. lv)

reach this new podium level, a large new flight of steps was created, which ran from the ambulatory beneath the Henry V chantry chapel to the landing in front of the planned new triple doorway into the chapel. On either side of this landing, small doorways were made to open into the extreme west ends of the new north and south aisles. The west walls of these aisles were made straight by cutting off the eastern buttresses of the thirteenth-century chevet chapels of St Paul (north) and St Nicholas (south) and blocking the eastern pairs of chapel windows. Rubble infill was needed here, as well as for blocking the ends of the old thirteenth-century wall passage.[44] At an early stage the triple portal from the ambulatory, which incorporates the slender piers that support the east end of the Henry V chantry, would have been built. This triple portal had as its counterpart on the east side a second triple portal (later to be filled with magnificent bronze gates),[45] and covering the whole area above the vestibule a four-centred north-south barrel-vault was also erected at an early stage. This, in fact, was almost certainly the only large vault to be built for the chapel in the first stage of the work, and the whole thing is very cleverly contrived to allow a light-well to be made above it (Fig. 13). The barrel vault is covered by a low-level shed roof, so that above it light could still get into the upper part of the Henry V chantry chapel, and, most importantly, so that a very large new west window could be made for the new chapel (Fig. 20).[46]

The arcades and outer walls

While the new vestibule and triple portal were being made, the arcades and then the outer walls of the new chapel were constructed, presumably working from west to east, though there is no clear evidence for this in the visible fabric. The arcade piers have a very complicated plan, and it is clear that from the beginning a very elaborate set of mouldings had been specified.[47] The aisles were made with four square bays on each side, with double doorways opening into extra half-bays to the west. These accommodated the passageways from the vestibule to the spiral staircases that were made in the two westernmost octagonal turrets (Fig. 2).[48] The turrets with staircases can just be distinguished externally by the small rectangular windows that light the vices. All the other turrets, which were made to support the flying buttresses, are solid. At the east ends of the aisles two solid stone walls were constructed which had stone altars and reredoses attached to their west faces. The walls themselves are over three

not quite aligned with the tomb above, and that it was made of very carefully cut blocks of Reigate stone. See Stanley, *Historical Memorials*, 524.

[44] Above, 190.

[45] As there was already an earlier fifteenth-century triple portal into the vestibule of the thirteenth-century Lady chapel, it is possible that there was a triple doorway into the original chapel, or (as at Windsor again) a central doorway flanked by blind openings.

[46] Even the new vestibule itself was able to be lit with windows under the barrel-vault in the north-east and south-east corners.

[47] All these moulding details are shown in Cottingham.

[48] The extreme north-west corner of the north aisle was given a stone screen not long afterwards (from the style of the masonry) to surround a small sacristy.

feet thick, and project well beyond the last octagonal turret making a very sharp re-entrant angle in the external face. The east ends of these walls then form the base-line for the five sides of the half-octagon that were planned to contain the new shrine. There is, therefore, a clear offsetting eastwards of the junction between the two parts of the chapel. As the plan (Fig. 2) shows, this was to have its consequences, probably not foreseen at this time, when the high vault came to be built.[49]

We have already seen how the plan of the eastern part of the chapel, with its five separate rectangular chapels and sharply pointed external bay-windows, was quite different from the nave and aisle part of the building. There was, however, one internal feature that bridged the gap between the two halves, and that was the bowed screens,[50] which were put into both the ends of the aisles, and in the most westerly of the 'chevet' chapels. Unfortunately the screens into the western ends of the aisles were completely destroyed in c.1732, when the stalls were extended eastwards for the Order of the Bath, while the upper parts of the eastern pair of screens were removed by Wyatt in 1806. Only by studying the fine engraving of c.1723 in Dart (Fig. 17)[51] do we see the original effect, which took the bow-shaped part of the design from the nave into the sanctuary area. Because of their destruction, we cannot be certain whether these screens were an afterthought, but the surviving fragments seem to suggest that they were not.

The outer walls to the chapel, and the internal arcades, with the sixty-nine statue niches above them,[52] must have been built rapidly, and as soon as they were complete all the aisle spaces must have been roofed over. Most of the original roofing-trusses survive over the north aisle,[53] and, as separate roof structures, over each of the five eastern chapels.[54] These trusses allow for a continuous shallow-pitched shed roof, and the rafters have always been covered in lead. In the spaces below the roofs and above the vaults, most of the external masonry on the internal walls (i.e. behind the statue niches) is unrestored (quite a lot of Reigate stone is used here), and this allows a constructional sequence to be worked out. Most interesting here are first, the indication that a series of lower tie-beams had to be removed from the roof trusses when the aisle vaults were put in, and secondly, that extra pilasters had to be added to the east ends of the aisles (on top of the east end walls of the aisles) when the upper clerestory wall was built. These pilasters are clearly secondary, as they butt up against the earlier masonry (Fig. 45), and have to accommodate the already existing roof-timbers. This must indicate that the aisle vaults (at least in their present form) were not planned at the beginning, and that the plan of the great upper pendant vault had, at the very least, not been fully worked out when the lower part of the chapel was being built. The upper clerestory wall, the flying buttresses and the amazing pendant vault do all, however, appear to have been built in one continuous campaign, so the evidence from

---

[49] Below, 202.
[50] In fact a central bow flanked by two smaller bows, which mirror the windows in the outer aisle walls.
[51] Dart.
[52] There are five niches per bay and two pairs of niches above the wider 'pier' between the nave and the sanctuary. See below, Fig. 38.
[53] Unfortunately the south aisle trusses have mostly been renewed.
[54] There were too few rings in the timbers to make dendrochronology worthwhile. For these roofs, see below, 213.

the fabric in the aisle roof area does seem to confirm that the chapel was designed and built in two separate phases, with a slight change of design, even if the gap in time between the two phases was short.

The designers of the Henry VII chapel

We can be fairly certain that all of the main fabric of the Henry VII chapel was built between the beginning of 1503 and the year of the king's death, 1509,[55] though the exact date of the completion of the whole building (i.e. of the vaults, in particular) is not known. Halfway between these two dates, in 1506, both Robert Janyns and Robert Vertue died, not long after both of them (with John Lebons) had made an estimate for the king's tomb.[56] In exactly the same year, June 1506, there is a well-known agreement for the making of the choir vault in St George's Chapel, Windsor, by John Hylmer and William Vertue, freemasons, and the agreement specifically states that this vault was to 'bee wrought more pendant and holower than the keyes or pendaunts of the body [i.e. nave] of the said college'.[57] Five years later, in December 1511, there is another surviving agreement with William Vertue to make a new stone vault over the Lady chapel of St George's, Windsor,[58] and though this vault was in fact never built, it too was meant to have the 'principal keyes [bosses] more hollowe than the keyes of the Boddy of the said Colege' (i.e the nave of St George's Chapel). Today the difference is still very apparent between the very wide nave vault (built before 1506) in St George's Chapel and the choir vault with its line of pendants, 'built more hollow' down the centre.

I would suggest, therefore, that the lower half of the Henry VII chapel was designed by Robert Janyns, but that in, or soon after, 1506 the design was modified by William Vertue to allow for the inclusion of the remarkable high vaults with their huge pendants.[59] William Vertue was also probably responsible for the vaults in the remarkable rebuilding of Bath Abbey, where Bishop Oliver King was able to boast that 'of the vaulte devised for the chancelle, there shall be noone so goodely neither in England nor in France'.[60] This could perhaps now be more appropriately applied to the Henry VII chapel's high vault, where a very skilled master mason, probably William Vertue, was able to produce a virtuoso design for both the vault itself, and for its supporting turrets and flying buttresses.

---

55 Henry VII's will of 31 March 1509 does not help us, as it merely says 'which chapell we have begoune to buylde of newe': see above, 113.
56 See discussion in Colvin, *HKW* iii, 214.
57 Salzman, *Building in England*, 562–3.
58 Salzman, 562–3.
59 For William Vertue see J. Harvey, *English Medieval Architects*, 1987, 307–10. Walter Leedy attributed the vaults to Robert Janyns, but did not study the whole building: 'The design of the vaulting of Henry VII's chapel, Westminster: a reappraisal', *Architectural History* 18, 1975, 5–11; in his later major study of fan-vaulting in England, *Fan-vaulting: a Study of Form, Technology and Meaning*, 1980, 214–17, he says merely 'the attribution of Henry VII's chapel to the Vertues is conjectural'.
60 J.A. Robinson, 'Correspondence of Bishop Oliver King and Sir Reginald Bray', *Proceedings of the Somerset Archaeological and Natural History Society* 60 pt 2, 1914, 4.

The upper walls, flyers and vaults

As we have just seen, the upper part of the chapel, with its remarkable new high vault, was probably built between c.1507 and 1510. The upper walls contain very large clerestory windows with double transoms which, unlike the aisle windows, tell us that we are dealing with a church rather than a Tudor palace. The large windows in the thin clerestory walls, together with the very large west window (of fifteen lights), were designed to let in the maximum amount of light, as in other late Gothic buildings. Above all of this is the quite extraordinary vault, which was first studied and drawn over 150 years ago by the Revd Professor Robert Willis (Fig. 4).[61] The best succinct modern description of the vaults are by the late Sir Nikolaus Pevsner, and one cannot do better than quote him:

> It seems a fan-vault of the most glorious richness and size, but it is not – it is a superbly ingenious fantasy on the theme of fan-vaulting. The vault is in fact a groin-vault divided into bays by strong transverse arches with a fringe of cusping. These are given a form similar to (and influenced by) the arched-braces of timber roofs. Thence also comes the openwork tracery in the spandrels. Then, however, at a certain height, these transverse arches disappear in the solid vault and only their cusping remains visible. The place where this change occurs is marked by huge pendants of fan shape. They are structurally in fact part of the wedge-stones of the arches or braces but appear like fans suspended in the air. The rest of the vault is panelled all the way through as if it were a normal fan-vault. One can call the whole design of the vault almost a design consisting of nave and aisles, but with the arcade piers removed. Technically it is all a spectacular tour de force.[62]

If one looks carefully at the masonry of the high vault, particularly the upper side, it is clear that there is one major area of discontinuity, and that is the section between the nave part of the vault and the sanctuary. This problem is studied in more detail below by Andrew Reynolds, but his findings can be summarised by saying that an additional great arch was inserted into the upper clerestory level and the vault while it was being built (see Plate IVA, Fig. 22A). This necessitated the reorganising and 'botching in' of the fan-vault masonry on the west side of the semi-octagonal sanctuary vault.[63] Presumably the panels of the whole vault were prepared first,[64] but when the time came to put them in, it was felt that the area between the two halves of the building was likely to be unstable, and hence an extra 'great arch' was needed. This would follow on from the decision to add an extra external pilaster at this point (mentioned above). Because there was a discontinuity (an offset to the west) in the flying buttress supports for the high vault at this point on either side, the builder must have feared that the vaults could break at this critical point, and that more support, in

---

[61] R. Willis, 'On the construction of the vaults of the middle ages', *Transactions of the RIBA* 1, 1842, 53–4.
[62] N. Pevsner, *London, i: The Cities of London and Westminster*, The Buildings of England, Harmondsworth 1973, 417–18.
[63] Professor Heyman in correspondence put it succinctly by saying 'to my mind the great arch must have been spatchcocked in as an afterthought'.
[64] The form of the original vault, as planned, is worked out by Andrew Reynolds, below, 210.

the form of the great arch, was necessary. The mass of decoration all over the undersides of the vaults, as well as on the great arch itself, successfully hides this change of plan, and it is only on the plain top side of the vault that the irregularities in the masonry are obvious.

The real novelty of the design of this vault is in having a series of masonry arches between each bay from which hang the pendants on either side of the vault. In the central upper part of the vault these arches disappear from below, because they pass through the vault to the top side above the panels of the fan-vaults, as Robert Willis's superb 1842 isometric drawings show (Fig. 4). A small-scale version of this clever device can be seen in the side-aisle vaults of the chapel where the diagonal cross-arches are only seen above the vault. The large pendants that hang below the fan-vault here are in fact also the keystones (bosses) of these diagonal arches (Fig. 25).

The vaults over the aisles, and over the five eastern chapels were clearly put in sometime after the lower part of the chapel had been built and roofed over. The best evidence for this is in the south aisle roof, where the lower tie-beams have had to be removed subsequently, to allow the panels of the vault to be fitted in.[65] This must indicate that the design of the vaults (at least in the aisles) had not been worked out when the roof was put in. The vaults over the four aisle bays on each side are square in plan, and are separated from each other by a series of arches. In the eastern chapels, by contrast, the vaults are rectangular in plan, and each vault is separated from its neighbour by a massive wedge-shaped block of solid masonry. Between all the vaults and the frieze-fenestration of the outer windows, there is an awkward empty space, which also indicates that when the windows were put in the ceiling vault above them had not yet been worked out. The vaults in the aisles and eastern chapels were perhaps the last solid masonry parts of the fabric to be built, and their construction probably took place not long before the death of Henry VII. Once again it seems likely that William Vertue was responsible for their design.

With the completion of all the vaults, the shell of the Lady chapel was complete, and the putting in of all the statues,[66] and the making of the stalls in the three western bays of the chapel was probably put in hand immediately. As Charles Tracy and Julian Munby have shown,[67] the stalls are still *in situ* in their original position, though modification to the original design perhaps took place in the course of construction. Of most interest, however, is the remarkable height above the floor of the back stalls. These stalls sit on large box-frames above the remains of the cut-down outer walls of the old thirteenth-century Lady chapel, and it is possible that these box-frames were constructed deliberately to act as 'sound boxes' (acoustic chambers) to amplify the voices of the singers in the professional choir of the Lady chapel. In other choirs trenches were dug beneath the choir stalls to act as acoustic chambers, but here this would not have been possible because of the thirteenth-century masonry.

After the death of Henry VII, and despite the instructions in his will, most of the

---

[65] See below, 216.
[66] See below, 276–92.
[67] See below, 254.

interior decoration of the Lady chapel was never carried out, though much painted glass was put in the windows.[68] It seems likely, therefore, that the statues, glass and stalls were all put in before the death of Henry VII, and that all the other decoration, specified in his will, was never carried out by his son.

[68] Richard Marks, 'The glazing of Henry VII's chapel, Westminster Abbey', in *The Reign of Henry VII*, 157–74.

An Archaeological Survey of the Vaults of Henry VII's Chapel

ANDREW REYNOLDS

Introduction

THE MAIN vault has been described as 'the climax not only of Henry VII's chapel but of the whole development of English late medieval vault design. In every way it is the most perfect existing example of a pendant fan vault, the most ambitious kind of vaulting current in the perpendicular period.'[1]

The first comprehensive survey of Henry VII's chapel was undertaken by L.N. Cottingham, during the substantial repairs and alterations of the early nineteenth century, and published in two fine volumes (1822–29). Further analysis of the construction of the vault was undertaken by Willis in 1842, his engraving of a section through the chapel being the most frequently reproduced illustration in any discussion of the subject (Fig. 4). Subsequently, general books on Westminster Abbey have described the vault[2] and the design has been reappraised by W.C. Leedy.[3] There has been no archaeological analysis of the vault and, with this very much in mind, further recording work was considered necessary.

The vault of the main chapel

The vault comprises two distinct parts, the eastern section over the apse and the western section over the nave, separated by the great arch. The vault consists of a series of jointed masonry cones supported by transverse arches which mark the bay divisions of the superstructure. Where the transverse arches pass through the cones, masonry pendants hang with startling effect into the nave and apse. After passing through the 9cm thick shell of the vault the transverse ribs of the western section run over the crest, which is characterised by five circular keystones running east-west and visible from below as the series of smaller pendants. The ribs of the six cones forming

---

[1] Wilson, *Westminster Abbey*, 77.
[2] F. Bond, *Westminster Abbey*, Oxford 1909; Wilson, *Westminster Abbey*.
[3] W.C. Leedy, 'The design of the vaulting of Henry VII's chapel, Westminster: a reappraisal', *Architectural History* 18, 1975, 5–11.

the eastern section meet at the apex of the vault at a keystone visible from below as the central pendant.

Above the vault the western section finishes in a pair of stilted cones which are well finished and appear to have remained largely undisturbed since being built. From above, the western section connects comfortably with the west facing edge of the great arch. In contrast, the junction between the eastern section and the great arch has an uncomfortable, untidy appearance.

The aisle vaults

Each side aisle vault consists of four panels with cross-ribs running to a cross-shaped keystone, visible from below as a pendant, in the centre of the bay at forty-five degrees to the ridges of the panels. The cross-ribs support a pendant independently of the vault cone. The blocks of the vault are generally well fitted and shaped and many have Lewis-holes.

Survey methodology[4]

The sample section of the main vault (Fig. 21) was selected to provide detailed information about the junction between the western and eastern sections of the vault.

Above the main vault a base line was set out along the east-west axis of its central ridge. Two further lines were offset from the base line to allow accurate plumbed measurements to be taken of the individual features and components of the vault. All plans and profiles were drawn at a scale of 1:20 whilst details of certain displaced moulded stones were drawn at full size.

A sample of the vault and roof structure above the north aisle was recorded using the same techniques. Level lines were fixed onto the roof structure and the timbers recorded by taking offsets. All joints were probed and the presence or absence of pegs and reused timbers was noted. The direction of observed saw marks on timbers is indicated by fine lines.

The main vault survey results

The results are discussed in two parts; in the first instance each observation is presented and its implications assessed; and, secondly, a summarised sequence of construction for the main vault of the chapel is proposed. Structural elements relevant

---

[1] The survey was carried out over a period of three weeks in September and October 1994 and was directed by the author with principal assistance from Paul Charlton, who provided part of a first draft on the north aisle roof structure. The recording of the north aisle vault and roof structure was undertaken by Sarah Semple and Rosie Edmunds. Thanks are due to Brian Bowen and his colleagues of Rattee and Kett for providing access to the survey areas, Tim Tatton-Brown for suggesting that the recording work be undertaken in the first place and Gustav Milne for advice and support. All illustrations were prepared for publication by Sarah Semple.

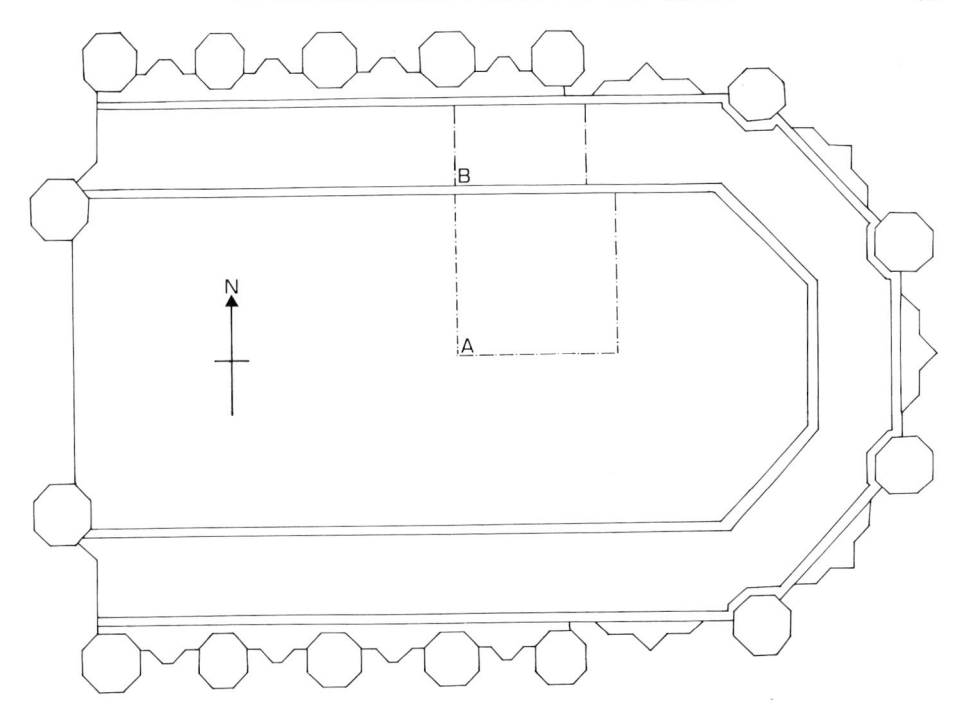

Fig. 21. Location of the sample areas.

to this discussion are numbered (in bold) in a running sequence in the text and all relate to Figure 22A.

The main vault: observations and implications (Figs. 22A–B)

It can be argued that, from below, the geometric pattern of the eastern vault is incomplete, giving the appearance of having been truncated by the great arch. If a full circle is described for each of the cones of the eastern section which meet with the great arch, it becomes a real possibility that this is what was either intended or what once existed. Furthermore, above the vault, the junction between the great arch and the eastern section (**1**) provides a startling contrast in finish, being untidy and awkward in relation to its western counterpart (**2**). It is suggested therefore, that the vault as we see it is an altered version of the original.

There is stratigraphic evidence which suggests that the great arch may have been inserted so as to encapsulate the end of the western section. This is clearly seen from above where the broken corner of one of the panels of the great arch has revealed the rib of the transverse arch sealed below it (**3**). This may be due to the two being conceived as a whole, but the proposed scenario does explain the rather awkward way in which the pendant boss visible below the stilted cone protrudes from the great arch itself.

The panels of what became the great arch seem to have been conceived as part of the original design up to the level of the springing of the vault. It is suggested here

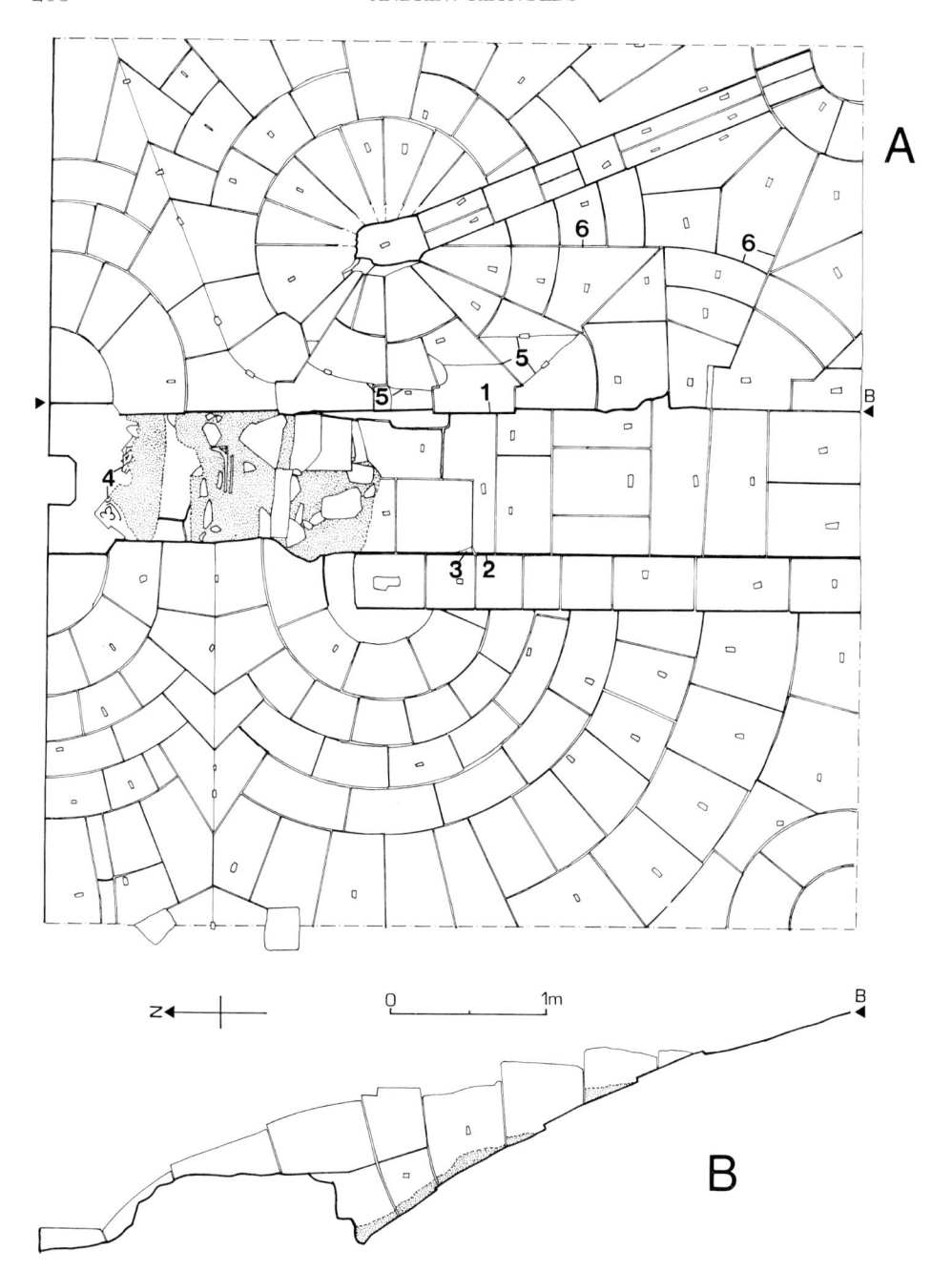

Fig. 22 (A) Plan of the main vault sample. (B) West-facing section of the junction between the western and eastern sections of the main vault.

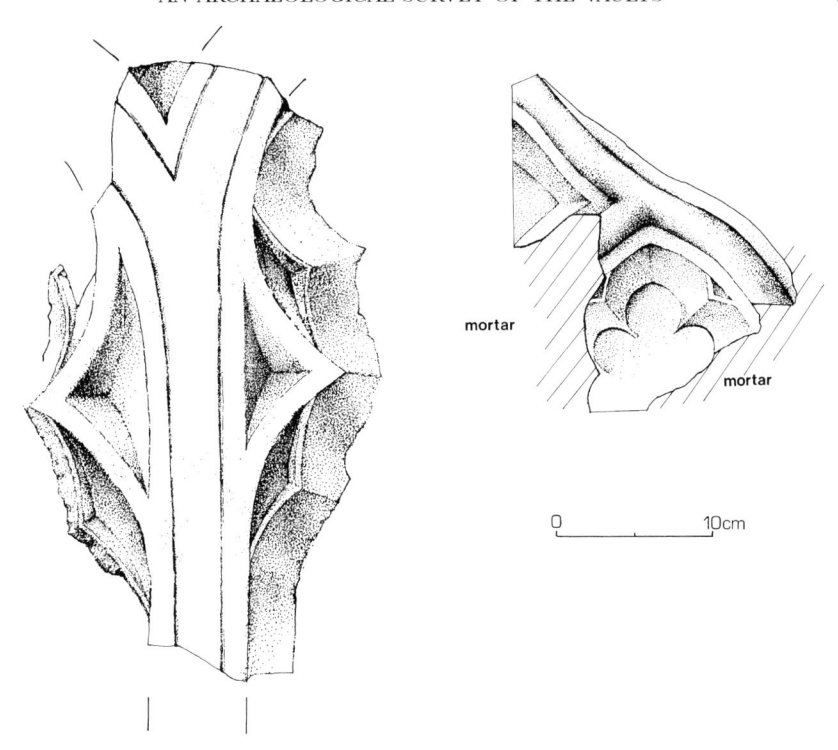

Fig. 23. Displaced moulding stones from infill above the northern springing of the great arch (see Fig. 22A (4)).

that the great arch itself was an afterthought, but was easily achieved by the upward continuation of the wide panels, hard against the west facing edge of the easternmost transverse rib of the nave vault.

Rubble infill incorporating fragments of displaced moulded stones (Fig. 23) **(4)**, some of which are exactly paralleled by those on the exterior of the chapel, is used to cap the great arch at its northern and southern extremities. That this rubble contains architectural detail, some apparently unused, suggests alteration of the building prior to completion.

The insertion of the great arch necessitated alteration of the terminal cones of the eastern vault. This is indicated by the untidy disposition of the stones of the vault cones where they meet the great arch. A number of the stones which make up the cones, where they come into contact with the great arch, are faced on several sides. Several of these stones appear to have been cut to form a ridge **(5)** and these are now disposed at all angles. Certain stones have Lewis-holes in their side faces, as seen in the west facing section of the junction between the western and eastern vaults (Fig. 22B). The sides of the cones where they meet with the great arch have the appearance of having been crudely steepened by the removal of some stones and the displacement of others as described above. Bad finishing of certain stones has been explained as the mason's forgetfulness[5] but this is an unacceptable explanation for the problems considered here.

[5] Bond, *Westminster Abbey*, 136.

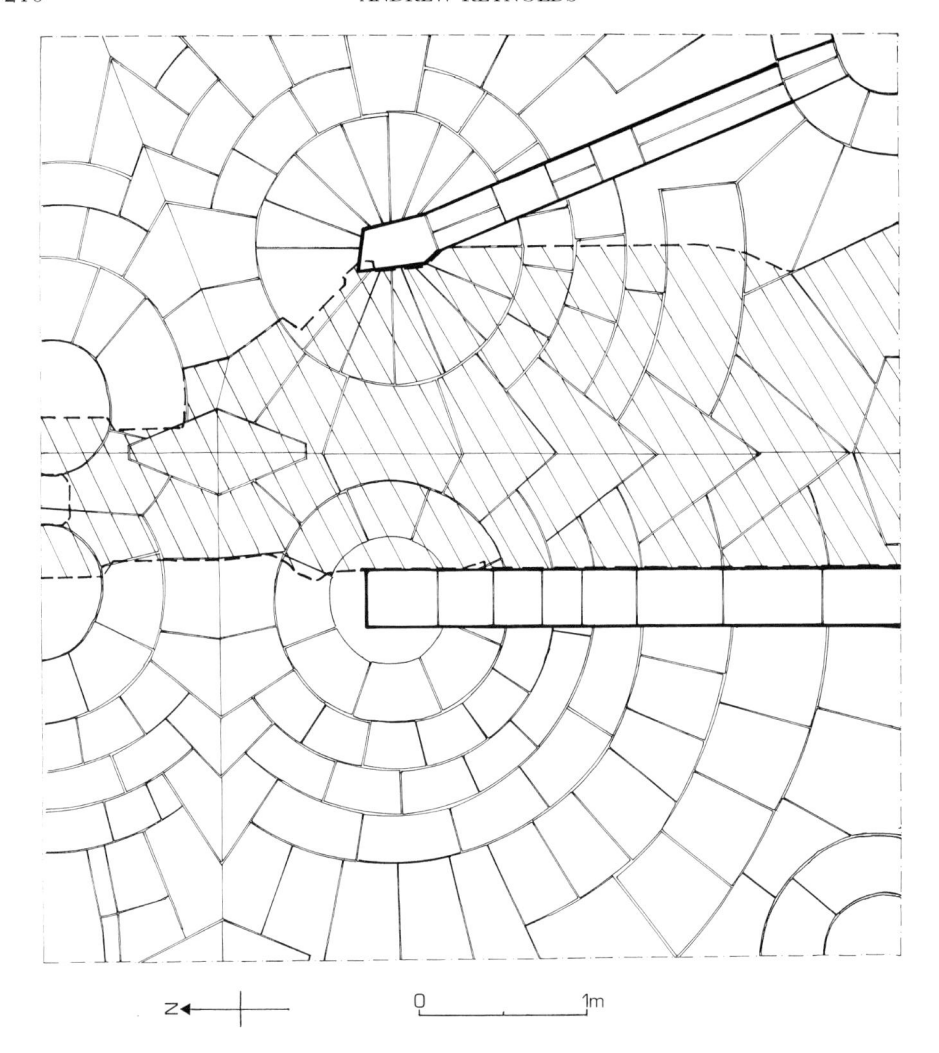

Fig. 24. Proposed reconstruction of the initial design of the main vault, with hatching showing extent of deconstruction.

The jointing of the terminal cones of the eastern section requires some attention as, although for their greater part the stones are put together so as to break joint, some constructionally very poor continuous joints can be seen **(6)** and may be used with the evidence described above to suggest the extent to which these cones were deconstructed (Fig. 24).

This is again thought to be due to the insertion of the great arch at a time after the completion of both the eastern and western vaults which, although now seemingly separate entities, were once part of a unified structure exhibiting geometric continuity (Fig. 24).

There is some slight evidence for structural settling in the north and south internal elevations at either end of the great arch above the vault. This shows as a series of staggered joints and in some cases as inserted masonry perhaps designed to even up the level of the building.

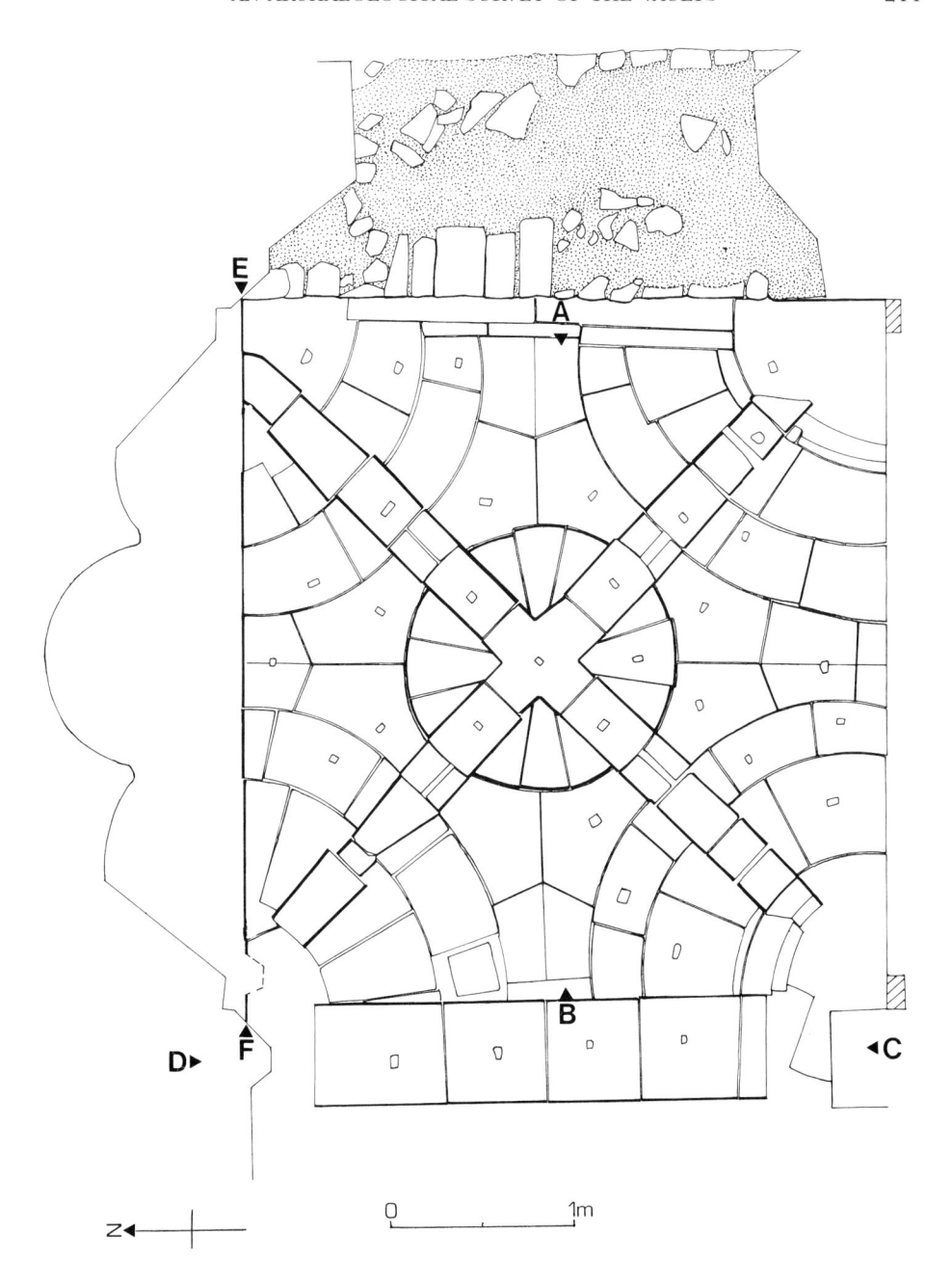

Fig. 25. Plan of the easternmost vault of the north aisle (letters indicate positions of roof structure drawings shown in Fig. 26).

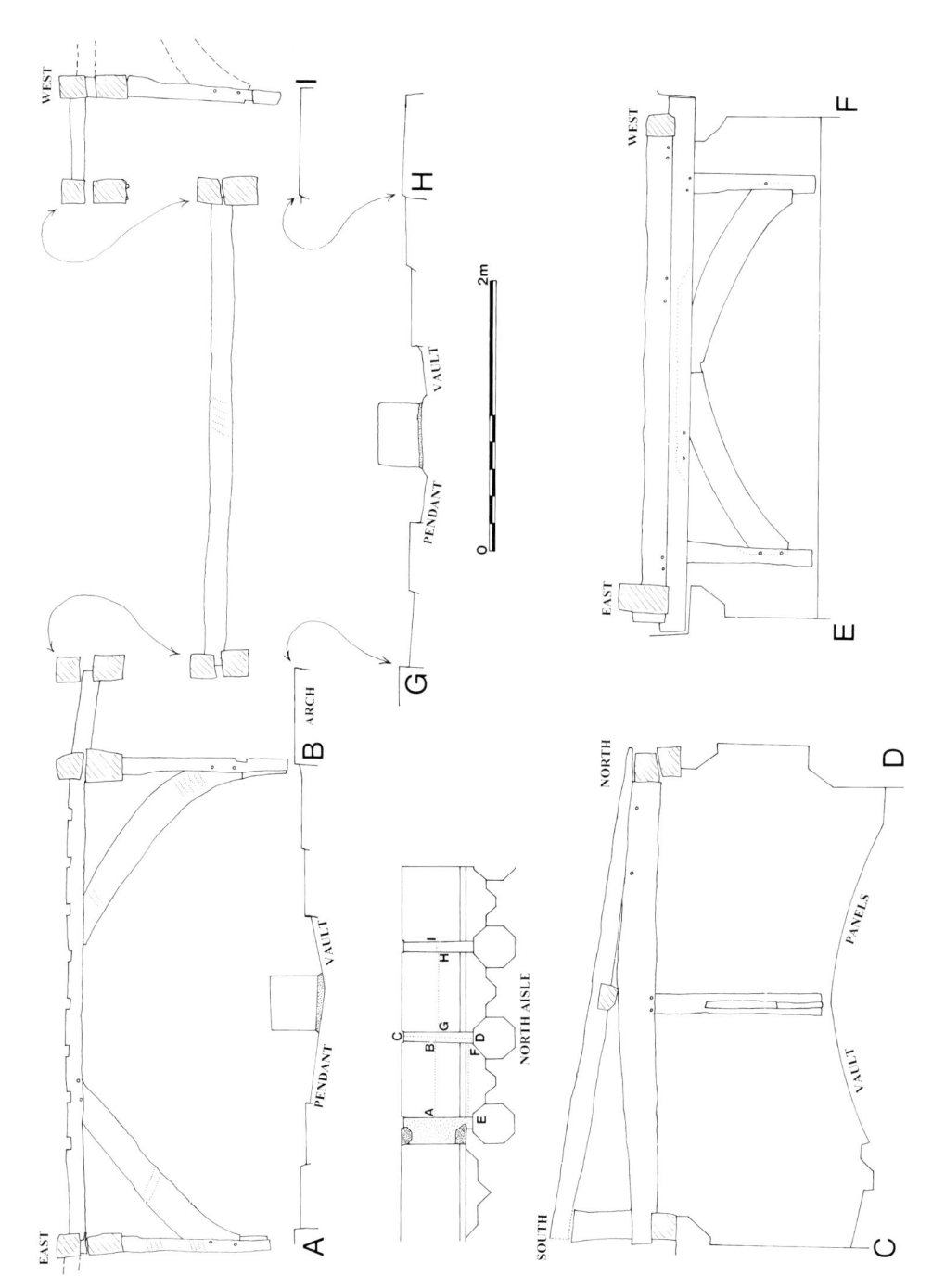

Fig. 26. The roof structure above the sample area of the north aisle.

The main vault: the construction sequence

(a) Superstructure built to wall plate level incorporating springing for transverse arches.
(b) Formers built for vault.
(c) Transverse arches built up from springing and large pendants dropped in place.
(d) Remainder of vault cones and transverse arches built up.
(e) Circular keystones/midline pendants dropped in and finishing of upper surface of vault.
(f) Potential for structural failure between nave and apse due to:
   i. removal of formers/scaffolding,
   ii. settling of superstructure, or, more likely,
   iii. initial design fault.
(g) Re-erection/replacement of formers/scaffolding.
(h) Insertion of great arch enveloping terminal cones of nave vault with loss of circular keystone/midline pendant.
(i) Rubble infilling at north and south limit of great arch incorporating moulded stones paralleled on chapel exterior, perhaps suggesting alteration of vault during infilling between octagonal piers of aisles.

Summary

The results of the survey suggest that the main vault has been substantially altered from its original plan, probably in the early sixteenth century, probably during construction.

The north aisle vault and roof structure survey results

The top of one bay of the vaulting of the north aisle was planned in detail (Fig. 25) and sections were recorded of the timber roof structure both above and to the west of the vault sample (Fig. 26). The rubble wall to the east of the sampled area is roughly faced with a core of mixed rubble and mortar including a few fragments of displaced architectural detail.

Some phasing of the structure was possible by examining the masonry and this largely served to confirm what is already known about the building, specifically that the aisle structure was a later addition onto the nave. This is evident where the vaulting meets the previously external wall of the chapel and butts against it, noticeably out of alignment with the existing ashlar courses in the wall. Much of the masonry in the wall shows signs of weathering, probably prior to construction of the aisle. The rectangular pilasters are contemporary with the construction of the nave wall whereas the semi-octagonal pilasters sit on top of the rib to the east of the sample area and abut the rectangular pilasters. In addition, the semi-octagonal pilasters encase some of the woodwork, indicating construction after completion of the vault roof.

The trusses are quite simple (Fig. 26A), although the survey recorded evidence for further timbers that no longer survive. They consist of tie-beams with principal rafters on either side of each bay. The tie-beams were slightly offset from each other by c.30cm in the sample recorded. In the area recorded there are central posts at either end of each bay tenoned into the tie-beams (Fig. 26B). There are no intermediate trusses; instead the structure is given stability by concave up-braces, slot-jointed and pegged into the collar purlin. The outer wall-posts sit on the shelf above the window bays (Fig. 26C), often supported by wooden wedges where there are voids. Rebates were cut into the central posts, with corresponding slots in the masonry, indicating the former presence of east-west cross-beams. The roof structure appears to have undergone running repairs throughout its life with episodic reconstruction probably being responsible for the lack of consistent evidence along the length of the north aisle to support any one interpretation.

Summary

The survey recorded evidence of the stratigraphic relationship between the aisle and chapel and showed how the roof structure had been subject to continual repair. The 'floating' central posts remain problematic.

The Roofs of Henry VII's Chapel

JULIAN MUNBY

Introduction

AS WITH SO MUCH of the chapel, documentation is too scanty to allow an attribution for the designer of the structural carpentry,[1] but it is almost inconceivable that the roof would not have been designed by Richard Russell, who worked elsewhere in Westminster Abbey between 1490 and 1516, and is recorded as being directly involved on the scaffolding, centering and roofing of the new work in the nave, where the roof was built after the vault was completed, in 1501–2.[2] Russell was also concerned in the second phase of constructional carpentry in the chapel of King's College, Cambridge, and was later to work for Cardinal Wolsey at York Place and Hampton Court. Had not Henry VIII dispensed with appointments, Russell would doubtless have succeeded Thomas Mauncey as the king's Chief Carpenter when the latter relinquished the post in c.1504 (and before Humphrey Coke became the king's carpenter in 1519).[3] The chapel roof was probably constructed towards the end of the building programme (1502–9), even if designed from before the outset, and the timber will have been felled, cut and shaped shortly before being brought to the chapel for erection.[4]

The main-span roof

The main timber roof of the body of the chapel has been lost, and the present one seems to have been a replacement of 1793, as Wyatt later reported to the Parliamentary Committee that £1,198 had been spent since that time.[5] The roof will have been one of a number of lead-covered late medieval and Tudor low-pitched roofs designed to cover a relatively flat fan-vault, and where the external design called for a parapet but not the view of a steep-pitched roof covering. Surviving examples include the chapel roof of King's College, Cambridge, and the nave roof of Bath Abbey, both

---

[1] See Colvin, *HKW* iii, 210ff.
[2] Harvey, *EMA*, 262–4.
[3] *Ibid.*, 263; see also John Harvey, 'The King's Chief Carpenters', *JBAA* xi, 1948.
[4] See, e.g., J. Munby, 'Wood', in *English Medieval Industries*, ed. J. Blair and N. Ramsay, 1991, 382.
[5] Cottingham, 7; C.A. Hewett reports the date of 1785 found in the roof: *English Cathedral and Monastic Carpentry*, 1985, 98.

with interrupted tiebeams and braced collar.[6] Alternatively, the roof may have had a tiebeam with a short kingpost supporting low-pitched rafters, as over the choirs of Bristol and Oxford cathedrals.[7]

The aisle roofs

The surviving parts of the original roof of the chapel are to be found in lower lean-to covering of the aisles and 'ambulatory' at the east end: most of the south side has been replaced, but much of the north side remains. These roofs are configured to the stone shell, but appear to have been adapted to the construction of the stone vault. The roof is supported on two wallplates, the inner one resting on a corbel table and the outer (double) one on separate corbels within the blank wall openings. Tiebeams at bay intervals are suspended between the wallplates, and at the inner ends carry short struts that support the low-pitched rafters (further struts stand on the inner wallplate and perform a similar function). The principal rafters carry a purlin at mid length, which is often trapped between the rafter and tiebeam, and itself provides support for the common rafters. The outer wallplates and the purlins are supported by a system of bracing, with pairs of long curved braces rising from posts to support the beams, and often forming a four-centred arch. The posts to the outer wallplates rest on the sills of the blank wall openings, but the posts for the purlin braces are suspended from the tiebeams in a manner that is not likely to have been intentional. The most obvious explanation for this is that the roof was built before the aisle chapels were vaulted, that the roof had a lower plate between the walls to support the posts, and that the arches between the vault cells were then found to be too high for the plate to remain.

The east end

The five eastern bays of the roof were necessarily different since the plan geometry required each cell to be separate from the next, and the plan of each roof cell is more trapezoidal than rectangular. Probably for this reason the posts supporting the middle purlins were dispensed with, and replaced by stout braces from the tie to the purlin, while the tie and rafter are here separated by a short strut. This seemingly ineffective support was in fact made more secure through the jointing method employed, double tenons on the end of the brace sloping downward into the tiebeams, a most unusual feature. The general appearance of this part of the roof, of purlins with dropped ends, can be paralleled in the late fourteenth-century roof of the abbot's hall (College Hall) at Westminster.[8]

---

[6] Hewett, *Carpentry*, 61–3; J. Munby, 'Cathedral carpentry', in *The Archaeology of Cathedrals*, ed. T. Tatton-Brown and J. Munby, Oxford 1996, 165–82.
[7] Hewett, *Carpentry*, 48; J. Ashdown *et al.*, 'The roof carpentry of Oxford Cathedral', *Oxoniensia* 53, 1988, 201.
[8] M. Wood, *The English Medieval House*, 1965, 313, pl. 21B.

Details

Apart from the double downward tenons just mentioned, there are no other remarkable aspects of the roof's construction. All the other supporting posts do however have double tenons, and the struts supporting the inner wallplates have both a tenon and an external spur clasping the plate. The timbers are well finished and the braces are all chamfered; numerous carpenters' marks survive.

Conclusion

This modest work, presumably carried out by the leading royal carpenter of the day, was carefully constructed to provide a totally braced frame on which the rafters could rest with minimum possibility of movement. The fact that the roof support has evidently been truncated suggests that it was here found necessary to put the roof in place prior to the vault construction, rather than the more practical method (used shortly before in the Abbey nave) of building the vaults first.

The Structure of the High Vault of Henry VII's Chapel[1]

JACQUES HEYMAN

A CLOSE inspection was made of the vault of Henry VII's chapel, Westminster Abbey, when it was scaffolded for repair and maintenance in 1994–5. Defects were seen which appear to be peculiar to fan vaults, and this paper attempts to explain these defects.

The four largest fan vaults were designed and built in little more than the first decade of the sixteenth century. The vault at Westminster, spanning 10.6m, was built in the campaign 1503–09, and the designers were possibly Robert (d.1506) and William Vertue, both King's Master Masons. The thickness of the vault is about 100mm, and in some places less. The Vertues had been the designers of the vault at Bath Abbey (c.1503, span 9.1m, thickness about 90mm). William Vertue paid at least three visits to King's College, Cambridge, during the final building campaign there of 1508–15, in the years 1507, 1509 and 1512; the date of the vault, for which the mason was John Wastell, is about 1512–13. This vault, the largest of the four at 12.7m, is about 120mm thick. Finally, the smallest vault of the four at 8.0m, and about 90mm thick, that of the retrochoir at Peterborough, may also be due to Wastell (on stylistic grounds); there is doubt about its date, which may be 1509, and thus a forerunner of King's College Chapel, or 1518, in which case it is derivative. All four of these vaults have a span to thickness ratio of about 100; the shell of a hen's egg has the same proportion. Peterborough, Bath and King's College Chapel are all constructed from rib and panel work in the lower parts of the fans, and jointed masonry in the upper parts and spandrels.

The vault of Henry VII's chapel differs in two major respects from the other three fan vaults. First, it is constructed throughout of jointed masonry; the ribs and panels are cut from a single stone, so that the ribs are effectively surface decoration, giving visual definition to the shape of the vault. Second, the fans spring not from the walls of the chapel, but from pendants placed about 2m from the walls; Fig. 4 gives Willis's view. The fans cannot, of course, actually be supported by the pendants; the intention to astonish and delight can be traced back immediately to William Orchard's vault of the Divinity School at Oxford, 1480. Indeed, a 'joke' of this sort may be seen in

---

[1] This is a shortened version of a paper published in *Architectural Research Quarterly* 4, 2000, 357–72.

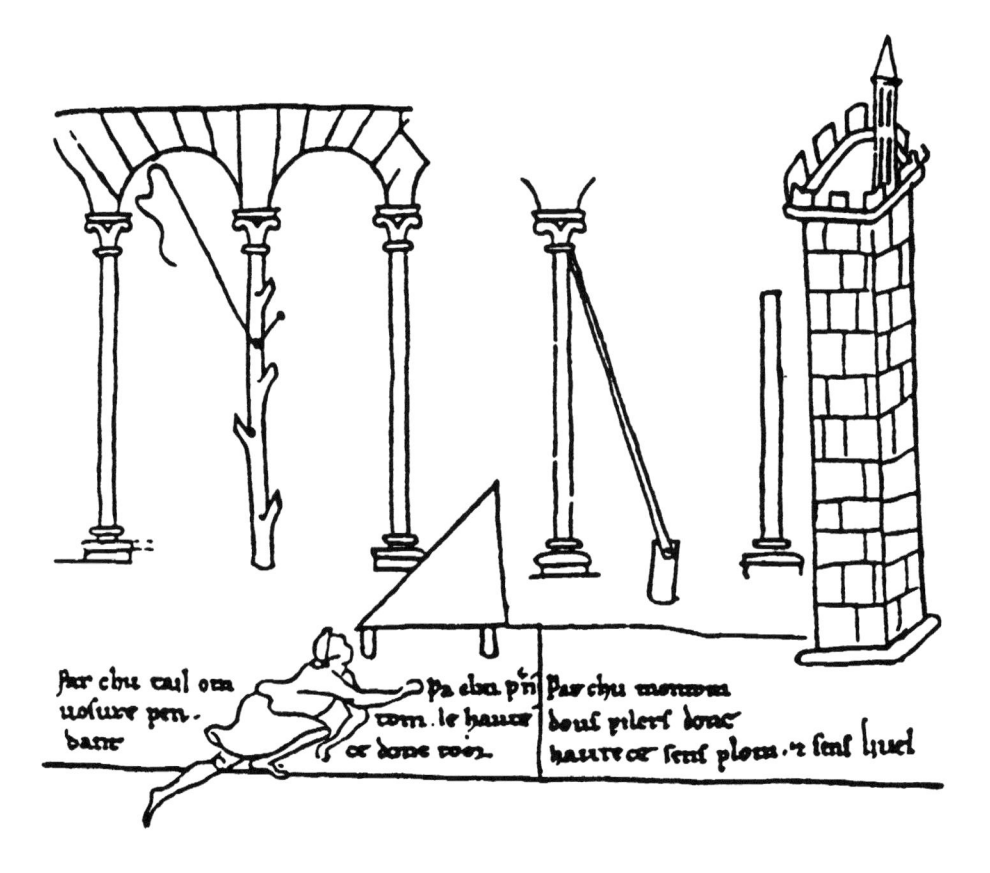

Fig. 27. When the construction has been completed the tree trunk may be removed to leave a hanging voussoir. (*Facsimile of the Sketchbook of Wilars de Honecort*, ed. R. Willis, 1859, fo. 20v)

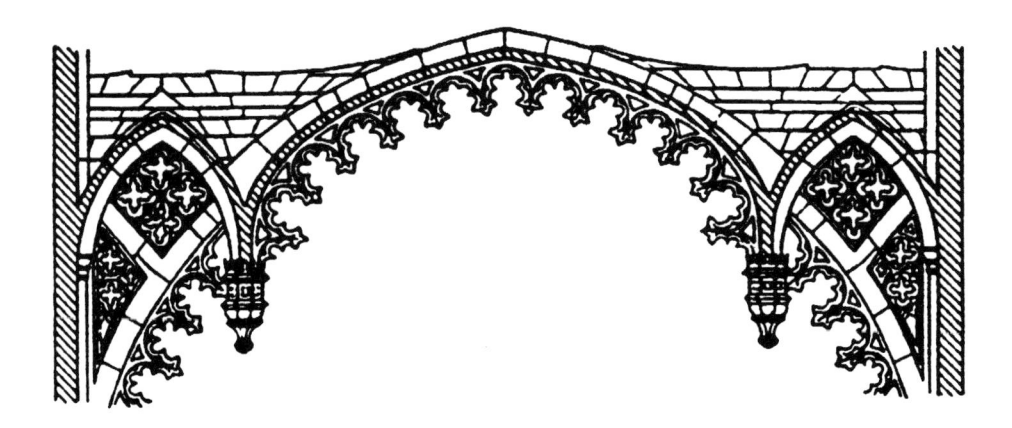

Fig. 28. Cross-section of the vault: the pendants are about 2m from the walls of the chapel. (From Colvin, *HKW,* after Willis)

Plate 17. Hinge in central arch of nave vault, just north of mid-span.

Villard's lodge-book of c.1235, Fig. 27; when the arcade under construction has been completed, the tree trunk may be removed to leave a hanging voussoir ('*Par chu tail om vosure pendant – Par ce moyen on taille une voussure pendante*').

The pendants in Henry VII's chapel are in fact elongated single stones forming part of the structural arches, as may be seen from Fig. 4. In the Divinity School William Orchard left the arches exposed; at Westminster, the Vertues made the arch 'disappear' through the vault, so that of its total thickness of 300mm about 100mm is 'buried' in the vault, leaving 200mm exposed on the top surface. Fig. 28 shows the cross-section of the vault; the fringe of decorative cusping has been excluded from the thickness quoted above. The photograph, Plate 17, is of the exposed 200mm of the arch above the top surface of the vault; the nave of the chapel has four bays, and the photograph is of the central arch just north of the central ridge. It will be seen that, in the foreground, one of the vault stones has slipped down (by about 50mm), and an iron bar has been attached in the nineteenth century (either Wyatt or G.G. Scott) to arrest any further movement that might occur. These and other defects are discussed more fully below.

It will be seen also in Plate 17 that a hinging crack has opened between the arch stones; the maximum hinge opening is 10mm in the depth of 200mm that is visible. This hinging crack corresponds to the hinging crack shown schematically for a quad-ripartite vault in Fig. 29. As with all vaults, the yielding buttress system has allowed the vault to spread, and the span of the nave has in fact increased by 200mm or more. The hinge pattern in the central arch at Westminster is, by observation, as sketched in

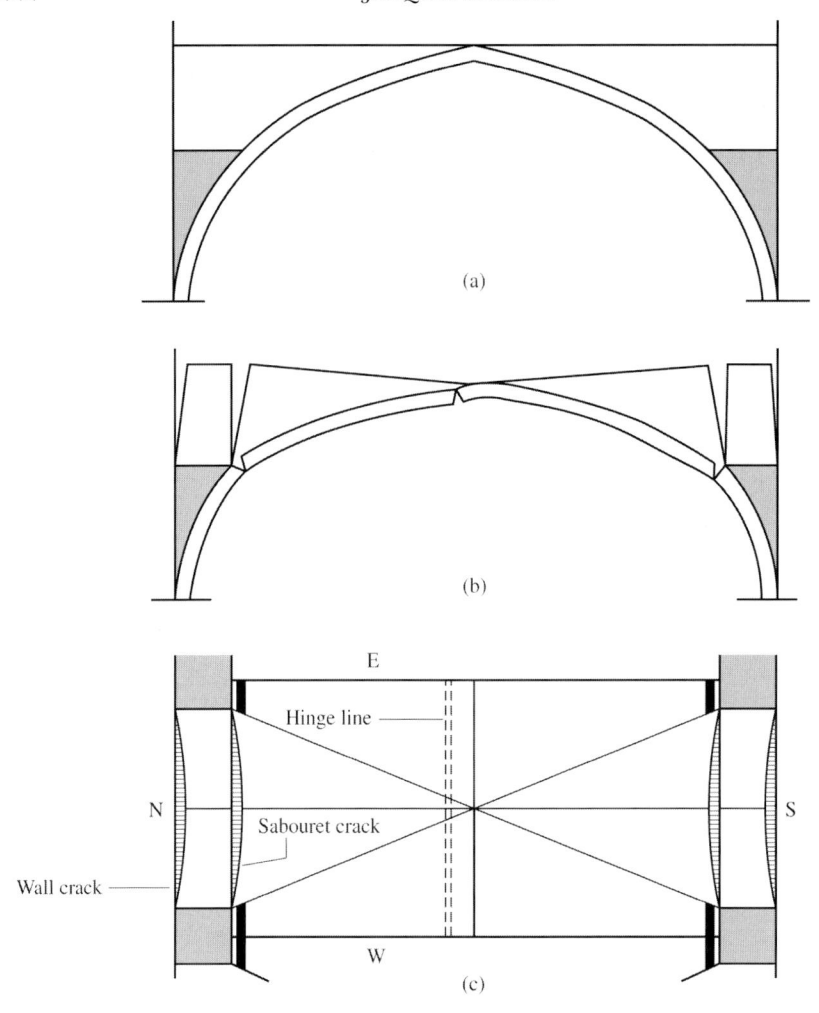

Fig. 29. Hinge and Sabouret crack in a quadripartite vault.

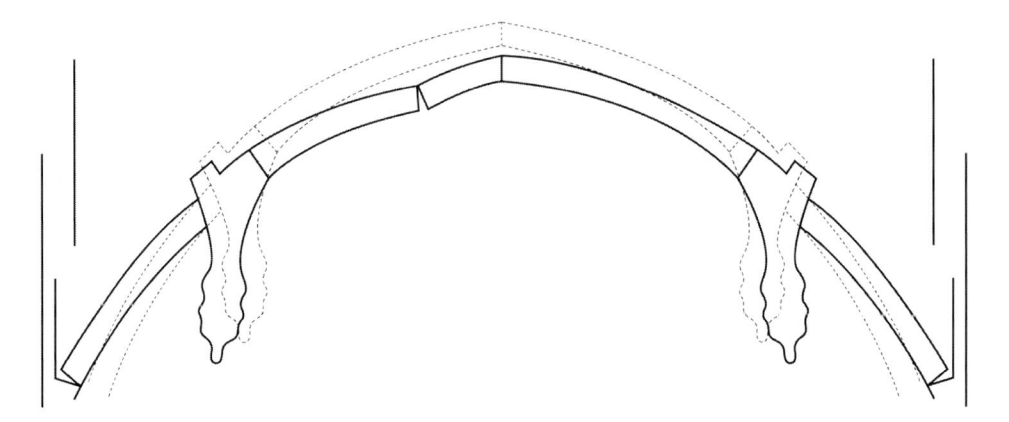

Fig. 30. Hinging deformation of central arch, with movements exaggerated by a factor of about three (north to left).

Plate 18. Northern pendant of central arch looking west, January 1995.

Fig. 30; the deformations are exaggerated by a factor of about 3 in this drawing. The photograph in Plate 18 was taken in January 1995; the northern pendant of the central arch is shown (looking west), and its inclination with respect to the vertical scaffold poles is evident. Similar inclinations may be detected in the other pendants of the vault. (The iron ties, of which there are four in the nave, are clearly intended to prevent further spread. The evidence of the present state of the vault indicates that there has been no substantial movement for the last century, and more particularly since 1933, when work to the vault was carried out by Tapper. Thus the ties appear to have been effective – or, of course, they were perhaps unnecessary, in that movement has effectively ceased since their installation. In either case, there seems to be no compelling reason to remove the ties.)

The sketch, Fig. 30, shows *only* the arch; missing are indications of the vault itself, and of the spandrel tracery including the quatrefoils enclosed by a lozenge (Plate 19).

Plate 19. Northern quatrefoil of the central arch looking east, January 1995: the topmost stone in the upper quatrefoil has dropped by about 50mm.

The movements implied by Fig. 30 cannot occur without severe distortion of this lozenge, and the photograph, Plate 19, shows this distortion (the same central arch, north side, looking east). The topmost quatrefoil has been severely distressed by a dropped vaulting stone, of which more will be said immediately, but the other quatrefoils indicate clearly the elongation of the lozenge in the north-south direction. The lower tracery indicates a similar pattern of movement.

The dropped vaulting stone in Plate 19 is the equivalent in the Henry VII fan vault of the Sabouret crack (Fig. 29). There is not enough material in the north-south direction to match the increased span of the vault; the main arch has developed hinges (Fig. 30), and the material of the vault itself tends to pull apart. In the quadripartite vault (Fig. 29) the north-south barrel is of substantially constant cross-section, and complete separation occurs along the lines of the Sabouret cracks. The surfaces shown in the isometric drawing (Fig. 4) are much more complex, being formed from partial fans; an attempt to pull the fabric apart does not result in cracks, but in dropped vaulting stones.

The pendants (Plate 18) are about 2m away from the walls; the critical sections are at the heads of the inner arches, about 1m away from the walls. The joints between the stones of the fans are normal to the surface of the vault, and at the heads of the inner arches these joints make angles of about 45% with the vertical, as may be seen from the cross-section (Fig. 28). Thus an attempt to open a 'Sabouret' fissure of 100mm will result in the dropping of a vault stone in this region; the movement is about 50mm (since the stone has two edges), and this is the order of deformation visible in the dropped quatrefoil stone (Plate 19).

The four bays of the nave vault were examined from above and below, and a

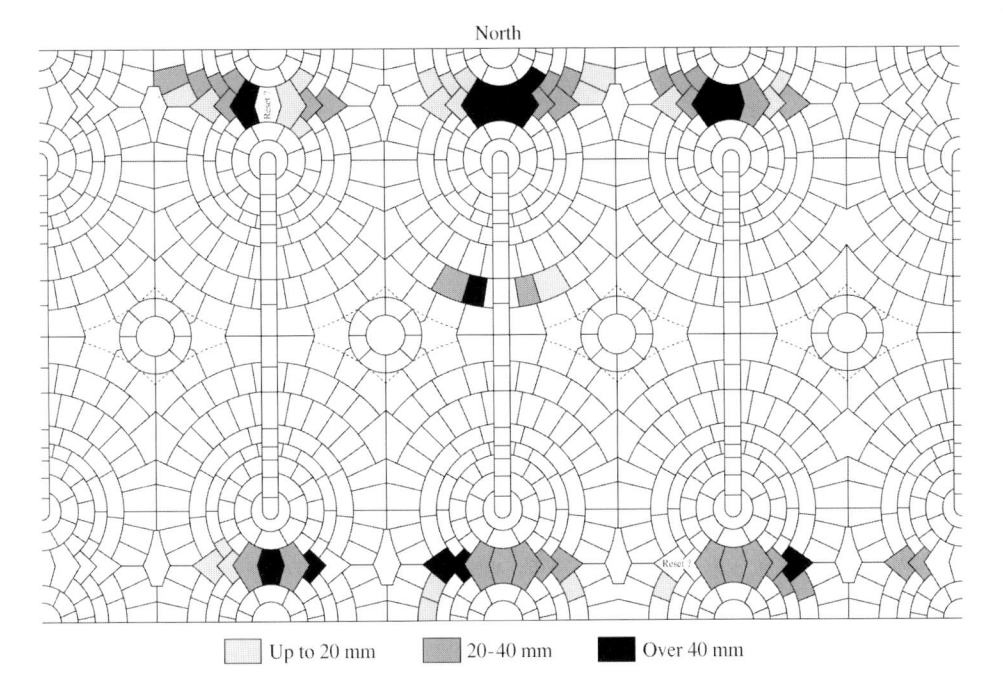

Fig. 31. Plan of top side of the four bays of the nave vault indicating dropped stones.

record was made of all stones which appear to have dropped in this way. An estimate was made of the amounts of displacement, but measurements were of course referred to adjacent stones, and the surfaces of the stones themselves are irregular; the recorded readings cannot therefore be regarded as accurate. Nevertheless, if the dropped stones are grouped into three classes, namely those that have dropped by less than 20mm, by between 20 and 40mm, and above 40mm, a strong pattern emerges. Fig. 31 is a plan view of the top surface of the four bays of the nave vault, and it will be seen that 'Sabouret' movements have occurred at each of the three main arches. At the west end the massive masonry has inhibited movement, and at the east end a substantial double arch divides the nave from the apsidal choir, where again there is little evidence of movement. In some places the mortar does not appear to be original, and some of the vault stones may have been reset (perhaps by Tapper in 1933).

These are marked in Fig. 31. Here, four dropped vaulting stones are marked which lie close to the centre of the central arch; the one with the greatest movement appears in the photograph (Plate 17). The hinge opening of 10mm in the visible depth of 200mm corresponds to an opening of 15mm in the soffit of the vault 100mm lower down, and it will be appreciated from a study of the inclination of the joints in Fig. 28 that such an opening of 15mm is consistent with a drop of say 50mm in the adjacent stone.

The defects shown in the accompanying photographs and sketches, and in the plan (Fig. 31), are all entirely explicable in terms of an increase of span of the vault. Such an increase in span results from the thrusts engendered by the masonry vault itself and also by the surmounting and protecting timber roof. The increase in span is visible in every major and minor church, and is related finally, and primarily, to movements of the foundations of the buttressing system. There is a timescale for consolidation of soil under pressure which is measured in decades, and major distortion of the masonry fabric is usually complete within this period; most geometrical deformation visible in an old building has remained virtually unchanged for centuries.

There is, however, a continuing source of minor distortion, which has been called the drift of masonry. The mechanism of drift stems from the nature of masonry as a unilateral material unable to accept tensile forces. A crack, once opened, cannot close, but will, on the contrary, be wedged open by dust. It is this slow development of perhaps disfiguring, but in reality harmless, hairline cracks which leads to the necessity of a more or less major overhaul of a masonry building at a period of a century or so.

The defects in the vault of Henry VII chapel seem to be ancient, and were, at a guess, virtually fully developed by say 1550. Since then, routine maintenance will have dealt with continued minor cracking. The vault was previously scaffolded some sixty years ago, and the 1994–5 campaign has not revealed any signs of new defects.

The Henry VII Chapel Stalls and their Eighteenth-century Re-modelling[1]

CHARLES TRACY
with an appendix on the carpentry by JULIAN MUNBY

A chronological history of the stalls

THE CLERGY STALLS at St George's Chapel, Windsor and the Henry VII chapel, Westminster, represent the peak of achievement for later English gothic ecclesiastical wooden furniture making.[2] Their manufacture was separated by some thirty years, but in both cases reflects strong Flemish influence in the architecture and decorative carving. Nonetheless they are English through and through.

Disappointingly for an English royal commission, the building accounts for the

---

[1] Since working on this furniture nearly fifteen years ago my interpretation of the joinery has changed in a number of important ways. I now accept that the area in front of the seats in the second block from the west almost certainly never accommodated substalls, an unique situation for English greater churches. I originally suggested that there had only ever been one campaign in the eighteenth-century extension, probably around 1760. A closer examination of the carving style of this work, in both the second block of substalls and the eastern extension, shows, however, that it was undertaken in two phases, probably in the 1730s and then possibly as late as the 1770s. Nonetheless the extension for the knights of the Bath was much more modest than had previously been thought, confining itself purely to the addition of substalls to the eastern block of early Tudor back stalls. I also suggested that the seats for the dignitaries were not returned in the first place. It is still difficult to be categorical about this, but my supposition now looks tenuous, although we may never know exactly how things were arranged at the west end. Finally I was rash enough to suggest that the stalls must originally have been in a straight line, as ubiquitously elsewhere in England, instead of fitted between the piers. Since then, a careful examination of the substructure has been carried out, an option not available at the time, and this supposition has proved to be groundless. Some of the technical problems are discussed in the Appendix, below, 253–7. I am most grateful to the Dean and Chapter of Westminster for giving me access to the choir-stalls, allowing me to take some photographs and to reproduce others. Other collections of photographs which I have drawn from are the Victoria and Albert Museum, the Courtauld Institute of Art, and Michael Denman RIBA. Tessa Murdoch, Michael Snodin and Marjorie Trusted generously offered their advice on the sculptural interpretation of the two phases of the eighteenth-century joinery campaign. I am indebted to the PRO for access to the eighteenth-century Office of Works accounts. Finally I would like to thank Tim Tatton-Brown and Hugh Harrison for their support, and Julian Munby for his invaluable insights on the carpentry and joinery.

[2] For a discussion of the St George's Chapel, Windsor, stalls see C. Tracy, *English Gothic Choir-Stalls, 1400–1540*, Woodbridge 1990, 48–51.

Plate 20. North range of choirstalls.

Henry VII chapel are lost. However, the stalls were probably completed by 1512, well after Henry VII's death.[3]

Originally at Westminster, there were twelve back and seven substalls on each side, together with the seats for the dignitaries at the west end, making a total of forty seats (Plate 20, Fig. 32).[4] The furniture ran across the first three western bays of the chapel, and was interrupted by an entranceway each side at the west end, and at the start of the third bay.[5] Unusually, the second block of back stall desking to the east had no substalls beneath them.[6] The additional space would, no doubt, have been required to accommodate Henry VII's tomb between the stalls. It has always been assumed, however, that the latter was eventually placed where it is now, two bays further to the east, on the originally intended site for a shrine for Henry VI. This would have been in defiance of the terms of the king's will, which stipulated that the 'chapel of Our Saviour', which was to accommodate at its west end the bodies of himself and his queen, Elizabeth of York, was to stand in the middle of the stalls. Therefore the absence of substalls at the east end of the Tudor furniture does seem to conform to

---

[3] C. Wilson, 'Henry VII's Chapel', in Wilson, *Westminster Abbey*, 70. Pevsner dated the stalls to c.1520, which is too late: N. Pevsner, *London* i, *Cities of London and Westminster*, Buildings of England Series, 3rd edn, Harmondsworth 1973, 438.

[4] For speculation on the original number of stalls, see Appendix, below, 253. For an exhaustive description of the screens, stalls and misericords see *Inventory*, 69–70 and pls. 216–20.

[5] See Britton's plan, Fig. 2.

[6] Admittedly the seventeenth-century sketch plan in the Thorpe collection (see Fig. 3) does show there to be substalls in the second block to the east. But it is considered by general consensus to be, in the words of Lethaby, only 'roughly sketched' and unreliable. See Lethaby, *Re-examined*, 172, and the woodcut in Scott, *Gleanings*, 82, and Appendix below.

THE STALLS AND THEIR EIGHTEENTH-CENTURY RE-MODELLING 229

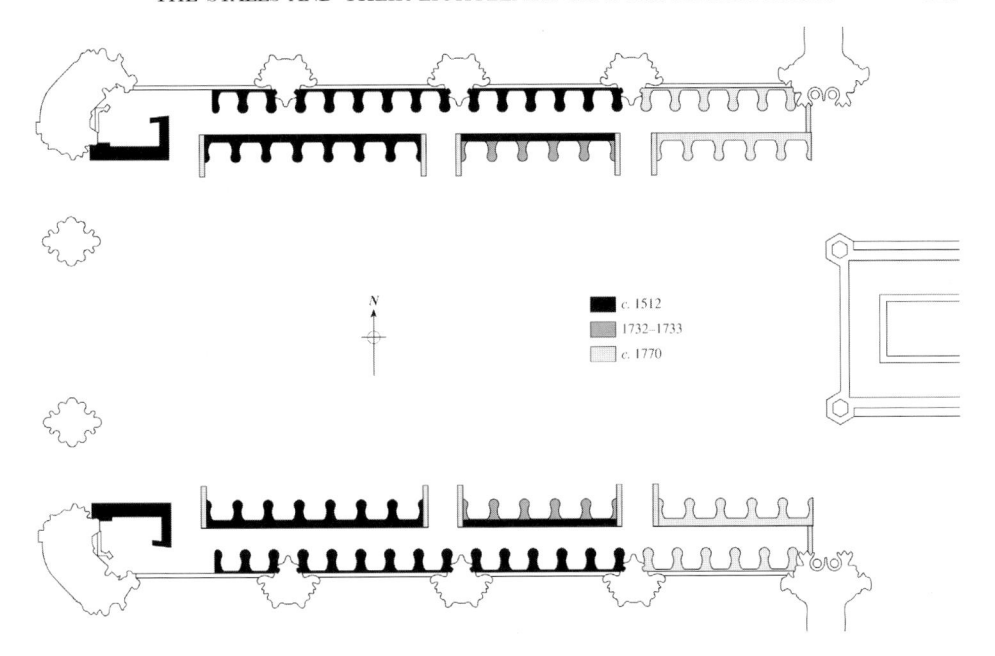

Fig. 32. Plan of the clergy stalls showing construction periods.

the royal testamentary vision. As is well known, many of the terms of the will in this respect were ignored, not least the translation of his predecessor's bones to Westminster. Indeed the tomb seems never to have been sited where specified, even though Hollar's engraving of 1665, appears to show otherwise.[7] We know that in the nineteenth century Dean Stanley found the bodies of Henry VII and his queen under the tomb where it is now.[8] Given that it seems at no time to have been sited between the stalls, it is surprising that the additional space for another ten substalls would not have been taken advantage of before the eighteenth century.

The decorated posts, which on the backs of the substalls ran down from the top of the book rests to the seat capping below, in the former eastern block, went right down to the ground, as can be seen in the engraving by John Dart of 1723.[9] The desk fronts in this portion would have been unencumbered. All the original back and substall misericords except one on the south side, which was replaced, probably by one from the thirteenth-century Lady chapel stalls,[10] are still *in situ*. The misericords in the extant block of substalls and throughout the eighteenth-century seating are very skilfully carved, and were made in two different campaigns (Fig. 32).

The canopies of the dignitaries' seats are problematical. The terminal angel figures on the western frieze cornice of the stone screen are hidden by them, and their size does not allow sufficient room for the canopy (now missing) over the westernmost of the straight seats (Plate 21). Both of these were removed on each side on the occasion of the 1812 installation of the knights of the Order of the Bath, and placed at the east

---

[7] Sandford ii, 442–3.
[8] Stanley, *Historical Memorials*, 520–6.
[9] See Fig. 18.
[10] P. Tudor-Craig, 'The medieval monuments and chantry chapels', in Wilson, *Westminster Abbey*, 139.

Plate 21. Dignitaries' stall canopy on south side.

end of the eighteenth-century back stalls, where they remain.[11] Also at this time another block of back and substalls was added at the east. It was subsequently removed. The dignitaries' seats were fronted by panelled desking, some of which is still extant (Plate 22). The shape of the enclosure seems to preclude the possibility that these seats were not originally returned (Appendix, below, 254).

There is no surviving desking for the substalls. Presumably because of the need to keep the furniture as much as possible out of the centre of the chapel, it was deemed that desking constituted an unnecessary encumbrance.[12]

---

[11] The reference to the moving of the terminal canopies at the west end is in Neale and Brayley, 49.
[12] Sandford ii, 442–3.

Plate 22. Front panelling of dignitaries' stall on south side.

The raising-up of back stalls a whole seat's height above the substalls, is not found elsewhere in England during the middle ages. If the tomb was originally to have been placed between the eastern block of stalls, such elevation would have improved the view for the occupants of these seats. The stalls were probably intended for use at the founder's anniversary services, stipulated in Henry VII's will.[13]

Howard Colvin has suggested that the two eighteenth-century blocks of five new back and substalls each side, which extend across the fourth arcade bay from the west, were added soon after the re-foundation of the Order of the Bath in 1725 (Fig. 32).[14]

[13] Colvin, *HkW* iii, 218.
[14] See J. Risk, *The History of the Order of the Bath*, 1972.

The Order gets its name from the ceremony of bathing practised at a knight's inauguration. Established in the reign of Henry IV, the last knights were created in the ancient manner at the coronation of Charles II in 1661. There is no reference in the royal accounts to any desired augmentation before the early 1730s. Even then it seems that the only alteration to be undertaken was the relatively minor one of providing five new substalls in front of the eastern portion of the ancient back stalls. This would have increased the total number of lateral stalls from thirty-eight to forty-eight. With the revival of the Order of the Bath, thirty-five knights were created, presided over by a Great Master, who was a Knight Companion.[15] The knights were administered by seven Officers – the Dean of Westminster (Dean of the Order), a Genealogist, King of Arms, Registrar, Secretary, Usher and Messenger. The letters patent and the statutes of the Order differ slightly as to the proposed number of knights. The former stipulates thirty-six, the latter thirty-five.

On 7 March 1732 an estimate 'for making 12 stalls for the Knights Companions of the Most Honourable Order of the Bath and 22 for Esquires' was approved, the estimated cost of which was later given as £716.[16] In his trawl of the accounts Colvin picked up the reference for the making of six new stalls (2 March). He seems to have overlooked the second entry (7 March), in which it is made clear that the number of new stalls required was much greater.[17] On 18 April it was 'Ordered that the same be forthwith proceeded on accordingly'.[18] The first entry (2 March 1732) reads: 'Received from the Treasury, a Reference relating to the Erecting Six New Stalls in His Majesty's Chapell at Westminster (commonly called the Hen: 7th Chapell) for the Installment of the Knights of the Bath, with their Esquires. Ordered that Mr Flitcroft forthwith prepare an Estimate thereof, and lay the same before the Board'. The second entry (7 March, 1732) reads: 'Agreed to the Estimate of £716 for making 12 Stalls for the Knights Companions of the Most Honourable Order of the Bath & 22 for their Esquires. In Henry 7th's Chapell, and Ordered a report to be made thereof, which was done and signed accordingly.' Not unreasonably, Colvin assumed that the expenditure statement in the royal accounts in respect of May of the following year, under the rubric 'Extras in H 7 Chappell' and amounting to £587 4s 5d, related to this project for extending the stalls.[19] However, the sum of money expended was

---

[15] *Ibid.*, 11, 15.
[16] PRO, Works 4/5, Minutes of Proceedings April 1731 – August 1733, entries for 2 and 7 March 1732.
[17] Colvin, *HKW* iii, 218 n. 7.
[18] *Ibid.*
[19] The Abstract of Accounts for May 1733 (PRO Works 5/58), referring to 'Extras in H 7 Chappell', amount to £587 4s 5½d, are made up as follows:

Thomas Lucas	56 00 03½	Thomas Churchill	3 19 03
	242 16 00¼	Andrews Jelfe	48 04 09
	12 16 06¾	John Thornhill	1 12 10
Sub-total	311 12 10½	John Willis	4 02 00
Richard James	34 00 00	GRAND TOTAL	583 18 00½
	178 09 00		
John Cleave	1 00 00		
	17 04		

The figure of £587 4s 5½d is also noted in the Payments Annual Accounts (PRO, Works 5/141) for the year ended 31 December 1733.

considerably less than had been allowed for, and none of the named craftsmen involved can be identified as joiners. The only identifiable protagonist is Andrews Jelfe, presumably the well-known master-mason and builder of that name.[20] It is true that, if so many new stalls had been made at that time a mason would have been needed for constructing the new foundations. Jelfe's contribution, at £48 4s 9d, was not inconsiderable.

However, if the only augmentation that was undertaken at this time was the addition of ten new substalls with their misericords, it is unlikely that even the sum of £587 would have been required. If we were to allow an average of 60p per day for the carving and joinery, the cost of making ten new seats with misericords would have been around £114. This is based on the assumption that the misericords would have each taken about three weeks to carve, and that the seats could have been made by two joiners in two months.[21] On the other hand, had all thirty-four of the new stalls, mooted on 7 March 1732, been made at this time, the cost would have been about three times this amount (£342) for the joinery, as well as additional sums for making and arranging the superstructure and necessary masonry work for the foundations. In these circumstances an expenditure of £587 would have been quite feasible.

The planned addition in 1732 of thirty-four new stalls seems to have been modified, however, so that it did not extend beyond the line of the earlier ones. The new blocks of stalls, which appear to have been added *later* in the century, amount to only twenty seats in total. The number of seats created in the eighteenth century in total is only thirty, compared to the thirty-four envisaged in 1732. Clearly the ambitious original scheme, which may very well have envisaged the extension of the line of the stalls by an additional bay, was abandoned for some reason.

One possible corroboration of the hypothesis that the stalls were re-modelled in two phases is to be found in the two Canaletto paintings of the interior of the chapel.[22] The artist came to England in 1746, and neither painting can have been executed until a few years later. In both versions the viewpoint is similar to that published by Dart in 1723.[23] Although the dignitaries' seats are out of the picture, the entire echelon of sixteenth-century furniture is visible, as is the easternmost of the two stone screens. This, of course, suggests that, at that time, the new block of twenty stalls had not yet been added. In one Canaletto version, substalls at the east end of the ancient stalls are visible.[24] Unfortunately these paintings are hopelessly inaccurate in their treatment of many of the architectural features, such as the oriels at the base of

---

[20] H.M. Colvin, *A Biographical Dictionary of British Architects 1600–1840*, 1978.

[21] Tradesmen's prices in the eighteenth century are usually quoted for the job. Thus the record that the mid-century carved and gilded console table from the Tapestry Room at Hinton House, Somerset, now in the Victoria and Albert Museum (Acq. No. W.35–1964) took eighty-nine days to make and cost £22 5s 5d for the joiner and £21 0s 0d for the carving is very useful for the purpose of estimating contemporary day rates. In this case Lock worked at it for fifteen days, the remainder being done by his assistants.

[22] The first painting is in the Museum of London (Acq. No. A 20964). See J. Hayes, *Catalogue of Oil Paintings in the London Museum*, 1970, cat. 27. The second is the version, possibly from the Samuel Dickinson collection, sold by Christie's, 12 March 1774. See W.G. Constable (rev. J.G. Links), *Canaletto: Giovanni Antonio Canal, 1697–1768*, 2 vols., Oxford 1989, ii, cat. 433, p. 422, pl. 80.

[23] See Fig. 18.

[24] It is much harder to make them out in the Museum of London version. See Tracy, *Choir-Stalls 1400–1540*, pl. 178.

Plate 23. North-west entranceway to stalls showing back and substalls, and eighteenth-century desk end.

the windows, the window tracery itself and the plan of the fan vaulting. This inevitably somewhat undermines the artist's credibility as a witness. The patent unreliability also extends to the pattern of the floor, which is depicted as chequer-board in plan. In fact the present diagonally-laid black and white marble floor is almost certainly the one given by Prebendary Killigrew in 1699. It nonetheless seems unlikely that Canaletto would have ignored the fact that one of the stone screens had by that time been destroyed on the basis that a new block of stalls had already been placed in the fourth bay from the west, unless he was relying wholly on Dart, which seems unlikely.

A similar view in oils of about 1760 in the Abbey library, once also thought to be by Canaletto, does, however, provide a record of the first stage of the subsequent late eighteenth-century metamorphosis. A wholly new block of five back stalls each side, with reproduction desking to match, has been thrown across the fourth bay from the west at the expense of the westernmost of the two sixteenth-century stone screens.

Plate 24. Eighteenth-century misericord in second block of stalls from west, north side.

Plate 25. Eighteenth-century misericord from back stall in third block from west on north side.

Interestingly, the painting shows no new substalls provided to match the new back stalls, although the mouldings and the style of the carving on the seats that are there now strongly suggest that this eastern extension to the stalls can have remained but a short time without any substalls.

The new work was separated from the earlier by a generously wide six-step gangway. The desking throughout, both old and new, was fitted at the same time with new desk ends *cum* stair guards, which are still *in situ* (Plate 23). These replaced the original desk ends, possibly with heraldic animals and poppy heads, shown in the Dart engraving. The entrances at the west end seem to have retained their ancient format of four solid steps.

It is sometimes suggested that parts of the modern furniture date from the nineteenth century. We know that new stalls were added at the east end for the 1812 installation, but there is no workmanship of this date anywhere now in the extant work.

The carving of the misericords on the new seats within the Tudor furniture

Plate 26. Eighteenth-century misericord supporter from back stall in third block from west, south side.

(Fig. 32) conforms to the style of the English rococo period. It is characterised by the naturalistic treatment of birds and animals in vigorous motion, with acanthus foliage similarly depicted caught in frozen animation. It is in a generously proportioned 'open style', with the misericord supporters almost reaching to the bottom of the seat. The acanthus foliage is spiky and untidy, and employs the double curve wherever possible (Plate 24).[25] The shape of the seat capping extensions is a direct copy of the sixteenth-century seats, using the trefoil plan on capping extensions and standard capitals and bases. As before there is a single column fronting the seat standards.

The misericords of the eastern block of substalls (Fig. 32) are, by contrast, in an 'enclosed' style. The carving is self-contained with the supporters characteristically about 11.5cm across, as against the 15cm width of the 'open style' supporters. Also the supporters of the later group finish well above the bottom of the seat (Plate 25).

[25] In *ibid.*, pl. 180, I showed one of the eighteenth-century phase 1 misericords as a sixteenth-century one.

The 'auricular' style, doubtless a nod to the mid sixteenth-century fashion, is seen exclusively here. The mouldings of both back and substalls is distinctively different from the furniture to the west, using a circular plan for capping projections, and seat standard capitals and bases. Three equal columns front the seat standards, instead of one on the sixteenth-century furniture.

The design sources for the earlier eighteenth-century campaign seem to have been contemporary trade cards, such as Henry Copeland's for Thomas Gardner.[26] The seated and standing figures of dogs are reminiscent of chimneypiece tablets carved by the workshop of Henry Cheere (1703–81).[27] He was appointed carver to the Abbey by the Dean and Chapter in 1743.[28] His career at the abbey spans both periods of the eighteenth-century choir stall construction. Although we have no record of him having carved in wood, it seems very possible that he designed both sets of misericords.

Those in the easternmost block of stalls probably date from the 1760s or even the 1770s. Similar decorative features occur on some of the architectural carvings at Somerset House, where the sculptor Joseph Wilton was working, with others, to the designs of William Chambers.[29] Moreover the satyr's heads on the misericords are classical in inspiration, the eyes being goat slit-eyes rather than medieval grotesques (Plate 26).[30] The printed sources for the later group of carvings were probably baroque ornamental prints reissued in the 1720s and 1730s such as Thomas Bowles, *A new book of Ornaments Proper for Jewellers, Painters, Gravers, Carvers etc*, c.1728, and *A Compleat Book of Ornaments*, c.1728.[31] It may be surprising to some that the seventeenth-century auricular style was being reverted to in the 1760s and 1770s. An example of the unfrivolous late Baroque material that appealed to these artists is the title page from *A Compleat Book of Ornament*, designed after Jean Bernard Honoré Toro and another artist (Fig. 33). The treatment of the cartouche at the bottom is particularly relevant in its flowing handling of foliage and the mask at the base.

It is curious that there is no mention of the making of the later stalls in the royal accounts. But as already noted, it is questionable whether the cost of the first extension to the stalls was recorded either. It is interesting to speculate what could have been the reason for the addition of the new block of stalls in the fourth bay from the west. It does seem that, as the century wore on, there was increasing pressure from the military for new members to be elected to the Order. This culminated in an additional statute, which was issued on 8 May 1812, 'removing all limitations on the number who could be admitted to the Order. The extra Knights were to succeed to stalls when vacant, by seniority.'[32]

Limited access to the foundations was afforded during the emplacement of a new heating system in 1995 (see Appendix, below, 253–7). It was found that the entire

---

[26] M. Snodin, 'Trade cards and the English rococo', in *The Rococo in England*, ed. C. Hind, Victoria and Albert Museum 1986.
[27] I am indebted to Tessa Murdoch for this suggestion.
[28] WAM Chapter Minutes, 26 April 1743.
[29] I am grateful to Marjorie Trusted for this observation.
[30] Information kindly supplied by Michael Snodin.
[31] I am grateful to Michael Snodin for this suggestion. See M. Snodin, 'Thomas Bowles and baroque ornament: some more printed sources for engraved brass inlay', *Furniture History* 1994, 86–91.
[32] Risk, *Order of the Bath*, 28.

Fig. 33. Title page designed after Jean Bernard Honoré Toro and another artist, c.1728. (V & A Picture Library, E1451–1983)

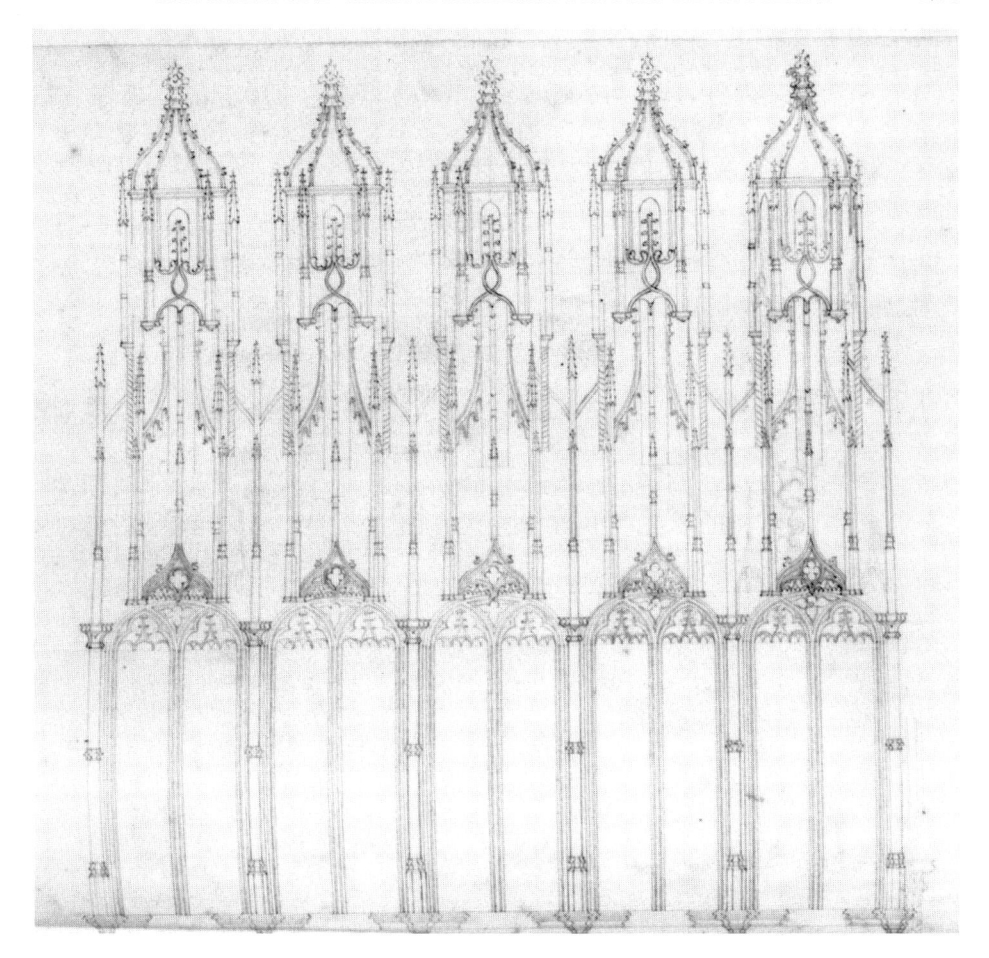

Fig. 34. Stalls, early eighteenth-century drawing by Nicholas Hawksmoor.

substructure of the sixteenth-century stalls rests on ancient undecorated glazed tiles. On the south side there are two layers of them. Both levels are very worn. There is no instance in England throughout the middle ages, to my knowledge, of a set of choir-stalls being set in this way. In the centre the tiles would have been visible right up to the line of the seat rail of the substalls. It has also been conjectured that this also happened on the fourteenth-century choir-stalls at Winchester Cathedral, but there the tiles went no further.[33]

The canopies for the ten new back stalls in the Henry VII chapel were taken from the backs of some of the others, which, in the first place were designed fully in the round. On the north side the original free-standing canopies from the first two bays from the west are still intact. The three central canopies in the next bay have been cannibalised. The other seven half canopies were taken from those on the south side.

---

[33] See the drawing by Corinne Bennett in C. Tracy, *English Gothic Choir Stalls, 1200–1400*, Woodbridge 1987, fig. 5.

Plate 27. Stall canopywork, detail.

Style and artistic provenance

The canopy design represents a re-working of the traditional English three-tier structure (Fig. 34, Plate 27). A band of decorative foliage carving is applied at the lower level to a series of alternating hexagonal and octagonal canopies. Above this, a four-sided traceried oriel, placed at 45 degrees to the front plane, is linked to the lower canopies by flying buttresses. Finally, the twisted columns which spring from the base of the lower canopies support domed hexagonal shrines supported on corbels. The design is of considerable originality and is aesthetically very successful. The horizontal zones are only subtly emphasised. The top and bottom layers catch the light and provide the necessary impression of architectural substance. The middle zone suggests a dark impenetrable depth.

The ancient decorative carving shows itself to best advantage in the lower canopies of the superstructure, on the misericords (Plate 28), the panelling of the dignitaries's stalls, and on the underside of the desk tops (Plate 29).[34] The overhanging desks for the back stalls do duty as canopies for the substalls. The care which was lavished on these substalls is one of the monument's most attractive features. Interestingly, the same design formula was used again on Henry VIII's second large-scale stall commission a quarter of a century later at King's College Cambridge.[35] As already mentioned, in the Henry VII chapel, originally there were uprights on the seat capping, since removed, which were fastened at intervals along the leading edge of the desking above (Plate 30). The backing of the substalls comprised two finely moulded

---

[34] There is carved wainscot panelling behind the stalls.
[35] C. Tracy, *Continental Church Furniture in England: a Traffic in Piety*, Woodbridge 2001, cat. M/7.

Plate 28. Pomegranate fruit and foliage misericord supporter (sixteenth-century).

Plate 29. Underside of desking: detail of Tudor badges.

Plate 30. Front edge of stall desking.

Plate 31. Backing of substalls: detail.

Plate 32. View of underside of stall desk tops: detail.

Plate 33. Tongres, Notre-Dame: retable with Life of the Virgin.

open arches filled with tracery in the apex (Plate 31). Underneath was a frieze of battlementing above a row of quatrefoils. As also at Cambridge, the underside of the desking is decorated with an elaborate net vault, inside the cells of which on the south side are cusp terminations comprising the badges of the Tudor dynasty (Plate 32).[36]

The ornamental vocabulary points unmistakably to the Low Countries for a stylistic ambience. Unfortunately, many Netherlandish choir-stalls were destroyed during the Napoleonic era. Their scarcity, and the complete absence of comparable canopywork, presumably accounts for the unwillingness of earlier writers to assign the Henry VII chapel furniture a definitive artistic status.

At the same time the Henry VII's chapel stalls, like their predecessors at Windsor, are deeply rooted in the English traditions of ecclesiastical joinery. The canopy work is uniquely English. Even by the second decade of the sixteenth century the motif of the large-scale 'ciborium-type' stall canopy had not been adopted on the continent. The architecture of the stalls is still the traditional English double-screen formula. The treatment of the seating and the misericords is typically English too. The major difference in this case is that the manufacture was probably the responsibility of Flemish craftsmen working under the close supervision of an English architect. Alternatively the work was created and executed by Flemish craftsmen who had lived in England long enough to have fully absorbed the native practice of choir-stall designing.

The retention of the English 'ciborium'-type canopy at the Henry VII chapel, Westminster, during a period of radical stylistic change, is remarkable tribute to the tenacity of English ecclesiastical joinery practice. It is interesting to note that even in the considerably later renaissance-style King's College, Cambridge, furniture, Anglicisation was again the rule. Certainly the making of large-scale architectural canopies in wood seems to have been an uniquely English contribution to the last two hundred years of the medieval Gothic period.

The decorative carving can be closely compared with contemporary Flemish work. Moreover prints by the German engravers Dürer and Israel van Meckenem inspired some of the subjects on the misericords.[37] Examples in Flanders of monuments using the same ornamental vocabulary are the Nôtre Dame, Tongres, retable with the Life of the Virgin, of about 1510 (Plate 33), the pulpitum at St Martin, Tessenderloo, of about 1500 (Plate 34), and the pulpitum in the Onze Lieve Vrouwkerk at Aarschot (Plate 35). It can also be seen on contemporary German engravings, such as those by van Meckenem.[38] It is noticeable that the decorative carving on the stalls is quite distinct from that on the interior stonework.

A few English monuments are sometimes cited as being related to the Henry VII chapel stalls, such as the Langton chapel and Lady chapel furniture at Winchester Cathedral,[39] and the Corporation benching at Southwold, Suffolk. The Langton

---

[36] *Ibid.*
[37] J.S. Purvis, 'The use of continental woodcuts and prints by the "Ripon School" of woodcarvers', *Archaeolia* 85, 1935, 124–6.
[38] For example, the foliate ornament design by Israel van Meckenem. See Max Lehrs, *Geschichte und kritischer Katalog des deutschen, niederländischen und französischen Kupferstichs im XV. Jahrhundert* ix, Vienna 1934, repr. New York, cat. 620.
[39] For both see C. Tracy, 'The Lady chapel stalls', in *Winchester Cathedral 1093–1993*, ed. J. Crook, Chichester 1993, 231–46.

Plate 34. Tessenderloo, St Martin: pulpitum.

Plate 35. Aarschot, Onze Lieve Vrouwkerk: pulpitum

Plate 36. Winchester Cathedral, Lady chapel stalls: decorative carving on desk front.

chapel woodwork was probably made towards the end of the first decade of the sixteenth century, and the Lady chapel stalls about five years later. Neither is directly comparable. The Spring chantry, Lavenham is dated by the will of Thomas Spring, d.1523.[40] The Corporation benching at Southwold must also be early sixteenth-century.

The Winchester Cathedral Lady chapel stalls are in a conservative perpendicular style little influenced by continental art. The decorative carving is of a high quality, and the treatment of foliage has a plasticity reminiscent of the Westminster misericords (Plate 36). The alternating semi-circular and angled canopies in the Langton chapel at Winchester (Plate 37) recall Westminster in a general way. The approach is patently more traditional as the canopy fronts are merely modified tracery panels, instead of the non-structural filigree work at Westminster.

Recently, some woodwork has been brought to my attention, which is unequivocally related to the Henry VII chapel material, namely the rood-screen at Ardingly church (Plates 38–9).[41] The latter is a small but ancient building, which is distinguished from it neighbours by its church tower with walls four feet thick, probably constructed at the end of the fourteenth century. Both the single-cell chancel and the aisled nave are short, and must be respectively of the thirteenth and fourteenth century. The church was granted to the Cluniac priory of St Pancras at Lewes by William de Warenne II, and remained with it until the Dissolution in 1537.

---

[40] N. Pevsner, rev. E. Radcliffe, *Suffolk*, Buildings of England, Harmondsworth 1974, 324.
[41] My thanks to Hugh Harrison for alerting me to the existence of this important screen.

Plate 37. Winchester Cathedral, Langton chapel: canopywork, detail.

Plate 38. Ardingly church, West Sussex: former rood screen still *in situ* in 1999.

Plate 39. Ardingly church, West Sussex: detail of dado panelling showing transom frieze above.

The rood stair with its upper and lower openings remains, thus marking the position of the original screen. The latter must have been replaced in the second decade of the sixteenth century by the one which was moved for the third time in 1999. At the 1853 restoration it was taken down and stored in the tower.[42] In 1887 it was retrieved and placed across the western side of the tower arch. Finally in 1924 it was restored to its original position. The recent decision to move the screen yet again was made in the Consistory Court. The east side of the tower is no longer available as an alternative site, because it is already 'taken' by the tailor-made and draught-excluding screen which must have been placed there in 1924. The only area remaining in which to store the screen was found to be at the *back* of the tower, which is in almost complete darkness. To fit into the narrow space the screen had to be 'returned' at right-angles into three sections. Because of the height restrictions the head of the screen had to be removed. This present position is a return to the immurement of 1853. It is in permanent darkness, facing away from any potential viewer, and in any case screened from sight by the structure on its west side. At least it has not been damaged in any way through its metamorphosis, and could perhaps one day be returned quite easily to its proper location and status as an unique English parish church rood-screen.

A number of idiosyncratic features on this screen recall the Henry VII chapel woodwork. There are the same prominent rounded mouldings everywhere. The

---

[42] *VCH Sussex* vii, 1940, 132.

Plate 40. Detail of tracery on front of dignitaries' enclosure, south side.

Plate 41. Stall backs, south side: detail of tracery head with scrolling foliage arch infill, with transom frieze above.

Plate 42. Stall backs, south side: detail of upper portion of dado panelling.

Plate 43. Ardingly church, West Sussex: detail of upper part of rood screen, showing pinnacles with flattened crockets. Only right-hand pinnacle is original.

flat-faced and intertwining mouldings of the 'tracery', in the door and panel arches at dado level (Plate 39), can be paralleled in the same position on the outside of the dignitaries' stalls at Westminster Abbey (Plates 22, 40). The foliage infilling of the dado tracery heads on the extensive panelling on the backs of the stalls in London (Plate 41) recalls Ardingly, as well as the ribbon-like treatment of the foliage on the dignitaries' enclosures. The treatment of this decorative carving recalls the Flemish late-gothic style. On the back of the stalls in London the panel on the transom rail is empty, but must surely have contained a decorative field as at Ardingly (Plates 39, 41). The handling of these transom friezes at Ardingly is somewhat inelegant, as the horizontal mouldings are allowed to overlap the posts. By contrast the moulding on the tracery head is neatly mitred at Westminster, and there is no overlapping. Finally both monuments share the same flattened frilly crockets on the arch pinnacles, capped by a polygonal or circular disc at the top (Plates 42–3).

The Ardingly screen is undated, but on stylistic grounds must have been made sometime during the second decade of the sixteenth century. The two local Wakehurst heiresses, Elizabeth and Margaret, were abducted as girls by the brothers Richard and Nicholas Culpepper in 1463, and forcibly married.[43] Margaret died in 1509, followed by her brother in law Nicholas a year later. Her husband died in 1516 and finally Elizabeth, having produced ten sons and eight daughters died some time after 1517. The Wakehursts had been benefactors of the church in the fifteenth century, and probably paid for the tower. There are memorial brasses to Richard and Margaret in the chancel, with the husband's date of death left blank. Another slab contains the brasses of Nicholas and Elizabeth, with their children below. Nicholas's death is recorded but not that of his wife. Clearly the first brass was made on the death of Margaret Wakehurst, and the second on the demise of Nicholas Culpepper. The insertion of a new rood-screen was very possibly in memory of some or all of these family members. A dating bracket for the manufacture of the screen of 1509–16, that is between Margaret and Richard's death, would seem to be reasonable.

---

[43] R. Harper, *Ardingly: a Brief History*, 1980, 11. The information given here about the Wakehursts and Culpeppers is based on material from this booklet.

Appendix

The Carpentry of the Choir Stalls

Julian Munby

This study of the carpentry of the stalls was undertaken at the request of Tim Tatton-Brown during renovation works in the chapel, in order to determine what evidence there was for the original character of them, and for any subsequent changes that might have been made. Before the structure of the stalls is described, it is necessary to discuss some key questions and propositions about their history.

The History of the Stalls

How many seats were there?
The primary arrangement is indicated both by surviving misericords and a plan of the chapel in c.1600 in the Thorpe collection. The Royal Commission on Historical Monuments inventory lists and illustrates forty original misericords and condemns the remainder as 'modern'.[44] The current disposition of the forty stalls is as follows: 5 + 5 + 2 and a return stall in the upper tier, and a single row of seven substalls, as shown in Colvin's reconstructed plan.[45] The plan in the Thorpe collection shows a minimum of sixty-four stalls (actually sixty-eight, but the rendering of the return stall is confused), arranged 8 + 8 below on each side. While the precise number may not be accurately represented, the plan can more certainly be used to confirm the extent of the stalls in that it shows them terminating at the third column, and two stairs on each side with a break in the stalling opposite. If the plan indeed indicates that there was a full set of substalls, then on the present plan the original total number would be increased to fifty arranged as follows: 5 + 5 + 2 above and 5 + 7 below, and two return stalls, i.e. with a substall matching each superior stall in the second bay. But if these five extra seats were removed in the eighteenth or nineteenth century it is unlikely that the misericords would have been disposed of, and the current total (forty) clearly does not include them.

The original stalls have not moved
Allowing for numerous alterations recorded (or not), from the seventeenth to the twentieth century (and including wholesale dismantling and removal in the last war), it is the evidence of the monument that must now be considered. The original misericords are placed in discrete runs of stalls, respecting the arcade piers. The stall ends adjacent to the piers only have a recess for a misericord on one side, showing that a

---

[44] *Inventory*, 70, pls. 216–20.
[45] Colvin, *HKW* iii, 212, fig. 6.

seat in front of the pier has not been removed, or that the stall ends are completely new.

The substructure (described in more detail below) consists of an oak box frame providing support for the stalls, integral with the superstructure, and built in discrete bay lengths (Fig. 35). The framing was certainly made for its present position, and seems to accommodate the western return stalls without modification, though the western stair has been renewed and its supports are additional to the frame.

The canopies over the stalls also form a consistent piece of design, with one continuous run of canopies end to end. To the confusion of artists drawing the interior of the chapel there are canopies over the breaks in the stalls below, with the canopy carefully set round the pier mouldings, and the individual cells in the miniature vaulting suggesting that this is primary work (although imitated in the Georgian phase, the refashioning of these original vaults at that stage seems rather unlikely). There are two more certain alterations that should be mentioned: firstly the removal of the rear half of several canopies to provide tops to the new Georgian stalls, and secondly the removal of two canopies in the north-west and south-west corners to the east end.[46] The remaining evidential problem is the non-appearance of the piers in early views of the stalls by Hollar and Canaletto. As already stated, the continuous line of canopies would have been misleading to the casual observer, and if the piers were panelled over or painted, they would hardly have been visible.

The return stalls have not been moved
That the large return stalls at the west end of the chapel have been repositioned has been suggested on the ground that they obscure the sculptured frieze above the west door; the alternative would be that they were in line with the other stalls, facing into the chapel. However, since the frieze runs from wall to wall it would be impossible to place stalling anywhere near it without causing some obstruction while, given the history of the chapel, it is by no means certain that it has the furnishing originally intended for it.

Although there can be no certainty about the original position of the return stalls, it is hard to see how the existing canopies could cover stalls in any other arrangement. The misericords are wider than all the others, and the canopies are bigger, so if they were originally laid against the side walls they would have to displace the canopies and standards of at least two of the three blank bays of the main run, and break the symmetry of the rear wall. Accommodating the desks would be equally difficult, for if simply turned then the panelled fronts are either hard against the wall or set only a short distance from it (the matter would be somewhat simpler if the desks were swapped from one side of the chapel to the other, so they were entered from the west end). These alternatives seem altogether too elaborate to explain something which is not really a problem. The stalling required at the time it was designed happens to cover some sculpture. Nevertheless, it is fitting, it allows the bronze side doors of the chapel to open properly, it matches other types of return stall (e.g. Windsor), and has a sub-structure which shows no signs of extensive rearrangement.

[46] Lethaby, *Re-examined*, 171.

APPENDIX ON THE CARPENTRY OF THE STALLS 255

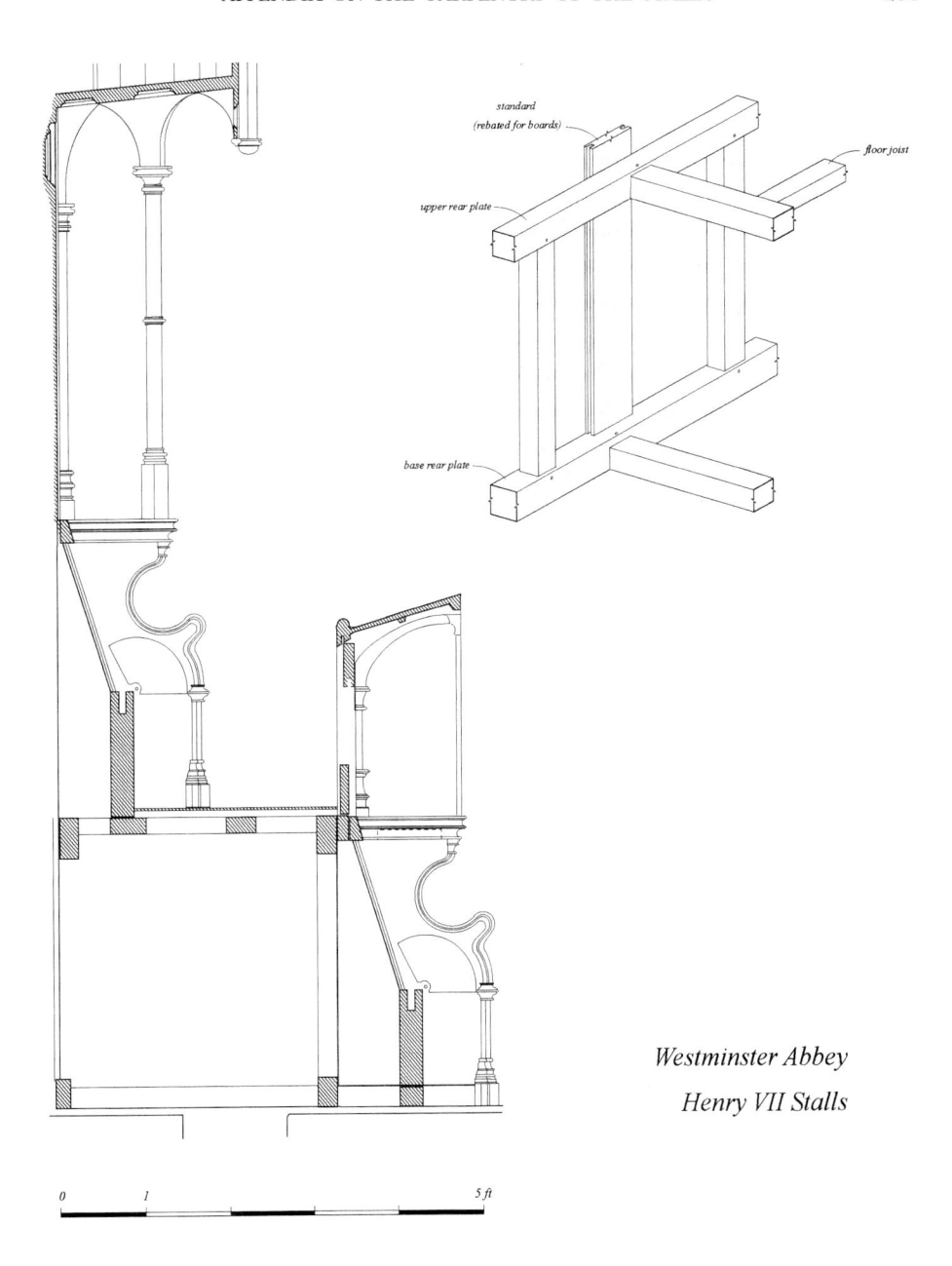

Westminster Abbey
Henry VII Stalls

Fig. 35. Substructure of stalls.

The end bay
New work can be distinguished by the use of plain moulded terminals on the canopy pendants, and generally by the use of round rather than polygonal mouldings (on the columns and stall bases). The substructure (described below) has a generally similar framing to the western part, but with different jointing and flooring arrangements. This proves that the eastern extension (assumed to be mid-eighteenth century) cannot be contemporary with a supposed moving back of the other stalls round the piers at the same time. Further proof of this is that there is also a clear straight joint between the last canopy attached to a pier and the first canopy of the new stalls on both sides.

The Substructure of the Stalls

The primary stalls
The original misericords are placed in discrete runs of stalls in the three western bays of the chapel, respecting the arcade piers (the bench ends adjacent to the piers only have a recess for a misericord on one side). As far as can be seen on each tier, the sides of the stalls (standards) are of normal form, supported on a substantial seat-rail, and with a sloping back board; the two tiers of stalls are brought together on a framed substructure that will be described next (Fig. 35).

The substructure consists of a box frame made of four horizontal plates supported by a series of square transverse frames coinciding with the stall standards. The carpentry, insofar as it is accessible amongst the heating arrangements, appears to be built in discrete bay lengths. That on the north side at the west end is most easily seen, where the first bay is carried on an oak frame between the piers, set on ground plates of which the back one lies on a stone plinth and the front one lies on the original tiled floor. The rear plate has two sets of uprights tenoned into it, first the main rear standards between each stall that rise to canopy level (consisting of a plank rebated on either edge to carry the panelling boards); and second the posts that meet an upper plate at the point where transverse joists for the floor of the upper stalls cross to the front upper plate. There are matching joists at ground level between front and back plates, while a post between the top and bottom plates at the front completes the square. On the upper level are pairs of secondary joists or trimmers running between the joists, and a similar pair of trimmers joins each frame to the next in front of the pier. The floor boards of the upper stalls are laid longitudinally on top of these joists.

The framed substructure does not require any internal bracing, but is given support by the rear standard and the substantial stall standards of the upper stalls, and at the front by the sub-stalls. The substalls are related to the frame at the lowest level, where the joists from the frame continue forward to meet the seat-rail; but the canopy and reading desk above are both carried on standards that rise from a capping rail independently from the back frame but at the level of upper floor (this is best seen in the centre of the south side).

This substructure is of oak, is entirely joined with pegged mortice-and-tenons (some of them with double tenons), and the only hesitation in declaring it to be original stems from its pristine condition. It was certainly made for its present location, since the framing is built to fit within each bay of the chapel, and it seems to accommodate the western return stall without modification, though the western stair has been renewed and its supports are additional to the frame.

The eastern additions

The substructure of the eastern bay, as viewed from the vent door at the east end of the north side, appears generally to have a similar framing to the original part, though is possibly not all of oak. Differences of detail are that the members are joined with diminished haunch tenons rather than the plain tenons used at the west end, and there are no secondary floor joists, while the floorboards run north-south (rather than east-west, as at the west end). These differences show that the east bay must be entirely distinct from the remainder.

'The singuler mediacions and praiers of al the holie companie of Heven': Sculptural Functions and Forms in Henry VII's Chapel

PHILLIP LINDLEY

Introduction: royal blood and relics

IN 1498, an extraordinary three-way lawsuit took place between the abbots of the monasteries of Westminster and Chertsey and the dean of Windsor for possession of the remains of King Henry VI, who had died a quarter of a century earlier. A series of rather geriatric witnesses – the youngest was in his sixties – gave depositions as to Henry VI's own choice of burial site some forty years before. Several remembered how the king had come on different occasions to Westminster Abbey, to select a place for his own tomb in the area round the Confessor's shrine, already crowded with royal monuments. Thomas Humfrey, aged sixty-eight, and now blind, recalled how Henry, after discussing the matter with the abbot, had finally decided on a spot between Henry III's tomb and the shrine. The king's master mason, John Thirsk, had been summoned to incise the precise dimensions on the *opus sectile* pavement in the king's presence. Henry had composed detailed instructions for the monument: John Dawson still remembered having once seen them in the office of the clerk of the king's works. The sixty-six year old marbler Thomas Fifelde, who had been an apprentice at the time, testified that his then master, John Essex, had been summoned with Essex's partner, Thomas Stephens, to contract with the king for the tomb.[1]

This eye-witness testimony won the expensive legal suit for the abbot of Westminster and helps explain an otherwise entirely uncharacteristic, dramatic, and massively expensive change of heart by King Henry VII. For the Tudor king now abruptly abandoned work on his nearly complete new Lady chapel at the east end of St George's Chapel, Windsor, which he had initiated only four years earlier, 'entending',

---

[1] Stanley, *Historical Memorials*, 506ff; Harvey, *EMA*, s.n.; T. Tatton-Brown, 'The pavement of the chapel of St Edward the Confessor, Westminster Abbey', *JBAA* 153, 2000, 71–84. Thanks are due to Donald Buttress, Dr Miriam Gill, Dr S.J. Gunn, Dr Richard Mortimer, Dr Sophie Oosterwijk, Professor Charles Phythian-Adams, Christine Reynolds, Tim Tatton-Brown, and Professor Greg Walker for all their help. This paper, an expanded version of my 1995 lecture, is intended as a precursor to more extended study of the freestone imagery of the chapel.

as he subsequently recorded, 'to have translatid the body of his said Uncle in to the same and nygh unto him within the said chapell to have be[en] buryed hymself'.[2] Richard III had removed Henry VI's 'bodie and reliques' from Chertsey to the splendid new Yorkist church at Windsor, to ensure that his remains could not become a focus of political opposition. Henry VII had planned to mark his own appropriation of the throne by placing a shrine for the last Lancastrian monarch close to a tomb for himself and Elizabeth of York in a newly constructed Lady chapel at Windsor.[3] Now, instead, the Tudor king decided to build a magnificent new chapel at Westminster, the most ostentatious act of royal patronage at the Abbey since the time of Henry III. The fact that the chapel was never completed as Henry VII intended, and the palimpsesting effect of its later history, have tended to erase the principal functions of the chapel as originally conceived.[4] Yet scrutiny of Henry's major objectives, which can be reconstructed by analysis of the king's will and of the indentures drawn up with the abbot and convent of Westminster in 1504, must underpin any attempt to interpret the seminally important sculptural programmes which adorned the chapel's exterior and interior.[5]

The new building was to serve as a Lady chapel, replacing that constructed on the site in the reign of King Henry III; as a chantry chapel for Henry VII and his wife, for his grandmother, Katherine de Valois (who had been buried in the earlier Lady chapel), his mother, Margaret Beaufort, and, perhaps, for his successors; and, finally, as the splendid setting for the shrine of King Henry VI, whose canonisation Henry was still seeking at the time he constructed the chapel.[6] Margaret Beaufort's cancellation in 1499 of her previous licence to endow Windsor with appropriations and lands – to support four chaplains in her proposed chantry there – in favour of Westminster Abbey, emphasises the abrupt finality of the royal transfer of patronage, and stresses the chief importance of the new chapel's chantry roles.[7] For the chapel's functions have to be located within the massive network of provisions made by Henry VII for his welfare in the afterlife. These arrangements included the foundation and endowment of almshouses at Westminster, close to the west end of the Abbey, the ordinances for which were to be set out in a panel to hang in the new chapel:[8] the thirteen

---

[2] W.H. St J. Hope, *Windsor Castle*, 2 vols., 1913, 479.
[3] Colvin, *HKW* iii, 308–9.
[4] For the documentary history of the chapel, see Colvin, *HKW* iii, 210ff; the best general surveys are those of Perkins, *Worship and Ornaments*; *Inventory*, and Wilson, *Westminster Abbey* and 'The designer of Henry VII's Chapel, Westminster Abbey' in *Reign of Henry VII*.
[5] The most recent study of the sculptural programmes is H.J. Dow, *The Sculptural Decoration of the Henry VII Chapel, Westminster Abbey*, Durham 1992, which is, unfortunately, unillustrated.
[6] Perkins, *Worship and Ornaments*, 149–52. For the development of chantries, see Colvin, 'The origin of chantries', *Journal of Medieval History* 26, 2000, 163–73. J.T. Rosenthal's important *The Purchase of Paradise: Gift Giving and the Aristocracy, 1307–1485*, 1972, excludes royal chantries from his purview, but see also G.H. Cook, *Medieval Chantries and Chantry Chapels*, 1963.
[7] *CPR 1494–1509*, 79 for the licence to endow Windsor, and 517–18 for the December 1506 licence to the abbot and prior of Westminster. However, an inspeximus of 1505 in *CCR 1500–1509*, 227–8, records a licence (not enrolled at the time) in the letters patent of May 1499 for Westminster to appropriate rectories and receive lands previously granted to Windsor. For the context of the transfers, see the lucid account in Jones and Underwood, 208–9. The establishment of Beaufort's chantry at Westminster in 1506 does not mean, as has often been uncritically assumed (e.g. Westlake ii, 361), that the chapel in Westminster was now physically complete.
[8] *CCR 1500–9*, 389, xi. For the almshouses, Colvin, *HKW* iii, 206ff.

almsmen were to assemble three times every day for masses at Henry VII's tomb, as part of the chantry provision. Nor should it be forgotten, in considering Henry's switch from Windsor to Westminster, that the Abbey's roles as the coronation church, in which Henry VII had received the unction as king, and as the repository of the tombs of his royal predecessors, were expressly mentioned by the king in his will. So, the construction of the new chapel at the east end of the Abbey should be construed as a deliberate and carefully structured plan to appropriate the past – represented above all by the great sequences of royal tombs and the shrine of St Edward – in the service of Henry VII, legitimising and naturalising Tudor power.

Helen Dow has convincingly argued that the chapel's intended functions affected both the disposition and the broad iconographic thrust of its freestone figure-sculpture.[9] As well as reconsidering the meaning of this sculptural programme, and some specific identifications, a preliminary analysis of the figures' stylistic context will be offered here. I shall suggest, contrary to Dow's view, that the programme was largely in the hands of sculptors from the Low Countries, and that Henry VII's chapel contains, in fact, the largest extant scheme of contemporary Netherlandish figure sculpture. Henry VII's patronage, and that of his court, was dominated, with the key exception of architecture, by foreign artists, and the figure-sculpture revealingly illustrates the abject failure of indigenous artists to respond to the challenge of continental European sculptors, notwithstanding the lavish patronage available in England.

The scanty documentary evidence for construction of Henry VII's chapel can be quickly summarised: all the fabric accounts have disappeared and there is no direct record of the progress of construction. From the king's will of 1509 it is clear that there once was a 'Plat made for the same Chappell, and signed with our hande'.[10] This 'Plat' or drawn design – it is clear from the context – will have included the intended location of the tomb, high altar and other major liturgical objects. Tantalisingly, as Sir Howard Colvin has shown, there still existed, in the early nineteenth century, approximately seventy drawings which contemporary antiquaries associated with this chapel, but these drawings cannot now be located.[11] Only the broad outlines of the building's progress are recorded in Royal Chamber Accounts from October 1502 onwards. On 24 January 1503 the foundation stone of the new building was laid and between October 1502 and April 1509 some £14,856 were spent on the chapel.[12] On 13 April 1509, eight days before his death, Henry entrusted a further £5,000 for the completion of the building and made provision in his will for his executors to provide even more money if this sum were insufficient.[13]

In his will, Henry refers to the stained glass of the chapel, 'as is by us redily devised and in picture [doubtless *vidimuses*] delivered' to the master of works, William Bolton, Prior of St Batholomew's, Smithfield, and continues that he desires that 'the Walles,

---

[9] Dow, *Sculptural Decoration*, 54–7; she goes on to state that 'the sculptures of the chapel express in stone what the funeral masses expressed in words and actions'.

[10] See above, 113.

[11] Colvin, *HkW* iii, 211; *Gentlemans Magazine* 77, 1807, 1189–90; 78, 1808, 286, 296, 399–400, for the argument involving John Carter as to the status of the drawings. The fact that the name of some of the buildings was written above the subjects suggests that the design for the monument to Henry VI, discussed below, may have been one of them.

[12] Colvin, *HkW* iii, 211–13; see above, 192, for annual expenditure totals.

[13] Above, 115–16.

Doores, Windows, Archies, and Vaults and Ymages of the same our Chapell, within and without, be painted, garnisshed and adorned, with our Armes, Bagies, Cognoissaunts, and other convenient painting, in as goodly and riche maner as suche a work requireth, and as to a Kings werk apperteigneth'.[14] There appears to be a very strong implication that although the glass had yet to be produced, the sculptural programme was already complete and in place, though still unpainted, at the time that the will was finally revised. The painting of niche imagery would seem often, perhaps even normally, to have occurred after the figure-sculpture was installed, as can be deduced, for instance, from the painted outlines of the images once housed in the Lady chapel of Ely Cathedral (completed in the mid-fourteenth century) and later removed by iconoclasts. The Ely Lady chapel, which is sometimes seen as the zenith of the image-filled Lady chapel, had successors in the fifteenth century: the Lady chapel of Gloucester Abbey, for instance, was also given a mass of sculpted imagery. Such evidence for the prior existence of extensive sculptural programmes in Lady chapels may be one reason for the extraordinarily dense sculptural freighting of Henry VII's new Lady chapel at Westminster. More significant, undoubtedly, was the increasing encrustation of chantry chapels with huge programmes of imagery, a proliferation of sculpture which almost overwhelms some contemporary chapels. One obvious precedent which was both a Lady chapel and a chantry chapel, encrusted with imagery, was Richard Beauchamps's chapel at St Mary's Warwick, with its magnificent gilt-bronze effigy of the earl.[15] If Henry's will shows that the freestone figure-sculptures of the chapel's interior and exterior were already probably in place by 1509, it is nonetheless clear that other figure-sculptural components of major significance had not yet been completed. It will be argued that their analysis is a necessary precursor to a study of the freestone statuary even though some were never produced and the others postdate the freestone figure-sculptures.

'The bodie and reliquies of our uncle of blissed memorie'

The first object to consider is the proposed shrine for King Henry VI. In the British Library is a drawing lettered in a later hand: 'The Monument intended for Kinge Henry the sixte' (Fig. 36). There is nothing, so far as I can see, to challenge this attribution for what is evidently a presentational drawing for the patron.[16] The background to the production of this drawing lies, of course, in Henry VII's attempt to secure the canonisation of Henry VI, who was already unofficially venerated as a saint.[17] By preferring Westminster to Windsor as the site of his new chapel, Henry VII benefited – as he explicitly recognised – from the proximity, in St Edward's chapel, of what had become the mausoleum of earlier English royalty, grouped round the

---

[14] See now R. Marks, 'The glazing of Henry VII's chapel, Westminster Abbey', in *Reign of Henry VII*, 157–74 for the glazing.

[15] For this chapel see Stone, *Sculpture*, 207–10, and for the effigy P.G. Lindley, *Gothic to Renaissance: Essays on Sculpture in England*, Stamford 1995, 62–6. For later chantry chapels see e.g. Bishop Alcock's chapel at Ely.

[16] The drawing is BL MS Cotton Augustus ii, 1.

[17] Hope, *Windsor Castle*, 480, citing the faculty for Henry VII to move Henry VI's body to Westminster. S. Anglo, *Images of Tudor Kingship*, 1992, chapter 3, is a helpful study of the context.

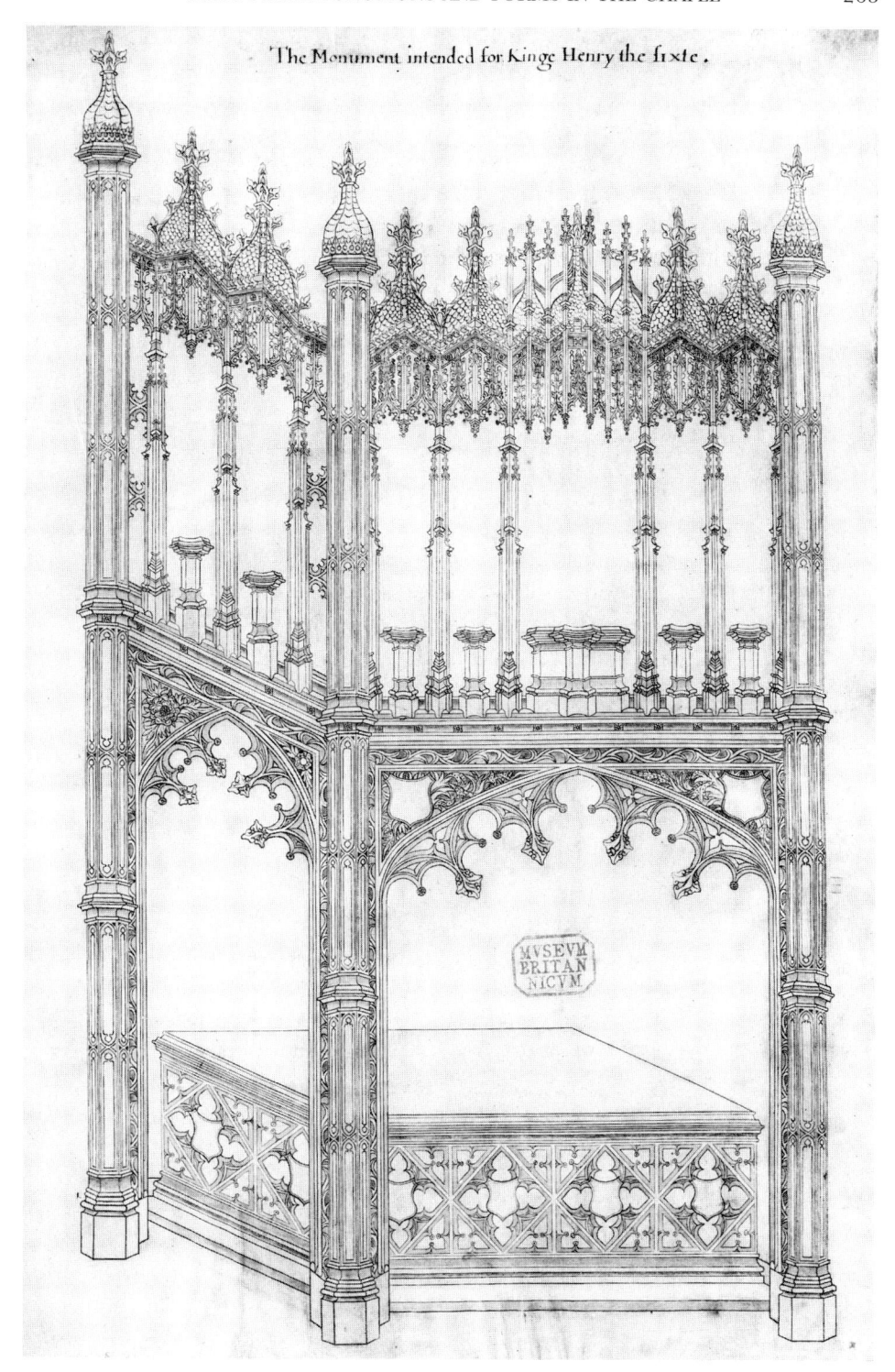

Fig. 36. Drawing of proposed shrine monument to Henry VI (BL MS Cotton Augustus ii, 1).

Confessor's shrine: Henry thus asserted continuity with previous monarchs, in the coronation church of the English monarchy – situated directly across the road from the palace of Westminster, which continued to house the Chancery, Exchequer, the common law and prerogative courts, and the High Court of Parliament. The format of the new chapel, with radiating chapels and aisles flanking the nave, represents a modernised emulation of the existing east end, with the important modification that the relationship of tombs to shrine and high altar is both rationalised and reconfigured into a coherent axial stress: Henry VII's own tomb was intended to dominate the 'nave' of the new building, standing to the west of the steps to the high altar, beyond which would be Henry VI's shrine.[18] The dominant linear axis in the church now read: high altar; Confessor's shrine; Henry V's chantry chapel, then Henry VII and Queen Elizabeth's tomb; Lady altar; Henry VI's shrine. The Yorkist monarchs were not, of course, represented by tombs at Westminster and the Yorkist chapel of St George at Windsor was now effectively relegated from Henry's concerns; after he transferred his financial support to Westminster, Henry VII seems largely to have left completion of the nave and choir of St George's 'to private benevolence'.[19]

Pope Julius II granted licence for the removal of Henry VI's remains to Westminster in 1504.[20] This makes it possible to narrow down a little more precisely the date when the design was drawn, for although Henry VII still expected the translation to take place in his will, there is little evidence to suggest that his successor pursued the scheme.[21] It seems likely, therefore, to antedate 1509. The drawing shows two sides of a structure whose precise functional antecedents – shrine or tomb – are, it is true, partially obscured by the absence of any figure-sculpture in the drawing, but it is a temptation to see this ambiguity as deliberate, a reflection of the uncertainties of the canonisation process. Its general appearance, as well as details such as the coats of arms decorating the base, is much closer to tombs than to conventional shrine-bases: one odd feature, the lack of contact between the tomb-base and the enclosing arches of the superstructure, has a precedent in Archbishop Bourchier's monument at Canterbury, although in Henry's monument the tomb-chest would have been very low.[22] There is no evidence for the location of a dedicated altar on the drawing, but one was certainly envisaged in Henry VII's will; this need not have been attached to the monument, merely in its immediate vicinity.[23] Pilgrimage was already taking place to Henry's tomb at Windsor, so no separate *feretrum* may have been envisaged and the distinction between tomb and shrine may be otiose.[24]

[18] Perkins, *Worship and Ornaments*, 151–2.
[19] Colvin, *HkW* iii, 312.
[20] Hope, *Windsor Castle*, 489–90.
[21] Anglo, *Images*, 71, comments that 'it was papal policy rather than Henry Tudor's parsimony which prevented the canonisation of Henry VI'. The canonisation was again mooted in 1528 but there is no evidence otherwise of Henry VIII's interest in the matter.
[22] C. Wilson, 'The medieval monuments', in *A History of Canterbury Cathedral*, ed. P. Collinson, N. Ramsay and M. Sparks, Oxford 1995, 484, n. 149, suggests it derives from Edward IV's tomb at Windsor. Numerous French tombs also had this feature. See also Alice Chaucer's monument at Ewelme, Oxon.
[23] 'The Aulter of or said uncle of blessed memorie King Henry the VIth' is specified in the will. Dow, *Sculptural Decoration*, 66, follows William Burges in Scott, *Gleanings*, 81, when she contends that 'the altar was to have been included in the top storey of this tomb structure', but this is impossible.
[24] Anglo, *Images*, 68–70, for the investigation of Henry VI's miracles. See also Hope, *Windsor Castle*, 415. There was an altar dedicated to Henry near to the tomb.

Stylistically, the rich architectural vocabulary of the structure seems very close indeed to that of the Westminster chapel itself, and it is therefore unlikely to antedate 1498. The designer has drawn a rectangular structure, with slender octagonal turrets at the corners – like those on which beasts are perched at the chapel's entrance, though here embellished with additional decoration – running the full height of the monument to terminate in ogee domes modelled on those of the chapel. The diagonally turned buttresses of the superstructure, separating the image niches, with subsidiary bases in the angles, find parallels in those between the niches of the chapels. The flying arches above the apices of the central trio of niches on the long-side are reminiscent of the arches which run into the pendants of the fan vaults, and the cusping of the arches is related to that of the main transverse arches. Other details – such as the flattened four-centred arches and the lozenges with trefoil terminations in the panelling of the turrets – can also be found in the chapel. Some of the detailing can also be closely paralleled in Provost Lupton's chantry chapel at Eton College (completed by 1515), which Harvey assigns to William Vertue – to whom, indeed, he also attributes this design.[25] If Vertue was indeed the designer of the Westminster monument, he is most likely to have undertaken the design after 1506. In an estimate for Henry VII's own tomb drawn up in the same year, William Vertue is not listed amongst the trio of 'king's master masons':[26] instead, Robert Vertue, his elder brother, was associated with Robert Janyns and John Lebons, one of the future designers of Wolsey's Cardinal College, Oxford.[27] Both Robert Janyns – according to Leedy and Wilson the probable designer of Henry VII's chapel – and Robert Vertue were senior to William and would probably have had precedence over him in such an important commission as a monument to Henry VI.[28] However, both of them died in 1506, after which year William's involvement becomes much more likely: in July 1510, when Henry VIII returned to the tradition of issuing a patent to one master mason charged with general responsibility for all activity within the king's works, William was named as master mason.[29] Very probably, then, the design should be dated between late 1506 and April 1509. Its stylistic proximity to Henry VII's chapel itself would be readily explained by the fact that Vertue was doubtless in charge of its completion from 1506.

The superstructure of the monument is full of niches for imagery:[30] fourteen spaces if the other two sides exactly replicated those shown in the drawing. The fact that no sculpture is drawn emphasises the separation of architectural design from sculptural production in late medieval England and the subsidiarity of the latter in works designed by master masons: on a drawing for Bishop Fox's chantry chapel, on which work was in hand in 1513, no sculpture is shown either.[31] Although the size of

---

[25] Harvey, *EMA*, 308.
[26] Harvey, *EMA*, 160.
[27] J. Newman, 'Cardinal Wolsey's collegiate foundations', in *Cardinal Wolsey: Church, State and Art*, ed. S.J. Gunn and P. Lindley, Cambridge 1991, 109.
[28] W.C. Leedy, 'The design of the vault of Henry VII's chapel, Westminster: a reappraisal', *Architectural History* 18, 1975, 5–11, and Wilson, 'Designer'.
[29] D.R. Ransome, 'The administration of the works: the earlier Tudors', in Colvin, *HKW* iii, 26. Henry VII may already have changed this at the end of his life: see under Vertue in Harvey, *EMA*.
[30] Lethaby, *Re-examined*, 165, points out that scale rules out this upper part being a chantry chapel – as Dow, *Sculptural Decoration*, 66, maintains.
[31] A. Smith, 'The chantry chapel of Bishop Fox', *Winchester Cathedral Record* 57, 1988, pl. 3. Some features

the proposed monument is surprising if it was intended to stand in the eastern chapel – for it would have been difficult of access for pilgrims[32] – the disposition of the sculpted images in the axial chapel, with Sts Thomas and Nicholas flanking a (till recently) empty niche with the letters HR for Henry VI facing Sts Edward the Confessor, Peter and Edmund (Plate 6), emphasises the intended proximity of the shrine.[33]

In the end, of course, the debate about the function of the monument and its planned location lacks finality because neither the translation nor the canonisation of Henry VI ever took place. Westminster's triumph over Windsor was an expensive Pyrrhic victory. Henry VI's corpse remained at St George's, beneath a tomb commissioned by Richard III, who had the body translated from Chertsey in August 1484; it was a low altar tomb with an effigy of Henry VI in armour, bearded, lying on it, at his feet the king's beasts, the leopard and antelope, the side of the tomb-chest decorated with a shield of his arms borne by an angel. Upon a bar over the figure were suspended the king's achievement (without the spurs, which were venerated as a relic). The whole monument was probably of alabaster and was unfortunately dismantled some time between 1598 and 1611.[34]

'Altogether the greatest sculptures ever wrought in England.'[35] Pietro Torrigiano's work in Henry VII's chapel

Today, the tomb of King Henry VII and Queen Elizabeth of York occupies part of the space originally intended for the chapel's high altar. The evidence for the series of abortive projects for Henry VII's tomb before the Florentine sculptor Pietro Torrigiano Torrigiani was awarded the contract in October 1512 is well known and has recently been reviewed by Alan Darr: accordingly it requires no more than a summary here. Between July 1501 and April 1502 over £78 had been disbursed on a first project for Henry VII's tomb at Windsor. In 1503 £10 was spent in bringing the

---

of the low base are repeated in a monument at Turvey (Beds.), F. Crossley, *English Church Monuments*, 1921, 100.

[32] Cf. Wilson, *Westminster Abbey*, 75. Pamela Tudor-Craig, *ibid.*, 136, follows Colvin, *HKW* iii, 219, in assuming that the tomb/shrine would have stood behind the high altar and not in the axial chapel.

[33] Tudor-Craig, *ibid.*, 134, appears to suggest St Thomas for this location: 'Henry VI . . . has . . . been suggested for the blank niche in the axial chapel, where "HR" appears on the pedestal. However, Thomas Becket ought to have stood there, between Denys and Paul.' This claim is difficult to interpret because the figures on either side of the central niche of the axial chapel are usually identified as Sts Thomas and Nicholas. Sts Denys and Paul flank another blank niche, in the reredos of the western chapel on the south side. Henry VI was commemorated with a statue at the Savoy and is shown on the lectern in King's College chapel, Cambridge. The figure on the Westminster return stalls, *Inventory*, pl.127, is doubtless Henry VI.

[34] See C.R. Beard, *The Tomb and Achievements of King Henry VI at Windsor*, Frome 1936. See BL Additional MS 6298, fo. 148. It hardly seems likely that Henry VII intended to have the alabaster effigy moved to Westminster (and that this is the reason why no effigy is shown on the design for the abbey monument).

[35] Lethaby, *Craftsmen*, 237. For Torrigiano's work in England, including detailed study of the Westminster tombs, see A.P. Darr, 'Pietro Torrigiano and his sculpture for the Henry VII Chapel, Westminster Abbey', unpublished Ph.D. dissertation, New York University 1980. The pertinent documentary evidence had been assembled by Sir Howard Colvin in *HKW* iii.

materials to Westminster.[36] Work on this tomb (if the references in 1501–2 are not rather to the metal grate to be discussed shortly)[37] must have soon been abandoned because in 1506 Guido Mazzoni provided a design for a new tomb which, as Meyer and Verdon have shown, was a splendid renaissance monument intended to surpass Mazzoni's recently completed tomb of Charles VIII in St Denis.[38] Various theories have been advanced why this grand monument with its kneeling figure of Henry VII in gilt-bronze, placed above two recumbent effigies of the deceased, also in gilt-bronze, should have been rejected.[39] One additional, practical, reason may be suggested. If constructed, it would have towered over the metal grate or chantry chapel enclosure which was then already under construction: for it seems certain that the intended site for Henry VII and Queen Elizabeth's tomb and the enclosing grate was in the new chapel's nave, between the choir stalls. Certainly, this is the location specified in his will where the king states: 'we wol that our Tomb be in the myddes of the . . . chappell before the High Aultar' and this must have been the location indicated in the missing 'platte'.[40] The original stalls only occupied three bays of the nave, their vertiginous height already necessitated by the requirement for their occupants to be able to see one another across the grate round Henry VII and Queen Elizabeth's tomb, intended to stand between them.[41] In such a position, the kneeling figure of Henry VII and the four flanking lords envisaged by Mazzoni on top of the tomb would have made it virtually impossible for some of the monks in the stalls on either side – even if they were standing – to see one another.

Although Mazzoni's scheme was abandoned, no work had taken place on the more conservative monument envisaged in the king's will – with images of saints in niches on the sides and ends and with recumbent gilt-bronze figures of the king and queen – at the time of his death. The image of the kneeling king from Mazzoni's design was transmuted into a votive figure of gold plate on a wooden core, to be placed on the shrine of Edward the Confessor.[42] A similar image of silver and gilt, presumably rather smaller, had already been presented by the king to be set before the shrine of the Virgin at Walsingham, and his will required a further one, holding a scroll with the words 'Sancte Thomae intercede Pro Me' and with an inscription 'Rex Henricus Septimus' on the table on which it knelt, placed 'as nighe to the Shrine of St Thomas as may bee'.[43]

---

[36] Hope, *Windsor Castle*, 481, and Colvin, *HKW* iii, 219.

[37] Lethaby, *Craftsmen*, 227, disputes Higgins' suggestion (p. 136) that this was for the grate. John Esterfeld could not have been the maker: he was a canon of Windsor, acting as paymaster (Colvin, *HKW* iii, 219).

[38] See B.M. Meyer, 'The first tomb of Henry VII of England', *Art Bulletin* 58, 1976, 358–67; T. Verdon, *The Art of Guido Mazzoni*, New York 1978, 137–8. The estimate is BL MS Harley 297, fos. 28–30.

[39] See Darr, 'Pietro Torrigiano', and Lindley, *Gothic to Renaissance*.

[40] Above, 113.

[41] A stone screen, like those of which there are remains further east, originally separated off the aisles from the main body of the chapel, but additional stalls and seats were added in the eighteenth century, when the chapel was fitted up as the chapel of the Order of the Bath: see Tracy, above. Since 1913, the banners of the knights of the Order hung over their respective stalls have again obscured the statuary and vaulting above them.

[42] Above, 133; Lindley, *Gothic to Renaissance*, 57–8.

[43] Above 134: these arrangements seem to have been based on those for Richard Beauchamp, Earl of Warwick, who wanted four gold images of himself sent to four churches (including St Albans and Canterbury).

Plate 44. Tomb figures of Henry VII and Elizabeth of York.

In the event, the traditional tomb-design outlined in the will was transformed in the hands of Pietro Torrigiano into the monument we now see (Plates IVB, VI; Plate 44). Not only was the monument subtly modified from Henry VII's specification, it was also placed in an entirely different position, behind the high altar, to the east. The reason for this change of site may have been, as has often been speculated, that Henry VIII wished to reserve the nave space for his own monument.[44] Certainly, in 1516, Torrigiano was already estimating for the cost of a double tomb for Henry VIII and Katharine of Aragon. The terms of this contract repeat much of the specification of Torrigiano's tomb for Henry VII and Queen Elizabeth in October 1512.[45] By that date Torrigiano's first major royal tomb, that for Margaret Beaufort (contract signed on 23 November 1511), to be situated before the altar at the east end of the south aisle, must have been nearing completion.[46] In the Beaufort project, Torrigiano had been constrained by the traditional working procedures imposed on him by the English patrons. Thus, although he was responsible for the design and execution of the touch-stone tomb-chest, with its renaissance detailing, the effigy and the niche within which it was housed (Plate VIIC), were designed by a painter named Meynard Vewick (the designs for the coats of arms of her parents and grandparents, of Henry V and Katherine of Valois, her husbands Edmund Tudor and Thomas earl of Derby,

---

[44] E.g. Perkins, *Worship and Ornaments*, 158. However, the terms in the document cited in the next note make it clear that in 1516 no precise location for the tomb had been determined.

[45] PRO, SP 1/18, pp. 2–5, for the draft indenture of covenants for the erecting of a tomb to the memory of King Henry the Eighth, rehearsing the 1512 indenture's details.

[46] Torrigiano had signed a contract on 23 November 1511 requiring the monument to be set up by 1 February 1513, with Prior Bolton as surveyor and controller of work, replicating his role in the chapel's construction: see R.F. Scott, 'On the contracts for the tomb of the Lady Margaret Beaufort, Countess of Richmond and Derby, mother of King Henry VII and foundress of the colleges of Christ and St John in Cambridge', *Archaeologia* 66, 1915, 365–76. Scott is not entirely reliable as to the accounts (see St John's College, Cambridge, MSS D 56 21 (the tomb contract); D 91 7 (the draft for the executors' accounts); D 91 24 (the executors' accounts); D 57 14 (the parcel of miscellaneous warrants); D 57 11 (Morgan Mores' memorandum); D 57 15 (Maynard Vewick's memorandum); Bishop Fisher's letter to Prior Bolton is D 57 17; Scott missed D 7 221, the bond for £500 referred to in the contract).

of Arthur, and of Henry VIII and Katherine of Aragon, were supplied by a herald).[47] The later tomb contract for Henry VII and his queen, and the evidence of the monument's appearance, reveal that for the first time one man, Torrigiano, was in charge of both design and execution. The tabernacle work which had flanked Margaret Beaufort's effigy was now abandoned.[48] The tomb-chest houses gilt-bronze tondi with pairs of saints along the sides (the deployment of saints rather than 'weepers' or coats of arms may be a debt to Richard II and Anne of Bohemia's monument), the upper level of the tomb-chest was self-consciously modified in the direction of Florentine sarcophagus design and with gilt-bronze angels, originally holding royal banners or the sword and scales for royal justice, perched on the corners (Plate VI).[49] Amongst the numerous departures from indigenous tradition, perhaps the most remarkable is the pair of naked putti suspending the coat of arms from ribbons on the east end of the tomb.[50] Margaret Whinney describes Torrigiano as 'the first artist to show the English something of the true renaissance style'.[51] Although the primary functions of the monument were entirely unaffected by its appearance in the vanguard of the greatest revolution in style for several hundred years, the up-to-date renaissance idiom and the employment of the new medium of white Italian marble must have impressed the court of Henry VIII, with its acute, if not always well informed, sensitivity to developments across the channel and in Italy.

It is worth considering the materials employed by Torrigiano a little more carefully. Whilst gilt-bronze effigies were, by reason of their enormous cost, restricted to the very wealthiest patrons, it would be wrong to view them as confined to sovereigns: for instance, Richard Beauchamp, Earl of Warwick and, most recently, Margaret

---

[47] Margaret Beaufort never recognised her first marriage, as a six-year-old, to John de la Pole, dissolved three years later in 1453: Jones and Underwood, 37. Nor is her third marriage, to Stafford, represented on the tomb. The arms are (from the west): France and England quarterly with Edmund earl of Richmond (her second husband) impaling Beaufort; France and England quarterly impaling de Burgh and Mortimer for Henry VII (her only child) and Queen Elizabeth; France and England quarterly impaling France for Henry V and Katherine of Valois, mother of her second husband (Edmund Tudor); France and England quarterly with a label (for Prince Arthur); the quartered coats of Stanley and Lathom quartering the legs of Man for Thomas earl of Stanley, her fourth husband, impaling Beaufort; Beaufort for John earl of Somerset, her grandfather, impaling England with a border, for Margaret Holland, her grandmother; Beaufort for John, first duke of Somerset, her father, impaling Margaret Beauchamp of Bletsoe, her mother. The now missing coat is that of Henry VIII and Katherine of Aragon, shown by Sandford, on the plate on p. 320.

[48] The tomb of Richard Beauchamp, quasi-regal in its magnificence and setting, in St Mary's, Warwick, provides a precedent for the absence of the enclosing 'canopy' but this is most unlikely to have been known to Torrigiano. It should be noted that important elements are missing from Beaufort's pinnacles and canopy superstructure, most importantly the front section which joined to the pinnacles and would have made the canopy even more elaborate (cf. A. Higgins, 'On the work of Florentine sculptors in England in the early part of the sixteenth century: with special reference to the tombs of Cardinal Wolsey and King Henry VIII', *Archaeological Journal* 51, 1894, 134, who has not understood this).

[49] The engraving between pp. 442 and 443 in Sandford shows them.

[50] Higgins, 'Florentine sculptors', 138–41; Lindley, *Gothic to Renaissance*, 59–62. For excellent discussions of Italian influences see D. Thomson, 'Henry VII and the uses of Italy: the Savoy Hospital and Henry VII's posterity', in *Reign of Henry VII*, 104–16, and, for a later period, C.M. Sicca, 'Consumption and trade of art between Italy and England in the first half of the sixteenth century: the London house of the Bardi and Cavalcanti company', *Renaissance Studies* 16/2, 2002, 163–201.

[51] Whinney, 31. If by artist she means solely sculptor, this assessment still seems fundamentally correct. For an alternative discussion of Torrigiano's tombs see A.P. Darr, 'The sculptures of Torrigiano: the Westminster Abbey tombs', *Connoisseur* 200, 1979, 177–84 and *idem*, 'Pietro Torrigiano'.

Beaufort's final husband, the earl of Derby, had gilt-bronze effigies.[52] Edward IV had in fact viewed gilt-bronze as distinctly second best to silver-gilt for his effigy at Windsor.[53] Edward had presumably ruminated on the precedent set by Henry V's effigy for silver-gilt and solid silver; but this was to remain an exception. At Westminster the gilt-bronze effigies of Eleanor of Castile, Henry III, Edward III and Richard II and Anne of Bohemia, collected round the Confessor's shrine, provided the model of opulent royal display which Henry VII explicitly favoured in his will.[54] We can be certain that these earlier tombs were kept closely in mind: the 1511 contract had explicitly required Torrigiano to ensure that the quality of gilding was as good or better than 'any ymage or ymages of any king or queyn within the Monastery of Westminster'.[55] By selecting the same or, at least, very similar materials, and by preferring Westminster to Windsor, Henry VII was implying a dynastic continuity which simply did not exist.[56] Given the desire to conform to an existing model, the changes made by Torrigiano in terms of medium as well as style, assume some significance. The replacement of Purbeck marble by touch-stone for the tomb-chests reflects Burgundian predilections for the material – most recently the tomb of Mary of Burgundy, from 1488 to 1501 – and constitutes one revision of the earlier tombs (though the tomb-chests of John of Eltham's and Philippa of Hainault's monuments did exhibit touch-stone as a backdrop to alabaster in the Abbey); but it was, of course, one already specified by Henry VII in his will.[57] In this context, it may be particularly significant that the polychromatic enhancement of Margaret Beaufort's effigy, which found no precise precedent in the earlier effigies at Westminster, was abandoned for the later two.[58] If we may judge from the emulation of some of his monuments' novel features, Torrigiano's modernisations of the royal tomb-format were quickly perceived as paradigmatic. He had managed to emulate the key elements of earlier royal tombs – polished 'marble' tomb-chests and gilt-bronze effigies with open eyes, lavishly gilded – and yet he had combined this retention of the 'recognition features'

---

52 Lindley, *Gothic to Renaissance*, 55 and 62–8.
53 Hope, *Windsor Castle*, 419. As early as 1467, parts of Henry V's effigy had already been stolen, which may be another reason for the choice of gilt-bronze by Henry VII.
54 P. Binski, *Westminster Abbey and the Plantagenets*, Yale 1995, 196. It is hard to agree with Binski that the first two tombs are 'masterpieces of restraint' (*ibid.*, 110).
55 Scott, 'On the contracts', 366.
56 See the discussion in Marks, 'The glazing', 173, who justly comments 'all of these artefacts [imagery, glass, tombs and vestments] were part of the same strategy: to signal that the new dynasty was the legitimate successor to the English throne'; see also D. Howarth, *Images of Rule: Art and Politics in the English Renaissance, 1485–1649*, Basingstoke 1997, 158. Janet Backhouse has associated a Parisian book of hours with Margaret Beaufort's patronage and describes it as 'heavily laden with family allusions looking to an illustrious past, in support of the right of the first Tudor king to occupy the throne of some demonstrably royal forebears': J. Backhouse, 'Henry VII's illuminated manuscripts', in *Reign of Henry VII*, 175–87.
57 E.g. Mary of Burgundy's tomb, for which see A.M. Roberts, 'The chronology and political significance of the tomb of Mary of Burgundy', *Art Bulletin* 71, 1989, 376–400. Darr, 'Pietro Torrigiano', 153ff provides evidence that this model would have been well known to Torrigiano.
58 H.J. Plenderleith and H. Maryon, 'The royal bronze effigies in Westminster Abbey', *Antiquaries Journal* 39, 1959, 89: 'her face, hands, cuff, wimple, and the lining of the cloak were painted: not gilt'. Perhaps the earl of Derby's lost effigy also featured polychromy, and it was certainly intended for the effigies of the Mazzoni project (Verdon, *Mazzoni*, 282). The effigies of Henry III and Eleanor of Castile were rendered like precious metalwork by the liberal use of stones imitating precious gems.

of the early tombs with a modish but subtle introduction of new media – white marble and touch-stone – and an overtly modern, renaissance, formal vocabulary.

The double tomb of Henry VII and Queen Elizabeth was housed inside the metal grate – forming a chapel-like enclosure within the larger chapel – under construction from 1505 if not earlier, and made by Thomas the Dutchman (Plate 14).[59] Henry VII's will desires that:

> by a convenient space and distance from the steps of the high altar of the chapel be made . . . a grate, in manner of a closure, of copper and gilt, after the fashion that we have begun, which we will by our said executors be fully accomplished and performed.[60]

The choice of material and the scale of the grate was another feature undoubtedly intended to surpass that of the incomplete tomb of Edward IV at Windsor, which featured iron gates and towers probably by John Tresilian, from 1477–83.[61] Henry's grate was still unfinished when he made his will in 1509, but it was doubtless complete when Skelton's poem *In praeconium Henrici Septimi epitaphium*, dated 29 November 1512, was composed. This was displayed near the tomb, inscribed on parchment tables or painted on a board. Skelton probably also composed the inscription on Henry VII's tomb beginning *Septimus hic situs*, just as Erasmus composed that on Margaret Beaufort's monument (for which he received £1).[62]

The king made provision for an altar within the grate, to be served by three chantry priests. The altar was to have a reredos overhanging the mensa by 6in. at each end and was to be 5ft high, with the image of the crucifix, Mary and John flanking Henry's 'advouries' (named earlier in the will as saints Michael, John the Baptist, John the Evangelist, George, Anthony, Edward, Vincent, Anne, Mary Magdalene and Barbara) 'as many . . . as the said table wol receive', with the twelve Apostles below, all to be of gold plate on a timber core. The altar was to be presented with a piece of the holy cross in a gold reliquary, and an Italian renaissance reliquary containing one of the legs of St George, presented to the king by the Cardinal of Amboise. Silver-gilt figures worth 20 marks each and representing the Blessed Virgin Mary, Saints John the Evangelist, John the Baptist, Edward, Jerome and Francis were also donated by the king.[63] It seems certain, therefore, that the gilt-bronze effigies and tondi images once intentionally resonated within a complex of precious metal figures, gathered round the chantry altar within the grate. These resonances were iconographic too. The gilt-bronze tondi set into the sides of the touchstone tomb-chest include, on the north: Mary Magdalene and Barbara; Christopher and Anne; Edward the Confessor

---

59 PRO, E 36/214, pp. 15 and 52; Colvin, *HKW* iii, 219. A detailed analysis of the grate is included in Darr 'Pietro Torrigiano', 223ff.
60 Above, 114; English modernised.
61 Hope, *Windsor Castle*, 428–9.
62 See W. Camden, *Reges, Reginae, Nobiles at alii in Eclesiae . . . Westmonasterii sepulti*, 1603. For Skelton's poems and the surely correct conjecture that he was the author of the inscription, see D.R. Carlson, 'The Latin writings of John Skelton', *Studies in Philology* 88, 1991, 115–21 (esp. 118 n. 15). I am indebted to Greg Walker for this reference. There are measured drawings of the grate in *The Architect* for 27 February 1875, and *The Builder* for 7 March 1885.
63 Above, 132. The choice of an image of St Francis reflects Henry's patronage of the Franciscans.

Plate 45. Saint John the Evangelist, from the tomb grate.

and St Vincent. To the south are George and Anthony; John the Baptist and the Evangelist; the Virgin and Child and St Michael. A spiritual continuum was thus evoked by the repetition of some saints on the reredos, as freestanding figures, and again on the sides of the tomb chest in a discreet gradation of precious materials.

With its declamatory poem beginning *Septimus Henricus*, surely also by Skelton, engraved right round the grate's interior, this chantry chapel seems to be a prime example of a 'privatised' space . . . 'enclosed and separate, intruding into the collective space of the church and disrupting its plural uses'.[64] Chantry masses are inherently private, of course, a colonisation of the mass in the interests of the testator, but such a view of *this* grate would be, paradoxically, superficial precisely because it pays too little attention to the superficies. For people other than those Henry VII explicitly required to pray within the grate enclosure – the chantry priests and almsmen – were always intended to be able to see the tomb and altar, and to witness the ceremonies. The traceried metal walls of the grate enable easy visual access to its precious contents, whilst ensuring that the latter remain secure from deliberate theft or casual damage. Margaret Beaufort's tomb was subsequently given an iron railing whose primary function must have been to protect the tomb. The care taken to address the external viewer is demonstrated by the repetition of the lengthy inscription poem on the grate's exterior, engraved, presumably, by an English brass engraver.[65] So, whilst a range of responses to the monument must always have been possible, it seems highly unlikely that contemporary viewers would have missed the point that a primary function of the building in which they stood was always to house this chapel within a chapel. The grate originally boasted an exterior complement of no fewer than thirty-two images (four to the west and east and twelve on each of the north and south sides, all arranged in two tiers), of which only six now survive (e.g. Plate 45).[66] These images could only be seen, of course, by those standing outside the grate. Three of the saints represented are also found on the tomb chest and figured on the reredos; two were further represented by silver-gilt statues. Lethaby suggested that the twelve apostles originally occupied the whole east end, and the lower range on the south, with prophets in the lower niches on the north, and with national saints in the upper range on the north, west and south.[67] This tidy-minded suggestion is perhaps undermined by the fact that the original upper figures (of which two survive) seem to have possessed semi-circular bases and the lower images (the remaining four) polygonal ones: if this was consistent – and there seems no reason to doubt it – only two

---

[64] Carlson, 'Latin writings', 118, for Skelton's putative authorship. Dow, *Sculptural Decoration*, 43, confuses Lethaby's reference, *Re-examined*, 180, to Skelton's 'In praeconium Henrici Septimi epitaphium', with the grate inscription. P. Binski, *Medieval Death: Ritual and Representation*, 1996, 120, for this description of 'cage-type' chantry chapels.

[65] Neale and Brayley, 60. Four huge candles, perpetually burned upon the grate, signalled the function of the chantry enclosure.

[66] They are: an unidentified bearded figure, perhaps St Basil; St James the Greater; St Edward the Confessor; St Bartholomew; St John the Evangelist (Plate 45) and St George. Helen Dow, *Sculptural Decoration*, 98, connects with the grate two directly related pipe-clay figurines in the Victoria and Albert Museum; she shows that one of St John the Evangelist is so close to the bronze that it is evident that the other figure – St James the Greater – must represent one of the lost images. The superb engraving by Hollar in Sandford, between pp. 442 and 443, shows eight statuettes. Dart i, 155, mistakenly says only four survive.

[67] Lethaby, *Craftsmen*, 236.

surviving figures belong to the upper tier, and the scheme seems less systematic, like the tomb and reredos. Whatever the case, they extend the intercessory role of the saints inside the chantry enclosure out into the larger chapel and provide a direct linkage with the freestone imagery of the lower and upper levels of the chapel. In material terms, too, these bronze figures, which seem themselves to have been gilded, provide a step in the gradation of materials used for sculpture from the most precious – on the grate's altar – to freestone in the Lady chapel's niches.

The position of the high altar identified in Henry VII's will was to the east of the grate; he left for its adornment the greatest image of the Madonna and Child in his Jewel House (in keeping with the dedication of the chapel) and a cross of plate of gold on timber worth £100.[68] No reredos is mentioned: a tall one would have obscured the shrine of Henry VI intended to stand to the east. No contract was awarded until March 1516 when Pietro Torrigiano signed it, agreeing that the altar would be erected in 1519; by this date Henry VII and Queen Elizabeth of York's tomb was complete and in its present position, with the high altar to be placed to its west. In fact, Torrigiano only began work on the altar in 1519 and it was still incomplete when he left England for Spain; it was set up, by Benedetto da Rovezzano, in 1526.[69] It was almost completely destroyed in 1644, but the contract, visual and documentary records (and the few original fragments incorporated into the present reconstruction) show that whilst its height and width were carefully moderated to relate it to the pre-existing grate to its east, it was of a design which was entirely unprecedented in England (Fig. 37).[70] Nine feet high and the same width, it featured kneeling pairs of terracotta angels holding gilt-bronze emblems of the Passion, flanking the royal arms on the canopy;[71] interestingly, the royal arms were supplemented by the arms of Henry VII and Queen Elizabeth and by the arms of England and Spain, stamping (as the inscriptions and arms did on the tombs) Henry VIII's place as reigning monarch. The white marble canopy was supported by pillars and capitals of gilt-bronze standing on bases of white and black marble. The basement of the massive altar-slab was of black marble, and the mensa itself was supported by four white pillars and by sixteen gilt-bronze balusters.

Under the altar was an image of the dead Christ, made of painted terracotta: a 'bakyn image of erthe coloured of Christ dede'.[72] This image was unique for a high altar in an English Lady chapel; it does not seem to have been indebted to the type of permanent Easter sepulchre which had just been constructed at Christ's College, Cambridge, Margaret Beaufort's foundation; there Ralph Bowman had carved an image of Christ, Mary, and the four knights, on the premises of the Carmelites.[73] Sadly, there is no visual record of Torrigiano's image, and it may be distantly

---

[68] WAM 6638*; Britton, 23–5. For the destruction of the high altar, Lethaby, *Re-examined*, 176, and Perkins, *Worship and Ornaments*, 182–3.

[69] Perkins, *Worship and Ornaments*, 163.

[70] Darr, 'Pietro Torrigiano', 239ff, provides a summary of what is known about the altar and its subsequent history. He also sheds light on its Italian sources.

[71] The angels were terracotta of the glazed della Robbia type, which had not been seen in England before. For the care taken to bring the altar into line with the grate, see Perkins, *Worship and Ornaments*, 166–7.

[72] Britton, 24.

[73] Jones and Underwood, 228–9 n. 94.

Fig. 37. High altar (Sandford, *Genealogical History*, 471).

reflected in the Netherlandish sculpture of the Dead Christ from the Mercers' Hall in London.[74] Holy Sepulchre and Entombment groups were increasingly popular in France, but even if he did not suggest the subject matter, the formal vocabulary was Torrigiano's choice.[75] In his altar's design and in its range of media, Torrigiano was moving his patrons much further still in the direction of Italian renaissance norms. The Florentine's altar ensemble was as revolutionary in early sixteenth-century Westminster as the Cosmati shrine-base of Edward the Confessor had been in the thirteenth century.[76] Unlike the cosmatesque work, though, Torrigiano's renaissance works at Westminster formed part of the vanguard of a major artistic revolution in sixteenth-century England, and his tomb monuments in particular were much more influential than has generally been appreciated.

At first sight, the image of the Dead Christ seems more suited iconographically to the chantry altar – dedicated to Christ – within the grate to the east, than to a Lady altar. And, in fact, it is interconnected iconographically with the reredos of the grate altar, which showed the Crucifixion. But the subject matter of the Lady altar was peculiarly suitable for a building which also possessed chantry functions: the dead Christ and instruments of the Passion are linked to the cross of gold on timber given by Henry VII to stand on the mensa, and to the great gilt-bronze dorsal relief of the Resurrection, which promised rebirth in Christ to the deceased within the chapel. The rear face, showing the Nativity, is similarly connected to the standing image of the Virgin donated by the king for the altar.[77] None of the individual liturgical objects should be considered in isolation.

'The holie companie of Heven': the freestone figure-sculpture

As Dr Wilson has shown elsewhere, Henry VII's chapel luxuriously revised features of St George's, Windsor.[78] Of all these enhancements, the additional sculptural embellishment is most distinctive. Even in a period notable for the massive proliferation of architectural figure-sculpture, Henry VII's chapel must always have seemed densely populated. The loading of the exterior of the building comprised, in addition to the luxurious encrustation of Tudor heraldic badges and beasts, a large complement of figure-statues in niches on the turrets. Each of the first four on either side housed three images, whilst all six of the more easterly turrets featured four.[79] If we may judge from the inscriptions (the pedestal for each figure bears a scroll with a name carved on it), the exterior of the chapel rather bewilderingly interspersed sculptures of Apostles and Evangelists with Old Testament types (subsequently echoed, more systematically, in the historiated typological schemes of the clerestory glazing). However, Micklethwaite was profoundly sceptical that the inscriptions, 'some of [which] are in

---

[74] For which, see J. Evans and N. Cook, 'A statue of Christ from the ruins of Mercers Hall', *Archaeological Journal* 111, 1954, 166–80.
[75] E. Mâle, *Religious Art in France: the Late Middle Ages*, Princeton 1986, chapter 3.
[76] P. Binski, *Westminster Abbey and the Plantagenets*, Yale 1995, 93–107; see also D.A. Carpenter, 'King Henry III and the Cosmati Work at Westminster Abbey', in *The Cloister and the World*, ed. J. Blair and B. Golding, Oxford 1994, 178–95.
[77] Higgins, 'Florentine sculptors', 145–7.
[78] See above, 171–2.
[79] Micklethwaite, 'Imagery', 361.

English, some in Latin, and some in neither', could be trusted accurately to reflect the original inscriptions.[80] Not a single one of these sculptures survives *in situ*. Lethaby reported that Sydney Lee possessed a drawing of Wren's time which showed a bay of the chapel with the statues and parapet and suggested the images were removed c.1720.[81] This seems consistent with the fact that Dart, writing in 1723, says that they had just been removed, apparently because they caused some offence to clerics.[82] Lethaby contrarily claimed that the apparently random mixture of categories of figure was deliberate and that care was taken to spread the various classes; even the three Hebrews of the Fiery Furnace did not appear as a group.[83] It seems possible that the so-called 'Abbot Islip's head' which was re-used in the Wren/Dickinson rebuilding of the north transept and rediscovered in the core of the north-east buttress c.1887, belongs to one of these exterior figures, though a sainted bishop does not obviously fit into the scheme. It therefore seems likelier that the figure came from one of the interior chapels where huge monuments obliterated the original sculptures: it might have been removed from the north-east chapel when the monument to John Sheffield (d.1721), first duke of Buckingham was erected: wherever it came from, though, it certainly belongs in the chapel's scheme.[84]

During the cleaning of the interior sculptures in 1995, Donald Buttress had two of the figures from the north aisle (now Elizabeth I's chapel) placed in the exterior niches, confirming that they were of identical size (c.5ft tall) and proportions to the lower sculptures of the chapel's interior; this conversely ruled out the possibility that any of the triforium figures could have been brought from outside the building.[85] It follows from this that the differential in the weathering of stone found in the interior

---

[80] *Ibid.*, 361–2. *Inventory*, 59, lists: Hosea, Joel, Amos, Nahum, Sem-ah (Shemaiah?), Philyp, Aggeus, Jehu, Micheah, Anamias, Malachy, Simon, Zakarias, Mathew, Abacuc, Daniel, Matthias, Paul, Azarias, Mark, Zephaniah, Elisha, Bartylmew, John, Nehemiah, Eliah, Samuel, Jude, Abdias, James, Ezechial, Michias, Esdreas, David, Petre, Jeremy, Jonas, Andrew, Nathan, Luke, Barnabes, Elizeas, Misall, James L, Esay, Solomon, John Baptist & Thomas. Dow, *Sculptural Decoration*, 5–6; her mysterious and confusing reference in n. 19 to Westlake i, 28–30, should be applied to Brayley (whose middle name was Wedlake), not to Westlake.

[81] Lethaby, *Re-examined*, 158; see also Lethaby, *Craftsmen*, 227 note, where he states 1712.

[82] Brayley, in the separately paginated section on Henry VII's chapel in Neale and Brayley, 30, footnote, quotes Dart, writing in 1722 (*sic*: I can only trace a 1723 edition) as saying they were 'by workmen . . . taken down, for fearful Reasons offered to some of the Ministry'. Brayley must be the source of the slightly different quotation from Dart offered by Lethaby, *Craftsmen*, 227. I have not been able to find the Brayley quotation in Dart who writes that the statues were removed (ii, 49) 'lest they should fall on the heads of those who attend the Parliament'. I am indebted to Dr Tony Trowles and Dr Richard Mortimer for helping to sort out my confusion here: Dr Mortimer suggests to me that the 'Ministry' could mean the government, in which case the two stories would converge.

[83] Lethaby, *Re-examined*, 159.

[84] L.E. Tanner, 'A carved stone head of an abbot from Westminster Abbey', *JBAA* 11, 1948, 79; and *idem*, *Unknown Westminster Abbey*, Harmondsworth 1958, 30. I would want to modify my position very slightly from that I espoused in 1995 as I now think it more likely that it came from an interior niche than from an exterior one. I am relieved to find that Dr Paul Williamson has independently come to the same view that the sculpture originated from the chapel and am indebted to him for discussion of the head. For the Wren/Dickinson restorations, which date from 1719–23, see Cocke, *900 Years*, 43, and Scott, *Gleanings*, 36. The Islip roll shows Islip's recumbent effigy beneath a table tomb: the 'Islip head' is clearly not that of an effigy and there is nothing specifically connecting it to Islip.

[85] I am indebted to Donald Buttress for a personal communication on this subject of 20 December 1995. See also Cocke, *900 Years*, 120.

sculpture is not because some figures have been brought from outside the building, but because they are carved from different types of stone. The same variation in surface survival is found in the thirteenth-century sculpture of the Abbey.[86] It anyway seems inconceivable that sculptures removed from the building's exterior to avoid offending protestant sensitivities would then have been redeployed inside the chapel.

Even more than on the exterior, the glut of carved Tudor badges and heraldry of the interior convey a proprietorial message on a remarkable scale, to be echoed in the main western entrance doors and in the heraldic glass of the chapels and aisles as well as on the tombs and grate (the badges include the Beaufort portcullis, the English lions, French fleur-de-lis, the Welsh dragon, falcon and fetter-lock and Tudor rose). The heraldic beasts above the chapels' and aisles' image niches are close relatives of those carved for the ante-chapel of King's College Chapel, Cambridge, between 1509 and 1515 by Thomas Stockton's team of sculptors, and the studding of the whole building with heraldry is analogous to that inside King's, where the ante-chapel's profuse heraldic imagery signifies a profound change of emphasis from the work begun by Henry VI.[87] In addition to the heraldic beasts, Tudor badges are held at Westminster by the frieze of orders of angels running below the image niches and across the west end, and the heraldry is also continued on the vaulting.[88] It was undoubtedly Henry VII's intention that all the Westminster heraldry and heraldic imagery should be painted, but there is no evidence that any of this decoration occurred in the sixteenth century. Indeed, the only painting of the chapel's interior heraldry took place in 1995 when the restoration programme (which also saw the application of several coats of coloured limewash to the vault and elevation and the limewashing of the angel frieze) included gilding and painting of the vault heraldry and pendant bosses.

At King's, it was still intended c.1515 to adorn the chapel's interior with forty-seven figure-sculptures, and the exterior doorways with six much larger figures calculated on the basis of 5s per foot.[89] Lawrence Stone noted that such an estimate tends to underline the difference in esteem for sculptors and sculpture between renaissance Italy and late medieval England, but of course it also enables us to calculate the cost of the figure sculpture at Westminster: judging the larger sculptures to be approximately 5ft tall each and the smaller, triforium ones 3ft, the total spent on the freestone figures must have been over £150.[90] Today, ninety-five images survive from the original complement of 107 images in the chapels, at the east end of the aisles and (sixty-nine of them) in the smaller roughly 3ft high images in the triforium and in the

[86] C.J.P. Cave and L.E. Tanner, 'A thirteenth-century choir of angels in the north transept of Westminster Abbey and the adjacent figures of two kings', *Archaeologia* 84, 1935, 64, and the comments of Neale and Brayley there cited.
[87] RCHM, *An Inventory of the Historical Monuments in the City of Cambridge* i, 1959, 102. It is also related to that at Windsor.
[88] The nine orders of angels may have once featured in the stained glass of the great west window together with the twelve apostles, bearing creed scrolls, and twelve prophets. Marks, 'Glazing', 165–6.
[89] R. Willis and J.W. Clark, *The Architectural History of the University of Cambridge and of the Colleges of Cambridge and Eton* i, 1886, 482. Including the stone, the cost at King's was estimated at £66 6s 8d.
[90] The seventy-eight large sculptures (forty-eight exterior, thirty interior) cost £97 10s; the interior seventy-seven triforium and arch ones £57 15s: compare the image-encrusted chantry chapels of men such as Bishop Alcock at Ely (whose openwork pendant fan-vault is a progenitor of the Westminster pendants).

Plate 46. Christ, from easternmost bay.

tiers of the 'chancel' arch. Some of the lost imagery may have disappeared between 1643 and 1645, when most of the stained-glass and the high altar were destroyed.[91]

The Westminster programme is the largest surviving ensemble of figure-sculpture from early Tudor England (Plate V). Some general observations should shape our enquiry into the iconography of the extant figure sculpture. First, the chapel's programmes all enlist the heavenly hierarchy to speed the patron's progress through Purgatory, a visual augmentation of the chantry endowment of personal masses. The king's will declares his trust in Jesus Christ, his faith in the intercession of the Virgin Mary and in 'the singular mediacion and praiers of al the holie companie of Heven; that is to saye Aungels, Archaungeles, Patriarches, Prophets, Apostles, Evangelists, Martirs, Confessours and Virgyns'. Lawrence Stone's view that the choice of some otherwise obscure Breton saints (such as St Armagil) whom Henry venerated proves that the programme had been fixed before the king's death is undoubtedly correct: indeed, in my view, the sculptures were all in place by then.[92] The king's will effectively outlines the general scheme of the figure-sculpture and explains its raison d'être. Specific identifications of the individual images were published by Micklethwaite and, with a few amendments, have been generally accepted (Fig. 38).[93] Secondly, as Dow has indicated, the original location planned for the monuments and liturgical furniture is the key to the programme's general disposition.[94] Thirdly, the space for the programme at triforium level was determined by the architect, evidently without much thought about the iconography of the sculpture. The five-light windows fixed the number of niches available below, creating awkward problems for the deviser of the sculpture programme's iconography. It is apparent that the programme is affected by the need to fit the images into these predetermined spaces; but it has already been argued above that this separation of architectural from sculptural design was ordinary procedure in the period.[95] Fourth, one should note that many of the subjects of the lower chapels are repeated in the triforium sculpture, continuing the tendency towards repetition seen in the tombs and altar imagery. Finally, had the images been painted as intended, identifying inscriptions would also have been added to the (separately carved) scrolls beneath all the triforium figures.[96]

I want to depart from scholarly precedent by considering the upper level of sculpture first. Christ is shown in the centre of the axial bay (Plate 46). He holds a book outwards in His left hand and His foot is on the earth. Christ neither shows His wounds nor is He seated in judgement, so this does not appear to be a conventional picture of the Last Judgement; nor can the flanking Gabriel and the Virgin of the Annunciation be taken, as Lethaby also claimed, as a Coronation of the Virgin. The fact that the angel carries a sceptre does not by itself imply a coronation: a sceptre is

---

[91] Marks, 'Glazing', 159.
[92] Above, 112, for the will. Stone, 228, views the images as c.1505–15.
[93] Micklethwaite, 'Imagery'. See also *Inventory*, 63–5 and Lethaby, *Re-examined*, 167–70; Dow, *Sculptural Decoration*, 7–13.
[94] Dow, *Sculptural Decoration*, 54.
[95] See above, 268.
[96] For earlier restorations of the building, see Cocke and Buttress in Cocke, *900 Years*. Matthew Beesley's report of 15 March 1994 shows that the figures were not originally painted as Henry VII had intended. Micklethwaite, 'Imagery', 368, for the painted dedication crosses.

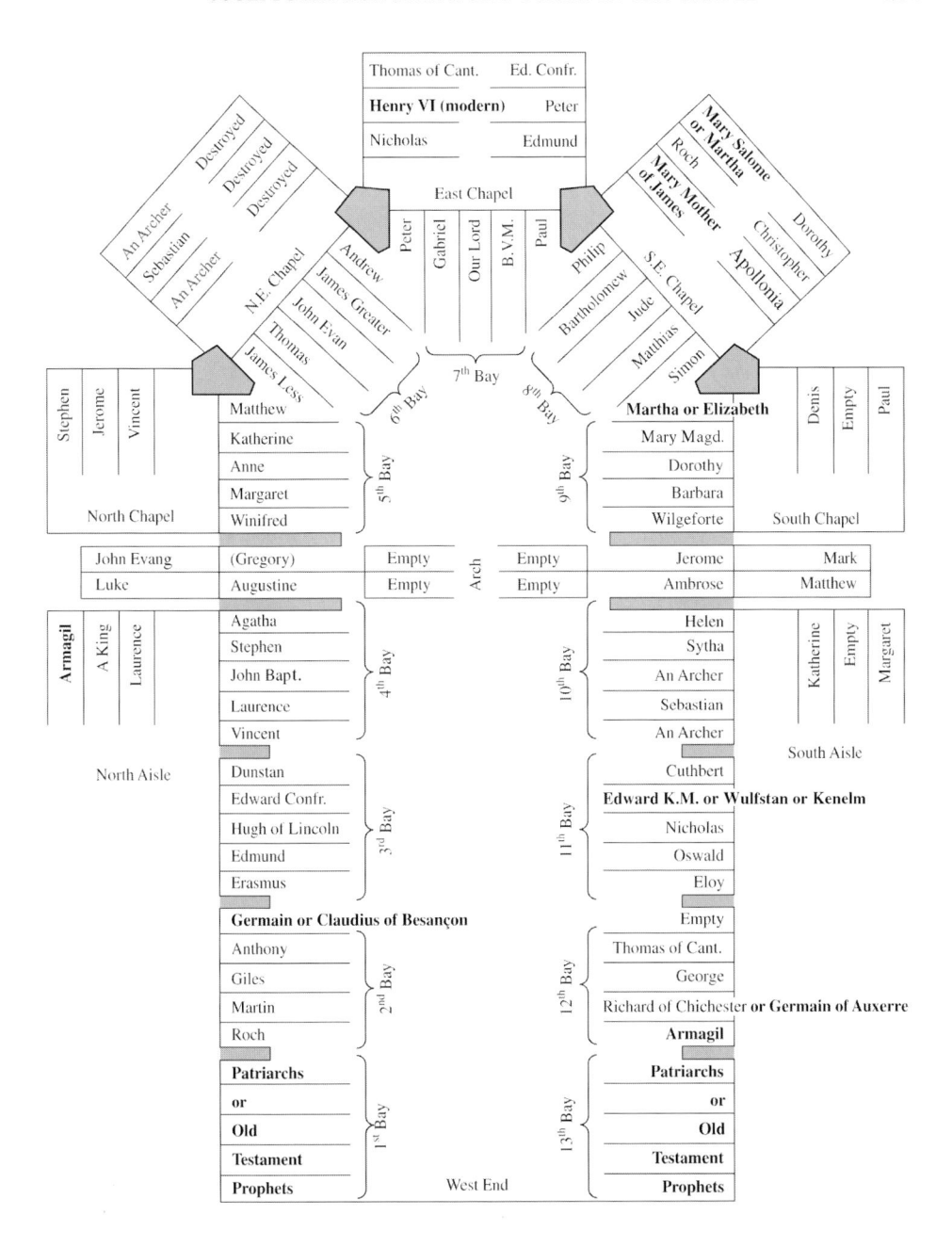

SCULPTURAL FUNCTIONS AND FORMS IN THE CHAPEL 281

Fig. 38. Plan showing figure sculptures. (Phillip Lindley after J.T. Micklethwaite)

shown in a woodcut of the Annunciation from Antwerp of 1491, for instance.[97] It is, in fact, in woodcuts that the likeliest model for the figure of Christ can be found: the Christ Blessing in Jan Veldener's *Fasciculus Temporum*, first printed in 1475 and based on a Cologne source, is a possible model.[98] When Torrigiano's high altar was put in place, the imagery of the resurrected Christ connected down to the gilt-bronze reredos, showing the resurrection, down below to the terracotta image of the dead Christ beneath the altar, and then to the Crucifixion on the chantry altar reredos. Torrigiano's high altar cannot, of course, have been planned when the freestone sculptures were put in place, but the chronologically sequential consistency of the scheme strongly suggests that the subject matter had already been anticipated.

The apostles are ranged on either side of the central trio and across the next two bays. The triforium images should, of course, be read not from west to east, but from the centre outwards, with the bays organised symmetrically *across* the chapel.[99] Female saints – including St Wilgeforte or Uncumber (Plate 47), of whom there was a famous image in St Paul's to which women might pray to rid themselves of their unwanted husbands[100] – were gathered further west but still close to the planned location of the altar. Flanking them were the four doctors of the church and the four Evangelists and, below, four empty niches. Micklethwaite had no idea what figures had originally been represented here. The four great prophets would be iconographically suitable, below the church fathers, above whom were the Evangelists, but it is also possible that four important saints – Edward and Edmund, Peter and Thomas, for example, all of whom had special resonances at Westminster – could have figured.[101] Beyond, to the west, above the place in the nave where the king and queen's tomb was intended to stand, are male saints, especially royal and military ones, most appropriate for a king who had won the crown in battle. Just as, in life, Henry had surrounded himself with statues of previous kings of England in the great hall at Richmond, in death he planned to be surrounded by his sainted predecessors. Charles Phythian-Adams has pointed out to me that the selection of kings and bishops gathered round the tomb provides fairly inclusive regional coverage of England, and this was doubtless deliberate. The ten western niches contain prophets (it seems far less likely that these are Pagan philosophers as Micklethwaite suggested, though it *is* a scheme contemporary with Raphael's School of Athens), flanking the west window. Iconographic connections with the schemes of the stained glass have been lost with the virtually total destruction of the glazing but, given that it had already been planned in detail by

---

[97] Lethaby, *Re-examined*, 167. On p. 168, he suggests that because Gabriel carries a sceptre in his hand, this scene represents the Coronation of the Virgin. For a woodcut showing the Annunciation where the angel carries a sceptre see, for instance, A.M. Hind, *A History of the Woodcut*, New York 1963, fig. 337, but this is commonplace in the period.

[98] Hind, *Woodcut*, fig. 317. I am indebted to Dr Miriam Gill for this suggestion.

[99] It is surprising that this has not been realised before, though Lethaby's correct (in my view) numbering of the apostles in the central bay (*Re-examined*, 169), outwards from Christ and the Annunciation implies it. The various different numbering systems currently used are chaotic and now retard even simple identifications of the sculptures.

[100] Micklethwaite, 'Imagery', 373; cf. F. Bond, *Westminster Abbey*, 1909, 216, who misidentifies St Helen as Wilgeforte.

[101] Cf. the comment of Mâle, *Religious Art in France*, 212, on late medieval art. An alternative suggestion would be Sts Benedict and Francis, Dominic and Bernard, which would also explain why they have been removed. Wilson, above, 150, suggests the Annunciation and the Visitation.

Plate 47. Saints Wilgeforte (right) and Barbara.

1509, must have been intended. The lower level of the chapel, the radiating chapels and aisles were, in the case of the chapels, glazed with royal badges and shields enclosed in cartouches and set in quarries, whilst the aisles contained only quarries featuring heraldry.[102] All the historiated glass was set in the upper windows of the chapel. The scheme can be reconstructed in outline because the extant programme of King's College Chapel, Cambridge, was to be modelled on it in 1526. Old Testament types, prefiguring anti-types in the New Testament, were separated by witnesses to the events portrayed.[103] The types and anti-types each occupied two lights, the messengers the central one. The western window was more visually co-ordinated with the triforium sculptures, since it contained tiers of figures under niches on an alternating red and blue background.[104] The figures represented the twelve apostles bearing articles of the creed, accompanied by twelve Old Testament prophets as counterparts. The nine orders of angels may have been represented in the remaining lights.[105] Thus the iconography of the figure-sculpture was both supplemented by the historiated clerestory glass and replicated and expanded in the west window. As the sculpted imagery was never polychrome as Henry VII intended, the glazing must, until its destruction, have visually dominated the still monochrome sculptural ensemble.[106]

Although the freestone image programme deserves more attention than is possible here, some of its iconographic peculiarities demand brief comment. The sculptors' deployment of an Annunciation on either side of a standing figure of Christ in the central bay was doubtless suggested by the reredos of Henry V's chapel, which has an Annunciation flanking what must have been (the image is now missing) the Trinity.[107] Secondly, as Micklethwaite noted, the arrangement of the apostles in the order in which they are named in the canon of the mass was upset in three cases, the most obvious of which is the mistaken placing of St Mathias (Judas's replacement) where St Matthew should stand.[108] The fact that St Paul is included in the central bay, balancing St Peter, leads to an overspilling of the apostles from the available spaces and also suggests that Henry VII had no time for the traditional rivalries between Westminster and London's cathedral. Another anomalous feature is the appearance of St Sebastian's executioners alongside the saint himself in Micklethwaite's bay 10. At Fairford, in the near-contemporary stained glass programme of the nave clerestory, persecutors of the church are placed on the north side, balancing champions of the Faith, Christian saints and martyrs on the south side.[109] St Sebastian is there shown flanked by female saints and one of his executioners seems to have been placed opposite. At Westminster though, the crossbowmen flank the saint. Micklethwaite thought this suggested loose control of the sculptors; perhaps, however, the designer of the iconographic scheme furnished the sculptors with a woodcut which they simply

---

[102] Marks, 'Glazing', 168.
[103] Lethaby, *Re-examined*, 178–9; Marks, 'Glazing', 161–3.
[104] Lethaby, *Re-examined*, 180–1.
[105] Marks, 'Glazing', 165.
[106] For the destruction of the glass see Buttress in Cocke, *900 Years*, and J.G. Noppen, 'King Henry VII Chapel: recent work of renovation', *The Builder*, 31 May 1946, 526ff. I owe this last reference to Mr John Clark.
[107] Tudor-Craig in Wilson, *Westminster Abbey*, 134.
[108] Micklethwaite, 'Imagery', 372–3.
[109] H. Wayment, *The Stained Glass of the Church of St Mary, Fairford, Gloucestershire*, 1984, 71ff.

Plate 48. Saints Catharine (left) and Margaret, from south aisle.

copied. It cannot have been accidental, for the whole group is repeated in the life-sized figures of the chapels below as is St Roch, like St Anthony (who also appears among the triforium figures) an important protector against the plague.[110] Edmund Tudor, Henry VII's father, had died of the plague and Margaret Beaufort owned a book of tracts on the subject; in a codicil to her will she directed that Malton manor be repaired as a plague refuge.[111] None of the royal family had attended Prince Arthur's funeral in April 1502 precisely because of their dread of the plague. The popularity of saints associated with protection from the plague in this period emphatically proves the ubiquity of fear of pestilence.

The larger sculptures are ranged below, in the chapels and aisles: both the aisles and the two western chapels had three images, over the altar; the three apsidal chapels have groups of three images on both east and west walls, making thirty large images in total. Study may conveniently begin with the south aisle, Beaufort's chantry chapel. An empty central niche is flanked by images of Sts Katherine and Margaret (Plate 48). The choice of her namesaint is obvious and after the countess's death St John's College, Cambridge (one of her foundations), was presented by her executors with a statue of St Margaret, from her private chapel. Her chapel also contained an altar cloth worked with the figure of St Margaret. Beaufort had a particular devotion to St Katherine, one of her chapel copes being worked with her image, and the countess owned a precious metal figure of the saint; Bishop Fisher recalled in his month-mind sermon that Margaret Beaufort's 'peculiar fasts of devotion' included St Katherine's day. St Katherine was the patron of scholars as the countess, a great patron of the university of Cambridge, would know: the Cambridge college dedicated to the eponymous saint had been founded in 1473.[112] The choice of the saint supports the view that it was Henry VII's intention to have Katherine de Valois reburied in this chapel (though the plan came to nothing). The central niche may have housed an image of the Virgin and Child (as Dow conjectures).[113] Below the niches, above the altar, is a large rectangular space which must have been filled by a precious reredos. The chapel was certainly lavishly endowed: in the schedule of bequests added to her will in February 1509, Margaret Beaufort left the Beaufort Hours, one of her most valued possessions, to be chained in the chapel and she also bequeathed service books, plate and vestments to her chantry.[114] In the niches of the corresponding aisle on the north, Micklethwaite was puzzled by a figure later identified by M.R. James and Henry Bradshaw as St Armagil (or Armil) of Brittany, venerated by the Welsh.[115] Between him and a statue of St Laurence is a figure which Lethaby thought represented Henry VI.[116] The loss of that saint from the apsidal chapel, where he was certainly shown (and has unfortunately been replaced recently with a modern image),

---

[110] Micklethwaite, 'Imagery', 367.

[111] Jones and Underwood, 220.

[112] Jones and Underwood, 177-8 and 190. A statue of St Katherine was also provided for the Savoy Hospital.

[113] Dow, *Sculptural Decoration*, 8. Margaret had a particular devotion to Our Lady of Pity but there was no room for a pieta in the niche.

[114] Jones and Underwood, 240.

[115] J.T. Micklethwaite, 'On an unexplained figure in Henry the Seventh's chapel', *Archaeologia* 47, 1883, 483–5, misidentified this figure as All Hallows.

[116] Lethaby, *Re-examined*, 170.

makes definite identification impossible, but it may have been Henry VII's intention that this chapel, which now houses his grand-daughters' monument, would be adopted by Henry VIII as his own burial chapel, in which case the Lancastrian king would be an obvious choice for the central image. The axial chapel itself had Henry VI flanked by Sts Nicholas and Thomas of Canterbury (an extraordinary survival if this identification is correct) facing St Peter between Edward the Confessor and Edmund (Plate 6). St Benedict must also have been prominently included somewhere in the programme. Three or four of the figures missing from the chapels are above the altars and may have been taken down following Cromwell's injunctions of 1536, which called for the removal of images before which lights had been placed; others were destroyed by the intrusion of the duke of Buckingham's monument.[117]

If I am correct in believing that the sculptural programme was in place by April 1509, the designer of the scheme must have received considerable input from Henry VII himself. Although the prior of St Bartholomew's, Smithfield, was the master of works, he is not likely to have been responsible for the iconography. The likeliest candidate is Bishop Fox of Winchester, who was mentioned in 1515 as responsible for the glazing scheme at King's College Chapel, Cambridge, itself based on the glazing at Westminster, and a widely consulted expert on artistic matters.[118]

Rather than iconography, it is the style of the images which has recently claimed scholarly attention. Micklethwaite saw them as the work of many hands which 'vary in quality from very good to very bad', but the great pioneers of the study of English medieval figure-sculpture, Prior and Gardner, devoted little space to the figures, perhaps rather blinded by their prejudices against late medieval sculpture in general.[119] All scholars are agreed, though, that these figures are by far the most important surviving architectural sculpture of early sixteenth-century England and the two most recently published studies spent some time investigating the workshop's stylistic formation. Professor Stone viewed the statues as part of a general stylistic trend in southern English art in the first decades of the sixteenth century, and pointed to the imagery of Prince Arthur's chantry chapel as an important link between the Divinity School statuary of Oxford University and the Westminster figures.[120] The Westminster figures were, he thought, generally 'characterised by an extreme boldness of carving in depth, by vigorous and often forbidding facial expressions, and by the extraordinary variety and intricacy of the headgear'. Although the qualities exhibited by the images were 'present in some degree in late fifteenth-century Low Countries sculpture . . . the closest parallels are with German art'.[121] Stone argued that the

---

[117] Micklethwaite, 'Imagery', 364–5 and 366–7. A statue of King Henry VI was also provided for the Savoy Hospital (A. Oswald, 'The glazing of the Savoy Hospital', *Journal of the Society of Master Glass-Painters* 11, 1951–5, 232).

[118] K. Harrison, *The Windows of King's College Chapel, Cambridge*, Cambridge 1952, 1; cf. Dow, *Sculptural Decoration*, 106–7.

[119] Micklethwaite, 'Imagery', 363. E.S. Prior and A. Gardner, *An Account of Medieval Figure-Sculpture in England*, Cambridge 1912, 416: 'the figures vary to some extent in quality, the most being of short proportion with large heads, and with the somewhat confused and crumpled draperies of the late fifteenth century'.

[120] Stone, *Sculpture*, 227.

[121] Stone, *Sculpture*, 229.

chapel's sculpture exhibited considerable stylistic variety, with 'the greatest sculptor' responsible for 'the rows of prophets in the westernmost bays of the triforium'. He seemed to identify this sculptor as the head of the workshop in describing other sculptors as 'his disciples' but – surprisingly in view of his identifications of stylistic parallels – he also strongly implied that the sculptor was English.[122] Dr Dow sought the sources of the Westminster style in wooden sculpture. She identified Thomas Stockton, master carver at King's Chapel and the king's joiner, as the head of the workshop, with his close relative, William Stockton, as his chief assistant, heading a team probably including Ralph Bowman, sculptor of the Christ's Easter Sepulchre group, and also employed at King's in 1512–1513. Other sculptors she linked to Westminster were John Moore, Richard Codeman, Robert Bellamy, Nicholas Delphyn and John Hudde.[123] Although she considered other candidates – such as the Swabian sculptor Lawrence Emler, who carved the head of Elizabeth of York's funeral effigy in 1503, and two Flemish sculptors working twenty years earlier in Windsor – Dow's conclusion was that 'it is hardly possible' that Flemish or other European sculptors were employed, because 'the images decorating the Westminster Lady chapel are basically English in type . . . It would be difficult, therefore, to trace a continental hand in the carvings of this chapel.'[124]

It is certainly true that there is considerable stylistic variation in the sculpture. Indeed, W.S. Weatherley, whose drawings illustrated Micklethwaite's paper, believed several figures – Sts Augustine, Katherine, Ambrose (Plate 49), Helen and Edward K.M. – to be stylistically earlier than the rest of the programme and to have been rescued from an earlier building.[125] Although there are cases in medieval English sculpture of the re-use of earlier figures, considerations of iconography, size and the lavish context of the overall building scheme in which they feature render it impossible that this is the answer here. What we are dealing with is, more plausibly, the work of a single, extremely distinctive, sculptor, working in a large shop of imagers.[126] Dr Dow would not, one suspects, agree. For her, it was 'entirely feasible on stylistic grounds that [all the freestone images in the chapel] were all done by one hand, a sculptor who developed gradually from the somewhat stilted traditionalism of the Christ figure in the Henry VII chapel to the powerfully Burgundian expression of its Patriarchs'.[127] She conjectured that the master sculptor, Thomas Stockton, designed all the figures on paper, with assistants blocking out the main details in stone and perhaps carving some of the details.[128]

Is it possible, in principle at least, that one sculptor could have been responsible for carving all 155 sculptures? Although it is hard to know how long it would take an early sixteenth-century sculptor to produce an image (and also difficult to know the average wage rate – massive differences in costs are shown in the 1506 estimates for executing Mazzoni's project for Henry VII's tomb), it may be worth conjecturing. The 155

---

[122] Stone, *Sculpture*, 229 and 228.
[123] Lethaby, *Craftsmen*, 230, anticipates Dow.
[124] Dow, *Sculptural Decoration*, 91. She continues 'except perhaps in the stalls, and more especially in the misericords', but these are not our concern here.
[125] Micklethwaite, 'Imagery', 378, note A.
[126] See Lindley in R. Deacon and P. Lindley, *Image and Idol: Medieval Sculpture*, 2001, 40–1, for references.
[127] Dow, *Sculptural Decoration*, 102.
[128] *Ibid.*, 104.

Plate 49. Saints Jerome (left) and Ambrose.

sculptures comprised at least 621ft of imagery (estimating the smaller sculptures at 3ft tall, though they are generally nearer 3ft 3in.). If we borrow the Cambridge estimate at 5s per foot, and assign as a daily wage to the sculptor as much as 10d a day, it suggests he would take six days to carve a foot of sculpture.[129] So, he could produce one of the smaller figures every eighteen days. 621ft at six days per foot, would take 3,726 days to carve, or ten sculptors over 372 days. Even if my estimate is wayward, it seems unlikely that an individual sculptor could have produced more than fifteen or sixteen images a year. Thus it would have taken one sculptor over a decade or at least ten sculptors over a year to have carved all the images; twenty would be needed if only six months were allowed. Even if two years had been permitted, then five or half a dozen sculptors would have been required, always supposing that they were not responsible for any of the angel friezes or heraldic sculpture. It actually seems unlikely that so long would have been allowed; the implication from King's is that the freestone figure-sculpture became a priority only when the building was physically complete or nearing completion. Further detailed stylistic analysis of the images is necessary, but as a working hypothesis, a workshop of half a dozen to a dozen sculptors was required. What we can definitively say is that it is impossible that we are dealing with the work of just one or two sculptors. If the group of five distinctive images classified by Weatherley as earlier than the rest represented most, or all, of one man's work, then the division of work may not be equal amongst the sculptors employed. That sub-group of images, interestingly, is carved of Reigate stone, not Caen (though this is also true of some of the larger figures), and could indicate that one sculptor had access to the less good quality stone.[130] It is tempting, but probably wrong, to view this as an oblique comment on the sculptor's ability by whoever assigned the material. Although they are close together in the chapel, Sts Augustine and Ambrose are not from the triforium level and are technically different from that range of images. This implies that the sculptor was working in the same physical environment as the other carvers: if he were an independent subcontractor, working elsewhere, it would be natural to assign him a single group of five images from the same bay of the triforium level to minimise potential problems. The workshop was probably within the precincts of the Abbey.[131] Interestingly, the left hand of St Edward was separately dowelled on, but this is not a technical peculiarity of one sculptor's work: there is some other evidence of dowelled-on features throughout the programme, most obviously in the crossbow of one of St Sebastian's archers; and the arrows in St Sebastian's body were also separate pieces of wood.

It has always been agreed that this small sub-group of images is deeply traditional in its formal repertoire: this is why these images have sometimes been thought to come from an earlier building.[132] Most of the rest of the sculpture is clearly in a

---

[129] This would seem rather high. The average skilled labourer would expect about 6d a day (H. Swanson, *Building Craftsmen in Late Medieval York*, York 1983, 27, for York freemasons), as Salzman, *Building in England*, 77, shows, and 8d was what the foreman mason was receiving at Westminster in 1532; at the same time, though, certain stone carvers, presumably highly skilled, were receiving 10d per day.

[130] Micklethwaite, 'Imagery', 378. This is supported by Matthew Beesley's recent conservation report.

[131] Torrigiano later employed unused pieces of the angel frieze in his Dr Yonge tomb, proving that he had access to the masons'/sculptors' yards, and Darr has established that his workshop was within the abbey precincts. Such an area would be free of the city of London's guild controls.

[132] See above, n. 121.

different stylistic idiom, although it also exhibits a wide range of handling. Several pieces of information suggest that these sculptors were not English. First, the English stylistic connections which have hitherto been proposed do not seem convincing: there is a gulf between works such as the monument to Sir Richard Croft (d.1509) – notwithstanding the appearance of saints such as St Roch and St Antony who are also found at Westminster – and the Tudor chapel's images.[133] Although the angel frieze at Westminster is clearly prefigured by that in St George's Chapel (whence some of the sculptors may have come), and the workforce may include the sculptors of the heraldry at King's College, Cambridge, the Henry VII chapel programme seems otherwise obstinately isolated in an English sculptural context. Iconoclasm has, of course, deprived us of the programmes of many great chapels – such as that of Bishop Alcock at Ely – which might have provided 'missing links', but the only two figure sculptures yet convincingly connected with Westminster are the Saints George and Edmund from Eton College, another royal foundation.[134]

An alternative route to the origins of the Westminster sculptors is provided by the – much remarked – very close stylistic comparisons between Henry VII chapel's figure-sculpture and the six surviving bronze statuettes from the grate.[135] The grate was the responsibility of a 'Dutch' smith, and the statuettes belong, too, in a Low Countries context, their closest connections being with the bronze figures from the 1476 Isabella of Bourbon monument (the weepers being now in the Rijksmuseum, Amsterdam) and related works.[136] Visually, they are also close to wood sculpture of c.1500 from Saint-Pierre-aux-Liens.[137] It seems perverse to deny that the bronze figures are by artists from the Low Countries. A sculptor will have carved the wooden models for the bronze caster and the implication is that the stone sculptors came from the same milieu and may well include the sculptor, or sculptors, of the grate statuette models. Stylistic comparisons suggest that some, at least, of the triforium image sculptors may have originated in the Limburg area.[138] If we look at woodwork in England, the closest comparisons are with the sculpture of the choir stalls at Windsor carved, apparently, some twenty years earlier, and certainly by Netherlandish sculptors.[139] The fifteenth and early sixteenth centuries saw a great influx of Low Countries craftsmen into London, and they dominated some crafts, such as stained glass painting. The style of glazing produced by indigenous craftsmen seemed old-fashioned by contrast with that of the immigrants and royal and court patronage decisively broke the stranglehold of the London guild. This led to long-running conflict between the Glaziers Company of the City of London and the alien glaziers, based outside their jurisdiction in Southwark. Most pertinently, the glazing of Henry VII's chapel itself and of the Savoy hospital was in the hands of Low Countries craftsmen.[140] J.L. Bolton

---

[133] This was proposed by B. Little in N. Pevsner, *Herefordshire*, The Buildings of England, Harmondsworth 1963, 108–9.
[134] Lindley, *Gothic to Renaissance*, 156ff.
[135] Dow, *Sculptural Decoration*, 78.
[136] See J.W. Steyaert et al., *Late Gothic Sculpture: the Burgundian Netherlands*, Ghent 1994, 138–41.
[137] *Ibid.*, 98.
[138] *Laat-Gotische Beeldsnijkunst uit Limburg en Grensland*, Sint-Truiden 1990, 40.
[139] Lindley, *Gothic to Renaissance*, 161ff, for discussion. Much of this sculpture looks early sixteenth-century to me, though the documentary evidence contradicts this.
[140] J.A. Knowles, 'Disputes between English and foreign glass-painters in the sixteenth century',

has estimated that there were about 2,700 long- and short-term alien residents in London and its suburbs in 1483–4, about 6% of the city's population, many of them artisans and craftsmen. In 1436, where their places of birth are listed, nearly half of all of them came from Holland and Brabant, from the towns and urban villages lying on or near the great river systems of the Low Countries, the Rhine and its tributaries and the territories between them, from Antwerp and Bruges in the west to Maastricht and Aachen in the east.[141] More research is needed, but it seems likely that sculptors from precisely these areas came to London and worked for Henry VII, just as, I have argued, their predecessors worked at Winchester Cathedral on the Great Screen, which backs the high altar on which Prince Arthur had been laid for his confirmation after baptism in September 1486.[142] Southwark, where so many of the Netherlanders congregated in London was, of course, in the diocese of Winchester, and Richard Fox, Bishop of Winchester in the early sixteenth century, would have been well placed to advise Henry VII on the selection of sculptors, as he guided his executors on artistic matters.[143] In exactly the same way that the work of English glaziers was rendered obsolete by Netherlandish workmen, so, perhaps, were English sculptures old-fashioned by comparison with Netherlandish images. It seems plausible to argue that the rather different style of one sculptor in Henry VII's chapel is that of an English-trained artist, whose work is as out of place in this ensemble as some of the full-sized figures (their heads alone seem to survive) were in Winchester Cathedral's great high altar reredos.[144]

The identities of the sculptors are even more elusive than their formation, but most of the names cited by Lethaby and Dow above, of sculptors who were working in the king's employ around 1500, sound like anglicisations of northern French or Netherlandish names. Professor Caroline Barron has suggested that even James Hales, who is usually thought of as English and who carved the wooden model for the earl of Derby's bronze effigy, came from the Netherlands.[145] He worked in London and for the court circle: perhaps he was at work in Henry VII's chapel too.

Antiquaries Journal 5, 1925, 148–57; and D.R. Ransome, 'The struggle of the Glaziers' Company with the foreign glaziers, 1500–1550', *Guildhall Miscellany* 2, 1960, 12–20.

[141] J.L. Bolton, *The Alien Communities of London in the Fifteenth Century*, Stamford 1998, 31.

[142] E. McClure, 'Some remarks on Prince Arthur's chantry in Worcester cathedral', *Associated Architectural Society Reports and Papers* 31, 1911–12, 539. The sculptures recently excavated in the cathedral of Sts Michael and Gudule in Brussels may provide close comparisons.

[143] Angela Smith, 'The life and building activity of Richard Fox, c.1448–1528', unpublished Ph.D. thesis, University of London 1988, 77ff.

[144] P. Lindley, 'The great screen of Winchester cathedral', *Burlington Magazine* 131, 1989, 612–14. See also G. Kipling, *The Triumph of Honour: Burgundian Origins of the Elizabethan Renaissance*, Leiden 1977, 52–66 for Maynard Vewick or Wewyck and the import of Flemish painting in England.

[145] C. Barron and M. Erler, 'The making of Syon abbey's altar table of Our Lady c.1490–96', in *England and the Continent in the Middle Ages: Studies in Memory of Andrew Martindale*, ed. J. Mitchell and M. Moran, Stamford 2000, 318–35. I am indebted to Prof. Barron for a copy of her paper prior to its publication.

Conclusion

The sculptural programmes of Henry VII's chapel represent the best visual evidence we have for the building's original functions and help to clarify Henry VII's intentions. The intended purposes of the chapel have been obscured by the fact that it was never completed as intended because Henry VIII abandoned the plan to canonise Henry VI, placed his parents' tomb in the space where the shrine should have been and left the nave empty, presumably because he intended to place his own monument in this central space (although he later changed his mind, ironically preferring Windsor). Just as the original glazing scheme was in the hands of Netherlandish artists, so too the freestone imagery of the chapel demonstrated the dominance of Netherlandish sculptors in the first decade of the sixteenth century. The tombs of Margaret Beaufort and Henry VII in the next decade, and the high altar, heralded a new influx of Italian, and specifically Florentine, renaissance taste.

As completed, Henry VII's chapel was the most impressive royal benefaction to the Abbey since Henry III had started its Gothic rebuilding. Henry III was of course, a very different patron from Henry VII, and our understanding of the thirteenth-century king's aims and objectives in rebuilding Westminster Abbey is – in spite of the many entries in the Liberate and Close Rolls[146] – profoundly affected by the statements of monastic chroniclers such as Matthew Paris. Henry VII, like his Plantagenet predecessor, spent on a gigantic scale, contributing to the completion of King's College Chapel, Cambridge, building at Windsor, at the Tower of London, undertaking substantial works at Pontefract Castle, in Calais, constructing the Savoy hospital and the almshouses at Westminster, and building, especially from the late 1490s at his houses of Woodstock, Langley and Sheen (it has been estimated that he spent over £20,000 on Sheen, to which he gave the name Richmond) as well as constructing his new chapel at Westminster Abbey.[147] There seem to be, though, fundamental differences between the two kings' motives for building at the Abbey. Again, our sources may bias our understanding of Henry VII's character. Yet it is hard to avoid the view that Henry VII thought of the monks of Westminster Abbey as essentially his servants. He employed them to supply his three chantry monks and to maintain the great machinery of intercession which he had set in motion.[148] The painstaking attention to ensure that they fulfilled every obligation, and the set of quadripartite indentures specifying penalties and elaborate procedures to check on them, leaves one with the impression that the king, for all his conventional piety, viewed the transaction as a commercial one, in which he bought salvation, and made sure that he got value for money.

---

[146] Colvin, *HKW* i, 94.
[147] Colvin, *HKW* iv, 1.
[148] *CCR 1500–9*, 532. It is, of course, true that as early as the fourteenth century safeguards against breaches of contract were customary.

The Royal, the Great and the Good: the History of the Later Monuments

JOHN PHYSICK

AS WELL AS the Torrigiano tombs of King Henry VII and Queen Elizabeth of York and of Lady Margaret Beaufort, discussed by Dr Lindley above, Henry VII's Chapel contains about twenty other monuments. Often by the leading sculptors of the day, they form a group of great significance. The chapel was in effect reserved for royalty until the burial in 1628 of George Villiers, duke of Buckingham, a favourite of both James I and Charles I; thereafter, though burials of members of the royal family continued down to the end of the eighteenth century, a number of other influential people were buried and allowed major monuments in the chapel. In the twentieth century a small number of commemorative wall plaques have been erected, to imperial administrators and military men, particularly those associated with the Order of the Bath. In addition, other monuments that might have been expected did not materialise. Most of the older monuments have suffered from damage and depredation. Partly this was caused on specific occasions, especially the scaffolding erected in 1725 for additional seating at the reintroduction of the Order of the Bath, but partly by visitors, who always appear to have felt the desire to take away something, presumably as a souvenir – as early as 1569 one Raymond was arraigned at Finsbury for stealing 'plates' from Henry VII's monument.[1] Here the enormous increase in tourism in the later twentieth century and the resultant crush did not help. But there have also been some general campaigns of repair and restoration which affected the monuments; we shall begin with these, going on to look at projects that were never executed, and finally examining the individual monuments and their restorations.

---

[1] WAM 38937. John Thomas, servant of Dean Goodman, asked for 12d for his boat hire and dinner to go to 'Fynnesbery' on 18 December 1569. Most of the earlier monuments in the Lady chapel are described and illustrated in Dart, Neale and Brayley, R. Ackerman and W. Combe, *The History of the Abbey Church of St Peter's Westminster, its Antiquities and Monuments*, 1812. Those monuments dated up to 1714 are described in *Inventory*. I am grateful to the Dean and Chapter for their permission to quote from their archives and to Dr Richard Mortimer, Keeper of the Muniments, Dr Tony Trowles, the Librarian, and Miss Christine Reynolds, Assistant Keeper of the Muniments.

General approaches to the care of the monuments

By the end of the eighteenth century, the condition of the monuments throughout the Abbey was causing comment and criticism. Sir Francis Chantrey recommended that the railings round them should be removed in order to prevent visitors from clambering about: some of these railings were eventually bought by John Bridge of the firm of royal goldsmiths, Rundell and Bridge. On 20 December 1821, the *English Chronicle* reported that the railings 'which obstructed the view of the monuments . . . are now removed preparatory to Mr. Theakstone the sculptor beginning his Herculean task . . .'. John Theakston (d.1842), a former assistant to John Bacon, John Flaxman, and E.H. Baily had been with Chantrey for nearly twenty-five years, and was to be paid an annual £60. Doubtless he concentrated on the monuments that had been damaged during the installations necessary for the coronation of George IV. Whatever he managed to achieve was probably undone at the coronation of Queen Victoria in 1838, after which Allan Cunningham, Chantrey's foreman, had noted that twenty-four fingers and pieces of drapery had been knocked off monuments, including that to Lord Mansfield, by Flaxman, then under the arcade in the north transept, and that a plank had fallen on a monument by Westmacott.[2]

Edward Blore, the surveyor of the Abbey, also recommended that someone should be appointed in order to clean and repair. He reported to the Dean and Chapter in June 1842:

> Having examined the state of the Monuments I find them in so dirty a state that the necessary process of cleaning will in the first instance be insufficient to remove the accumulated dirt with which they are disfigured. I should therefore recommend that a cleaning liquid such as is generally used by sculptors under similar circumstances should be applied to remove this dirt and as a general principle afterwards that they should be well cleaned and washed annually and dusted every alternate half year. That to perform these duties a competent person should be appointed and that in addition to the above duties he should be required to make annual reports to the Dean and Chapter of the state of repair and general condition of the monuments especially pointing out those which are in a dangerous or dilapidated state. That the Dean and Chapter may if they think it desirable communicate with the representatives of the individual whose monument has been allowed to fall into that state.
>
> I should consider it indispensably necessary that the person appointed to fulfil the above duties should be a sculptor of some repute and who unites to professional reputation a private character.[3]

Upon the suggestion of Blore, John Ternouth was appointed at the same salary as that enjoyed by Theakston. A competent sculptor, Ternouth's major contribution in London is the large bronze relief of the battle of Copenhagen on the base of Nelson's Column.

Blore resigned as surveyor in 1849 (the year of Ternouth's death) and was succeeded by (Sir) Gilbert Scott who, after the appointment in 1864 of A.P. Stanley as

---

[2] *Report from Select Committee on National Monuments and Works of Art*, House of Commons 16 June 1841, 89.
[3] WAM 66361. Vouchers for payments to both Theakston and Ternouth, and from 1849 to Henry Poole, are in the Muniments.

Dean, together with him undertook a great deal of rearrangement and reduction in size of monuments. In the main, the monuments in Henry VII's chapel escaped their attentions, although Dean Stanley sought, and was given, government assistance for the cleaning and repair of the royal monuments, both in that chapel and the Confessor's chapel. Scott employed Henry Poole as the Abbey mason who looked after monuments.

On 13 February 1869, George Russell, the secretary to the Office of Works, asked the council of the Society of Antiquaries for 'a list of such Regal and other Historical Tombs in Cathedrals, Churches, and other public Places and Buildings, as in their opinion it would be desirable to place under the protection and supervision of the Government, with a view to their proper custody and preservation'.[4] The Society decided that the monuments should be limited to those who had died not later than 1760, and eventually listed 531. Dean Stanley compiled that of the Abbey's monuments, and this included fifteen in Henry VII's chapel.

Gilbert Scott, together with Dean Stanley, Augustus Franks (a Vice-President of the Society of Antiquaries), Dr Percy, James Fergusson, Edmund Oldfield and others, met the First Commissioner of Works, Austen Layard, on 12 April 1869 to discuss the condition of Henry VII's monument. Among the principal points they talked about were the steps to be taken to remove the dirt that encrusted the gilding, whether missing portions, including shields and the inscription, should be remade, and what should be done to arrest decay.[5] It was unanimously agreed at first that the whole monument should be cleaned with soap, water and ammonia, although Dr Percy warned that the gilding might be removed. So it was decided that as gilding had to be preserved, Poole was authorised to undertake only a little cleaning with a brush, but not with any chemicals. So far as missing parts of the architectural portion were concerned, the committee thought that they could be restored. No missing sculpture was to be replaced, although the missing inscription could be restored in a different material from the original in order 'to obviate any risk of future confusion' and that all rusting iron cramps ought to be removed.

Moving on to inspect Lady Margaret Beaufort's monument, which generally was in the same deplorable condition, Poole 'pointed out a portion which he had cleaned some years since, removing the coating of dirt with a knife, and exposing the gilding underneath'.[6] Gilbert Scott thought, and the committee agreed with him, that no knives should be used, and suggested that rather than experiment on Henry VII, soap, water and ammonia could be tried out on Lady Margaret Beaufort.

As Layard wished to limit repairs only to those which were necessary, the Treasury was asked for £5,000. Poole presented his bill in June 1870, when he charged £382 15s for the repair and cleaning of Henry VII's monument, including the screen, and £31 for cleaning Lady Margaret Beaufort. Later Poole was hauled over the coals, as an Office of Works official thought that he had washed the Beaufort effigy without authorisation.

However, the government changed in 1870 and Layard was replaced as First Commissioner by the Radical member for Tower Hamlets, Acton Smee Ayrton. The

[4] *Report of the Sepulchral Monuments Committee*, Society of Antiquaries of London, 1872, 2.
[5] WAM 57127.
[6] Ibid.

new First Commissioner was convinced that architects, painters and sculptors were making a fine living on government funds and was determined to bring this to an end. He is probably best remembered today for dismissing E.M. Barry as architect to his father's Palace of Westminster, and for having locked Alfred Stevens, the sculptor of the long-unfinished monument to the duke of Wellington in St Pauls' Cathedral, out of his studio and seizing the contents. So far as the Abbey was concerned, nothing further was done about the list from the Society of Antiquaries. Dean Stanley asked Ayrton on 6 June 1870 if he would consult Gladstone to see if the cleaning of the royal monuments could continue, as the Dean had every reason to believe that Gladstone was sympathetic.[7] Ayrton, in his memorandum to the Prime Minister, explained that once such a monument was placed in position, there was nothing to indicate that the Crown was further involved, but if the Crown were to exercise that duty, then legislation would be necessary – so nothing was done, although the Treasury continued to allocate funds until 1872, after which time the Office of Works involvement came to an end.[8]

During the cleaning of Henry VII's tomb, Dean Stanley recorded that

> In removing the effigies ... from the structure of the tomb ... there were found in the hollow space beneath, some gilt ornaments, evidently belonging to the gilt crown which once encircled the head of the Queen, and also the name of an Italian workman, apparently *Fr. Medolo*, which must have been scratched on the wall at the time Torrigiano erected it.[9]

There was a suggestion during the 1930s that the grille round Henry VII's tomb should be repaired and partially restored. The firm of Bainbridge Reynolds estimated that to do this, and to replace a considerable amount of missing bronze parts, the cresting and inscription among them, would cost £1,700: but the proposal was abandoned.[10]

During the 1939–1945 war, the effigies and much of the other bronze work of Henry VII's tomb, as well as that of Lady Margaret Beaufort, were with the other royal effigies removed for safety to the riding school and stables of Mentmore in Buckinghamshire. Late in 1945, they, together with other sculpture from the chapel, were exhibited in the Victoria and Albert Museum, and returned to the Abbey in the following year.[11]

Only a limited amount of cleaning was undertaken throughout the building until the 1950s, when the interior of the Abbey and all the monuments were spruced up in preparation for the nine hundredth anniversary of the Abbey in 1966. The Surveyor who undertook this was Stephen Dykes Bower. 'The grime', he later wrote, 'which gradually darkened and discoloured the entire interior, had so totally obscured the conjunction of stone and marble that these two materials were indistinguishable',[12]

---

[7] WAM 57129.
[8] PRO, Work 20/75.
[9] Stanley, *Historical Memorials*, 525 n. 1.
[10] WAM (P) 656 and A–D.
[11] See below, 341.
[12] E. Carpenter, ed., *A House of Kings*, 1966, 400.

and this criticism applied equally to the monuments, as anyone who saw them at the time can well remember. In order to preserve at least one dirty patch, the writer was told at the time that a portion of the wall was left uncleaned by the doorway into the Jerusalem Chamber, at the west end of the south nave aisle.

Proposals for monuments never executed

Edward VI was buried at the head of his grandfather's tomb, beneath the altar, but although a monument was later designed, it was not erected. In the Bodleian Library, Oxford, there is a design for his tomb attributed to Cornelius Cure. This tall structure consists of ten corinthian columns (between each is a balustrade) supporting a flat ceiling, beneath which lies the effigy of Edward VI, crowned and in armour, upon a sarcophagus: above are allegorical figures, crowns and the Tudor heraldic achievement. The drawing[13] has been dated to the 1570s but could well be of some years later. No position for the monument is indicated, but presumably it would have been above, or adjacent to, the king's grave.

No monuments seem to have been contemplated for Henry Frederick, Prince of Wales (d.1612) or Anne of Denmark (d.1619), although their effigies, dressed in robes, were displayed in the chapel for a while. A drawing of 1786 by John Carter in the Abbey's library, shows them when they stood in Henry V's chantry chapel.[14] Seriously damaged, fragments of them still survive.

Although William III and Mary II were both buried in the chapel, they have no monument. Grinling Gibbons drew one for Mary II (d.1695)[15] and then another for both the king and the queen.[16] Each design is for a very large monument and either would have stood in the nave at the eastern end of the stalls, then not so extensive as they are now. Such enormous baroque constructions in the chapel, with their array of life-sized standing or recumbent marble figures, would not, perhaps, have aroused criticism at the end of the seventeenth century, when the adjective 'gothic' had been coined to describe what was considered barbaric – but we may feel the building was lucky to escape. Some of the figures, those representing Justice and Prudence, were later used by Grinling Gibbons for his monument to the first duke of Beaufort at Badminton, Gloucestershire.[17]

Just as enormous as Grinling Gibbons' designs was that by Edward Pierce for a projected monument to George Villiers, the second duke of Buckingham

---

[13] Bodleian Library, Oxford, Gough Maps 45, no. 63. Illustrated in *Architectural Drawings in the Bodleian Library*, ed. H.M. Colvin, 1952; J. Physick, *Designs for English Sculpture 1680–1860*, 1969, fig. 3; Colvin, *HKW* iii, pl. 8; Whinney, fig. 18.

[14] WAM, Langley Collection, IX (I), illustrated in A. Harvey and R. Mortimer, *The Funeral Effigies of Westminster Abbey*, Woodbridge 1994, 22, 59–71.

[15] Designed by Sir Christopher Wren. Oxford, All Souls' College, Wren Drawings, I, no. 5; D. Green, *Grinling Gibbons: his Work as Carver and Statuary, 1648–1721*, 1964, 74, 164; E. Croft-Murray and P. Hulton, *Catalogue of British Drawings* [in the British Museum], i, 1960, 333; Whinney, 124–6; G. Beard, *Grinling Gibbons*, 1989, 200.

[16] British Museum, no. 1866–6–11–164. L. Stainton and C. White, *Drawings in England from Hilliard to Hogarth*, British Museum exhibition catalogue, 1987, 195, 196.

[17] Whinney, 124–6.

Fig. 39. Design by Edward Pierce for a monument to the second duke of Buckingham, d.1687, British Museum, Dept of Prints and Drawings, 1881–6–11–176.

(d.1687) (Fig. 39),[18] which was, according to the scale on the drawing, about 25ft (over 8m) in width and 20ft (nearly 7m) high. This, one supposes, was intended to stand on the north side of the nave, blocking the arch that then led into the north aisle.

Following the death in 1879 of the Prince Imperial (the son of Napoleon III), who had been killed while with the British army in Africa, a monument to him, with a recumbent effigy, commissioned from Sir Edgar Boehm, was proposed by a committee headed by the Earl Sydney, and agreed by Dean Stanley for the chapel. But the Dean soon found that public opinion was against him. A limited but vociferous opposition culminated in a vote in the House of Commons against the monument being in the Abbey. A letter of 21 July 1880, was published in the *Daily Telegraph*,

---

[18] British Museum, no. 1861–6–11–176. Whinney, 105, 106, 441 n. 33; E. Croft-Murray and P. Hulton, *Catalogue*, i, 1960, 451–5; Stainton and White, *Drawings*, 168–9.

and in it Dean Stanley defended his decision and criticised the House of Commons. The latter, he wrote, had defeated ministers and has the effect of throwing upon the House the responsibility of a defeat. 'The resolution to have its full effect should have assumed the usual form which alone could give it legal validity – that of an address to the Crown as visitor of the Abbey.' Dean Stanley ended the letter by stating that he had recently 'caused to be recorded on the floor of Henry VII's chapel the only act in which a precedent to the recent action of the House of Commons is sought to be found – the disinterment of the magnates of the Commonwealth under the pressure of the strong outburst of party passion which followed the Restoration. Posterity will judge how far the ungenerous spirit which governed the Parliament of 1661 still, under an altered form, survives in the Parliament of 1889.' Boehm's monument to the Prince Imperial was later erected in St George's Chapel, Windsor.[19]

The monuments: accretion and restoration

The first monument to appear after those by Torrigiano, placed at the west end of the chapel's south aisle, was in fact to a grand-daughter of Henry VII, Margaret, Countess of Lennox, who died in 1578. On the tomb-chest is her recumbent effigy, with kneeling figures of her sons and daughters on the sides, together with heraldic shields and panels of inscription. Photographs taken in the late nineteenth century and even between the two wars, show considerable damage – missing hands, broken or missing marble obelisks, dirt and faded colouring. From 1956, Stephen Dykes Bower employed Abbey workmen to carry out a preliminary cleaning, and then in the following year, specialist marble workers, Messrs. Earp & Hobbs, made good the missing alabaster, marble and other parts. W.J. Butchart[20] who had been commissioned by the Surveyor, undertook the recolouring, while C.W. Scott Giles advised on the heraldry and 'many other features'.[21] An insurance claim was submitted in 1962 for making good missing hands on kneeling effigies, and this work was carried out by Messrs. J. Whitehead. However, the surveyor was forced to write in 1970 that 'Wilful damage has been suffered by the Countess of Lennox more than any other', hands had once again disappeared from one of the kneeling figures on the south side and another on the north, and unicorn heraldic supporters had lost their horns. A kneeling son on the south side of the tomb-chest represents Henry, Lord Darnley, the husband of Mary, Queen of Scots, and was, as the epitaph states (in capitals) 'K of Scotts/ and Father to James the 6 Now King This Henry/ Was Myrthered At The Age Of 21 Yeares. . .'. Consequently, above his head was a crown, one of the details replaced in 1957/8. A few years later, Stephen Dykes Bower noted that its cross had been broken off and taken.[22] A photograph in the Abbey's muniments shows an inscription, now no longer visible, recording that the countess's monument had been

---

[19] A draft of a similar letter by Dean Stanley is WAM 57118. For Sir Edgar Boehm see M. Stocker, 'The church monuments of Joseph Edgar Boehm', *Church Monuments* 8, 1993, 66–9. Earl Sydney's own monument in St Nicholas, Chislehurst, Kent, was commissioned from Boehm, but was completed by (Sir) Alfred Gilbert.
[20] Of West Croydon. According to his letter-head, he was an 'Ecclesiastical Decorator, Gilder, etc.'
[21] WAM, Audit Report, 1957.
[22] WAM, Audit Report, 1970.

Plate 50. Princess Sophia, monument by Maximilian Colt, 1606: detail.

erected by her executor, Thomas Fowler. During the 1960s, there was correspondence about some railings bought by John Bridge and installed at the school in Piddletrenthide, Dorset, that had been built by the Bridge family. Nicholas MacMichael, keeper of the muniments, suggested that these might have come from the monument to the countess of Lennox.[23]

The countess's grandson, James VI and I, commissioned four monuments, two in the north aisle to two young daughters, Sophia (d.1606) (Plate 50) and Mary (d.1607); an enormous construction in the north aisle to Elizabeth I from Maximilian Colt (together with the sergeant-painter, John de Critz), completed in 1606, and then in the

[23] Letters and reports, 1962–9, WAM nos. 65078 (1–12).

Plate 51. Mary queen of Scots, monument by William and Cornelius Cure, 1612: detail.

south aisle, the equally towering monument to his mother, Mary, Queen of Scots, from Cornelius Cure, completed some years later by William Cure (Plate 51).[24] Both these monuments are in the form of a triumphal arch, with an effigy on a sarcophagus beneath. Even though the stalls in the nave at that period extended one bay less to the east than they do today, for a long while the chapel, its very restricted aisles and the nave as well, must have resembled a building site, with scaffolding, and bricklayers and masons erecting these huge constructions.

There was at least some sporadic maintenance: during the reign of William III and Mary II, a man spent several days cleaning the tombs of the 'quenes maiesties grete grandmother', Mary, Queen of Scots, and charged 35s.[25] But generally damage has predominated, and it is difficult to discover when the damage to these monuments happened. The early engraving by J. Cole in Dart's *Westmonasterium* (Fig. 40) shows only the cross on the orb of Elizabeth I missing, but it is known that the crown disappeared quite early. E.W. Brayley remarked that her gilded Garter collar was removed

---

[24] For the monuments to Elizabeth I and Mary, Queen of Scots, see Whinney, 52–5, 60, 433 nn. 47–9; A. White, 'Westminster Abbey in the early seventeenth century: a powerhouse of ideas', *Church Monuments* 4, 1989, 16–53; A. White, 'England c.1550–c.1660: a hundred years of continental influence', *Church Monuments* 7, 1992, 34–74. For Colt and De Critz see M. Edmund, 'Limners and picturemakers', *Walpole Society* 47, 1980, 144–74.

[25] WAM 66400.

Fig. 40. Elizabeth I, monument by Maximilian Colt and John de Critz, 1606. (Dart i, 171)

after the railings had been taken away.[26] In a complaint in March 1895 by E.R. Robson to the president of the Society of Antiquaries about the state of the royal monuments 'in the charge, but scarcely in the care of the Dean and Chapter', the Surveyor, J.T. Micklethwaite, replied concerning the monument to Elizabeth I, that among various losses, 'only one badge, that of the thistle, remains in the middle of the north side [whereas] there was probably one on each of the four sides. These badges were only heralds' stuff, and to judge from the one that is left were more disfigurements than ornaments to the tomb.'[27]

In the course of time there were various breakages, and eventually all the Tudor and Stuart monuments had become extremely dirty. Stephen Dykes Bower noted that the recently completed work to the large monument to Elizabeth I's first cousin, Lord Hunsdon, in the chapel of St John the Baptist, was now 'an exemplar of what monuments of its period should be – the marble repolished, the ornament gilded and coloured'.[28] He wrote that the tomb of Elizabeth I 'has been partially cleaned and polished. But so many parts of its design are missing and need to be supplied that, until a decision can be taken on its proper restoration and painting', he had transferred the cleaners to other monuments in the chapel. The following year, he stated that

> the monument to Queen Elizabeth, the most important undertaken this year, exemplifies the type that we cannot tackle unaided. Its splendour depends on its decoration, but this decoration could not be renewed until the large number of missing features in marble and alabaster, vital to the design, had been supplied. Even now the full effect is marred because some are lacking: the queen's effigy lacked its crown, collar and sceptre, the emblem – the crowned lion – that, on the north side, should balance the thistle surmounting the south, and several coronets over royal and ducal arms are absent.[29]

It was not until 1972 that Dykes Bower was able to record that the sceptre and the cross on the orb had been replaced. Restoration was carried on by his successor, Peter Foster, assisted by private donation. After discussion with Hubert Chesshyre, then Rouge Croix Pursuivant, Sah Oved (Mrs Hughes) was asked to design a replacement for the missing collar of the effigy. This, of gilded copper, was put in place in 1976. Two years later Arthur Ayres made and painted the crest of England on the south side of the summit, to a design supplied by C.W. Scott Giles. In 1981, Mr Furneaux was working on replacement railings to enclose the tomb incorporating copies of the original emblems that had been discovered by Claude Blair in the possession of the Armourers' Company. Arthur Ayres also made a replacement crown of gilded wood, which was placed on the effigy's head in November 1986. A few days later it was wrenched off by a visitor and stolen: a metal replacement was made in 1987.[30]

Stephen Dykes Bower was able to report in 1958 that W.J. Butchart had 'restored' the painting of the two princesses and that he had cleaned and gilded the monument,

---

[26] *Select Committee on National Monuments* (1841), 114, paras. 2223–4.
[27] *Proceedings of the Society of Antiquaries*, 9 May 1895.
[28] WAM, Audit Report, 1955.
[29] WAM, Audit Report, 9 April 1956.
[30] Peter Foster, Audit Report.

designed by Sir Christopher Wren and made in 1674 by Joshua Marshall, master mason to Charles II, which contains the supposed bones of Edward V and the duke of York found in the Tower of London.

Dean Ryle told the Chapter on 21 July 1914 that the iron grille originally round the tomb of Mary, Queen of Scots, which had been removed in 1820 and sold, had been recovered, and offered to the Abbey by the National Art Collections Fund, in order that it could be replaced. The Chapter gratefully accepted the offer, provided that the authenticity of the grille could be proved beyond question. Nothing further was done however, until 1921, when the Chapter reviewed the matter. It was then thought that if the grille were to be re-erected, it would obscure the effigy, block the passage in the aisle and also, the marble plinth would have to cut into and damaged. So it was decided that the grille would be put up in the Undercroft Museum instead. The Surveyor in 1958 stated that the grille had at last been fixed round the monument, and also that a replacement for the missing sceptre, once held by the heraldic lion at the feet of the effigy, had been made and placed in position.

Ludovic Stuart, duke of Richmond and Lennox, a cousin of James I, was commemorated after his death in 1624 by a stupendous bronze and marble monument by Hubert Le Sueur, with four allegories, Faith, Hope, Charity and Prudence, supporting a metal canopy, on which stands Fame with two trumpets; it was erected by the widowed duchess. The secretary of state to Charles I, Lord Conway, wrote to the Dean on 17 September 1628 that the duchess of Richmond had petitioned the King

> to order that a partition of stone, wherein there is a door and a window, at the entrance into the little chapel, in Westminster Abbey, where the duke of Richmond's tomb is placed, may be removed, and an iron gate placed instead thereof. The king is ready to do honour to the memory of that duke, but requires to understand what [the Dean and Chapter] conceive of the request.[31]

There are no records in the Abbey, and no mention in the chapter acts of the reaction of the Dean John Williams, but certainly the wall has at some time been lowered (Fig. 8). Apart from a few loose gilded bronze fittings, such as garlands and urns, little damage is now apparent, but by the nineteenth century the condition of the monument had deteriorated. The mason, Henry Poole, wrote that in 1875 'the order came from the earl of Darnley to entirely repaint and restore the monument of his ancestors . . . It had been barbarously demolished and despoiled of its metalwork, but much was left, giving authority for its restoration . . .'. At the east end of this monument is a tall obelisk, standing on skulls, on top of which is an urn containing the heart of the boy duke, Esme Stuart, who died in Paris in 1660.[32]

Damage is visible on the equally large first non-royal monument in the chapel, on the north side, also by Hubert Le Sueur, to George Villiers, Duke of Buckingham, who had been assassinated at Portsmouth in 1628. Above the gilded bronze effigies of

---

[31] *Calendar of State Papers, Domestic, 1628–9*, 1859, 329.
[32] Whinney, 86, 438 nn. 7, 8; C. Avery, 'Hubert Le Sueur, the "Unworthy Praxiteles" of King Charles I', *Walpole Society* 48, 1980–82, 42ff. There is one earlier heart burial in an urn on an obelisk in the Abbey, that to Ann Harley (d.1605) in the chapel of St Nicholas. See White, 'Continental influence', 41; H. Poole, 'Westminster Abbey. Annals of the masonry carried out', *RIBA Journal*, 3 April 1890, 281.

Fig. 41. George Villiers, duke of Buckingham, d.1628, monument by Hubert le Sueur. (Dart i, 165)

the duke and duchess, is a marble group of their children, by Isaac Besnier.[33] At each corner is a large bronze seated figure; Mars, Neptune, Pallas and Bounty. A writer on the Abbey in 1909 commented acidly that these 'are the first of the host of heathenish figures which disgrace the church'.[34] The engraving by J. Cole in Dart's *Westmonasterium*, shows that many of the gilded monograms and other devices have now disappeared, as has the trumpet of Fame at the feet of the effigies (Fig. 41).

During the Commonwealth, Oliver Cromwell and several of his prominent companions were buried in the chapel, but not for long, as they were all disinterred by command of Charles II at the Restoration. Only one monument to any is known, that to Cromwell's son-in-law, Henry Ireton (d.1651). This monument, with two effigies, was by William Wright, of Charing Cross, and dated from about 1653. Wright was paid £120 for the work which was hoped would be 'to the good contentment of Your Highness [Cromwell] and the most skilful beholders and to the well-deserved fame of the said lord deputy'.[35] No record seems to have survived of the monument's appearance, but an epitaph that might have been part of it, was printed in *The Antiquities of Saint Peter's or the Abbey Church of Westminster* by J. Crull.[36] It was Cromwell who really created the Abbey as a national Valhalla, for, when Robert Blake died off Plymouth in 1657, Cromwell caused 'him to be brought up by land in all the state that could be; and to encourage his officers to venture their lives, that they might be pompously buried, he was, with all the solemnity possible, at the charge of the public, buried in Henry VII's chapel'.[37]

Two supporters of the Stuarts and of George I are commemorated in the north aisle, an appropriate location. The first, with a relief portrait medallion, is to George Savile, Marquess of Halifax (d.1695), Lord Keeper of the Privy Seal in the reigns of Charles II, James II and William III. The other is to Charles Mountague (Montagu), created Earl of Halifax in 1714 by George I; statesman and financier, founder of the Bank of England, he died in May 1715.

William III and Queen Anne are both buried in the chapel without a monument, but are now commemorated by a small bronze plaque in the south aisle, presented in 1966 by the Trinity church of New York; William III, as the plaque reads, 'in 1697 granted a charter and a generous gift of land to Trinity Church, establishing it as the first Anglican Church in the City of New York', and Queen Anne granted to the church the queen's farm and garden on Manhattan Island, in 1705.

During the eighteenth century, sculpture in England was dominated by four sculptors, Peter Scheemakers and Michael Rysbrack from the Low Countries, Louis-François Roubiliac from France and the Englishman, Sir Henry Cheere. Although

---

[33] P. McEvansoneya, 'A note on Hubert Le Sueur and Isaac Besnier', *Burlington Magazine* 135, 1993, 532–4.

[34] F. Bond, *Westminster Abbey*, 1909, 220.

[35] Quoted in Carpenter, *House of Kings*, 175.

[36] Appendix to the third edition, 1722. William Wright's other monuments in the Abbey, chapel of St John the Baptist, to Colonel Edward Popham (d.1651), also has no inscription. Tradition has maintained that, at the Restoration, this was either removed, or the marble slab simply reversed. In order to check the latter, Stephen Dykes Bower had the tablet removed and found no trace of an inscription, WAM, Audit Report, 1955. A slip of paper among the Muniments, WAM 42404, is Wright's bill for 2s on 2 June 1643 for work on the communion table. He signs as a 'Graver in stone'.

[37] Edward, Earl of Clarendon, *The History of the Rebellion and Civil Wars in England*, 1826 edn, vii, 215.

Plate 52. John Sheffield, duke of Buckingham, d.1721, monument, designed by Denis Plumier and sculpted by Laurent Delvaux and Peter Scheemakers.

Plate 53. George Monck, duke of Albemarle, d.1670, monument by Peter Scheemakers, c.1746.

there are many monuments by these four artists in the Abbey, only Scheemakers and Rysbrack (a minor one) appear in Henry VII's chapel.

In the north-eastern chapel is the large monument to John Sheffield, Duke of Buckingham (1721), innovatively designed by Denis Plumier, who made several models of the figures before his own death in 1721 (Plate 52). The figure of the duke in Roman armour reclines on the sarcophagus, with the duchess in contemporary dress seated at his feet. Above the main figures, Time carries medallion relief portraits of their children. According to George Vertue, Scheemakers sculpted the figure of the duchess, and his partner at the time, Laurent Delvaux, that of Time and possibly the duke.[38] The monument was erected by the duchess, an illegitimate daughter of James II. She died in 1743 and her funerary figure in coronation robes is among those now on display in the Abbey's museum.[39]

Less well-known is Scheemakers's monument, designed by William Kent, to George Monck, first duke of Albemarle, at the eastern end of the south aisle, which has the distinction of being one of the very few monuments placed in the Abbey with no identification (Plate 53). Monck, who died in 1670, remained without a memorial until well into the eighteenth century. On 1 March 1740 (New Style), the Dean 'acquainted the Chapter with the Request of a noble Lord for putting up a monument in one of the East windows of King Henry the seventh Chapel for the late General Monk. It is the unanimous Opinion of the Society that, no Monument should be put up in the said Chapel, as it will necessarily deface or hide some of the curious workmanship thereof',[40] but just over two years later the Chapter 'ordered that leave be given to put up a monument in the South Isle . . . upon payment of Thirty guineas'.[41] Although Monck is not mentioned in the inscription, the monument was commissioned under the will of his son, who had died so long before as 1688, and shows the figure of the general in armour standing before a rostral column with, on one side, a seated mourning woman holding a portrait relief medallion of the second duke. Monck's face is based on a head by John Bushnell (now in the Library), itself probably based on a death-mask, while the armour used on his funeral effigy is on display in the Museum.[42] The fine was not paid until the end of 1746 and the inscription seems to record all the then living members of the family, as well as the designer and the sculptor. For some reason there always seems to have been confusion about the date of the memorial. The Abbey's Official Guide recorded it as 1720, while Rupert Gunnis in his *Dictionary of British Sculptors 1660–1851* gave it as 1730. However, there is a clue on the monument itself as, among the names is that of Earl Gower, a title not created until 1746.

Adjacent to Monck is the standing figure of Modesty by Filippo della Valle, after a Roman original, which was erected to the memory of the first wife, Catherine

---

[38] Design in Sir John Soane's Museum, no. AL. 31E, 46. C. Avery, 'Laurent Delvaux's sculpture in England', *National Trust Studies 1980*, 1979, 150–6; Whinney, 157–9; I. Roscoe, 'Flemish sculpture and adjustments for the English market: the case for Peter Scheemakers', *Church Monuments* 7, 1992, 75–94; I. Roscoe, 'Peter Scheemakers', *Walpole Society* 61, 1999, 178–80.
[39] Harvey and Mortimer, *Funeral Effigies*, 147–53, colour plate XVII.
[40] WAM, Chapter Acts.
[41] WAM Chapter Acts, 29 October 1742. Designs are in the Victoria and Albert Museum, no. D. 1050–1887, and Sir John Soane's Museum, no. AL. 31E; Roscoe, 'Peter Scheemakers', 214–15.
[42] For Monck's funeral effigy, see Harvey and Mortimer, *Funeral Effigies*, 72–8.

Plate 54. Antoine Philippe, duc de Montpensier, d.1807, monument by Sir Richard Westmacott, detail.

(d.1737), of Sir Robert Walpole. Modesty stands on a pedestal designed and almost certainly sculpted by Michael Rysbrack. Lady Walpole was buried at Houghton, Norfolk, and consequently the Dean and Chapter charged only half burial fees of £24 12s 9d and a further £21 for their permission to put up the monument. Lady Walpole's son Horace, paid the total of £45 12s 9d in 1739. In today's values this would be probably about £3,000, and drew a waspish comment from Horace Walpole that the Dean and Chapter 'sell their church over and over again'.[43]

No other monument was placed in the chapel until the early nineteenth century. The Duc de Montpensier, brother to Louis-Philippe of Orleans (later king of the French), died in England in 1807, and was buried outside the chapel at its entrance. Not long afterwards, the prince's body was moved into a vault under the south-eastern chapel, and an inscribed stone was placed on the northern wall. A monument by Sir Richard Westmacott, signed and dated 1830 and exhibited at the Royal Academy, was commissioned by Louis-Philippe and placed in the chapel (Plate 54); the earlier inscription (which still remains on the wall) was copied for the tomb-chest.[44] In the Abbey muniments is a letter from Westmacott, dated 31 October 1819:[45]

---

[43] See pl. 4 in W.S. Lewis, *Horace Walpole* (Mellon Lectures 1960), 1961; WAM, Funeral Fees Book. Walpole's comment is quoted in E.T. Murray Smith, *The Roll Call of Westminster Abbey*, 1903, 323.

[44] The etching by R. Sands, after a drawing by J.P. Neale of 1822, Neale and Brayley i, pl. LVI, shows the duke's tomb slab, and the earlier inscription.

[45] N. Penny, *Church Monuments in Romantic England*, 1977, 122; P. Ward-Jackson, 'The French background of royal monuments at Windsor and Frogmore', *Church Monuments* 8, 1993, 64, 65.

I have wished to see Lord Farnborough [chairman of the Committee of Taste] upon some points relative to the Duc de Montpensier Monument and as I had communicated with the Dean personally upon the site &c, I did not consider the dimensions so immediate. I have the pleasure now to send them, general dimensions are 6ft. by 2ft. 6. The extreme length at base 7ft. by 2. 8.

Dean Stanley noted that there had been earlier indecision about whether anyone who was not a member of the British royal family could be buried in Henry VII's chapel. 'Even the Dean [John Ireland] seems to have been ignorant of the burial of any person of inferior rank, except the duchess of Richmond and the two dukes of Buckingham. There are, in fact, not less than seventy.'[46]

In the south-eastern chapel is the recumbent effigy of Dean Stanley, who died in 1881, sculpted by Boehm on the tomb designed by John Loughborough Pearson, the Abbey's surveyor of the fabric. The Dean was buried in Henry VII's chapel by permission of Queen Victoria, and Boehm's first model for a seated figure, is in the Abbey Library. At some time the effigy's nose had been damaged, for Stephen Dykes Bower noted in 1965 that it had been necessary carefully to graft on a new portion.[47]

The Dean's monument is the last free-standing memorial in the chapel, although a few wall tablets have later been placed in position. In 1917 and 1918, the Chapter considered a request for a memorial to the first earl of Cromer, and agreed that it could be placed on the then blank wall on the right side of the entrance to the south aisle: this position, it was decided, was to be used only for members of the Order of the Bath. Sir Goscombe John met the Dean, Herbert Ryle, and the Chapter, together with the Lord Cromer memorial committee, and placed *in situ* a model which was approved, and the finished memorial was unveiled in 1920. Beside it was placed a medallion portrait of the first viscount Milner (d.1925), by Gilbert Ledward,[48] and a tablet by Sir Bertram Mackennal to the Marquess Curzon of Kedleston (d.1925), Viceroy of India, but not a member of the Order of the Bath. It was at this time that members of the Chapter complained that the monument was being erected without their knowledge. 'After discussion it was agreed that the Dean [Foxley Norris] should put forward his views as to the duties and powers of the Dean and the Dean and Chapter respectively in such matters.'[49]

At the east end of the same aisle Detmar Blow designed an altar of black marble for Sibell, Countess Grosvenor, in memory of her son, Percy Wyndham, and of Earl Kitchener of Khartoum as well, both killed during the First World War. It is dated 1924 and was first used on 24 July 1929 (Fig. 6).

The High Commissioner for Southern Rhodesia on 12 October 1951, suggested to the Dean, Dr Don, that the Abbey might have a memorial to Cecil Rhodes, who had died in 1902. Dr Don and the Surveyor met the High Commissioner together with L.S. Amery and Sir Dougall Malcolm, and after they had inspected several possible sites, settled on the south aisle of Henry VII's chapel. Presumably the Dean and

---

[46] Stanley, *Historical Memorials*, 171.
[47] The model of the seated figure of Dean Stanley is illustrated in Cocke, *900 Years*, 152. WAM, Audit Report.
[48] WAM no. 58732A.
[49] WAM, Chapter Acts, 8 July 1930.

Chapter had no remembrance of the Chapter's earlier decision, as Rhodes was not a member of the Bath, but Stephen Dykes Bower had reservations about the limitations of the site. He recorded that it would be unwise to place another memorial in this rather restricted area but, however, the Milner plaque was raised slightly and the small Ancaster stone tablet to Rhodes, designed by Dykes Bower, was unveiled by L.S. Amery on 3 December 1953.

The latest of the memorials in the chapel commemorates the Royal Air Force leaders of the Second World War, all of them Knights Grand Cross of the Bath: Marshal of the RAF Lord Douglas of Kirtleside; Air Chief Marshal Lord Dowding; Marshal of the RAF Sir Arthur Harris; Marshal of the RAF Lord Newall; Marshal of the RAF Lord Portal of Hungerford; and Marshal of the RAF Lord Tedder. The lettered tablets which run beneath the east window of the Battle of Britain chapel were designed by the surveyor, Donald Buttress, and placed in position in 1989.[50]

---

[50] Until the early 1980s, there was on the north wall of the south aisle, adjacent to the monument to Lady Margaret Beaufort, a bronze roundel with a relief portrait of Sir Thomas Lovel by Torrigiano. This was formerly above the gateway of East Harling Manor in Norfolk and in 1903 was presented to the Dean and Chapter by Sir Charles Robinson. As it was not a memorial, as such, it has been removed to the Abbey's museum.

Henry VII Chapel: the Royal Connection

THOMAS COCKE

I have left the Repository of our English kings for the Contemplation of another Day, when I shall find my mind disposed for so serious an Amusement. (Addison)[1]

THE OTHER articles in this volume cover every major aspect of the fabric and furnishings of the Henry VII chapel. So much survives of the original design that even the relatively few losses can be reconstructed. This paper will argue that such survival is not merely a matter of good fortune but has been powerfully assisted by the use of the chapel for the first three centuries of its existence as a royal mausoleum and, from 1725, as the spiritual home of the revived Order of the Bath. These noble connections have proved of enduring benefit.

I will not be describing the later restorations of the chapel, a task that has been accomplished elsewhere.[2] Neither will I discuss the design of the great tombs, first the royal monuments of the Tudors and early Stuarts and then, from the duke of Buckingham onwards, those to the aristocracy; instead I will consider the effect they and their associated burial vaults had both on the fabric itself and on people's attitude to the chapel as a whole. Similarly the renaissance high altar, spared at the Reformation, only to fall victim to the civil wars, and the marble lozenge floor of 1699 given by Henry Killigrew, will only be mentioned as they have been affected by royal burials.

The focus of this paper is on functions of the chapel which were addressed with attention in the eighteenth and nineteenth centuries but which are often ignored today, its uses as a royal mausoleum and, after 1725, as the seat of the Order of the Bath. Standards of respect alter. Prints of the late Stuart and then of the Hanoverian royal vault, showing the location of each coffin, were put on public sale whenever a royal death provided a market, something which would now be thought ghoulish and over-commercial.[3] Today, while we pry into living royalty relentlessly, we shun them dead.

---

[1] *Spectator* no. 26, published 30 March 1711: *The Spectator*, ed. D.F. Bond, Oxford 1965, 111.
[2] See below, 327–55.
[3] A startling example of this candour is the publication in *Philosophical Transactions* 52, 1761–2, of two engravings of George II's heart in an article written soon after the king's death by his physician, Frank Nicholas. I owe this reference to Palmira Fontes da Costa, 'In quest of monsters', *Darwin College Magazine* 12, 1997, 75–6.

Fig. 42. Entrance to the tomb of Henry VII, 1869, from a drawing by George Scharf. (Stanley, *Historical Memorials*, frontispiece)

For three hundred years the Henry VII chapel was the usual burial place of English monarchs and their families. In a society which remained, despite the civil wars, firmly monarchical, this gave a unique aura to the building, an aura strong enough to endure even changes of dynasty and changes in religious practice.

The standard account has been that the chapel was built by Henry VII as a 'lasting Honour to himself and his Descendants whose Burying place (exclusive of all others) he intended it should be'.[4] It has been questioned, however, whether Henry VII intended his chapel to become a dynastic mausoleum. The slight misalignment between the vault below and Henry's tomb above, noted by Dean Stanley when he inspected the vault in 1869, might suggest a change of plan but the careful construction in ragstone, again noted by Stanley, indicates that the vault was not inserted but was intended from the first foundation (Fig. 42).[5] The burial in the south aisle of the chapel, only two months after Henry's death, of his mother, Lady Margaret Beaufort, shows that Henry himself or those near him expected the chapel to contain the remains of other members of the royal family. It can also be argued that raising the body of the chapel so high over what is virtually a basement storey suggests that the substructure was planned for more funerary vaults than only that for the founder and his wife.[6]

The later choice by Henry VIII to revert to Windsor, burial place of his Yorkist grandfather, can be explained on grounds of expediency, whatever it might also say about his attitude to his father. The kind of tomb envisaged when he commissioned a design from Torrigiano in the early years of his reign would have been suitable in scale for a place at Westminster. Once Henry had commandeered the disgraced Cardinal Wolsey's vast tomb project, Westminster simply did not have room for the whole composition to be set up there, whereas the tomb house at Windsor offered ample space.[7] The various elements prepared by Benedetto da Rovezzano and his successors remained at Westminster, where presumably they were made, until the 1560s.[8] It is surely significant that in the tense political and religious circumstances surrounding the burial of Edward VI, it was decided to revert to Westminster and to place his remains literally at the feet of Henry VII's tomb in a shallow vault extending west from the entrance to the earlier vault.[9] The dynastic link must have outweighed the irony of laying the protestant prince under Torrigiano's rich altar canopy.[10]

James VI and I made every effort to establish the Stuart dynasty physically at Westminster, not only by building the showpiece tombs to Elizabeth I and Mary, Queen of Scots, but also adding the much smaller but evocative memorials to his infant daughters, the princesses Mary and Sophia. Although no permanent monument was erected to any of the Stuart kings or queens, the only break in the series of their burials at Westminster was when the victorious Parliament ordered that the body of Charles I be laid at Windsor.[11] Yet that decision did not mean rejection of the Abbey by the

---

[4] Neale and Brayley i, 18 (section on Henry VII chapel).
[5] Stanley, *Historical Memorials*, 524.
[6] Other factors presumably influenced this element of the design, in particular the preceding early thirteenth-century Lady chapel.
[7] *Cardinal Wolsey: Church, State and Art*, ed. S.J. Gunn and P. Lindley, 1991, 270, 279.
[8] Colvin, *HkW* iii, 320–1.
[9] Stanley, *Historical Memorials*, 514–17, 520.
[10] Similar tensions as to the ceremonial and liturgical arrangements delayed Edward VI's funeral.
[11] Designs exist for tombs to Mary II and, jointly, to Mary II and William III, which appear to have been intended to stand approximately over the later Royal Stuart vault at the east end of the south aisle, but they remained on paper. The only royal memorial actually erected by the later Stuarts was the tablet to the princes in the Tower, placed in 1678 by order of Charles II at the east end of the north aisle. It is noteworthy both that the princes' tablet (and their remains) were laid at Westminster, not with their father Edward IV at Windsor, and that they were sited by the little princesses' tombs, suggesting a thematic grouping of the memorials in the chapel. *Wren Society* 5, ed. A.T. Bolton and H.D. Hendry, Oxford 1928, 13.

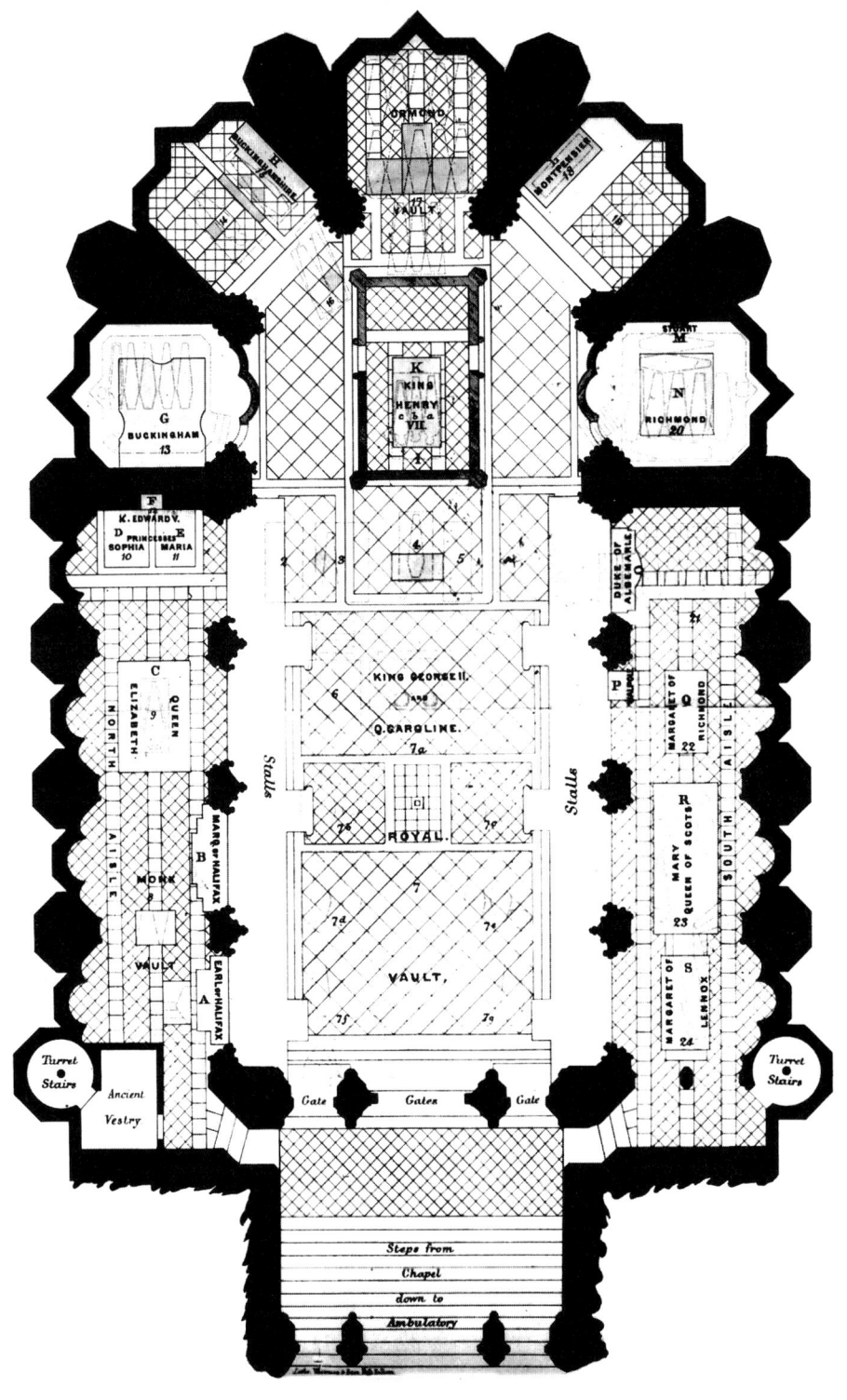

Fig. 43. Plan showing burial vaults, by Hubert Poole, c.1870. (Dean and Chapter of Westminster)

Parliamentary regime. In the 1650s the church was turned into a kind of English Valhalla by the interment there of state heroes such as Pym. The Abbey was also employed to cast some air of dynastic sanction to the rule of Oliver Cromwell by the burial of his relations in the Henry VII chapel, culminating in that of the Protector himself at the east end. The place of Cromwell's burial, like the royal splendour of his lying-in-state at Whitehall, was intended to mark him as the successor of kings.

The peaceful transition from Stuart to Hanoverian did not alter the status of the Henry VII chapel as the royal mausoleum. Indeed, as I will demonstrate, the change of dynasty enhanced the role not just of the chapel but of Westminster Abbey as a whole in national life. George I was buried in his native Hanover but in 1737 his son constructed the largest and most sophisticated vault yet created in the Abbey for himself and his family (Fig. 43).[12] George III continued this tradition for the major part of his reign.

It is important to distinguish between the emotional impact produced by the function of the chapel as a cemetery and the artistic interest created by the presence of monuments. Curious as it may seem today, I suspect that in the seventeenth and eighteenth centuries people were more inspired by the general idea of the 'royal dust' under their feet than by seeing a complete set of memorials. Even at a coronation the congregation could be urged to 'think how much Royal dust and ashes is [sic] laid up in yonder chapel'.[13] The message of *memento mori* thus stimulated could be given both to the sovereign who mounted his throne 'o'er Pavements where his predecessors lay' and to the tourist who should turn his mind 'from the loud Living to the silent dead'.[14] The tombs to Elizabeth and Mary, queen of Scots, acquired special significance for their respective religious parties but this was the exception, not the rule.[15] A visitor to the chapel would presumably be supplied with sufficient information from the stories told by their guide or from their own knowledge concerning the famous figures buried beneath their feet, not to need a monument to each one. The display of the royal funeral effigies may also have supplied the roles of tomb and epitaph. In the eighteenth century the exceptionally lifelike wax effigy of Charles II stood in the south aisle of the chapel, approximately over his coffin.[16]

It is not only in Great Britain but also in the great monarchies of the Continent, that we find few monumental tombs to reigning sovereigns after the sixteenth century. Instead they created royal vaults such as that of the Hapsburgs in the Capuchin church in Vienna where the lead sarcophagi of the Imperial family were laid out in orderly fashion for family devotions. George II's vault, with its convenient staircase for access, large marble sarcophagus for himself and his much-loved wife and generous compartments for future burials, was not dissimilar.

The stimulus to erect tombs and to exploit them for propaganda seems generally to have been a change in the ruling family. It was surely the insecurity of Henry VII on the throne that led to such a grandiloquent statement of royal status in his tomb. The

---

[12] There is some evidence that vaults intended for royal burials were excavated in the north-eastern part of the chapel c.1728 since the Stuart vaults were known to be full, but these continued the small scale and haphazard arrangement of the past. Stanley, *Historical Memorials*, 505.
[13] Stanley, *Historical Memorials*, 525 n. 2. Sermon by Bishop Turner at the Coronation of James II.
[14] Dart, xi.
[15] Stanley, *Historical Memorials*, 155.
[16] *The Funeral Effigies of Westminster Abbey*, ed. A. Harvey and R. Mortimer, Woodbridge 1994, 80–4.

way in which the plan of the Henry VII chapel, with a central tomb and chapels opening off an ambulatory, reflects that of the Abbey itself, has been noted by several commentators. If the plan to create a shrine for a canonized Henry VI had been successful, the mingling of dynastic and religious piety would have been yet more potent. After the arrival of the next dynasty, a century later, James I was evidently determined to have his remains placed in the same vault as the founder of the chapel, since it took great effort to achieve this.[17] James perhaps felt that, by sharing the vault with the first of the Tudors, the first of the English Stuarts would be more acceptable. It is also noteworthy that, just as the tomb of Lady Margaret Beaufort, erected soon after the death of Henry VII, was a precedent hardly followed in succeeding Tudor reigns, so the tombs of Elizabeth I, of Mary, queen of Scots, and of the infant princesses were all erected in the first decade of James's reign. Once a dynasty felt secure, it felt less incentive to spend money on erecting expensive pieces of sculpture.

The Hanoverians behaved in a similar way, making deliberate and careful use of Westminster Abbey in general and the Henry VII chapel in particular. A comprehensive restoration of the structure had been under way since 1699, in part financed by public funds on the grounds that it was 'the place of the Coronation and of the Sepultures of many of the nobility and gentry'.[18] By the time of Anne's death in 1714, the work on the eastern arm and the south side had been completed and the altarpiece from James II's Roman Catholic chapel at Whitehall had been installed in the sanctuary but much remained to be undertaken, especially on the north and west fronts. Periodic financial crises arose, as in 1717 and 1724, when Parliament proved reluctant to vote further funds, but they were overcome and the restoration continued to its successful completion in 1745.[19]

It should not be surprising that the Abbey was given such prominence during the reigns of George I and George II. J.C.D. Clark has demonstrated that this period, far from witnessing a collapse of traditional ideas concerning throne and altar, saw a successful re-statement of them in terms which could accommodate the new Newtonian thinking.[20] Rationality in science was allied to Anglican rationality in religion and Hanoverian rationality in politics. To understand this aspect of the eighteenth-century monarchy, it is necessary to discount those memorable contemporary sources, Lord Hervey and Horace Walpole. Their feline malice against their royal masters has coloured all subsequent historiography. Horace Walpole's description of the funeral of George II in November 1760, the last burial of a reigning monarch at Westminster, is so vivid and so tempting to quote that its bias is usually forgotten. He begins:

> Do you know I had the curiosity to go to the burying t'other night; I had never seen a royal funeral. Nay, I walked as a rag of quality, which I found would be, and so it was, the easiest way of seeing it.[21]

[17] Dean Stanley discovered by painstaking investigations that James's body was not buried next to his wife in a vault to the north of Henry VII's tomb, though ample space remained, but was placed next to Henry VII and Elizabeth of York: *Historical Memorials*, 522–5.
[18] WAM 34807; draft of a petition to Parliament of c.1740.
[19] Cocke, *900 Years*, 45–54.
[20] J.C.D. Clark, *English Society 1688–1832*, Cambridge 1985, 175–7; J. Gascoigne, *Cambridge in the Age of the Enlightenment*, Cambridge 1989, 147.
[21] Horace Walpole, *Correspondence*, ed. W.S. Lewis and R.S. Brown, Yale 1941, ix, 321.

Our lips smile in sympathy with Walpole at his condescension and we understand how as fellow-sophisticates we should view the event as theatre without going any deeper below the surface. Yet even Walpole admitted that it was 'absolutely a noble sight', consciously arousing the image of past centuries of royal and religious ceremonies.

The royal family, contrary to the standard image of the early Georges, was closely involved in the process. When John Dart published his definitive survey of the Abbey in 1723, he dedicated the two elaborately illustrated volumes to the heir apparent, George, Prince of Wales, the future George II. Dart commented:

> As no church can boast sepulture of so many great Personages as St Peter's, Westminster; so the greatest among these are Your Royal ancestors. To You then, Great Sir, we may justly address the following History of this Religious Structure. Hither You are led to contemplate the Actions of those glorious British Heroes, to whose Lasting Honour most of these Monuments were erected and whose Virtues You both Emulate and Inherit.[22]

There rapidly followed the revival in 1725 of the Order of the Bath and the decision to give it a permanent home in the Henry VII chapel, with the Dean of Westminster as its presiding cleric. This initiative has usually been discussed in utilitarian terms, as a cynical device by Robert Walpole to increase the amount of patronage available to the Crown.[23] However, the careful way in which it exploited mediaeval pageantry and mediaeval architecture points to a more subtle understanding of the situation by both monarch and minister.

The celebrated herald, John Anstis, admitted in 1731 that he had drawn up the statutes of the Order 'with much hurry', using those of the Garter as a model.[24] Even so, he retained an uncompromisingly traditional model for the vigil and the profession of a knight, including the ceremonial bath itself. In practice, the Great (*sic*) Master granted a dispensation for most of the archaic detail but the solemn procession through the Abbey and the elaborate administration of the knightly oath in the chapel were highly visible tokens of continuity with the past. The extension of the stalls in the 1730s, discussed above by Charles Tracy, re-using canopies and recreating misericords, was a complex and expensive operation, not an exercise in economy or vandalism. The choice as principal Knight of the Order of the young Prince William (the future duke of Cumberland) and the prominent part he played in the first Installation, despite his tender age, show the intense importance attached to the Order by the reigning house. While George I kept his elder grandson Frederick, later Prince of Wales, firmly in Hanover, William was the first surviving prince of the new dynasty to be both English-born and English-bred.

Altogether eleven Installations were held between the refoundation of the Order and its major revision and enlargement in 1815, which weakened the links between the Order and the Henry VII chapel for a century. The ceremonies were conducted with great splendour. They began with a procession from the Prince's Chamber in the

---

[22] Dart, dedication.
[23] Horace Walpole, *Reminiscences*, ed. P. Toynbee, Oxford 1924, 46–7.
[24] N.H. Nicolas, *History of the Orders of Knighthood of the British Empire*, iii, 1842, 237–8, n. 7.

Fig. 44. Installation of Knights of the Bath, 1812. (Stanley, *Historical Memorials*, 83)

Palace of Westminster (a signal mark of royal favour since this was the room retained for royal ceremonial use when Parliament had absorbed the rest of the building) around the exterior of the Abbey[25] and then up the nave, around the ambulatory and into the chapel. The Installation of the newly created knights was followed by Divine Service with prayers and anthems and the day was concluded by a solemn banquet. Surviving illustrations of the installations of 1725 and of 1812 show that these occasions rivalled coronations in the rich clothing and their elaborate ceremonial and also in their very public nature (Fig. 44). The man in the street could admire the processions to and from the Abbey and those who could procure a ticket could witness the ceremony from elaborate boxes constructed for the occasion, again like the coronation, even over the tomb of Henry VII. Although the sovereign was absent, the installations were presided over by the Great Master, who was, except for the second duke of Montagu, a royal prince, and were attended by the queen and other members of the royal family.[26] This deliberate use of archaic ceremonial and of well advertised royal favour helped to rid the Order of the Bath of its initial taint of party favouritism and to raise it and the chapel which formed its focus into major icons of the new British Empire.

Royal interest in Westminster Abbey did not diminish with the accession of George II and his queen, Caroline. Their joint coronation in October 1727, the first complete ceremony with a queen consort since that of James I and Anne of Denmark, was notable for its splendour.[27] In honour of the occasion, Handel composed anthems which have become so familiar as part of the coronation ceremonial that their wholehearted royalism can be forgotten, especially as it conflicts with the usual interpretation of the Hanoverians as German nonentities. A celebratory ode by a Westminster scholar linked the new king both with the mediaeval fabric of Westminster and the protestant succession: 'That sacred roof which rose of old so high/ And stood the Wonder of the Gazers' Eye,/ That which for numberless successors spread/ Its proud Pavilion o'er th'anointed Head . . . thus pays, O George in an auspicious Hour/ The Church her Homage to thy Regal Power/ And none shall Now of Rome's Pretension dream/ St Peter's Self confesses Thee Supreme/ With Edward's Ensigns while St George is decked/ Your unfaded Majesty they still reflect.'[28]

Less than ten years later the west front of the Abbey was recast under Nicholas Hawksmoor who refaced the perpendicular fabric in Portland stone and completed the towers to a new design. The iconography of the shields on the exterior of the west front and of the stained glass in the great west window gave prominent stress to the royal role at the Abbey, an emphasis confirmed by the name of George II inscribed in large letters over the west window. As the visitor entered the newly refurbished west door, he or she would see at the further end of the nave a mediaevalizing screen, further evidence of royal munificence.[29] On the occasion of his coronation, George II

---

[25] At least until 1761 when the procession was shortened to enter through Poets' Corner.
[26] Princess Charlotte of Wales made her first State appearance at the 1812 Installation: J. Perkins, *The Most Honourable Order of the Bath: a Description and Historical Account*, 2nd edn, 1920, 104.
[27] The coronation of James II and Mary of Modena in 1685 had to be curtailed because of the monarchs' Roman Catholic allegiance.
[28] Anon., *Verses at Westminster School*, 1761, 8.
[29] Cocke, *900 Years*, 48.

gave a new organ which entailed re-designing the entry into the choir from an opening flanked by piers to an arch to carry the instrument.[30] In the key spaces to north and south of the archway to the nave, commemorative tombs were erected to Sir Isaac Newton, the great thinker, and Earl Stanhope, the prominent statesman. They function as reformed equivalents to the traditional altars which traditionally flanked the rood screen door and as modern exemplars of the contemplative and the active life.

The culminating evidence of George II's commitment to the Abbey was his commissioning of a new royal vault under the Henry VII chapel. Whereas the Stuarts had allowed their funerary vaults to be created in an informal and even chaotic manner, the new mausoleum was built in a much more careful way.[31] The documents appear to indicate that both the vault and the royal sarcophagus were conceived and built in the three weeks or so between the death of Queen Caroline on 20 November 1737 and her funeral the next month: the Board of Works minute of 23 November 1737 ordered that the new vault was to be made 'out of hand' and Flitcroft had to provide the plan by the next morning.[32] Yet the vault is a sizable construction of three square bays with equal 'aisles' to north and south, a larger bay at the east end and an entry stair and vestibule at the west. Not only would it take some time to build, but there must have been some careful preparatory work to establish the practicability of such a major excavation under the delicately poised vault of the chapel and to protect the stalls and re-lay the marble pavement.[33] Certainly the master sculptor, James Richards, was given only a fortnight to carve 'in statuary marble the Crowns, Palm branches and Sceptres' for the sarcophagus.[34] Perhaps there had already been discussions as to the desirability of a new royal vault when the chapel was being altered by the extension of the stalls earlier in the decade.

The plan of the vault was by Henry Flitcroft but the style is that of William Kent. According to one of the few people in the twentieth century to view the vault, it resembles that of the arcade through the Horseguards in Whitehall, a few hundred yards to the north, designed by Kent though erected after his death.[35] Kent was closely involved with the king and queen throughout the ten years of their joint reign. He had designed the bold triumphal arch in Westminster Hall at their coronation; as a painter, he had created for Queen Caroline small-scale mediaevalizing paintings from the life of Henry V and as an architect he had built for her both an elegant classical library at St James's Palace and a rustic philosopher's hermitage at Kew. Kent was present at all the meetings of the Board of Works during the weeks between the

---

[30] *Ibid.*, 127–8.

[31] The opening of the late Stuart vault in 1977 confirmed that the coffins were tightly spaced within the vault, with no provision for access around them.

[32] PRO, Works 4/7. Minute of Meeting of Board of Works on 23 November 1737.

[33] Perkins noted that the variation in the pattern of the central part of the marble pavement of 1699 was presumably caused by its removal to create the vault: *Worship and Ornaments* ii, 186. The provision of a permanent stair into the vault obviated the need to take up the floor again at any but the grandest funerals.

[34] PRO, Works 4/7: Minute of Meeting of Board of Works on 1 December 1737.

[35] L.E. Tanner, *Recollections of a Westminster Antiquary*, 1969, 178: Tanner also described the 'immense and rather fine black marble sarcophagus and bronze handles rather like a mediaeval cope chest' and the 'magnificent' and well-preserved coffins of the other burials in the vault.

queen's death and her funeral so he may well have played a part in the design, not only of the architecture of the vault but of the great sarcophagus in black and yellow marble, 7ft long and 4ft 4in. wide, which was erected to contain the remains of the royal pair.[36] The master mason, Andrew Jelfe, who was responsible for making the tomb, worked with Kent both at Houghton and Holkham.

The closeness of the royal connection with the Abbey at this date is confirmed in less edifying fashion by the row which developed after the funeral when the Lord Chancellor tried to claim that the chapel belonged to the Crown, not to the Dean and Chapter. The latter had to defend themselves using both the major argument of Elizabeth's charter of 1560 which transferred all the site and appurtenances of the former monastery to the new foundation and such minor points as the willingness of kings to pay burial fees to the Chapter.[37] Sensitivity on the subject was still apparent at the funeral of Frederick, Prince of Wales, in 1751, when officers of the Office of Works were told by the Dean that 'they had no business there'.[38]

It was therefore no blind compliment when George II was hailed in a eulogy after his death as another Edward the Confessor in devotion.[39] His perception of the central position of the Abbey in national life determined him to create a physical commemoration of his dynasty there. Not until the Stuart pretenders were virtually extinct did the royal family decide against Westminster as a fitting princely mausoleum and retreat to Windsor; it was only then, too, that the chapel received a comprehensive restoration as a national monument. Yet its role as spiritual home to the Order of the Bath (a role revived in 1913) ensures that royal involvement is no historical footnote but continues five hundred years after Henry VII's foundation.

---

[36] PRO, Works 4/7: Minute of Meeting of Board of Works of 29 November 1737; Stanley, *Historical Memorials*, 167, recorded that in 1871 the adjoining sides of the coffin were seen to have indeed been removed at the king's burial so that the royal couple would rest together.
[37] Neale and Brayley, 18.
[38] PRO, Works 21–5/2.
[39] T. Smollett, *History of England*, v, 1800, 372.

The Earlier Restorations

TIM TATTON-BROWN and RICHARD MORTIMER

HENRY VII and his masons bequeathed to posterity a work of striking and soon famous beauty, but executed with great elaboration in soft stone. Exposed to smoke from the houses around it, and eventually to the high levels of pollution to be found in central London, its subsequent history has been a more or less constant battle against deterioration.

The condition of the fabric was already poor in the mid-seventeenth century.[1] Sir Christopher Wren commented on the poor quality of the stonework, particularly the Reigate stone: he called the chapel a 'nice embroidered work perfected in tender Caen stone'.[2] Some minor works like the removal of the external statues, had to be carried out 'lest they should fall upon the heads of those who attend Parliament'.[3] We also hear that in 1739 'the lower windows at the east end, which are so near the ground that they are always broken', were to be filled up with stone.[4]

The early nineteenth-century restoration (TT-B)

By the end of the eighteenth century, much of the external stonework of Henry VII's chapel was in very poor condition indeed. Unlike the rest of the Abbey, which had been much restored in the first half of the eighteenth century with moneys granted by Parliament, no repair work had yet taken place on the Henry VII chapel. Estimates for the restoration work here had been made by both Wren and Hawksmoor, as part of the overall costings, but no major works had yet been done.[5]

Then in 1793, when James Wyatt was surveyor (he was given this post, aged only thirty, long before in 1776), work was put in hand to repair the high roof, and do some trial restoration work above the high east window.[6] The king-post roof, which still exists above the high vaults, must be a completely new roof put in in 1793. Two years

---

[1] For a survey of the defects in the chapel c.1650 see WAM 24854.
[2] C. Wren, *Parentalia*, 1750, 295–302.
[3] Dart ii, 49.
[4] WAM 54517, fo. 27.
[5] Cocke, *900 Years*, 57.
[6] WAM 24880–2. The new roof is shown in S. Ware's 1810 section of the chapel: see Cocke, *900 Years*, 143.

after this, a chapter order of 19 January 1796 tells Wyatt 'to survey King Henry VII's Chapel . . . and make an estimate of the repairs necessary to be done thereto'.[7] Unfortunately just after this James Wyatt, the king's 'favourite architect', was appointed Surveyor General and Comptroller of the King's Works,[8] and as a result Wyatt had many more important things to do. From this time also, Wyatt had far too many other projects to deal with, and his work for the Abbey inevitably suffered.[9] The chapter persisted, however, and five years later, on 4 March 1802, he was again 'ordered to survey the fabrick and report such repairs as if neglected will prove detrimental'. On 15 March 1803, he gave the chapter a first estimate 'for repairing each window of King Henry VII's Chapel'. Two months later a revised estimate for the repair of the windows was given, and he told the chapter 'that two turrets of King Henry VII's Chapel in a decayed state [should] be taken down as far as necessary and capped'.[10] These were the high western stair-turrets flanking the great west window, which were covered in timber and lead. They were taken down, but the work was interrupted by a serious fire in the lantern of the Abbey on 9 July 1803, which meant that all further work was curtailed. The cost of repairing the lantern, and putting in a new plaster vault,[11] was £3,848 and this effectively used up all the money in the 'Fabric Fund' set aside for the repairs to the Henry VII chapel as Wyatt himself later told the Parliamentary 'Committee of Taste'.[12]

Just before this, in December 1802, the chapter appointed Thomas Gayfere master mason to the Abbey, jointly with his father (of the same name, master mason at the Abbey since 1766, and now over eighty years of age; he died in 1812).[13] The younger Gayfere was also a skilled artist, and he was to be the key figure throughout the restoration of the Henry VII chapel, and retired in 1823 after its completion.[14] When the western turrets were taken down in 1803 John Britton (writing in 1808) recorded that

> Mr Gayfere, the mason, made accurate measurements and sketches of them before they were displaced. And if the restoration of the whole building be determined on by Committee of the Taste; it will be an easy task to have these re-erected.[15]

The accurate recording of the masonry of the chapel and of its architectural decoration, both before and during the restoration, was a very unusual feature of the work, and we are exceptionally lucky in having a published series of engraved drawings of the Henry VII chapel in 1808 and 1822.[16]

---

[7] WAM Chapter Minute, of that date.
[8] J. Mordaunt Crook, 'The surveyorship of James Wyatt, 1796–1813,' in *HKW* vi, 47–75.
[9] In 1796 he also started to build William Beckford his immense new house at Fonthill Abbey in Wiltshire. For Wyatt's career see H. Colvin, *A Biographical Dictionary of British Architects, 1660–1840*, 1995, 1107–21.
[10] WAM Chapter Minute, 21 May 1803.
[11] WAM 66093–4. The vault made of 'stucco on lath coloured and jointed to imitate stone', was designed by Wyatt and made by Francis Bernasconi.
[12] Cottingham i, 7.
[13] Colvin, *Biographical Dictionary*, 395–6.
[14] *Ibid*. Gayfere later reconstructed the north front of Westminster Hall (in 1819–22), using Bath stone. He died on 20 October 1827, aged seventy-two.
[15] Britton ii, 49.
[16] The 1808 measured drawings are by F. Mackenzie, J.R. Thompson, J.C. Smith and others for John

The work on repairing the lantern tower, and in putting in the elaborate new plaster vault above the crossing of the Abbey was finished by 16 March 1805, and Wyatt reported to the chapter that the new work was 'agreeable to his directions'.[17] The funds were now almost exhausted, but this did not stop Wyatt's reporting on 17 April 1806,[18] that the 'screen or stonework in front of the two little chapels at the east end of Henry VII's chapel is much decayed'. He therefore 'recommended the removal of the same and that an iron railing be put in its place'. This was, alas, duly carried out and now only the plinths of the magnificent curved screens survive.[19]

A new era was now dawning for both the country and for the restoration of the Henry VII chapel. William Pitt died on 23 January 1806, just a fortnight after Lord Nelson's magnificent funeral in St Paul's Cathedral, and it was the new Prime Minister, Lord Grenville and his 'Ministry of All the Talents' who were to start the process of providing large new sums of state money for the complete restoration of the chapel over the next fifteen years. The important point of contact here was the Dean, William Vincent (1739–1815), who had previously been headmaster of Westminster School (1788–1802). Between 1697 and 1743 about £100,000 had been voted by Parliament for 'repairing and finishing' the Abbey, and all this work was complete by March 1745, when a final account was laid before Parliament.[20] However, as this had not included the restoration of the Henry VII chapel, it was felt reasonable to make an application to Parliament for this work for a second time.

At the same time, it should be noted that the earlier restoration of the Abbey culminated in the clearance of all the houses on the north side of the nave, and the opening up and improving of the St Margaret's churchyard and Broad Sanctuary areas by the 1740s.[21] Now all the houses around St Margaret's church itself were being demolished, and the external walls of the church were being repaired, opening up and exposing the north side of the Henry VII chapel.[22] All this work came under the Westminster Improvements Commission and the very large sum of £228,497 had been spent on this work by 1810. It had created a new 'Garden Square' (now Parliament Square) to the north of St Margaret's church,[23] and a new open setting for Westminster Hall. Just behind this, and directly opposite the east end of the Henry VII chapel James Wyatt was erecting his new façade to the House of Lords, which was now in the old Court of Requests. Between 1800 and 1812 Parliamentary grants for the reconstruction of the Houses of Parliament totalled £180,229 12s 4d, and as

Britton. The much more detailed series of drawings was made by L.N. Cottingham and published in 1822 and 1829.
[17] Chapter Minute, 24 May 1805.
[18] *Ibid.*, 5 June 1806.
[19] These screens are well shown in earlier eighteenth-century interior views of the chapel, like Dart.
[20] WAM 34915. See also Cocke, *900 Years*, 50. At the end of this work, in the 1730s, Parliament was giving £4,000 a year in grant aid, see Cottingham, 8.
[21] Parliament had, in fact, discontinued the Abbey's repair grant in 1735 until the houses against the nave were pulled down, because of their 'annoying with smoke, disfiguring and endangering by fire the said church'. See H.F. Westlake, *St Margaret's, Westminster*, 1914, 23. For a view of the north side of the nave before the removal of the houses see Cocke, *900 Years*, 134.
[22] All the houses here had gone by 1808.
[23] See Colvin, *HKW* vi, 515–16.

Professor Crook has pointed out, Wyatt was receiving 5 per cent commission on all of this.[24]

This then is the background to the Dean and Chapter's first approach, via the Dean, Dr Vincent, in October 1806 to the lords of the Treasury. It was

> accompanied by a letter requesting permission to state to them different proposals which had been made for its repair as also to give in an estimate of expense, in order to procure their recommendation of the matter to Parliament

to quote Cottingham's detailed account of the negotiations between the Abbey and Parliament.[25] This was agreed to, and the matter was referred by the lords of the Treasury on 5 December 1806, to the Committee for the inspection of Models for National Monuments, etc. This body of grandees, connoisseurs and some artists was set up by the Treasury in 1802, with the responsibility for the allocation of public money, choice of artists, designs, and other matters. It was popularly known as the 'Committee of Taste', and among other things was allocating large sums of money to great national monuments for war heroes.[26] This body, chaired by the Rt Hon. Sir Charles Long, then became the intermediary with the Abbey, and its letters and minutes are quoted extensively in the introduction to Cottingham's book.[27]

In June 1807 a petition was prepared and presented to the House of Commons, and the Chancellor of the Exchequer told them that the king had seen the petition and 'recommended the same to the consideration of the house'. This petition asked for a grant of £1,000 per annum and an extra £1,000 in the first year for 'immediate exigencies'. The Dean and Chapter also asked

> to be placed under the directions of the Lords of the Treasury, and hoped to receive their instructions from the same authority; and they would be ready annually, or whenever required, to deliver in an account of their proceedings and expenditure.[28]

James Wyatt and the chapter clerk, George Vincent, were then examined and, as already shown, they told the committee of the Dean and Chapter's lack of funds because of the fire of 1803. Wyatt estimated that about £14,000 would be needed for the repair of the masonry of the chapel and £10,400 more for the ornamental work, and that the work 'might be completed in about three years'. The report was ordered 'to lie on the table and to be printed' and the House agreed to grant up to £2,000 towards the initiation of the work.

A detailed series of questions about the masonry and stone types were then put by the Dean and members of the Chapter to Thomas Gayfere, and his answers are recorded fully in Cottingham.[29] There is much discussion about the possible stone types for the repairs, and the extent of the repairs required, and on 3 February 1808

---

[24] *Ibid.*, 518.
[25] Cottingham, 6.
[26] For example £6,300 for Lord Nelson's monument in St Paul's Cathedral: see M. Whinney, *Sculpture in Britain, 1530–1830*, 1st edn, 1964, 199.
[27] Cottingham, 6–24. He gives a full list of the committee members, which included the artists Flaxman and Westmacott.
[28] Cottingham, 7, and Chapter Minute, 6 June 1807.
[29] Cottingham, 8–9.

the Committee of Taste were invited to a meeting by the Dean at his house, with Wyatt and Gayfere in attendance. The Committee felt that Bath stone should be used for all the repairs (except that Hopton Wood stone should be used for the, window-sills), and then sent Gayfere to Bath to inspect and price the stone (and work out the method of transportation). He was also sent to St Alban's Abbey and Woburn Abbey 'to form a judgement as to the nature and durability of the Totternhoe stone used in the buildings'.[30] Gayfere's tour took place between 29 February and 9 March and his most interesting and detailed report is also printed by Cottingham.[31] Bath stone, from the Combe Down quarries, was finally agreed by the Committee, and an immediate order was put in for 150 tons in March 1808, so that work could start in the spring. Unfortunately when the stone was taken down the river Avon from Bath to Bristol no ship could be found to bring it to London, because of the 'demand of transports for the service of government'. When a ship was eventually procured in December 1808, she was wrecked with all her cargo of stone off the Isle of Portland, and it turned out that the ship was not insured. No work was therefore started in 1808, and it was agreed that in future a regular supply of Combe Down stone would be brought to London down the newly opened Kennet and Avon canal and the river Thames.[32]

All this was communicated to Parliament on 23 February 1809, and further discussions took place about the finances, and the methods for doing the repairs. They were also told that 'chiselling of the lower part of the building was done at Gayfere's suggestion, by the order of the Dean, and with the approbation of Mr Wyatt, the surveyor'. Gayfere went on to say that this did not impair the strength of the building, and that 'about half an inch has been taken off from the superfices of the building'. Gayfere proposed to restore the upper part of the fabric

> by scraping off the surface, and adding stones where wanting. That every moulding and ornament was proposed to be restored as if new, and one compartment finished as a specimen of the work. That he thinks the ornamental repair necessary to the durability of the building, as far as the flying buttresses are concerned; and that many of the windows are almost decayed and gone.

There was also discussion about the siting of the masons' workshop, which because it was a 'disagreeable object' had been moved from the north side of the chapel to the 'north-west grass plot'. This, however, meant that 'the expense of the rough materials would be a halfpenny per foot greater, and the expense of labour considerably more'.[33]

When all this was put to a committee of the House of Commons they were not at all happy, and further displeased that it had been sanctioned by the Committee of Taste. They therefore drew up a set of resolutions which were sent to the Dean and Chapter. These were the main points:

---

[30] Cottingham, 10.
[31] Cottingham, 10–12.
[32] The Kennet and Avon canal (from Bath to Reading) was started in 1795, but not finally completed until 1810.
[33] Cottingham, 12.

That it was their opinion, that the south-east buttress, which was represented to be in the most decayed state, should be rebuilt in its original form.

That the window to the south, which was most decayed, should be repaired so as to restore it to a substantial state, but without removing any of the old mullions and transoms which were not in a state of decay, and without working any part of the surface of the old work.

That the south-east turret should be repaired in such a manner, and to such an extent only, as was rendered necessary for its security by its present state of dilapidation; without attempting to restore the ornamental parts, and without reworking any part of the surface.

That the plinth of Kentish stone should be left in its present state, without reworking any part of its surface. That no part of the surface of the old work be reworked or refaced.

And, that the shed or workshop, now erected on the north-west grassplot, should be removed to a more convenient place for carrying on the work.[34]

These resolutions are quoted in full because they are an exceptionally early example of Parliament's trying to insist on the minimum repair necessary, in fact a sort of 'conservation' programme for the chapel. This was, of course, mainly to save money, but they were also being influenced for the first time, after many years of lobbying, by Richard Gough, John Carter, John Milner, Thomas Kerrich, and others at the Society of Antiquaries of London. Between 11 May and 1 June 1809, Kerrich delivered a series of lectures at the Society of Antiquaries, calling for the preservation of 'even the smallest fragment' of Gothic architecture, when great medieval buildings were being restored.[35] This was at exactly the time when Parliament were sending their resolutions to the Dean and Chapter.

Cottingham's account tells us that Dean Vincent, as soon as he received the resolutions, gave the formal order to Mr Gayfere, on 11 May 1809, to proceed with the work as already agreed, and to ignore Parliament's resolutions 'unless stopped by the injunction of the House of Commons'. His justification for this was that these resolutions were 'completely at variance with the former directions' of the Committee of Taste, and that 'he was bound to act in conformity to their wishes'.[36] The work on the restoration of the first turret, that on the south-east (sometimes referred to as the 'White Turret') then began on 15 July 1809, and was finished by 31 March 1810.

On 13 February 1810 the Dean and Chapter submitted a new application to Parliament for a further grant of money towards the next stage of work. Six days later, a Parliamentary committee was held to look at the new application. It started, however, by asking why the resolutions of the previous year had been disobeyed, and Thomas Gayfere, the Dean, chapter clerk and receiver at Westminster Abbey were all thoroughly examined (and cross-examined) by the committee, and asked to justify their actions. The questioning continued for over a month (at committees held on 19 and 26 February and 8, 15 and 22 March 1810), and all aspects of the restoration were discussed.[37] Towards the end of this, Wyatt was called in for examination, and

---

[34] Cottingham, 13.
[35] Quoted in J. Frew, 'The "Destroyer" vindicated? James Wyatt and the restoration of Henry VII chapel, Westminster Abbey', *JBAA* 134, 1981, 100–6.
[36] Cottingham, 13.
[37] The questions and answers are fully given in Cottingham, 14–21.

he was asked very detailed questions about the stability of the building and how the restorations would make the structure more stable. The committee then concluded their work, and issued a report, which laid out in full all the monies donated by Parliament to date (£3,000), and exactly how it had been spent. They reviewed the direction of the work, under the Committee of Taste, and retained oversight from their own committee, and finally agreed a further sum of £1,500 for the next stage of the work.

The upshot of all this was that the Dean and Chapter's view (and those of the Committee of Taste) prevailed, and they were able to carry out a very thorough repair to the outside of the chapel with all the decayed work being replaced in new Combe Down stone. All the turrets and flying buttresses were completely rebuilt, but some small areas of original masonry were left untouched in the main walls. The new work, despite Gayfere's and his masons' skills, was much more mechanically cut, and this too has been very heavily eroded in the highly polluted atmosphere of later nineteenth- and twentieth-century London. It was almost entirely Gayfere's Bath-stone work that had to be restored again in the 1990s.[38] Parliament also, to a certain extent, 'won' by insisting that no 'improvements' whatsoever should take place, and that all the new masonry should, as far as possible, copy the old work. It also kept a close eye on the finances. As a result, the project was almost entirely carried out by Gayfere and his masons, though under James (and after his death, Benjamin) Wyatt's oversight. As with all their other work, the Wyatts signed the annual accounts for Parliament, and took their 5 per cent.[39] By 1810, however, James Wyatt himself was in debt, due to the incompetent management of his own affairs. He was also living a very frenetic life, moving around his very many jobs at Windsor, Westminster, Fonthill, Wilton or Ashridge, and many other places.[40]

On 31 March 1810 work began on rebuilding a second turret, that on the north-east side of the chapel. This work, according to Cottingham, was finished on 13 October, and was followed immediately by the rebuilding of the great east window of the chapel, which work was in turn finished on 26 January 1811. By this time the money was once more running out, and another petition was made to Parliament, on 19 February 1811, for further aid. Once again, detailed accounts were submitted, and it was stressed that they were urgently in need of more stone, as the supply in the yard was nearly used up. They therefore asked permission to order new stone as soon as possible.[41] They were also keen to have money for glazing the east window, which was finished. £1,500 was needed immediately, followed by another £1,500 for the next stage. Parliament duly agreed to grant a sum not exceeding £3,000 'to his majesty towards defraying the expenses of Henry VII Chapel'. The elderly king, George III, was at this period going through one of his phases of madness, and it was exactly at this time, on 6 February 1811, that the Prince of Wales was sworn in as Prince Regent.[42]

[38] See below, 348–9. For early twentieth-century comment on the restoration see Lethaby, *Craftsmen*, 229.
[39] James Wyatt died in 1813, and was replaced as Surveyor of the Abbey by his elder son, Benjamin Dean Wyatt (1775–1855): see Colvin, *Biographical Dictionary*, 1104–5.
[40] Crook, 'Surveyorship of James Wyatt', 50–2.
[41] Cottingham, 22–3. All the Combe Down (Bath) stone would now have come by canal.
[42] C. Hibbert, *George III, a Personal History*, 1998, 398. The money from Parliament for the Henry VII chapel was always officially given to the king because of the Abbey's royal peculiar status.

During this period of negotiation with Parliament, work continued on the lower east window (or 'angular window at the east end' as Cottingham called it), and this was completed by 11 June 1811, when work started on the upper parapets for the first time. Here there was a problem because all the original parapets and upper pinnacles had been removed long before.[43] Wenceslaus Hollar's engraving of the 'North Prospect' of the Abbey (made in 1654) was consulted, and in this tall, crocketed pinnacles are shown with an elaborate parapet in between.[44] The exact details of the parapets could not be made out, so a completely new design was made for them by James Wyatt which was drawn up by his drawing assistant John Dixon.[45] This design is with lozenge-shaped openwork, containing pointed quatrefoils. It cannot have been like the original parapet work, and this new design survives on the chapel.[46] It is perhaps worth quoting in full Wyatt's letter to Gayfere on this, as it is a rare glimpse of James Wyatt's direct involvement in the work:

Dear Sir,
I have just received your letter as to the upper battlement of Henry VII's Chapel which Dixon says you were to have sent to the offices for, and which certainly has been finished ever since the day I saw you last: I have ordered it to be sent you. There can be no doubt that the one drawn out by Dixon is preferable to the other. For though *our forefathers paid but little regard to strict regularity* [thus italicised], yet, whenever that regularity can be obtained without sacrificing effect, it must always be desirable. And in this particular instance, the parapet as drawn out by Dixon must have a good effect. The mouldings of course will be according to those first intended.
I am sir, yours, etc., etc.
Windsor, March 11, 1811   JAMES WYATT[47]

After this, Cottingham goes on, 'other remaining parts were begun and finished with the like dispatch until the year 1821'. No more details are given, but we know that the work was continued westwards, bay by bay, alternating between the north and south sides. A date was marked on the rear face of the turrets (just above the roof), or on the flat top of the lower parapets, and these dates are shown on the roof plan.[48] At the end of 1811 work started on the next turret to the south-east to be followed in 1812 by its opposite number to the north. In 1813 the turret at the south-east corner of the south aisle was started, while in 1814 it was the turret on the north-east corner of the north aisle. Work then continued westwards on all the other turrets, a bay at a time until 1821, when the final work at the west end if the chapel was put in hand. The last stage of the work was the complete rebuilding in stone of the two upper stair-turrets at the west end. These were the turret-tops which were originally of timber and lead, and were dismantled in 1803. This work was completed in 1822 (Fig. 45).

---

[43] See for example Thomas Malton's view of the east end of the chapel in 1796 (Plate IB): there are no traces of the high parapets, or of the parapets above the eastern chapels.
[44] See D. King, *The Cathedrall and Conventuall Churches of England and Wales*, 1672, 18.
[45] For John Dixon see Colvin, *Biographical Dictionary*, 306.
[46] 'The lower parapet designs copy the design on the neighbouring octagonal turrets, while the pinnacles are said to have been copied from fragments of the old ones, found on the spot': see Cottingham, 24.
[47] Cottingham, 24.
[48] As can be seen from the plan, there are some irregularities in the order of the work at the west end.

THE EARLIER RESTORATIONS 335

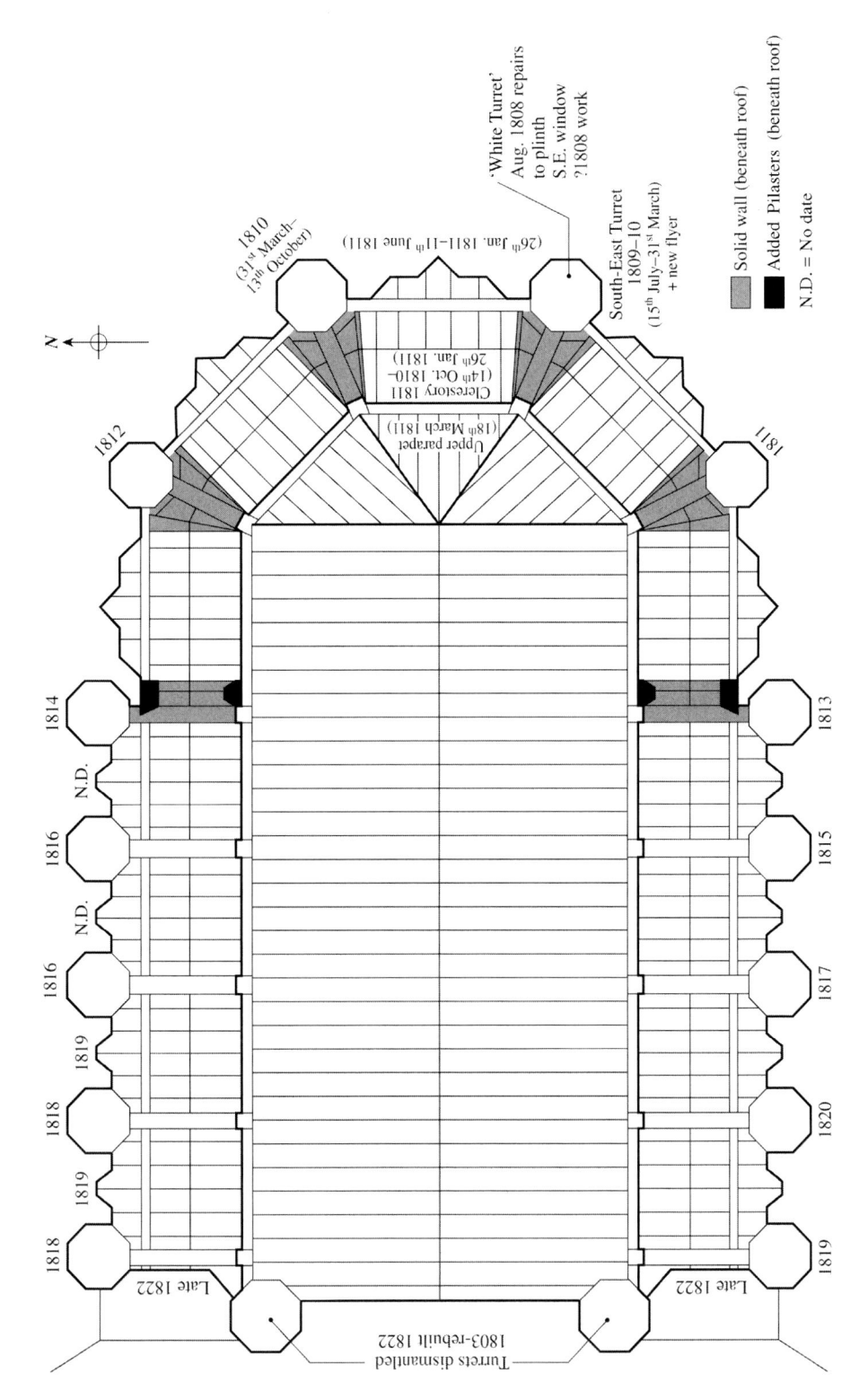

Fig. 45. Plan of the roof showing sequence of repairs.

An abstract of the annual accounts for the work were 'prepared for the Dean and by him were sent to the Treasury', usually in February, and these can be found in the Abbey muniments.[49] The grants made by Parliament each year from 1812 to 1821 are also recorded by Cottingham,[50] and after a grant of £4,700 in 1812, between about £2,500 and £3,500 was granted each year. More detailed Paper Books of bills relating to the repair work can also be found in the Abbey muniments,[51] and it is perhaps worth looking in more detail at the accounts for just one year, 1819. They are given as follows:

Abstract of bills for sundry works at K-H.7. Chapel – under the direction of Mr. Benjamin Wyatt, architect, from 1 Jan to Dec 31 1819

Carpenter – Jeffry Wyatt		£32. 4. 8¾
Mason – Thos. Gayfere		£2,334. 4. 3
Plumber – Jas. Edzard		£49. 14. 8
Painter – Pitt Cobbett		£1. 12. 3½
Glazier – Willm. Miles		£57. 13. 10
Smith – Saml. Tansly		£117. 0. 6
Stationers – Vacher and Davis		16. 0
Clerk of Works – Jeremiah Glanville		£54. 12. 0
Labourer in Trust – Edward Tooth		£81. 18.
Stone Merchant – Bath stone – J. Greenway	£169. 1. 6	
Stone Merchant – Kentish Rag – Jn. Yates	£30. 5. 0	
Freightage from Bath to London – Geo. Yates	£306. 2. 1½	
Delivering at the Wharf by Geo. Buckham	£15. 8. 4	
Cartage to the Abbey by Jeremiah Glanville	£23. 8. 5	
		£544. 5. 4½
		£3,268. 1. 7¾
To Commission on the above bills at 5 per cent		£163. 8. 0¾
		£3,431. 9. 8½

(Signed) Benj. Wyatt

As can be seen, by far the largest sum is for the mason's work, and in the Paper Books full details of this work are recorded. For 1819 there is:

To working upper panelling, frieze, cornice, open parapet, and pinnacle. Hoist and set windows jambs and tracery in head, panelling, frieze, cornice, open parapet and pinacle of last N.W. turrett. Take down scaffold and erect do. to lower circular windows, take down and lower old stone from do. work ashlar base, cap and battlement, muntens, transome, panelling, cornice and open parapet to N.W. circular windows. Hoist and set do. down scaffold, cut out old to S.W. stair tower, cut out for, and assist carpenters shore buttress down, and lower old buttress and stair tower, work Ashlar base, cap and battlement, panelling, cornices, niche, canopies, dome of flying buttress, Hoist and set do. take down scaffold and erect

---

[49] Feb. 1813 – WAM 54156; Feb. 1814 – 54157; Feb. 1815 – 54158; Feb. 1816 – 54159; and 31 Dec. 1819 – 6 Mar. 1821 – 54160. They were signed by the receiver to the Dean and Chapter.
[50] Cottingham, 23–4. He also records that Parliament had given £4,288 by 31 Dec. 1810.
[51] For 1809–10 – WAM 54135; 1811 – 54137; 1812 – 54139; 1813 – 54140; 1814 – 54141; 1815 – 54128; 1816 – 54142; 1817 – 54129; 1818 – 54130; 1819 – 54131; 1820 – 54132; 1821 – 54133; and 1822 – 54134.

to last N.W. turrett. Work ashlar base, cap and battlement and panelling for do. and get in Stow stone.

This shows how the masons cut and carved the Bath stone in the masons' sheds on the north side of the chapel, and how it was then taken up the scaffold and set in place. The 'circular windows' are the wonderful bow windows on the north side of the north aisle. In 1819 two of these windows were being rebuilt, as well as the outer turret on the extreme south-west of the chapel. The 'ashlar base' is the lower plinth and this was made originally, and repaired, in Kentish ragstone.

The numbers of man-days of work in the year by all the masons, labourers and carvers is then given, and we see that the carvers are the most highly paid (at 12s 6d or 9s), followed by the masons (at 5s 9d). The labourers were paid 3s 4d. There are then the lists of (and prices for) the number of bags of fine plaster, of hods of Vauxhall stone lime, hods of common mortar, hods of lime and hairs, and hods of blue mortar. Expenses are also given for files for saws, and various other tools, as well as for coals, wood, resin, white lead, and oil.

After these detailed accounts of the masons' work, we have shorter entries for the other craftsmen. The carpenters are recorded as repairing tools and moulds for the masons, repairing the hoarding on the south side of the chapel, and putting up 'outside shutters'. They also 'shored up' the bottoms of gutters, and worked with the masons and plumbers on repairing the gutters. Finally the carpenters 'sett the centres [i.e. the wood centring] to the flying buttress, and made wedges for the masons on the south side'. This was a very important job, as each of the very elaborate flying buttresses had to be taken down and rebuilt with new masonry.

We also read of six lead ingots, each weighing 5cwt, being delivered to the plumber, James Edzard, for use on the chapel (each ingot cost £87 0s 11d). This was probably mainly used for the aisle roofs. During the re-roofing work in 1993 it was found that the small lead roofs over each window bay had all been re-formed in the early nineteenth century to slope inwards, to an internal gutter and downpipe.

The painters are recorded as painting the bars to the new windows on the north side of the chapel. These are the iron glazing bars in the bow windows made by the smith, and they covered the diamond lattice glazing put in by the glaziers. All the lower (aisle and eastern chapel) windows had external glazing bars, while the clerestory windows had their glazing bars on the inside. All the glazing was renewed at this time, except for the glazing in the tracery work at the tops of the windows, where quite a large amount of the original coloured glazing was allowed to survive. Unfortunately much of this was the destroyed in the Second World War.[52] Cast iron downpipes were also put in for the first time in the early nineteenth century, but these had become very rusted and were completely replaced in 1993–4.

By the end of 1822, all the restoration work on the chapel had been completed after nearly fifteen years continuous work. About £42,000 had been provided by Parliament by this time, and the restoration had been very well done, even if the

---

[52] Much of the glazing in the main lights had been smashed in the Civil War period: see Lethaby, *Re-examined*, 174–83, and R. Marks, 'The glazing of Henry VII's Chapel, Westminster Abbey', in *Reign of Henry VII*, 157–74.

outside of the building did look like a new early nineteenth-century structure. Later in the nineteenth century William Morris was to say that Wyatt had 'managed to take all the romance out of the exterior of this most romantic work of the late middle ages',[53] though this is more than a little harsh, and in Morris's time, the exterior was already very heavily covered in soot and pollution. There is no doubt that the early nineteenth-century restoration protected the interior of the chapel from the extremely polluted atmosphere of later nineteenth- and twentieth-century London.

The hero of the restoration was the Abbey's master mason, Thomas Gayfere, as Cottingham himself pointed out in the preface to his book. Gayfere was

> the gentleman by whose skill, and under whose able superintendence, the whole has been restored in a manner that not only entitled him to the thanks of every person of taste in the country, but will make his name remembered as long as the building itself shall last.[54]

Later restorations, 1822–1994 (RM)

The restoration by Wyatt and Gayfere ensured the physical integrity of the chapel for a certain length of time, but the effect of the ever more polluted London air was inexorable. As early as 1852 Gilbert Scott noted

> Here again the stone is decaying and in some parts its details are obliterated so that in the course of another century it may again be reduced to a mere mouldering mass, while the restorations much more recently executed in Caen stone are already in a state of rapid and miserable decay . . .[55]

Nevertheless nothing was done to the exterior for some time, though heating was installed in the interior by Scott in 1867,[56] and in 1871 he placed the renovated Abbey font at the west end of the chapel and designed a new cover the following year.[57] In 1870 Scott recommend releading the roof, but nothing appears to have been done. In the long run it was the exposed roof structures, the balustrade pinnacles and the caps of the turrets, that decayed first. By 1878 J.L. Pearson was suggesting that 'the decayed parts may be cleaned off and further decay arrested by some external application'.[58] It is not clear if this was followed by action. A similar proposal was made by Pearson's successor as surveyor, Micklethwaite, in 1898: he suggested limewashing the external surfaces, and made an experimental start at the west end. Some of the lower roofs also caused him anxiety: then covered with cement, he

---

[53] Quoted by Lethaby, *Craftsmen*, 228.
[54] Cottingham, ii.
[55] WAM 57797, report of 11 Dec. 1852. I should like to thank Christine Reynolds and Tony Platt for their help with this section.
[56] WAM Chapter Minute, 28 June 1867.
[57] Perkins, *Worship and Ornaments* iii, 41–3, for the history of the font; Chapter Minute, 12 February 1872, 170.
[58] Letter of June 1878, WAM RCO 6.

suggested asphalting them.[59] In 1912 electric lighting was installed by the surveyor, W.R. Lethaby.[60]

The first systematic campaign of repair and conservation since that of Wyatt was begun in 1929 by the then surveyor of the fabric, Walter Tapper, and addressed the perennial problem of decay to the external stonework. On 5 February 1929 he wrote 'something should be done at once to stop the disintegrating effect of the London atmosphere and dirt'.[61] Masonry repair must have started that year and by July 1930 all but four bays had been completed. The exterior was then limewashed, and by 4 February 1932 the job was nearing completion, as Tapper reported to the Dean and Chapter:

> All the sooty deposit on the stone of this last section has been removed down to ground level, and the work of making good the decayed stones, and raking out and repointing the jointing of the old masonry is well advanced. The application of the lime preservative will be proceeded with as soon as weather conditions are suitable for it . . .[62]

Whether he had intended to or not, Tapper soon had to turn his attention to the interior of the chapel. On 29 August 1932 one of the cusps, weighing 10 pounds, fell from the roof in the vicinity of the altar. The chapel was closed immediately, and could not be reopened until repairs were finished. The surveyor estimated that the work would take two and a half years: 'The raking out and refilling of joints of ribs and panels can only be done . . . in small sections at a time for fear of causing movement'.[63] By the time of his next annual report Tapper was able to chronicle good progress:

> Raking out and refilling all the joints from the roof-space above the vaulting has made a very sound and successful work, and has greatly strengthened the vault. All the jointing of the cusps has been renewed and strengthened with copper bands, and the fractures in the spandrils have been stitched with copper, and the fixings of the pendant bosses have been secured. The ends of the tie rods, which were fixed during the surveyorship of Mr Pearson[64] have been rearranged to relieve the masonry of any pressure or vibration. Almost all the works of structural repair of the main vault have been finished, and the cleaning has been commenced.

Work continued apace during the ensuing year, and is summarised by Tapper:

> The work on Henry VII chapel since my last report, has been largely concerned with surface repairs and cleaning of the inside walls. The structural repairs of the main vault have already been reported upon, and following these repairs, the vaulting of the five radiating side chapels at the east end, has been consolidated in the same way as the main vault was done, by cutting out the disintegrated joints of

---

[59] Audit report, 10 May 1898. The Surveyors' Audit or annual reports are sometimes dated by the day, sometimes only by the month.
[60] Chapter Minute, 5 February 1912.
[61] Audit report of that date.
[62] Audit report of that date.
[63] Audit report, 6 Feb. 1933.
[64] No evidence has been found of this and the rods are usually believed to be of the Wyatt/Gayfere period.

all the stone panels separately, and refilling and grouting them by working from the roof space above the vaulting as well as from below.

The walls were limewashed and the statues below the windows were taken out and 'cleaned and treated'. This thorough overhaul extended to the vestibule to the west of the main chapel, and to the furniture:

> The fine stepped and barrel vaulted entrance to the chapel has been repaired and cleaned and renovated like the chapel itself, and the ceiling of this entrance has been decorated in gold and colour . . . The stalls and their canopies are being cleaned and waxed, and the making of the new altar, in reconstruction so far as possible of Torrigiani's altar, is well advanced.[65]

Tapper died in office on 21 September 1935; by November his successor (Sir) Charles Peers, had been appointed. Work was proceeding in the south aisle of the chapel, which

> shows in its fan-vaulting the same evidences of initial settlement that were seen in the main vault of the chapel. As a rebuilding to the true lines would have been needless and very costly, the dislocated masonry has been grouted and pointed up as it is, and there is no reason to fear any further movement.[66]

The rest of the stonework was in very good condition, but needed to be 'freed from its encrusted dirt' and some of the quarries in the windows 'which had been set in side out' were turned round. Peers also proposed to renew the lead roof over the aisle, which was in a poor state.

Later that year Peers began work on the north aisle, which had been coated with soot by a stove, then long disused, in the vestry at the west end of the aisle. As in the south aisle

> the dislocation of the vaulting is much in evidence, but more severe than the rest, some of the stonework having dropped as much as four inches, while the fan-vaulting springing from the pendants is nearly falling outwards on the north side. What has happened is that the thrust of the high vault transmitted by the flying buttresses has pushed out the top of the north wall of the aisle, and everything suggests that this was an initial settlement. No serious repair has ever been made, but the worst cracks and splintering have been filled in with rough plaster and no signs of subsequent movement are to be seen. The date 1817 on the stonework records such a repair. What has now to be done is to run the open joints with cement from the back of the vault, and to secure loose stonework where necessary. A few of the most marked dislocations can be modified by resetting, but no attempt to restore the original profile need be made.[67]

The work in the north aisle was completed that year, the Savile and Elizabeth I monuments cleaned and loose pieces fixed and some glass repairs carried out.[68] It was during this work on the chapel interior that the present altar was installed, in time for an installation of knights of the Bath in June 1935. It replaced an altar erected in

---

[65] Audit report, 14 Feb. 1935.
[66] Audit report, 18 Feb. 1936.
[67] Audit report, Feb. 1937.
[68] Audit report, Feb. 1938.

1870 by Dean Stanley and Gilbert Scott, which incorporated a piece of the frieze of Torrigiano's original baldachino which Stanley had discovered in the passage leading to Henry VII's burial vault. The new altar of 1935 was designed by Tapper, incorporating two further pieces of Torrigiano's original altar which had been in the Ashmolean Museum at Oxford. The new altar framed a painting of the Madonna and Child by Bartolommeo Vivarini, dating from c.1480, presented by Lord Lee of Fareham.[69]

Barely was the work complete when precautions had to be taken for the protection of the chapel at the start of the Second World War. The statues were taken down from their niches, and the Vivarini painting removed. The precautions proved necessary, for, as Sir Charles Peers reported,

> At 12.15 on September 27th (1940) a heavy bomb fell in Old Palace Yard . . . This blew out nearly all the glass in the chapel windows, except for that in the tracery of the clerestory, and the masonry at the east end of the chapel was battered with flying stones, so that parts of the window tracery were knocked out and the openwork parapets over the east ambulatory chapel were splintered and blown off their beds. No doubt the whole chapel was considerably shaken, but except for the fall of two pendants from the roof no trace of serious movement is at present to be seen. . . . The windows have been filled in with opaque materials, and Henry VII's chapel shut off from the rest of the church.

It would not seem to have been until 1941 that fuller precautions were taken, following a Government grant of £5,000: the effigies from Henry VII's tomb, the screen round it, the Chapel gates, all the removable stone statues and the stalls were evacuated to Mentmore, Bucks.; the Bath stall plates were removed and stored in the Chapter House crypt.[70] Fortunately the chapel sustained no further damage during the war.

Plans for reinstatement were being laid even while the war continued. The damaged easternmost chapel was assigned as a memorial to the members of the RAF killed in the Battle of Britain, and a memorial committee chaired by Lord Trenchard came into existence.[71] After the war Henry VII's chapel was the first priority, and by April 1947 Peers was able to report that the statues were back in their niches, the effigies were again on the tomb 'in their bronze chapel', and that he hoped to complete the masonry repairs by the end of the summer. The worst damage was to the glass; the one remaining whole panel, in the middle light of the eastern clerestory window, 'was blown to pieces, and not a trace of it is now to be found'.[72] The Battle of Britain window, designed by Hugh Easton, was unveiled and the chapel dedicated on 10 July 1947, by which time the stalls were back in position but without the canopies. These were finally reassembled in 1952–3, at the same time as the reglazing was completed: the remaining original quarries, bearing the letters H and E, were brought together and set in the centre lights of the aisle west windows.[73]

---

[69] See the account in Perkins, *Worship and Ornaments* ii, 206–10, now supplemented by WAM Lapidarium Inventory, by Tony Platt, to whom I am grateful for his help in this matter.
[70] Audit report, March 1942, and Schedule of War Removals attached.
[71] Audit report, July 1944.
[72] Audit report, April 1947.
[73] Audit reports, 26 March 1952 and June 1953.

Thus reconstituted, the chapel continued with minimal intervention – some roof beams were treated against beetle in 1963 – until 1967, when the pinnacles along the balustrade, except for four round the apse, were taken down, having become precarious: 'they have given trouble for a long time, owing to the inherent weakness of a cross-sectional area only 6 inches by 6 inches for pinnacles carrying relatively tall crocketed spires'.[74] It was not until 1975 that Peter Foster, the surveyor, replaced them with new ones in Portland stone.[75] In the following years the work was extended to the crocketed turrets and the flying buttresses, and some of the heraldic beasts were recarved; gilded weather vanes, the gift of the Royal Institute of Chartered Surveyors, were added as the turrets were completed.

[74] Audit report, March 1968.
[75] Audit report, 4 March 1975.

Restoring the Chapel, 1991–6

DONALD BUTTRESS

A CORRESPONDENT to *The Gentleman's Magazine* in 1808 wrote a postscript to a letter as follows:

> It afforded me much pleasure to find that Henry the Seventh's Chapel is to be restored to its original architectural state. All the decayed and dilapidated parts are to be renewed with stone and all the carvings and ornaments to be imitated from analogous members. This work will be worthy of a great Nation, and will be the best refutation of the garrulous invectives of those who delight only in finding fault.

At that time there were proposals, under the general direction of James Wyatt, then the surveyor of the fabric of Westminster Abbey, for a thorough restoration and repair of the exterior, the state of which was increasingly felt to be an affront to our national pride. After all, by the turn of the eighteenth century the weather-worn fabric was three hundred years old and in a serious state of dilapidation. Over a century earlier Wren had found the structure decayed and in need of attention, but forced by more pressing problems on the transepts and buttresses of the nave and choir, had had to be content with minor patching and the probable removal of loose and the more threateningly damaged parts of the rich external ornament. During the course of the eighteenth century the external statues were removed as a danger to passers-by.

By 1800 it was clear that something had to be done and, subject to the oversight of a special 'Committee of Taste', a certain amount of government money was provided within the context of other works of improvement to the environs of the Abbey, Old Palace Yard and what is now St Margaret's Street.[1] Up to the beginning of the nineteenth century the east end of the chapel protruded into what was essentially a quiet residential street; earlier still, the area was quite literally a 'yard' or a series of enclosures or gardens only gradually opened up as the old Palace of Westminster was extended and improved to give better government offices. Thomas Malton's view of 1792 (Plate IB) shows the unrestored chapel surrounded by domestic property and modest official buildings before clearance took place gradually over the next hundred years.

---

[1] See above, 327–8.

James Wyatt was one of the most influential exponents of the early gothic revival, and like others generally favoured the English late medieval styles of the fifteenth and sixteenth centuries. Amongst nationalists, and scholars both amateur and professional, there was a similar preference. For this reason Henry VII's chapel was greatly admired, and came to be so much so that it was a natural source of inspiration in the 1830s for Pugin's facades of Charles Barry's new Houses of Parliament across Old Palace Yard. There was therefore great popular interest in the proposals for repair; many individuals wanted a say, as they always will when any great project is under consideration. Talk could have been endless had not the matter been taken in hand by the resolute Dean Vincent and made possible by the coincident availability of a superb master mason and an architectural draughtsman of outstanding skill – Thomas Gayfere and L.N. Cottingham. The work of external repair undertaken between 1809 and 1822 was a masterpiece of late Georgian masoncraft, enabled and assisted by Cottingham's series of measured drawings, published in two parts soon afterwards.

It is necessary to discuss the Wyatt restoration in some detail, before we can move on to describe the recently completed restoration of 1991–6, for two reasons. Firstly it explains the state of the fabric before we began work, why it was like it was and the problems which had to be faced; and secondly because restoration is not only a practical matter but does involve art historical and archaeological considerations. It is worth adding here that these factors should illuminate and guide restoration, but in the end real repair, on which the well being and integrity of a building ultimately depends, has its own imperatives and should never be circumscribed by limited and specialist academic considerations. Repair is practical and must follow sound craft-based practices if it is to be properly carried out. That happened in 1809–22, and that again is what has happened during the most recent work.

Surviving drawings, such as that of Malton, show the chapel with significant parts missing – parapets, pinnacles and the like (Plate IB). When Wyatt's repair began there were no surviving parapets and the niches on the external octagonal buttress piers appear to have been shaved and cut back. Certainly the present parapet design(s) are wholly Wyatt/Cottingham in appearance and appear too puny to be a copy of their Tudor originals. Similarly the cupola statue canopies (empty since the mid-eighteenth century) as they now exist do not appear to be authentic late Tudor designs but rather to be re-interpretations, based upon similar internal canopies which of course had survived in a good state. There are a few other less prominent features of the Georgian rebuilding which may also owe more to Gayfere and his carvers than to damaged surviving details.[2] There are few engraved examples of old stone carving in Cottingham's plates and where the early nineteenth-century grotesque heads and beasts still survive they have an unmistakable late Georgian flavour, since all new carving work partakes of its own period and character. For example one fascinating mask on the north side, in the blind stone panelling, has a Chinese-style head and a mandarin hat which would not be out of place in the chinoiserie of Claydon Hall in Buckinghamshire dating from the mid-1760s!

---

[2] J. Frew, 'The "Destroyer" vindicated? James Wyatt and the restoration of Henry VII's chapel, Westminster Abbey', *JBAA* 134, 1991, 101–6.

Wyatt's, or rather Gayfere's, late Georgian work consisted in the replacement of most of the external Tudor fabric in a Combe Down Bath stone of superb colour and quality. Earlier writers have said the Gayfere recasing was total but during the recent work it became clear that this was not so. Some of the original medieval window tracery remains (the west window all is old) skilfully repaired by piecing in re-used Caen stone in mullions, panels and in plain ashlar work. During the dismantling and reconstruction of the external cupolas (1992–95) a great deal of re-used rubble was removed and returned to the cupola cores. Several carved details of sixteenth-century panelling and mouldings emerged which confirmed the accuracy of Cottingham and Gayfere's profiles. Much of this core filling was similarly of Caen limestone, which suggests that much of the original exterior was of this material. Altogether the late Georgian reconstruction was of the finest quality and withstood the weather of a heavily polluting nineteenth century reasonably well except that the Bath stone did not last well on the more exposed features such as the cupolas, the parapets and the pinnacles, and it was these which had to be dealt with again during this latest restoration. Gayfere dismantled all the great buttressing cupolas, rebuilding them and the panelled flyer-arms. Presumably to guard against possible outward movement during the progress of the work, wrought iron tie bars were inserted across and just below the internal vaulting, where they still exist.

Since the time of J.L. Pearson (1878–97) and J.T. Micklethwaite (1897–1906) as surveyors at the end of the nineteenth century it had become customary for nearly all repairs at the Abbey to use Portland stone, because of its superior weathering properties in the dirty air of London. It had of course a history going back longer than that, to Hawksmoor in the early eighteenth century. He used it to complete the western towers, as did John James, whereas Wren had generally followed a more conservative line, using for the most part a brownish-cream Oxfordshire stone from Burford and Taynton, which he perhaps felt went well with the older medieval Caen stone, Magnesian limestone and the softer Reigate. Whilst Portland has fine weathering qualities, provided it is well chosen and bedded, it looks best in larger areas. Used for sporadic repair it can contrast unpleasantly with older, darker weathered material. But use of two or more contrasting stones, especially where they are used together for different purposes, has a long medieval pedigree. At the Abbey it was possible in 1992 to discover that the lowest medieval face of the north-west tower hidden beneath its eighteenth-century casing was composed of blocks of greenish grey Reigate contrasted with harder, much lighter Caen stone string courses. This clearly demonstrates that in this sense medieval masonry could have a two tone aesthetic using each stone for its best properties, with the softer one being used for flat ashlar walling where it survived well, especially when periodically limewashed, and the harder, lighter-coloured stone being reserved for weathering parts and carved work. This self-evident ancient practice became the rationale and justification for the decision in 1991 to use two contrasting stones for the complete external masonry overhaul of the outside of the Lady chapel of Henry VII.

The late twentieth-century restoration of the exterior of the Abbey was carried out with funds raised by the Westminster Abbey Trust, chaired for nearly twenty-five years by HRH Prince Philip, Duke of Edinburgh. £5 million was the first estimated cost; in the end, as a result of inflation, over £25 million was raised and spent up to 1997. For the whole of that time the Cambridge-based firm of Rattee and Kett were employed with a workforce that varied, but at its peak exceeded seventy masons, craftsmen and labourers. The repairs began on the north side of the Abbey in 1973, moving from the north transept, round the apse and on to the south transept and the south side of the nave where the urgency of work on the great flying buttresses there and the realisation that Henry VII's chapel would be excessively expensive meant that work on the Lady chapel was stopped in the early 1980s. Directed by Peter Foster, then Surveyor, it went only as far as some exploratory repairs to the upper parts of four bays on the south side. These provided valuable information for the later work of 1993–5, undertaken after the very extensive repairs to the west front and its towers had been completed.

About 1991 it was clear that the cleaning and repair of the chapel would be an expensive and yet essential part of the late twentieth-century programme of external repairs. As the five year long campaign of work on the west front neared completion in 1991/92 three bays on the north side of the chapel were fully scaffolded for the work to be assessed, planned and costed by extrapolation, multiplying the number of bays by the average cost of these three. Three estimates were prepared for £4 million, £5 million and £6 million, based on limiting the work to the upper parts (i.e. above aisle parapet level) in the middle estimate of £5 million and in the lowest estimate making use of cast stone for those elements, such as the flyer-arm beasts, which might lend themselves to such treatment. After all there was the Georgian precedent of Coade Stone. Wisely, however, the artificial stone option was rejected and expenditure on the middle option at £5 million was approved by Westminster Abbey Trust early in 1992. As work went on over the next three years the agreed sum increased to £6 million to take account of a modest element of inflation and to deal with unexpected and very severe decay at the south-east corner which had been exacerbated by weather exposure and wartime bomb damage. This extra work required the total replacement of a further two bays of the upper frieze in hard Portland stone to accord with the four similarly re-made in the late 1970s. It had always been intended to relay the lead roof at high level and on the aisles. In the course of this, severe timber decay in the gutters and roof members especially on the south side again added further cost which eventually brought the total expenditure to the highest original estimate. But this in the end also included the total cleaning and repair of the inside of the chapel, not originally envisaged as essential. A sum of about £250,000 provided by the Dean and Chapter, largely from the Dean Ryle Fund, was augmented by a further £100,000 provided by the Trustees. The only element left untouched at the end of work in 1995/96 was the proper reclamation of the former contractors compound, repaving and the repair and re-alignment of the railings, matching similar work done at the west end in 1994.

The aims of the recent restoration were threefold. Firstly, to repair the external fabric thoroughly to withstand the weather and atmospheric attack for at least one hundred years. Secondly to replace and redesign where necessary the richly ornamented decorative carved features, lions, talbots, dragons and other Tudor emblems found on parapets, in string courses, but above all, on the cupolas and flyer-arms, to regain the full integrity of the chapel as a complete work of art and architecture. Such work should not be constrained by excessively stringent notions of conservation: a living building is not a museum object and should not be thought of or treated as such. Thirdly it was necessary to ensure that the chapel was structurally sound by the detailed examination of all its parts and by the necessary reconstruction of certain elements, notably the massive cupola tops or domes, on which its stability very substantially depends.

Once these three objectives were firmly grasped, one other aim and purpose could also be accomplished – namely to use the recarving programme, of unprecedented extent at least in the twentieth century, to the benefit and for the revitalisation of the stone carving trade. In the end it may be this by-product of the restoration which could bring the most long lasting benefits as the carving team, which included up to twenty-five or so members between 1991 and 1995, have spread out into the wider building industry. This dispersal is exactly what happened historically as lodges of masons travelled out from large, important medieval building projects.

Before giving a general description of the work, divided for convenience into sub-headed sections, one more general comment is necessary. It is this. In the climate of regulation and control which now embraces and surrounds the construction industry, logical planning of the work is essential. Scaffolding must remain safe and be moved and adapted methodically; expenditure and cost planning are vital if expenditure is to be measured against estimates and costs are to be contained, and above all the momentum of a large building project must be sustained. The relative, and thus merciful, absence of too much committee interference made possible by the independence of the Abbey enabled this to be achieved, combining firmness of intention with the best traditional masonry practice.

The chief elements of the work have been as follows:

The roof and leadwork

The high roof is late eighteenth-century, almost certainly that put in by Wyatt in 1793. Tudor trusses survive over the north aisle and the eastern chapels, supplemented by Georgian and later timbers. On top of these are two-inch thick deal boards which until 1994 supported cast lead laid down with solid timber rolls in the early nineteenth century and repaired only in a few places since.

On the upper roof most timbers were sound and only required repair at gutter level where leaks had softened the wood and encouraged repeated beetle infestation. Beam ends were scarfed with new oak in a few cases, defective deal boards replaced and a new widened gutter formed with better steps, falling into a number of sump outlets, all more easily cleaned, and protected by a full set of duck boards to take foot traffic. For better ventilation the upper roof was remade with 'open' rolls and fitted with a number of ventilation 'noses' on the windward side.

Several eaves beams, about 12 inches square, on the south side of the lower roof were replaced in matching new well seasoned timber, avoiding all forms of steel splinting and shoes. To form a new, widened straight gutter the old layout following the zig-zag lines of the parapets and running around each cupola turret was abandoned. Extra softwood joists were built up on top of the Georgian timbers and then boarded and covered with recast lead, this time with solid timber rolls to reduce future damage from foot traffic.

Following the practice generally in other parts of the Abbey, lead has been dressed over all the cills of the clerestory windows lapped on to the lead roof flats. The original Georgian rainwater heads and pipes were generally too small. Following the moulded profiles of the old heads and pipes, new ones were formed, all much larger and decorated with casts of the original rosettes and fleur-de-lis. In all cases the enlarged heads were fitted with overflow chutes to minimise damage caused by occasional blockage.

Following war damage the whole chapel had been reglazed in plain diamond quarries in the early 1950s. All this was in good order and has been cleaned, and the ferramenta, which are mostly of Tudor date, have been wire brushed and repainted.

The upper parapets
These were totally replaced in hard Portland limestone to the former Wyatt/Gayfere design very slightly thickened up to achieve greater stability and better weather resistance. By 1988 all but one short section of the former parapet and all but one pinnacle had fallen or been removed, and what remained was used as the model for the new. The heraldic frieze beneath, of rosettes, fleur-de-lis and portcullises, has similarly been remade; four bays on the south side were done around 1980, under Peter Foster with carvings designed under the direction of Arthur J.J. Ayres (1902–85). When work restarted in 1992 these were considered a little overlarge and stiff and the new ones were, as with the new heraldic beasts, loosened up more in design to shake off vestiges of their late Georgian stiffness.

The upper frieze panels
Three of these had been renewed in Portland on the south side in 1975–6. Two more had to be replaced on the south side and the eastern facing panel heavily repaired, partly in Portland but mainly in new Bath stone matching the repaired body of stone generally. Two blind panels in each frieze bay have been opened up and filled with wire guards to provide strong cross-ventilation of the upper roof space.

The cupola tops
Four of these, towards the west of the south side, were repaired piecemeal by Tapper as early as the 1930s: clearly these must have been the most decayed. These four have now been further repaired, without dismantling them, and the older Portland stone heavily limewashed for continued protection. The other ten cupolas at the lower level and the two larger cupolas which terminate the western stair turrets have been dismantled completely and rebuilt with Portland stone obtained from the Perryfield quarry, which in 1992 could offer us a large quantity of smallish blocks of fine-grained stone, largely free of shells and very suitable for the lavish new carvings we required.

The Wyatt/Gayfere cupolas were all severely decayed; the majority of their animal carvings, surface scale ornament and crockets had lost outlines at least; at worst whole features were missing. Architecturally the profiles on which the completeness of the whole design depends were greatly compromised. But the decayed ornament was not the only reason for a decision to dismantle and rebuild. The structural integrity of the cupolas was in question and, because they were tackled from expensive scaffolding, the repairs had to be effective for another century. Although the Georgian masons had rebuilt the cupolas soundly, the relatively small component rings of stones had decayed, split and opened up and were admitting rainwater. The cramping and bonding devices used from around that time were primitive and had become ineffective in holding the increasingly loose masonry together. During demolition it was calculated that the temporary removal of between ten and twelve metric tonnes of stone, one cupola at a time, would not seriously risk outward movement of the flyers and thus the vaulting. This danger was probably why the four internal iron ties were introduced. As a modern precaution, however, the arms adjacent to a particular cupola during its reconstruction were braced to resist any tendency to buckle and move outwards as the dead load on top was temporarily removed.

Inside the Georgian Bath casing of the cupolas we found that much of the core material was the re-used rubble from the former medieval outer facing and nearly all of it was again packed back into place. A few interesting carved bits (some with pre-Regency period soot encrustation, which showed pre-industrial pollution) were salvaged and together with representative carvings of the Gayfere period have found a permanent place in the new Lapidarium in the northern triforium gallery – itself a valuable by-product of the 1973–96 restoration.

To achieve maximum and lasting stability each new cupola top was rebuilt with integral rings of stainless steel reinforcement and a 2.5 metre long central vane rod anchored into the octagonal pier below and post-tensioned from the top before it was topped off by way of celebration and decoration with a large gilded weather vane, the gift of the Royal Institute of Chartered Surveyors. Thus was design linked in this way to utility.

The flyer arms
These had been reconstructed totally in Bath stone by Thomas Gayfere and whilst weathered badly, on the south side more than the north, they needed only sporadic repair of their geometric webs. The flyer caps however were all severely weathered, open jointed, and would have deteriorated further without serious attention. Virtually all their surmounting beasts, seven to each arm, had decayed and at least half of them were shapeless lumps or had gone altogether. Here then it was vital to combine new weatherings with new carved beasts to regain an important element of the outline of the design. Following the soundly based principle that hard stone is needed for a hard job, the new flyer caps were remade in Portland limestone with each new beast set into a pocket on top, so that the re-capping could precede the carving of the animals which would clearly take longer to produce.

The new external carvings
The new sculptures, over 350 in number, must certainly represent the most complete and extensive such commission since the end of the nineteenth century. Once clay models of examples had been produced, trial carvings were made and tested in place as plaster casts. Samples of all stages of the production have been selected and will be permanently stored as a record of the scope and method of this prodigious carving project. When carvings were approved and the parameters of style had been set, individual carvers were allowed increasing freedom to model and carve in their own way, adding originality without novelty, being encouraged especially to express individual styles of hand-tooled finish. Smooth, over-finished surfaces were generally discouraged. The result is there to be seen, a major contribution to late twentieth-century art, fresh, vibrant and alive, restoring the chapel exterior to a vigorous character which a sterile and academic approach to the strict conservation of the old surviving figures would never have achieved. The chapel as a work of architecture is alive, when it

could so easily have been deadened by over-zealous adherence to fashionable conservation dogma.

The lower parapets
Whilst in better condition generally than those at high level, some short sections had already been replaced in Portland in the past but these sadly could not be reused. The reason for total replacement was twofold, besides the well-intentioned desire to make a uniform effect, with white parapets top and bottom. Firstly, since the configuration of the lower gutters was to be totally changed, it was necessary to construct a new series of low timber roof slopes behind the lower parapets to throw water into the new, wider straight gutters. This meant that the lower two sections of open work on the stone parapets needed to be blind and not pierced, to cover the extra depth of roof timbers. So the old sections of parapet could not be easily re-used even if in reasonable condition. Secondly, and this was an important factor, the lower 'zig-zag' parapets sheltered a valuable range of late Georgian beasts and heraldic carvings, a high proportion of which could be repaired and conserved rather than be replaced. Rebedding new parapets allowed a lead flashing to be introduced at this level, bedded under the re-set stones which could then be dressed over the conserved carvings to shelter them in the future. This technique had been very successfully employed to save and shelter important carving in a similar location along the Jerusalem Chamber parapet in 1992/93.

Where new heraldic and animal carvings were required in this running frieze below the renewed parapet, they were carved in a style deliberately intended to harmonise with Georgian examples alongside. In many cases Gayfere carvings which could remain undisturbed were given new features, heads, limbs and rear ends, where these were missing.

Tracery and plain walling
Almost all of the surface of the body of the chapel, that is excluding the cupolas, flyers and parapets already described, is composed of glazed or blind tracery work. Except on the lower plinth and in the western light well, there is almost no plain ashlar work. A number of intrusive 'ad hoc' repairs had been made over the past sixty years in white Portland stone. Where it was unwise or too expensive to remove them they have been left undisturbed, but a number have been taken out and replaced in a compatible new Bath stone (from the Box Ground quarry) as close to Gayfere's Combe Down as possible. The use of 'like with like' has been a principle firmly adhered to since 1988 for chemical and weathering reasons and to avoid at all cost a spotty surface effect which in the end breaks down the architectural and visual integrity of the whole.

A small amount of surface repair, certainly far less than 5% in all, has thus been carried out in matching Bath stone. Besides this, and especially where cutting out and serious disturbance could not be justified, there has been a certain amount of what is often called 'plastic' repair, which is the removal of surface decay and the building up of new areas of stone with lime and sand and stone-dust based mortars, later rubbed down after an initial period of setting. This is an old, well tried technique, both cost-effective and durable, especially suitable for the repair of less exposed items or features which are decorative rather than structural such as the tiny crenellations below the window tracery.

Limewashing

If medieval buildings were built of rough rubble stone then they were invariably finished and protected by an initial and then regular coats of limewash. Even finely constructed ashlar structures were usually given a surface 'dressing' in this way to help with protection and probably to let the new masonry 'cure' and achieve a harder surface conducive to a more prolonged life. The Georgian refacing of the chapel of Henry VII was no exception and during the repairs evidence of at least one external ochre coloured limewash was detected, preserved in the crevices of more protected places. It was this fact, as much as a belief in limewashing as a valuable preservative, which informed the decision to cover all the surviving and renewed Bath stone areas with a two- or three-coat application of a traditional lime based casein and tallow-enriched limewash, stained to an ochre colour with earth pigments as close to the Georgian original as possible (Colour Plate IA). New stones will mature under this protection and the older Bath stone, opened up by light abrasion and washing, will thereby have its stone pore structure strengthened in the process. In time the new ochre limewash will thin and wash off to a great extent, matched by a corresponding darkening of the new white Portland stone elements. In short, the exterior may begin to look even better after, say, ten years, with a less dramatic contrast of colours. In the meantime the contrasted colouring expresses its purpose and is not an aesthetic matter alone.

Internal repairs

The erection of a mass of scaffolding inside the chapel presented two main risks – firstly that the wood might be set alight; so the planks and the plywood used to make level surfaces had to be treated before use with a fire retardant, and at all times from September 1994 to June 1995, a period of ten months, there was a strict regime of control of access, extra fire precautions, the sole use of low voltage lighting and power tools and rigid rules for supervision and security to safeguard one of the gothic world's most valuable masterpieces. Secondly there was danger of mechanical damage and theft. Two large steel cabins were placed on the floor below the first major deck level and used for storage; all removable items were photographed, listed and regularly checked. One cabin became a temporary conservation workshop for the cleaning of special items such as the Bath banners and helms and eventually several of the internal groups of statues. The external roof access afforded to visitors was an unusual opportunity; but the opportunity for close examination of the whole interior was a unique, once-in-a-century chance for scholars and others with a more general interest. During the ten months the chapel was closed for repair, many special individual visits were arranged, no reasonable request for access being refused.

The first task was the vacuum cleaning, aided by soft brushing, of the entire wall and vaulting surfaces; in places dust laid down in over fifty years was up to 1.5 inches thick. Next the masonry was carefully washed by hand-worked sprays of de-ionised water and mopped off by clean cotton and wool rags.

At an early stage the first flat platform of the scaffolding was used as the base for a photogrammetric survey of the vaulting conducted by a team under Professor Ian Harley from University College, London, to produce rectified photographs.[3] This was

---

[3] See L.D. Blank and A.L. Alan, 'Henry VII's chapel at Westminster Abbey: photogrammetric recording and survey control', *Survey Review* 34 no. 270, October 1988, 517–27.

followed by a photographic and a hand-measured survey[4] of the top surfaces of the main vault and those over the side aisles which will provide useful data on which to assess future movements of the masonry, and a series of drawings on which past movement and interventions can be plotted as a record. Close examination showed several expected but significant movements and patterns of settlement of the thin shell-vaulted structure, all of which seemed to have taken place within a short time of the building's completion.[5] There was interesting evidence of the manner of using the original centred support-structure of timber, how it might have been removed and how initial movements were in several places corrected by 'trimming in' of the smaller mouldings and hollowed cusps to acceptable visual alignments.

Structurally there was much evidence of Walter Tapper's excellent consolidation work of the early 1930s by means of pointing, joint packing and the use of non-ferrous straps put in place to secure vulnerable sections of carved ornaments, notably the free standing cusps and crockets of the five great transverse arches which pierce the shell of the vault. Two of the larger great pendants were a little loose on their iron and bronze rods in that slight rotation was possible, presumably because the original or later lead caulking had been incomplete. Rather than risk disturbing the cores the slightly open joints were secured by means of injected epoxy based resin stone adhesives. The four transverse Georgian iron tie rods appeared on testing to be under modest tension only, which suggested that there had been no significant movement outwards since the 1820s. Whilst it was reassuring to think that the ties were not now necessary neither the surveyor nor Professor Jacques Heyman, the consultant engineer, could find a compelling reason to remove them. Hence they were 'painted out' and are at most times hardly visible in most lights when observed from below.

In 1932 Walter Tapper had cleaned the interior and applied a warmly tinted limewash to the vaulting and the internal masonry, and this process was repeated again for two reasons. Firstly the limewash would perform the function of isolating the Tudor masonry from the corrosive effects of traffic pollution and the damp produced by the many human visitors. The nasty cocktail thus present is best kept away from the old Caen stone and other stone surfaces. Secondly, the whole interior has been limewashed many times and underneath is rather dirty. It would hardly be possible, even with brisk, determined, and damaging abrasion, to reach a uniformly clean and attractive surface. Limewash therefore provides a useful and practical means of giving the sophisticated and intricate interior a uniform and pleasing surface covering. Since there is little coloured glass, strong, harsh sunlight has been softened by the choice of a warm honey-coloured wash (applied in two and in places three sprayed and brushed thin coatings) in pleasant and harmonious contrast with the rich brown shades of the woodwork (Colour Plate V). During the cleaning of the walls and vaulting no trace of any original polychromatic scheme of decoration was found, although it is almost certain that, but for the interruption to the work after the death of Henry VII in 1509, the whole vault would have been fully coloured as, for example in the choir of Gloucester Cathedral. In the event it was decided to gild the main pendants of the central and secondary vessels (Colour Plate IVA) as a celebra-

---

[4] See above, 205–14.
[5] See above, 226.

tion of the redecoration of early 1995 and to emphasise their function in the structural virtuosity of this unique late gothic vault.

Lower down, the almost complete range of statues in the wall niches presented some problems, as well as the opportunity for the first time for over fifty years to examine and photograph them at close quarters. Again few traces of polychrome decoration were evident, but all the statues retained significant amounts of what appeared to be a gesso dressing intended as the base for painting, probably never carried out. The statues closest to the east end had the most traces of black tallow staining from a probable concentration of candles at that end around the altars and the shrine enclosure. The canopies and insides of the statue niches were cleaned and limewashed but the fine detail of the statues themselves was not reduced further; they were washed and protected by means of a very thin shelter coat of lime water.

The slightly larger statues in the side chapels are surprisingly different, a little different in style and with differences in weathering. This needed explanation and requires further work in the future. By the painstaking removal of many thick layers of limewash from three of the statues at the east end of the north aisle, unsuspected detail was revealed. Certain crudities and a lack of perfect fitting suggest the distinct possibility that some, or even most, of these lower statues are the remains of the outside suite of forty-six removed during the mid-eighteenth century.[6] A detailed look at the two iconographical schemes, inside and outside, and individual examination of each statue in turn might decide the truth of the matter.

A number of the lower internal niches lack figures, but in 1997 it was possible to fill the important one intended for a statue of Henry VI on the north side of the central eastern (RAF) chapel; it was modelled by Tim Metcalf and carved by Matthew Hyde from funds provided by King's College, Cambridge, Eton College and Hoare's Bank.

As the access scaffolding was removed for the chapel to be reopened in June 1995 all the memorials were washed and gently polished with microporous organic wax. The medieval wooden stallwork revealed a few more of its secrets.[7] It had long been known that the stalls had been ingeniously extended in the mid-eighteenth century but the full extent of the Georgian supplementation of the carvings, even some misericords hitherto described as Tudor, was a surprise. Careful study of documents and a minute survey[8] have produced more evidence still for what is really a key example of the work of the early gothic revival, paralleled only in extent by John Thornton's restoration of timber and stone carving, often mistaken for medieval, at Beverley Minster.

Finally, on the purely practical front, the opportunity of closing the chapel for ten months made it possible to install improved heating under the back stalls and to install simple, dimmed halogen uplighters at clerestory window level, accessible through glazed hopper lights from the aisle roof level.

As the restoration of the Lady chapel drew to a close, the surveyor of the fabric suggested that stained glass might be introduced to commemorate the achievements since 1973 and to compensate for the almost total loss of the surviving coloured glass

---

[6] See above, 277–8.
[7] See above, 253–7.
[8] See above, 227–52.

during the 1939–45 war. Major donations, many of them from North America, were recorded by the introduction of small lozenge-shaped panels low down in the apsidal chapels; these introduced heraldic and personal emblems of the donors set within the discipline of the plain diamond-shaped post-war glazing, and were designed by Alfred Fisher of Chapel Studios, Hertfordshire. The colours generally used were chosen to harmonise with Hugh Easton's Battle of Britain window of 1951.

An ambitious fully heraldic west window was donated by Sir John Templeton, a Trustee, and unveiled by HM the Queen on 19 October 1995. Devised by the surveyor, with the heraldic assistance of Hubert Chesshyre, at that time Chester Herald, it was made by the firm of Goddard and Gibbs and largely carried out by John Lawson, designer, James Weatherley, glass cutter, and Bill Smith, painter. The design includes the armorial bearings of the Sovereign, Prince Philip and the Prince of Wales, the three deans in office during the restoration from 1973, Abbey officers, Trustees, and in numerous small lozenges the initials of workmen, clerks of works and contractors – in all, nearly a hundred persons.

Following the success of this window, Sir Philip (later Lord) Harris offered to pay for an east window in the central bay of the apse, with the intention that two others, one either side, might eventually complete the scheme. Proposals for a central figure of the Blessed Virgin Mary and surrounding heraldic devices were set aside in 1996 by the Architectural Advisory Panel. In the end a much more expensive and intricate design was approved and unveiled in 2001, the work of Alan Younger. Its greater design density reduces some of the eastern glare from the plain glass, but as yet it awaits its flanking windows to complete the composition.

Every restoration project finds its place in the continuum of history since nothing can be seen or understood in isolation. Recording what has been done between 1973 and 1996 on the Abbey exterior has been meticulous and full. There are several thousand drawings generated by Rattee and Kett, reduced for ease of storage onto acid-free paper and bound in accessible volumes. There are thousands of progress photographs, complete runs of relevant minutes of site meetings, Trustees' meetings, Chapter Audit Reports and a mass of supporting loose documents. All these will find their place in the Abbey muniments. In addition, due to the energy of Mr Tony Platt, an impressive archive of stone fragments, woodwork, metalwork and plaster casts has been assembled and is now displayed in the newly constructed Lapidarium housed in the north east triforium gallery. A public exhibition, with access to the work in progress, attended by nearly 100,000 visitors between June and October 1995, was permanently recorded by means of an illustrated catalogue.[9] The present book, initiated by a full day seminar held at the Society of Antiquaries in October 1995, completes the record of what has been done. Thus this latest of many great Restorations will be without doubt the most fully recorded ever for the information and enlightenment of our successors, a responsible action taken today to assist those in the future who will have the great responsibility of caring for the chapel of Henry VII and the great Abbey church and its precincts, of which it is a glorious part.

[9] Cocke, *900 Years*.

The Trustees of the Westminster Abbey Trust during the period of work on the Lady chapel of Henry VII were:
HRH The Duke of Edinburgh (Chairman)
Lord Catto, Sir Philip Harris, the Very Revd Michael Mayne (Dean), Sir John Quinton, Lord Robens, Canon Colin Semper, Rear Admiral K.A. Snow (Secretary), H.R. Sykes, Sir John Templeton, Sir Peter Walters, the Duke of Westminster, G.H. Weston.

Donors to the restoration commemorated by windows:
Walter J. Annenberg, Lord Catto, Derek Crowson, Sir Harry Djanogly, Josephine Gargiulo, Lord Harris of Peckham, Lucina Ho, Stanley Ho, Leopold Muller, Governor and Mrs J.A. Noe, Linda Noe Lane, Christel McRae Noe Lane, Captain John Latsis, Lord Robens of Woldingham, M. and J. Sackler, L.J. and Mary Skaggs, Gordon Southam, Jean M. Southam, Hugh Ridley Sykes, Sir John Templeton, Vella Handly Templeton, the Duke of Westminster, Colin Williams, Messrs. Wogen, John Zochonis

Donors to the restoration commemorated by plaques in the vestibule:
Hugh Leander Adams; Mary Trumbell Adams; Alexander, Elisabeth and Margaret Chisholm; David Croft; Robin Stormonth Darling; Wilfred Thomas Edwards; the Esmee Fairbairn Charitable Trust; the Fishmongers Company; Glaxo Wellcome plc; Mena Lee Griffiths; Christopher B. Mitchell; Bette and Al Moorman; E. Leslie Peter; the Rank Group plc; Dr and Mrs Mortimer Sackler; the Sainsbury Family Charitable Trusts; Christopher, Virginia and Susan Templeton; Harvey Maxwell Templeton; Heather Erin Templeton; Irene Reynolds Butler Templeton; Jennifer Ann Templeton; Sir John Templeton; John and Josephine Templeton; Judith Dudley Folk Templeton; Susan Judith Templeton; Vella Handly Templeton; Anne D. Zimmerman; Gail D. Zimmerman; Rhonda, Michael, Mitchel and Renee Zimmerman.

Contractors for the restoration were Messrs. Rattee and Kett, whose staff included Vic Franklin (Restoration Director), Brian Bowen (Project Manager), Tim Crawley (Senior Stone Carver), Matthew Beesley (Conservator), Nigel Hudson (Draughtsman). The Quantity Surveyor was Christopher Norris, the Consultant Engineer Professor Jacques Heyman. The Trust office was run by Eileen Sly.

Index

Aachen 292
Aarschot, Onze Lieve Vrouwkerk 244; *Plate 35*
Abingdon abbey 95
Abyndon, Henry 57
Agarde, Arthur 101
Albemarle, George Monck duke of 311; *and see* Westminster Abbey, Lady chapel of Henry VII, tombs
Alcock, John, bishop of Ely 124–5
Alkborough (Lincs) 82
Amadas, Robert 106
Amboise, cardinal of 132, 271
Amery, L.S. 313–14
Amiens cathedral 191
Andre, Bernard 92
Anne of Bohemia, queen 16 *and see* Westminster Abbey, church, tombs
Anne of Denmark, queen 299, 323
Anstis, John 321
Antiquaries, Society of 297–8, 305, 332, 354
Antwerp 292
Ardingly (Sussex) church, rood screen 247, 249, 252; *Plates 38–40, 43*
Arthur, Prince 268, 286, 292
  chantry chapel of 287
Arundel, Thomas earl of 125, 137
Arundel, Thomas, bishop of Ely 41
Ashridge 333
Astle, Thomas 99, 109
Atwater, William 119
Audley, Edmund, bishop of Salisbury 125, 127–8, 137
Ayres, Arthur 305, 348
Ayrton, Acton Smee 297–8

Bacon, Francis 1
Bacon, John 296
Badminton (Gloucs) 299
Baily, E.H. 296
Bainbridge, Christopher, archbishop of York 137
Bainbridge Reynolds, Messrs 298
Barnes, Dr 193
Barons, William, bishop of London 127
Barry, E.M. 298
Bath abbey 146, 201, 215, 219; *Fig. 9*
Bath and Wells, bishop of, *see* King, Oliver
Bath, Order of the 200, 229, 231–2, 237, 295, 313, 315, 321, 323, 325, 340; *Fig. 44*
Bayeux cathedral 191
Beatrice, daughter of Henry III and Queen Eleanor 12

Beaufort, duke of 299
Beaufort, Margaret 81, 84, 87, 104, 109, 137, 143, 175, 187, 260, 274, 286, 317
  chantry 84, 173, 260, 286
  funeral 60
  household chapel 52
  tomb, *see* Westminster Abbey, Lady chapel of Henry VII, tombs
Beawpee, Piers 26
Bedford, Jasper Tudor, duke of 124
Bellamy, Robert 288
Bergavenny, George, Lord 82–4
Berkeley, Maurice, Lord 82–4
Bermondsey abbey 95
Besnier, Isaac 308
Beverley Minster 353
Blair, Claude 305
Blake, Robert, Admiral 308
Blore, Edward 296
Blount, Sir James 125
Blow, Detmar 313
Blythe, Geoffrey, bishop of Coventry and Lichfield 127
Boehm, Sir Edgar 300–1, 313
Bolingbroke (Lincs) 126
Bolton, William, prior of St Bartholomew Smithfield 193, 261, 287
Bond, Francis 1
Bonvisi, Lorenzo and Ieronimo 68
Boston, St Botolph's church 52
Bosworth, battle of 103
Bothe, Dr 84
Bourbon, Isabella of, monument 291
Bower, Stephen Dykes 298, 301, 305, 313–14
Bowman, Ralph 274, 288
Brand, Matilda 15
Bray, Sir Reynold 84, 125, 193
Bridge, John 296, 302
Bristol cathedral 215
Britton, John 1, 328; *Figs 7, 8*
Broadwater (Sussex) 82, 84
Bruges 292
Buckham, George 336
Buckingham, Catherine duchess of 311
  Edward duke of 127, 141, 181
  George Villiers first duke of 295 *and see* Westminster Abbey, Lady chapel of Henry VII, tombs
  George Villiers second duke of, proposed monument 299–300; *Fig. 39*
Burgundy, Mary of 270 *and see* Charles

Burton Stather (Lincs) 82
Bushnell, John 311
Butchart, W.J. 301, 305
Buttress, Donald 314

Calais 293
   Staple of 136
Cambridge, Carmelites of 274
   Christ's College 274, 288
   King's College 61, 65–6, 71, 81, 104, 107, 128–9, 215, 219, 240, 244, 278, 284, 287–8, 291, 293, 353
   St Catherine's College 286
   St John's College 286
   University 81–3, 88, 93–5, 105, 120, 286
      hearse cloth 82
Canaletto, paintings by 183 n81, 233–4, 254; *Plate III*
Canterbury 107, 124, 139
   archbishop of 79, 95, 137–9 *and see* Courtenay, William; Morton, John; Warham, William
   cathedral 160, 192
      shrine of St Thomas Becket 134, 156
      tombs in: Black Prince 177
         Bourchier, Archbishop 264
         Henry IV and Joan of Navarre 264
   Friars Observant of 130–1
   prior and convent of 79–80, 96
   St Augustine's abbey 81, 96
Capell, William 80
Carmarthen, Grey Friars of 88, 120
Caroline, queen 323–5
Carter, John 299, 332; *Fig. 9*
Carthusians 104 *and see* Champmol; London, Charterhouse; Sheen priory
Castile, Philip king of 92
Caxton, William 192
Chambers, William 237
Champmol, Charterhouse, tombs in 181
Chancellor, Lord 87, 90, 325 *and see* Warham, William
Chantrey, Sir Francis 296
Chapel Royal 37, 40, 42, 44–5, 49, 52, 54, 57, 153
Charles I, king 295, 317
Charles II, king 232, 306, 308
   funeral effigy 319
Charles VI, king of France 63
Charles VIII, king of France 267
Charles of Burgundy 104, 135–6
Chaucer, Geoffrey 27, 192
Cheere, Sir Henry 237, 308
Chertsey abbey 60, 192, 259–60, 266
Chesshyre, Hubert 305, 354
Chester, bishop of, *see* Blythe, Geoffrey
   rood of 105
Cheyney, Sir John 125
Chios, Cyo, Greece 132
Claydon Hall (Bucks) 344
Clitheroe, Clidrowe 125
Cobbett, Pitt 336
Cobham, Sir Reginald 179
Codeman, Richard 288
Coke, Humphrey 215
Cologne 282
Colt, Maximilian 302; *Plate 50; Fig. 40*

Colvin, Sir Howard 2, 189, 231–2, 253, 261
Coningsby, Humphrey 74, 83–4, 127
Conway, Lord 306
Cope, William 83
Copeland, Henry 237
Corpus Christi, feast of 28
Corsi, Antonio, of Florence 68
Cottingham, Lewis N. 1, 205, 328 n16, 330, 332–4, 336, 338, 344–5
Courtenay, Peter, bishop of Winchester 124
   William, archbishop of Canterbury 179
Coutances cathedral 191
Coventry 123
   bishop of, *see* Blythe
Critz, John de 302; *Fig. 40*
Croft, Sir Richard, monument 291
Cromwell, Oliver 308, 319
Culpepper, Nicholas 252
   Richard 252
Cunningham, Alan 296
Cure, Cornelius 299, 303; *Plate 51*
   William 303; *Plate 51*
Cutte, Sir John 84, 137

Dalbroke, Anthony 164
Darley, Dr Brian 89
Darnley, Henry Lord 301
Dart, John 1, 200, 229, 233, 235, 277, 303, 308, 321; *Figs 17–18*
Daubeny, Giles Lord 92, 125
David Bruce, king of Scotland 75
Dawson, John 259
Delphyn, Nicholas 288
Delvaux, Laurent 311; *Plate 52*
Derby, Thomas Stanley earl of 83, 268, 270, 292
Dixon, John 334
Don, Dean Alan 313
Drope, Robert and Alice 29
Dudley, Edmund 78, 84–5, 118–19, 137
Dunstan, St 6, 46
Dürer, Albrecht 244
Durham, bishop of *see* Ruthall, Thomas; Sever, William
   cathedral 156–7; *Fig. 11*
   prior of 131
Dynham, John Lord 125

Earp and Hobbs, Messrs 301
Easthampstead 171
Easton, Hugh 341, 354
Ede, Richard 57
Edward I, king 12
Edward II, king 171 *and see* Gloucester cathedral
Edward III, king 171 *and see* Westminster Abbey, church, tombs
Edward IV, king 26, 29, 68, 103, 171, 192, 270–1
Edward VI, king 94, 164
   burial of 187, 299, 317
   proposed monument 299
Edward, Lord, the future Edward II 12
Edward the Confessor, St 5, 11 *and see* Westminster Abbey, church, tombs
Edzard, James 336–7
Eleanor of Castile, queen 12, 20, 62, 93, 175 *and see* Westminster Abbey, church, tombs

INDEX

Eleanor of Provence, queen 12
Elizabeth I, queen 94, 187 *and see* Westminster Abbey, Lady chapel of Henry VII, tombs
Elizabeth II, HM queen 354
Elizabeth Woodville, queen 26, 192
Elizabeth of York, queen 69, 81, 87, 91–2, 113–14 *and see* Westminster Abbey, Lady chapel of Henry VII, tombs
    funeral effigy 288
Ely, bishop of, *see* Alcock, John; Arundel, Thomas
    cathedral 38, 262
        Bishop Alcock's chapel 291
Emler, Lawrence 288
Emson, Sir Richard 118, 127, 137
Erasmus, Desiderius 271
Essex, John 259
Esyngton, William 83
Eton College 265, 291, 353
Exeter, bishop of, *see* Fox, Richard

Fairford (Gloucs) 284
Farnborough, Lord 313
Fava, Lewis de 69
Fen (Lincs) 83
Fergusson, James 297
Fifelde, Thomas 259
Fisher, Alfred 354
Fisher, John, bishop of Rochester 118, 137, 180, 286
Fisher, Robert 105
Fitz James, Richard, bishop of London 118
Flanders, *see* Low Countries
Flaxman, John 296
Flitcroft, Henry 232, 324
Florence 134, 185
Fonthill abbey 333
Foster, Peter 305, 342, 345, 348
Fowler, Thomas 302
Fox, Richard, bishop of Winchester 79–80, 83, 118, 125, 127–8, 137, 157, 287, 292
Franciscans, Observant 104–5, 119, 130–1 *and see* Canterbury, Greenwich, London, Newcastle, Richmond, Southampton
Franks, Augustus 297
Frederick, prince of Wales 321, 325
Frowyk, Thomas 84, 127
Furneaux, Mr 305
Fyneux, Fineux, John 78, 118 n34, 127, 137

Gardner, Thomas 237
Gayfere, Thomas, the elder 328
    the younger 194, 196, 328, 330–4, 336, 338, 344–5, 349
George I, king 319, 321
George II, king 319–21, 323–5
George III, king 319, 333
George IV, king 296
George de Samford 15
Germany 183, 287
Gibbons, Grinling 299
Giles, C.W. Scott 301, 305
Gladstone, W.E. 298
Glanville, Jeremiah 336
Gloucester abbey, cathedral 262, 352
    tomb of Edward II 177
Goddard and Gibbs, Messrs 354

Gough, Richard 332
Greenway, J. 336
Greenwich palace 92, 124, 146
    Friars Observant of 130–1
Grenville, Lord 329
Grosvenor, Sibell countess 313
Guildford, Guldeford, Sir Richard 125

Hales, James 292
Halton (Lincs) 82
Hamme, Robert 54
Hampton Court 215
Handel, G.F. 323
Hanover 319, 321
Hanworth 105
Hardwicke, earl of 108
Harris, Lord 354
Hateclyff, William 29
Hawksmoor, Nicholas 323, 327, 345
Henry III, king 5, 14–15, 23, 25, 93, 160, 175, 189–90, 259–60, 293 *and see* Westminster Abbey, church tombs
Henry IV, king 17, 37, 43, 44 n84, 192, 232 *and see* Canterbury cathedral
Henry V, king 43–5, 49, 62–3, 83, 105, 109, 175, 268, 324 *and see* Westminster Abbey, church, chapels and tombs
Henry VI, king 27, 60–1, 63, 81, 85, 90, 92, 113, 128, 132, 145, 153–4, 164, 192, 229, 259–60, 264, 278
    canonisation of 60–1, 154, 156, 188, 260, 262, 266, 292–3
    shrine of 30, 49–50, 60, 63, 154, 156–7, 159–60, 167, 183, 187–8, 192, 200, 260, 261 n11, 262, 264–6, 274, 320; *Figs 6, 12, 36*
Henry VII, king
    burial of 59, 64, 104, 113–14, 116, 118, 187 n97
    chantry and obituary services for 30, 61–2, 64, 66–9, 81–3, 85–93, 104, 114, 116–18, 120, 123, 173, 175–7, 179–80, 185–6, 231, 261, 271, 293
    death of 59, 103, 114, 203–4, 228; *Plate 3*
    intentions regarding Lady chapel and contents 30–1, 49–50, 59–69, 93, 113, 118, 120, 131–4, 143, 146, 153–4, 164, 174–5, 181, 188, 192, 228–9, 259–60, 264, 267–8, 284, 287, 292, 316–17, 319
    Mary, daughter of 65, 135–6
    mother of, *see* Beaufort, Margaret
    tomb of, *see* Westminster Abbey, Lady chapel of Henry VII, tombs
    will of 59–60, 63–8, 83, 86, 93, 99–140, 143, 150, 156, 160, 176–7, 181, 185–6, 203–4, 228, 260–1, 264, 270–1, 274, 280; *Plate 2*
    saints named in:
        Anne 113
        Anthony 113
        Barbara 113
        Edward 113, 132–3
        Francis 130, 132
        George 112, 132–3
        Jerome 132
        John Baptist 112, 132
        John Evangelist 112, 132
        Mary Magdalene 113
        Michael 112

Peter 134
Thomas of Canterbury 134
Vincent 113
Virgin Mary 112, 132–3
Henry VIII, king 60, 65, 68, 84, 93, 105, 124, 137, 186–7, 215, 265, 268–9, 274, 287, 292–3, 317
will of 101
Henry Frederick, prince of Wales 299
Herbert, Charles Somerset, Lord 118, 127, 137
Heron, John 65, 74, 83
Hervey, Lord 320
Heyman, Jacques 352
Hoare's Bank 353
Hobart, James 127
Hobbes, Thomas 79
Hody, William 91
Holinshed, Raphael, chronicle of 193
Holkham Hall (Norfolk) 325
Hollar, Wenceslas 9, 229, 254, 334
Hornby, Henry 180
Houghton (Norfolk) 312, 325
Hudde, John 288
Huddlestone (Yorks), quarries 194
Humfrey, Thomas 259
Husee, Sir William 125
Hyde, abbot of 80
Hyde, Matthew 353
Hylmer, John 201

Innocent IV, pope 189
Innocent VIII, pope 154
Ireton, Henry 308

James I, king 295, 302, 317, 320, 323
James II, king 311, 320
James, John 345
Janyns, Robert 193, 197, 201, 265
Jelfe, Andrews 233, 325
John, tailor of Charing 15
John, Sir Goscombe 313
Julius II, pope 264

Katharine of Aragon, queen 187 n97, 268–9
Katharine of Valois, queen 27, 30, 63, 113, 260, 268, 286
tomb of 192 *and see* Westminster Abbey, old Lady chapel, tombs
Kebill, William 106
Kennett and Avon canal 331
Kent, William 311, 324–5
Kerrich, Thomas 332
Kew 324
Killigrew, Henry 234
King, Oliver, bishop of Bath and Wells 125, 146, 201
Kingsmill, John 74, 80, 83–4, 127
Knaresborough, Knaresburgh (Yorks) 126

Lancaster, county palatine of 125
duchy of 65, 83–4, 103–4, 125–6
chancellor of, *see* Emson, Sir Richard
Langley, 293
Lavenham (Suffolk) church, Spring chantry 247
Lawson, John 354
Layard, Austen 297
Lebons, John 201, 265

Ledward, Gilbert 313
Lee of Fareham, Lord 341
Leland, John 1
Le Sueur, Hubert 306
Lethaby, W.R. 2, 9, 193, 273, 277, 339
Lewes (Sussex), St Pancras priory 247
Lichfield cathedral 191
Limburg 291
Lincoln, bishop of, *see* Smith, William
cathedral 38, 154 n29
dean and chapter 131
Lingfield (Surrey) 179
London,
Armourers' company 305
Austin friars 96
bishop of 92 *and see* Barons, William; Fitz James, Richard; Ralph de Stratford
Carmelites 96
Charterhouse 81, 96, 130–1
city of 14, 20, 94–7, 116–17, 121, 138, 194, 292
friars 81
Friars Preachers, Dominicans 96
guilds 291
Grey Friars, Franciscans 96
Holy Trinity Aldgate 37, 93, 96
mayor and commonalty of 66, 78–81, 87, 91 *and see* Capell, William
Mercers' Hall 274
Nelson's colunm 296
St Bartholomew Smithfield, prior of 115 *and see* Bolton, William
St Botolph 50
St James's palace 324
St Martin le Grand 61, 83, 89
St Mary Graces 96
St Michael Cornhill 29
St Olave 50
St Paul's cathedral 66, 78, 80, 95–6, 121–2, 282, 298
Dean *see* Sherborne, Robert
St Paul's Cross 88
Somerset House 237
Temple church 191
Tower of 101, 146, 293
Victoria and Albert Museum 298
Long, Sir Charles 330
Long Bennington (Lincs) 126
Louis IX, king of France 63
Louis XII, king of France 132
Louis-Philippe, king of France 312
Lovell, Sir Thomas 118, 125, 137, 314 n50
Low Countries, Netherlands, Flanders, influence and workmen from 181, 183, 227, 244, 252, 261, 274, 287–8, 291–3, 308
Luffield priory 61, 83

Maastricht 292
Mackennal, Sir Bertram 313
MacMichael, Nicholas 302
Maidstone (Kent) 194
collegiate church 179
Malton, manor of 286
Malton, Thomas 344; *Plate IB*
Manewden (Essex) 84
Margaret, duchess of Savoy 135

INDEX

Marshall, Joshua 306
Mary I, queen 94, 101, 164, 187
Mary II, queen, proposed monument 299, 317 n11
Mary, daughter of Henry VII 104
Mary, queen of Scots 301 *and see* Westminster Abbey, Lady chapel of Henry VII, tombs
Master of the Rolls 87, 91 *and see* Barnes, Dr; Yonge, John
Matthew Paris 293
Mauncey, Thomas 215
Maximilian, emperor 135
Mazzoni, Guido 267, 288
Meckenem, Israel van 244
Mentmore (Bucks) 298, 341
Metcalf, Tim 353
Micklethwaite, J.T. 2, 276, 280, 284, 286–7, 305, 338, 345
Miles, William 336
Milner, John 332
Monck, General *see* Albemarle, duke of *and* Westminster Abbey, Lady chapel of Henry VII, tombs
Montagu, duke of 323
Montgomery, Sir Thomas 125
Moore, John 288
Mordaunt, John 127
Morris, William 338
Morton, John, archbishop of Canterbury 124
Mundy, John 74, 106

Napoleon III, emperor of France 300
Nelson, Admiral Lord 329
Netherlands, *see* Low Countries
New York, Trinity church of 308
Newark, Friars Observant of 131
Newcastle, Friars Observant of 130–1
Norfolk, county of 126
   duke of 164
Norris, Dean W.F. 313
Norwich cathedral 38

Odo the goldsmith 15
Oldfield, Edmund 297
Orchard, William 219
Osbert of Clare, *see* Westminster Abbey, monks of
Osmund, St 189
Oved, Sah 305
Oxford, Ashmolean Museum 341
   Cardinal college 265
   cathedral 215
   Divinity school 219, 287
   university 53, 81–3, 86, 88, 96, 105, 120
      hearse-cloth 82
      scholarships at 89, 120
Oxford, John earl of 125

Paris 306
   Sainte chapelle 191
Parliament 264, 327, 329–33, 336
Parliamentary Committee 215, 313, 328, 330–3, 344
Pearson, J.L. 313, 338, 345
Peers, Sir Charles 340–1
Pembroke, Mary de St Pol countess of 13
Percy, Dr 297
Perkins, J.H.T. 2, 143, 157, 177, 179; *Fig. 12*

Peterborough cathedral 219
Pevsner, Sir Nikolaus 202
Philip, HRH Prince 345, 354
Philippa of Hainault, queen 12 n31
Pickering (Yorks) 126
Piddletrenthide (Dorset) 302
Pitt, William 329
Platt, Tony 354
Plumier, Denis 311; *Plate 52*
Plumstead (Kent) 84
Pontefract, Pountfret (Yorks) 125, 293
Poole, Henry 297, 306
Pope, papal curia 83
Poulet, Quentin 74
Poynings, Sir Edward 127
Prince Imperial, of France 300–1
Purbeck marble 270
Pym, John 319
Pynson, Richard 30, 86, 88

Ralph de Stratford bishop of London 10
Raphael 282
Rattee and Kett, Messrs 345, 354
Raymond 295
Rede, Sir Robert 118 n34, 137
Remenham (Berks) 82–4
Richard II, king 16, 37, 40, 42, 49, 62, 68–9, 83, 93, 108–9, 171, 175 *and see* Westminster Abbey, church, tombs
Richard III, king 192, 260
Richards, James 324
Richmond, palace 92, 105, 107, 112, 115, 124, 129, 135, 173, 293; *Fig. 16*
   Friars Observant of 130–1
Richmond, Esme Stuart duke of 306 *and see* Westminster Abbey, Lady chapel of Henry VII, tombs
Risley, Sir John 125
Robson, E.R. 305
Rochester, bishop of *see* Fisher, John
   cathedral 96
Rome 30
Rotherham, Thomas archbishop of York 124
Roubiliac, Louis-François 308
Rovezzano, Benedetto da 274, 317
Russell, George 297
   Richard 193, 215
Ruthall, Thomas bishop of Durham 118, 127, 137
Ryle, Dean H.E. 306, 313
Rysbrack, Michael 308, 311

St Albans abbey 81, 95, 331
St Denis 266
St Martin le Grand *see* London
St Pierre-aux-Liens 291
Salisbury, bishop of *see* Audley, Edmund
   cathedral 145 n8, 189, 191
Savage, Sir John 125
   Thomas achbishop of York 126, 128
Savoy, hospital of the 61, 65–7, 71, 93, 104, 107, 121–2, 291, 293
Scheemakers, Peter 308, 311; *Plates 52–3*
Scott, Sir George Gilbert 221, 296–7, 338, 341
Scrane (Lincs) 83
Sever, William bishop of Durham 127–8

Sheen, king's house at, *see* Richmond palace
    priory 97, 130–1
Sherborne, Robert 79
Shrewsbury, George earl of 118, 125
Simeon, Geoffrey 127
Skelton, John 271, 273
Smith, Bill 354
Smith, William bishop of Lincoln 127, 137
Southampton, Friars Observant of 130–1
Southwark 291–2
    St George's church 124
Southwold (Suffolk) 244, 247
Spring, Thomas 247
Stanley, Dean A.P. 1, 229, 296–8, 300–1, 313, 317, 341 *and see* Westminster Abbey, Lady chapel of Henry VII, tombs
    James 83
    Thomas, *see* Derby, earl of
Star Chamber 77, 80
Stephens, Thomas 259
Stevens, Alfred 298
Stockton, Thomas 278, 288
    William 288
Suffolk, county of 126
Surrey, Thomas earl of 91, 118, 125, 137
Surveyors, Royal Institute of Chartered 342, 349
Sydney, earl 300
Syon abbey 75 n86, 81, 97

Talbot, Sir Gilbert 125
Tamworth (Staffs), college 89
Tansly, Samuel 336
Tapper, Sir Walter 223, 225, 339, 341, 348, 352
Taylor, Dr 84
Templeton, Sir John 354
Ternouth, John 296
Tessenderloo, St Martin's church 244; *Plate 34*
Theakston, John 296
Thirsk, John 259
Thomas the Apostle, St 11
Thomas Becket of Canterbury, St 11, 47
Thomas the Dutchman 271
Thomas of Hereford, St 13
Thomas de London 15
Thornton, John 353
Thorpe, John 181, 253; *Fig. 3*
Tickhill, Tykhull (Yorks), college 83
    honour of 126
Tonbridge (Kent) 198
Tongres, Notre-Dame 244; *Plate 33*
Toro, Jean Bernard Honoré 237; *Fig. 33*
Torrigiano, Pietro 187 n97, 266, 268–70, 274, 276, 282, 295, 314 n50, 317, 341
Treasurer, Lord 87, 90 *and see* Dynham, John Lord; Surrey, Thomas earl of
Trenchard, Lord 341
Tresilian, John 271
Tudor, Edmund 88, 268, 286
    Owen 63
Tutbury (Staffs) 126
Twylly, Edith 13, 20
    John *see* Westminster Abbey, Lady chapel, clerk
Tyler, Sir William 193

Underwood, Edward 79

Valle, Filippo della 311
Vannes, Brittany 113 n4
Vernon, Sir Henry 127
Vertue, George 311
    Robert 146, 193, 201, 219, 265
    William 143, 201, 203, 219, 265
Vewick, Wewyck, Maynard 268, 292 n144
Victoria, queen 296, 313
Vienna, Capuchin church 319
Villard de Honnecourt 221; *Fig. 27*
Vincent, George 330
    Dean William 329–32, 344
Virgin Mary, cult of *see* Westminster Abbey, Lady chapel
Vivarini, Bartolommeo 341

Wakehurst, Elizabeth 252
    Margaret 252
Wall, Dr 193
Walpole, Horace 312, 320–1
    Sir Robert 312, 321
Walsingham, shrine of Our Lady at 134, 267
Wanley, Humphrey 109
Warenne, William II de 247
Warham, William, archbishop of Canterbury 79–80, 91, 107, 118, 126, 128
Warwick, St Mary's church 171, 179, 183 n82, 262; *Plate 12*
    earl of, Richard Beauchamp 262, 269
        Thomas Beauchamp 171
Wastell, John 219
Weatherley, James 354
Welles, John viscount 125
    Richard 105
Westlake, H.F. 2, 8, 23, 187 n97, 190
Westmacott, Sir Richard 296, 312–13; *Plate 54*
Westminster (Middlesex) 7, 14, 18, 20, 27 117
    Improvements Commission 329
    places in:
        Eye 15
        Long Ditch 15
        Old Palace Yard 341, 343–4
        Palace of 29, 101, 192, 264, 298, 323, 329, 343–4
        St Margaret's church 47, 56
            churchyard 329
        St Stephen's chapel 45, 53, 66, 78, 80–1, 95–6, 171
        Tothill 15
        Whitehall Palace 320
        York Place 215
Westminster Abbey
    abbots of 81, 88, 91, 104, 114–15, 117, 120, 185, 259
        George Fascet 61–2, 68
        George Norwich 29
        John Estney 47
        John Islip 31, 61–2, 68–9, 76, 82–5, 92–3, 127, 173, 193
        Nicholas Litlyngton 37, 39
        Richard de Berking 14–15, 25–6, 189
        Simon Langham 27
        William Colchester 39, 45
        William Humez 5, 7–8, 14, 29
        William Postard 8 n12

INDEX

almoner 39 n44, 47
almonry 47, 52
   school 48
cellarer 17, 39 n44
chamberlain 39 n44
church (except Lady chapel) 8, 10, 23, 87, 130, 145, 167, 175, 196
   altars in 8–9, 12, 150, 152, 175, 191, 264, 320
   chapels
      Henry V chantry 177, 199, 264, 284, 299
      St Benedict 27, 87
      St Edward 156, 177, 259, 262
      St Faith 150; *Plate 5*
      St John Baptist 305
      St Nicholas 199
      St Paul 199
      St Thomas 47
   east end of 189–91, 196, 264; *Fig. 13*
   Edward the Confessor, shrine of 10–13, 16, 20, 63, 67, 89, 133, 159–60, 191, 259–60, 264, 267, 270, 276; *Fig. 1*
   Lady altar in 5, 7–11, 14, 29
   lantern 328–9
   liturgy in 14, 18–19, 22, 33–4, 40, 47, 51, 87, 175
   music in 44, 46–7, 56
   nave 8–9, 16, 29, 191, 215, 217
   north door 8–9, 13, 29
   organ 44, 47, 324
   restoration of, 1973–95, 346
   St Mary Magdalen image 27
   tombs and monuments 261–2
      Edward III 270
      Eleanor of Castile 270
      Henry III 259
      Henry V 270
      Hunsdon, Lord 305
      John of Eltham 270
      Mansfield, Lord 296
      materials of 269–71
      Newton, Sir Isaac 324
      Philippa of Hainault 270
      Richard II and Anne of Bohemia 269
      Stanhope, Earl 324
   west front and towers 323, 345
   white hart painting 171
confraternity 14
Customary, Consuetudinary 6, 8–10, 18, 21, 25, 33 n4, 34, 36 n20, 49
Dean and Chapter 232, 237
infirmarer 39 n44, 43 n77
Lady chapel
(i) *as an institution*
   almshouse of Henry VII 59–61, 66–7, 74, 88, 91, 94, 120, 179, 260, 293
      almsmen 62, 76–8, 87, 91, 120, 179, 261, 273
      poor women 120
   books in 18–19, 23, 35–6, 40, 44, 46, 54–6, 67, 132, 160, 286
   choir 16–17, 37–57, 203
      boys 16, 28–9, 38–9, 41–3, 48, 51, 53–4, 57
         clavichord for 54
         master of 48, 51
         Peter Best 50
         Richard Bemond 50
         William Fynnes 50
      masters, cantors 16–17, 22, 26, 28, 37, 42, 49, 51–3
         George Thaxton 51, 53
         James —— 51
         John George 51
         John Kemp 51, 53
         John Sylvester 51, 53
         John Tyes 16 n56, 23 n90, 41–3, 57
         Robert Penn 51–3
         Roger Cricktoft 51
         Thomas Watson 51–2
         Walter Braytoft 37–9
         Walter Whitby 16, 37–9
         William Cornysh 51–2, 54–5
            Joan his wife 52
         William Green, Grene 51, 53
         William Park 51–2
         —— Mason 51
      singing-men 16, 22, 26, 28–9, 39–49, 52–3, 56–7
         Henry Drayton 39–40
         John Barbour 46
         John Barker 41, 57
         John Browing 41, 57
         John Byfeld 41–2, 57
         John Grede 41, 43, 57
         Lewis Mugge 54
         Nicholas Ludford 53
         Peter Pleford 41, 57
         Richard the singer 39
         Richard Pridias, Prideaux 46
         Roger Empson 53–4
         Thomas Thomas 45
         Thomas Wharleton 54
         Thomas Youell 54
         William Causton 41–2, 57
         —— Coks 54
         —— Roger 54
   clerk, warden's assistant 20–1
      John Chaundhors 21 n83
      John Twylly 20–1, 29 n120
      Richard 20
   cult of the Virgin at 5–14, 35, 48, 63–4 *and see* relics, below
      feasts of the Virgin 5–7, 22, 25, 28, 34, 46–7, 56, 87
      images of the Virgin 8–11, 13–14, 25–6, 35, 67, 132, 150, 164, 274, 276, 286, 341
   endowment of 7, 14–18, 30, 34, 60–2, 67, 76, 82–5, 89, 120
   hearses 68–9, 90, 175–7, 180–1
   indentures 59–62, 66–82, 87, 89–90, 94–7, 99, 114–15, 117, 143, 170, 174–5 185–6, 260, 293; *Plates VIIA–B, VIII*
      chests for 75–6
   indulgences 12, 29–30, 60, 64, 88
      Scala Coeli 30, 88, 90–1, 179
   inventories of 19, 23, 25–6, 35–6, 48, 55, 64 n26, 90
   liturgy in 2, 5–7, 14, 18–19, 21–2, 25, 28–30,

364 INDEX

33–6, 42, 46, 49–51, 66, 68, 85–91, 152–3, 175, 185
music in 19, 22, 33–57, 152–3 *and see* choir, above *and* organs, below
offerings 13
relics 10–14, 25, 67, 104, 132, 271
rota 22, 28–9, 152
vestments and textiles 6, 18, 21, 23, 25–6, 28–9, 64, 67–9, 71–2, 82, 90, 104, 132–4, 160, 185–6; *Plate 1*
wardens of 14–15, 17–23, 25, 27–9, 34, 38, 39 n44, 42, 46, 152
   Henry de la Rye 19
   John Waterden 19
   Peter Combe 19–20
   Ralph de Gloucester 15
   Reginald de Hadham 19
   Thomas Arundel 19
(ii) *the old Lady chapel, building and contents* 2, 33, 63, 185, 196, 203, 260
ambitus 25, 150; *Fig. 5*
appearance of 23, 25–6
construction of 5, 8, 14, 23, 189–92
demolition of 50, 193, 196
desks 50
domestic quarters 22–3
garden 22, 25, 27, 192
lecterns 26
Mary Magdalen, St, image of 27–8
organs 26, 36, 42, 44, 46, 56, 192
plan of 23–7, 190; *Fig. 5*
pulpitum 19
retable, reredos 25, 150; *Fig. 5*
St Erasmus, chapel of 26, 192–3; *Fig. 5*
tombs 28
   Abbot Berking 25–7, 96; *Fig. 5*
   Katherine of Valois, queen 27, 63, 196; *Fig. 5*
vestry 23, 192
   records in 23
(iii) *Lady chapel of Henry VII, building and contents*
altars in 25, 50, 61, 64, 66, 113–14, 131–2, 143, 145–6, 150, 151 n18, 152–4, 156, 160, 162, 164, 167, 169–70, 175, 179, 181, 186–9, 191, 199, 261, 264, 266–8, 271, 274, 276, 282, 315, 340–1; *Figs 1, 3, 6, 37*
burial place 1, 186–8, 295, 299, 313, 315–17, 319
burial vaults 2, 190, 197, 319, 324, 341; *Figs 42–3*
chantry chapel, grate and altar 30, 64, 71, 87, 90–1, 114, 131–2, 159 n36, 175–7, 179–81, 185–8, 267, 271, 273–4, 276, 278, 291, 297–8, 341; *Plates II, IVB, 14, 45; Figs 6, 42*
closets and screens 167, 169–71, 173, 186, 200, 306, 329; *Figs 8, 17*
construction of 2, 50, 59, 66–7, 93, 104, 113, 141, 190, 192–204, 261; *Fig. 19*
designer of 193, 201
figure sculpture 1–2, 60, 131–2, 150, 163–4, 181, 203–4, 261–2, 271, 274, 276–92, 340–1, 344, 351, 353; *Plates V, 6; Figs 15, 38*
   Christ 280, 282, 284; *Plate 46*
   Gabriel 280
   Henry VI 286–7, 353
   'Islip' head 277
   St Ambrose 288, 290; *Plate 49*
   St Anthony 286, 291
   St Armagil 286
   St Augustine 288, 290
   St Barbara *Plate 47*
   St Benedict 288, 290
   St Edmund 266, 287
   St Edward the Confessor 266, 287–8, 290
   St Helen 288
   St Jerome *Plate 49*
   St John Evangelist *Plate 45*
   St Katharine 286, 288; *Plate 48*
   St Laurence 286
   St Margaret 286; *Plate 48*
   St Mathias 284
   St Nicholas 266, 287
   St Paul 284
   St Peter 266, 284, 287
   St Roch 286, 291
   St Sebastian 284, 290
      executioners 284, 290
   St Thomas 266
   St Thomas of Canterbury 287
   St Wilgefort (Uncumber) 282; *Plate 47*
   Virgin Mary 280
floor 315, 324
font 338
foundation stone 50, 62, 193, 261
gates 64, 94, 199, 254, 278, 341; *Plate 16*
glass 64, 115, 181, 204, 261–2, 278, 284, 287, 327, 333, 337, 340–1, 348, 353–4
graffiti 164; *Plate 8*
heraldry 64, 73, 94, 115, 133–4, 169, 171, 244, 269 n47, 276, 278, 284, 291, 301, 305–6, 342, 346, 348–50, 354; *Plates 4, 10*
layout, internal 145–6, 150, 154, 156–7, 159–60, 164, 177, 179–81, 183, 187, 228, 261, 266–7, 280, 320; *Figs 1–2, 6, 12*
limewash 338–40, 345, 348, 351–2
mats 50
organs 56, 153
parapets and pinnacles 334, 336, 338, 341–2, 344, 348, 350; *Plates IA–B*
praise of 1, 327, 338
RAF chapel 341; *Plate 6*
restorations of:
   1809–22: 327–38, 344–5; *Fig. 45*
   1929–35: 143, 223, 225–6, 339
   1991–6: 226, 343–55; *Plates IA, IVA, V*
      donors to 355
      staff engaged on 355
roofs 194, 196, 199–200, 203, 213–17, 225, 327, 337–40, 342, 347–8, 350; *Fig. 26*
Second World War, impact of 253, 337, 341, 346
stalls, desks 50, 115, 152, 169, 177, 179–81, 183, 185–6, 190, 200, 203–4, 227–57, 267, 321, 324, 340–1, 353; *Plates III, 4, 15–16, 20–3, 27, 29–32, 41–2; Figs 3, 6, 17–18, 32, 34–5*
   misericords 181, 229, 235–7, 240, 253–4, 256, 321; *Plates 24–6, 28*

stall plates 341
tiles below 239, 256
steps 50, 145
stone types
   Bath, Combe Down 194, 196, 197 n39, 331, 333, 337, 345, 348–51
   Burford, Taynton 345
   Caen 193–4, 196, 197 n39, 290, 327, 338, 345, 352
   Hopton Wood 331
   Huddlestone, magnesian limestone 194, 196, 197 n39, 345
   Kentish rag 193–4, 197, 317, 337
   Portland 342, 345–6, 348–51
   Reigate 194, 196, 200, 290, 327, 345
   Totternhoe 331
tablets, tables 88, 271
tombs and monuments
   Albemarle, George Monck duke of 311; *Plate 53*
   Anne, queen 308
   Buckingham, George Villiers first duke of 306, 308; *Fig. 41*
      John Sheffield duke of 277, 287, 311, 315; *Plate 52*
   Cromer, earl of 313
   Curzon, marquess 312
   Edward V and Richard duke of York, supposed 306, 317 n11
   Elizabeth I 187, 302–3, 305, 317, 319–20, 340; *Figs 1, 40*
   Halifax, Charles Montagu earl of 308
   George Savile marquess of 308, 340
   Henry VII and Elizabeth of York 49–50, 59, 64, 66, 71, 90, 104, 113–14, 120, 159, 175–6, 179–80, 185, 187, 192, 201, 228, 264–71, 273–4, 293, 295, 297–8, 319, 323, 341; *Plates IVB, VI, 44; Figs 6, 12*
   Lennox, Margaret countess of 301–2
   Margaret Beaufort 173, 180, 192, 268–71, 273, 293, 295, 297–8, 320; *Plate VIIC; Figs 1, 6*
   Mary, princess 302, 305, 317, 320
   Mary, queen of Scots 303, 306, 317, 319–20; *Plate 51; Fig. 1*
   Milner, viscount 313
   Montpensier, Antoine-Philippe d'Orleans duc de 312–13; *Plate 54*
   not erected, see Buckingham George Villiers second duke of; Edward VI; Henry VI, shrine of; Mary II; William III
   RAF leaders 314
   repairs and restorations of 296–8
   Rhodes, Cecil 313–14
   Richmond and Lennox, duke of 306
   Sophia, princess 302, 305, 317, 320; *Plate 50*
   Stanley, Dean AP 313
   Walpole, Catherine 311–12
   William III, king 308
   Wyndham, Percy, and Earl Kitchener 313

turrets, cupolas 328, 332–4, 337–8, 342, 345–9; *Plate IA*
vaults 2, 194, 200–3, 205–13, 219, 221, 223–6, 339–41, 351–2; *Plates II–IVA, V, 17–19; Figs 4, 21–5, 28, 30–1*
lay brothers, *conversi, converses* 68, 89, 91, 120
Litlyngton missal 33 n4, 34 n5
monks of 16–17, 28, 47, 68, 91
   Alexander de Pershore 36
   Edward Botiller 49
   Henry Jones 86 n149
   John Ashley 86 n149
   John Flete 11, 26–7
   John Walden 44
   Osbert of Clare 6
   Philip de Brightwell 29
   Richard of Cirencester 11
   Robert de Molesham 7, 17, 22
   Robert Humfrey 86 n149
   Robert Wynwyk 36, 40
   Stephen de London 8, 10
   Thomas Barton 89
   Thomas Gardiner 160 n36, 188
   Thomas Jay 89
   William Bothe 89
monk-bailiff 17, 19, 86
pilgrims 7, 13, 29
places in, cemetery 192
   chapter house 62, 77, 101–3, 192, 341
   Cheyneygates 61
   College hall 216
   infirmary 22
   Jerusalem chamber 350
   Pyx chapel 101
   refectory 19
   Sanctuary yard 46, 52, 329
precentor 17–19, 22, 49
prior 86, 89, 185
relics at 12–14, 20
sacrist 9, 12, 17, 20, 25, 39 n44, 47
service books 22
shrine-keeper 12
sub-sacrists 13
succentor 22, 28, 152
treasurer 56
Trust 345–6, 355
warden of the churches 39 n44
Whitehead, Messrs J. 301
Widmore, Richard 1
Wild, Charles *Plate II*
William III, king, proposed monument 299, 317 n11
William, prince 321
Williams, Dean John 306
Willis, Robert 1, 202–3, 205, 219; *Fig. 4*
Wilton 333
Wilton, Joseph 237
Winchester, bishop of 78, 95 *and see* Courtenay, Peter; Fox, Richard
   cathedral 41, 43, 292
      Bishop Fox's chantry 265
      Lady chapel 244, 247; *Plate 36*
      Langton chapel 244, 247; *Plate 37*
      stalls 239
   prior and convent of 78–80, 97, 131

Windsor, castle 92, 124, 173, 197, 333
    St George's chapel 37, 45–6, 53, 61, 68, 81, 83, 88, 97, 104, 133, 154, 160, 170–1, 173, 187, 193, 201, 227, 244, 254, 259–60, 264, 266, 270–1, 276, 291, 293, 301, 317; *Plate 13*
        Lady chapel 23–4, 60, 153–4, 156, 191–2, 197, 201, 259–60; *Fig. 10*
Woburn Abbey 331
Wolsey, Thomas, Cardinal 105, 215, 265, 317
Woodstock 293
Worley, Nicholas 106
Wren, Sir Christopher 306, 327, 343, 345
Wright, William 308
Wyatt, Benjamin 333, 336
    James 200, 215, 221, 327–34, 338–9, 343–5, 347
    Jeffrey 336

Yates, George 336
    John 336
Yonge, John 108, 118, 137, 139
York 123
    archbishop of, *see* Bainbridge, Christopher; Rotherham, Thomas; Savage, Thomas
Younger, Alan 354